CW00544754

"Hopwood has assembled a fascinating array assessment luminaries about their personal an ences, their life- and career trajectories. In es erativity. This treasure chest of narratives will personality assessors to find their visions and carve out their unique paths.

—**Radhika Krishnamurthy, PsyD, ABAP;** *Clinical Psychology Professor, Florida Institute of Technology; Former President, Society for Personality Assessment*

"People who understand people know that scientists are not inert ingredients in their research. Chris Hopwood has curated a master list of the most accomplished and influential living personality assessment scientists and practitioners to share their professional journeys, which have left an indelible mark on the field. The result is a brightly illuminating volume that will be a must read for those who want to understand how we come to understand people."

—**Aidan Wright, PhD;** *Associate Professor of Psychology at the University of Pittsburgh*

The Evolution of Personality Assessment in the 21st Century

This edited volume provides readers with a deeper knowledge of the growth of personality assessment in North America over the past 40 years through the autobiographies of its most notable figures.

Experts provide insights into their professional backgrounds, training experiences, their contributions and approaches to personality assessment, their perceptions of current trends, and their predictions about the future of the field. Each chapter explores topics of deep significance to the writer, fluidly intertwining theory and personal narrative.

Beginning clinicians, scholars, and students will gain a better understanding of the major empirical advances that were made during the last generation regarding key questions about the nature of people, the structure of personality traits, and the connections between personality and mental health.

Dr. Christopher J. Hopwood is Professor of Personality Psychology at the University of Zürich. He is a fellow and former board member of the Society for Personality Assessment and Associate Editor of the *Journal of Personality Assessment* and the *Journal of Personality and Social Psychology*.

The Evolution of
Personality Assessment
in the 21st Century

Understanding the People who
Understand People

Edited by
Christopher J. Hopwood

Routledge
Taylor & Francis Group

NEW YORK AND LONDON

Cover image: © Getty Images

First published 2022
by Routledge
605 Third Avenue, New York, NY 10158

and by Routledge
4 Park Square, Milton Park, Abingdon, Oxon, OX14 4RN

Routledge is an imprint of the Taylor & Francis Group, an informa business

© 2022 Taylor & Francis

The right of Christopher Hopwood to be identified as the author
of the editorial material, and of the authors for their individual
chapters, has been asserted in accordance with sections 77 and 78
of the Copyright, Designs and Patents Act 1988.

Library of Congress Cataloging-in-Publication Data
A catalog record for this title has been requested

ISBN: 9780367477431 (hbk)
ISBN: 9780367477424 (pbk)
ISBN: 9781003036302 (ebk)

DOI: 10.4324/9781003036302

Typeset in Bembo
by codeMantra

Access the Support Material: www.routledge.com/9780367477431

I dedicate this book to the *Society for Personality Assessment*.

Contents

Figures

Tables

About the Contributors

Robert P. Archer was the Frank Harrell Redwood Distinguished Professor and Director of Psychology, Department of Psychiatry and Behavioral Sciences, at the Eastern Virginia Medical School, Norfolk, Virginia and he is currently a member of the Bay Forensic Psychology group in Virginia. Dr. Archer is the author of numerous books, articles, and book chapters related to psychological assessment.

Donna S. Bender is a psychologist, psychoanalyst, and Director of Strategic Initiatives for the Division of Computer Science and Engineering, University of Michigan.

Lorna Smith Benjamin is an American psychologist best known for her innovative treatment of patients with personality disorders who have not responded to traditional therapies or medications.

Yossef S. Ben-Porath is a Professor of Psychology at Kent State University and is recognized internationally as a foremost expert on the MMPI instruments.

Ety Berant is the director of the clinic of the school of psychology. She received her PhD in psychology from Bar-Ilan University. During the years 2008–2010, she was the vice head of department of psychology in Bar-Ilan University. Ety is a senior clinical psychologist and a licensed supervisor in psychotherapy and personality assessment. She is the founder of the Israeli Rorschach association.

Robert F. Bornstein is a Professor at the Gordon F. Derner School of Psychology, Adelphi University.

Virginia M. Brabender currently works at the Institute for Graduate Clinical Psychology, Widener University. She is recognized as a Widener University Distinguished Professor (2017–2020). Virginia does research in Abnormal Psychology, Psychoanalysis, Ethics, Group Psychotherapy, and Psychological Assessment.

Lee Anna Clark is a Professor and William J. and Dorothy K. O'Neill Professor of Psychology in the Department of Psychology at the University of Notre Dame in Notre Dame, Indiana, USA.

Phebe Cramer was a clinical psychologist and Professor of Psychology, Emerita at Williams College. Best known for her research on defense mechanisms, body image, and narcissism, and for her creation of a manual for coding defense mechanisms for purposes of psychological testing and personality assessment.

Stephen E. Finn is the President and founder of the Center for Therapeutic Assessment, and is a licensed clinical psychologist in practice in Austin, Texas, USA.

Roger L. Greene is a Professor at Palo Alto University. He received the Bruno Klopfer Award in 2010. He worked on self-report measures of personality, particularly the Minnesota Multiphasic Personality Inventory.

Christopher J. Hopwood is a Professor of Personality Psychology at the University of Zürich.

Nancy McWilliams is a Visiting Full Professor at the Graduate School of Applied and Professional Psychology at Rutgers University. She has written on personality and psychotherapy. McWilliams is a psychoanalytic/dynamic author, teacher, supervisor, and therapist.

Leslie C. Morey is a Professor of Psychology at Texas A&M University. He received his PhD in Clinical Psychology from the University of Florida, and has served on the faculty at Vanderbilt University, Harvard Medical School, the Yale University School of Medicine, and the University of Tulsa.

D. S. Moskowitz is a Professor Emerita of McGill University. Her research concerns patterns of behavior and affect and the relation between behavior and affect across time and situations.

David S. Nichols is retired. Formerly Staff Psychologist, Oregon State Hospital, and Adjunct Professor, Pacific University.

Aaron L. Pincus is a Professor of Psychology at Pennsylvania State University.

Irving B. Weiner is an American psychologist and Past President of Division 12 of the American Psychological Association and Past President of the Society for Personality Assessment.

Thomas A. Widiger is an American clinical psychologist who researches the diagnosis and classification of psychopathology. He is a Fellow of the Association for Psychological Science, Editor of *Personality Disorders: Theory, Research, and Treatment*, and Co-Editor of the *Annual Review of Clinical Psychology*.

1 Understanding People Who Understand People

Christopher J. Hopwood

When I was about ten years old, I spent one of the sleepless nights that have been common throughout my life generating a detailed description of one of my classmate's personalities. I still remember what I found interesting about him, and could more or less reproduce that description in the form of a psychological assessment report today. Until I was eight and my sister was born, I was an only child in a rural community so small that there were no other children my age, so I spent a lot of time alone. During much of that time, I would arrange GI Joe figures in such a way that they would play out 11 on 11 football games, and I would compile detailed statistics in meticulously organized notebooks. One particular fullback was remarkable for having zero variance in rushing attempts – he gained exactly eight yards on every carry. I had an extensive and meticulously organized collection of sports cards, magazines, and books; trivial details like Joe Morris' rushing yards in 1986 (1,516), Pedro Guerrero's home run total in 1987 (27), or Charles Barkley's rebounding average in 1988 (12.5) took up far too much space in my prepubescent memory bank. Only with hindsight is it obvious that these eccentricities foreshadowed my interest in personality assessment. At that time, I had no idea that a person could make a living doing these sorts of things.

If you take a sheep dog who has never seen sheep to a field with sheep in it, they will herd the sheep until they are exhausted, seemingly unable to care about or focus on anything else. I don't know what this is like on the inside, but from the outside they look like they are living the best version of themselves. In my view, the responsibility of the person with a liberal education is to find their sheep so that they can be the best version of themselves. My students sometimes feel ashamed for not having found their sheep yet, but that seems natural to me. It took me until my mid–20s to find mine. A few salient post–pubescent memories picked up the thread from those sports statistics, real and imagined. In high school, I found myself reading up on the content I felt was missing in class. As an undergraduate, I observed with curiosity and confusion the bored responses of other students to a class about Nietzsche, Hobbes, and Rousseau. When I was teaching overseas, I observed myself reading Freud and Sullivan when my roommates would come home late from a night at the bar. In

DOI: 10.4324/9781003036302-1

my master's program, I found myself at a reception enrapt by conversations about research design with the faculty, whereas many of my fellow students perseverated on how hard graduate school was. In each of these experiences, my peers' behaviors seemed really odd. The sheepdog doesn't notice their lather.

It was during that master's program that I read a chapter by Les Morey in which he said, more or less, that he had noticed with curiosity that he was one of the few students in his psychometrics class who found quantifying peoples' behavior with psychological tests exciting – everyone else somehow thought that was tedious. I thought: that's it! Like a good test item, he had captured my inner experience exactly. Personality assessment was my sheep. Now I just needed to find the people who were good at it. This book showcases some of those people, in their own words.

Some of the people who taught me how to understand people

I used three main criteria to select authors. First and most important, the people I asked to contribute to this book have had a major impact on personality assessment science and practice.

Second, each of the authors have been influential within the *Society for Personality Assessment* (SPA), as board members, journal editors, award winners, keynote speakers, and/or presenters. SPA has been a home conference for my entire career. Early on, SPA was an encouraging environment where I could observe the masters in action. As I continued attending SPA and other meetings, I became aware of SPA's uniqueness in providing a forum for clinicians and researchers to interact. For this reason, SPA is singularly important for the integration of research and practice in personality assessment. But SPA also offers a highly personal experience of warmth, intellectual stimulation, compassion, and communion. I wanted this book to give the reader something like the experience of being at the conference because that is the best way I can think of to encourage people to be involved with and support personality assessment. My relatively small share of the proceeds from this book will be donated to SPA, as a modest gesture of gratitude.

Third, it was important for me to invite as many women as men. Women have comprised the majority of my fellow students, supervisors, and teachers, yet they are in the minority in the journals, books, and academic conference programs. This dynamic is multiply determined but the root cause is uncomplicated; several women spoke to their experiences of institutional sexism in this volume. In contrast, people of color and non-binary gender have played essentially no role in my training; I never had the opportunity to be supervised by a non-white, non-cis-gendered person. It is a shameful reality that people of color or non-binary gender are rare in psychology training, in general. Recent meetings about this issue have made it clear that, within SPA, this is at least partly because of structural issues that make people from underrepresented groups feel alienated and unwelcome. These barriers to diversity contributed to a major limitation of my training and continue to reflect a profound problem for our profession and society. I am hopeful that SPA is beginning to do something about it.

Many people are not in this book but could have been, based on their impact on personality assessment and on my own development and career. This includes my internship supervisor Mark Blais, my personality assessment instructors Jim Roff and Doug Snyder, many excellent colleagues with whom I served in my role as an SPA board member, including Paul Arbisi, Ginger Calloway, Barton Evans, Ron Ganellan, Giselle Hass, Steve Huprich, Jan Kamphuis, Nancy Kaser-Boyd, Radhika Krishnamurthy, John McNulty, Greg Meyer, Joni Mihura, Carol Overton, Piero Porcelli, John Porcerelli, David Streiner, and Jed Yalof, and many, many others. I must also mention Bob Erard and Bruce Smith, both of whom we lost too soon.

That said, this a fairly representative and extraordinarily impressive sample of people who have spent the last few decades trying to understand people. By way of introduction, I presently share some brief anecdotes that I hope communicate the essence of their impact on me and on the field.

Stephen Finn

I cry often and often enjoy it. I am usually more likely to remember the things that happen to me when I cry because they meant something important to me at the time. A few people can reliably make me cry: Aretha Franklin, Carl Rogers, Lauryn Hill, and Fred (Mr.) Rogers. The only person I know personally who reliably makes me cry is Steve Finn. I think that has to do with the same inner essence – a kind of authenticity that resonates deeply with people – that has made Steve's work so impactful. People who know him or read his enclosed chapter will know what I mean, even if they don't cry as easily as I do.

Donna Bender

Donna Bender is the foremother of the Levels of Personality Functioning Scale (LPFS), which serves as Criterion A of the Alternative Model of Personality Disorders. The LPFS not only accounts for the covariation among different PDs but also provides clinicians a vehicle with which to be curious about their patients, including their strengths, capacities, and inner experiences as social beings. Donna has emphasized this latter point in a number of places, including the enclosed chapter. But I want to set the record straight; I didn't invite her to contribute only because of influential work on the LPFS. I have come away from my handful of encounters with Donna with the sense that she is one of those people whose path I wished to have crossed more often. She enlivens her environment, wherever she goes, by being herself. This quality enabled her to breathe life into the *DSM-5*, and inspires courage to follow one's heart.

David Nichols

During my first SPA board meeting, as a graduate student representative, the board learned that a new contract with the publisher of the *Journal of Personality Assessment* (JPA) had left the society poised for a fairly dramatic revenue increase. The suggestion was raised, at first as a kind of jest that became, briefly, a serious consideration, that we might want to increase our reimbursement for the previous night's dinner in light of this revelation. Dave Nichols said plainly and sternly that he wouldn't go along – we had ordered the previous night with a particular arrangement in mind and the right thing to do was to stick to that. Everyone immediately knew that he was right. Even a brief brush with Dave's work shows that he is kind and sharp and has a way with words, but his serious and abiding concern for the difference between right and wrong as he sees it is the quality that stands out for people who know him.

Ety Berant

Reading Ety Berant's chapter, an idea crystalized that had been in the back of my mind the last few times I have met with one of the students I described above, who feel ashamed about not having yet found their sheep. These students often have the narrow focus of racehorses with cheekpieces that concerns me – they want to be psychotherapists of a particular kind, in a particular setting, and with a particular degree, and don't want to think about other possibilities. I get the impression that they want to narrow down the type of program to apply to so as to reduce information overload, and they want me to justify this kind of narrowing, help them do it, and give them the formula for how to succeed therein. A wish surges within me to slow the conversation down, and a fear emerges that anything I might say will be taken too seriously. Contrast this constricted feeling with how I felt after reading Ety's chapter: a kind of calm, warm admiration. Ety strikes me as wise in a way that I would like to be with these students. She has had diverse and multilayered career and life, with a mix of responsibilities related to practice, clinic administration, research, and training. These roles have been synergistically woven together into a coherent gestalt, balanced against her personal priorities. Ety sets an example of how to live a life so as to achieve what many of my students hope for.

Irving Weiner

Irv Weiner is the only person in this book who has already written an autobiography. But how could I not ask him? At SPA, he is like the patron saint and guardian angel, the keeper of the history and peak of the pile. He has been the person that the people I look up to look up to since I began coming to SPA. When Irv speaks people listen, and that gives him space to speak softly and slowly. As one develops, these pedestaled people tend to come down to earth. But in Irv's case, the aura persists for me, and in my observation of the social dynamics of SPA, it seems to persist for everyone else, too. Irv documents in this chapter, in his understated way, the impact he has had on mental health research, training, and practice, which has reached well beyond personality assessment and SPA. The winding path of Irv's illustrious career would be nearly impossible to replicate. But this presence seems tied to something more universal, the essence of a revered person, whose legacy has been to leave the many things they have touched better off than before.

Virginia Brabender

Virginia Brabender uses English real good. You might think, if you read her work but had not heard her speak, that she writes in her decorative way for effect, thesaurus by her side. But in fact, she makes English sound good all the time. Indeed, I have never personally known a North American who can flourish as well as she can. I get a similar experience when Virginia writes or talks as I do from people like Toni Morrison or Christopher Hitchens. There were times when Virginia and I served on the SPA board together, that I thought she could charm us all (well me, at least) into nearly anything with one of her stirring soliloquys. The incredible thing to me was that these were contemporaneous. They seemed written in advance, but in point of fact her linguistic swirls and ribbons are just cuts from the fabric of her lovely personality.

Robert Bornstein

Bob Bornstein is one of the most distinctive and interesting people I know. His application of process dissociation to personality assessment is among the most important ideas in the last few decades in the field of personality assessment. It provides a principled, empirical, and profound vision for how to get us out of the horse-race model of test comparison to a more nuanced and sophisticated way of thinking about psychological assessment. It is embedded not only in his thorough knowledge of psychometrics, certain tests, and constructs like dependency, but also a much deeper theoretical foundation that can be linked, in his capable hands, with the work of Heisenberg, Kandinsky, and Rorschach. He is extraordinarily interesting to talk to, and I have been lucky to have the opportunity to do so fairly regularly over Manhattans at SPA, and more recently over the phone. It is sort of unusual to find an intellectual giant who is also a modest and charming person, with good taste in life partners, music, and cocktails. What more could a person want in a friend and colleague?

Nancy McWilliams

Nancy McWilliams is the only author of this book with whom I have not interacted personally, and thus her influence on me has been entirely indirect. But I'm not the only one: she is perhaps the most impactful personality assessment teacher – from the perspective of metrics like book sales – of her generation. I knew from reading her books that Nancy is a good writer, and holy moly, please see below. Her capacity to write elegantly about deeply painful experiences, to express strong feelings or controversial positions with warmth and sensitivity, and to build momentum to highly memorable lines, is breathtaking. Nancy's chapter exemplifies how to reflect on how one's own psychology impacts the way one thinks about the psychology of others. I was left wishing I could have gotten to know her better.

Robert Archer

Bob Archer was one of the SPA presidents during the time I was on the board. For reasons of confidentiality and tact, I cannot give all of the specific reasons that I admire him. But suffice to say that there was a lot going on while he was president. The thing I admired about Bob was that he kept the ship steadily steered in the right direction – a skill he has presumably mastered while sailing on the actual sea. There were several times I saw him gracefully take lumps that rightfully belonged to others, for the sake of the society. He was always good humored and serious, measured and thoughtful. I thought to myself, if by some great mistake some poorly informed group of people ever entrust me with the responsibility for something as important as SPA, Bob would be my role model for how to conduct myself.

Yossef Ben-Porath

Yossi Ben-Porath was the first person featured in this book whom I met in person. It was in Hawaii, at the *American Psychological Association* session in which I presented my first poster (on my master's thesis, having to do with the reliability of scoring the WAIS-IV). He encouraged me to submit the paper to *Assessment*, where he was an editor, and where the paper was ultimately published. I was naturally awestruck, and shocked that he would find this level of value in my work. I was struck in reading his chapter that he had had an experience similar to mine as a child informally assessing his classmates' personalities. I suppose our futures seem to have a funny way of revealing themselves, if we listen closely enough. Yossi has been one of the most programmatic and influential scholars in applied personality assessment as researcher, mentor of an impressive number of influential scholars, editor, and workshopper during the last few decades. His career exemplifies the payoff of sticking to a good plan.

Phebe Cramer

Nothing to see here, no big deal, just a world war and rationed shoes, a childhood cross-country trek, a world record in swimming, some trail-blazing within some of the pillars of male-only academia. Just the most influential scholar of her generation on defense mechanisms and narrative assessment – in her *second* career. Phebe's understated approach to her autobiography belies a career and a life that is so extraordinary that I cannot imagine it being replicated. I admit to feeling some level of intimidation when having interacted with Phebe at SPA but insist that it is because of my great admiration for her work and her life. I am very sorry that, because Phebe passed away shortly after contributing this chapter, that I will miss out on future such interactions.

Thomas Widiger

Tom Widiger's highly influential program of research has arguably done more to promote personality assessment in clinical practice than that of any other person of his generation. He has developed a variety of tests, edited a number of influential books and journals, published an astonishing number of empirical articles, and trained a broad network of highly influential personality assessors. But what I admire most about Tom is that he is both a dogged and tenacious promoter of his beloved five-factor model of personality traits and disorders, and also an open-minded, self-critical, and highly genial editor, mentor, and colleague. In a world in which many people believe in dialectics until it is their turn, Tom's ability to keep different agendas in his head at the same time is, like his career, extraordinary and distinguished.

Lee Anna Clark

If I could have chosen the president in last year's US election, my choice would have been Lee Anna Clark. There seem to be no limits to her wisdom, generativity, attention to detail, and, apparently, time. Along with Tom, Lee Anna has been one of the most productive and impactful scholars of her generation, including being the only person to serve on both the DSM and ICD personality disorder committees, which have revolutionized personality disorder diagnosis. But she also somehow finds time to promote the careers of people like me in ways that are unusually time consuming. Lee Anna, one of the most principled people I have ever met, taught me and many others how to conduct oneself in a professional setting. She has also given me some of the most helpful and specific advice I have received, about how to frame one's work, how to prioritize tasks, how to draft a recommendation letter, and how to be sure to drink one glass of water for every glass of alcohol at conferences. Personality assessors should feel lucky she didn't go into politics (yet).

Roger Greene

At one of my first SPA meetings, Roger Greene gave a presentation that caused a bit of a stir. He said something like, the next generation of personality assessors are not going to be asking their clients to answer long lists of true-false or multiple-choice questions. I guess the hubbub was about the fact that this was coming from an MMPI guru, and it sort of signaled a revolution from the inside, which could have perhaps been interpreted as a kind of treason. At that time, I was cutting my teeth on the ins and outs of the PAI, which is also, from the perspective of the respondent, a long list of questions. But what Roger had said seemed perfectly natural, albeit prescient, to me. Even then, I had the sense that we could do better, and that using different kinds of methods, and in particular passively assessing people repeatedly in their actual lives, was the future of personality assessment. I have never forgotten that moment, in the first instance because it gave a narrative to the direction in which I felt we ought to be pushing ourselves, and because the reaction among the people I spoke to afterwards surprised me. As you can read below, Roger is full of surprises – and on that particular point, I am completely confident that time will prove him right, even if it might take a little longer than he or I had hoped back then.

D.S. Moskowitz

Why do I say that time will prove Roger right? Because the most exciting thing happening in personality assessment research is the study of personality dynamics. How do people change from one situation to the next, and what kinds of things affect those changes? How can you distinguish people based on their patterns of changes across situations? It is difficult to find an issue of a leading assessment, personality, or psychopathology journal that doesn't include some form of dynamic personality assessment (one hopes that we will soon say the same about clinical assessment batteries). Debbie Moskowitz was the pioneer of these techniques. Her chapter illustrates the incisive thinking style that has powered the revolution. It also highlights vividly the context of sexism in which these ideas were colored, but thankfully not fully constrained. It is astonishing and absurd that a person like D.S. Moskowitz would go six years without a proper position, or a career without a gendered name. It is a testament to Debbie's sustained attention and methodical approach that her work has been, nevertheless, transformative and groundbreaking.

Lorna Smith Benjamin

Lorna Smith Benjamin lives her life a few steps ahead of everyone else. Or, at least, you feel behind when you are with her, or when you read the things she has written. I experience her as a kind of archetype of the kind of woman one had to be to survive 20th-century academia. Imagine: a woman working in Harlow's lab with expertise in mathematics and computer science, shut out of the standard opportunities by sexism, births one of the most elegant and sophisticated evidence-based models of human behavior on the market, translates it to a fully integrated mental health care system that focuses in particular on the most difficult patients, and applies it directly to treat these most difficult patients and to train students. Her blend of tough, sensitive, and smart generates one of the most disquieting interpersonal experiences one can have, and I am enormously lucky to have had it. One can learn from Lorna to pay attention to everything with a critical eye because the patterns are there if you look hard enough.

Leslie Morey

I am not sure if I knew I should be Les' doctoral student when I read his work in my master's program and had the uncanny impression that we were cut from the same cloth, or whether it was when I first saw him on stage playing bass to ACDC's "You shook me all night long," or whether it was during my interview with him when we spent a half an hour talking about the limitations of coefficient alpha that felt like half a minute. What I know for sure is that he was the perfect mentor for me, and he will always be the person in psychology I look up to the most; it is deeply ironic that what I learned from Les, the master of measurement, seems to me immeasurable.

Aaron Pincus

In graduate school, I struggled to integrate what I was learning in classes, my own research, and my clinical work. I was looking for a way to integrate assessment data, theories of psychopathology and intervention, and my experience of interacting with patients. I wanted a system that gave me reliable heuristics for what to do, and when, and also what not to do, during my actual interactions in the consulting room. Then I read the single most formative paper I have ever read: a chapter by Aaron Pincus on Contemporary Integrative Interpersonal Theory. It offered just the kind of model I was looking for – it was evidence-based, theoretically rich, experience near, and specific. I set out to meet him soon after reading it, and that turned out to be one of the turning points of my career, one of the great privileges of which has been to have Aaron as informal mentee, collaborator, and friend.

My hope for this book

That meeting with Aaron occurred at the *Society for Interpersonal Theory and Research*. At the same meeting, Steve Strack presented a newly published book of autobiographies by eminent personality assessors, which collated papers that had been previously published in JPA. That book had an intense influence on me. I read it front to back on the flight home and have read several of the chapters several times since. At that point, I was familiar with the work of all of the authors, but that book revealed a more personal perspective, and helped me see that the theories and research that I had been vigorously digesting came from *people*. Actual people who, on some level, were like me. They had their own motives and backgrounds, strengths and weaknesses, penetrating insights, and blind spots. I found particular interest in the way these authors approached the task. Some of the chapters were agentic, focused on their scientific impact in a way that was even, in some cases, self-congratulatory, bitter, or diminishing of others. Others were communal, with little mention of accomplishment but significant attention to the relationships the author had developed over their careers, and their gratitude for having been a part of the profession, sometimes in a way that was a little diminishing of their own contributions. Some were somewhere in between.

The opportunity to understand these people, who had themselves been pioneers in the science and practice of understanding people, was fascinating to me. I understood why everyone loved Paul Lerner and Len Handler so much. Jane Loevinger offered me a glimpse of what it must have been like to be a woman academic in the middle of the 20th century. I appreciated why an expression of interest in your work from Jack Block provoked fear rather than pride. I realized how fun it would have been to hang out socially with Marv Zuckerman, or to sit in on a lecture by Ted Millon. That book shaped the way I thought about the profession and my goals within it. I was moved and inspired.

As I say in the abstract, my motives for the current book were largely selfish. I wanted to read the personal stories of the people who had influenced me, both personally and professionally. I wanted to see what they would focus on and how they would approach the task because I wanted to think about how their approach and their lives provide texture to their influential scholarly work. I wanted, in some sense, to replicate my experience of having read that earlier book of autobiographies, but this time with people by whom I had been more directly influenced. As before,

I was moved and inspired, and I am very grateful to the authors of this volume for having taken me up on my invitation.

But I also hoped that this book would stimulate young scholars who are in a position similar to my own, a decade and half ago, and that it would provide a historical document of value to future scholars interested in interpreting the work of these authors in a fuller context. With this goal in mind, I asked each of the authors to discuss three things: (a) personal and professional aspects of their life and career, (b) their approach to personality assessment, and (c) how their own personality and experiences have contributed to that approach. I invited them to address these topics in any order and proportion they see fit, and to include other topics as well if they wished. The idea, not unfamiliar to personality assessors, was to provide a standardized task within which the authors could show who they really are and how they are different from others, using both the content and the process of their response.

As I read through the chapters, I was struck by the subtle differences in content, such as the emphasis on agentic vs. communal themes, professional vs. personal focus, and the nature and contents of the reference section. But differences in process were even more striking: the degree to which people hewed closely vs. deviated from my request the arrangement of headings, the use of various kinds of humor, or the degree to which the prose was colorful or straightforward. Each chapter spurred a slightly different feeling for me, which was, of course, highly textured by my own experiences, personal and professional, of each of the contributors. Even if this project had not been completed during a pandemic that saw the cancellation of one SPA meeting and an online version of another, reading these chapters would have been a highly sentimental experience for me. I hope you enjoy reading them as much as I did.

2 The Development of Therapeutic Assessment

From Shame and Isolation to Connection and Love[1]

Stephen E. Finn

Early years and challenges

I was born on January 8, 1956 to Edward Finn (age 33) and Dawne (age 24) Merrill Finn, who lived in Canastota, New York—a largely Italian Catholic village 25 miles east of Syracuse. From what I have pieced together, my parents had been in love when they married three years earlier, but by the time I arrived their relationship was already on a downslide. My father had Bipolar Disorder—undiagnosed at the time and rampant in his Irish-Catholic family—and I believe my mother married him while he was in a hypomanic period: charming, romantic, energetic, and promising her the moon. My mother was a quieter, insecure, anxious woman, and although it soon became apparent that my father had promised more than he could deliver, she did not have the self-confidence to leave and became depressed and withdrawn.

Fortunately, before I started school, often my father would take me to my maternal grandmother's house on his way to work in Syracuse, giving my mother a break and me a safe haven. Grandma Jessie was a nurturing presence, and she and I had a special relationship. I was a sensitive boy who loved animals. We couldn't afford to have pets; thus, I befriended all the dogs in the neighborhood and spent hours playing with them. Apparently, when I was four, my father took my sister and me to visit a friend who lived on a farm, and I got to ride my first horse. I'm told they had a hard time getting me to leave, and that afterwards I resolved to save every piece of money that came my way to purchase my own horse. Eventually, my mother explained that even if I could buy a horse, we couldn't afford to keep one. I'm told that I cried for days.

My parents, and especially my father, didn't know how to handle my sensitivity, and I was called a "cry baby" because I didn't like rough-and-tumble play or loud noises and would often break into tears. I also remember happy times as a small child. My father loved nature and novelty and one time he took my sister and me on an excursion to the Catskill Game Farm, an outdoor zoo four hours from us where we fed baby deer and giraffes. My mother loved to sing and taught my sister and me a series of rounds, including one in French (Frère Jacques) that I can sing to this

DOI: 10.4324/9781003036302-2

day. My mother had studied French in high school and she would teach me what she could remember. Also, her father, my grandfather George, learned a number of different languages, including French, Spanish, German, Portuguese, Russian, and Chinese. I was fascinated and would ask him to teach me words in the different languages. Unfortunately, he died when I was 12 years old. I would like to have known him better.

Elementary school

I was delighted when I was enrolled in half-day kindergarten at age 5, and I would come home and regale my mother with all that had happened during the morning. Sometimes I would embellish the stories to try to get her to smile; at other times I would come home and find her still in bed, depressed. I think it was around first grade that school became a refuge for me. I was an excellent student, and teachers generally liked me and would give me special projects to do. Some teachers would invite me to their homes on the weekends, perhaps sensing that I needed extra support. I loved to read and would take home seven to eight books each week from the public library and devour them. Also, starting in kindergarten, I began writing and illustrating my own small books. I have several in my possession still.

I also became more involved with music in elementary school, singing in the school choir and performing in the concert band, where I soon became the first-chair clarinet. I still love listening to all kinds of music and believe my experiences playing music with others taught me about collaboration and having a strong individual "voice" while also blending with others. Music also developed my nonverbal skills and helped me become more emotionally attuned and balanced.

Spiritual leanings

My other solace as a young boy was the Catholic Church. I became an altar boy in second grade, and for many years, I would get up at dawn and ride my bicycle the mile to church to assist with the early mass. I think I might even have gone on to be a priest, except for an incident when I was 13. With a lot of anxiety and confusion, I told the head priest in our parish that I thought I might be "homosexual." He asked me a few questions, then told me that I had to stop being an altar boy. In retrospect, I believe he was afraid—perhaps of himself—but of course, I took his reaction as a sign that something was terribly wrong with me. I hid in my room for several days, and then stubbornly refused to go to Sunday mass after that. I remember being quite depressed at the time and feeling there was something terribly wrong with me. Soon after I went to Quaker Meeting with my grandmother Jessie when I was visiting her, and I liked it. I would go whenever I could.

Growing up gay

In retrospect, apart from family struggles, one of the hardest parts of my childhood was that by the standards of the Italian immigrant community, I was a "sissy." I was not athletic and didn't like sports. The older boys in the neighborhood taunted me mercilessly, boys at school bullied me, and I dreaded gym class, where other children and certain teachers would ridicule me. My father was ashamed of me, and my mother would try to protect me from him, which then led him to accuse her of coddling me.

Of course, even though I was called a "sissy," I really had no idea what it meant to be gay. Then when I began to have sexual feelings around age 12–13, I realized they involved other boys, did some furtive reading, and concluded to my horror that what I had been accused of for years was actually true. I hid my sexuality from all but one close friend throughout high school. Fortunately, he did not reject me. Still, the enormous shame I felt was crushing, and I struggled with depression. Looking back, this was one of the most painful times in my life, and it is no coincidence that one of my professional interests in recent years has been to help people heal from shame.

Academic achievement and staying busy

I realize now that I coped with the pain of my early years by staying busy and devoting myself to achievement. In high school, I was in Boy Scouts, concert band, marching band, jazz band, model UN club, Spanish club, National Honor Society, and co-editor of the high school newspaper. I wrote and published poetry and short stories, worked most days at a local Italian restaurant, read avidly, took piano lessons, composed music, and occasionally did volunteer work. I did have several close friends, especially through band and the restaurant, and I began to mature socially. I was away from home a lot but was still close to my mother, who basked in my achievements and lived through me vicariously. I was particularly successful in music, math, and languages (like my maternal grandfather) and starting in seventh grade I won prizes each year in the National Spanish Examinations. I also studied French in high school and began to think about being a Romance language teacher. I was a finalist in the National Merit Scholarship competition and graduated Valedictorian of my high school class in 1974. These accomplishments were a way to feel better about myself and address my deep shame, and they worked to some extent. Other ways of healing had to wait.

College years

I feel fortunate now because it was almost by accident that I enrolled in Haverford College in the fall of 1974. As a National Merit finalist, many colleges recruited me, but I didn't know one from the other, there was no one in my high school to advise me, and both my parents were mystified by college, having never been themselves. Because I had attended Quaker meetings with my maternal grandmother I became interested in Haverford, which was founded by the Society of Friends, and at one point, I flew on my own to Philadelphia to interview there. I was awestruck by the stunning beauty of the campus and impressed by the college's honor code, which granted so much respect and responsibility to students. I was excited also that I could be close to the Philadelphia Orchestra and attend their weekly concerts. Haverford offered me a full scholarship, and after some thought, I chose to go there.

There are many ways that my years at Haverford affected me deeply. For the first time, I was in an academically challenging environment with top-notch professors and other accomplished students. This caused me anxiety at first, but I worked hard and found I could hold my own academically, and this helped my confidence enormously. Originally, I aspired to become a professor of Romance languages, and I spent part of my first two years studying abroad in both Spain and France. These experiences broadened my views and helped me learn about and appreciate other cultures. But, after taking a psycholinguistics course my sophomore year, I became interested in psychology, took a number of basic courses, and decided to major in that field. One psychology professor, Douglas A. Davis, took a special interest in me, and I began to do research with him on personality. Davis was an expert on Harry Stack Sullivan and on psychodiagnosis, and he and I spent hours in his office discussing both topics. I also began to study statistics and found it easy and interesting. A friend, Mona Cardell, and I did our senior psychology projects together, studying sex roles in heterosexual, lesbian, and gay male couples. We were supervised by Jeanne Marecek of Swarthmore College, an internationally recognized feminist social-clinical psychologist.

My sophomore year, I also came out publicly as gay. This was easier than it might have been because the Dean of Students at Haverford had recruited a social work graduate student from neighboring Bryn Mawr College to start a gay and lesbian student organization, called Gay People's Alliance (GPA). I remember attending my first meeting with a great deal of fear, but almost immediately I felt at home in a way I never had before. Over the next few years, I had several boyfriends and began to learn about romantic love and intimacy. I still remember the thrill of going to New York City in June 1976 to participate in the gay pride parade. After having felt so alone and ashamed for years, it was a thrill to walk up Fifth Avenue in the company of hundreds of thousands of gay, lesbian, and transgender people and our supporters.

Around this time, I also sought out psychotherapy, first at the Haverford student counseling center, and then at several community clinics in Philadelphia. I was terribly insecure and wanted to feel better about myself.

Haverford College paid for my sessions and my transportation. The therapists I saw were generally psychiatry residents or psychology interns and probably were not the most skilled. But they listened and asked questions and helped me learn about myself. One more seasoned therapist I saw was trained in Gestalt Therapy, and I had some eye-opening sessions involving more experiential techniques. Years later, when I was developing Therapeutic Assessment, I incorporated some of these powerful Gestalt techniques and experiences.

Finally, it is clear to me that the Quaker values of acceptance, respect, service to others, and openness "seeped" into me at Haverford, and these are embedded in Therapeutic Assessment. I remember one incident that affected me profoundly. My senior year, my boyfriend from Philadelphia stayed over one night in my dorm room. I had a white board on the outside of my door where friends could leave messages. When I came out the next morning, I saw that someone had written "Filthy Faggots!" in large letters on the white board. But there were numerous other messages also—from people in the dorm—supporting me and confronting the original writer. All that day, people stopped by in person to express support for me and my boyfriend. I felt so touched and held by the community, and the event helped me heal from the bullying I had experienced earlier in my life. Also, I learned first-hand that traumatic events can be transformed if we get enough support at the time from people who care about us.

I graduated from Haverford with a B.A. in psychology in May 1978 and spent almost a year after that in Göttingen, West Germany, where I had a friend from when I studied in France. I traveled a great deal around Europe and perfected my German. I had the fortune to land a job helping to teach beginning statistics to psychology students at the University of Göttingen. This was my first teaching experience, and I enjoyed inventing ways to make statistics alive and relevant for others. I decided I wanted to be a psychology professor and applied to graduate school in clinical psychology in the USA. I was accepted and decided to study at the University of Minnesota. I was awarded a full scholarship, and I began in the fall of 1979.

Graduate training at the University of Minnesota

A "dream team" of brilliant faculty taught clinical psychology at the University of Minnesota in the early 1980s, including Auke Tellegen, Paul Meehl, James Butcher, Steven Hollon, Philip Kendall, Irving Gottesman, David Lykken, and Norman Garmezy. Clinical students also took courses with other "giants" in the psychology department, including Kenneth MacCorquodale and Thomas Bouchard. Generally, applied clinical courses were taught by highly skilled adjunct faculty, most of whom were University of MN graduates and practicing clinicians. The combination of research and clinical training was stimulating and well-coordinated. I fell in love with personality assessment, which combined my interest in statistics with my growing fascination with people. Of course, James Butcher and Auke Tellegen taught us the MMPI, and an adjunct faculty member, Nancy Rains, taught us the Rorschach, using Exner's Comprehensive System. We were given the opportunity to take both tests before we learned them, and I was impressed by how accurately they captured me. The summer after my first year, I had my first practicum placement at the adult inpatient psychiatry ward of Hennepin County Medical Center (HCMC). This was an important and moving experience that influenced me in many ways.

First, as a student, I was allowed to participate in team meetings and case conferences for the psychiatric inpatients I worked with. Since my undergraduate studies with Douglas Davis, I had been fascinated with psychodiagnosis, and I got to see diagnosis in action in these meetings. I began work on a paper that was published in the *Journal of Abnormal Psychology* my third year of graduate school, "Base Rates, Utilities, and DSM-III: Shortcomings of Fixed-Rule Systems of Psychodiagnosis" (Finn, 1982). This article grew out of my observations at HCMC, and it was my first time navigating the review process at a major psychology journal on my own. By that point I had asked Auke Tellegen to be my doctoral advisor, and he supported me a great deal. The published article received a fair amount of notice, and Thomas Widiger (who has a chapter in this volume) wrote a challenging comment to which I was invited to respond. Again, Auke Tellegen helped me write a clear and balanced reply. This entire experience with writing and publishing taught me a lot about academic clinical psychology and supported my burgeoning goal to seek an academic position after I got my Ph.D.

Second, in my practica at HCMC and in others during graduate school, I began to have striking experiences of the utility and power of psychological assessment. I wrote about one of these events in my book, *In Our Clients' Shoes* (Finn, 2007, pp. 17–20), where my giving Rorschach feedback to a man with chronic schizophrenia transformed both him and me. This experience impressed me so much that I returned to the University of MN and asked Butcher, Tellegen, Meehl, and others if anyone had ever written about the therapeutic aspects of psychological assessment. At that time, assessment was taught exclusively as a way to diagnose and label clients, so as to plan interventions or track the efficacy of an intervention. My academic mentors were intrigued but did not know where to point me in the literature. I had more success talking to the senior psychologists at HCMC during two practicum placements, my internship, and two-year fellowship there.

Psychology internship and fellowship at Hennepin County Medical Center

Ada Hegion and Kenneth Hampton were my main supervisors at HCMC, and both were wise, highly skilled clinicians with a broad view of the value of psychological assessment. I remember one early assessment where

I administered the WAIS to a young man who was seeing Dr. Hegion for therapy; he was having trouble at work because his boss saw him as "lazy and not trying hard." I remember carefully scoring the WAIS and telling Dr. Hegion that the man had a Verbal IQ of 105 but a Performance IQ of 85, "which is highly statistically significant." She praised my newfound competence and then asked, "What do you think it's like to be a person with scores like those?" I was completely dumbfounded, as none of my assessment professors had ever asked a question like that. Dr. Hegion then led me through an interesting thought process—inquiring whether I thought that Verbal IQ or Performance IQ was more relevant when we informally estimate how intelligent someone is. I guessed it might be Verbal IQ, and she agreed. "Then what would happen," she queried, "if we believed someone was of average intelligence, but then asked him to do a task that required non-verbal skills—not knowing his Performance IQ was low average?" I exclaimed with excitement, "We might see him as unmotivated or as not trying," suddenly understanding something important about our mutual client. This was the first time I grasped how psychological assessment could help us "get in someone's shoes" in a new way, and it transformed my view of assessment as a potential "empathy magnifier." That view is fundamental to Therapeutic Assessment.

Kenneth Hampton, my second major supervisor, was a brilliant Rorschacher and clinical interviewer. He taught me how to listen "with my third ear" to clients, and he sensitively helped me sort through the myriad of personal reactions I had to the clients on the inpatient ward. Years later, I wrote about one of these experiences—and Dr. Hampton's wise supervision—in a paper called: "How Psychological Assessment Taught Me Compassion and Firmness" (Finn, 2005). In fact, it was through my work at HCMC that I began to understand that if I were committed to doing meaningful psychological assessments, I would need to face and learn about aspects of myself that I had never explored.

Besides training us in psychological assessment, Ken Hampton, Ada Hegion, and the Chief of Psychology, Zigfrieds Stelmachers, also supervised our psychotherapy cases, listening to audiotapes we made of our sessions. This was incredibly helpful, and they also gave our intern class a gift by frequently letting us observe sessions they did with clients. It was only much later in life that I realized how rare this opportunity was, and how generous and brave these three supervisors (and their clients) were. Years later, when I developed TA, I was convinced that showing videos of my work with actual clients was essential for training others, and I also developed the practice of conducting live Therapeutic Assessments while others observed.

More psychotherapy

Thankfully, in my second year of graduate school, I had the courage to ask Ada Hegion to help me find a psychotherapist, and for the next 3.5

years I worked with a highly skilled psychologist, Dr. Millie Huttenmaier. Although as mentioned, I had seen several therapists during my college years, this was my first time connecting with someone who could lead me into deep emotional work. In our sessions, I began to name and unpack the enormous shame I carried from my childhood and from being part of a despised group (gay men). And with Dr. Huttenmaier's support, I began to grieve—in a way I had never done, and this was essential to my healing. The whole experience was mysterious and transformative, and I began to reap the benefits.

For instance, I began to date more compatible men. (My early relationships had been pretty disastrous.) In 1982, I met Jim Durkel in a gay men's support group, and over time we became partners. Jim was a speech-language pathologist and audiologist working in the St. Paul public schools. He loved animals, weird theatre, and food—just as I did. We moved in together in early 1984, and Jim was a huge emotional and practical support as I wrote my dissertation and applied for academic jobs. I also began to reconnect with my parents and siblings, from whom I had been distant for years. They all loved and accepted Jim, and this helped me feel closer to them and more "whole" myself.

Working at Lesbian/Gay Community Services

Another important experience during graduate school was working part-time at a newly formed gay and lesbian community mental health center in Minneapolis called Lesbian/Gay Community Services (LGCS). Although I was a novice therapist, I was paid to see individual clients under supervision. (Ken Hampton at HCMC was also willing to help with me these clients.) I met a young social work therapist in the LGCS supervision group, John Driggs, and we became friends. I was surprised when I found out that John was heterosexual, as he had a lot of understanding of the lives of gay men and lesbians. Besides seeing individual clients, for several years, John and I ran a series of short-term (eight to ten week) gay men's support/therapy groups. Most of the men were dealing with issues of shame and its effect on their relationships, and in classic fashion, as John and I worked to help our clients with these issues, I also reaped huge benefits. My long friendship with John has sustained me through some difficult times.

Before I left the Twin Cities in 1984, John and I decided to write a book for gay men about all we had learned doing our groups, and we eventually published *Intimacy Between Men: How to Find and Keep Gay Love Relationships* (1990, Dutton). Working on this book was very important in multiple ways. First, our editor took John and me in hand and taught us how to write in a way that was more accessible and impactful. This "writing school" has served me well ever since. Second, the book hit a chord among gay men and was quite popular. With the publisher's support, John and I traveled the country giving talks and workshops, and this helped me grow more comfortable as a public speaker and teacher. Third, the book was financially successful, which gave me the funds I needed later to start an important venture.

As I neared the end of my doctorate, I was faced with the decision of what kind of position I wanted after graduate school. I had come to love clinical work and the feeling of helping people; thus, I seriously considered applying for work in a hospital or clinic. But I also loved research and writing and decided in the end to look for an academic position teaching clinical psychology. Luckily, I had several offers from excellent programs.

Being a faculty member at the University of Texas

In August 1984, my partner Jim and I moved to Texas, and in September, I began as an Assistant Professor at the University of Texas at Austin. Like many clinical psychology programs at the time, UT saw itself as training mainly academics and researchers, and many of the clinical faculty had not worked with clients in years. Nevertheless, most of the clinical program's graduates took clinical jobs, so the faculty also wanted to ensure they were trained adequately. I was hired as a young psychologist who loved research, was a good statistician, and thought rigorously about clinical matters—and hence was respected—but who also loved clinical work and could teach applied clinical courses. The role served me well at the time, and before long I was promoted to being the Associate Director of Clinical Psychology. One of my tasks was to develop and coordinate student practicum placements in Austin, and in this way, I came to know many fine clinicians in Austin.

In retrospect, teaching core psychological assessment courses for UT clinical students was an absolute gift, as I was forced to clarify and advance my ideas about psychotherapy and psychological assessment as a potential intervention. I began to lecture to first-year students on what I called an "interpersonal model of psychological assessment" (tipping my hat to Harry Stack Sullivan), and remembering my supervisors at Hennepin County Medical Center, each year I would assess clients live as students watched from behind a one-way mirror. I also saw the assessment classes as opportunities for graduate students to learn and grow, and I intentionally structured the assessment sequence so it paralleled a psychological assessment of the students themselves. After some years, I wrote a chapter about this way of teaching a core assessment class (Finn, 1998).

The years at UT were also an opportunity to experiment with new ways of practicing psychological assessment and to do research in this area. I was lucky to work with several talented graduate students, and in particular with Mary Tonsager and Hale Martin, both of whom served as my teaching assistants for the clinical assessment courses. Mary did her Master's thesis on the therapeutic effects of collaboratively giving clients feedback on the MMPI-2, and this was one of the first studies to document the direct interventional power of psychological assessment (Finn & Tonsager, 1992). Mary and I also wrote an article laying out fundamental features of the Therapeutic Assessment paradigm (Finn & Tonsager, 1997). Hale and I have collaborated many times in writing (e.g., Finn & Martin, 1997), and he is now a Professor of Psychology at the University of Denver, where he teaches and writes about Therapeutic Assessment (see Martin, 2018). Jan Kamphuis, now Professor of Psychology at the University of Amsterdam, came to UT a bit later but proved to be another able writing partner. Like me, Jan is "good with numbers" and we wrote a chapter explaining base rates to practicing clinicians (Finn & Kamphuis, 1995). Also, much later, Jan and his doctoral student, Hilde de Sager, conducted an important study on Therapeutic Assessment with clients with severe personality pathology (De Saeger et al., 2014).

I also met several colleagues during this time who greatly influenced my thoughts about assessment. William Swann, a social psychologist at UT, was doing groundbreaking work on *self-verification theory*, which helps to explain the human tendency to take in information that confirms our self-views and reject information that does not (Cf. Swann, 1997). Swann and I discussed the implications of self-verification theory for providing assessment feedback to clients, and we did research together that led to my concepts of "Level 1, Level 2, and Level 3 information" (Cf. Finn, 1996, 2007).

While I was at UT, I began a small private practice with another faculty member from the School Psychology Program, Deborah Tharinger, and this was instrumental in my continuing to formulate a model of assessment as a brief therapeutic intervention. I coined the phrase Therapeutic Assessment for this new approach, which was still taking form. I began watching videotapes of all my assessment sessions with clients and experimenting with different ways of using tests as therapeutic tools. One practice seemed extremely useful, of asking clients at the beginning of an assessment to pose questions about what they wanted to learn about themselves, and this was incorporated into the Finn and Tonsager (1992) study I referred to earlier.

During these years I also expanded my clinical skills by reading and getting advanced training in multiple interventions, for example Self Psychology (with Ernest Wolf), Systems Centered Therapy (with Yvonne Agazarian), and Control Mastery Theory (with Elayne Lansford). I also had the great fortune to study Family Therapy with Carol Middelberg, a former faculty member of the Chicago Family Therapy Institute who had moved to Austin. Carol was instrumental in my developing Therapeutic Assessment with children, Therapeutic Assessment with adolescents, and Therapeutic Assessment with couples, and in my understanding how assessment could be used as a systemic intervention. I "appropriated" useful concepts and techniques from all these and other psychotherapy schools and incorporated them into Therapeutic Assessment, and this helped TA become more flexible and powerful.

Attending the Society for Personality Assessment for the first time

In 1992, James Butcher asked me to submit a workshop for the annual meeting of the Society for Personality Assessment (SPA). (He was CE chair.) Somehow, I had never heard of SPA before, but I was honored, and in 1993 in San Francisco I presented a one-day training entitled "Using Psychological Assessment as a Therapeutic Intervention." Little did I know that this event would be a turning point in my life. The conference program was full of famous assessment psychologists such as John Exner, Philip Erdberg, Irving Weiner, and Paul Lerner. And there was one person I longed to meet: Constance Fischer. Some years earlier, a friend had given me a copy of Fischer's (1985) book, *Individualizing Psychological Assessment*, and I had stayed awake all night reading it with awe and excitement. Fischer went far beyond my fledgling ideas about assessor–client collaboration, articulating a coherent philosophy of science based in phenomenological psychology that grounded many of the assessment practices I had been developing on my own. The next morning, I told my partner, Jim, "This book is 30 years ahead of its time!" (I think history has borne me out.) When I arrived in San Francisco I left a message for Dr. Fischer at the conference hotel asking if I might invite her to lunch. She was kind enough to come and greet me the morning of my workshop and apologized for not being able to attend. I gave her a copy of my handouts, and we agreed to have lunch the next day. When we met, I found out that that Fischer had read all my handouts that night and had been excited and moved by the way I was integrating her work. That lunch was the beginning of a lasting friendship and a thrilling collaboration. Until she retired, Connie and I would have dinner together each year at the SPA annual meeting and plot "how to take over the world for Collaborative Assessment." Over the years, Connie and I did many presentations together at SPA, APA, and all over the world at the congresses of the International Society for Rorschach and Projective methods. I also had the honor of helping compile a volume of her collected papers, *On The Way to Collaborative Psychological Assessment* (Fischer, 2017). Connie inspired me and many of us in the psychological assessment community with her clear thinking, elegant writing, and palpable humanity. Although she is retired now, we still speak frequently, and I am still grateful for her friendship and mentorship.

Another person I met at SPA who influenced me and my work was Leonard Handler, a brilliant and innovative clinician, teacher, and writer. I heard Len speak at SPA in the mid-1990s about his "Fantasy Animal Drawing and Storytelling Technique" and was completely captivated. Len invited me several times to lecture on TA to his students at the University of Tennessee at Knoxville, and it was through Len that I met J. D. Smith, Len's last graduate student, who is now an expert in TA and has done a great deal of important research on TA. Besides bringing us J.D., Len influenced many of our practices in Therapeutic Assessment, especially regarding TA with children. He also co-edited the Collaborative/ Therapeutic Assessment casebook (Finn, Fischer, & Handler, 2012) with Connie and me. I remember Len as someone who deeply respected the wisdom of his clients, believed in the power of psychological assessment to change people's lives, and brought creativity and playfulness to psychological assessment. He also had a willingness to judiciously "bend the rules" of traditional assessment in order to help his clients. For example, Len used playful techniques to understand clients' test responses, such as asking them (after the standardized administration of the Rorschach), "If this monster on Card IV could talk, what would he say?" Len coined the word "Extended Inquiry" for this technique, and we have incorporated both the term and the practice in TA.

Back to SPA, my association with this organization was crucial to my developing TA and spreading it to others. First, having an opportunity to interact with world-class assessment psychologists and researchers helped me develop my ideas and grow personally. Over the years, I consulted with people such as Irving Weiner, Philip Erdberg, Paul Lerner, Carol George, Julie Cradock O'Leary, and Yossi Ben-Porath when I needed help with clients, and I always learned a great deal. Second, it was incredibly exciting to present on Therapeutic Assessment and other topics in symposia, workshops, and round tables at SPA annual meetings and to have people be interested in my work. In fact, many of the chapters in my book *In Our Clients' Shoes* (Finn, 2007) were adapted from presentations I gave at SPA meetings or first published in the society's journal, *The Journal of Personality Assessment (JPA)*. And people who heard about TA for the first time at SPA meetings or by reading *JPA* went on to attend TA trainings in Austin, or invited me and my colleagues to present workshops in their local areas. SPA also published a DVD in 2009 called *Pioneers of Collaborative Assessment*, which helped spread the word about TA. It contains lectures by me, Connie Fischer, and Len Handler and a discussion facilitated by Dr. Radhika Krishnamurthy, who has long been a supporter of TA. Third, I had the opportunity to serve on the SPA Board from 1996 to 2005, first as Representative-at-Large and then as President-elect, President, and Past President. I learned a great deal from this experience about managing organizations, and this helped me when I founded the Therapeutic Assessment Institute in 2009. Fourth, SPA gave me two Martin Mayman Awards for publications in *JPA* (Finn, 2003, 2011) and greatly honored me in 2011 with the Bruno Klopfer Award for Distinguished Lifetime Contributions to Personality Assessment. Of course, it always feels good to receive awards, but the Klopfer Award had special meaning to me; it affirmed that TA was a valuable paradigm shift and helped quiet my inner doubts, which stemmed in part from criticisms that had been levied against me and TA over the years.

More psychotherapy: A deep dive into restructuring my character

On the personal front, the late 1980s and 1990s were a time of rapid personal growth and transformation, spurred by several things. First, in 1984, just after we arrived in Austin, my partner Jim tested positive for HIV, while I tested negative. Jim's having HIV was a huge blow for both of us, and it greatly stressed our fledgling relationship. We literally expected that Jim might die at any time (although his health was generally good), and this terrified us both and affected our relationship. I realized later that I reacted as I had to my difficult family situation growing up—by withdrawing into myself, striving for achievement, and keeping busy. Understandably, Jim felt alone and got depressed; this reminded me of my depressed mother, and I pulled back further. The good news is that these events spurred us to seek couples therapy, which we did for almost eight years, and I also went into individual and group psychotherapy. Gradually I went deeper into a process of self-exploration than I had in any of my previous psychotherapies. For three to four years, I did individual therapy two to three times a week, group therapy one time a week, couples therapy with Jim once a week, and I was in various consultation/training groups that also stretched and supported me. With such a broad emotional "safety net" in place, my character defenses—which had helped me survive a difficult early life—loosened, and I let myself "fall apart" to some extent. I was still able to work and help others, but I became aware of shame, depression, and grief that I had successfully held at bay for years. For several months I was plagued with daily thoughts of suicide. I got through this period thanks to my support network, learned a great deal about myself (and the process of long-term psychotherapy), and gradually transformed into a humbler, less serious, more playful and relational person; all this greatly influenced my work with clients and the development of Therapeutic Assessment.

Another event deepened my work in psychotherapy and led to an important breakthrough. In 1995 I discovered that my office manager had embezzled a large amount of money from me over the course of a year. There had been many small signs that something was amiss that I had completely ignored, and in fact, I had a long history at that point in my life of being taken advantage of in various relationships. I remember walking into my therapist's office and saying, "I want this to be the last time I let something like this happen to me," and him saying, "I've been waiting." In our subsequent work, I discovered how I had dealt with my early traumas through denial and being overly "positive" about people; I also had largely dissociated my assertiveness and anger, which set me up to be repeatedly victimized. I slowly reclaimed my anger and assertiveness, became less naïve, and I haven't been taken advantage of in a major way since. I also learned about dissociation of affect states, and this has informed a great deal of my work in Therapeutic Assessment (e.g., see Finn, 1996b, 2011).

A similar transformation was that I became less of a "rescuer," both in my life and with clients. I think like many clinicians, I so enjoyed "helping" that I didn't always confront or "contain" clients enough. I came to see that being overly compassionate was not respectful and did not help my clients (Finn, 2005).

This round of psychotherapy also improved my ability to be in an intimate relationship, and Jim and I grew closer and we stopped waiting for him to die. We realized the best way to live was to hold mortality in mind and build the kind of loving relationship we wanted. We affirmed our hope for our relationship by applying to the Austin Quaker Meeting to be married. (At that point, Quakers had been performing marriages for same-sex couples for many years.) On November 2, 1991, almost 200 friends and family gathered in a Meeting for Worship at Austin Friends Meeting to watch Jim and me take our vows. That day stands out to me still as one where I felt accepted and loved. Jim and I also reaped the benefits from all our work in therapy. I learned what it means to hold someone in mind and to love them, and what it feels like to have this in return. Our relationship changed me profoundly and made me a better person and clinician. Also, Jim helped me in so many ways that I am certain I could not have developed Therapeutic Assessment without his support.

One other experience with Jim also affected me and my work. Both Jim and I loved children, and we had initially planned to be parents; but we abandoned this idea when he was diagnosed with AIDS. This was a big loss, and we were excited and honored when our friends, Ray Condon and Dale Rudin, asked us to be "godfathers" when their daughter, Tessa, was born in August 1995. Although being a godfather is much easier than being a parent, my relationship with Tessa over the years has given me some of the same experiences I would have had with my own children—such as "losing it" occasionally out of frustration and needing to repair. As a result, I have more empathy for parents and less anger at my own parents, and this helped me especially as I developed Therapeutic Assessment with children and families.

I am very aware that I was incredibly privileged to have had the opportunity to do extensive psychotherapy with excellent therapists, and it has left me a firm believer in the power of psychotherapy to transform lives. Of course, when anxious, I can still become dismissing or start working compulsively. But these things happen much less frequently now, and most days I feel present, happy, and full of energy and gratitude.

My life with horses

Not infrequently when I show videos of myself doing TA with challenging clients, someone asks how I became so good at balancing kindness and firmness. Often, I reply "from horses!" In 1996, when I was 40 years old, in part because of the therapy work I just described, I began to cut my work hours and get in touch with other needs and interests. As I wrote about earlier, my whole life I have felt drawn to animals and to horses in particular, and I thought, "Well, I'm not getting any younger! I would like to ride horses." It was not hard to find a riding teacher in Austin, and after a few tries, I discovered a woman who used a method called Parelli Natural Horsemanship (PNH). This way of working with horses is based on ethology and teaches humans how to read and respond to horses, so they perceive you as a strong, benevolent "herd leader." I began studying PNH and loved the experience, and in 1998, I bought my first horse, Harley. One year later, I bought a second horse, Lefty, and Jim and I purchased land and moved to Elgin, a small town 25 miles outside of Austin (Figure 2.1).

Learning to be a competent rider helped me tune into and "make friends" with my body, quite a task after the awful experiences of sports bullying I had as a child. And training my horses taught me patience and empathy, and helped me integrate my assertiveness and aggression in a way I never had before. As just mentioned, these were issues I was working on in psychotherapy also, but they came to the fore with horses, who are incredibly sensitive "biofeedback machines" for the people around them. I not only became a skilled horseman, but the lessons I learned via horses helped me personally and in my work with traumatized clients. I truly believe that Therapeutic Assessment would not be what it is today without

Figure 2.1 With Harley and Lefty in 2001.

my relationship to horses. I still ride two to three times a week and cherish the hours I spend with my horses.

Leaving UT and Establishing the Center for Therapeutic Assessment

In 1993, I became more and more aware of my discontent with my academic position at the University of Texas, and I decided to resign and go into private practice. This was a difficult decision, as there were many things I liked about being at UT. However, I felt called to develop and spread Therapeutic Assessment, and most of my time was consumed by the duties of a fulltime faculty member. In addition, as I healed in therapy and in relationship with Jim, I felt a strong urge to help others directly. Last, in retrospect, there were things about the UT department that made it hard for me to feel at home. For example, one day, one of the Full Professors called me and several senior faculty into his office to show a "hilarious" clip from the Johnny Carson show. The skit was callously demeaning of gay men, and while they all were sniggering, I felt confused and upset. They all knew I was gay and had met Jim. How could they think I would find this video amusing? In today's language, this was a "micro-aggression," and experiencing it (and others) has given me empathy for people in despised groups. I also understand how helpless such events make one feel; because of my shame and internalized homophobia, I said nothing that day and went to my office and stared at the wall. I had no way to confront these men, and I began to think seriously of leaving.

Of course, all my colleagues at UT thought I was "crazy" to give up a tenure track faculty position, but I felt it was right thing to do. In September 1993, I rented and furnished a large office in Austin (using my earnings from the publication of *Intimacy Between Men*) and opened the Center for Therapeutic Assessment. I was invited to become an adjunct faculty member at UT, a position I still hold, and this has allowed me to continue to work with graduate students and take part in university life. During the summer of 1993, I invited several well-established clinicians to lunch whom I had met in my role as practicum coordinator for clinical psychology graduate students. I told these colleagues about Therapeutic Assessment and invited them to refer their "hardest clients" to me for a free TA. Several of them did so, and they were impressed by how much TA helped their clients. Soon, referrals began to pore in. I had opened the Center with two assessors: myself and Mary Tonsager. Seven months later, there were seven Ph.D. psychologists learning and practicing TA under my supervision, and we had a 9-month waiting list. We became a professional community as well as a center, and this was necessary because of the mutual support we needed to do TA at a high level. I worked long hours, but I didn't mind; I was thrilled by the chance to experiment with and develop TA further, especially its application to child and adolescent assessments and to couples. The word about TA spread, and our Center began to do training courses on TA and on the collaborative use of different psychological tests. I also continued to write and published a brief manual on using the MMPI-2 as a therapeutic intervention (Finn, 1996a).

In retrospect, the success of TA during this period was remarkable in that traditional psychological assessment was facing huge challenges from 3rd-party payers, who asserted there was no evidence that assessment led to better outcomes for clients or more effective or efficient interventions. Many hospitals had stopped doing psychological assessments on their psychiatric inpatients, and assessments of outpatient clients were increasingly limited, causing a crisis for many psychological assessors. I confronted this situation at the Center for Therapeutic Assessment by spending hours with insurance gatekeepers explaining how Therapeutic Assessment was different than traditional assessment and how it might save them money. After witnessing the outcome of our assessments, several large insurance companies made exceptions from their usual practices to fund TA.

Building on this success, Hale Martin and I wrote a chapter about TA under managed care (Finn & Martin, 1997). Perhaps because of this work, in 1996 I was invited to chair the Psychological Assessment Work Group (PAWG), an ad-hoc committee convened by the Practice Directorate of the American Psychological Association. The group's charge was to document challenges to psychological assessment at the time and compile evidence of the validity and utility of psychological assessment. I enlisted Gregory Meyer, a brilliant colleague I had met at SPA, and one result was an article documenting the reliability and validity of psychological tests compared to medical tests (Meyer et al., 2001). The piece has been widely cited, and I believe it had some impact on assessment reimbursement.

The CTA moved to its present Austin location in 2000 and reorganized into a collective, so I am no longer everyone's boss. This restructuring recognized that all CTA members are highly trained in TA and have areas of expertise that complement my own. We meet bi-weekly for peer consultation and often work together on complex assessments; I seek input on my TA cases as does everyone else. The current TA certified members of the CTA are Lionel Chudzik, Marita Frackowiak, Melissa Lehmann, Dale Rudin, Pamela Schaber, and Kate Thomas.

TA starts to spread

Starting in the mid-1990s, I also began to get invitations to travel and teach about TA, both nationally and internationally. This did not always go smoothly, and early on several colleagues walked out of TA workshops and demanded their money back. It seemed they were incensed by the very idea of blending assessment and therapy. Other audiences were more receptive. For example, two colleagues from SPA, Caroline Purves and Barbara Mercer, invited me to present at WestCoast Children's Center

(WCC), a community mental health clinic in Oakland, CA. My initial visit led to a fruitful collaboration with WCC over the years, including a series of live TA workshops co-taught by myself and Carol Middelberg, Caroline Purves, and Barbara Mercer. WestCoast clinicians pioneered adapting TA to economically disadvantaged, diverse families with high levels of trauma, and I learned a great deal from working with WCC colleagues and clients. Also, WCC clinicians have produced a series of moving publications about their work with TA (e.g., Mercer et al., 2016).

Starting in the mid-1990s, the Swedish Rorschach Society invited me for a number of years to present on TA in Stockholm, and this led to trainings in Gothenburg, Copenhagen, Helsinki, and Oslo, and several live TA workshops in Stockholm. I learned that the core values of TA fit well with Scandinavian culture, and I worked closely with Lena Lillieroth, a psychologist from Stockholm who learned and then helped teach TA in Sweden, Finland, and Denmark. During this time period I also was invited to do TA workshops in Melbourne, Australia, and in Amsterdam.

The Therapeutic Assessment Project (TAP) at the University of Texas

In 2002 my colleague and friend, Deborah Tharinger, and I began a multi-year research project at UT on TA with children (TA-C) and TA with adolescents (TA-A). The study clinicians were doctoral students in the School Psychology Training Program. This research led to many refinements in TA-C, such as the practice of inviting parents to watch testing sessions of their child over a video link or from behind a one-way mirror. We found this allowed clinicians to "scaffold" new narratives about the child and family as the assessment progressed, rather than presenting them to parents all at once at the end. We also "borrowed" and refined a practice illustrated in Connie Fischer's (1985/1994) book, of writing feedback fables for children at the end of a TA-C. I am grateful to Deborah Tharinger for her leadership and collaboration on this project and the many articles that came out of it (e.g., Tharinger et al., 2009).

Publication of *In Our Clients' Shoes*

In fact, although I love writing and am excited by this mysterious process, I am not a fast writer. I used to feel bad that I have not written down more of what I know. But now I generally accept that I have my own pace and have to live with that. For years I aspired to write a "how-to" book for adult TA that went far beyond my 1996 MMPI-2 manual, and I did write a number of chapters but never finished it. Finally, as a stopgap, I collected a number of paper presentations and articles on TA, wrote several new pieces to fill out the model, and in 2007 Erlbaum and Associates published my book, *In Our Clients' Shoes: Theory and Techniques of Therapeutic*

Assessment. I am pleased by how this work has been received, including being translated and published in Italian, Korean, Japanese, French, Spanish, and Portuguese. Many people have been introduced to TA through this volume, and I am currently working on a sequel comprised of papers and articles I have written since 2007.

Shortly after *In Our Clients' Shoes* was published, I stopped seeing clients at the CTA in Austin to concentrate on supervision, training, and writing. My colleagues at the CTA threw a huge book release party for me, and coincidentally, I received a request from several Italian psychologists to visit me in Austin. I invited them to the book party, and I still remember greeting Drs. Patrizia Bevilacqua and Filippo Aschieri at the door to the CTA and spontaneously embracing them, although we had never met before. I have never felt so immediately at ease with two people. The two of them stayed for the festivities and spent several days in Austin learning about TA. They were enthusiastic, and in January 2008, Filippo came to Austin for a three-month internship at the CTA. With his fluent English and excellent training in psychological assessment and family therapy, Filippo took to TA like a duck to water.

TA spreads further internationally

Bevilacqua and Aschieri invited me to Milan to do an introductory TA training in April 2008, and I began to go there twice a year, presenting at Catholic University of the Sacred Heart. Milanese clinicians received me warmly, and in 2010, with the support of Professor Vittorio Cigoli at Catholic University, I co-founded the European Center for Therapeutic Assessment (ECTA) in Milan, with Bevilacqua, Aschieri, and a number of Bevilacqua's former students as our staff. We began to see clients at the ECTA and to do TA trainings all over Italy, and *In Our Clients' Shoes* was published in Italian. I gradually learned Italian, and Jim and I began taking our vacations in this beautiful, historic country. Perhaps, because I grew up in a village with second-generation Italian immigrants, I felt both excited and "at home" in Italy. The ECTA flourished and is still going strong at the time I write this chapter. Filippo Aschieri is now Associate Professor at Catholic University of the Sacred Heart, and he and Francesca Fantini, another ECTA Board member, have made many substantial contributions to the TA literature. Most important, I learned that TA could be adapted to yet another culture, and that people around the world are more similar than different. As I write, the current staff of ECTA (all certified in TA) are Drs. Filippo Aschieri, Cristina Augello, Camillo Caputo, Cristina Corvi, Erica Dell'Acqua, and Francesca Fantini (Figure 2.2).

Several other European developments also created new opportunities for TA. In 2008, at the International Rorschach Congress in Leuven, Belgium, Jan Kamphuis introduced me to Hilde De Saeger, a gifted clinical psychologist on staff at the Viersprong Institute, a clinic in the Netherlands

Figure 2.2 With the staff of the ECTA, Milan, 2015.

specializing in the treatment of persons with severe personality disorders. Hilde was fascinated with TA and invited me to train her assessment team at the Viersprong. I visited multiple times and did supervision of the team over Skype. Then, Hilde and her team conducted the first Randomized Controlled Trial of the full TA model for Hilde's Ph.D. at the University of Amsterdam (De Saeger et al., 2014). Since that time, Hilde has overseen the creation of a robust TA program at the Viersprong, where adults and adolescents are now assessed. In addition, De Saeger and Kamphuis regularly provide training on TA to Dutch psychologists.

In 2009, I met Dr. Alessandro Crisi in Prague at the Summer Seminar of the International Society for Rorschach and Projective Methods. There I learned about his work with the Wartegg Drawing Completion Test (WDCT), a performance-based personality test of the same vintage as the Rorschach. I was impressed with Dr. Crisi's wisdom and humility, and I learned that he had done for the Wartegg what John Exner did for the Rorschach—standardizing its administration and coding system, collecting norms, and conducting many validity studies on WDCT scores and indices. The resulting Crisi Wartegg System (CWS) intrigued me, and Dr. Crisi invited me to administer the test to one of my clients and send it to him to interpret blind. I still remember the amazement when I read his report to my colleagues at the Center for Therapeutic Assessment. As a result, in 2010, the CTA invited Crisi to Austin to teach us the CWS, and eventually many of us traveled to Rome, Italy, for advanced training. Many of us find the WDCT to be a valuable tool that fosters collaboration with TA clients, and that Extended Inquiries of clients' drawings often lead to breakthroughs. CWS workshops have now taken place all over the USA, and Crisi has taught at the University of Denver after being invited by Hale Martin. One of the members of the American TA community, Jacob Palm, has worked with Crisi in collecting American norms, running training seminars, and in publishing the CWS manual in English. And along the way, Alessandro became a dear friend, got excited about TA, and helped sponsor TA trainings in Rome.

Another international development around this time was the interest in TA in Argentina spurred by Isidro Sanz. My first workshop there was in 2010, and recently Ernesto Pais is carrying the TA torch farther. Also in 2010, I received invitations to present on TA in Japan, thanks to Noriko Nakamura, whom I had met through Rorschach Workshops and the International Society for Rorschach and Projective Methods. And Lionel Chudzik, a friend of Filippo Aschieri who lived in France, began attending TA trainings in Milan and brought TA back to France to his work with clients in mandatory treatment for aggressive and sexual offenses.

The Therapeutic Assessment Institute is formed

As TA began to spread further, I began to think about how to ensure its longevity and foster its development. So, in 2009, I gathered a group of people who had studied and were passionate about TA, asking them to think with me about further developing and spreading TA. Rich Armington, a friend and colleague who was a trainer in Systems Centered Group Therapy facilitated the meeting. The discussions were exciting, and we agreed to form the Therapeutic Assessment Institute (TAI). I proposed a group project, and in June 2010, we held our first TA Immersion Course, a five-day TA "boot camp" involving lectures, videos, and role plays, where participants practiced collaborative assessment under close supervision. The intensive format, with 13 "faculty" and 36 "students," was successful, and many of the attendees from that first training are still involved in the TA community today. In addition, the TAI has held seven TA Immersion Courses since then and two international conferences (in 2014 and 2017), training hundreds of psychologists in the TA and fostering connections between assessors from all over the world.

The fledgling TAI also took on other projects that have helped TA, including a twice-yearly online newsletter, *The TA Connection*, which is under the able editorship of J. D. Smith. The newsletter has provided a venue for many useful articles on TA, as well announcements of upcoming trainings and recent publications concerning TA. The TAI also undertook a major revision of the TA website I had put up in 2009, www. therapeuticassessment.com, and it now includes a "landing video" explaining TA to the public and to professionals alike.

The TAI was formally incorporated as a non-profit in 2014, with the following Board of Directors: myself, Filippo Aschieri, Lionel Chudzik, Hilde De Saeger, Diane Engelman, Barton Evans, Francesca Fantini, Marita Frackowiak, Jan Kamphuis, Lena Lillieroth, Melissa Lehmann, Hale Martin, Noriko Nakamura, Dale Rudin, J. D. Smith, and Deborah Tharinger. There has been some turnover since then, but I now feel that when I die, TA is in good hands. I look forward to our Board retreats each year and to working with this fine group of people. In 2016, the TAI created the possibility for people in the Collaborative/Therapeutic Assessment community to become TAI "members," which gives them discounts to TAI trainings and case supervision, and access to the TA list serve. At the current time, there are over 200 TAI members.

Personal crisis and discovering resiliency

In June 2011, while we were on a flight from Italy to Austin, Jim experienced severe abdominal pain that eventually led to his being diagnosed with multiple myeloma—a type of blood cancer. The state-of-the-art treatment at the time was a bone marrow transplant, and in December 2011, Jim and I moved to San Antonio, TX, for a month, so he could have this procedure. Our friends supported us a great deal, and we felt uplifted by them. Jim responded well, and by March 2012, he was declared to be in remission. We were relieved and elated. Then suddenly in April, small things began to go wrong. Jim had a good 56th birthday on May 13, but on May 21 I rushed him to the hospital with difficulty breathing. The initial diagnosis was pneumonia, but he worsened rapidly, and the next day Jim was sedated and put on a respirator. It turned out the multiple myeloma had mutated and returned. Jim never was conscious again, and on May 28, 2012—our 30th anniversary as a couple—I gave permission for Jim to be disconnected from life support. It was the hardest decision I have ever made. A group of close friends joined me in the ICU that morning around Jim's bed, and we sang, talked, and caressed him as he passed. It was a moving experience, and of course, I was completely devastated and in shock. After years of fearing that Jim would die from AIDS, and the initial reports of his remission from multiple myeloma, I was not prepared to lose him. I relied heavily on the support of friends and family, and eventually got back into psychotherapy. I also faced other losses, for I realized quickly that I could not care for the horse farm without Jim, and in December 2012, I found a place to stable my horses and moved back into Austin.

Losing Jim was the hardest event I have faced in my adult life, but I also relearned something incredibly valuable I mentioned before: with enough support, people can come through terrible losses and be stronger and more resilient in the end. All of this has deepened my work with clients, and I am more focused on helping them build support networks in their personal lives.

After Jim died, I thought it unlikely that I would ever be partnered again. To my surprise and relief, however, later in 2012, I found myself more and more drawn to an old friend of Jim's and mine, Hal Richardson. We began dating, slowly and cautiously, as I processed my grief, and one day I realized I was in love. Hal was too. We moved in together in 2014 and got legally married on September 5, 2015, shortly after the landmark Supreme Court decision on same-sex marriage. It has been a remarkably easy and happy relationship for me, and I count myself lucky to have had two great loves in my life.

New professional breakthroughs

As I recovered and grew following Jim's death, I found renewed energy and passion, and selectively took on new TA projects that have proved meaningful.

Workshop on helping clients heal shame

At the urging of Filippo Aschieri, in 2012, I began developing a two-day training on, "Working with Shame in Psychological Assessment and in Psychotherapy." The workshop uses lecture, videos of actual clients, role plays, and other experiential exercises to teach clinicians about the neurobiology and functions of shame and how to help clients heal shame. This was a personal project for me because of my own efforts to deal with shame, and it incorporated my many years of reading about shame and experimenting with ways of helping clients with deep shame. I presented this training for ECTA in Milan in late June 2012, and it was well received; since then I have presented it many times all over the world. Many participants have told me that this workshop not only affected their work with clients, but also changed them personally.

Co-Founding the Asian-Pacific Center for Therapeutic Assessment (ACTA)

Earlier I mentioned Dr. Noriko Nakamura, my colleague in Tokyo; I laugh at myself now when I remember our first face-to-face meeting, which took place at the ISR Congress in 1996 in Boston. I had submitted a symposium on TA for the meeting, and I was happy when it was accepted. Then, when the conference program arrived, I was incensed to see that someone—named Noriko Nakamura—had been added to the symposium without my being consulted, and she would be talking about a method she called the "Rorschach Feedback Session." Luckily, I kept my own counsel, and I was humbled at our symposium when Noriko presented a beautiful paper describing a touching example of Collaborative Assessment using the Rorschach. After this, Noriko and I came to know each other better, and often I would invite her to be part of symposia I organized at SPA or ISR Congresses. At one point, she and I had discussed possibly opening a TA Center in Tokyo, but I had given up the idea when Jim became sick in 2012. After Jim passed, Noriko and I spoke again, and in November 2014, the Asian-Pacific Center for Therapeutic Assessment (ACTA) opened in

Tokyo, with me, Noriko, and her psychiatrist husband, Dr. Shin-ichi Nakamura, as co-directors.

ACTA has been enormously successful, conducting training workshops on TA for hundreds of psychologists from across Japan, and sponsoring several Live TA workshops. I was unsure whether TA would "fit" with Japanese culture, and as elsewhere, we have had to make adaptations. In the process, I have learned a great deal about life in a "collectivist" culture, and how it is different than in the West. As I write, our ACTA group is composed of Seiji Mabuchi, Mitsugu Murakami, Sachiyo Mizuno, Hisako Nakagawa, Noriko Nakamura, Shin-ichi Nakamura, Yasuko Nishida, Masamichi Noda, Naoko Ogura, Mituse Tomura, and Sho Yabugaki. We continue to promote TA in the Asian-Pacific region (Figure 2.3).

Video for APA Psychotherapy Video Series

In 2015, I was invited to record a video on TA with adults for the APA Psychotherapy Video Series. Hal and I went to Chicago in August for the taping, and in between my work, Hal and I explored Chicago and shopped for clothing for our upcoming wedding. APA staff had found three clients for me; they recorded sessions with me talking to each about their scores on the MMPI-2-RF, and eventually selected one for the published video. Ron Ganellen, President of SPA at the time, led a panel discussion, and I am very proud of the resulting DVD (Finn, 2016). Also I am glad to have a video of me working with an actual client that can be viewed by people interested in TA.

Figure 2.3 With Jan Kamphuis and the staff of the ACTA, Tokyo, 2019.

Awards from APA

To my surprise, recently I have been the recipient of several meaningful awards for my work with TA. In 2017, Section IX (Assessment Psychology) of Division 12 (Clinical Psychology) of APA presented me with their Distinguished Contributions to Assessment Psychology Award. Then, in 2018, I received the Carl Rogers Award from Division 32 (Humanistic Psychology) of APA for "outstanding contributions to the theory and practice of Humanistic Psychology." I was touched when I realized that Connie Fischer was a previous recipient of this second award.

The reassessment of Madeline G

In 2017, two colleagues from SPA, Christopher Hopwood and Mark Waugh, invited me to take part in an exciting project. They planned to update Jerry Wiggins' (2003) landmark case study book, in which a group of experts in personality assessment had used different psychological tests to assess an interesting woman, "Madeline G." I was asked to lead a reassessment of Madeline, and I agreed on two conditions: (1) the evaluation would be conducted as a full Therapeutic Assessment, and (2) Gregory Meyer would join me in Austin for the sessions with Madeline and administer and code the Rorschach. My proposal was accepted, and the resulting volume (Hopwood & Waugh, 2019) documents one of the most fascinating TAs I have ever done. Madeline is a remarkable woman—highly traumatized but incredibly resilient—who readily accepted the TA frame for the reassessment. Working with her was both challenging and exciting, and in my chapters in the book, I comment that this is an example of "TA pushed to its limits." Greg and I were able to help Madeline at a difficult time in her life, and to do so in a way that we respected her dignity while bringing in a lot of "Level 3 information" about herself. I believe the assessment was successful partly because Greg and I are friends and have worked together before, and we combined our respective strengths in working with Madeline.

Epistemic trust

One noteworthy part of my personality is that I am high on excitement seeking and generally need to be doing something new to feel happy. In 2016, Jan Kamphuis helped satisfy this need of mine by introducing me to a novel area of literature in evolutionary psychology and suggesting we apply it to Therapeutic Assessment. The major concepts—Epistemic Trust and Epistemic Hypervigilance—were new to me, although others had written about them for over five years. I dove deep into the topic and read everything I could, and Jan and I had a series of stimulating discussions. Our resulting publication (Kamphuis & Finn, 2019) feels to me like a major development in Therapeutic Assessment theory. Basically, we explain how the values and techniques of TA emphasize assessors "mentalizing" their clients (i.e., "getting in clients' shoes"), and how, when clients feel seen and understood, they become more open to taking in relevant information (Epistemic Trust) and modifying their working models of self and the world. Also, by involving clients as active collaborators, TA reduces skepticism (Epistemic Hypervigilance) and reaches clients who do not respond well to other therapies. In short, Kamphuis and I lay out a rationale for why TA works so well and so efficiently with a wide variety of clients who have diverse problems in living.

I have developed a new workshop for clinicians to teach them about mentalization, Epistemic Trust, Epistemic Hypervigilance, and how and why TA is effective. I am excited to bring this workshop to clinicians around the world.

Current situation and closing

As I type these closing words, Austin is under restrictions because of the COVID-19 pandemic, and I am working from home. Although the pandemic has forced me to cancel many workshops and presentations around the world and to change my way of working drastically, I still feel blessed to be alive and doing work that I believe in and love. My colleagues and I have learned that TA can be successfully implemented with clients remotely, and we are developing and presenting online trainings. I ride my horses two to three times a week, and Hal and I enjoy cooking, reading, and watching movies at home. I stay in regular contact with friends and colleagues over Zoom, and I now have more time to think and write. In fact, Deborah Tharinger, Dale Rudin, Marita Frackowiak, and I are now writing a book on TA with children, and Filippo Aschieri, Francesca Fantini, Hale Martin, Raja David, and I are writing one on TA with adults. It feels good to have help with these projects I long felt overwhelmed by. Also, I am working on the sequel to *In Our Clients' Shoes*. Finally, I am moved by the growing awareness in our society of the deadly effects of prejudice, racism, and hate—spurred by the death of George Floyd. People's responses to this tragedy around the world give me hope for future generations, and the TAI Board and I are considering how we can contribute to this movement. For example, we have established the Leonard Handler Fund, which will finance Therapeutic Assessments for clients who cannot afford them.

I feel privileged to have been invited to reflect on my life and work by writing this chapter, and doing so has given me a sense of wonder and gratitude for all the opportunities I've had and all the people who have helped me along the way. An overarching theme I see in my life is how shame and isolation can be healed by connection and love. And quite fittingly, this is the main goal of Therapeutic Assessment.

Note

1 I am grateful to Carol Middelberg, Martha A. Penzer, Dale Rudin, Hal Richardson, and Deborah Tharinger for their comments on an earlier draft.

References

De Saeger, H., Kamphuis, J. H., Finn, S. E., Verheul, R., Smith, J. D., van Busschbach, J. J. V., Feenstra, D., & Horn, E. (2014). Therapeutic assessment promotes treatment readiness but does not affect symptom change in patients with personality disorders: Findings from a randomized clinical trial. *Psychological Assessment, 26*(2), 474–483.

Finn, S. E. (1982). Base rates, utilities, and DSM-III: Shortcomings of fixed-rule systems of psychodiagnosis. *Journal of Abnormal Psychology, 91*(4), 294–302.

Finn, S. E. (1996a). *A manual for using the MMPI-2 as a therapeutic intervention.* Minneapolis: University of Minnesota Press.

Finn, S. E. (1996b). Assessment feedback integrating MMPI-2 and Rorschach findings. *Journal of Personality Assessment, 67,* 543–557.

Finn, S. E. (1998). Teaching therapeutic assessment in a required graduate course. In L. Handler & M. Hilsenroth (Eds.), *Teaching and learning personality assessment* (pp. 359–373). Mahwah, NJ: Erlbaum.

Finn, S. E. (2003). Therapeutic assessment of a man with "ADD." *Journal of Personality Assessment, 80,* 115–129.

Finn, S. E. (2005). How psychological assessment taught me compassion and firmness. *Journal of Personality Assessment, 84,* 27–30.

Finn, S. E. (2007). *In our clients' shoes: Theory and techniques of therapeutic assessment.* Mahwah, NJ: Erlbaum.

Finn, S. E. (2011). Journeys through the valley of death: Multimethod psychological assessment and personality transformation in long-term psychotherapy. *Journal of Personality Assessment, 93,* 123–141.

Finn, S. E. (2016). *Therapeutic assessment with adults.* DVD published as part of the Systems of Psychotherapy Video Series. Washington, DC: American Psychological Association.

Finn, S. E., Fischer, C. T., & Handler, L. (Eds.) (2012). *Collaborative/therapeutic assessment: A casebook and guide.* Hoboken, NJ: Wiley.

Finn, S. E., & Kamphuis, J. H. (1995). What a clinician needs to know about base rates. In J. N. Butcher (Ed.), *Clinical personality assessment: Practical approaches* (pp. 224–235). New York: Oxford University Press.

Finn, S. E., & Martin, H. (1997). Therapeutic assessment with the MMPI-2 in managed health care. In J. N. Butcher (Ed.), *Objective psychological assessment in managed health care: A practitioner's guide* (pp. 131–152). New York: Oxford University Press.

Finn, S. E., & Tonsager, M. E. (1992). Therapeutic effects of providing MMPI-2 test feedback to college students awaiting therapy. *Psychological Assessment, 4,* 278–287.

Finn, S. E., & Tonsager, M. E. (1997). Information-gathering and therapeutic models of assessment: Complementary paradigms. *Psychological Assessment, 9,* 374–385.

Fischer, C. T. (1985/1994). *Individualizing psychological assessment.* Mawah, NJ: Routledge. (Originally published by Brooks-Cole.)

Fischer, C. T. (2017). *On the way to collaborative psychological assessment: Selected papers of Constance T. Fischer.* New York: Routledge.

Hopwood, C., & Waugh, M. (Eds.) (2019). *Personality assessment paradigms and methods: A collaborative reassessment of Madeline G.* New York: Routledge.

Kamphuis, J. H, & Finn, S. E. (2019). Therapeutic assessment in personality disorders: Toward the restoration of epistemic trust. *Journal of Personality Assessment, 101*(6), 662–674.

Martin, H. (2018). Collaborative/therapeutic assessment and diversity: The complexity of being human. In S. R. Smith & R. Krishnamurthy (Eds.), *Diversity-sensitive personality assessment* (pp. 278–293). New York: Routledge.

Mercer, B. L., Fong, T., & Rosenblatt, E. (Eds.) (2016). *Assessing children in the urban community.* New York: Routledge.

Meyer, G. J., Finn, S. E., Eyde, L. D., Kay, G. G., Moreland, K. L., Dies, R. R., Eisman, E. J., Kubiszyn, T. W., & Reed, G. M. (2001). Psychological testing and psychological assessment: A review of evidence and issues. *American Psychologist, 56,* 128–165.

Swann, W. B., Jr. (1997). The trouble with change: Self-verification and allegiance to the self. *Psychological Science, 8,* 177–180.

Tharinger, D. J., Finn, S. E., Gentry, L., Hamilton, A., Fowler, J., Matson, M., Krumholz, L., & Walkowiak, J. (2009). Therapeutic assessment with children: A pilot study of treatment acceptability and outcome. *Journal of Personality Assessment, 91,* 238–244.

Wiggins, J. S. (2003). *Paradigms of personality assessment.* New York: Guilford.

3 Personality

The Heart of the Matter

Donna S. Bender

"I think we should try to ride the elevator," I said to my new patient as we sat in my office at New York Columbia-Presbyterian Hospital. I was working at my psychology internship and one of the rotations I had opted to take was behavior therapy. Rosa had become afraid to use several forms of transportation, including elevators, and she was no longer able to ride the buses or subways in her Upper Manhattan neighborhood. My supervisor had instructed me to stick to the behavioral exposure protocol, starting with the elevator in the building. My patient was having none of it. I fairly quickly figured out that I had to pivot to establish a working alliance or we were going to go nowhere in this treatment and she may well just leave. Rosa needed to tell me her story so I would know about her abusive father (a major source of her fear and current inhibitions) and how things were going with her new boyfriend. She wanted to talk about her interactions with family and friends in her largely Dominican circles and her hopes for her future. So, much to the consternation of my supervisor, I spent most of our sessions for a while getting to know Rosa, building our relationship, communicating my interest and appreciation of her and her culture, and an understanding of why her young life might be so difficult. I got the sense she didn't have many opportunities to be seen in this way. We eventually did ride that elevator, and we took the bus down Broadway. A year after we ended our work together, Rosa wrote to tell me how well she was doing and expressed her gratitude for my being with her on her journey.

I had taken that behavior therapy rotation to make myself maybe more employable because I was worried about getting a job after finishing my doctorate. What I ended up learning was that I needed to honor my identity as a psychodynamic therapist instead of trying to be what I thought somebody else might want. Behavior therapists use specific actions as their data, cognitive-behavioral therapists add conscious thoughts and maybe feelings, but psychodynamic/psychoanalytic therapists use everything as data, the whole person. The latter approach fit my character and my convictions.

In March 2019, I had the honor of delivering the Paul Lerner Memorial Master Lecture at the Society for Personality Assessment annual conference. I titled my talk "Personality: The Heart of the Matter" because it is my firm belief that how we think about ourselves and others is at the core

DOI: 10.4324/9781003036302-3

of who we are and how we fare in life. So-called "symptom disorders," such as Rosa's phobia, have meaning beyond the criteria used to mark them as pathological; they arise from within the substrate of personality and subjective experience. Moreover, every type of clinical interaction will be affected by the patient's and clinician's self-other proclivities. I share with Paul Lerner (2005) the belief that it is imperative we understand that individuals have a fundamental need to tell their stories, and be seen and understood as whole individuals:

> ...the ultimate purpose of an assessment is not the achieving of a diagnosis and the assigning of a diagnostic label. Instead, many of us are appreciating that one assesses with the intent of understanding the other in his or her totality, complexity, and uniqueness so that such an understanding can then be used as a basis for making decisions and suggesting interventions that will be beneficial to that individual.
>
> (p. 271)

I believe I have been invited to contribute to this volume in large part because of the latest and perhaps best-known aspect of my work, the DSM-5 Level of Personality Functioning Scale (LPFS; American Psychiatric Association, 2013). The LPFS, a component of the Alternative DSM-5 Model for Personality Disorders, is a measure for assessing personality using definitions for capacities common to all humans: identity, self-direction, empathy, and intimacy. Based on decades of research conducted using a number of instruments exploring constructs such as mentalization, emotion regulation, and self-esteem (Bender et al., 2011; Morey et al., 2011), the LPFS delineates five levels ranging from little or no impairment to extreme. It is one of the very few elements of DSM providing a definition of healthy or adaptive functioning.

Some have observed that the LPFS was developed using psychoanalytic object relations concepts. Whether remarking on that is a compliment or an insult depends upon the individual's particular theoretical biases and/or academic political aspirations. Notions such as identity and empathy are pervasive across a number of psychology frameworks, as well as in areas such as literature, anthropology, philosophy, artificial intelligence, and social media. We are hard-wired to construct mental models of self and others from our earliest days as a way of learning to adapt to a social world. As Freedman (1998) has noted, "the process of symbolization is propelled by the intrinsic wish to connect" (p. 87).

So, it seems logical, at least to me, that to help people have an easier time of it we need to understand their beliefs, conscious and implicit, about themselves and their relationships. How are our internal lives populated by identifications and representations of others? What are those unconscious burdens and unproductive narratives we end up with about ourselves and our place in the world of other people? How have developmental capacities such as identity formation and the ability to know one's thoughts and feelings been shaped and perhaps damaged by life experiences?

Then it is no surprise, given my own beliefs, stated at the outset, that I came to the DSM-5 enterprise with certain broad hopes for the contribution I might be able to make: to bring back something more psychological to the tome, and provide a vehicle for clinicians to help patients tell their stories and be seen as whole people rather than as their anxiety or depression or personality disorder. I had long been concerned about the possibly dehumanizing effects of diagnostic labeling and an increasing trend in the field toward very narrow symptom-focused assessments and treatments. I have heard of too many instances of individuals seeking treatment and having been speedily diagnosed and hurried out with a prescription, or given homework for one habit or behavior, without the clinician considering the complexities of the person's history, circumstances, and personality. Handing someone the identity of being "mentally ill" stacks the deck in a certain kind of way, often based on significant misassumptions and biases on the part of the clinician, and forecloses on many conversations that should otherwise have occurred in the service of self-discovery, connection, and empowerment. Having grown up in a society and a family that were often very invested in their own version of my identity did not leave me kindly predisposed to such trends in my profession.

So, to understand how I got to the place of self-appointed advocate for the mistreated of the world and the need to understand others' stories and minds, I will talk a bit about my own tale navigating a family and a culture with an interesting and sometimes oppressive mix of values, expectations and shortcomings. It is not necessarily a path I am eager to re-trace, as I have invested a great deal of effort in working through and moving forward. As Satchel Paige is quoted as saying, "Don't look back. Something might be gaining on you."

In the heart of PA Dutch country

"It's been a hard day's night and I've been workin' like a dog," sang the Beatles in 1964. My three-year-old-self danced around the living room, laughing like crazy at the notion of a working dog, and I played that tune over and over on my kiddy turntable. My parents' record collection, especially those discs in the magical red 45 box with the front clasp closure, helped to get my lifelong dance party started. One of the upsides of being born to teeny bopper parents.

I arrived in the world on Christmas Day, 1960, kind of a lousy day to have a birthday. "Here, pick one of these Christmas presents for your birthday." I didn't much like that approach, but I had discerned very early on that I had better behave and attend to my caretakers' expectations, which meant learning from the beginning how to read people and figure those out. Thus, began my training as a psychoanalyst, working on my empathy and mentalizing skills.

My very young parents had a number of personal challenges trying to negotiate all of life's responsibilities without having had great parenting themselves, and I had to grow up very early in some ways. From birth, I went back and forth between households, often cared for by my maternal grandmother, who was a very helpful, but also a fraught, presence. Her own history was filled with trauma and loss. She had many siblings, who ended up in orphanages after their mother died young and their father was gassed in WWI, spending a large portion of his life in a VA hospital. My grandmother was the eldest and ended up living with an aunt, and was so poor, when she married my grandfather in her teens, he had to buy her shoes. He was a talented man who founded a tool and die business and was a stabilizing influence, but died in his 40s. He was a role model for me, calm and funny, and I remember having a conversation with him when I was in elementary school about why we don't convert to the metric system in the US. I have a sister who is six years younger and a brother, ten years my junior. They both turned out to be successful and lovely people in spite of the family challenges. Nevertheless, I always felt very responsible for them, another contributing factor to my personality, driving me toward the road to the helping professions (Figure 3.1).

Figure 3.1 Donna in a poofy dance dress, circa 1964.

The town of Ephrata, Lancaster County, Pennsylvania, where I grew up, was populated originally by people from religious sects in Germany and Switzerland seeking more religious freedom. The Amish and the Mennonites and other inhabitants of the area, many engaged in farming the green rolling countryside, in general are collectively referred to as "Pennsylvania Dutch." It is Dutch, as in Deutsch, as in German. The Amish continue to speak high German when they gather to worship and they and some of the Old Order Mennonites still drive horses and buggies. Electricity is not used even today by some of these families. There are a number of variants of these religious traditions, as well, such as the Brethren, the "black bumper" Mennonites (they paint their car bumpers black to cover the worldly chrome), and other "Plain People." There are also various other fundamentalist churches and the region overall might be considered a "Bible Belt" of sorts. The local speech pattern ("Dutchified English") can be heavy, a sort of drawling German accent, a mix up of v's and w's, j's as ch's, and a switching around of word order.

Of course, there were some in the county who did not belong to one of these religious groups, including my immediate family. There was a fair amount of in-group/out-group prejudice, but I will get to that more in a bit. Gender roles were quite traditional, and in the '60s and '70s, some children were not educated past the eighth grade. One can see how the origins of the area led to Ephrata being in the 1960s demographically almost exclusively white and Christian. To my knowledge, we had one Jewish family and one Black family during the time I was growing up, and that was about it for diversity. Oh, and my friend Tom, who was of Italian heritage and had moved there from New York. I heard virtually nothing about the civil rights movement as a child of the '60s, and there certainly was no mention of first wave feminism. My high school advanced government seminar teacher refused to discuss fascism, and I don't recall learning anything in school about World War II and the Holocaust. The good news is the teaching was strong in reading, writing, and arithmetic so I did get solid training in the basics.

I also spent a lot of time from little on up hanging out in the public library. I remember being incredibly excited when they moved it from kind of a creepy and cramped old house to a brand new bright and spacious building. So many books! My mother even enrolled me in a summer program where I would read selections and meet with the librarian to talk about them. I was pretty shy and it wasn't easy to interact with a grownup like that, but it gave me a sense of accomplishment and reinforced my love of stories, adventures and places out in the world. Nancy Drew was one of my favorites and I still read mysteries today!

As one might gather, people in my area were quite conservative (provincial?) in a number of ways. As my father would joke, even as he was one who would join in, "the people here would vote for Mickey Mouse if he ran Republican." (Events of the past decade actually led to my father renouncing that party, which is an incredible development, and a testimony to human potential for growth throughout the lifespan.)

On the other hand, my mother was one of the few Democrats in town. She had finally pursued her college degree when I was a teenager, getting up very early in the morning to do her school work before her three kids were even awake. She then taught biology for a few years in a middle school in the city of Lancaster, where her class was comprised predominantly of Black students who had been placed in a remedial section. She would bring home stories reflecting her enjoyment of the funny and wonderful things her students would do and say that reflected a culture different from ours. She modeled appreciation of those differences, while also expressing outrage at how under resourced her classroom was for meeting the learning needs of these young people. Social justice was not in common parlance, and many surely did not share my mother's view of Black people.

Earlier on, my mother was employed in a variety of unfulfilling jobs, and she and my father, who started his lifelong career as a wastewater treatment plant manager soon after high school, did the best they could to make ends meet. They communicated in a lot of different ways the need to work hard (and always have health insurance). I don't think my mother ever felt like she fit, though, and because she was unable to realize her own ambitions to become a doctor, she was determined that I would not get stuck in Ephrata, Pennsylvania. The message was clear: you don't belong in this limiting place and you will go away and get an education (preferably as a doctor).

This idea of not fitting in and needing more was to some extent reinforced by my elementary and high school experiences. When I was perhaps in second grade, I was identified as gifted and participated in "Creativity Classes," a district-wide program bringing together once per week children from several schools to learn such things as oil painting, physics, and advanced mathematics. (In high school there was a small group of us who took all of the advanced college prep classes.)

These educational opportunities were invaluable to my development and sense of identity as a person of some intelligence. However, at times I surely got messages that a girl should know her place. Boys who resented my opportunity to spend an afternoon at Creativity Class told me they didn't know why I got to go and they didn't because they are smarter than I am. In chemistry class in high school when I would produce answers to the teacher's questions in class, one of my male friends would shout from the back, "D. Bender! Kitchen chemistry!" I laughed and took it in stride at the time, but I was keenly aware throughout those years that I was too smart, too tall, too slender, too "worldly," and really just not the right kind of Ephrata female.

I was also part of the wrong religion. Back in those days, and maybe still now, if you met a new grownup, they would ask who your parents are and what church you attend. My answers did not check the right boxes. My mother converted to Catholicism when I was six and had me baptized as well. While my circle of high school friends and I would sit at the lunch table and debate various aspects of Christianity such as the idea of predestination, most of them were not allowed to set foot in my church. They were taught that Catholics have sinful ideas and practices. Adding insult to injury, I would go to dances and polka lessons at my church. Fortunately, in the school cafeteria we were largely able to put aside these differences and had a lot of laughs about various goofy things when we weren't talking about the fate of our souls.

This détente wasn't always possible, however. My junior year boyfriend was president of his church's youth group and the adult advisor said I had to leave my church or my boyfriend had to step down from his position because he set a bad example (getting rid of me was another obvious but unspoken option). To his credit, (and with his parents' full support) my boyfriend quit the position. But little wonder the one close high school friend I still have today is Grace, who at the time wore the cape dress and head covering typical of her Mennonite branch, but who was not afraid to join me at mass. Neither one of us belongs to our respective churches anymore, however, and she is now married to a woman who is not welcome to come along when Grace visits her family back in Ephrata.

Another thing that was different about me is I am part Hungarian. My mother's father's parents emigrated from what was then Austria-Hungary early in the 20th century. My great grandmother was a formidable presence in some ways when I was a girl and I enjoyed the visits to that branch of the family, who lived in a different county. She brought a rich culinary tradition from Europe and I remember when she would fill the kitchen with wooden boards covered with spaetzle dough pieces. Her cookies and pastries, goulash, paprikash, and palacinta are still part of our lives today.

I skated across a number of social circles, but my sense of belonging was never really secured because each group had some issue with one of the aspects of my identity. I was varsity cheerleading captain and Future Farmer of America. I was a yearbook editor and president of the 4-H sewing club. While many of my friends went to churches that didn't allow them to dance, I was on the prom committee and drove to Philadelphia to buy my dress with my gay friend (nobody talked about that aspect of his identity, especially him) who eventually became a designer, and to Washington, DC, to get my high heels. I donned the simple all-white outfit mandatory to show in competition the dairy heifer my best friend who lived on a farm lent to me, and had a modeling gig where my long hair was cut short and dyed and I danced with a punk rocker hired for the show. Yep, a worldly weirdo alright.

And that tendency I had necessarily cultivated to understand how people tick could at times be a bit too intense and earnest for some. My mother would get frustrated with my "analyzing" the family dynamics. "Stop staring!" she whispered on one occasion as I gazed at my rarely encountered relatives, trying to figure out how they could be so different from us. As the varsity cheerleading captain, I had the opportunity to participate in the county cheerleader queen contest. To compete, the girls had to compose and deliver a speech entitled, "What Service to Mankind Means to Me." I lectured on the importance of making sure you understand and improve your own circumstances so you could be at your best to help others. That went over like a lead balloon, as they say, and the girl who won delivered a poem about the necessity of being "sugar and spice and everything nice" (true story). At least one of the parents came over and privately told me my speech had been meaningful for them. This was long before anybody talked about self-care, but I could already see that lots of people needed some help.

One more important influence worth mentioning is my history as a Girl Scout. I started as a Brownie in first grade and went all the way to First Class Scout (equivalent to Eagle in Boy Scouts) my senior year of high school. I had some wonderful adult leaders as figures of identification and learned so much by taking trips, making crafts, going camping, selling cookies (I hated that part), and singing. I am grateful for these opportunities and the central touchstone that has shaped my life's journey to this day: *leave anyplace you go better than how you found it.* That fit really well with my oversized sense of responsibility for things, and has guided my decision-making up to today.

So off I went to college to figure out how to fix the world. With no models of how one actually successfully goes away to college, and not really having enough money to easily finance it, as my parents contributed none, I set off with high hopes anyway. Sometimes you don't know what you don't know.

Not a doctor at heart

My interest in psychology combined with the pressure I felt to become a medical doctor, led me to conclude I would become a psychiatrist. In 1978, I started as a pre-med student at Dickinson College, a small liberal arts school about an hour west of my hometown. Here I met students who had grown up in places like New York who had much more expansive views of the world and certainly had had the chance to study ideas and topics that were just not available in my small-town high school. For the first time I took a serious history class and a wonderful anthropology course and realized there were many more fun things to study outside of the standard pre-med curriculum.

I also had to adjust to behaviors that were not previously part of my life. I did not drink and was shocked at the levels of drunkenness that were an institutionalized aspect of college. I managed to learn how to navigate socializing as the only sober one in a group of drunk friends, and

I did identify the fraternity where I could count on a good dance party. The culmination of sorority rush found me pledging as a Kappa Kappa Gamma, the "cool" national sorority that had recently started a new chapter at Dickinson and billed itself as an alternative to the drinking club focus of the other organizations. In spite of being socially shy and relatively sheltered, I found ways to have fun and sort of fit in.

What was more difficult for me to reckon with was the "weed out" approach to the pre-med courses and the cheating behavior of some of my classmates. I also didn't find the pre-med classes very interesting. On top of that, Psych 101 was dreadful, and I was running out of money. Since it was clear I didn't want to be pre-med anymore, psychology did not appear to be a good option, but I wasn't sure what I wanted to do, I ended up taking off a semester and sewing in a factory. During that time, so as not to fall behind on my education, I took some classes at Franklin and Marshall College, a sister school of Dickinson not far from home.

One of those classes was an intro economics course taught by a bona fide Italian Marxist. People exploited as extensions of machines? The proletariat robbed of the means of production? For god's sake, I was spending my days sewing nightgowns, never making enough to earn beyond the very bare minimum! Of course Marxism made sense to me! And I was already a card-carrying empath, concerned for the oppressed everywhere. Long story short, I transferred to Bucknell University to major in economics (where there was another Marxist economist), took my German language skills to study abroad in Vienna, worked for a year as an economist, and went on to get a Master's in City and Regional Planning at Rutgers University, a hotbed of Marxism in that department at the time.

Planning was a good choice for me in a lot of ways because it combines a number of different skills and disciplines where one can make an impact: design, transportation, environmental policy, regional systems, etc. I remember having to create a city bus system as one project, and loved being on a team that worked late into the night on many occasions developing our design for revitalizing downtown Trenton, NJ. I concentrated on developing nations, but was counseled by my professors as I was finishing my degree in 1985 that there were few jobs in that area, particularly for an American woman. Fortunately, my transportation professor, who really liked my bus system, connected me with the Director of Planning at the Port Authority of NY and NJ and I went to work in that department in World Trade Center One in lower Manhattan.

So, in the latter half of the '80s, I worked in regional planning for the Port Authority, the State of New Jersey, and a tri-county nonprofit in Princeton. The thing about city and regional planning is that it brings together a variety of constituencies with often conflicting interests, peppered with the complications of individuals and organizations with very unequal power and resources. When I was working at the Port Authority, I wrote a piece on the growing economic inequality of the region.

That was 1986. It takes a long time to change these things and clearly the revolution was not coming in America anytime soon.

In trying to understand how to at least try to make some incremental progress, I was always drawn to the impacts of the personalities and group dynamics of these situations where governments, corporations, public interest groups, and powerful people vied to shape the future. I was also the one colleagues sought out to discuss both professional and personal issues. One of my co-workers joked I was the "planners' analyst." Clearly, my interest in psychology had persisted, and by this point I had also experienced my own personal psychotherapy. I decided perhaps I could be more effective at changing the world one individual at a time, and, as I wasn't getting any younger, I commenced making all the preparations to apply to clinical psychology doctoral programs, including taking undergraduate psychology classes at Rutgers. I already knew I was interested in a psychodynamic perspective, having read some Freud and a few other analytic writers, independently and as part of my course work, so I focused my applications on appropriate programs. I learned fairly quickly that in choosing to pursue this school of thought, I was not going to easily fit in with much of the rest of late 20th-century American psychology. Nevertheless, being used to, if not loving, the sense of not fitting in, I committed in 1991 to beginning my PhD adventure at the Columbia University Teachers College clinical psychology program in New York.

Following my heart

The first week of graduate school at Columbia, I marched into clinical psychology chair Barry Farber's office and asked if there were any research projects I could join. This was a fateful encounter that ended up shaping my path for the rest of my academic career, and for that I am very grateful. Barry had been working for quite some time with Jesse Geller, who was at Yale, studying the nature of how patients think about their therapists and the implications for treatment process and outcome. The basic idea is that mental representations of self and others are at the heart of how psychotherapy is "taken in" as a transformative experience.

The instrument Barry and Jesse had been utilizing was the Therapist Representation Inventory-II (TRI; Geller et al., 1989). Because the TRI is not a widely known instrument, but offers rich material for understanding how people may internalize their therapy and therapist and was important to my evolution, it is worth a minute to go into further detail. Underscoring the observation that patients use therapist images during times of separation, and that improving our understanding of the nature of these dynamics might yield important insights into pathology and treatment efficacy, the TRI focuses particularly on patients' symbolization of the therapy process outside of the therapy hour. Asking patients about their extra-session or post-termination thoughts and emotions regarding their therapist and the therapeutic experience, it was designed to yield a detailed profile of various characteristics of the therapist and therapy relationship, including content, forms, and functions of the representations. Content is assessed, in part, through asking the patient to provide an open-ended description of the therapist, an unstructured task that is projective in nature. The TRI also taps the forms—verbal or visual, for instance—that patients characteristically utilize in constructing mental images of therapy. In addition, a central component of the TRI is the exploration of the functions served by the therapist introjects, such as continuing the therapeutic dialogue or imagining interacting in an aggressive manner.

So, given that context, I will say that my collaboration with the Yale-Columbia research group, in many senses, had the greatest impact on how I think about formal personality assessment. First of all, the focus of the research on mental representations dovetailed very nicely with the attunement to others' thoughts and emotions I had been obliged to hone as a child. Secondly, it was also reinforced by the object relations–orientation of the doctoral program, which resonated with me very deeply. Third, one of my favorite things to do throughout my career has been working on a collaborative team of smart people figuring things out. And, I had tremendous fun singing along to songs on the radio with Barry on our drives to New Haven and back. We also presented at the Society for Psychotherapy Research conferences, where they often had good dance parties.

The task we were pursuing at Yale was refining the Thematic Patterning Scale of Object Representations-II (Geller et al., 1992), an instrument that fit within the central paradigm of the TRI and measures developed by Sid Blatt's group (e. g., Blatt et al., 1992; Blatt, et al., 1992). The basic assumption is that symbolization of self and significant others evolves cognitively, intellectually, and emotionally over the course of development. In the absence of significant impediments and trauma, a well-adjusted adult will have a rich internal life populated with predominantly positive, multi-dimensional and well differentiated internal representations that underpin adaptational functioning. However, things don't always unfold in an optimal way and an individual may end up with problematic beliefs about self and others that cause difficulties that may bring them for therapy. Our research was aiming to help better understand the nature of these representational challenges, and possible ways the therapist might be internalized into pre-existing schemas.

The Thematic Patterning Scale was designed to assess descriptions of others using eight dimensions: Complexity, De-Illusionment, Embodiment of the Other, Need Gratification/Frustration, Psychological Being, Temporality, Uniqueness of the Other, and Structural Cohesiveness. Each is rated on a scale ranging from 1 (least elaborated) to 5 (most illustrative) of the nature of the construct. Our discussions and reliability scoring practices were intended to improve the anchor descriptions for each of the five levels for all eight dimensions. The written descriptions we were using for this work were obtained with the prompt, "Please describe your (mother/father/therapist/self) (take 5 minutes)." To illustrate the Thematic Patterning Scale, the following are definitions of the construct and scale definitions for Psychological Being (Geller et al., 1992):

This scale is scored in terms of the degree to which it portrays the psychological world of the other person, including feelings, attitudes, values, ideals, motives, and world view.

At Level 1, the description is restricted solely to the visible, tangible external attributes and observable activities of the person. The focus is likely to be on demographic characteristics, physical attributes, or with no attempt to extrapolate the subjective meaning the attribute has for the person.

At Level 2, psychological characteristics, subjective state, emotions, and attitudes are attributed to the person in an amorphous, global, overgeneralized way, as though they were invariant across all situations and in all contexts. No effort is made to distinguish between situation specific psychological states and enduring personality traits.

At Level 3, a few specific psychological qualities or states of the particular person are described, based on generalizing from publicly available behavior. There are rudimentary attempts to convey variations in the person's psychological state and to understand the subjective meaning certain behaviors have for the person.

At Level 4, some feelings, attitudes, values, interests, and/or stylistic qualities of the person are described. Moreover, some aspects of the person's conscious wishes, conflicts, and/or motives are understood and conveyed with greater depth and elaboration of details than are those found at Level 3. These attributes may either be deduced from the person's behavior or empathically perceived.

At Level 5, the person is understood in terms of a complex organization of psychological states and enduring qualities. These descriptions characterize the person in terms of conscious and unconscious motivation, consistencies and contradictions, and both publicly accessible and private aspects. There is evidence that the person's psychological world is both affectively shared and cognitively understood (p. 8).

The dimension that in many ways struck me as somehow the most profound and has continued to influence me to this day is De-illusionment (Geller et al., 1992):

This scale assesses the extent to which the description reveals constructive acceptance of the flaws, contradictions, and disappointments in the person and/or in the relationship. In contrast to disillusionment, de-illusionment is not accompanied by despair, radical transformation of belief, or impotent rage. Rather, it entails an element of forgiveness and contemplative appreciation of imperfections and conflict. Disillusionment represents a solution based on splitting off and ignoring or rejecting parts of the person; de-illusionment is a synthetic, integrative achievement.

(p. 3)

Given the ways in which my upbringing was often not a very facilitating environment and the internalizations of significant others in my life were mixed at best, my own personal development needed to traverse this de-illusionment process. I had to work over the years to come to terms with my family members' inability to show up in ways I needed, and the judgmental culture of my childhood that conveyed the message of not being and doing the right thing. When I began practicing as a therapist, I met individuals with significantly greater challenges in this arena, internal worlds riddled with splits and trauma, and I was glad to have this concept as a reference point.

For my dissertation research, I gathered data in the Columbia Teachers College outpatient clinic over a period of three years. Patients were assessed after approximately five sessions and again after four to six months of treatment. Written descriptions of parents, self, and therapist were scored using the Conceptual Level Scale (Blatt et al., 1992; Blatt, Chevron et al., 1992) and the De-illusionment, Frustration/gratification, and Uniqueness dimensions of the Thematic Patterning Scale (Geller et al., 1992). Self-reported improvement and attributes of intersession therapist images were assessed using the TRI (Geller et al., 1989). Personality psychopathology dimensions came from the Millon Clinical Multiaxial Inventory-II (MCMI-II; Millon, 1987), and five attachment dimensions were utilized from the Calgary Attachment Questionnaire (West et al., 1987). The resulting product was *The Relationship of Psychopathology and Attachment to Patients' Representations of Self, Parents, and Therapist in the Early Phase of Psychodynamic Psychotherapy* (Bender, 1996).

I will share a few quick highlights of the findings (Bender, 1996; Bender et al., 1997, 2001). First, the conceptual levels of the descriptions of mother, father, self, and therapist were positively correlated. Higher conceptual levels were associated with being able to see the therapist as a separate, unique, potentially helpful individual, while also being able to tolerate flaws or disappointments that come up in treatment. In addition, patients who remained preoccupied with negative aspects of therapy between sessions had worse outcomes, while those who were able to mentally continue the therapeutic dialogue between sessions were more likely to improve. Elevated character pathology dimensions were associated with lower-level descriptions (e.g., inverse: borderline and mother; paranoid and father and therapist). Mother and father description ratings were significantly linked to overall functioning. This research was a significant part of the inspiration for my later work creating the DSM-5 Level of Personality Functioning Scale.

My heart was won

Graduate school gave me many things, but without a doubt the most important is my husband, John Rosegrant. As a student I was asked to assist in the coordination of a psychoanalytic conference at Teachers College. It was an excellent two-day program focused on three analysts' experiences with treating adults they had originally worked with as children. I was staffing the front desk registering attendees and I noticed John when he signed in. I remember thinking to myself that he is good looking, but cynically concluded he is likely married but doesn't bother to wear a wedding band. However, he apparently noticed me as well, wasn't married, and came over to talk at the cocktail hour at the end of the day. I was standing with some of my New York-raised grad student friends who rolled their eyes at John's midwestern humor. I thought he was delightful, and learned he was a psychologist in private practice and had moved to New York from Michigan to pursue psychoanalytic training. (Coincidentally, his doctoral training at Yale had overlapped with Barry Farber's grad school time there.) The next day he asked for my number and, fast forward, we were married the following year, 1995.

Because John had established his practice and committed to training in New York, I decided to focus my internship applications to local options. I ended up at Columbia Presbyterian/New York Psychiatric Institute (NYSPI). During internship I got to know Dr. Lisa Mellman, a psychiatrist/psychoanalyst who became interested in the TRI. She ended up being the outside reader on my dissertation, and knew about my interest in personality psychopathology, and so the day of my defense she told me about a new study focused on personality disorders commencing at NYSPI. She connected me with Principal Investigator Dr. Andy Skodol, who hired me right out of graduate school to set up and run the operations at the Columbia site of an NIMH-funded multi-site ten-year collaboration with PIs at Brown (Tracie Shea), Yale (Tom McGlashan), Harvard (John Gunderson), and Vanderbilt (Les Morey, later at Texas A&M). This large enterprise was named the Collaborative Longitudinal Personality Disorders Study (CLPS) (Skodol et al., 2005). It was the first study of its kind (and perhaps the last) to follow a large cohort of individuals (about 750) in several different personality disorder categories over a decade assessing such things as functioning, treatment, and the course of "Axis I and Axis II" pathology. John Oldham, who was the head of NYSPI at that time, was also a Columbia collaborator. My research career in personality and personality disorders was launched in Summer 1996.

Like the Yale-Columbia project, CLPS called for road trips for the sites to gather to advance the work. With Andy Skodol the driver this time, we motored to New Haven and Providence. Andy and I shared foodie interests, so the highlight of these trips were the restaurants we attended with our colleagues after long days of meetings. Our group could be a bit boisterous at times, and we were on the edge of being thrown out of the place from time to time.

The CLPS generated an enormous amount of data about the individuals we followed over those ten years and the study collaborators were tremendously productive. My most impactful work, from a mainstream PD research perspective was first authoring two papers on treatment utilization (Bender et al., 2001, 2006). However, remaining committed to challenging, in my way, the application of personality disorder categories, I cultivated the opportunity to conduct an ancillary study in this population using the TRI. I wanted to explore the internal lives of our study participants in the context of mental health treatment, as all those entering the study were required to have had. Results showed that individuals with major depression and no personality disorder diagnosis most often endorsed never wanting to be in therapy again. Patients in the borderline group hoped their therapists would be proud of them, and those with obsessive–compulsive and avoidant PDs most often wanted to try and solve their problems the way they had worked on them with their therapists (Bender et al., 2003).

To me the most striking finding of this work emerged for the people diagnosed with schizotypal disorder. If one examines the DSM-IV/5 categorical criteria (APA, 2013), the obvious conclusion would be that these "odd, paranoid" people with no "close friends or confidants" would have a very hard time thinking positively about their therapists. This is not what we saw in the therapist descriptions we asked participants to provide. Individuals from the schizotypal group expressed thoughts such as wanting to be married to the therapist who would "always be in my soul and thoughts," "I love to see him and wish we could hang out," and "She turns me on and I desperately want to make love to her eternally" (Bender et al., 2003, pp. 231–232).

Clearly, there were wishes for deeper connections, even if the ability to traverse interpersonal interactions was significantly compromised. We saw evidence of this as well in these individuals' encounters with our CLPS clinical interviewers. Even though the follow-up interviews were very infrequent (once yearly after the second year of the study), our clinicians reported that a number of the individuals categorized as schizotypal were quite attached to them and valued the opportunity to come and talk about what had been going on in their lives over the prior year. All of this validated my firm belief that people need to tell their stories and be seen and appreciated. Building therapeutic alliances, even with people with significant interpersonal challenges, is foundational. This is done most effectively by understanding individuals' inner worlds and how they might view themselves-in-relation-to-others (Bender, 2005; Bender, 2011). As Sheldon Bach (2016) so aptly observed:

> Perhaps the primary problem in engaging the difficult patient is to build and retain what Ellman (1991) has called analytic trust... These

patients have lost their trust not only in people but also in the environment as a reliable place that will hold them safely. So one task we have
is to restore this faith, and to rebuild it again and again...

(p. 217)

I took it all to heart

Soon after finishing graduate school I started a private practice in addition to my CLPS work, and I decided to begin psychoanalytic training
in 1997. I interviewed at two different organizations, but chose to attend
the Institute for Psychoanalytic Training and Research (IPTAR), in part
because of the "research" component. IPTAR was founded in 1958 by
psychologists during the time when the American Psychoanalytic Association controlled US institutes that were part of Freud's International
Psychoanalytical Association (IPA), and they would not train non-MDs to
become practicing analysts. IPTAR was a participant in the lawsuit that
was eventually brought, becoming one of the first institutes admitted to
the IPA in 1989.

The point of departure of IPTAR was contemporary Freudian and
I was trained in the "widening scope" of psychoanalysis, studying a number of important contributions across psychoanalytic theoretical traditions. The medical institutes, who, in my opinion have a lot to account
for in the damage they have historically done in the name of psychoanalysis, often refused to treat people in analysis whom they deemed as
having difficulties that were beyond those who were "Oedipally organized." Freud (1926/1959) spoke to the limited and rigid application of
psychoanalysis when he stated, "For we do not consider it at all desirable
for psycho-analysis to be swallowed up by medicine and to find its last
resting place in a textbook of psychiatry under the heading "Methods of
Treatment" (p. 248).

IPTAR taught us the means to understand all individuals and adjust
the analytic endeavor to meet the person where they are. My supervisors on my training cases, Drs. Steve Ellman and Irving Steingart,
supported my evolving ability to work with more deeply troubled
people with narcissistic and borderline difficulties using a "self and
object Freudian" perspective (Ellman, 1998). My training at IPTAR,
and my own personal analysis along the way, was absolutely invaluable
and transformative.

During those years I also had the opportunity to participate in the psychoanalytic research aspect that had drawn me to IPTAR. Dr. Norbert
Freedman had gotten to know Jesse Geller over the years and so our team
set out to evolve our previous work on how patients internalize their
therapists. We created the Schedule of Therapy Remembered Interview
(STR; Geller et al., 2011a) and the Representations of the Therapeutic
Dialogue Coding System (RTDCS; Geller et al., 2011b) to study patients'

narratives about therapy post-termination. We recruited participants who had recently ended therapy with one of the clinicians affiliated with IP-TAR's outpatient clinic. The STR begins with the prompt to talk for five minutes about the person's therapist or therapy, or anything that seems important in that moment. They are then asked to explain what brought them to therapy, what their life was like at that time, and any significant others they wish to speak about. Using an approach from the Adult Attachment Interview (Main & Goldwyn, 1990), participants were next instructed to provide five words describing their relationship with their therapist, followed by examples for each word. The final sections of the interview focus on good and difficult moments in therapy, perceived outcome, and an opportunity to describe any dreams they had during therapy that featured the therapist.

All of the interviews were recorded and then transcribed, so the research team could code them using the RTDCS. Profiles for each patient were developed by scoring such attributes as the form of remembering the therapeutic dialogue (recalled, inhibited, longed for, imagined), the presence of positive or negative feelings attached to the recollections, and whether the therapist introject seemed benign or problematic. We were learning about how specific clinically meaningful aspects of reconstructions of the therapy relationship mediate treatment outcome. Again, what are important dimensions of how people symbolize self-in-relation-to-others?

Our meetings at Bert Freedman's apartment on the Upper West Side always included good food and camaraderie. Bert was a brilliant, kind, and engaging mentor to many and working with him and Jesse on this project was a compelling experience. It was very moving to be able to witness and think deeply about individuals' stories of their therapists and therapy experience.

I also accidentally got feedback about myself as a therapist. We began to go through the transcript of a woman who had recently ended therapy. There were aspects of her description that were sounding familiar and it turned out she was my former patient. I had worked with her for a year and the process was enormously challenging. She had quickly gone through a number of other therapists before landing with me, and described every one of them as stupid and deficient in some way. She had trained in the field, although had not successfully worked in it, and was often scornful and mocking of me, lecturing me on technique and demeanor. We had to navigate many alliance ruptures. That she stayed with me for a year was a testament to something, perhaps my own masochism, but when she got up yet again to storm out of the room, I didn't coax her back. Given some other life circumstances and a number of other difficult treatments I was doing, I had reached my limit. So, I was flabbergasted when her description of me was one of admiration and gratitude. She had a sense that I was able to survive her attacks without retaliating and that I cared about her enough to show up and keep trying. It is really difficult for many people to form positive introjects and her internal world was populated by attackers. The fact that she was able to think about me in positive and helpful ways was quite something.

My heart skipped a few beats

Being the worldly person that I am, I have always loved to travel, an interest John and I share. Our annual big trips to places in Australia, Europe, South and Central America, and around the US have often occurred in August. Our visit to the Yucatan in Mexico in 2001 turned out to be the most momentous of all. It was there we discovered we were expecting a child, an outcome we were not so sure would ever happen. Suddenly, I had to begin to navigate the process of adding mother as another aspect of my identity.

The next month came the 9/11 attacks. I can still picture clearly getting word as I was sitting in my office in upper Manhattan. Everyone was hurrying to the NYSPI auditorium to watch the big screen, but I refused to leave my seat. My brother and his fiancée worked in a building directly across the street from the World Trade Center. This was before iPhones, so instant contact with anybody and everybody was not yet a thing, nor was streaming the news on your desktop computer. I needed to be there to watch my email, my mother was writing, my sister was writing, my mother-in-law was writing. "Have you heard from Mike?" Never before was I so appreciative of Blackberry when finally my brother managed to get off a message, "We're ok. Just crossed the Brooklyn Bridge. Heading home. Be home in 1.5 hours. Both buildings collapsed. It's chaos here."

It was a surreal time to be pregnant and I was grateful I lived on the Upper West Side away from the noxious air of the invasion's aftermath. John's cousin Elizabeth who lived downtown came up to stay, and having her there was a bright spot as we all struggled to process this horrendous event. We still mark that date with her every year.

While many things never did go back to "normal," such as airport security, John and I focused on getting ready for the new addition to our family. Our son Joseph arrived on an unseasonably hot day in April and the blossoms on the trees in Riverside Park burst out in their pink puffball glory. This was the start of one of the biggest adventures of all (Figures 3.2 and 3.3).

From a self-other representation perspective, there ain't nothing like becoming a parent. Every developmental phase you help your child navigate brings up whatever was going on for you at the same age, although that isn't always obvious so one needs to be on the lookout. And just when you think they will never stop doing that worrisome/annoying/exhausting thing, or will never be capable of walking/talking/using the bathroom, they move on to the next phase. These are lessons I have been able to share with patients who have young children.

Figure 3.2 Joseph and Donna surrender to the Dark Side.

Figure 3.3 John, Joey, and Donna in the Austrian Alps.

Our son is 18 now and is a very interesting and fun person. We have taken him far and wide on our travels and he is an expert on history and geography. Already decidedly a citizen of the world, Joey is in his first year at the University of Oxford, studying archaeology and anthropology.

Changing hearts and minds?

Having gone through the Manhattan experience of our toddler son having to compete to get into preschool, including "interviews" at age 18 months, we started to wonder if we were really prepared to put him (and us) through the intelligence testing requirements and pressure cooker process of kindergarten applications. Even though we loved our New York life in many ways, we were having a hard time figuring out how we might raise a child there. We reckoned it might be time to move to America and started thinking about where that might be. We wanted a reasonably affordable place (that ruled out California) with outdoor beauty (preferably with mountains), a university, and a psychoanalytic community. Our research, followed by an August monthlong visit, landed us in Tucson, AZ. During the time we lived there (2007–2014), I established a private practice, served on the University of Arizona faculty supervising psychology doctoral interns, became president of the local psychoanalytic society, and taught at the analytic institute. I also worked with Andy Skodol who, through a strange sequence of events had ended up in Phoenix, at two nonprofit research organizations. The second, the Sunbelt Collaborative, was founded by Andy and myself, with help from John Oldham and Les Morey, to support the work we were doing as part of the DSM-5 Personality and Personality Disorders Work Group. Let me return to that saga.

Andy chaired that work group, which got going in earnest in 2007. We embarked on our collaboration with excitement, having been charged by the DSM-5 process chairs with leading the way into a new era by crafting a dimensional approach, a shift that was in line with where other a number of medical disciplines had already gone. Our team was assembled including psychiatrists and psychologists with decades of collective experience working in the field of personality disorders. Some were veterans of past DSM processes and had made contributions to the categorical system we were now set to challenge, while others, such as myself, were already invested in dimensional assessments.

As I mentioned previously, I was hoping to somehow use my research and clinical perspectives to shape this new approach into something more humane and psychologically meaningful, and personality functioning proved to be an opportunity to do this. The work group's early discussions led to the conclusion that a severity of impairment measure applicable to personality was needed that went beyond simply adding up the number of PDs for which a person meets criteria. The self-other perspective that eventually was incorporated in the Alternative DSM-5 Model for Personality Disorders, emerged from work that had been ongoing by several members of the group. Besides the earlier work I discussed above, I had already weighed in on the notion that personality psychopathology emanated from disturbed internal object relations in a paper I wrote with Andy Skodol about borderline being a self-other representational disorder (Bender & Skodol, 2007). Other members had also made significant contributions to this perspective (e. g., Livesley & Jang, 2000; Morey, 2005; Morey & Bender, in press; Verheul et al., 2008).

Those who followed the DSM-5 PD process will know that things became embattled and tempestuous, within the work group, across the PD field more broadly, and ultimately in responses from the APA leadership. Some work group members wanted their own approaches to be wholesale adopted as the model (often so similar to one another it left one to stand in awe of the narcissism of small differences), other PD experts were invested in their favorite diagnoses or assessment approaches so waged attacks, and ultimately the APA was not ready to evolve past categories. Traits scared some people and, regarding the proposed self-interpersonal framework, we were straight up told at one point by one APA official that "self" is not a viable concept. The early fun of a creative process morphed into soldiering on in the face of continuous conflict and controversy. Frankly, it was often miserable. That is all I will say on this aspect of the experience; interested readers can find a more detailed account elsewhere (Skodol et al., 2013).

At the end of the day, we came to a compromise in the Alternative Model. The Level of Personality Functioning Scale provides a means of engaging with fundamental self and interpersonal capacities of identity, self-direction, empathy, and intimacy, and offers the only definition in the AMPD of what it looks like to approach life with little or no impairment. (We also had been working on a set of adaptive traits that did not make the cut.) People with an affinity for pathological trait psychology get their needs met with the facets and domains, and those who still want to utilize a particular PD diagnosis can do so, but need to think about self-other constructs and traits in the process.

It is gratifying that there has been a great deal of interest in the Alternative Model in our field, with many research groups testing various aspects. Andy Skodol, John Oldham and I joined with Michael First to develop SCID instrument modules for assessing LPFS, traits and domains, the personality disorder types (First et al., 2018). Each begins with eight questions designed to facilitate the interviewee in telling their self-other story. I have had the great opportunity to collaborate with colleagues all over the world, including conducting training with research groups in Norway and Denmark. Not surprising, though, the controversy continues and there are factions determined to prove the LPFS should go away.

I heart NOLA, y'all

After wrapping up the Sunbelt Collaborative DSM-5 work, it felt like time to look for my next professional adventure. Long story short, I was hired at Tulane University in New Orleans to build a new student counseling center. I had a long-time love for that city, having first gone there on my honeymoon in 1995. There is no place else like it anywhere, and one gets the sense of being in a different country. The Big Easy is not actually always so easy, with a troubled and storied history, but it has soul in ways that are hard to describe. I think you either get it or you don't. I arrived in January 2014 to begin my new big project.

I won't say a great deal about my job at Tulane, except that it was a tremendous learning experience. (That's what people often say when things were pretty rough.) If you know anything about the mental health landscape these days for students at university, you are aware that pressures are high and needs are great. Couple that with seven student deaths my first full academic year there in the midst of new leadership starting all the way at the top with the president and no prior Tulane experience in responding to this kind of trauma. Nevertheless, I really did learn a lot about managing and operations and strategic planning, and about the most pressing issues in higher education. I had some great colleagues as well.

I also got to live in a lovely house in the Garden District and do creative New Orleans activities. I joined a dance troupe and performed renditions of such classics as the Can Can, Charleston, and Go Go. As part of Mardi Gras parade groups, I was decked out as a pirate, a wisteria fairy, Star Wars characters, and Anne Boleyn. I also became a potter (Figure 3.4).

Then the pandemic. As I write this, we are all still in it and we all have our own tales to tell. In my little family's version, we fast forwarded to our long-term plans of returning north from whence we came, and moved to the Ann Arbor, Michigan, area to be near some of John's family. We now live by the Huron River in Ypsilanti and the snow is glorious. I am working for the University of Michigan from home, and John's practice is all remote here in the house too. Joey is conducting his Oxford studies online in the basement. All in all, we have been very fortunate during this difficult era, and I am interested to see what the future will bring when the world opens up again.

On being a therapist: not for the faint of heart

It has been a privilege to be part of the lives of my patients, and they have taught me so much about life, human resilience, and myself. Because my practice has often been comprised of people with more serious personality challenges, whose histories are threaded with heartbreaking deprivations and trauma, it has been absolutely vital that I have been able to draw on my long years of training, my own analysis, and my research about how

Figure 3.4 Donna still favors poofy dance dresses.

people think about themselves and others. The task is to creatively find ways to be the therapist each person needs so together you can discover the stories they live by and craft a narrative for a less painful and more fulfilling way of being. One of my patients described her process:

> I'm going deeper and deeper into uncharted territory. I'm not sure I want to see those things, but if I don't, I will always be afraid of what's down there. So, if it is a matter of confronting anger and envy, I'd rather know about it. So many fairy tales and stories have to do with going underground to find things, like Harry Potter. No one wants to go down there, but if you do, you'll find the treasure, but first you have to overcome danger to get it.

Accompanying each patient into uncharted territory, providing the light to help illuminate the way, and demonstrating you will be there to help them find themselves and make it through to a better place, requires stead-fastness. These journeys can be arduous, requiring a great deal, but as my analytic supervisor Irving Steingart (1995) put it, "This analyst love is not only real but extraordinary. And what makes it extraordinary follows directly and naturally, from the altogether extraordinary nature of the psychoanalytic relationship" (p. 106). Building this relationship serves as the crucible in which new possibilities for living are forged. It's both very difficult and very simple. As humans, who we are and how we are comes down to those basics of identity, self-direction, empathy, and intimacy (Bender, 2019). Cultivating a flourishing self with meaningful connec-tions really is the heart of the matter.

References

American Psychiatric Association. (2013). *Diagnostic and statistical manual of mental disorders* (5th ed.). Arlington, VA: American Psychiatric Association.

Bach, S. (2016). On treating the difficult patient. In S. Bach (Ed.), *Chimeras and other writings: Selected papers of Sheldon Bach* (pp. 217–228). Astoria, NY: International Psychoanalytic Books.

Bender, D. S. (1996). The relationship of psychopathology and attachment to patients' representations of self, parents, and therapist in the early phase of psychodynamic psychotherapy. In *Dissertation abstracts international: Section B: The sciences and engineering* (Vol. 57, Issue 5-B, p. 3400).

Bender, D. S. (2005). The therapeutic alliance in the treatment of personality disorders. *Journal of Psychiatric Practice, 11*(2), 73–87.

Bender, D. S. (2019). The p-factor and what it means to be human: Commentary on "Criterion A of the AMPD in HiTOP." *Journal of Personality Assessment, 101*(4), 356–359.

Bender, D. S. (2011). Therapeutic alliance. In A. E. Skodol & J. M. Oldham (Eds.), *The American psychiatric publishing textbook of personality disorders* (3rd ed., pp. 311–334). Washington, DC: American Psychiatric Publishing.

Bender, D. S., Dolan, R. T., Skodol, A. E., Sanislow, C. A., Dyck, I. R., McGlashan, T. H., Shea, M. T., Zanarini, M. C., Oldham, J. M., & Gunderson, J. G. (2001). Treatment utilization by patients with personality disorders. *American Journal of Psychiatry, 158*(2), 295–302.

Bender, D. S., Farber, B. A., & Geller, J. D. (1997). Patients' representations of therapist, parents, and self in the early phase of psychotherapy. *Journal of the American Academy of Psychoanalysis, 25*(4), 571–586.

Bender, D. S., Farber, B. A., & Geller, J. D. (2001). Cluster B personality traits and attachment. *Journal of the American Academy of Psychoanalysis, 29*(4), 551–563.

Bender, D. S., Farber, B. A., Sanislow, C. A., Dyck, I. R., Geller, J. D., & Skodol, A. E. (2003). Representations of therapists by patients with personality disorders. *American Journal of Psychotherapy, 57*(2), 219–236.

Bender, D. S., Morey, L. C., & Skodol, A. E. (2011). Toward a model for assessing level of personality functioning in DSM-5, part I: A review of theory and methods. *Journal of Personality Assessment, 93*(4), 332–346.

Bender, D. S. & Skodol, A. E. (2007). Borderline personality as a self-other representational disturbance. *Journal of Personality Disorders, 21*(5), 500–517.

Bender, D. S., Skodol, A. E., Pagano, M. E., Dyck, I. R., Grilo, C. M., Shea, M. T., Sanislow, C. A., Zanarini, M. C., Yen, S., McGlashan, T. H., & Gunderson, J. G. (2006). Prospective assessment of treatment use by patients with personality disorders. *Psychiatric Services, 57*(2), 254–257.

Blatt, S. J., Bers, A. B., & Schaffer, C. E. (1992). *The assessment of self description.* Unpublished manuscript.

Blatt, S. J., Chevron, E. S., Quinlan, D. M., Schaffer, C. E., & Wein, S. (1992). *The assessment of qualitative and structural dimensions of object representations.* Unpublished manuscript.

Ellman, S. J. (1991). *Freud's technique papers: A contemporary perspective.* Lanham, MD: Rowman & Littlefield Publishers, Inc.

Ellman, S. J. (1998). The unique contribution of the contemporary Freudian position. In C. S. Ellman, S. Grand, M. Silvan, & S. J. Ellman (Eds.), *The modern Freudians: Contemporary psychoanalytic technique* (pp. 237–268). Northvale, NJ: Jason Aronson Inc.

First, M. B., Skodol, A. E., Bender, D. S., & Oldham J. M. (2018). *User's guide for the Structured Clinical Interview for the DSM-5 Alternative Model for Personality Disorders (SCID-5-AMPD).* Arlington, VA: American Psychiatric Association Publishing.

Freedman, N. (1998). Psychoanalysis and symbolization: Legacy or heresy? In C. S. Ellman, S. Grand, M. Silvan, & S. J. Ellman (Eds.), *The modern Freudians: Contemporary psychoanalytic technique* (pp. 79–97). Northvale, NJ: Jason Aronson Inc.

Freud, S. (1959). The question of lay analysis. In J. Strachey (Ed. and Trans.), *The standard edition of the complete psychological works of Sigmund Freud* (Vol. 20, pp. 183–250). London: Hogarth Press. (Original work published in 1926)

Geller, J. D., Behrends, R., Hartley, D., Farber, B., & Rohde, A. (1989). *Therapist representation inventory-II.* Unpublished manuscript.

Geller, J. D., Bender, D. S., Freedman, N., Hoffenberg, J., Kagan, D., Schaffer, C., & Vorus, N. (2011a). Patients' representations of the therapeutic dialogue: A pathway towards the evaluation of psychotherapy process and outcome. In N. Freedman, M. Hurvich, & R. Ward (Eds.), *Another kind of evidence: Studies on internalization, annihilation anxiety and progressive symbolization in the psychoanalytic process.* (pp. 17–28). London: Karnac Books.

Geller, J. D., Bender, D. S., Freedman, N., Hoffenberg, J., Kagan, D., Schaffer, C., & Vorus, N. (2011b). The RTD Coding System and its clinical application; a new approach to studying patients' representations of the therapeutic dialogue. In N. Freedman, M. Hurvich, & R. Ward (Eds.), *Another kind of evidence: Studies on internalization, annihilation anxiety and progressive symbolization in the psychoanalytic process* (pp. 29–54). London: Karnac Books.

Geller, J.D., Hartley, D., Behrends, R., Farber, B., Andrews, C., Marciano, P., Bender, D. & Brownlow, A. (1992). *Thematic patterning scale of object representations-II.* Unpublished manuscript.

Lerner, P. M. (2005). Red beavers and building bridges between assessment and treatment. *Journal of personality assessment, 85*(3), 271–279.

Livesley, W. J. & Jang, K. L. (2000). Toward an empirically based classification of personality disorder. *Journal of Personality Disorders, 14,* 137–151.

Main, M. & Goldwyn, R. (1990). Adult attachment rating and classification systems. In M. Main (Ed.), *A typology of human attachment organization assessed in discourse, drawing and interviews.* New York: Cambridge University Press.

Millon, T. (1987). *Millon clinical multiaxial inventory-II.* (Available from NCS Professional Assessment Services, P. O. Box 1416, Minneapolis, MN 55440).

Morey, L. C. (2005). Personality pathology as pathological narcissism. In M. Maj, H. S. Akiskal, J. E. Mezzich, & A. Osaka (Eds.), *World psychiatric association series: Evidence and experience in psychiatry* (pp. 328–331). New York: Wiley.

Morey, L. C. & Bender, D. S. (In press). Articulating a core dimension of personality pathology. In A. E. Skodol & J. M. Oldham (Eds.), *The American psychiatric publishing textbook of personality disorders, 3rd ed.* Washington, DC: American Psychiatric Publishing.

Morey, L. C., Berghuis, H., Bender, D. S., Verheul, R., Krueger, R. F., & Skodol, A. E. (2011). Toward a model for assessing level of personality functioning in DSM-5, part II: Empirical articulation of a core dimension of personality pathology. *Journal of Personality Assessment, 93*(4), 347–353.

Skodol, A. E., Gunderson, J. G., Shea, M. T., McGlashan, T. H., Morey, L. D., Sanislow, C. A., Bender, D. S., Grilo, C. M., Zanarini, M. C., Yen, S., Pagano, M. E., & Stout, R. L. (2005). The collaborative longitudinal personality disorders study: Overview and implications. *Journal of Personality Disorders, 19*, 487–504.

Skodol, A. E., Morey, L. C., Bender, D. S., & Oldham, J. M. (2013). The ironic fate of the personality disorders in *DSM-5. Personality Disorders: Theory, Research, and Treatment, 4*(4), 342–349.

Steingart, I. (1995). *A thing apart: Love and reality in the therapeutic relationship.* Northvale, NJ: Jason Aronson Inc.

Verheul, R., Andrea, H., Berghout, C. C., Dolan, C., Busschbach, J. J., Van Der Kroft, P. J. A., & Fonagy, P. (2008). Severity Indices of Personality Problems (SIPP-118): Development, factor structure, reliability and validity. *Psychological Assessments, 20*, 23–34.

West, M., Sheldon, A. E. R. & Reiffer, I. (1987). An approach to the delineation of adult attachment: Scale development and reliability. *Journal of Nervous and Mental Disease, 175*, 738–741.

4 My Hobby

Listening for the MMPI's Questions

David S. Nichols

When Chris asked me to prepare an autobiography for this collection, my first reaction was, "Why me?" Over the many years that the *Journal of Personality Assessment* was under the editorship of Bill Kinder and Greg Meyer, I relished the autobiographies that appeared there as an opportunity to learn about the lives and contributions of luminaries in the personality assessment community. Some were known to me only by reputation; others, as colleagues with whom I had enjoyed relationships over many years.

But why me? Unlike the careers of many others in this collection, mine was centered in the hospital, not the academy. My assessment "career" has always been more in the nature of a hobby than a trajectory of university employment. In this sense at least, my life in personality assessment does not conform to the more familiar pattern of most of the others who have shared their lives on these pages.

So, contemplating the invitation to contribute to this series has given me the opportunity to reflect on my career from the standpoint of its difference from others, the kind of difference the great Samuel Butler had in mind when he titled one of his books, *Luck or Cunning* (Butler, 1920). As you will see, my own story owes far more to the former than to the latter, and I content myself that this may, at least for the generously inclined, be a sufficient answer to the 'Why me' question.

I was born at 7:10 AM, Pacific War Time, on February 3, 1943, the day that Hitler made a national broadcast from his headquarters to announce that the German Sixth Army had been destroyed at Stalingrad. It was the turning point of the war in Europe. On the same day, the US Army troopship Dorchester was torpedoed and sunk by German U-boat 233. Among the 674 men who lost their lives were four chaplains, a Methodist, a Jew, a Roman Catholic, and a Dutch Reformed, all of whom had given their life vests to other soldiers when the supply of vests ran out. Stateside, it was on this day that the War Relocation Authority (WRA) began distributing loyalty questionnaires to the Japanese-Americans interned at the Manzanar and Tule Lake concentration camps. The hit song on that day was Tommy Dorsey's "There Are Such Things." Nobody much remembers it now…

DOI: 10.4324/9781003036302-4

Among the other events that year: Iraq declared war on Germany, Italy, and Japan. The Pentagon was dedicated, as was the Jefferson Memorial. Race riots erupted in Detroit. Selman Waksman coined the word 'antibiotics.' Casablanca, with Humphrey Bogart and Ingrid Bergman, won Best Picture. George Harrison of the Beatles was born. The Psychological Corporation acquired the rights to the distribution of a new personality inventory, the Minnesota Multiphasic Personality Inventory, and its chief developer, Starke Hathaway, turned 40.

My parents, Ambrose R. Nichols, Jr. (1914–2000), and Barbara Adele Seward (1913–2006), had married in 1938. Following the completion of his PhD at the University of Wisconsin, my father was hired by San Diego State College (SDSC) the next year as their first physical chemist. My mother had taught Fourth Grade in Fontana, California, before their marriage. My sister Debbie followed my birth by two years; my other sister, Eleanor, by eight.

The economy of the San Diego of my youth (pop. 330,000 in 1950, 570,000 in 1960) was dominated by the military and the aircraft industry (Ryan Aeronautical had built the Spirit of St. Louis for Charles Lindbergh in 1927). I grew up in the postwar atmosphere of confidence, optimism, and relief. The adults around me, having lived through the Great Depression and World War II, had reached the sunny side of life. They now looked forward to lives of relative ease and even abundance, their hope clouded only by the threats of nuclear attack and communism, "The Red Menace." It was also a period of deference to authority and mostly willing conformity in dress, demeanor, and expression – a time when any adult could tell me what to do.

I was a happy, curious, and adventurous child, one well cared for, but also one given to providing my mom, herself an only child, a generous amount of on-the-job-training. I enjoyed climbing and running into the street, activities the enthusiasm for which she did not share. Once, left in our 1934 Chevrolet while she ran into the grocery for milk, I became curious about the gearshift, a lever I'd seen her manipulate many times. When I did so, however, the car began to move toward a three foot drop off just above the sidewalk, gathering speed. I remember her running out of the store in a panic, yanking open the door and jumping in the car to mash the brake as the car came within inches of jumping the retaining curb at the precipice.

Apart from a voice raised more in fright than in anger, I don't recall being punished for this 'experiment.' Indeed, it was the policy of both of my parents not to overreact to their children's transgressions. In the word of the time, my parents would have been described as 'permissive.' In this, my mom tended to follow my dad. If he believed in anything, he believed in education; yet he almost never offered precept. He must have thought example was better but would have been uninclined to say so. His values were humanistic and democratic. His approach to discipline, and later governance (see below), was laissez faire: he believed in muddling through. He never thought he knew enough to tell others what to do; he believed others would mature in their own way. This policy of noninterference extended to his own kids. To me, he would say things like, "It's OK to go ahead and flush the toilet after using it."

In September, 1947, the first period of my childhood came to an abrupt end. Attending the birthday party of a peer down the street, I began to feel a fatigue so extreme that I could not hold up my head. My mom took me home and, when my dad returned from work, I was taken to San Diego County Hospital where I was diagnosed with polio. It was the same year that Jonas Salk accepted a position in Pittsburgh at a new medical laboratory funded by the Sarah Mellon Scientific Foundation.

Although known for at least two millennia, polio was first described clinically in the late 18th century. It was much in the public mind in the immediate postwar years which had seen serial epidemics of about 20,000 new cases annually. Franklin D. Roosevelt was thought to have contracted it in 1921, and at his death, as a gesture acknowledging the premiere polio charity of the time, the March of Dimes, the head of the dime was changed to show his portrait. My reaction to being struck was more one of interest and curiosity than of fright or tragedy, at least initially. I regarded my stay in the hospital as a kind of unscheduled adventure as I drew the attention of doctors, nurses, and other staff, all asking me questions, examining me, writing notes in my chart, bathing me, bringing me meals. It was only a week or two later, when I was discharged, that I began to appreciate that things had changed.

I was assigned to a young orthopedist, Chester K. Barta, who prescribed my braces and crutches, my physical therapy, and saw me through several subsequent surgeries to correct my posture, and my convalescences therefrom. The only pain I can recall was that stemming from the physical therapy, but even that was leavened by the kindness of my young and pretty therapist, Mary Ballard, and the comforting presence of my mom as Miss Ballard worked on me.

In most ways my development proceeded normally. I enjoyed the support and confidence of my family who treated my condition matter-of-factly, but my surgery convalescences occasioned a subtle shift in my family position, with my sister Debbie assuming an elevation in rank and status as I became an 'honorary second-born' (Sulloway, 1996). This shift was painless, both at the time and after, but it had a large influence on my educational development, as Debbie grew into the role of bright, conscientious, and achieving student with grace and relative ease, while I carved out a student role of underachievement, one that followed me all the way through graduate school, of haphazard motivation and uneven performance, the kinds of things that find expression on grade slips as "shows difficulty organizing and completing work," and "achieving below his potential."

Out of school, I was obviously disadvantaged, unable to run, jump, and keep up with my peers. Although I continued to feel mostly accepted by them, I remember calling to them with anguish and frustration, "Hey, wait for me!" In school, however, apart from recess, I enjoyed a level playing field socially, if not academically. In the classroom my peers were as tied to their desks as I was. A captive audience! School became for me an apprenticeship in what might be called sit-down comedy, and at this I was an eager learner. My dad had a good and clever sense of humor, often in the vein of Ambrose Bierce and Victor Borge, and was especially fond of puns. I took after him in this way, though not as skillfully, and my mom, in response to my efforts, I can recall saying "Don't laugh, it only encourages him," on more than one occasion.

Although in many ways quite insecure for reasons related to my disability, I genuinely liked others, following my parents' example. This extended especially to the girls in my classes because they seemed, at least on balance, less physically competitive. They seemed to enjoy my humor, sometimes shameless clowning, and I appreciated them for their gentle humor, their grace and beauty, their kindness or at least tolerance, and their spirit. I fell in love for the first time in the second grade. Sharon Barrows had a wonderfully crisp voice, and the prettiest hands I'd ever seen. When she became my date at the senior prom ten years later, I felt triumphant.

Apart from the 1951–1952 academic year we spent in Oak Ridge, Tennessee, for my father's leave of absence to work at the Oak Ridge National Laboratory, my family lived near San Diego State; for the last eight years of my time in San Diego, close enough for my father to walk to work. And apart from the diverse circle of friends my parents met or entertained at home for cocktails, supper, bridge, or dancing, my childhood was spent in neighborhoods and schools that were white and middle-class as far as the eye could see. These were neighborhoods where the fathers 'worked' and mothers stayed at home as 'housewives' or 'homemakers.' With two sisters and the active social life my parents enjoyed, my mother was the center of our household, available, interested, and competent; she was our family's CEO. To paraphrase Mary Chapin Carpenter, "She makes his coffee, she makes the bed, she does the laundry, she keeps him fed... she does the car pool, she PTAs, doctors and dentists, she drives all day...." My father did the taxes, mowed the lawn, did the dishes, took us camping, occasionally made fudge, and never got over his amazement at my mother's ability to run our household.

I was extraordinarily lucky in my choice of parents. Although their areas of interest and competence were often complementary, both were broadly interested in others, in the arts, and in world events. My father had played clarinet in his high school and college bands; my mother played the piano and had once, at about age 15, drawn the attention of Vladimir Horowitz and played a private duet with him during a visit to Lake Arrowhead. I remember my mother sitting me down in front of the television (new for us) to watch such things as the coronation of Queen Elizabeth and the Army McCarthy Hearings. To the extent that I can claim these traits, I get being sober, reflective, and witty from my father; and being expressive, loving, and occasionally outrageous from my mother.

Neither of my parents was especially religious. Although my father's family were Methodist, he was not much invested in religion of any kind. I don't really know the 'why' of this, it's just the way he was. He basically expected people to behave themselves. I came to call him a Football Methodist, meaning that he might go to church if there was no football game on TV. My maternal grandmother was a devout Christian Scientist but had inflicted an emotional injury on my mom in the First Grade. Mom had befriended a girl in her class who was Catholic, her first close school friend. When my grandmother found out about this friend a month or so later, she forbade my mom from ever speaking to the girl again, and my mom complied. I'm afraid I was an indirect beneficiary of this cruelty in that I'm sure that it weakened my mother's attachment to Christian Science, and left her less conflicted about the treatments that attended my polio infection and its aftermath than she might have been otherwise.

Until I was seven or eight, my family went to the Christian Science Church most Sundays but, following an incident of insensitivity to one of my peers by our Sunday school teacher, I told my parents that I no longer wished to go. They may have made me go another time or two, but then it was over. We all stopped going to Sunday services, and it was probably a decade before I set foot in a church again, and then only because, following my father's appointment as President of the new Sonoma State College (SSC), we moved from San Diego to Santa Rosa, California, and I was suddenly without a peer group. Carl, the son of a professor my father hired away from San Diego State, had been an acquaintance in my high school graduating class, and his family were devout Baptists. They promptly joined a church in Santa Rosa that had a youth group to which Carl invited me. I gratefully accepted and attended their weekly meetings for the next three years, by which time I had made many new friends.

My parents were both well spoken, and my mother, in particular, was attentive to my grammar, correcting it as necessary into her 90s. She never swore, and it was exceedingly uncommon for my father to do so. Neither used obscene language or racist or other degrading epithets. In fact, the first time I ever heard such speech ('shit') was in the third grade, and it made no particular impression then. One day in the fifth grade, while walking back to class from the school cafeteria with my friend Margo, our teacher, Mr. Rodarte, mistakenly overheard me to say "shit" as we passed by our classroom window. He immediately called me in for a vigorous scolding, and my truthful denials of having said what he overheard fell on deaf ears.

This event was painful because I was especially fond of Mr. Rodarte, as were my classmates. An unusually effective teacher, he was also affectionate, respectful, and had a fine spirit of fun, with a steady good humor that was often self-effacing and occasionally flamboyant. We all loved him, and the prospect of my falling in his esteem was distinctly painful because I liked him so much. To find him unmoved by my sincere statements of innocence was at once puzzling, hurtful, and disappointing. But it was also my first real lesson in the power of language, and it inaugurated me into the habit of salty speech that continues to this day and, more broadly, to a rebellious turn of mind strongly at variance with my previous pattern of conformity in both conduct and sentiment. My father had always been passionate about justice and the misuse of power but, after this incident, I came to understand these values in a more personal way.

My preadolescent and adolescent years were largely uneventful. I went through the Cub Scouts, Indian Guides, Boy Scouts, Explorer Scouts, but without any zeal when it came to earning badges and ranks, though I did enjoy the crafts, events, trips, and campouts these memberships afforded. My major preoccupations through these years were guns and cars, both of which I've psychologized as relating to my problems with mobility through the idea of action-at-a-distance. My interest in guns fell dramatically after I shot and killed a small bird while on an Explorer camping trip. I had anticipated feeling triumphant for my marksmanship as this bird fell from its limb, but was instead surprised by a combined sense of shame and sorrow.

Beginning at about age 12, my folks sent me to a YMCA camp, Camp Marston in northeast San Diego County, for a week or two each summer. After a couple of years, and for reasons unknown to me, the Camp Director, Chet Chappell, took a liking to me and hired me for the full summer camping season as a junior staff member to assist in the camp store and, in following summers, as a counselor. These summer jobs ended abruptly at age 17 when I and two older camp counselors were fired for drinking.

An event during my first camp season proved especially influential. While working as the assistant storekeeper my first summer at Y-camp, I lived in a large cabin with the kitchen staff, the wrangler, storekeeper, pool lifeguard, and other non-counselor staff. All were older than I was, and two had relocated from Indiana to enroll in San Diego State. One day they took off to spend the weekend in San Diego, about 60 miles away. When they returned they brought with them a copy of Allen Ginsberg's *Howl and Other Poems* (1956). I noticed it on the table around which many of us played Hearts in the evening. One morning, while alone in the cabin I picked it up and, idly thumbing through it, stopped at the poem, "America." My eyes fell on the line, "Go fuck yourself with your atom bomb." I was dumbstruck. I had never before encountered a package of syntax so disorienting; it was my second major lesson in the power of language, and I read this little book from cover to cover at once. It was a few more years before I returned to Ginsberg, but that initial encounter was a true turning point. It opened a chest of questions, reflections, and contemplations, with which I've been preoccupied ever since. Allen Ginsberg became the first of my heroes on that day.

My only passionate interest for most of my adolescence was in drag racing and hopping up cars. With a couple of running mates I spent many idle hours hanging around a gas station near us. I must have felt at the time that it was either this or homework. Like a few of my peers, I subscribed to *Hot Rod* magazine and loved to work on cars when opportunities to do so arose.

My 16th birthday was later known as "The Day the Music Died," the day the light plane with rock and roll musicians Buddy Holly, Ritchie Valens, and "The Big Bopper" took off from Lubbock, Texas, at 1:00 in the morning and crashed in a cornfield near Clear Lake, Iowa, killing all three plus the 21-year-old pilot. This event hardly registered with me because I was so focused on obtaining my driver's license. Walking on braces and crutches made it impossible to ride a bike, but the prospect of driving meant that, for the first time in my life, I would be able to cover ground in a manner more or less equal to that of others, and I could not realize this promise quickly enough.

The achievement of my license and the purchase of my first car, a 1955 Packard Patrician through the sale of my coin collection, gave me not only a new means of personal transportation but also a focus for my mechanical interests and aspirations for speed. Car ownership also seemed to elevate my status among my peers as I could now keep up with them, for example in drag races on Highway 94 in San Diego, or an abandoned airstrip in Tecate, Mexico. When not in school, my time – and money – was spent on the car's engine to increase its horsepower and torque. The success thereby achieved was happily realized in minor street drag racing victories, the occasional admiration of peers and, less happily, in a succession of blown automatic transmissions (I couldn't drive a standard shift) until I could no longer afford replacements and had to sell the object of my mechanical devotions for junk. Nevertheless, the experience of these years made me aspire to a career as a mechanical engineer.

In high school, although not maladjusted in any significant sense, I was quite uncertain of my place and, I think, alienated, at least inwardly. I had friends, but would not have in any sense been considered popular. I generally ate lunch with the 'brain' group, who tolerated me fairly well but mostly because I could make them laugh. Dirty jokes, mostly. I did not qualify for the most distinctive groups in high school; the ones we referred to then, respectively, as the "soshes" (long o) and the "jocks," but was not especially avoidant of or avoided by them, either. Still, high school was, on the whole, an uncertain and occasionally unhappy time.

Following my father's appointment as President of the new Sonoma State College (SSC), we moved from San Diego to Santa Rosa, California, only a week after I'd graduated high school in 1961. I spent the summer getting oriented to my new surroundings. Our home was on the outskirts of town and I was without a car. Within weeks I found and purchased a 1954 two-door Oldsmobile; I also discovered a local business, Bing's Speed Shop, which proved a comfortable hang-out.

That I would go to college was a given, at least as far as my parents were concerned. As my father observed: "No one is going to hire you as a mechanic." This was my tacit assumption as well. However, my academic performance in high school was so lacking in distinction that my grades were insufficient to meet the – by no means exalted – entrance requirements of the California State College System. I would have to go to the Santa Rosa Junior College. Although I performed well in an auto shop class (my instructor, Mr. Emmenegger, opined, "Nichols is the best bench mechanic I've ever seen!"), by the end of my first year I had managed to fail or drop chemistry, trigonometry, mechanical drawing, graphics, and advanced algebra. I was typically performing at an average level or below in my other courses, had a D+ average, and was on academic probation.

That summer, I had my first good idea. It went something like this: "Dave, if you're managing to flunk the courses related to things you think you know something about, maybe it's time to take courses in subjects about which you know nothing." The next term I enrolled in psychology, sociology, and anthropology. And voila! I enjoyed my classes and my grades improved. I was captivated. I haven't changed a spark plug since.

My first great psychology teacher was Bill Radtke. He had been a paratrooper and interrogator in World War II, and he returned to attend college and complete the Master's Degree at the University of Florida. His thesis was a translation of Lipot Szondi's *Experimentelle Triebdiagnostik* (Szondi, 1947). We took a liking to each other ("You get my jokes," he said), often talked after class, and occasionally met at the quirky Apex Book Store, my new hang-out just off the square in Santa Rosa where, over time, I discovered an interest in literature. Joyce, Miller, Dostoevsky, Vonnegut, Camus, Nietzsche, Heller, Steinbeck…. Radtke was and remained a great raconteur, but also wise in ways I couldn't fully appreciate at the time, e.g., "You don't own your possessions, they own you." He taught me how to administer and score the Szondi Test (my introduction to personality assessment), and I proceeded to test as many of my peers at the Apex as would sit still for it.

The next year I entered SSC to complete my degree in psychology. At that time, the Psychology Department was humanistic-existential in its orientation. Rogers, Maslow, and May were considered titans by the faculty, and all visited the college during my time there. I even had breakfast with Carl Rogers one morning during one of his visits. Although their names came up frequently in lectures, and we were strongly encouraged to familiarize ourselves with some of the writings of existential philosophers like Kierkegaard, Sartre, Heidegger, and others, I can't recall these ever being assigned. I do remember that in my first year there I thought to try to make a good impression on one of my professors by reading Heidegger's newly translated *Being and Time* (1962). However, after only a very few pages, I experienced something that I can only call a kind of cognitive choking, and put the book down for good.

The mantras of the Psychology Department were the shoulds of being "real" or "genuine," being "open to experience," holding others in "unconditional positive regard," being a "fully functioning person" and, conversely, not being a "phony." Having spent little time heretofore in introspection, these desiderata came across to me more as commandments than as aspirations, and I vaguely recall many times being in situations wherein I would put questions to myself of the type, "How should I respond in order to come across as genuine (or "open")." In short, how to fake being real was not an infrequent preoccupation at the time. Personality assessment was not only not valued within the department, but more or less actively disparaged as 'labeling,' and 'pigeonholing.' It wasn't the sort of thing nice (or "real") psychologists did. I put up my Szondi cards.

I remember a woman named Norma Rosenquist. She was at least a decade my senior and in many of my psychology classes. She had worked as an RN at the Palo Alto VA hospital for many years and had been personally acquainted with Carl Rogers for at least a few of these. But when she spoke up in class, she would often mention an experience or quotation from one of her colleagues there, Gregory Bateson. Eventually, I found myself sufficiently intrigued to look up his writings – initially his *Perceval's Narrative* (1961); then *Communication: The Social Matrix of Psychiatry* (Ruesch & Bateson, 1951). Bateson's writings gripped me in a way few others had. They set my sights on a more distant horizon, made possible connections that were novel for me at the time, and made the notions of context, difference, and pattern vivid and rich in ways they'd not been before. I was truly entranced. Bateson became my second hero. While I can no longer recall how, it was through Bateson that I was introduced for a second time (after Ginsberg) to William Blake, this time, specifically, to his *Marriage of Heaven and Hell* (1965). Like Bateson – and Ginsberg before him – I added Blake to my permanent mental furnishings; he became my third hero.

Two teachers from my time at Sonoma State stand out. Stanford Lyman was a young sociologist fresh out of Berkeley who taught a course called Contemporary Civilization. The course text was arranged into pairs of chapters taking opposite positions on such social issues as abortion and capital punishment. Assigned one issue per week, each Friday we were to turn in a paper arguing for our personal position. Each Monday these were returned heavily marked up, calling our attention to non sequiturs, logical fallacies, latent assumptions, and any other failures of reason Lyman could detect. In my case, such flaws were bountiful, and my first several papers were duly graded F. But I persisted and struggled to think more critically about each issue and the arguments I mounted to support my positions. And I remember the sense of elation I felt when a paper came back marked

D+. I was making progress! And though I don't recall my final grade, whether B or C, this course was another turning point for me. Previously, I am embarrassed to say, my views of mind and brain were laughably naïve. Intelligence, as I saw it, was immutable. Learning was akin to filling up a filing cabinet with information. And thinking amounted to little more than the retrieval of the material therein stored. After this course, thanks to Lyman, I was able to see that one's thinking and reasoning could be expanded and improved by dint of *effort*. No doubt many, probably most, of my peers has already figured this out, but I had not.

A different kind of influence came in my first course in abnormal psychology. Hobart "Red" Thomas was a deep believer in student-centered teaching, but I found his nondirective style in class more than a little frustrating as most of the discussion among my classmates centered on the behavior of their children, spouses, parents, in-laws, neighbors, and co-workers, whereas I was eager to learn about the seriously abnormal, "crazy," and such. So, after two or three classes I made an appointment to see Thomas to convey in the least offensive way I could that I thought his class sucked, and why I thought so. To his credit, he simply asked "What would you like to do?" I told him that I'd like to read the text (White, 1964) and perhaps write papers and talk with him, but felt that going to class was a waste of time. He then asked if I'd like to actually see some patients with mental disorders. I told him I would. "Well, suppose I arrange for you to visit Mendocino State Hospital, would you be willing to go up there, make observations and write about patients?" I said "Yes" again, whereupon he picked up the phone and called Wilson Van Dusen, the Chief Psychologist there. After a few minutes, the arrangement was set pending the permissions Van Dusen would need to secure from the hospital administration.

The next Friday I drove up to the hospital, about 60 miles from my home, met with Van Dusen for his approval, and moved into the psychiatric technicians' quarters for the weekend. I would have access to the staff library and a few of the general psychiatric wards at the convenience of the staff, and return home Sunday afternoon. I would write a brief paper each week, and class was waived. I was thrilled!

Van Dusen himself was a brilliant and fascinating man. He had also had polio, but walked with only a slight limp. He had an unusual and unusually broad set of interests, including Zen Buddhism, LSD therapy, Emanuel Swedenborg, schizophrenia, and, in particular, hallucinatory phenomena of all kinds. Van, the name he went by, had completed the PhD (summa cum laude) at the University of Ottawa in 1952. His dissertation, Mind in Hyperspace (see Van Dusen, 1965), focused on Einstein and the question of what constituted the fifth dimension. His Committee required that Einstein personally review and approve his reasoning and calculations, which he did! At the time I met him, Van had a reputation for doing something most unusual in psychotherapy with schizophrenic patients. He would first seek to discern whether the patient could distinguish between his/her own identity and the phenomena (voices, visions, etc.) that constituted his/her hallucinatory experience. For those who could do so, he would try to interact directly with the hallucinations described by the patient, using the patient as an intermediary/interpreter. He would thereby seek to establish an empathic relationship with both the patient and his/her hallucinatory personages.

On the one occasion I observed him do this, he was careful not to judge the reality of phenomena that the patient reported, assuming, apparently, that if they were real to the patient, they were real enough for him. He would typically speak directly to the entities that the patient reported or, if a response was not forthcoming, would ask questions or make observations and request that the patient convey them to the voices or whatever verbatim, and ask that the patient report the entity's response with like precision. It was an impressive and fascinating performance, and one that appeared to bring a degree of comfort to the patient.

My weekly visits to Mendocino continued through the end of the semester, and provided numerous opportunities to converse with a variety of patients on many topics. Although these conversations occasionally involved expressions of psychopathological interest, on the whole they were more ordinary that otherwise. I knew I was not skilled or knowledgeable enough to pursue psychotherapeutic aims with these patients, nor was it my place to do so. But I found that even though I often felt awkward in these interactions, I truly enjoyed them, both intrinsically and for the questions they brought to mind. Perhaps most importantly, after a few days my initial apprehensiveness subsided and I achieved a sense of comfort and confidence, and even a degree of spontaneity in my conversations with these patients. They were, in most ways, a lot like me.

As with so many psychology majors of the time, it was through Freud that I caught my first peek into the psychotherapist's chamber. I no longer recall through which of his writings this introduction came about, but it rapidly led to his other writings and shortly, thanks to the gift of Jones' (1957) biographical opus from my parents one Christmas, my trajectory as a psychologist was set: I would become a psychotherapist. Soon I was reading the psychoanalysts by the busload. The appeal was less a source of principles that one could apply to the understanding of human psychology and its vulnerabilities than it was the sense of mystery and suspense that came with each new case history. It was Sherlock Holmes transplanted from the moors to the mental universe. I had my magnifying glass and calabash pipe, and I was in training.

However, I was often dismayed by the "solutions" analysts arrived at. These could feel forced or "canned," and were too often proffered dogmatically. The chains of evidence for a given interpretation sometimes seemed more arranged than organic and compelling. In this context, the humanistic-existential orientation at SSC was refreshing. The approach to human problems taken by the faculty there seemed more open and exploratory, and the client rather than the therapist was treated as the authority. But there were frustrations here as well. I received the promotion of qualities of authenticity, being real, in the moment, fully present, unguarded, etc., etc., as rather precious on the one hand, and as an oppressive catalog of desiderata on the other. Barely out of my teens, what the hell did I know about "being real?" If these attributes were to be taken as the measure of my own maturity, it was pretty clear to me that I was not making the grade. It is not merely that I was unable to appreciate these qualities as virtues, virtues worth encouraging in others as my teachers sought to encourage them in me. It was more that after being exposed to the intellectual drive and resourcefulness I so enjoyed and appreciated in the analysts, I was left wondering, in the words of the advertising jingle that was to come two decades later, "Where's the beef?" Imagining myself across the desk from a psychotherapy client, I felt I had little to offer beyond "How do you feel?" and "Can you tell me more about that?" I wanted more.

To be sure, the faculty and student environment at SSC were good for me. Academically, I gained a degree of confidence and involvement in my classes that I'd mostly failed to achieve earlier, and felt comfortable and successful enough to resolve to pursue graduate studies. At a more personal level, however, apart from the usual extracurricular activities and relationships I enjoyed, I failed to achieve a comfortable fit with the humanistic-existential ethos of the Psychology Department. But I was likewise discontent with my reading of the analysts. The humanistic-existential stuff felt gossamer and too often trite and/or cloying; the analytic material too magical, like treasure-hunting or pulling rabbits from hats. Both were humorless.

I wanted a psychotherapy mentor and, quite by chance, happened upon Sullivan's *The Psychiatric Interview* (1954), and thence to his other writings. In Sullivan I found what was then, and what has remained, a compatible spirit. The appeal of his writing was in its happy accord with my own observations and understandings, in its quality of search, and in its harmony with what I had been reading of Bateson. His thinking and commentary were agreeable for me on the grounds of being less abstract and complex than the psychoanalytic writings I had consumed, and more practical and realistic than the vague and airy-fairy humanistic-existential orientation to which I'd been (over)exposed at Sonoma State. In my later practice with patients, the writings of Sullivan and related thinkers like Frieda Fromm-Reichmann and Harold Searles were always close at hand. I was, I decided, a Sullivanian.

By the start of my last semester I was tired of school. I planned to apply for graduate school to pursue my studies, but felt the time was not right. So after spending the summer studying German at a school in Monterey, California, to complete my undergraduate credits, I applied to the Sonoma County Department of Social Services to become an Aid to Families with

Dependent Children (AFDC) welfare worker, and was hired. Just as I had had little contact with members of racial and ethnic minorities growing up, so I had virtually no contact with the poor. My caseload of about 60 families, all within a small semirural area, was quite varied. It included some single mothers with infants, some intact families, and a number of arrangements in between. Often one or more of the adults in these households were physically disabled or abused alcohol. When employed at all, my clients usually worked only part time or in menial jobs, or both. Virtually all were only a month or two from eviction. Despite the fragility of their lives, many were surprisingly generous in the way they looked out for each other, including watching others' children, lending each other money to make rent, repair a tire or buy groceries. A minority approached their financial struggles exploitatively by shoplifting, stiffing landlords, hiding income, and other means. And, to be sure, many in both groups had histories of being themselves exploited.

This job ended after ten months when I received a call from one of my Sonoma State professors. John S. "Jack" Robinson was a comparative psychologist who had done a postdoctoral fellowship with Roger Sperry. He needed two assistants for his perception research laboratory in Sonoma State Hospital near the home of Jack London, and called me looking for my great friend, Steve Fish. When he learned that I was also available, he hired us both! I let him know that I'd be available only temporarily, that I intended to return to school, and that my interests in psychology were primarily clinical. These did not deter Jack; he may even have considered them plusses, for I had been on the job less than a week when he burst into my office exhorting, "You must read Meehl!" Up to that moment I had no idea that he harbored any interest in clinical psychology, but he had just finished reading Meehl's *Clinical vs. Statistical Prediction* (1954), and thought so highly of it as to see it as essential reading for me.

It wasn't the first I'd heard of Meehl. I'd read his case of catatonic schizophrenia (1947), and one of my junior college friends who'd transferred to Berkeley had pressed his chapter on Tolman with MacCorquodale (MacCorquodale & Meehl, 1954) into my hands at one of our get-togethers. But he hadn't really registered as a figure. *Clinical vs. Statistical Prediction* changed that.

By this time I'd come across any number of authors who impressed me as thinking better than I did, or could, but these were mostly outside psychology. In philosophy, for example, I'd read Russell, Moore, Wittgenstein, and always with profit. I'd also happened on Levy's *Psychological Interpretation* (1963) another book that opened a new door for me to think about clinical psychology. Part of its appeal was his comment about those "who luxuriate in obscurantism and esoterica," from which I got a nasty thrill as I related it (somewhat unfairly) to my experience of psychology at SSC.

But nothing had prepared me for *Clinical vs. Statistical Prediction*. To this point, I had considered statistical issues only in the context of experimentation and would have, if asked, denied any *intrinsic* relationship between statistics and the activity of the psychologist within the consulting room. Meehl made it clear to me that sound practice in the gathering of clinical information – and in its combination with other information – entailed choices about which failing to think statistically made the clinician vulnerable to error and misjudgment at best and, at worst, courted catastrophe. He also clarified for me that prediction and decisions in the context of practice were both pervasive and unavoidable, notions that were previously only inklings. Looking ahead, I could see that these lessons stood to save my bacon when and if I ever worked as a psychologist, and I figured I had a great deal more to learn from Meehl. He became my fourth and last hero (Figure 4.1).

My time at Jack's lab afforded me both time and colleagues to explore previously unexplored areas of psychology. One of these was the Rorschach. Of course I had been nominally familiar with this test from my conversations with Bill Radke and had actually taken it from Red Thomas, but these interactions had not led to actual study. The supply of stimulus materials in the lab included the blots, and I began reading about the test. It the course of this study, I wrote to Martin Mayman to request a copy of his recent, unpublished form-level scoring manual, which he generously sent me.

By the fall of 1967 I was ready to return to school. I had married earlier that year and, with my wife, Mary, who had been my supervisor at the welfare department, and my two stepsons, Mel and Rod, ages 8 and 6, I returned to San Diego to begin studies toward the Masters' Degree at

Figure 4.1 Paul Meehl and Dave Nichols.

San Diego State. We were able to rent a small house only a few minutes from the campus for $90 a month. The boys attended a nearby elementary school (where the Principal was my wonderful second grade teacher, Ima Newberry!). We were supported by Mary's employment at a social services agency in Chula Vista that served mostly Black and Hispanic clients, as she pursued her MSW, and by monthly $100 checks from my folks.

If psychology at SDSC had an overall orientation, I was unable to detect it. With 35 or so faculty, the Department was many times the size of that at SSC, and enormously more diverse in terms of faculty interests. These ranged from the philosophy of science to operant behavior to evoked potentials to game theory to the social psychology of race relations to signal detection theory to experimenter effects to existentialism to the orienting reflex. Psychology at SDSC was for me a splendid hors d'oeuvres tray; my first real introduction to its breadth, research strategies, and substantive domains. Looking back, I can't think of a single class that I did not enjoy and profit from. However, one stands out. Theories of Learning was taught by Virginia Voeks. A graduate advisee of both Edwin Guthrie and Clark Hull, she understood and was able to communicate the material of this course in astonishing depth, and in terms readily understandable from her students' ordinary experience. Moreover, she related to her students on the assumption that all were exceptionally bright and engaged. Although this assumption in my own case left something to be desired, I certainly exceeded my own expectations in terms of the bounty of value I took away from this course. Although I could not have known so at the time, throughout my working career I would draw on that value more often, and with greater benefit, than from any other single course in my graduate training. The section of our text (Hilgard & Bower, 1966) on learning sets ("learning to learn"), particularly caught my attention. I was reminded again of Norma Rosenquist's mention of Bateson's double-bind, an idea then being discussed as a risk factor for schizophrenia (Bateson et al., 1956).

These years also overlapped with the Viet Nam war protests and the emergence of the Black Panther Party, and I remember vividly an evening in one of the classrooms at the college while sitting with perhaps 6–8 others in the company of Eldridge Cleaver. We listened as he related some of the history of that movement, of the oppression of Black citizens by the Oakland Police Department, and of his aspirations for his party and race. I had, of course, heard a great deal about Cleaver before that evening, but was quite unprepared to find him so soft-spoken and gentle in his manner, even as his language occasionally bore the color of the time (e.g., "white pigs of the power structure oinking in the faces of the people," and "if they keep this up, we going to have to barbecue some pork"). And he was just breathtakingly handsome! Later that year, and at a large public event I heard Bobby Seale, who was much more animated and vehement.

Another time a younger friend of many years who was an English major invited me to join him at one of his classes to hear Allen Ginsberg. He knew well of my affection and esteem for Ginsberg, and this afternoon proved the gift of a lifetime. Ginsberg spoke for perhaps two hours of his life in Patterson, of his mentor William Carlos Williams, of his love for William Blake, and of his 'beat' adventures in Paris, India, Morocco, and elsewhere, reading his poems and talking about poetic forms in other parts of the world, occasionally breaking his narratives up by chanting or singing while accompanying himself on his harmonium. I found it thrilling from start to finish, and was in a distinct and profound 'high" as I made my way back to my car afterward.

My last year in San Diego was largely devoted to my clinical practicum at an inpatient service that included group therapy and supervision, record keeping, and a great deal of informal interaction with both patients and staff. This site also served as my first real exposure to the MMPI, as the setting and source of participants for my Master's Thesis: Form-level and the MMPI: A construct validational study of Mayman's form-level scoring method.

I applied to PhD programs in clinical psychology that year, and was accepted outright by the University of Portland (UP). UP proved a serendipitous and happy partner in my graduate studies. In part, this was because the course offerings were similar but less demanding than those I had completed at San Diego State. There was little or no research activity for the majority of the faculty. With few exceptions, my teachers were generally agreeable and supportive, often stimulating, but not particularly demanding. In retrospect, it would be fair to judge the UP program as third-rate. On the other hand, I was no more than a third-rate graduate student, so the program was a good fit. Moreover, my graduate student peers were a considerably varied and interesting lot, and I think many were, as I was, somewhat surprised to find themselves surviving in this "advanced" academic setting. We were all at least a little afraid of failing, and this fear happily translated into mutual interest and support. There was no spirit of competitiveness that I could detect.

And Portland itself proved to be an attractive, interesting, and comfortable setting. In some ways a smaller version of San Diego. We could afford housing close to the University, close to the mental health clinic where Mary found a position as a psychiatric social worker, and close to the boys' school. The cultural and entertainment life of the city was both plentiful and convenient.

I remember learning somehow that Allen Ginsberg would be coming to Cinema 21, a locally owned movie theater. Mary and I arrived a few minutes later than we had planned, and found that seats were no longer available in the center section. We therefore went down the right aisle to find a couple of seats that were still open in the third row, about three seats from the wall. Once we settled into our seats, I noticed that Ginsberg himself was in the row immediately in front of us, and just one seat to the right. I wanted to reach to him, touch his left shoulder, to let him know how surely he had reached me, of my gratitude, and to extend my love and care to him. But I did nothing, and this failure of my moral courage is what emerged as the lesson of the evening. I resolved to do better.

Four months after our arrival, a shock came in an announcement from university administration that, due to a budget shortfall, the graduate program in psychology would close at the end of the academic year. Our class filed a lawsuit for breach of contract, but this was a panicky time for us. Several months passed before the university relented and agreed that we would be allowed to continue under the terms of our contract at the time of admission, amounting to three years of coursework, after which the program would close. Although this agreement gave us an enormous sense of relief, the message it sent to the faculty was that they were now passengers on a sinking ship, and while most were in no evident rush to leave, the air of those remaining was tentative. Happily, I was able to complete my coursework well within these time limits and, in my second year, even teach an introductory psychology course at a suburban community college. My dissertation (on a learning topic) was completed efficiently.

That left only internship. I applied and was accepted by the Department of Psychology at Dammasch State Hospital, a fairly new 12 ward, 400 bed psychiatric facility about 18 miles south of Portland in Wilsonville. Shortly before my first day, I learned that I had also been accepted for a half-time psychometrist position in a new, government grant funded alcohol treatment program at the hospital that included an assessment component under which each admission would be administered the MMPI and the Edwards Personal Preference Schedule. The most novel feature of the program was the employment, in addition to the usual hospital staff, of several case managers who were hired to reduce recidivism rates by providing enhanced care for the patients assigned to them in hospital, but also to follow them into the community upon discharge to strengthen their connections there. The remaining hours of my internship were divided among psychodiagnostic assessment referrals and their completion under supervision, attending treatment team meetings, occasional participation in group therapy sessions, informal ad lib meetings with patients on wards, consultations with other staff, making progress notes in patient charts, and Psychology Department meetings.

Within only days it became clear to me that I would be spending a great deal of time with the MMPI. My duties on the alcohol program centered on it, and it was routinely at the center of referrals to the Psychology Department, as it had been for more than a decade before my arrival. Although the MMPI was by no means unfamiliar to me, given my exposure to it in graduate school and my practicum in San Diego, I felt the need to hit the books and did so at once. The Psychology Department library had at least ten MMPI books, the hospital library had more, and I had already purchased a few of my own (largely unread). I dove into this reading as a necessary chore, something I simply needed to endure in order to do, more or less competently, what was expected of me.

I can no longer recall what it was that fired off the first spark in me, whether one or another case in Hathaway and Meehl's *Atlas* (1951), or in one of the comparisons in Marks and Seeman's (1963) book of codetypes, but I shortly found myself cognitively engaged in a way that I had never been before. Prior to this point the idea of a personality test as a species of autobiography had not crossed my mind. But reading *Atlas* cases caused a spark that placed the MMPI in the context of testimony, in contrast to the Szondi, the Rorschach, TAT, and other tests that populated the universe of performance. I felt myself bursting with curiosity, with a seemingly endless stream of questions, and a keen desire to pursue their answers and clarifications, in other books, in journal articles that I could request from the Oregon State Library, in reprints I could solicit with a post card, and in letters I could write seeking unpublished materials and manuscripts. I was off!

At the turn of the year I received an announcement that the 9th Annual Symposium on Recent Developments in the Use of the MMPI would be held in late February at the Holiday Inn in Westwood LA. About half of the names on the program were already familiar to me, but one stood out: Alex Caldwell. I no longer recall how I had first heard of Caldwell, but he'd been spoken to me as "the MMPI guru." I had tried to track down his publications, but without success, and this was only another reason to attend these MMPI meetings.

Most of the MMPI luminaries of the time were there: Jerry Wiggins, Grant Dahlstrom, Phil Marks, Jim Butcher, Wendell Swenson, Mal Gynther – all people I had known of and read, but had never seen before. And then there was Alex who, I was shortly to learn, was less a guru than the MMPI Rock Star.

I arrived at the hotel the afternoon before the meetings, noticing that The Exorcist was playing in the theaters we passed on the way in, had a light meal, read myself to sleep, awoke early, had breakfast, and waited in the lobby to register for Caldwell's advanced workshop. Facing the entrance, I saw a new bright blue sedan pull up and a man and younger woman exit to come into the hotel. The man, roughly 15 years my senior was striking because of his energetic gait and his blonde, leonine hair, and I wondered, "Is that him?" It was. The rock star. He truly looked the part. While the other mavens there stood out because they were all knowledgeable and accomplished, Alex stood out because he was passionate about the MMPI, the passion that I had so recently joined.

Our friendship started slowly, but it started. All of the other greats there were accessible, indeed welcoming, and with some I developed wonderful and lasting friendships. But Alex was especially accessible. He seemed to sense my hunger for something to feel fully engaged by, something that could secure a lasting curiosity. That something turned out to be the MMPI, and Alex was my bridge. And in the years following, our friendship never lapsed. We visited each other, stayed in each other's homes, and enjoyed countless hours of conversation by phone and at meetings. After I had achieved some level of proficiency with the MMPI, our conversations were usually peppered with the spice of lively argument. And this worked because Alex never allowed his mentorship to overshadow his friendship, a friendship I have worn with a kind of pride and gratitude that words alone cannot express.

Following the second day of the meetings, there was a reception in Alex's room with a man behind a counter serving wine. He would pour a three-quarters of an inch or so serving of red or white into a plastic cup. I don't know how many servings I consumed but, leaning against a credenza of some kind, I began to list and was unable to right myself. I fell to the floor, landing on my nose. Others nearby picked me up and restored me to my feet, and Bernard Glueck, a psychiatrist, helped me into the bathroom to treat my bleeding. Once that was taken care of, I was escorted back to my room and put to bed by Glueck, Grant Dahlstrom, and Mal Gynther.

The next day, no one uttered a word to me about my faux pas of the night before, nor did anyone later in the meetings. "These people have manners," I thought! This kindness sealed the decision I made that year, to continue to attend these MMPI meetings, as I did for the next 30 years.

Returning to the hospital after these meetings, I realized that I'd had a change of heart about my future career plans. Although never set in stone, I had always considered my career in terms of an independent practice with a primary emphasis on psychotherapy, and with psychodiagnostics only secondary and incidental. The effect of the MMPI meetings was to reverse these priorities. I left them feeling affirmed that my fascination with the MMPI and the multitude of questions its study raised in me was not a fluke but a direction, and one that would endure at that. A few months after my return, my first MMPI article was published (Nichols, 1974).

At the end of my internship I was hired by the hospital as a staff psychologist and became licensed at the end of 1975. Walter Klopfer headed my oral exam committee and, a few months later, invited me to join the Society for Personality Assessment (SPA) and to contribute to its Journal, of which he was then editor.

The settling of my career trajectory and the dissolution of my marriage were coincidental but otherwise unrelated. Mary and I had enjoyed many happy years as a team as we made our way through school and into careers, but this spirit had more recently been on the wane – for both of us – and we decided to separate. I found a small apartment in the staff quarters on the hospital grounds, and lived there for the next 18 months until I met Cathy. She had just completed her nurse practitioner training and had come to the hospital to try to learn about family therapy. As I was the only psychologist with a family in treatment at the time, our Chief Psychologist assigned her to me.

We were married only a few months before the international MMPI meetings were to open in Rome! Apart from occasional but infrequent trips to Tijuana and Tecate in northern Mexico, I had never been out of the US, although Cathy had done a year's missionary work in Liberia a few years before we met. I was apprehensive about language and communication; Cathy about having her bottom pinched or her purse snatched. We therefore arranged to depart Rome as soon as possible after the meetings ended, and press on to London via Paris. However, and rather to our surprise, our time in Rome was splendid, captivating, and insufficient. Cathy did site-seeing during my time in meetings at the University of Rome, and I joined her in walks near our hotel, in the area around the University, the Vatican, and at other sites. In all, the greatest surprise for me was my response to the Italian language as we were in its midst. I had taken German in high school and college, but in both venues found it alien and a chore. By contrast, because of its phonetic nature, Italian was familiar. Its music was enchanting, and its comprehension unnecessary for its enjoyment. Italian was, in short, a great and happy find for me.

Following the meetings, we stopped in Paris for two days on our way to London, staying at the Le Meridien near Piccadilly Circus. Although we found, much to my surprise, that our communications were not appreciably more reliable than they had been in Rome, we enjoyed our stay, and I was able to place my hand on the marble head of William Blake in Westminster Abbey. We vowed to go to Europe for future MMPI meetings, and did so – to Copenhagen in 1983, Brussels in 1987, and Bruges in 1992. In all cases we used these meetings as occasions for more extended travels to Portugal, Spain, Holland, France, Germany, England, and always Italy. Having the time and funds to afford travel in these years and since, I count as an enormous blessing of good fortune. With experience, I began to recognize a distinction between what I called "places to be" versus "places to see." What most reliably separated the former from the latter was the desire to return rather than their respective amenities, monuments, landmarks, and so on. And on this basis, it is locations in Italy that have always stood out for me in particular: Rome, Lucca, and Siena.

My MMPI focus through the rest of the '70s and '80s was on the patients I was assessing and treating at the hospital. Often in the evenings I would go back to review the case records and MMPIs of patients from many years earlier. More often than not, their MMPIs had been hand scored for only the standard validity and clinical scales, so I would score these protocols for the more transparently autobiographical Wiggins Content Scales, and often the Harris and Lingoes subscales as well, in order to better appreciate and reconcile the test results with the case history.

Paying closer attention to the Wiggins and Harris scales, and to the items comprising them, sharpened my apprehension and appreciation of the problems and issues patients were seeking to communicate via the test: "Hey, I'm taking this test to tell you about myself; are you listening?" Within a few months I began to notice an improvement in my interactions with those patients I was assessing and/or treating. Specifically, I was able to pose the kinds of questions to patients that better communicated a sense of care and understanding, and these resulted in a greater sense of closeness and candor in their responses. And there were times when, at the outskirts of this or that topic with a patient, just the right MMPI item would dance into my consciousness in a way that enabled us to move more rapidly and directly into the opening of an important topic or issue that would ben-efit from better, deeper focus. In terms of my assessment activities, these changes in my sensitivity and alertness amounted to a kind of drift roughly in the direction Steve Finn would later map out comprehensively in his therapeutic assessment innovation.

I also noticed that there were cases that would show clear clinical scale elevations and profile/codetype patterns, but *without* corresponding, at times any, elevations among the Wiggins or Harris scales. To be sure, these were a distinct minority of cases, but they refreshed for me the difference between assessment via the path of conscious self-report, and the differ-ent form of self-revelation that assessment via empirically developed scales provides, a difference analogous to what people say they do, and what they may be observed to do.

After attending the regular annual MMPI Symposium meetings every year, including the international events in Rome in 1976, and Puebla, Mexico, in 1978, I was invited to present a brief workshop on the clini-cal interpretation of the Wiggins scales for the 1983 MMPI meetings. At some point in the workshop one of the attendees asked me an off-topic question about validity. I responded by referring the questioner to the work of Roger Greene on the Carelessness Scale (1978, a precursor, if not the inspiration for the MMPI-2's Variable Response Inconsistency Scale – VRIN) on this topic, adding that I had never met Dr. Greene, but would like to someday. As the workshop ended, Roger approached me and intro-duced himself, and we agreed to meet for dinner that evening.

I dwell on this event because it was decisive in my future MMPI en-deavors. In the first place, Roger and I got along well, found each other agreeable company. But we also shared a keen interest in MMPI/MMPI-2 validity, an interest that has remained lively for both of us through the present day. Another appeal Roger had for me was his academic appoint-ment and its research-related resources, to say nothing of his sophistication in statistics and research methodology, areas in which he was much more sure-footed than I was. What most brought us together as colleagues, however, was that we shared a persisting curiosity about the test, and a skepticism about its "received wisdom." We both wanted to ask the MMPI lots of questions, and the answers to mine sometimes came in 50-pound boxes of computer printout sent from Roger's Texas Tech University, and generously carried to my office by one of the hospital mailroom staff, often with a quizzical expression!

My practice with the MMPI in the hospital continued to develop in the direction of an increasing interest in individual test items. There were instances where a single item might help me to dramatically resolve diagnostic uncertainty. I remember a man in his early 20s who was brought to the hospital by the police following an incident at a Denny's Restaurant wherein he had suddenly erupted at the friend he was seated across and struck him in the face with a Ketchup bottle, breaking a tooth. The MMPI he completed a week or so later showed an only modestly elevated profile with an equivocal, 8–9 code pattern. The answer sheet, however, was notable for the line this patient had drawn through both the True and False response spaces for item #476: "I am a special agent of God," immediately below which he had written, "I am God," with the "am" double underlined and, for me, this set the diagnostic switch to mania.

The idea that a single test item may contribute mightily to the resolution of a diagnostic uncertainty cannot be novel, although such instances must certainly be rare. But a great many of the MMPI/MMPI-2 items shed light on what might be called the patient's *story*. To have been suspended from school, hurt by criticism, had trouble making friends, been afraid of the dark, preoccupied with one's looks, suffered a convulsion or beatings as a child, been misunderstood or looked at critically, to have never been in love, to give up quickly, to feel sinful or unattractive, to have had a nervous parent, any and all of these are, in addition to test items, threads of the patient's living biography, the patient's story. Each and any item may touch one or another of these threads to potentially enrich the interview through the patient's narration of recollection, or similar or related narratives, and through the ways in which these narratives may be framed, whether by the patient or the clinician. So for me, the MMPI became a kind of lantern, bringing a bit of light to parts of a patient's history that I might have otherwise passed without notice.

I had spoken of the importance of these item-biography connections occasionally in my MMPI/MMPI-2 workshops and in the classes for the Oregon Graduate School of Professional Psychology (OGSPP) I had been teaching since 1979, but it would be another decade and more before I would have the opportunity to articulate these notions in print. One Sunday morning in early 1992 I was reading the newspaper with the TV on when I looked up to see an MMPI profile on CNN. The story switched off to another almost at once, but at that time CNN repeated many of its stories in the subsequent half hour. So I waited. The story was repeated, a report of the sanity hearing of Jeffrey Dahmer, and the psychologist presenting Dahmer's MMPI findings to the Milwaukie Court was Samuel Friedman. Although I could not recall ever seeing or hearing of him at the MMPI meetings, I was able to look him up in the APA Directory, learning that he had received his PhD from the University of Minnesota in 1950. So I phoned him, introduced myself, mentioned seeing him on CNN, and asked if he might share Dahmer's MMPI with me. To my complete surprise, he readily agreed, adding that he had two additional Dahmer MMPI protocols that he would be happy to send me as well! The MMPI that Friedman had presented at Dahmer's sanity hearing provided me the opportunity to illustrate my notions of the role that MMPI items can play in opening important understandings in a life story (Nichols, 2006a).

Changes were occurring in my own life story. Cathy and I were productive and content in our professional lives and in the course of our marriage had enjoyed many blessings including, among others, many European travels together. I remember the speed and competence she showed in adapting to driving in England, both city and highway, on our three stays there. Over time, however, our passion for one another had moved in the direction of the fondness of friendship. We had grown into something like roommates, roommates with declining mutual interests. We decided to try a period of separation, but ultimately to divorce. Happily, we remained close friends until her death in 2004.

Within months I found Diane. She had been recently hired as a social worker at the hospital, and we were frequently in treatment team meetings together. We found that we were both quite good at making each other laugh. There was also an element of mystery about her that I found mildly intriguing: She was a convert to Judaism. Of course, I had known of Judaism since childhood, and had had Jewish friends and teachers all along the way since. But I had never been to a Jewish service. Diane was observant and had been attending Jewish services weekly since her conversion, and she wanted me to join her for Shabbat at her Temple. It was clear to me that my attendance was a condition of our relationship, and I agreed to comply on those grounds. But after only two or three Fridays, I was hooked! Except for weddings, funerals, the Baptist youth group in Santa Rosa, and a few cathedrals on travel, I had hadn't set foot in a house of worship since I was eight years old. But for reasons still far from clear to me, Jewish services found a venue in me that had been previously vacant. Singing and praying in transliterated Hebrew was more than agreeable; I liked both and looked forward to them. Of course, I had no idea whatever of the meanings of the lines issuing from my own throat on these evenings, but that did not seem to matter and, since the first service I attended with Diane, I have attended only Jewish services and consider myself at this point an uncredentialed Jew.

As Diane and I moved along it became clear to me that a future as a couple really was not in the cards. That she wanted and would have children was a given for her, but for me it was a source of painful conflict. For one thing, I did not feel that I had been better than a kind of cut-rate parent to Mel and Rod when Mary and I were married, but by this point in my career I had troubling doubts about both my capacity and desire to be a sufficiently devoted and generous parent, and to pursue my MMPI work successfully. There were certainly minutes here and there at the hospital to attend to my MMPI interest on the job, but it was obvious to me that the bulk of my MMPI work would have to be drawn from "family time."

Diane was understanding about my priority here, and extraordinarily generous in enabling the shift in our relationship that freed her to pursue her longing for a child, and allowed me to remain with her as a dear and committed friend instead of a romantic partner. Within a short time, she arranged for her pregnancy and, nine months later, invited me to be present as her son Ben came to light, and honored me as Ben's Godfather! This is a role I have cherished and tried to honor, joyfully, ever since, just as he has honored me by being my main Movie Buddy.

The decade of the 90s brought more work with Roger Greene. We continued to be interested in response style issues, and these had taken a boost for both of us with Paulhus (1984, 1986) distinction between *impression management* (IM), the calculated creation of an inflated positive self-description, and *self-deception* (SD), a positive self-presentation/appraisal but without the dissimulation aspect. This resurgence in our interest led us to review several earlier MMPI scales that could be readily assigned on the basis of their patterns of intercorrelation to the IM or SD groups. We then set about to construct new scales for each of these constructs, partly on the basis of the frequency with which items were included across scales within a given category. These efforts resulted in two new scales, Other Deception (Od, 33 items, Nichols & Greene, 1991) and Positive Mental Health, version 4 (PMH4, 36 items, Nichols, 1992). Both scales appeared to perform as well as related scales in subsequent research (Baer et al., 1995; Bagby et al., 1997), but neither demonstrated clear advantages over its peers.

Having summarized our thinking about what we were later to call "dimensions of deception" in the MMPI (Nichols & Greene, 1997), Roger and I turned our attention to our separate interests. This was not to last long, however. During our times at SPA meetings, we were both hearing the words "structural summary" regularly issuing from the Rorschach side of the aisle, and these took root in Roger's thinking with the idea of a structural summary for the MMPI-2.

At the time the second volume of the Dahlstrom, Welsh, and Dahlstrom *Handbook* (1975) came out, scales developed for the MMPI numbered not less than 495, and by the end of the following decade the number of MMPI/MMPI-2 scales would comfortably exceed the number of the test's items. Or, to put the matter differently, the test had become immensely cumbersome. Between validity scales, clinical scales and their subscales, content and supplementary scales, and codetype patterns, the task of collecting, organizing, integrating, and summarizing the information from the MMPI-2's 111 *routinely* scored scales had become unwieldy, excessively time-consuming, and error prone. The MMPI-2 Structural Summary (Greene & Nichols, 1995; Nichols & Greene, 1995) was designed to help organize and keep track of the clinical implications of test scores and patterns on the basis of thematic categories (e.g., cognition, interpersonal relations) determined on the basis of item content, but also reinforced by the intercorrelations of the components within each category.

Another colleague, Alan Friedman, and I had been in touch for many years through the SPA meetings. His awareness of my interest in item content and both the Wiggins and MMPI-2 content scales led him to invite me in late 1997 to join him and his co-authors for his *Psychological Assessment with the MMPI-2* (Friedman et al., 2001, 2015).

Then, in the summer of 1998, I received a phone call from someone at the Wiley publishing company who told me that Alex Caldwell had recommended me to write the MMPI book for their *Essentials* series. Although we were in touch in person or by phone a half-dozen times or more per year, Alex had said nothing to me about this. But I was obviously flattered by his confidence in me, and interested in exploring this possibility.

The publisher wanted a manuscript within one year and I agreed. But as the months went by, my progress increasingly lagged my expectations. I became discouraged. There just did not seem to be enough time at the end of a full day's work to make enough progress on my manuscript to live up to my agreement with Wiley. Then something completely fortuitous happened. It was my lunch hour and a couple of my favorite colleagues dropped in to let me know that they had both decided to retire shortly. Happy news for them, of course, and over a matter that I had never given a moment's thought. I expressed my pleasure in their plan and prospects, but bemoaned my own troubles in making progress on my writing obligation. Whereupon one of them said, "Why don't *you* retire?" They encouraged me to explore this possibility with my state retirement system and, when I did, I learned that after 27 years in state service my retirement income would at least equal what I was earning on the job! It was an easy decision and, albeit a year late, the book got done (2001)!

But the adjustment to retirement was not easy. I had many colleagues both within and outside the Psychology Department who I respected and enjoyed, and I missed them. However, I found that, somewhat to my surprise, I missed seeing patients even more. Their histories, their conflicts and dilemmas, their voices; most of all, their stories! And the moments when an inspiration, a tear, a guess, an eyeroll, a faux pas, would bring part of a patient's story to life, to open it or to enable a new perspective, to turn a corner. Compared to the hospital in these moments, my life in retirement felt a kind of desert. It took me a few years to make this adjustment.

For many, the prospect of retirement promises to allow indulgence in a hobby beyond the time constraints imposed by one's working life, and so it has been with me. Now, as for the last 20 years, my MMPI hobby has been at the center of my daytime hours, occasionally in consultation work or writing projects of various kinds, but more typically in the leisure of awaiting a new question, idea, or strategy to enter my thoughts. And in these I have continued to be blessed by my long partnership with Roger.

In my early days of retirement I spent a good deal of time simply thinking about the items, considered one at a time, and asking of each, "What is its topic, range, reference, implication?" My purpose here was first of all to simply better familiarize myself with the item pool's range and coverage of content, but also to take note of items' elements of individuality, to identify any that might be "one of a kind."

This exercise proved a useful precursor for identifying what Roger and I called packets, small sets of 2, 3, 4, or 5 items of highly similar content. We both went carefully, and semi-independently, through the item pool, looking for content-related items that could be given a packet label. The purpose here was partly to troll for items that, in combination, might constitute a new scale. One of the packets that resulted from this search we labeled Guilt, a seven-item scale partially overlapping with Pd5, but better focused (Nichols & Crowhurst, 2006).

Another inspiration came upon reading a report by Roger and some of his students on what they called the Suicidal Potential Scale (SPS), a set of six items with explicit suicidal ideation content (Glassmire et al., 2001). I remembered returning to the test files of a couple of patients who had committed suicide while on hospital pass, but who had not endorsed any of the Koss-Butcher critical items for Depressed Suicidal Ideation or from the DEP4 subscale, Suicidal Ideation. It occurred to me that my experience was almost certainly not unique, and that patients who went on to complete suicide but who had avoided endorsing the MMPI-2's explicit suicide items, while exceptional, were not especially rare. Thus, I wondered if a scale could be created to serve as a more subtle predictor of suicidality. A search of the aggregated Rouse et al. (2008) sample for MMPI-2 items meeting two conditions: (1) achieve correlations with each of the SPS items of .2 or greater, and (2) form a coherent theme with high internal consistency yielded twelve items that accorded well with a theme of hopelessness, a construct that had found abundant prior support as a precursor of suicide by Beck and his colleagues (e.g., Beck et al., 1990). Thanks to the generous cooperation of my Italian colleagues, Maurizio Pompili, Marco Innamorati, and Denise Erbuto, the validity of the MMPI-2 Hopelessness Scale (Hp) has now been supported in a sample of 153 psychiatric inpatients (Nichols et al., 2021). Another, and less happy preoccupation in my retirement was my felt need to inform attorneys involved in personal injury cases about a new MMPI-2 scale purporting to detect malingering in such cases (Lees-Haley et al., 1991) that gained considerable popularity among defense attorneys seeking to discredit plaintiffs as malingerers. Only 3 years earlier however, Lees-Haley (1988) had asserted that more than half of the items on his MMPI-2 scale described symptoms reflecting the stresses intrinsic to the person's involvement in litigation, rather than to malingering (Nichols & Gass, 2015; Nichols, 2017).

So retirement has been in most ways a continuation of the ways I spent much of my leisure time when employed. The main difference is that I am now able to embrace writing and other kinds of opportunities as they, like this one, come along. I am now with Connie, my partner of the last decade, who shares my love of travel. I have continued to attend the SPA meetings and, more often than not, present the MMPI projects to which my curiosities have led me over the previous year, but my primary motivation for these meetings is to enjoy again the company of my far-flung colleague friends, to burnish and celebrate these connections in the moments we have together, and to make tentative plans for next year!

And as I write this now, I think back on the many, many opportunities these kinds of meetings have provided me to visit, and often stay over with my MMPI and SPA friends: Grant and Leona Dahlstrom, Bob and Eva Jane Colligan, Bob and Linda Archer, Irv and Carol Gottesman, Jim Butcher and Carolyn Williams, Steve Finn and Jim, Barton and Judy Evans, Alex Caldwell, Alan Friedman, Richard and Linda Levak, Jane Rosen and Harold, Heather Cattell, Phil Marks, Paula Garber and family, Monica and Mike Tune, Harrison Gough, Paul Meehl and Leslie Yonce, Jerry Wiggins and Krista Trobst, Jane Sachs, George and Mary Ritz, Kevin and Dianna Bolinskey, Anita Boss and Darren, Brenton Crowhurst and Michelle Ranson, Peter Schmolk, Diana and Louis Everstine, Allessandro and Stefania Crisi, Carlo and Mimma Leone, Joe and Mary Finney, Lew Goldberg, Claudia Norcia and family, Stuart and Marcia Greenberg, and of course many, many times to Roger Greene and his family (Figure 4.2).

Happily, the questions keep coming. One of my chronic retirement years' preoccupations has been the Psychasthenia (Pt) scale, Scale 7.

Figure 4.2 Paul Costa, Jerry Wiggins, Dave Nichols, and Lew Goldberg.

McKinley and Hathaway (1942) were candid in their reservations concerning their criterion sample for Scale 7, a small group of 20 patients, at least 3 of which may have been inappropriate. Additionally, because the items that discriminated the criterion and two normal control samples were considered too few to form a final scale, item correlates from the remainder of the MMPI item pool were then gathered from a normal and a general psychiatric sample. "These data combined with the original comparison data of criterion and normal cases permitted us to select a final scale of 48 items" (p. 618). However, the items that originally separated the criterion from the normal groups ("the preliminary scale") were not provided in McKinley and Hathaway's report, nor was even the *number* of these items. A subsequent internal consistency evaluation of Scale 7, as Dahlstrom et al., note (1972, p. 212), found it to be saturated with general maladjustment (i.e., First Factor) variance. (They also note the relative *absence* of items (see, e.g., 193, 322, 356, 392, 397, 447 – True; 118, 186, 245 – False) with more or less manifest obsessive, compulsive, and phobic content. Thus Scale 7 has been significantly flawed from the beginning in terms of its construct validity and has, virtually entirely, functioned as simply an alternative marker for the MMPI/MMPI-2 First Factor (r >.9 with A, PK, Mt, Sc, DEP, WRK, ANX, etc.; see, e.g., Nichols, 2006b, p. 130). In a search of the vast MMPI literature I could find no evidence demonstrating specificity for Pt scores in relation to the obsessive–compulsive disorder (OCD) construct. Beginning with the small but non-trivial number of MMPI-2 items listed above that both manifested face validity for OCD and did *not* overlap Scale 7, I decided to follow a content strategy, gathering the item correlates of these items in a large body of samples. These explorations resulted in a preliminary scale of 23 items of which 14 manifest at least some degree of obsessive/compulsive face validity, the remaining 9 suggest defensive content consistent with OCD (e.g., reaction formation; 183, 189, 222, 260 [all keyed False]), and its saturation with the First Factor is considerably reduced (r = ~.50). On the basis of its apparent face validity, this scale, provisionally labeled OCD (Nichols & Greene, 2020), appears to show sufficient promise to warrant further investigation in samples in which the frequency of OCD diagnoses is nontrivial.

Finally, it recently occurred to me that the percentage of items endorsed True (T%) regularly appears on automated scoring and interpretive reports for the MMPI-2, but the MMPI-2 *Manual* and interpretive guidebooks offer little, if any, textual guidance for the interpretive significance of this value, and no numerical guidance whatever. Helping me to gain at least modest additional perspective on this value, Roger provided me the MMPI-2 normative values for T%, enabling me to pass them along here: Males: M = 38.19; SD = 7.21. Females: M = 38.32; SD = 6.76. Note that the gender difference is tiny, such that T% levels of 45 and 52 will translate into T-scores of 60 and 70 for *both* men and women. And yet another question answered; all in all, a good, happy, and incredibly lucky life!

Note

Access to the Support Material for this chapter can be found at: www.routledge. com/9780367477431.

References

Baer, R. A., Wetter, M. W., Nichols, D. S., Greene, R., & Berry, D. T. R. (1995). Sensitivity of MMPI-2 validity scales to underreporting of symptoms. *Psychological Assessment, 7*, 419–423.

Bagby, R. M., Rogers, R., Nicholson, R. A., Buis, T., Seeman, M. V., & Rector, N. A. (1997). Effectiveness of the MMPI-2 validity indicators in the detection of defensive responding in clinical and nonclinical samples. *Psychological Assessment, 9*, 406–413.

Bateson, G. (1961). *Perceval's narrative. A patient's account of his psychosis 1830–1832.* Stanford, CA: Stanford University Press.

Bateson, G., Jackson, D. D., Haley, J., & Weakland, J. (1956). Toward a theory of schizophrenia. *Behavioral Science, 1*, 251–264.

Beck, A. T., Brown, G., Berchick, R. J., Stewart, B. L., & Steer, R. A. (1990). Relationship between hopelessness and ultimate suicide: A replication with psychiatric outpatients. *American Journal of Psychiatry, 147*, 190–195.

Blake, W. (1965). *The complete poetry and prose of William Blake.* Berkeley: University of California Press.

Butler, S. (1920). *Luck or cunning, as the main means of organic modification? An attempt to throw additional light upon Darwin's theory of natural selection* (2nd ed.). London: Fifield.

Dahlstrom, W. G., Welsh, G. S., & Dahlstrom, L. E. (1972). *An MMPI handbook: Vol. I. Clinical interpretation* (Rev. ed.). Minneapolis: University of Minnesota Press.

Dahlstrom, W. G., Welsh, G. S., & Dahlstrom, L. E. (1975). *An MMPI handbook: Vol. II. Research applications.* Minneapolis: University of Minnesota Press.

Friedman, A. F., Bolinskey, P. K., Levak, R. W., & Nichols, D. S. (2015). *Psychological assessment with the MMPI-2/MMPI-RF* (3rd ed.). New York: Routledge.

Friedman, A. F., Lewak, R., Nichols, D. S., & Webb, J. T. (2001). *Psychological assessment with the MMPI-2.* Mahwah, NJ: Lawrence Erlbaum Associates, Inc.

Ginsberg, A. *Howl and other poems* (1956). San Francisco, CA: City Lights.

Glassmire, D. M., Stolberg, R. A., Greene, R. L., & Bongar, B. (2001). The utility of MMPI-2 suicide items for assessing suicidal potential: Development of a suicidal potential scale. *Assessment, 8*, 281–290.

Greene, R. L. (1978). An empirically derived MMPI carelessness scale. *Journal of Clinical Psychology, 342*, 407–410.

Greene, R. L., & Nichols, D. S. (1995). *The MMPI-2 structural summary* [computer software]. Odessa, FL: Psychological Assessment Resources.

Hathaway, S. R., & Meehl, P. E. (1951). *An atlas for the clinical use of the MMPI.* Minneapolis: University of Minnesota Press.

Heidegger, M. (1962). *Being and time.* New York: Harper & Row.

Hilgard, E. R., & Bower, G. H. (1966). *Theories of learning* (3rd ed.). New York: Appleton-Century-Crofts.

Jones, E. (1957). *The life and work of Sigmund Freud.* New York: Basic Books.

Lees-Haley, P. R. (1988). Litigation response syndrome. *American Journal of Forensic Psychology, 6*, 3–12.

Lees-Haley, P. R., English, L. T., & Glenn, W. J. (1991). A fake bad scale on the MMPI-2 for personal injury claimants. *Psychological Reports, 68,* 203–210.

Levy, L. H. (1963). *Psychological interpretation.* New York: Holt, Rinehart & Winston.

MacCorquodale, K., & Meehl, P. E. (1954). Edward C. Tolman. In W. K. Estes, S. Koch, K. MacCorquodale, P. E. Meehl, C. G. Mueller, Jr., W. N. Schoenfeld, & W. S. Verplanck, *Modern learning theory: A critical analysis of five examples* (pp. 177–266). Appleton-Century-Crofts.

Marks, P. A., & Seeman, W. (1963). *Actuarial description of abnormal personality: An atlas for use with the MMPI.* Baltimore, MD: Williams & Wilkins.

Meehl, P. E. (1947). Schizophrenia, catatonic form. In A. H. Burton & R. E. Harris (Eds), *Case histories in clinical and abnormal psychology* (pp. 71–83). New York: Harper.

Meehl, P. E. (1954). *Clinical vs. statistical prediction.* Minneapolis: University of Minnesota Press.

Nichols, D. S. (1974). The Goldberg rules in the detection of MMPI codebook modal diagnoses. *Journal of Clinical Psychology, 38,* 186–188.

Nichols, D. S. (2001). *Essentials of MMPI-2 assessment.* New York: Wiley.

Nichols, D. S. (2006a). Tell me a story: MMPI responses and personal biography in the case of a serial killer. *Journal of Personality Assessment, 86,* 242–262.

Nichols, D. S. (2006b). The trials of separating bathwater from baby: A review and critique of the MMPI-2 restructured clinical scales. *Journal of Personality Assessment, 87,* 121–138.

Nichols, D. S. (2011). *Essentials of MMPI-2 assessment* (2nd ed.). New York: Wiley.

Nichols, D.S. (2017). Fake bad scale: The case of the missing construct, a response to Larrabee, Bianchini, Boone, and Rohling. *The Clinical Neuropsychologist, 31,* 1396–1400.

Nichols D. S., & Crowhurst, B. (2006). The use of the MMPI-2 in inpatient mental health settings. In J. N. Butcher (Ed.), *MMPI-2: A practitioner's guide* (pp. 195–252). Washington, DC: American Psychological Association Press.

Nichols, D. S., & Gass, C. S. (2015). The fake bad scale: Malingering or litigation response syndrome – Which is it? *Archives of Assessment Psychology, 5*(1), 5–10.

Nichols, D. S., & Greene, R. L. (1995). *Interpretive manual for the MMPI-2 structural summary.* Odessa, FL: Psychological Assessment Resources.

Nichols, D. S., & Greene, R. L. (1997). Dimensions of deception in personality assessment: The example of the MMPI-2. *Journal of Personality Assessment, 68,* 251–266.

Nichols, D. S., Innamorati, M., Erbuto, D., Pompili, M., & Ryan, T. A. (2021). An MMPI-2 hopelessness scale. *Journal of Affective Disorders Reports, 3C*(2021) 100057.

Paulhus, D. L. (1984). Two-component models of socially desirable responding. *Journal of Personality and Social Psychology, 46*(3), 598–609.

Paulhus, D. L. (1986). Self-deception and impression management in test responses. In A. Angleitner & J. S. Wiggins, (Eds.), *Personality assessment via questionnaires* (pp. 143–165). New York: Springer-Verlag.

Ruesch, J., & Bateson, G. (1951). *Communication: The social matrix of psychiatry.* New York: W.W. Norton.

Sullivan, H. S. (1954). *The psychiatric interview.* New York: W. W. Norton.

Sulloway, F. J. (1996). *Born to rebel: Birth order, family dynamics, and creative lives.* New York: Pantheon Books.

Szondi, L. (1947). *Experimentelle Triebdiagnostik.* Bern, CH: Hans Huber.

Van Dusen, W. (1965). Mind in hyperspace. *Psychologia: An International Journal of Psychology in the Orient, 8,* 81–90.

White, R. W. (1964). *The abnormal personality* (3rd ed.). New York: Ronald Press.

5 Personality Assessment Land

Ety Berant

I was born in Israel to Holocaust survivor parents, which I believe made them sensitive and alert to their surroundings. They were pleasant and friendly but at the same time watchful, and attentive to subtle shifts in conversations. They were especially attentive to signs of dissatisfaction or negative emotion. Conversations thus conveyed verbal content but an implicit hidden message at the same time. They were opiniated people and could render sharp portraits of the traits of others. These survival instincts continued to affect them throughout their lives. I believe I inherited this dual awareness of language, without its ominous overtones.

As new immigrants to Israel from Czechoslovakia they faced formidable hurdles: they did not speak Hebrew and needed to adapt rapidly to the Israeli culture of the 1950s that differed so much from the European mentality and values they were used to. As a child, I lived in a bilingual world with one foot in Israeli culture and the other in the culture that my parents had left behind, a world that was a combination of beauty and destruction. Strikingly, people often told me that they did not think I was born in Israel. I was raised on stories about their peaceful life before the Holocaust, but of course was exposed to their sorrows and what they endured during the Holocaust. I believe that I was my parents' bridge between the old world of Europe that had been destroyed forever, and the new world of Israel with its promise of building a normal, peaceful life. This role was not easy at a time when newly independent Israel was in the midst of building the new country and was not tolerant of other cultures. No one had heard of the concept of post-trauma and the tragedy of Holocaust survivors was pointedly ignored until Holocaust survivors testified in recorded hearings that were broadcast in the radio in Israel during the Eichmann trial in 1961. Until then, the notion of victimhood as psychological trauma was unheard of.

In the 1950s, all new immigrants were required to Hebraize their names, even though this negated the fact that a person's name is part of his or her identity. My parents told me how hard it was to register me with a foreign name (I was named after my grandmother who perished in the Holocaust). I remember as a child being asked to produce my ID card to prove that Ety was my official name. This governmental and societal attitude left very little room for cultural differences. Newcomers were

DOI: 10.4324/9781003036302-5

expected to conform to Israeli norms. I believe that this duality contributed to my tendency (perhaps as a coping strategy) to see both sides of the coin, an attitude which I consider to be one of the building blocks of personality assessment. Inside the four walls of our house, I was raised in a cultured atmosphere that included a love of music, opera, and reading. My parents had a highly developed appreciation of the arts and esthetics. My father was a talented painter and I wonder whether this sense of esthetics is also related to my fondness for the Rorschach.

I believe that my early experiences as a child contributed to my listening with the "third ear" to clients' utterances when treating or assessing them. My childhood taught me that a picture is more than the sum of its parts. These were the first seeds of my integrative attitude toward personality assessment. When later, I encountered the world of clinical psychology, personality assessment and the Rorschach, I was fascinated with its richness and depth, the range of languages available to analysis and the comprehension of the human being as a whole.

After graduating from high school, like all my classmates I was drafted into the Israel Defense Forces, which is mandatory in Israel. I served as a medical secretary in a military hospital in the Institute of Speech Therapy. This institution was initially built to treat soldiers but very quickly turned into an institution for civilians. There I had my first chance to see and experience the points of view of clients, doctors and therapists. I was fortunate to learn about speech therapy from the director of the clinic. A few months following my arrival, he asked me to help him with the intake of children who had problems pronouncing words, or who stuttered. This early experience taught me the value of good intake. This was the start of my career as an assessor where I saw first-hand how complex it can be: the way parents describe their children's problems, their attitude towards these problems, the process of diagnosis of speech problems, differentiating between two types of stuttering, etc. I also learned how important empathy is when interviewing parents about their children's difficulties and when explaining their children's problems to them. What a wound it is for a parent to have a child who stutters! How threatening even a minor speech pronunciation problem can damage parents' views of themselves when they are low on self-esteem. However, as I became more qualified in this field, I felt that I wanted to delve deeper into the emotional world of individuals who suffered from stuttering, their self-esteem, their families' handling of their stuttering. I remember that I wondered why parents try to minimize their children's symptoms or find it difficult to engage in speech exercises with them. Similarly, I wondered why some parents exaggerate their children's problems. At this juncture I wanted to go beyond assessing and observing by combining assessment with treatment, and so decided to become a clinical psychologist.

After my stint in the army, I enrolled in the Psychology Department at Bar-Ilan University (where I earned my three degrees) and was captivated by psychopathology, child development and personality theories. Graduate school was a natural continuation. My first personality assessment teacher was a European gentleman who taught us the Piotrowski system. Mr. Edelstein had immigrated from Europe and his Hungarian accent still inflected his Hebrew. He was strict about administering, coding and writing in a very structured manner, but on the other hand was very creative and had a deep dynamic understanding of clients. His classes were inspiring. I felt that when I was conducting personality assessment and especially the Rorschach, clients did not have to tell me about themselves because their subconscious and inner world was opening up in front of me like a fan when they responded to the Rorschach (as in the line from the poem "subconscious opens like a fan" by Yona Wallach) as though their inner world revealed itself without my needing to ask many questions. The Rorschach or TAT (Thematic Apperception Test) content rise to the surface, enabling the assessor to infer the clients' stream of thoughts, feelings and object relations.

At end of my residency in clinical psychology I was recruited to be on the staff of the Bar Ilan University graduate clinical program in the Department of Psychology. I taught the clinical practicum, psychopathology and personality assessment. In the clinical practicum I combined personality assessment and psychoanalytical and psychodynamic theories. When supervising my students, I stressed the importance of formulating a diagnosis before beginning therapy. I felt that besides the DSM (Diagnostic and Statistical Manual of mental disorders, 2013) diagnosis, clinicians must be familiarized with the clients' core conflicts defenses, and coping styles. This can be derived from a thorough intake and from tests. Since that time, I realized that the fields of psychotherapy, psychopathology, and personality assessment are interconnected and it was fascinating to find the key to a dynamic understanding of the clients on the Rorschach or the TAT or even at times on the Wechsler. I served as the chairperson of the adult clinical program for three years and focused on the improvement of assessment courses and psychotherapy.

In the 1990s, while I was teaching a personality assessment course, I was introduced to the Comprehensive System (CS; Exner, 1993) when one of my colleagues who immigrated from the USA and was a student of John Exner told me about the CS and its advantages as compared to the Piotrowski (1957) system. She even agreed to teach me and supervise me on the Comprehensive System. I remember how much we had struggled with scoring on the Piotrowski. This came at a good time since some personality assessment specialists in Israel adhered to the Piotrowski school but others to Klopfer (Klopfer et al., 1954), or Beck (Beck et al., 1961). So even then, in such a small country as Israel, there was a Tower of Babel regarding Rorschach systems. The CS coding and its structured analysis of the Rorschach made personality assessment easier and clearer. The fact

Figure 5.1 The author with John Exner and members of the Israeli Society in Sweden.

that the CS determinants are based on empirical evidence added to its value (Figure 5.1).

Later while attending a European Rorschach Association (ERA) conference in Madrid I met Irv Weiner who was giving a workshop and got to know Phil Erdberg who delivered a lecture at that conference. This conference was a Eureka moment despite the 100-degree heat in the non-air-conditioned auditorium where the conference was held. When I got back from Madrid, I decided to concentrate on personality assessment and in particular the Rorschach. Afterwards I invited Irv Weiner to Bar Ilan University where he gave a two-day workshop which was a great success with a high turnout and mind-bending content. I believe that this workshop (and workshops I have attended since then) taught me how to think about personality assessment and most notably the Rorschach. These workshops also taught me how to teach the Rorschach, and how to convey complex concepts in a simple, clear, and coherent way. Irv Weiner, Barry Ritzler, and Bruce Smith, whom I invited to Bar Ilan, gave inspiring examples of how to appraise and analyze the Rorschach, which were very helpful in forming an integrative and coherent personality picture. Barry Ritzler's visit cast the Rorschach in a very different light. The Israeli folk dances that Barry never missed every night after the workshop gave him an instant following (Figure 5.2).

Figure 5.2 The author with Irv Weiner, Nancy Kaser–Boyd, and friends.

The advent of the internet suddenly enabled us to become a one big personality assessment community. It is rewarding to ask a scoring question or to write about my doubts about an assessment in the morning and get the appropriate responses from the masters (Irv Weiner, Barry Ritzler, Phil Erdberg and Greg Meyer) that evening. These consultations made us feel that we were on the cutting-edge of knowledge. I believe that their availability and their generosity in sharing their knowledge furthered my motivation. I have learned two lessons from these exchanges. The first is that one should be generous with knowledge, and the second is to convey it with the joy and passion we ourselves experience while assessing. I learned that our enthusiasm and love of personality assessment is contagious (Figure 5.3).

In these years, in addition to my academic activities, I was also conducting Rorschach workshops for psychology institutes and psychiatric hospitals in Israel. Clinical psychologists who had specialized in other systems wanted to get up to date and work with the CS. I felt that these workshops were important in upgrading our profession by enabling the psychological community to kept abreast of advances in the field. Very soon afterward all universities in Israel switched to the CS one right after the other. In the late 1990s my colleagues and I attended and presented in conferences first in Europe and then also in the US. In the summer seminars, we were fortunate to meet John Exner in person (a privilege, since these seminars were limited to 35 participants). Exner was charismatic and insightful

Figure 5.3 The author with Joni Mihura, Greg Meyer, and Joav Stien.

in his delivery of the Rorschach. We later founded the Israeli branch of the International Society. My colleagues and I felt very welcome at these meetings. I felt that these meetings enlivened the materials and gave them a personal touch that contributed to knowledge and to teaching. In the meetings of the Israeli Society we presented case studies and learned about new developments in the field (presented by members who had gone to the personality assessment conferences abroad). I am the Head of the Israeli group and was also on the Board of the ISR–International Society of the Rorschach and other Projective Methods (for three years) which gave me a perspective on what happens behind the scenes

However, there always surprises and unexpected events in life. Just as I thought that the Rorschach had been firmly established, the "sky of the Rorschach darkened" with criticism of its reliability and the validity and the legitimacy of using the Rorschach in the clinical and forensic fields. The voices of Wood (2003) and colleagues were heard loudly, and Rorschach scholars mustered its forces to defend the test.

As though this were not enough, the event that shocked and upended the assessment society was the death of John Exner in February 2006. Many members of the society felt that they had lost their leader or even symbolically their "father." Unfortunately, when some of Exner's closest collaborators who were also on the board of the research council wanted to continue developing the Rorschach, a bitter dispute broke out between them and Exner's family. The result was the founding of the R–PAS—Rorschach Performance Assessment System group (Meyer et al., 2011). Even before this group was set up, I had been in touch with Greg Meyer, Joni Mihura and with Phil Erdberg. I felt that going further with the new developments they suggested was the right thing to do and the right direction to take. I considered that the developments they suggested (with Don Viglione and the late Bob Erard) provided solutions to a number of problems related to administering the Rorschach that had not been resolved with the CS, and which had led to certain coding and conclusions that did not make sense to some clinicians. I thought that the R-PAS system was less time consuming and more parsimonious to administer and code, which allowed for more time and latitude for a deeper interpretation of the Rorschach. Joni Mihura and Greg Meyer came to Israel (as my guests) three times to give R-PAS workshops to the Israeli academic and clinical communities. I believe that the R-PAS enabled us to make the changes needed in the academic and clinical field with respect to the use of the Rorschach. Since the time allotted to teaching personality assessment had been curtailed in curricula, the fact that the R-PAS took less time to learn and to administer ended up being a good response to the opponents of the Rorschach who also claimed that too much time and effort was being invested in personality assessment. The empirical basis of the R-PAS was also a plus.

Six years ago I was asked by Prof. Mario Mikulincer, the founder and first Dean of the Baruch Ivcher School of Psychology at the Interdisciplinary Center Herzliya, to join and be a member of the new post-graduate clinical program and develop a research practice-oriented clinic for the community that would treat children and adults. I accepted this challenge, and we became the first academic program in Israel to offer the R-PAS (soon followed by other academic institutions in Israel). The clinic that I head operates on a large scale. We provide various kinds of psychotherapy to 300 clients per year. The clinic is research-oriented in that the psychotherapy sessions are videotaped, which allows for tight supervision and provides recorded data for research purposes. Clients also complete self-report questionnaires on their mental state. Being the Head of the clinic has allowed me to refine the assessment process. We integrate self-report tools into the standard battery of tests. We also use computerized programs to detect attention issues. In addition to my academic activities, I supervise psychotherapy and personality assessment to make sure that therapy is tailored to the needs of each client. We work according to the therapeutic assessment principles of S. Finn. Our clinicians constantly tell us how meaningful this process is for them, and the extent to which the personality assessment matters in the life of their clients. This is especially true for neglected children from broken homes who are referred to assessment by the welfare department. As one of my supervisees told me: "I felt that in the assessment it was the first time that professionals had taken the child's problems seriously." The children themselves felt that their life mattered, and that someone is listening and seeing them. The social welfare authorities take our recommendations seriously, which is a source of great satisfaction for us the staff members of the clinic.

In concluding the more personal part of this chapter I would like to mention that during my undergraduate years I married Michael, who is a pediatric cardiologist. We have 3 children. Ron is a physician and the Head of the ER unit at Schneider Medical Center for children, Jonathan is an Associate Professor in the School of Computer Science at Tel-Aviv University and Dafna is currently a resident in the Schneider Medical Center for children. We have six sweet grandchildren aged 2–16 who give us a lot of joy and mean that we often go to concerts, museums, and other outings. During all these years of raising our children and helping out with the grandchildren my priority has been my family. I know that it is not easy for women to excel in both demanding fields. I always felt that my contribution was worthwhile to my family, and value my family life as much as I value the clinic and my academic career. The importance of building a family was tightly bound up with my internal dialogue with my generous and loving parents. My family in a sense repaired the threads of the family cloth that had been ripped apart.

Professional aspects of my life

At the start of the new millennium, besides doing clinical work and teaching, I started to work with Mario Mikulincer and Phil Shaver, who are prominent researchers in attachment theory. They were curious about the psychodynamic world of insecurely attached individuals. Interestingly, at that time while delving into the life of the founders of attachment theory, I discovered that Mary Ainsworth, who was famous for her empirical "strange situation" studies (Ainsworth et al., 1978) (i.e., an experiment that gave empirical validity to Bowlby's [1982] attachment theory) had worked with Bruno Klopfer before meeting Bowlby. After World War II, Ainsworth took part in Rorschach workshops with Bruno Klopfer, because she had been asked to teach a personality assessment course. These workshops resulted in an influential collective volume on the Rorschach by Bruno Klopfer, Walter Klopfer, and Robert Holt entitled *Developments in the Rorschach techniques* (1954). Because of her background in the Rorschach, Bowlby hired her to be the head of his lab in London to conduct empirical studies on attachment when she relocated there with her husband (Rudnitsky, 1997). In the last interview before she died, Mary Ainsworth stated that she initially believed she could integrate the Rorschach with Bowlby's empirical work. However, by the end she concluded that this was not possible. "…when I got there, I thought this was not a feasible thing to do. I used it as a clinical psychologist as a diagnostic tool after I left London, but I have never settled down to make a new system of analysis that would fit the attachment theory" (Rudnytsky, 1997). I wonder what Mary Ainsworth would think today about the large body of research on the Rorschach and fMRI (Porcelli & Kleiger, 2016; Giromini et al., 2019)!

My focus on attachment theory together with my clinical work encouraged me to integrate the two. I was encouraged by the real interest on the part of Mikulincer and Shaver in the unconscious world of secure and insecure individuals, and their belief that dynamic patterns should be researched when studying attachment orientations. I have encountered many clinicians who feel there is a contradiction between research and clinical practice. I think it is the duty of clinical psychologists to prove to researchers that their work can be based on empirical data and research.

In addition to their specific orientation, clinical psychologists can be divided into two camps: (a) those who are more psychoanalytically oriented, who believe in the strength of the Rorschach and other performance-based tools, and (b) those who prefer explicit measures such as self-report scales. The more psychoanalytically and dynamically oriented camp tends to dismiss the usefulness of self-report tools by claiming that individuals who do not disclose their pain, flaws and conflicts when they are asked directly about them and become defensive about disclosing conflicts or problems will not respond honestly and openly on self-report tools. Rather, they will be influenced by social desirability bias and self-censorship that prevents these individuals from responding authentically. I think that we should integrate the self-report questionnaires with performance-based tools.

Most attachment theory studies have been focused on conscious manifestations of secure, anxious or avoidant coping strategies rather than the implicit subconscious processes theorized to be part of what Bowlby (1969/1982) called the "attachment behavioral system." In an attempt to respond to the controversy on the ability of self-report attachment orientation questionnaires to capture differences in underlying unconscious processes, Mikulincer, Shaver and I decided to study the associations between self-report tools measuring attachment related anxiety and avoidance and theoretically selected markers of these attachment dimensions on the Rorschach test (1921/1942). The aim was to fill the empirical gap in adult attachment by determining whether individual differences in self-report attachment scales reflect the implicit underlying hyperactivating and deactivating strategies of affect regulation. The results showed that self-report attachment dimensions are indeed coherently associated with theoretically chosen Rorschach markers. In addition, the Rorschach markers of attachment orientation were correlated with each other but not with Rorschach markers of other attachment orientations. The findings thus supported the claim of an association between attachment self-report measures and Rorschach markers (Berant et al., 2005). The findings also challenged the claim that the Rorschach test is empirically invalid (Wood et al., 2003). The results thus confirmed the validity, theoretical relevance and utility of the Rorschach.

In my opinion, these results added depth and meaning to the psychodynamic world of insecurely attached individuals. For example, one interesting psychodynamic explanation that relates to the interpersonal aspect of attachment theory addresses the tendency of anxiously attached individuals to give more CF responses. Based on Schachtel's theory (1943), Overton (2000) contended that the dominant attitude of people who display CF is highly subjective and mainly based on their emotional experiences rather than attention to the other. This is consistent with studies indicating that individuals who are anxiously attached tend to minimize cognitive distance from the other by creating an illusion of closeness and projecting their own self traits onto the other (Mikulincer & Horesh, 1999).

Our findings suggested that anxiously attached individuals are attracted to emotionally laden situations (they have a higher affective ratio). They also showed that individuals who scored high on attachment anxiety had a complex, ambivalent and confused emotional world in which negative emotions crowded out positive feelings (Color Shading Blend). What complicates the situation is that anxiously attached individuals seem attracted to emotionally laden experiences, somewhat like a moth to flames. Previous studies have found that this Rorschach score (Color Shading Blend) is associated with depression and suicidal tendencies (Appelbaum & Colson, 1968; Weiner, 2003; Exner & Erdberg, 2005). This finding coheres with Mikulincer and Shaver's claim (2016) based on their empirical studies, that the hyperactivating attachment strategies used by anxiously attached individuals produce a chaotic mental architecture pervaded by unregulated negative emotions. Relatedly, habitual resorting to hyperactivation may lower the threshold for triggering the sympathetic nervous system and diminish the capacity to exert cortical control over emotional reactions (Wallin, 2007). Attachment anxiety interferes with the downregulation of negative emotions and leads to intense and persistent distress. As a result, people high on attachment anxiety experience an unmanageable stream of negative thoughts and feelings which contribute to cognitive disorganization and fuel chronic worries and distress (Ein-Dor et al., 2010). This finding also contributes to a better understanding of the dynamics of the interpersonal dimension of attachment anxiety. They reasoned that hyperactivating strategies favor the spread of negative affect throughout working memory, and that subsequent to positive mood induction, anxiously attached individuals seem to be reminded of the downside of previous positive experiences and especially attachment relationships that somehow ended painfully.

Anxiously attached individuals tend to experience high levels of distress (Y and m). The findings of elevated levels of m and Y among anxious people that reflect their current experience of situational stressors and a sense of helplessness (m, Y) contributes to clarifying the relational dynamics behind the hyperactivating strategies used by anxiously attached individuals. Mikulincer and Shaver (2016) claimed that the frequent feeling of being overwhelmed by feelings of distress, vulnerability and helplessness is not only an unwanted reflection of difficulties in emotional regulation but also an instrumental means of eliciting others' love and support, which is the main purpose of the anxious individual's hyperactivating strategies.

This line of theorizing is supported by the tendency of these individuals to give Rorschach responses related to food (fd), indicating their passive and dependent position in life (Exner, 2000), and by their propensity to display MOR responses that reflect their vulnerable self-image and perception of themselves as weak, helpless and unworthy. This pattern of Rorschach scores is coherent with Mikulincer and Shaver's (2016) contention that the overly negative self-characterization of anxiously attached individuals is sometimes an attempt to elicit other people's compassion and support. This study thus pointed to the dynamics underlying self-reports of attachment anxiety. Rorschach scores help clarify the complex emotional world of the anxiously attached individuals and in particular the pain caused by reliance on hyperactivating strategies, together with the secondary gains of eliciting others' compassion.

Similarly, self-reports of attachment-related avoidance were thought to reflect the deactivation of attachment needs and were associated with Rorschach scores theorized to reflect lack of acknowledgement of need states, a disengaged orientation to the world (high L), and maintenance of a grandiose self-façade (reflection, Cg). This disengaged orientation was interpreted as reflecting the main goal of deactivating strategies, namely, to keep the attachment down-regulated to avoid the acute pain and distress caused by potentially demanding or threatening person-environment exchanges.

The high number of reflections and Cg Rorschach scores which were thought to reflect an exaggerated sense of self-worth, the use of narcissistic defenses, and a tendency to maintain a façade (Exner, 2000) converged with Mikulincer and Shaver's claim that avoidant individuals' perception of themselves as competent and powerful was a defensive façade that helped them handle distress and convince others that they do not need help or support. The Rorschach scores also emphasized the split in avoidants' mental representations that consists of showing an arrogant face and never allowing themselves to feel needy or personally involved with others. These findings are important because they were obtained on the Rorschach test, which is presumably less influenced by social desirability and other self-report biases.

Afterward, I extended the findings of this study beyond its structural elements to examine the associations between the individual's attachment orientation and content-based dimensions of ego-boundary representations (Fisher & Cleveland, 1968) and defensive processes. These dimensions were investigated through projective material, because these specific contents convey clients' authentic experience more closely than some of the structural determinants (i.e., Y, m, FM, Color Shading Blends). The results showed that self-reported attachment anxiety was associated with increased rates of penetration related percepts on the Rorschach, the use of projective identification, and the tendency towards cognitive slippage (INC and FAB) indicating boundary blurring (Berant & Wald, 2009).

These associations further clarified theoretical and empirical data on hyperactivating strategies used by anxiously attached individuals (Mikulincer & Shaver, 2016). The findings also contributed to a better understanding of anxious attachment dynamics by accounting for the fragile "equipment" they have at their disposal. Not only do they exaggerate their and stress, they also express metaphorically that they have a "thin skin" which is manifested by their Penetration score (Fisher & Cleveland, 1968). Such sensitivities make them particularly vulnerable as though they do not have a "protective shield" so that even a minor hassle turns into a major threat that can result in disordered thinking (Rapaport et al., 1945; Blatt & Ritzler, 1974). This study indicated that anxious individuals tend to use more projective identification, a defense that allows them to project their own characteristics and feelings onto an external object, thus controlling the others and driving them to "role compliance." The Rorschach findings suggest that presenting a weak façade, something that might be considered a manipulation, does not only serve to keep their objects close to them and force their partners into role compliance to prevent desertion. Rather, the Rorschach findings point to their vulnerability and their weak ego functions (as demonstrated by the penetration scores, the cognitive slippage indicating boundary blurring and the use of the less mature defense of projective identification).

Beyond the richer picture of the mental world of insecurely attached individuals, these studies also increased my interest in the integration of results from self-report measures with the Rorschach, and more specifically, the weak association reported in the literature between self-report measures and Rorschach scores (Archer & Krishnamurthy, 1993b). In an extension to work by Meyer (1997) and Bornstein (2000), my colleagues and I (Berant et al., 2008) examined the moderating role of self-disclosure on this association between dimensions examined by self-report and their corresponding indices in the Rorschach. That is, we looked at whether individuals who are prone to self-disclose are likely to complete self-report measures in a sincere manner and openly report their feelings, thoughts and opinions. We predicted that they would be more open about revealing their emotional pain and would be less threatened by exposing their mental distress. We expected they would be in a state of greater internal harmony. The participants were divided into high and low disclosure groups that was measured with Self Disclosure Questionnaire (Jourard & Lasakow, 1958). We found significant associations between the self-report scales of suicidality (Suicide Risk Scale; Plutchik & van Pragg, 1986), depression (Beck Depression Inventory; Beck & Steer, 1987) and loneliness (revised UCLA Loneliness Scale; Russell et al., 1980) and the corresponding Rorschach markers of psychological distress (suicidality, depression and loneliness) among high self-disclosers but not among low self-disclosers. The correlations between self-report (BDI and UCLA Loneliness scale) and the Rorschach markers of depression and loneliness were stronger in the high self-disclosure group than in the low self-disclosure group. These findings suggested that when participants were more relaxed about self-disclosure, there was a match between their deliberate and conscious reports of their psychological distress and the corresponding subconscious materials in the Rorschach. This may imply that self-disclosure is a facilitating factor in the convergence of self-report scales and the corresponding Rorschach scores (Meyer, 1997; Petot, 2005). These findings are consistent with Finn's (1996) comment that "when MMPI-II (Butcher et al., 1992) (Minnesota Multiphasic Personality Inventory) and Rorschach agree, it is because there is no hidden underlying disturbance, that is the clients' problems are quite evident in their day-to-day functioning, they are aware of these problems and are willing to report them on MMPI." These findings also have clinical implications. As noted by Meyer (1997), clients with a concordant response style may be ready to address their problems or conflicts earlier in treatment than clients with discordant response styles who may be more resistant to acknowledging the existence of conflicts, doubts or difficulties.

The findings did help me in clinical assessment and especially when discussing treatment planning with therapists. It was useful for the clinicians to understand that their clients were experiencing difficulties to disclose. This implied that in therapy they should first work on their fear to disclose before beginning to work on their presenting problems and conflicts. It seems to me that this kind of information that the client is experiencing disclosure problems helps the therapist to insist on continuing therapy, since if the working alliance becomes stronger, the client will be less anxious about self-disclosing and the therapy will unfold. Alternatively, therapists could choose to work with clients about the sources of their low self-disclosure.

My encounter with research on the Rorschach and my clinical work also underscored the importance of culture differences. Several writers including Ritzler (2004) have claimed that the Rorschach is a relatively culture-free method. I was fortunate to take part in a very large-scale project that involved collecting Rorschach norms from around the world (Shaffer et al., 2007). In this study (Berant, 2007) the sample was composed of 150 non-patient young people ranging in age from their early twenties to their early thirties. One of the most interesting findings was that only 39 of them gave the T response on their Rorschach, a determinant that was thought to emerge in every Rorschach of a mentally healthy person. This study also highlighted the importance of being attentive to the cultural differences in Israeli society such as the population that emigrated from Russia, Ethiopia, in addition to Palestinian and other minority groups. Over the years I have also found that cultural differences can impact the assessment process itself, for example when an Israeli born woman examines Ethiopian born man. This is also true for the Ultra-Orthodox population, where for example certain TAT (Thematic Apperception Test; Murray, 1971) cards that might be offensive should not be shown (Card 13MF).

While making the transition to the R-PAS, I was lucky to be involved in an R-PAS project that was designed to respond to the criticism that R-optimized administration radically alters the Rorschach task as compared to CS administration (Mattlar, 2011; Ritzler, 2011). In order to address this criticism, Meyer conducted a study that investigated the extent to which Rorschach protocols differ when administered using different guidelines. This study meta-analytically examined the impact of modified administration on the 51 CS-based variables that are found on Page 1 and Page 2 of the R–PAS profile pages, which are all the R–PAS variables that overlap with or can be easily calculated from CS variables. This was done by combining data from the six existing studies (I conducted one of them) that have examined participants assigned to standard CS administration versus an R-Optimized alternative. The metanalytic results indicated that the procedure had its intended effect of slightly increasing the average R and substantially decreasing its standard deviation (Hosseininasab et al., 2017). In addition, there were secondary decreases in the standard deviation of two variables derived from R. Variability in the percentage of R given to the last three colorful cards (R8910%) decreased substantially, and variability in Complexity decreased moderately. The findings also indicated that R-PAS variables (Viglione et al., 2014), and variables obtained using an R-optimized administration (Dean et al., 2007) are as valid as or more valid than their CS counterparts. No other reliable differences were observed.

However, it remained unclear whether changes in administration procedures affect the frequency of potential projective variables. The second study extended the first by evaluating to what extent R–optimized administration might affect the potential projective material in responses, as identified by three types of responses likely to carry projective material namely; movement, distortions, and embellishments (Exner, 1989; Weiner, 2003). Here again, there were no difference between CS and R-optimized administration related to potential projective material in the protocols. I felt that these two studies provided me with good empirical responses to critics of the R-PAS.

A significant part of my clinical work is dedicated to assessment of children, in particular children who are at high risk. Clinicians and researchers aspire to understand the well-being and inner world of children who suffer from significant health problems. There is a consensus that physical illness has a mental cost. However, it is well known that it is difficult to administer self-report questionnaires to young children especially under the age of 10, and in such cases their parents report on their children's well-being or problems. However, these reports can be inaccurate or there can be discrepancies between the parents' reports and the children's report on themselves (Briggs-Gowan et al., 1996; Mascendaro et al., 2012). Parents may over-report or underreport their children's difficulties, which is often attributed to parental distress or depression (Youngstrom et al., 2000). It is understandable that parents of children with severe health problems are under high levels of stress. This motivated us to devise a way to obtain an authentic picture from the children themselves.

Since studies had indicated a relationship between parental characteristics and their children's well-being, My colleagues (Mikulincer & Shaver) and I wanted to have a more comprehensive picture of the ways in which the dynamics and mental state of children who suffer from a life-threatening health problem was associated with their parents' personality traits. We investigated the contribution of parental attachment insecurities to their children's coping with life adversities. We examined children diagnosed at birth with Congenital Heart Disease (CHD) when they were seven years old and the contribution of their mothers' attachment orientation (examined immediately after their child's diagnosis) to their mental health. We studied the effect of the severity of children's CHD and their mothers' attachment insecurities on their children's emotional well-being and their representations of their caretakers (Berant et al., 2008). The cognitive abilities of these seven year olds are not sufficiently developed to enable them to understand their past and ongoing medical procedures, which might cause anxiety. This accounts for their need for their mother's mediation to explain their medical condition and health status to them as well as their repeated medical procedures. In addition to using self-report questionnaires, the psychodynamic structure of these children was assessed through the stories they generated in responses to CAT (Children Apperception's Test; Bellak & Bellak, 1986) cards. The stories shed light on these children with CHD implicit perceptions of themselves and their mothers, their interpersonal anxieties, and the nature of their psychological defenses (Haworth, 1996). These stories revealed their negative perception of their anxiously attached mothers; that is, their internalized negative image of their mothers. What emerged is that their mothers, who are anxious and pessimistic because of their attachment orientation, were perceived by their children as not "good enough mothers" (Winnicott, 1951), because they could not soothe their anxieties or regulate their emotional state. Children whose mothers were avoidantly attached shortly after their child's birth were revealed in their CAT stories to have a negative self-image, negative affect, and low-level defenses for managing distress. Consistent with research and the clinical literature (Mikulincer & Shaver, 2016), the children's stories indicated that being a child of an avoidantly attached mother was more detrimental to their mental health than being a child of an anxiously attached mother. Interestingly, this negative psychodynamic structure was mainly found in children who suffered from severe CHD. The stories in response to the CAT cards revealed more of these children's inner world. These children may have felt that they were not really loved by their avoidant and emotionally distant mothers, which in turn may have contributed to their negative self-perception, negative affect, the negative representations of their mother and their maladaptive modes of coping with frustration and pain. The children's stories also revealed their vulnerability when their mothers displayed anxious attachment and they had severe CHD. The clinical implications were important: we recommended that attention be paid to mothers' attachment insecurities especially if their child was suffering from severe CHD. We considered that identifying these mothers and supporting them could help children in general feel more at peace with themselves when they have a severe health problem. The children's CAT's stories exemplified that having a health problem does not necessarily have detrimental effects on children's mental health, unless the child suffers from a severe problem and his or her mother is insecurely attached. The example below discusses a CAT story in response to card 4 told by a girl with severe CHD whose mother was avoidantly attached.

> The mother is in a big hurry to go to on a trip. She is not waiting for her eldest child. The mother is angry at her eldest son because he is not hurrying. The eldest child is sad because his mother is not waiting for him. In the end they go on the trip, but the child is sad because his mother was moving very fast and did not wait for him.

Here we see the unavailability and inattentiveness of the mother to her child's wishes and needs. Furthermore, the mother is not responsive to the child's signals of distress and sadness but rather is angry with the child. This story corresponds to the Ainsworth et al. (1978) description of inattentive maternal behaviors.

The following story illustrates some of the CAT features associated with having an anxiously attached mother. This story was told by a seven-year-old boy diagnosed with CHD in response to CAT card 1:

> Here is a mother hen and she prepared a meal for her chicks. They knocked on the table, and suddenly their mother disappeared. She disappeared to the sky, perhaps she died. The chicks couldn't eat because they didn't have a mother to feed them.

The mother's behavior in the story is remarkably like that of anxious children's mothers in Ainsworth's home observations (Ainsworth et al., 1978). The mother is described as inconsistently present for her children, despite her efforts to be nurturing (i.e., preparing food). When her chicks express (possible) impatience or a demand (rapping on the table), she disappears and the children are left alone, helpless, and unable to thrive (Berant, 2009).

In an extension of the study above I found that clinically, the Rorschach and TAT are good sources of information for learning about children who find it difficult to convey their distress. For example, when children lose one of their parents at a young age, this event shakes the family, the school and the surroundings, not to mention the child. Since most of us refrain from dealing with the subject of death, these children are left alone is many cases. They feel that they are expected to return to normal life as quickly as possible, partly because they do not want to upset or burden the surviving parent. Even if they are in therapy it takes them time to open up to tell the therapist what is on their minds and in their hearts. In these cases, the Rorschach can reveal the dynamics of these children.

The vignette below describes eight-year-old twins (a boy and a girl) who lost their mother to leukemia when they were six. During her illness she was in quarantine most of the time partly because of a bone marrow transplant that eventually failed. Two years after her death the twins were referred to assessment. Dan was described as the problematic one of the two. He did not obey his nanny and fought with his twin and his sisters. Although he was a good student, if he did not like the teacher, he would disobey. In his after-school program, he got into fights with boys and felt insulted. His sister was described by the father as not having any special problems: she was a good student and sometimes domineered her girl-friends. However, he still wanted to know whether she had problems he could not detect.

Dan's Rorschach results (administered and analyzed with the R-PAS) as well as his twin sister indicated that most of their coping assets relied on intellectual and cognitive resources. This is problematic for children, especially young ones, since most of their interactions are emotionally laden. Both were very attentive to every detail in their environment. She was extremely attentive to other people and needed feedback from them, probably to make sure that she did not cause any trouble. She appeared to be preoccupied with showing her family and father that she was fine, happy, not angry and coping.

The contents of the twins' Rorschach revealed the children's distress and their troubled inner world. There were themes of negative and broken representations of the self and object, guilt feelings, being preoccupied with what happens after death and the impression that they had to be ac-robats to show the family and their father that they were coping well. The striking feature was their negative representations of the maternal object and the anger that could be directed to her but was not allowed to be ex-pressed, causing them feeling guilty.

More specifically Dan's Rorschach themes were devils, ghosts in the nursery, scary animals and a person with a scary face. He found it difficult to express his anger and saw a leg kicking a stone, not a whole human doing so. Interestingly, he saw the kicking leg in response to card VII where typically respondents see a feminine or maternal figure. Afterward he saw zombies; i.e., creatures that are brought back to life after dying that are scary. Playfulness was reflected by animals riding on a unicycle. The animals appeared to be performing acrobatics. His last response was bones (another somatic concern) that was perhaps associated with the bone marrow that failed and caused the mother's death (in Hebrew, it is the same word). The contents of the Rorschach revealed that this child was still preoccupied with his mother's death, but also contained the hope that she will return, which was also scary for him, along with his anger that his mother left him so that all is left for him is to kick her stone.

Dana's responses revealed a damaged feminine object of a woman without a head (which may have been a hint that her mother could not take care of her when she was sick). However, the show that she puts on is captured in a man doing ballet. As she continued to respond to the Rorschach the façade appeared to crack, and she saw a servant holding a skeleton in his hand. She tried again to focus on a positive representation by suggesting two people giving each other the high five. However, she failed to escape and saw afterwards a monster and a man seized and taken. The hard work she engaged in to preserve the façade of a happy and coping child was evident in particular in a man doing sprints (she only saw the legs and not the body). However, there was a collapse of these manic and narcissistic defenses because afterwards she saw a man being burned. Her farewell response again showed the manic nature of her defenses and her wish that all would end well: the fox is doing ballet.

The twins' Rorschach revealed the distress they were feeling, and how they were still thinking about their mother's death. The responses related to animals who do the acrobatics provided a sense of the difficulties they were experiencing while leading a normal life. They compared themselves to acrobats. The Rorschach demonstrated that even though the girl was coping better, she had the same concerns and distress as her brother. This assessment revealed that the children expressed implicit anger about their mother who was no longer there for them; these children tried to hide that they were still mourning for their mother and could not express it openly to avoid burdening their father and grandparents. In sum, as shown here, the Rorschach and the TAT are very useful to detect children's distress, feelings, and conflicts that they do not disclose (Berant et al., 2017).

In the last six years I have been directing the clinic in the school of psychology. In the clinic we train students and first- and second- year residents. It is a challenge to train young professionals, and to facilitate their development. The supervisors of the clinic and myself dedicate much attention to the training, which we believe is an important mission in the facilitation of their becoming professionals. We encourage them also to conduct research, and some of them engage in it willingly. They are curious about their clients' self-reports regarding their symptoms and the working alliance. We use personality assessment as an integral part of the clinical work. Besides doing assessment for the welfare authorities, schools and other agencies, we refer our clients to assessment in order to tailor their treatment to suit their needs, or when ruptures are experienced, and therapy is not progressing.

My approach to personality assessment

I define myself as a clinician and researcher. Thus, my approach to personality assessment considers these two fields to be intertwined. I believe that personality assessment should incorporate three core components: (a) constant familiarization with the most recent empirical and clinical knowledge; (b) integration of all sources of information about clients; and (c) training of students and young psychologists.

Updated empirical and clinical knowledge

When conducting personality assessment, therapists should avail themselves of cutting-edge, validated tools and update themselves constantly on recent empirical findings in psychopathology, tools that can better respond to the questions we ask about our clients, as well as the latest in personality theories and psychotherapy techniques. Keeping up to date with psychotherapy techniques makes it possible to recommend the most highly adapted therapeutic intervention. The implementation of empirical evidence in personality assessment allows us to appraise our test findings more accurately and with greater confidence. As is the case in all other sciences, personality assessors and supervisors must accept the fact that the field is in evolution, and that they cannot "rest on their laurels"; they need to devote to maintain an equivalent level of assessment and supervisory skills. A good example is the advent of the R-PAS or new versions of the Wechsler test. Conducting empirical studies also sheds new light on clinical topics. For example, in one study (unpublished) we examined the associations between attention disorders and R-PAS scores and indices. For this purpose, we approached students who had been diagnosed by a psychiatrist or neurologist as having an attention disorder and were under medical care, and a control group of students who stated they had no attention disorders. All completed the World Health Organization's adult ADHD Self-Report Scale; ASRS (Adler et al., 2003) to detect attention disorders and hyperactivity. To our surprise, several students diagnosed with attention disorders had no symptoms at all as determined by their questionnaire responses, whereas attention deficits and hyperactivity symptoms were found in some of the control students, which demonstrates the complexity of accurately assessing attention disorders on self-report scales. Constant updating enables us to keep abreast of empirical and clinical data that impact all the facets of assessment.

Integration of all assessment data

To have a comprehensive picture of the clients we appraise, data need to be collected from as wide a range of sources as possible, since each source facilitates interpretation from a different angle. These include structured interviews (e.g., SCID-II; Structured Clinical Interview for DSM; First et al., 1997), self-report questionnaires (e.g., MMPI; Butcher et al., 1992, ECR; Experiences in Close Relationships scale; Brennan et al., 1998), and the "classic battery" of performance-based tests such as the Rorschach, the TAT, and the Wechsler. When assessing children, we rely on information from significant people in these children's lives (parents and teachers) obtained through self-report tools (e.g., Conners et al., 1998).

The integration of self-report tools with performance-based tools such as the Rorschach can lead to a more comprehensive and revealing picture of the client. The Rorschach and the TAT enhance the clinician's understanding of the client's psychological state, coping, self-perception, defenses, interpersonal relationships and related psychodynamic processes. The Rorschach often circumvents the avoidance and guardedness displayed by certain clients in interviews and self-report scales. The Rorschach stimuli force the clients to rely on their internal store of associations, thereby decreasing the influence of social desirability and personal censorship. The TAT performs the same function by using pictures rather than inkblots to evoke partially subconscious motives and cognitive predispositions. The Rorschach and TAT give clients free reign to describe their perceptions and associations without the pre-imposed structure of a standard interview or the limited and closed answer alternatives of a questionnaire. Performance-based instruments can sidestep conscious attempts to distort or withhold information. Thus, studying the associations between performance-based tools and self-report scales can clarify and increase our understanding of the dimension measured on the self-report tools.

When the self-report questionnaires and the performance-based tools are aligned, this is gratifying for the assessors, and makes the assessment productive. However, when self-report tools do not converge with the picture derived from the Rorschach and the TAT, this can be frustrating. It is even more frustrating when the self-report tests do not match the clinical picture of the clients, especially when the self-report tests reveal a "healthier" personality portrait than suggested by the clinical picture and the Rorschach and TAT.

This can take place when clients find it difficult to self-disclose. They may have an underlying pathology that emerges in emotionally laden, regressive interpersonal or unstructured situations. I view this similarly to S. Finn. He argued that these clients function relatively well in familiar, structured situations when they can use intellectual resources to cope. These clients are often unaware of the full nature of their difficulties and hence have a problem reporting them on a questionnaire. They are often referred for assessment by therapists who are frustrated with their client's slow progress in therapy (Finn, 2007).

The integration of a variety of tests allows the therapist to observe and define the boundaries of what constitutes these clients' "safe space". It provides a container where they can cope well, and deal with contents they are comfortable talking about. The therapist can use this information to help these clients introspect into their world by focusing first on subjects that are less intimidating for them such as the themes that they felt comfortable mentioning on their self-report scales. These are the first subjects we should focus on in therapy, and only later delve into contents and themes that emerged in the Rorschach and TAT that these clients are less comfortable with.

Clients who suffer from somatic complaints constitute a special case of patients whose self-reports and Rorschach/TAT do not coincide. These clients are puzzled when their physicians suggest that their physical complaints may be an expression of psychological difficulties or conflicts. For these clients, performance-based tools can provide them with a better understanding of their physical symptoms and the conflicts or dilemmas they are not in touch with, repress, or deny. McDougall (1989) argued that in psychosomatic conditions, the body reacts to a psychological threat as though it were a physiological one. She suggested that there is a split between the body and mind deriving from a disconnection of consciousness from the person's emotional state. Mental states that are unable to achieve representation as ideas or feelings, are represented corporally. In these cases, the Rorschach and TAT may reveal these denied and repressed emotions and conflicts. This is exemplified when their self-reports give the impression of a relatively healthy picture that does not reflect their repressed mental state which is nevertheless manifested in their somatic complaints.

This is especially true for clients who are intelligent and can mask their emotional ineptness. A good example is the case of a client who suffered from unexplained abdominal pains and was referred for psychological treatment as a last resort. Her Rorschach findings were clearly related to a psychodynamic preoccupation with the body. The high volume of anatomical responses were combined with a paucity of M responses (a single immature *M*) and a single immature *H*. Difficulties in affect regulation, depressed mood, a high number of blood and sex contents, as well as the propensity for atypical and unconventional perceptions revealed that this client's immature personality was masked by her high intelligence (IQ = 131). The R–PAS pointed to the fact that on the surface, she appeared to have enough resources to cope with life, but these resources were dependent primarily on affect and a paucity of mentalization; that is, the ability "to see ourselves as others see us, and others as they see themselves" (Holmes, 2006). Her affective world was also immature in that she could not regulate, a factor that also contributed to her difficulties in mentalization, since she was readily flooded by her emotions and reactions. Her Rorschach contents revealed that she was preoccupied with themes of bodily concern, more specifically related to femininity and sexuality. The results also suggested it would be difficult to reach her because of the lack of representations of cooperating human beings. The Rorschach revealed the important "take-home" message that the therapist's interpretations should be as accurate as possible given the client's view of the world through an exclusive lens as well as her inability to mentalize (Berant, 2018).

Mentalization is addressed in attachment theory and Rorschach studies (Meyer, 2017). The ability to mentalize is a quality that develops out of secure attachment relationships characterized by affective attunement and accurate mirroring from caregivers and the facilitating of affect regulation. The Rorschach M manifests a deep understanding of the subjective experience of another person and the self (Porcelli & Kleiger, 2016). The *M-* (minus) manifests a difficulty in understanding people and social interactions, and indicates deficient empathy (Weiner, 2003). Integrating the *M-* with attachment insecurity can be valuable in therapy. For example, anxiously attached individuals' difficulties in mentalizing has mainly to do with their inability to escape long enough from their own intense affects, such as fear of abandonment or losing other person's love, to be able to step back and reflect on the source of these feelings and fears, thus impairing narrative coherence. Difficulties mentalizing as observed in the *M-* is also displayed in TAT stories, since it impairs clients' ability to compose a story for a card because of the emotional connotations and conflicts it has for them. For example, card 7GF (that can be termed the attachment card) exemplifies Bion's concept of "electric shortcuts" (Bion, 1962). Bion claimed that in order to avoid pain, a person may avoid thinking by repressing painful material or by "creating short circuits" in the process of learning and interpreting external reality. This is seen when clients say: "I do not have a story to go with this card," or "what's going on in the picture?" In these cases, it is worth inquiring how these clients' performance on the Wechsler Comprehension test and Picture Arrangement test that might shed light on their grasp of interpersonal social situations that requires mentalization. Do they know how to respond to questions about normative social conventions and behaviors as are asked on the Wechsler Comprehension test: "what should one do if?" Or put the pictures in the right order, or construct a coherent story that goes with that order (Picture Arrangement)?

There is also value in integrating the sequence of defenses from the Rorschach and the TAT with self-report questionnaires. For example, on Card I, which is termed the visiting card (Weiner, 2003), one client first responded by saying it was a carnival mask, and then mentioned that the mask was black, and in the end said it was the mask of a murderer. This suggests that the client used a manic defense to begin with the joyous image of a carnival, but was immediately caught up in the contents of depression and sadness (black mask) and finally the aggression (note that carnival masks are also used as disguises for aggressive acts, rather than as costumes). This sequence may indicate that when the defense of being cheerful failed and depressive contents crept in, and when the client found it difficult to contain the depression and sadness, it turned into murderous wrath. In cases like these, aggression should be examined on the MMPI. Hence, information about clients' self-reflection on their ability to be in touch their aggression can come from several sources.

Training

One of the key components in personality assessment is training students and young psychologists. This involves nurturing love and passion for our profession, in addition to developing their mastery of assessment skills. Today this mission is even harder given the ongoing criticism of performance-based tools.

Training in personality assessment should be the interface between diagnosis, empirical findings, psychotherapy, and clinical applications. For instance, starting the first time we teach the Rorschach, we need to connect almost every determinant to the world of psychotherapy and its clinical implications. This includes explaining for example, the meaning for the therapeutic process of having a client with a Rorschach protocol with Color-Shading Blends, its influence on the therapeutic alliance, or the meaning of treating a person who has difficulties holding onto good feelings when doubts and negative emotions penetrate. These clients might have difficulties "celebrating" their little triumphs in therapy and will keep returning to the downside of these experiences. One cannot understate the extent to which these clients frustrate therapists. Keeping these findings in mind can "protect" the therapist from feeling disappointed about their clients' inability to say a good word about their therapy.

While supervising, we can kindle the curiosity of our supervisees or students by asking them which Rorschach determinants that they expect to find when clients are referred to the clinic with certain problems, and which problematic Rorschach determinants are expected to decline after one year of therapy. This means that teachers and supervisors must keep up to date on the latest developments in assessment, psychopathology and outcome studies exemplify it.

Training is a complex process. It involves the "technical" aspects of administering the tests and the coding but attending to them in most cases is not only technical since they are infused with the characteristics of the examiner and the examinee. For example, some assessors tend to be more "generous" in coding the Wechsler test or deciding on the form quality on the Rorschach. A specific examinee can cause the examiner to be "generous" or "stingy" while coding the Wechsler. These behaviors can reveal the examiners' general attitude toward the people they appraise, or can be an example of the activation of projective identification of the client that causes the examiner to take the role of saving the patient by assigning more points on the Wechsler or favoring the u when debating between form quality of – and u. We need to keep in mind that although there are very detailed instructions for administering tests in a standard way, it is still essentially an interactive process between examiner and examinee (Berant et al., 2005).

During supervision, it is worth recalling that the supervisory process entails intersubjective and psychodynamic elements. The supervisee must come to the realization that in order to understand the client, both the clients' and the examiner's interplay of thoughts, feelings, and expectations need to be evaluated. By the same token, the supervisors must be aware of this interplay between them and their supervisees. The relationship between supervisor and supervisee often reflects parallel processes between examiner and examinee (Handler & Clemence, 2003). Deering (1994) defined a parallel process in the context of supervision as "an unconscious process that takes place when a trainee replicates problem of clients during supervision with the purpose of causing the supervisor to demonstrate how to handle the situation" (p. 102). The supervisory relationship is also influenced by social issues such as power, authority, gender roles, social and economic status, and certain cultural issues. All supervisory work is subject to cultural variability, even when both participants speak the same language (Rapp, 2000).

Writing an integrative report is one of the most difficult tasks in training, which some students and supervisees find almost impossible. The supervisor needs to show a great deal of patience and empathy. For those who find it difficult, the supervisor should provide examples of reports and show how to extract information; for example, by demonstrating what tests and self-report tools can contribute to an understanding of the client's self-perception, and how the data can be integrated into a meaningful paragraph that accurately depicts the examinee.

One training task that is closely connected to therapeutic work is the feedback or the summary of findings about the client. The supervisor should train the supervisee to give feedback in an empathic way, as recommended by Finn (2007). I agree that the word feedback is less relevant these days, especially for those of us who practice relational psychotherapy. Hence discussing the assessment results is better cast as a summary or discussion session. In my experience, training our supervisees to have a meaningful conversation about their client's appraisal results is one of the most noteworthy experiences in the supervisory process. If done the right way, our supervisees will enter the next supervision session with shining eyes, telling us about the moving and meaningful session they had with their clients. Those who have had these experiences will cherish these sessions and the supervisory processes that facilitated their ability to discuss their clients' pain and conflicts with them in a meaningful way. The summary of appraisal findings can be defined as the outcome of the procedure in which the examiner processes, organizes, contains, and returns the material to the examinee in a tolerable way. This resembles a "reverie":

the special mental state of the mother who perceives and contains the distressed feelings of her infant by giving them meaning, and thus transforming them in a way that makes them tolerable (Bion, 1962).

Conclusion

My experience with conducting personality assessment, teaching, and supervising underscore the importance of two processes. The first is being attentive to all the sources of information gathered about a client. The second is to integrate this vast body of data into a meaningful picture for the clients and their therapists. Last, but not least is to deliver the summary or report it in an empathic manner that will give the clients the impression that their feelings are validated, and that the examiner is empathic with respect to their conflicts, and difficulties. This process should go hand in hand with retrieving information from empirical sources and theoretical psychodynamic formulations. My life experience since childhood has exemplified the importance of paying attention to the specific world of each examinee and trying to empathize with their world.

References

Ainsworth, M. S., Blehar, M. C., Water, E., & Wall, S. (1978). *Patterns of attachment: A psychological study of the strange situation.* Hillsdale, NJ: Erlbaum.

Adler, L. A., Kessler, R. C, & Spencer, T. (2003). *Adult self-report Scale, ASRS-V1.1 screener.* New York: World Health Organization.

American Psychiatric Association. (2013). *Diagnostic and statistical manual of mental disorders* (5th ed.). Author.

Appelbaum, S. A., & Colson, D. B. (1968). A reexamination of the color shading Rorschach test response and suicide attempts. *Journal of Projective Techniques and Personality Assessment, 32*(2), 160–164.

Archer, R., & Krishnamurthy, R. (1993b). A review of the MMPI and Rorschach interrelationships in adults' samples. *Journal of Personality Assessment, 61*(2), 277–293.

Beck, A. T., & Steer, R. A. (1987). *Manual for the beck depression inventory.* San Antonio, TX: Psychological Corporation.

Beck, S. J., Beck, A., Levitt, E. E., & Molish, H. B. (1961). *Rorschach's test. I: Basic processes* (3rd ed.). New York: Grune & Stratton.

Bellak, L., & Bellak, S. S. (1986). *Children's Apperception Test (CAT).* Larchmont, NY: CPS. (Original work published 1949).

Berant, E. (2007). Rorschach comprehensive system data for a sample of 150 adult nonpatients from Israel. *Journal of Personality Assessment, 89*(S1), 67–73.

Berant, E. (2009) Attachment styles, the Rorschach and the TAT: Using traditional projective measures to assess aspects of attachment. In J. H. Obegi & E. Berant (Eds.), *Attachment theory and research in clinical work with adults* (pp. 181–206). New York: Guilford Press.

Berant, E. (2018). Being in pain. Using R-PAS to understand the (non-) dialogue of body and mind. In J. L. Mihura & G. J. Meyer (Eds.), *Using the Rorschach Performance Assessment (R-PAS)* (pp. 366–383). New York: Guilford Press.

Berant, E., Cohen, M., & Kord-Beilsky, M. (2017, July). *"Twins losing their mother"*. Paper presented at the 21th International Society of the Rorschach and other Projective Methods Congress, Paris, France.

Berant, E., Mikulincer, M., & Shaver, P. R. (2008). Mothers' attachment style, their mental Health, and their children's emotional vulnerabilities: A 7-year study of children with Congenital Heart Disease. *Journal of Personality, 76*(1), 31–66.

Berant, E., Mikulincer, M., Shaver, P. R., & Segal, Y. (2005). Rorschach correlates of self-Reported attachment dimensions: Dynamic manifestations of hyperactivating and deactivating strategies. *Journal of Personality Assessment, 84*(1), 70–81.

Berant, E., Newborn, M., & Orgler, S. (2008). Convergence of self-report scales and Rorschach Indices of psychological distress: The moderating role of self-disclosure. *Journal of Personality Assessment, 90*(1), 36–43.

Berant, E., Saroff, A., Reicher-Atir, R., & Zim, S. (2005). Supervising personality assessment: The integration of intersubjective and psychodynamic elements in the supervisory process. *Journal of Personality Assessment, 84(2)*, 205–212.

Berant, E., & Wald, Y. (2009). Self-reported attachment patterns and Rorschach related scores of ego boundary, defensive processes, and thinking disorders. *Journal of Personality Assessment, 9*(4), 365–372.

Bion, W. (1962). *Learning from experience.* London: Heinemann Medical.

Blatt, S. J., & Ritzler, B. A. (1974). Thought disorders and boundary disturbances in psychosis. *Journal of Consulting and Clinical Psychology, 42*(3), 370–381.

Bornstein, R. F. (2000). A process dissociation approach to objective-projective test score interrelationships. *Journal of Personality Assessment, 78*(2), 47–68.

Bowlby, J. (1982). *Attachment and loss: Vol. 1. Attachment* (2nd ed.). New York: Basic Books. (Original Work published 1969).

Brennan, K. A., Clark, C. I., & Shaver, P. R. (1998). Self-report measurements of adult attachment: An integrative overview. In J. A. Simpson & W. S. Rholes (Eds.), *Attachment theory and close relationships* (pp. 46–76). New York: Guilford Press.

Briggs-Gowan, M. J., Carter, A. S., & Schwab-Stone, M. (1996). Discrepancies among mother, child, and teacher reports: Examining the contributions of maternal depression and anxiety. *Journal of Abnormal Child Psychology, 24*(6), 749–765.]

Butcher, J. N., Williams, C. L., Graham, J. R., Archer, R. P., Tellegen, A., Ben-Porat, Y. S., & Kaemmer, B. (1992). *MMPI-II* (Minnesota Multiphasic Personality Inventory-II). *Manual for administration, scoring and interpretation.* Minneapolis: University of Minnesota Press.

Conners, C. K., Sitarenios, G., Parker, J. D., & Epstein, J. N. (1998). The Revised Conners' Rating Scale (CPRS-R): Factor structure, reliability and criterion validity. *Journal of Abnormal Child Psychology, 26*, 257–268.

Dean, K. L., Viglione, D. J., Perry, W., & Meyer, G. J. (2007). A method to optimize the response range while maintaining Rorschach Comprehensive System validity. *Journal of Personality Assessment, 89*(2), 149–161.

Deering, C. (1994). Parallel process in the supervision of child psychotherapy. *American Journal of Psychotherapy, 48*(1), 102–110.

Ein-Dor, T., Mikulincer, M., Doron, G., & Shaver, P. R. (2010). The attachment paradox: How Can so many of us (the insecurely attached) have no adaptive advantage? *Perspectives in Psychological Science, 5*(2), 123–145.

Exner, J. E. (1989). Searching for projection in the Rorschach. *Journal of Personality Assessment, 53*(3), 520–536.

Exner, J. E. Jr. (1993). *The Rorschach: A comprehensive system. Vol 1: Basic foundations* (3rd ed.). New York: Wiley & Sons.

Exner, J. E. Jr. (2000). *Primer for Rorschach interpretation.* Asheville, NC: Rorschach Workshops.

Exner, J. E. Jr., & Erdberg, P. (2005). *The Rorschach: A comprehensive system. Vol 2: Advanced interpretation* (3rd ed.). Oxford: Wiley & Sons.

Finn, S. E. (1996). Assessment feedback integrating MMPI-2 and Rorschach findings. *Journal of Personality Assessment, 67*(3), 543–557.

Finn, S. E. (2007). *In our clients' shoes: Theory and technique of personality assessment.* Erlbaum.

First, M., Gibbon, M., Spitzer, R. I., Williams, J. B., & Benjamin, I. S. (1997). *User's guide for the Structured Clinical Interview for DSM I-V Axis II personality disorders (SCID-II).* Washington, DC: American Psychiatric Press.

Fisher, S., & Cleveland, S. (1968). *Body image and personality* (2nd ed.). New York: Dover.

Giromini, L., Viglione, D. J., Pineda, J. A., Porcelli, P., Hubbard, D., Zennaro, A., & Cauda, F. (2019). Human movement responses to the Rorschach and mirroring activity: An fMRI study. *Assessment, 26*(1), 56–69.

Handler, L., & Clemence, A. J. (2003). Education and training in psychological assessment. In I. B. Weiner (Series Ed.) and J. R. Graham & J. A. Naglieri (Vol. Eds.), *Handbook of Psychology: Vol 10. Assessment psychology* (pp. 181–207). Hoboken, NJ: Wiley.

Haworth, M. R. (1966). *The CAT: Facts about fantasy.* New York: Grune & Stratton.

Holmes, J. (2006). Mentalization from psychoanalytic perspective: What's new? In J. G. Allen & P. Fonagy (Eds.), *Handbook of mentalization-based treatment* (pp. 31–50). West Sussex: Wiley.

Hosseininasab, A., Meyer, G. J., Viglione, D. J., Mihura, J. L., Berant, E., Resende, A. C., & Mohammadi, M. R. (2017). The effect of CS administration or an R-Optimized alternative on R-PAS variables: A meta-analysis of findings from six studies. *Journal of Personality Assessment, 101*(2), 199–212.

Jourard, S. M., & Laskow, P. (1958). Some factors in self-disclosure. *Journal of Abnormal and Social Psychology, 56*(1), 91–98.

Klopfer, B., Ainsworth, M. S. D., Klopfer, W., & Holt, R. (1954). *Developments in the Rorschach technique: I. Technique and theory.* New York: World Book Company.

Mascendaro, P. M., Herman, K. C., & Webster-Stratton, C. (2012). Parent discrepancies in ratings of young children's co-occurring internalizing symptoms. *School Psychology Quarterly, 27*(3), 134–143.

Mattlar, C. E. (2011). The issue of an evolutionary development of the Rorschach Comprehensive System (RCS) versus a revolutionary change (R–PAS). Retrieved from http://www.rorschachtraining.com/category/articles

McDougall, J. (1989). *Theatres of the body: A psychoanalytic approach to psychosomatic illness.* London: Free Association Books.

Meyer, G. J. (1997). On the integration of personality assessment methods: The Rorschach and MMPI. *Journal of Personality Assessment, 68*(2), 297–330.

Meyer, G. J. (2017). What Rorschach performance can add to assessing and understanding personality. *International Journal of Personality Psychology, 3,* 36–49.

Meyer, G. M., Hosseininasab, A., Viglione, D. J., Mihura, J. L., Berant, E., Reese, J., & Resende, A. M. (2020). The effect of CS administration or an R-Optimized alternative on potential projective material in Rorschach responses: A meta-analysis of findings from six countries. *Journal of Personality Assessment, 102*(1), 135–146.

Meyer, G. J., Viglione, D. J., Mihura, J. L., Erard, R. E., & Erdberg, P. (2011). *Rorschach Performance assessment system: Administration, coding, interpretation, and technical manual.* Toledo, OH: Rorschach Performance Assessment System.

Mikulincer, M., & Horesh, N. (1999). Adult attachment style and the perception of the others: The role of projective mechanisms. *Journal of Personality and Social Psychology, 76*(6), 1022–1034. https://doi.org/10.1037/0022-3514.76.6.1022

Mikulincer, M., & Shaver, P. R. (2016). *Attachment in adulthood: structure, dynamics and change* (2nd ed.). New York: Guilford Press.

Murray, H. A. (1971). *Thematic apperception test.* Cambridge, MA: Harvard Press. (Original work published 1936).

Overton, C. G. (2000). A relational interpretation of the Rorschach color determinants. *Journal of Personality Assessment, 75*(3), 426–448. https://doi.org/10.1207/S15327752JPA7503_05

Petot, J. M. (2005). Are the relationship between the NEO PI-R and the Rorschach markers of Openness dependent on the patient's test taking attitude? *Rorschachiana, 27,* 11–29.

Piotrowski, Z. (1957). *Perceptanalysis.* Macmillan.

Plutchik, R., & van Pragg, H. M. (1986). The measurement of suicidality, aggressivity and impulsivity. *Clinical Neuropharmacology, 9,* 380–382.

Porcelli, P., & Kleiger, J. H. (2016). The "feeling of movement": Notes on the Rorschach human movement response. *Journal of Personality Assessment, 98*(2), 124–134.

Rapaport, D., Gill, M., & Schafer, R. (1945–1946). *Psychological diagnostic testing.* Chicago: New Year.

Rapp, H. (2000). Working with difference: Cultural competent supervision. In B. H. Lawton & C. Feltham (Eds.), *Taking supervision forward* (pp. 93–112). London: Sage.

Ritzler, B. A. (2004). Cultural aspects of the Rorschach, Apperception tests, and Figure drawings. In M. J. Hilsenroth & D. L. Segal (Eds.), *Comprehensive handbook of psychological assessment* (pp. 573–575). Hoboken NJ: Wiley.

Ritzler, B. A. (2011). A critical review of the R–PAS manual. Rorschach Training Programs, Inc. Newsletter, 3(5). Retrieved from http://www.rorschachtraining.com/category/newsletters/page/3/

Rorschach, H. (1942). *Psychodiagnostik* [Psychodiagnostics]. Bircher. Original work published 1921.

Rudnytsky, P. L. (1997). The personal origins of attachment theory. An interview with Mary Salter Ainsworth. Interview by Peter L. Rudnytsky. *The Psychoanalytic Study of the Child, 52,* 386–405.

Russell, D., Peplau, L. A., Cutrona, C. (1980). The revised UCLA loneliness scale: Concurrent and discriminant validity evidence. *Journal of Personality and Social Psychology, 39*(3), 472–480.

Schachtel, E. G. (1943). On color and affect. *Psychiatry, 5*(4), 393–409.

Schachtel, E. G. (1966). *Experimental foundations of the Rorschach test.* Basic Books.

Shaffer, T. W., Erdberg, P., & Meyer, G. J. (2007). Introduction to the JPA special supplement On international reference samples for the Rorschach comprehensive system. *Journal of Personality Assessment, 89* (S1), S2-S6.

Van IJzendoorn, M. H. (1995). Adult attachment representations, parental responsiveness and infant attachment: A meta-analysis on the predictive validity of the adult attachment interview. *Psychological Bulletin, 117*(3), 387–403.

Viglione, D. J., Giromini, L., Gustafson, M., & Meyer, G. J. (2014). Developing continuous variable composites for Rorschach measures of thought problems, vigilance, and suicide risk. *Assessment, 21*(1), 42–49.

Wallin, D. (2007). *Attachment in psychotherapy.* New York: Guilford Press.

Wechsler, D. (1997). *Wechsler adult intelligence scale* (3rd ed.). San Antonio, TX: Psychological Corporation.

Weiner, I. B. (2003). *Principles of Rorschach interpretation* (2nd ed.). Mahwah, NJ: Erlbaum.

Winnicott, D. W. (1951). *Playing and reality.* New York: Basic Books.

Winnicott, D. W. (1971). *Therapeutic consultation in child psychiatry.* New York: Basic Books.

Wood, J. M., Nezworski, M. T., Lilinfeld, S. O., & Garb, H. N. (2003). *What's wrong with The Rorschach? Science confronts the controversial inkblot test.* San Francisco, CA: Jossey – Bass.

Youngstrom, E., Loeber, R., & Stouthamer-Loeber, M. (2000). Patterns and correlates of agreement between parent, teacher, and male adolescent ratings of externalizing and internalizing problems. *Journal of Consulting and Clinical Psychology, 68*(6), 1038–1050.

6 The Sands of Identity Keep Shifting

Late-Life Career Developments

Irving B. Weiner

Past history

My history in psychology began while I was an undergraduate at the University of Michigan intending to major in economics and go to law school. Captivated by some psychology courses I was taking, I changed course and decided that clinical psychology was the career for me. Subsequently in the doctoral program at Michigan, I had the benefit of a superb educational and training program highlighted by instruction and mentoring by some distinguished figures in psychology. I was a research assistant to Wilbert McKeachie and took a course on qualitative research methods co-taught by Lowell Kelly and Donald Marquis, all three of whom had served as APA presidents. My supervisor during a two-year half-time internship at the university counseling center and the chair of my doctoral committee was Ed Bordin, a prominent author, journal editor, and originator of the concept of the therapeutic working alliance. My experience in the counseling center resulted in my first publication, a 1959 article on "The Role of Diagnosis in a University Counseling Center."

After completing my doctorate in 1959, I took a position as Instructor in the Psychology Division of the Department of Psychiatry at the University of Rochester Medical Center. My primary interest, continuing from my training at the University of Michigan, was in doing psychotherapy, and I had the good fortune to have two years of postdoctoral psychotherapy supervision from Paul Dewald, a widely published psychoanalytic author who later headed the Psychoanalytic Institute in St. Louis. But then three events altered my identity as a psychotherapist. First, the Psychology Division was often called on to provide diagnostic testing of patients, both in outpatient and inpatient services. I consequently became more involved in psychological assessment than I had previously, particularly with respect to Rorschach testing and the identification of schizophrenia. I soon began to identify myself more as an assessment psychologist than psychotherapist, and my experience led to some Rorschach research articles (e.g., Weiner, 1962) and the 1966 publication of my first book, *Psychodiagnosis in Schizophrenia* (Weiner, 1966).

DOI: 10.4324/9781003036302-6

In the mid-1960s I became friendly with a pediatrician on the medical school faculty who was organizing a multi-specialist adolescent clinic and invited me to join the group as a consulting psychologist. My participation in this clinic stirred a particular interest in problems of adolescence that led to the 1970 publication of my second book, *Psychological Disturbance in Adolescence* (Weiner, 1970). Then in the 1970s I had the good fortune to become acquainted with David Elkind, a psychology professor at the University of Rochester and a nationally known child psychologist. Our friendship and collaboration produced two books, the Weiner and Elkind (1972) *Child Development* and the Elkind and Weiner (1978) *Development of the Child*. My professional Identity had now moved from psychotherapist to assessment psychologist to adolescent specialist to developmental psychologist. Each of these identities persisted in later book publications on *Principles of Psychotherapy* (Weiner, 1975), *Principles of Rorschach Interpretation* Weiner (1998), *Child and Adolescent Psychopathology* (Weiner, 1982), and *Adolescence: A Developmental Transition* (Kimmel & Weiner, 1985).

Finally with regard to my earlier career publishing, I became interested in editing as well as writing professional works. My edited works included *Clinical Methods in Psychology* (Weiner, 1976), Wiley's 12-volume *Handbook of Psychology* (Weiner, 2003), and *Adult Psychopathology Case Studies* (Weiner, 2004), and I served as Editor of the *Journal of Personality Assessment* from 1985 to 1993.

As for my employment history, by the 1970s I had advanced to Full Professor in Psychiatry and Pediatrics, I was head of the Psychology Division, and all was going well. The Psychiatry Department atmosphere was comfortable and intellectually stimulating, the Psychology Division was striving and providing both predoctoral and postdoctoral training opportunities, and I was totally satisfied with who and where I was. However, there came a fly into the ointment. I had become involved with Ron Fox and some other colleagues in organizing what subsequently became the Association of Psychology Postdoctoral and Internship Centers (APPIC), and Ron and I collaborated as initial advocates for a uniform date for extending internship invitations (Weiner & Fox, 1971). With my interest in training, especially in psychological assessment, I became increasingly distressed by having practicum students and interns come to us poorly prepared in assessment and even having been taught that it was of little value.

I had little success in attempting to convince psychology department colleagues to beef up their assessment curriculum, and I concluded that I could exert this influence only by becoming myself part of a psychology department. It happened at the time that Case Western Reserve University (CWRU) was looking for a clinician to chair its Psychology Department. I applied for this position and in 1972 went off to Cleveland, where after 12 years comfortably settled in the identity of a medical school psychologist and clinical practitioner, I then became an academic psychologist concerned with the welfare of students rather than patients.

The story could have ended here, with my new identity as an academic psychologist and department chair firmly in place, but the sands had not stopped shifting. I soon became involved in the issues and concerns of other departments in the university and more broadly interested in higher education than I had been previously. This new interest eventuated in my becoming Dean of the School of Graduate Studies at CWRU and adopting a new identity as a university administrator. Although I continued as a senior person teaching assessment and supervising psychotherapy in the Psychology Department, I was now a novice in academic administration interested in opportunities to advance. Such an opportunity arrived, and after seven years in Cleveland, I moved westward in 1979 to become Vice Chancellor for Academic Affairs at the University of Denver (DU).

I enjoyed my administrative responsibilities at DU and was for the most part well-received by students, faculty, and the deans and directors who reported to me. Regrettably, however, I did not see eye-to-eye with the Chancellor to whom I reported, which led to my resigning after four years in office and looking elsewhere for an academic position. I subsequently accepted appointment as Vice President for Academic Affairs at Fairleigh Dickinson University (FDU) and in 1985 moved to New Jersey. I enjoyed my work at FDU, which included academic oversight of campuses in Teaneck, Rutherford, and Madison, and I believe I acquitted myself reasonably well in discharging my responsibilities.

I was also able during my years of university administration to remain active as a psychologist. I regularly attended and presented at Society for Personality Assessment (SPA) meetings, continued to serve as Editor of the *Journal of Personality Assessment* (JPA), published a second edition of my edited book *Clinical Methods in Psychology* (Weiner, 1983), co-authored with John Exner Volume 3 of the *Rorschach Comprehensive System* (*Assessment of Children and Adolescents* (Exner & Weiner, 1982), and co-edited with Allen Hess the *Handbook of Forensic Psychology* (Weiner & Hess, 1987).

My time at FDU became problematic, however, with my once again having some differences with the university president to whom I reported. I concluded that, despite its many rewards, academic administration might no longer be the life for me. In 1989 I resigned from my FDU position and began looking for an opportunity as a psychologist. My job search resulted in my being appointed Professor of Psychiatry and Behavioral Medicine at the University of South Florida (USF) and Director of Psychology in the USF Psychiatry Center, and I headed south for Tampa.

One of the first and smartest things I did on my arrival in Tampa was to hire my wife Frances, a former high school English teacher whom I had married in 1963, as my Editorial Assistant for JPA. She served ably in this position during the remainder of my term as Editor and through the editorial term of my successor, Bill Kinder. In the process, Fran became as much a part of SPA as I was and regularly came with me to society meetings to meet and talk with JPA authors.

As for my professional identity, I was now, after a 17-year hiatus as a psychology department faculty member and university administrator, back where I had begun my career, as a medical school psychologist in a psychiatry department. I was fortunately able to re-capture my pleasure in doing clinical work, supervising psychology trainees and psychiatry residents, and interacting with colleagues whose major professional interest, like mine, was facilitating mental health. I soon became more heavily invested than ever before in the practice and teaching of psychological assessment and began again to consider myself primarily as an assessment psychologist.

Along with my successful transition back to working as a clinician, however, the advent of managed care in the 1990s sharply reduced my department's income from its 80-bed psychiatric hospital. Although I was a tenured faculty member, declining funding for the psychology division tempered my pleasure in running it. And so it was that I took early retirement from the university in 1994 and opened an office for private practice. As a practitioner I became actively involved in forensic consultations and once more had the good fortune to be mentored by a distinguished psychologist, in this instance former APA President Ted Blau, who showed me the forensic ropes and chaired the examining committee for my forensic board certification. An ABPP in clinical psychology since 1964, I received my forensic ABPP in 1996 and began to identify myself as a forensic as well as an assessment psychologist.

I kept my practice small in order to allow time for my writing, editing, and organizational work. My writing included second editions of my *Principles of Psychotherapy* (Weiner, 1998) and *Principles of Rorschach Interpretation* (Weiner, 2003). My editing included serving as Editor of *Rorschachiana* from 1990 to 1997 and Editor–in–Chief of Wiley's 12-volume *Handbook of Psychology* (Weiner, 2003). My organizational work included beginning six years as President of the International Rorschach Society in 1999 and serving from 2002 to 2005 on the Board of Directors of APA Division 12 (Clinical Psychology) as representative of its Section IX on Assessment.

Recent history

This past history career account runs up to the 2005 publication of my previous JPA autobiography (Weiner, 2005), at which time my identity had once more become firmly in place, now as an assessment and forensic psychologist and an independent practitioner. Soon thereafter, however, the sands of my identity began shifting once more. I was asked to run for President of the SPA, a position I had held previously in 1976–1978, and I was elected to serve a 2005–2007 term. During this term I became increasingly interested in devoting my time and effort to organizational activities. I was influenced and guided in this respect by two other former APA presidents, Norman Abeles and Charles Spielberger, whom I had come to know as assessment colleagues (see Weiner et al., 2003) and who encouraged me to become active in APA governance. This encouragement led to my running for President of APA Division 12 (Society of Clinical Psychology) and being elected for a 2008–2009 term. The following year I ran for President of APA Division 5 (Quantitative and Qualitative Methods) and served in this position from 2009 to 2010. These presidencies were followed by election to the APA Council of Representatives, on which I served from 2011 to 2014. With this new identity as an organization person and more time for writing and editing projects, I retired from my 14 years of independent practice in 2008.

As for late life career developments, the years following my 2005 autobiography were initially saddened by the 2006 loss of John Exner. John had been my closest friend for over 40 years, and we had been presenting Rorschach workshops together several times yearly since 1971. My workshop days were now over, although I continued until most recently to present at SPA meetings and since 2005 have had opportunities to discuss Rorschach assessment abroad, in Argentina, Belgium, Brazil, Israel, Japan, Spain, Switzerland, and Turkey.

The years since my 2008 retirement from practice have also been busy with publishing projects on diverse topics and with new collaborators. Roger Greene and I published two editions of our *Handbook of Personality Assessment* (Weiner & Greene, 2008, 2017). With Robert Bornstein as co-author, a third edition of my *Principles of Psychotherapy* appeared in 2009 (Weiner & Bornstein, 2009). I edited a second edition of Wiley's 12-volume *Handbook of Psychology* (Weiner, 2013). Together with Edward Craighead I edited a fourth edition of *Corsini's Encyclopedia of Psychology* (Weiner & Craighead, 2010), and I collaborated with Randy Otto to produce a fourth edition of the *Handbook of Forensic Psychology* (Weiner & Otto, (2014). Working with two Israeli colleagues, I wrote a book on the Rorschach assessment of adolescents (Tibon-Czopp & Weiner, 2016) and another on the Rorschach assessment of senior adults (Weiner et al., 2019). At the time of this writing I am working with James Kleiger on editing a book on *Psychological Assessment of Disordered Thinking and Perception* to be published by APA Books. When all is said and done, then, I am and expect to remain a retired assessment psychologist and an active contributor to the literature.

Perspectives on personality assessment

It seems fitting to conclude this autobiography with some observations on the nature of personality, how it is assessed, the utility of assessing it, and its future prospects in contemporary tines. Personality is generally considered to consist of abiding dispositions to think, feel, and act in certain ways. These dispositions are commonly referred to as traits, and several constellations of traits have been formulated to account for the entirety of an individual's personality characteristics. Most notable among these are the Five Factor Model (FFM) (Neuroticism, Extraversion, Openness to Experience, Agreeableness, and Conscientiousness; Costa & McCrae, 1992) and the HEXACO (Honesty-humility, Emotionality, Extraversion, Agreeableness, Conscientiousness, and Openness to experience; Ashton & Lee, 2005). A recent meta-analysis has demonstrated a substantial relationship between FFM and HEXACO trait scales and the subjective sense of well-being (Anglim et al., 2020).

As for how it is assessed, there is widespread agreement that personality characteristics are best identified by some multimethod combination of interviews, behavioral observations, historical records, collateral reports, and self-report and performance-based test measures (see Groth-Marnat & Wright, 2016; Kumar, 2016; Weiner & Greene, 2017). When adequately measured, personality assessment derives utility from facilitating decision-making when psychological traits have a bearing on conclusions to be drawn or actions to be taken. In clinical practice such personality-related decisions involve differential diagnosis and treatment planning; in forensic practice they play a role in identifying competence to stand trial, criminal responsibility, and suitability to parent; and in organizational practice they often guide personnel selection and promotion.

With respect to its prospects, three developments identify personality assessment as a growing field of study and practical application. The first of these developments that speak well for the future is a burgeoning literature. Each of the four assessment journals I regularly read—*Journal of Personality Assessment, Psychological Assessment, Assessment,* and *European Journal of Psychological Assessment*—has since my 2005 autobiography expanded in size and continued under able leadership to sustain its high quality. As a companion item of information about concerning its visibility, a PsycINFO search shows that since 2005, 317 books have been published with *Personality Assessment* in their title.

A second important development is a modification of diagnostic criteria for personality disorder in the forthcoming ICD-11 (International Classification of Diseases). As reviewed in a special section of *Psychological Assessment* edited by Bagby and Widiger (2020), this modification replaces categorical personality syndromes with a dimensional trait classification (negative affectivity, detachment, dissociality, disinhibition, and anankastia) that resembles the FFM and HEXACO models. The greater extent to which differential diagnosis becomes based on personality traits, and not only on signs and symptoms of disorder, the more relevant personality assessment will become in mental health practice.

Third, as recently elaborated in a special section of articles in the *Journal of Personality Assessment,* personality assessment is becoming increasingly utilized as a guide to practice in health care settings (Marek et al., 2020), and Bleidorn et al. (2019) have more broadly observed that "Personality traits are powerful predictors of outcomes in the domains of education, work, relationships, health, and well-being" (p. 1056). Personality traits accordingly have implications not only for psychological theory, research, and practice but also for public policy in such areas as health care status and needs, instructional goals and methods, civil planning, and business and government management. Recognizing this substantial relevance of personality traits to public policy as well as to individual well-being seems likely to enhance the perceived value of personality assessment and foster increasing demand for the services of capable assessment psychologists.

References

Anglim, J., Horwood, S., Smillie, L. D., Marrero, R. J., & Wood, J. K. (2020). Predicting psychological and subjective well-being from personality: A meta-analysis. *Psychological Bulletin, 146,* 329–323.

Ashton, M. C., & Lee, K. (2005). Honesty-humility, the big five, and the five factor model. *Journal of Personality, 73,* 1321–1353.

Bagby, R. M., & Widiger, T. A. (2020). Assessment of the ICD-11 dimensional trait model: An introduction to the special section. *Psychological Assessment, 32,* 1–7.

Bleidorn, W., Back, M. D., Hinecke, M., Jokela, M., Lucas, R. E., Oth, U., Wrzus, C., Hill, P. L., Jaap, J. E., Christopher, J. H., Kandler, C., Luhmann, M., Wagner, J., & Zimmerman, J. (2019). The policy relevance of personality traits. *American Psychologist, 74,* 1056–1067.

Costa, P. T., & McCrae, R. R. (1992). The five factor model of personality and is relevance to personality disorders. *Journal of Personality Disorders, 6,* 343–359.

Elkind, D., & Weiner, I. B. (1978). *Development of the child.* New York: Wiley.

Exner, J. E., & Weiner, I. B. (1982). *The Rorschach: A comprehensive system.* Volume 3, *Assessment of children and adolescents.* New York: Wiley.

Growth-Marnat, G., & Wright, A. J. (2016). *Handbook of psychological assessment* (6th ed.). Hoboken, NJ: Wiley.

Kimmel, D. C., & Weiner, I. B. (1985). *Adolescence: A developmental transition.* Hillsdale, NJ: Lawrence Erlbaum Associates.

Kumar, U. (Ed.) (2016). *The Wiley handbook of personality assessment.* Hoboken, NJ: Wiley.

Marek, R. J., Markey, C. H., & Porcerelli, J. H. (2020). Assessment of personality and psychopathology in healthcare settings. *Journal of Personality Assessment, 102,* 149–152.

Tibon-Czopp, S., & Weiner, I. B. (2016). *Rorschach assessment of adolescents.* New York: Springer.

Weiner, I. B. (1959). The role of diagnosis in a university counseling center. *Journal of Counseling Psychology, 6,* 110–115.

Weiner, I. B. (1962). Three Rorschach scores indicative of schizophrenia. *Journal of Consulting Psychology, 25,* 436–439.

Weiner, I. B. (1966). *Psychodiagnosis in schizophrenia.* New York: Wiley.

Weiner, I. B. (1970). *Psychological disturbance in adolescence.* New York: Wiley.

Weiner, I. B. (1975). *Principles of psychotherapy.* New York, NY: Wiley.

Weiner, I. B. (Ed.) (1976). *Clinical methods in psychology.* New York: Wiley.

Weiner, I. B. (1982). *Child and adolescent psychopathology.* New York: Wiley.

Weiner, I. B. (Ed.) (1983). *Clinical methods in psychology* (2nd ed.). New York: Wiley.

Weiner, I. B., (1998). *Principles of Rorschach interpretation.* Mahwah, NJ: Lawrence Erlbaum Associates.

Weiner, I. B., (2003). *Principles of Rorschach interpretation* (2nd ed.). Mahwah, NJ: Lawrence Erlbaum Associates.

Weiner, I. B. (Ed.). (2003). *Handbook of psychology* (Vols. 1–12). Hoboken, NJ: Wiley.

Weiner, I. B. (Ed.). (2004). *Adult psychopathology case studies.* Hoboken, NJ: Wiley.

Weiner, I. B. (2005). The shifting sands of a professional identity. *Journal of Personality Assessment, 85,* 103–111.

Weiner, I. B. (Ed.) (2013). *Handbook of psychology* (Vols. 1–12; 2nd ed.). Hoboken, NJ: Wiley.

Weiner I. B., Appel, L., & Tibon-Czopp, S. (2019). *Rorschach assessment of senior adults.* New York: Routledge.

Weiner, I. B., & Bornstein, R. F. (2009). *Principles of psychotherapy* (3rd ed.). Hoboken, NJ: Wiley.

Weiner, I. B., & Craighead, W. E. (Eds.) (2010). *Corsini's encyclopedia of psychology* (4th ed., Vols. 1–4). Hoboken, NJ: Wiley.

Weiner, I. B., & Elkind, D. (1972). *Child development: A core approach.* New York: Wiley.

Weiner, I. B., & Fox, R. E. (1971). Uniform dates for announcing internships: A goal of the APIC. *Professional Psychology, 2,* 199200.

Weiner, I. B., & Greene, R. L. (2008). *Handbook of personality assessment.* Hoboken, NJ: Wiley.

Weiner, I. B., & Greene, R. L. (2017). *Handbook of personality assessment* (2nd ed.). Hoboken, NJ: Wiley.

Weiner, I. B., & Otto, R. K. (Eds.) (2014). *Handbook of forensic psychology* (4th ed.). Hoboken, NJ: Wiley.

Weiner, I. B., Spielberger, C. D., & Abeles, N. (2003). Once more around the park: Correcting misinformation about Rorschach assessment. *The Clinical Psychologist, 56,* 8–9.

7 Reports of My Being an Extravert Are Greatly Exaggerated

Virginia M. Brabender

Personal and professional aspects of my life and career

The early years

A typical classroom in the 1950s might have 50 children with a single teacher. As I look back at my childhood class photos, taken at Blessed Sacrament in Erie, Pennsylvania, I see that some were as large as 60. We were the abundant products of our parents' joy that WWII had ended. Still, in our vastness, we created a continual specter of chaos. At any moment, our robust ranks could overwhelm the local powers. Expectedly, teachers, other authority figures—egged on by then-popular Dr. Spock—saw firm discipline as the means of managing us. Picture a large hall, filled with the entire population of the grade school, eating lunch in absolute silence while the principal looked on from her seat on the stage. Her eyes carefully scanned the room, and her deputies (the eighth graders) walked up on down the rows of tables, carrying out her commissions. Forget food fights—merely vocalize in any way and you will find yourself vacating both your table and your lunch while being consigned to stand in the front of the room for the duration of the period. *Nicholas Nickleby's* Mr. Squeers could not ask for more (Dickens, 1839).

Overall, I was an enthusiastic, but ill-behaved child. Although I think I was parted with my lunch only on a single occasion, it nonetheless was the case that I vexed the nuns inordinately. I was not of the hoodlum variety, but rather suffered a strange excess of energy and disorganization that led to many problems—my cluttered desk, my constant sidebar comments to classmates, my tendency to be working on the wrong assignment at any time. One day, my second-grade-self walked into the classroom only to find my desk and that of another student overturned with all of its contents on the floor. Sister said its state of messiness was so objectionable to her that I must take the morning to straighten it. Were I a child today, I'm certain I would have received a biochemical assist (possibly to my long-term detriment). Part of the problem for me was that I was considerably younger than everyone in my class, it being the practice of the day to include a very wide age swath in any one grade. Fortunately, for me, at bottom, the nuns

DOI: 10.4324/9781003036302-7

were kind people (in fact, very far from Mr. Squeers) and I never received the harshest of treatments. I suspect they realized I could not help myself.

Being a child who gets in trouble for rambunctiousness is bothersome, but it does have its merits. In a large sea of classmates, I was noticed. It brought not only chastisement but also, a kind of approbation. Imagining what they were seeing as an extreme case of extraversion, they provided me with public-speaking opportunities aplenty. I yearned to perform as a dancer or singer in our various revues and performances but was always found bereft of talent in these areas and assigned to emcee duties. This role ended up being lifelong: For a time I thought I might pursue an acting career and in fact did a great deal of acting in high school (Essie in "You can't take it with you") and college (Miss Madrigal in "Chalk Garden"). I loved the romance of the theater and the camaraderie among the cast, technical crew, and all involved in a production. Yet, I knew that acting was not where my real ability resided. I had an easier time landing a role than developing it—I was acutely aware that my Miss Madrigal was pretty flat, a difficult recognition in the midst of a performance. My ability is and has always been public speaking. Both acting and public speaking require mentalizing another person. However, whereas public speaking requires that the speaker mentalize the audience, acting requires that the performer mentalize the character and the audience, a more complex endeavor.

Beyond the opportunities being an unruly child afforded me, the more significant effect of my regular skirmishes with authority was that I inured myself to this type of conflict. I was spared the seduction of striving to maintain a steady stream of approbation and became increasingly comfortable holding my ground, something in my adult life I have had to do on many occasions at faculty and board meetings. During my adolescence, my prosecutor dad who bore an alarming resemblance to Perry Mason (Raymond Burr, not Matthew Rhys) provided multiple opportunities to hone these skills further. With authority figures, I was not so much oppositional as eager, if not insistent, to say what I thought. Once this element of my make-up crystallized, it has been ever present—to my benefit and detriment.

Transitioning to adulthood

Obviously, I moved (somewhat) beyond that rambunctious kid. In those early years, I was fortunate to have a mother who devoted endless hours helping this dillar, dollar, ten o-clock scholar[1] to attend and focus (Opie & Opie, 1951). By college, I was a thoroughly committed student with a double major in philosophy and psychology. Maturation is a wondrous process, and the freer environment of college suited me. I discovered in myself an ability to focus on my studies for endless hours. The picture I had constructed of myself of having an endless need for social stimulation turned out not to be the case at all. I was happily content working in my carrel in the library, listening to Brahm's Concerto No. 2 in B flat major (still my favorite 50 years later), and working on my next paper. Rest assured that vestiges of my old self remained: I still ran afoul of authority, primarily through my writing in various on-campus outlets. An article in the campus newspaper decrying mandatory physical education credits did not go over well with the physical education staff. In retrospect, I was wrong in my stance. I contributed a review of the Glass Menagerie in which I assailed the faculty-director's interpretation of Amanda Wingfield, and unsurprisingly, he was piqued. Today, I would never presume to write a review of a play, but in college, everything was a possible target of my critical spirit. Of course, given that this was the late sixties and early seventies, criticism of authority was *de rigueur* on college campuses.

What was a boon to my college life was that I was certain about my life direction—I began my college education knowing I wanted to study psychology and I never veered from that aim. However, initially, my interest was not in clinical psychology, an area about which I had many misconceptions. My undergraduate experiences taught me that I liked research and teaching and so, I planned for myself an academic career, the foundation for which would be laid at Fordham University where the emphasis was on research and teaching. At Fordham, I had the opportunity to become acquainted with the giant of psychological assessment, Anne Anastasi, who at that time was the chair of the department. I've often heard assessment faculty elsewhere complain that assessment is an area devalued by their colleagues, and ultimately, the student population. Not so at Fordham! The importance of assessment was recognized consistently throughout the faculty and student body. Although at that time, I was not pursuing psychological assessment as an area of concentrated study, I would have been astonished to learn about the devaluation of this activity elsewhere. In fact, wherever I have found myself, including in my current academic home, Widener University, psychological assessment has been regarded as a thoroughly worthwhile enterprise. Beyond my internalizing this value, I also was deeply influenced by my access to such a powerful female figure. Dr. Anastasi was formidable and indomitable—no one—not even the most senior faculty member—thought otherwise or, for that matter, crossed her.

My primary research interests as a graduate student were in the areas of perception, cognition, and psycholinguistics. I probably would have designed a study in the area of psycholinguistics, based on the work of Noam Chomsky whose notion that our generative grammar is innate, was utterly intriguing to me. Unfortunately, the one faculty member who was most aligned with this area re-located to another university. Happily, a new faculty member arrived, Dr. David Landrigan, who assisted me in finding another direction. Inspired by the work of Michael Posner and other cognitive psychologists, I conducted my dissertation research on the kinds of problem-solving situations that would induce a person to use verbal as opposed to visual information. It presaged my long-term interest in black box questions—what sequence of processes—both automatic and deliberate—are launched when an individual is presented with a problem, particularly when required to process stimulus information at different levels of complexity. My lifelong interest in the Rorschach represents a straight line from my original scholarship in perception and cognition.

Even though I did not study the Rorschach while pursuing my Ph.D., I was exposed to it. In the early seventies, boundaries were not what they are now. In universities across the country, it was not unusual for senior graduate students to assess their junior compeers. Perhaps this practice still takes place in some programs now but, undoubtedly, incorporates more safeguards. I vividly recall that when the assessor handed me each card, I had a panicky moment of fearing that perhaps I would not be able to see anything. I have carried this experience with me into many years of administering the Rorschach. As I tell my students, it's an anxiety-provoking task we're giving our clients, a phenomenon one of my students demonstrated many years later using biofeedback measures (Momenian-Schneider et al., 2006). I did try to procure my protocol years later, but apparently, it vanished. I also took the Thematic Apperception Test, which was far more pleasurable for me. Now the tables were turned: It was I who challenged the assessor by the extreme length of my stories.

It was two years later that I obtained clinical training through a year-long post-doctoral experience at Case Western Reserve University and an internship. Inducing me to make a transition were two years of teaching at St. Lawrence University in Canton, NY. More to the point, though, this appointment entailed running a community psychology program. I placed undergraduate psychology majors in various community organizations and agencies and conducted a weekly seminar in which we talked about their experiences in the field. I became intrigued with how personality and context interact. For example, I would place a highly agentic, take-charge student in a particular agency where the student fared poorly because these personality characteristics were interpreted as impudence. If I moved the student to a setting with a culture that contrasted with the first, the setting appreciated the student greatly, regarding the student as exhibiting positive leadership qualities. This involvement drew me closer to the clinical realm and whet my appetite to make some kind of contribution to the struggles of folks in the community. I continued to be an impassioned teacher and especially enjoyed research collaborations with students, but some component seemed to be missing. Given my somewhat aimless state, one direction seemed obvious: I needed to go back to graduate school.

A psychological assessor is born

We finally arrive in this narrative to my immersion in psychological assessment, a development launched when I began a respecialization program at

Case Western Reserve University, unpoetically dubbed "retread" by some members of the community. I could not have been more fortunate with the assessment training I had at Case. Most of the coursework was taught by Sandra Russ who is a nationally recognized psychological assessment scholar, particularly known for the use of play as an assessment tool. In her lectures, she nicely blended the science and poetry of psychological assessment, and I still remember some of the cases she discussed in class. Irving Weiner, then chair of the department, provided an extremely memorable and captivating lecture in which he described the history of the Rorschach, characterizing not only the seminal leaders' intellectual positions but also their personality qualities that intersected with and shaped these positions. He had a wonderful delivery! It made it even more meaningful to us knowing that he played an important role in that history. Somehow, I inherited an audiotape of that lecture and I listened to it many times in later years, especially in preparation for my own lecture on the same topic.

The structure of the assessment training at Case was excellent and stands in contrast to programs in many other doctoral programs today, programs that have suffered from a devaluation of psychological assessment, and especially, personality assessment (Krishnamurthy & Yalof, 2009). In the Case program, by the time we administered instruments such as the WISC or the Rorschach to an actual client, our administration and scoring had been checked out thoroughly. A phalanx of well-qualified senior graduate students put us through our paces with the various instruments and their associated tasks. None of us contemplated not memorizing the WISC instructions. I remember preparing for the Rorschach check-out. The side-by-side seating arrangement proved my undoing. Apparently, I was so tense while I was practicing that once I completed my check-out, I found I could not turn my head, and that debilitating condition continued over a five-day period. Once we were deemed "good-to-go" with respect to test administration, we were sent to a clinical venue, a pediatric inpatient facility in my case, where we conducted several assessments over the semester. Both the on-site supervisor and the Case faculty supervised these assessments. It allowed for deep, close supervision. Yes, we were helped with the integration of data, but supervisors also focus granularly on basic skills such as coding Rorschach responses.

The Case program qualified our cohort well to apply for internship given the priority internship directors place on assessment competence (Piotrowski & Belter, 1999). I went to Connecticut Valley Hospital, which was a very luxurious situation for psychological assessment. The institution boasted an extensive assessment library, qualified supervisors, and well-functioning treatment teams eager to receive the insights of the psychological assessor. Most of the individuals whom we assessed lived in the institution, and consequently, were quite accessible to interns, and we were not pressured by an approaching discharge date. We also had the time to develop a relationship of substance. What was invaluable was the opportunity to work with individuals at the lower end of the continuum of ego functioning in all of their variousness. I came to appreciate the utter insufficiency of the diagnosis of, say, schizophrenia, in my ability as an assessor to capture the person's individuality and develop a plan for treatment likely to be effective.

What made my internship year somewhat of an inflection point was a seemingly trivial step I took—an action on the level of a butterfly flapping its wings in Brazil (Lorenz, 2000)—that brought me into connection with the Society for Personality Assessment. Remember, I began as an assistant professor who, like assistant professors everywhere, committed myself to writing projects. When I went into my respecialization training, I continued to write, seeking any and every opportunity, to what end I'm not sure. The *Journal for Personality Assessment* put out a call for book reviewers, and I volunteered myself. I received an invitation to review a book that was a rather peculiar choice for *JPA*—Julie Rogers' *How to be your very own shrink*. Yes, it was a self-help book, but, given that I was in the beginning of my career, I felt I was in no position to decline. And frankly, at that time, I was unabashedly glad to have a free book, apparently no matter what it was. Had I read that book more closely, I might have saved the expense of my analysis. I submitted the review and several weeks later, received a lovely handwritten note "From the desk of Paul Lerner." He thanked me for my review and said he just happened to notice that I was not a member of the Society. Would I consider joining?

Full-fledged, pretty much

I responded in the affirmative to Dr. Lerner's invitation. The most immediate advantage of membership was the opportunity to add the most charming, petite issues of *the Journal for Personality Assessment* to my bookshelf. By the time those journals began filling my mailbox, I was fully ensconced in my first full-time position in clinical psychology (although the designation of "licensed psychologist" would await a year of postdoctoral experience, a bevy of completed forms, and a state and national examination). The position I accepted was that of staff psychologist at Friends Hospital, the oldest private psychiatric hospital in the United States, located in Philadelphia. Some new professionals find that although psychological assessment might have been an emphasis in their graduate training (and that is decreasingly the case), it is an activity rarely if ever requested by the setting. Not so, for me: Psychological assessment was the most critical service performed by staff psychologists, followed by group psychotherapy. To know me is to know that these two areas have been the emphases of my career—again, that Brazilian butterfly flapping its wings.

My assessment work over my ten years (1980–1990) at Friends Hospital was rich and vast. All of the psychology staff at the institution were housed together, and we had referrals from all over the hospital—all age ranges and levels of ego functioning. One week, I might assess a teen-age girl to determine whether the aggressive behaviors are rooted in depression, or evidence of a burgeoning personality disorder. The next week, I might assess a young adult male who was in the midst of a depressive episode, but some evidence suggested bipolarity. This heterogeneity was a great boon to my development as a new assessment psychologist because it enabled me to place the qualities of individuals on broad continua. I was able to see, for example, that thought disorder is not an element present in a highly circumscribed group of individuals but manifests itself in varying degrees in different people.

A couple other features of inpatient assessment practices in the 1980s are noteworthy. We still had the luxury of conducting a comprehensive assessment in inpatient and partial hospital settings. In those days, we used the term "battery" rather than multi-method approach, but we seemed to ascribe to the spirit of the latter term. No battery was deemed complete unless in included cognitive testing, performance personality instruments, narrative techniques, and omnibus self-report instruments. The Personality Assessment Inventory had not yet been published, so our major alternatives were the MMPI and the MCMI, the latter being seen as especially helpful in the diagnosis of personality disorder, thereby enabling us to address a common referral question. Although Diagnostic-Related Groups came on the scene in 1982, their use lagged in inpatient facilities. Most patients who came to the hospital enjoyed 28 days of coverage, a feature offering psychology staff with a reasonable timeframe in which to carry out robust assessments.

However, these extensive assessments were of uncertain utility. It is doubtful that they had much usefulness to the client because if any feedback at all was given to the patient, is was dispensed by the patient's psychiatrist. What benefit these reports had to the referral source, the psychiatrist, was also a mystery because we never talked about it. We sent out these reports like so many flying lanterns launched into the July night sky and moved on to the next patient. Very occasionally, one of the psychiatrists from the adolescent unit would say, "Nice report," or even, "I'm surprised you didn't find a thought disorder." It didn't occur to any of us that we might have had a conversation about the assessment.

Whether psychological assessors working in inpatient and partial hospital settings have clarity about how their reports are received, I do not know, but I am certain of one thing: Psychological assessors as a group need a better understanding, born out of research, as to how a psychological report is processed by the target group. To achieve such understanding, I believe that qualitative methodologies might be most helpful, such as that employed by my former dissertation student Robin Ward (2008) who looked at the experiences of assessor-client pairs following their participation in feedback sessions, and the complex reactions they had to one another as well as the feedback itself. Studies that explore the intentions of assessors as they wrote reports and how the material in those reports was received and used is necessary for us to whether our work is hitting its mark. To what extent does referring to the actual test data increase the reader's confidence in the findings? How does the heavy use of subheadings affect ease of reading? To what extent does discussion of evidence related to rule-outs add confusion or clarity in the diagnostic section? Beyond what point does the extensiveness of the recommendations section overwhelm the reader? These and a host of other questions could be usefully pursued, and probably most usefully, on a context-specific basis.

Back to the academy

Within the Philadelphia area, I quickly became known for my knowledge of the Rorschach Comprehensive System (RCS; Exner, 2005), a development that was a matter of sheer luck. Within this region, individuals who earned their doctorates locally were by-and-large trained in Zygmunt Piotrowski's system. Dr. Piotrowski had taught at Temple for many years, and then, at Hahnemann University. Individuals who had been trained elsewhere but practiced in the Philadelphia area would be likely to use another system. We had the very phenomenon John Exner talked about in Volume 1: No one could seem to understand anyone else. Consequently, psychologists and graduate students were quite eager to learn about this new comprehensive system that purported to take the best from each system. I began giving workshops and teaching courses on the RCS in local graduate programs. In the Hahnemann program, even though students would learn the RCS in their fourth year of graduate training, they would master the Piotrowski system in their second year. The students were clearly in a state of Rorschach overload. This arrangement continued for at least five years. During several semesters, my Rorschach course occurred in a room adjacent to Dr. Piotrowski's course, enabling me to experience his renowned amiability and urbanity. Even when he asked me to borrow a piece of chalk from my classroom, which he did frequently due to a widespread chalk deficiency within the building, he did so with élan.

These various forays into the classroom, even as I was working as an inpatient psychologist, eventually led to an invitation to apply for a position of Director of Internship Training in the Doctor of Psychology program at Hahnemann University. The program (now at Widener University) has an integrated, half-time, two-year internship in which all Doctor of Psychology students are placed in a multitude of sites in the tri-state (Pennsylvania, New Jersey, Delaware) area. Picture 60–70 students simultaneously placed in internship rotations. The sites hosting the rotations were greatly varied from college counseling centers to medical units of hospitals to schools to psychiatric hospitals (see Mangione et al., 2006 for a further description of this type of internship). While students are on internship, they also take a full-time course load. One noteworthy feature was that the kinds of assessment conducted by students were highly heterogeneous—full psychological assessments for treatment planning, rapid screening assessments for diagnostic purposes, extensive neuropsychological assessments, forensic assessments, and assessments performed in the context of organizational consultations As one of our assessment faculty, I knew I had to help our students recognize what core principles underlie all of these assessment activities, as well as discern how assessors must adapt to the demands of their contexts. For example, all of our students needed to recognize the importance of integrating data within a multi-method approach while also recognizing that in what section the integration occurs might differ in a forensic assessment versus an assessment written for psychotherapy planning.

Thirty-one years have passed since I took on the position of faculty member and director of the internship. A year after I joined the faculty, the Doctor of Psychology program moved from Hahnemann University to Widener University; the Ph.D. program remained at Hahnemann. The process was an ordeal. When the Psy.D. faculty made the decision to re-locate in order to reside in an institution whose mission was more compatible with ours, great uncertainty existed as to whether our students would accompany us or remain at Hahnemann in a reconstituted program. Fortunately for us, our entire group of 150+ students migrated with us. Still, I had never thought that entering academia would mean living on the edge.

Teaching

Since that time, I have been fortunate to teach in those areas that have always commanded my passion—psychological assessment and group psychotherapy. Early on I taught the RCS. I aimed to make this course as experiential as possible. For example, I found it extremely helpful in the beginning of the Rorschach course to have the students make their own inkblots. After one year in which I got in trouble with the University for the mess my students made in a classroom, I moved the operation outside where students could drop dollops of paint on sheets of paper to their hearts content. Years later, alumni tell me that many still have the framed inkblots decorating their abodes. But, in addition to wanting them to be alive to the playful aspects of psychological assessment, an awareness that has always enriched my assessment work, I sought to create a more thoroughly experiential appreciation of the importance of the stimulus properties of the blots. I had them analyze their own and their classmates' blots in terms of the well-known dimensions of chromaticity, shading, wholeness versus fragmentation, and so on. I discuss this and other teaching strategies in Handler and Hilsenroth's *Teaching and Learning Psychological Assessment* (Brabender, 1998; Figure 7.1).

In recent years, I have taught two required assessment courses that I think are relatively unique in relation to doctoral program offerings but

Figure 7.1 The author teaching personality assessment.

contribute greatly to strengthening students' assessment skills. The first course is titled Advanced Differential Diagnosis and enables students to integrate their prior work in the areas of personality, psychopathology, and assessment. Students take this course in the spring semester of the third year, well after the time that they fully mastered the DSM system (American Psychiatric Association, 2013). For my students, I think being in this course is a bit like an experience I had when I was in the ninth grade. I had taken piano lessons for years, and I began taking lessons from a new instructor. She was strict. In our first moments together, I played a polonaise for her. She shuddered. She proceeded to take me back to elementary pieces, the practicing of which would enable me to focus on fingering, pedaling, and other essential elements. I was outraged, but ultimately, compliant. In my course, I take them back to assessment basics. We talk about the psychometric properties of assessment tools and focus intensively on diagnostic systems. I share with them different ways of thinking about diagnosis and offer them the critique of descriptive diagnostic schemes such as the DSM-5 (American Psychiatric Association, 2013). They learn how to diagnose using the *Psychodynamic Diagnostic Manual* (Lingiardi & McWilliams, 2017) and get an introduction to more fully continua-based systems such as the Hierarchical Taxonomy of Psychopathology (Kotov et al., 2017). We then consider traditional categories of psychopathology, identify their personality forerunners, and link those forerunners to psychological test variables. In the end, the course is just as much about epistemology as clinical psychology, and if they leave with more uncertainty about the diagnostic enterprise than when they began, I feel I have been successful.

The other course is an assessment case conference which focuses on students' honing the skill of being able to explain their clinical decision-making in regard to all aspects of the assessment to others. Each student in this class of generally 12 students presents an assessment case. These students are placed in a variety of different assessment contexts, which enables the class to see the breadth of psychological assessment activities and to appreciate how the assessment must be adapted to the context. A week prior to the presentation, the class receives all of the de-identified raw data and report. Those students not presenting must prepare lists of questions and I do the same. Our questions are far-ranging from coding decisions, to justification of inclusion or exclusion of instruments in the battery, to the effects of identity facets of the client, to investigation of the student's way of resolving data splits, to exploration of ethical issues raised by the case. After approximately 90 minutes of vigorously questioning the presenter, we ask the individual to leave the room, and we discuss feedback we want to provide. Then, the student returns and receives the feedback from a peer (a challenging task for the peer). At the end of the course, the student drafts a developmental plan specifying the steps needed to be taken for the student to progress as a psychological assessor. I have observed that students leave this experience with a much more cohesive sense of themselves as psychological assessors.

Scholarship

Of course, as an academician, I am constantly thinking about translating my clinical and academic experiences into papers that would enable me to have a conversation with a broad group of scholars. For the most part, my focus has not been on research although I co-conducted a study (Singer & Brabender, 1994) based on my experience at Friends Hospital of noticing that treatment team members struggle to differentiate unipolar and bipolar depression, a distinction with major treatment implications. Our finding that individuals with bipolar depression have very significant cognitive slippage and difficulties with reality testing, born out by later research, seemed counter-intuitive at the time.

Currently, my scholarly writing in the area of personality assessment has focused on training, ethics, and diversity topics, often in their relationship to one another. For example, I edited a special series on the ethical issues that arise in particular assessment settings (see Brabender & Bricklin, 2001, for an overview), a series that emerged from my observation, particularly in relation to our psychology interns, that school psychologists, for example, face ethical problems that are quite different from those encountered by forensic psychologists. No basic ethics course could possible cover all of the issues that crop up, and so I felt that it was important that assessment psychologists, and especially trainees, have access to a resource tailored for them. In the series, I co-authored an article with Jed Yalof

(Yalof & Brabender, 2001) in which we discussed our view that often, instructors and supervisors of assessment are so focused on solving ethical problems that emerge with students that they miss important opportunities to strengthen students' ethical muscles. My prior description of my own experiences as a graduate student revealed examples of such ethical problems. Should advanced students assess their junior compatriots? If they do, what are the feedback requirements if any? By discussing with students the steps of ethical decision-making in relation to these questions, we argued, students achieve the skills to solve new problems that will inevitably arrive in their assessment practices.

My interest in diversity as it pertains to assessment was launched by a personal experience—the adoption of our daughter, Gabi, from Honduras. In this process, we saw quite directly how cultural factors—if ignored—can lead to an assessment that goes awry. Here is a very simple example. My husband and I were required to go Honduras to be interviewed by various human service professionals. Although before I left, I took an MMPI, more evaluation was going to occur abroad. The Honduran mental health professionals (I'm not certain that they were psychologists) decided to waive my involvement in assessment tasks because of my background in assessment. However, my husband was required to perform various tasks including the rendering of human figure drawings. When my husband was asked if he could speak Spanish, he responded in the affirmative despite the fact that his Spanish was quite rusty at the time. Nonetheless, because of his claim, all of the tasks were administered to him in Spanish. Of course, he was extremely anxious given his recognition that his performance would affect their view of his adequacy as an adoptive parent. He realized after he left that when he was instructed to draw a man, he drew a woman, and vice versa. In a country that that was, and likely still is relative to the United States, organized according to extreme prescriptions vis-à-vis gender and gender roles, we thought his comprehension error could create difficulties for us. In the end it did not but it gave me an appreciation for the disadvantage individuals are under when they are responding in other than their primary language, especially under anxiety-producing circumstances.

My personal involvement with adoption led me to immerse myself in the adoption literature and then, to form a research group specifically to learn about the bonding process. Our work ultimately led to a number of research articles and the co-edited text *Working with Adoptive parents: Research, Theory, and Therapeutic Interventions* (Brabender & Fallon, 2009). In the process of pursuing that research, my colleagues and I interviewed members of many adoptive families. I also began to conduct psychological assessments on members of adoptive families. What I learned was that the experience of being adopted is highly shaping of life experiences and psychological features such as attachment style. I also learned that being adopted is an identity status that is often accompanied—like many features that distinguish a person from most of the population—with a panoply of stressors. It became increasingly obvious to me that any adequate assessment or intervention with this population needed to take account of the additional burdens carried by marginalized populations. Reciprocally, I found that the adoption literature—and likely the literature about other minority populations—did not do justice to individual differences with respect to personality. In both assessment and intervention, consideration given to personality differences and their implications for how a person wends a way in the world is nigh on absent.

My awareness of the poverty of the psychological assessment literature in addressing the distinctive experiences of marginalized populations shaped my response when Routledge approached me, asking me to write a book on gender and psychological assignment. By no means did I think the psychological assessment literature had exhausted the topic of gender, and that no further contributions were needed. However, I did believe that the concept of gender had become far more complex than the traditional male-female comparisons that typified extant literature. Our conceptions of gender are extremely multi-faceted with gender identity, gender expression, femininity-masculinity, and sexual orientation all being part of the picture. The field of psychology is moving further and further away from the notion of the gender binary (Hyde et al., 2019). And yet, I was aware that the psychological assessment research was thin, fitting my notion that the accumulated findings on some marginalized groups— as some sexual and gender identity statuses are—barely exist. Therefore, I was faced with the dilemma that the book that was most needed might be one that could not be written at present. Yet, I reasoned that psychological assessors all over the country had individual experiences working with persons of various identity statuses and together, we could make a beginning in this area. I invited Joni Mihura to join me in this endeavor and we surprised ourselves by developing a text, *The Handbook of Gender and Sexuality in Psychological Assessment*, with 27 chapters, a large number of which were case studies and theoretical expositions rather than research reviews. Eventually, we were able to see that psychology does know a considerable amount about the life satisfaction, mental health concerns, and strengths of gender and sexual minorities. What we do not know is about the performance of various minority population on psychological tests. The chapters pointed to the work that the field of psychological assessment needs to do going forward.

My approach to personality assessment

My approach to psychological assessment is characterized by four features, the first of which is my aim to understand people in their fullness. I would imagine that most psychological assessors would establish this aim for themselves. For me, though, this effort entails grasping all of the identity statuses that are most important to the individual, particularly those tied to minority stress, and being aware of any intersectional spaces that exert influence on experience and behavior (Brabender & Mihura, 2016). Lamentably, I have not always embraced this feature. I recall that during the years I performed psychological assessment as an inpatient psychologist, I frequently encountered individuals who were first-generation Russians who had lived in the Unites States for many years. A common situational stressor for this group was being confronted by their young adult children engaging in life courses that were viewed by their parents as at odds with their values. My recollection is that at that time, I did not think with sufficient depth about acculturation phenomena. Assessing individuals today, I look at immigration status and nationality as critical elements in understanding a person who is immersed in multiple cultures. Specifically, in conceptualizing a case, I draw upon the theoretical literature on this topic (Roysircar & Krishnamurthy, 2018), consult the research pointing to mental health challenges and resources in a given immigrant population, as well as incorporate tools capable of providing information about a person's acculturative stress. Particularly in my assessment case conference described previously, I also help my students to explore these dimensions by using a framework such Comas-Diaz's system (2012) presented in her text *Multicultural care*, which includes a wide array of identity dimensions. With such a wealth of instruments related to acculturation and other identity dimensions, students require assistance in knowing how to choose among the instruments to find one appropriate to their cases.

Second, like most other psychological assessors today, I ascribe to the multi-method approach on the notion that different methods have sources of error that other instruments do not share. Moreover, different types of instruments are better at capturing particular types of psychological phenomena. For example, whereas performance instruments can tell us about basic ego functioning, self-report instruments are particularly good at phenomenological states and symptom patterns. As noted above, self-report instruments are also helpful for looking at identity elements as well as positive psychological features such as resilience. Even though many psychological assessors might regard the multi-method approach as the gold standard or even standard of practice, my experience with my students working in so many clinical sites tells me that that standard is often unachieved due to many factors such as time exigencies and the biases of supervisors. As we continue to attempt to persuade all psychological assessors of the benefits of this approach, we also need to help them recognize what limitations they are placing on the statements about personality and psychopathology they can make when the type of data is limited. Also, it could be advantageous to help assessors gain more performance information from data that are typically treated as self-report data. For example, assessors might be trained to attend more assiduously to how a client behaves in a clinical interview rather than noting merely the content of responses.

Third, for many years, I have written reports endeavoring to show how the individual's personality features set the stage for the kinds of psycho-pathology the person manifested. I find my efforts in this regard are now facilitated by the availability of empirically based models such as the Hierar-chical Taxonomy of Psychopathology (Kotov et al., 2017) showing links be-tween clusters of psychological symptoms and underlying continuum-based personality traits. I now feel better equipped in helping students to see that their task in the personality section is not, as they sometimes think, to talk about symptom patterns but to sketch out what undergirds the symptom patterns. One gap in the literature that I would imagine affects many psy-chological assessors is that the kinds of personality factors that are repre-sented in a model such a HiTOP are those gleaned largely from self-report data. A number of variables such as those captured by the Rorschach have an uncertain status with this model. For example, does reality-testing relate primarily to p, the general psychopathology factor, or would it also enter into the thought disorder factor? In any case, in my view, any adequate per-sonality section captures both the kinds of trait identified in the Five Factor Model, the general ego functions delineated in Axis M of the *Psychodynamic Diagnostic Manual* (Lingiuiard & McWilliams, 2017), the core conflictual issues, as well as a communication of what it feels like to the person to be that person, to be with others, and to be in the world.

Fourth, I generally write my psychological reports in a novelistic way. We have all read reports that are sterile, technical, reductionistic, and for-mulaic. Most reports I read contrast with the character sketches of Dickens, Hardy, Wharton or even lesser talents unfavorably. Too often, I believe, the authors of psychological reports are encouraged to use a very limited vocabulary on the notion that the report must be instantly comprehensible to a client. To me, the report is primarily for the referral source and should serve the referral source's needs. Given the variety of human presentations, we need language to make the appropriate distinctions and to capture sub-tleties. For the client, I generally write a letter (as is often done in Thera-peutic Assessment; Finn et al., 2012) and in this context use language most suitable for that client.

When composing a psychological report, I encourage in myself and my students a style of writing that does not shortchange what the English language can do, a crafting that should begin with the Behavioral Obser-vations. Consider, for example, Dickens' description of one of his most famous characters Bill Sikes of *Oliver Twist*:

> A stoutly-built fellow of about five-and-thirty, in a black velveteen coat, very soiled drab breeches, lace-up half boots, and grey cotton stockings which enclosed a bulky pair of legs, with large swelling

calves;--the kind of legs, which in such costume, always look in an unfinished and incomplete state without a set of fetters to garnish them. He had a brown hat on his head, and a dirty belcher handkerchief round his neck: with the long frayed ends of which he smeared the beer from his face as he spoke. He disclosed, when he had done so, a broad heavy countenance with a beard of three days' growth, and two scowling eyes; one of which displayed various parti-coloured symptoms of having been recently damaged by a blow.

A psychological report is not a novel, and were our prose to be this lush, we might be accused—correctly or not—of self-indulgence. Yet, we can see Dickens striving to draw and picture of the person, and we should do the same. To this end, I aim to use descriptive language and imagery, often the client's, but sometimes my own if I can develop a potent metaphor. In the therapeutic assessment movement (Finn et al., 2012), imagery has been used to excellent effect; this resource should be tapped for report writing. Unquestionably, I have been able to take this approach to report-writing because I am almost always writing reports for psychotherapists who are in private practices. They crave the detailed and rich depictions they have the time to read. What concerns me is that sometimes psychologists become so accustomed to working in a short-term time frame that when they have the opportunity to write in a less antiseptic, economical way, they fail to realize that another type of product is possible. Along the same lines, what my referring sources value is a personality portrait characterized by figure and ground. That is, what creates an impression is the identification of those personality traits that most significantly drive individuals' experiencers and behaviors.

How personality and experiences have affected my approach

Accounting for one's views on any matter, especially on matters of long-term importance in one's life, entails an acknowledgment of both character and situation, as well as their interplay. Among the situational (butterfly flapping) factors are the following: completing a respecialization program at Case Western Reserve where a major emphasis was on psychological assessment in general and the Rorschach Inkblot Method specifically; taking a position in Philadelphia where psychologists were eager to learn the Comprehensive System; having a teaching background that enabled me to take advantage of the aforementioned opportunity; and being the beneficiary of an adjunct teaching opportunity that would lead to an academic career in teaching and writing in the area of psychological assessment.

Of course, it is my family of origin that had the most to do with shaping my personality. My mother—introduced earlier in this essay as the person who helped me with my early studies—did not have a college degree to her great chagrin. I suppose my own accomplishments could plausibly be regarded as a compensation for her sense of deprivation. In any case, what I believe was more important than my mother's own frustrations was her enjoyment of, and facility in exploring the psychological lives of those around us. She was a master mentalizer, as Fonagy (Fonagy & Allison, 2014) might talk about it, and she invited me into her ponderings during our kitchen table chats. Her interest extended to the important players in my life, helping me to cope with difficult situations by gaining insight into them, and recognizing the humor in them. In short, my mother grew my *M*. Her labors bore fruit: At a very young age, adults sought me out for my opinion on matters psychological and social. My conversations with her were as important as any psychology course I took or any supervision situation in which I participated. The psychological features cultivated in my home environment might be seen as ones enlivening those processes tapped by the Engagement and Cognitive Processing cluster of the Rorschach, interpreted within a psychodynamic paradigm (Wiggins, 2003; Meyer et al., 2020). Staying within the Engagement and Cognitive Processing cluster, I must add that another aspect of my personality style is to immerse myself in a stimulus (Complexity), uncover all of its facets (Blends), and see their interrelationships (+). Whether it's a 600-page novel, a complicated mosaic of my creation, or an extensive scholarly involvement, I have always preferred big projects (W); I savor the feeling of full, protracted absorption (M again). That part of me that, as a freshman, enjoyed sequestering myself away in a carrel and study, is still present. As I described in the last section, when I write a report, I like to plumb the data deeply, lingering over the client's interesting word choices and revealing images. I think about the case not only when I am sitting and writing, but also when I'm jogging or making dinner with each activity affording different insights.

At the same time, my approach to my work is not wholly meditative. Since that time when I received an invitation from Paul Lerner to join the Society for Personality Assessment, my work in this area has been a social affair, rich in fruitful collaborations. If that graduate student who tested me decades ago found a plenitude of cooperative responses, that finding would make sense to me. Still, the psychological quality attached to the Space Reversal response is one to which I resonate. Perhaps it's a feature derived from my grade school encounters, or from my adolescent need to stand up to my powerful, prosecutorial dad, or none of the above, but I find myself ineluctably drawn to what is missing or what does not fit in current conceptualizations in psychological phenomena. In fact, a tension between an inclination to cooperate and an opposing wish to disrupt is one of my core conflicts with my behavior in any moment revealing different positions taken to resolve it. I credit my interest in exploring diversity issues as they pertain to personality assessment as a manifestation of the disrupting side and my continual engagement in co-authoring the agreeable, cooperative side. Connecting this trend to management of affect, much like Madeline G^2 (Meyer et al., 2020), I am highly prone to impatience when others seem to be moving, in my estimation, too slowly, creating in me a bouquet of negative experiences that undoubtedly stoke the members of my Stress and Distress cluster. These negative reactions, though, do not lead to any exciting eruptions from me; even as I egg others on, I tend to be pragmatically organized and controlled. Moreover, most of the time, I find ways to reconcile the need to disrupt with as strong an impulse to cooperate. For example, writing an edited volume involving a rather large cast of contributors represents a harmonization of the two forces.

I have touched upon the Self and Other Representations when I mentioned the tension between my cooperativeness and disruptiveness. An element of Self Representation, of course, is identity. I wish to leave this dive into my background, my personality, and my views on psychological assessment with this thought. I have been involved with psychological assessment over four decades. I have enjoyed productive, enriching relationships with other psychological assessors who have made a similar commitment to this area. For me, psychological assessment is a core aspect of my identity and a continuous sustainer of my well-being.

Notes

1 For those unfamiliar with the nursery rhyme, a dillar–dollar scholar is an unwilling student, one highly inclined to procrastinate.
2 Madeline G. is an individual who participated in two psychological assessments, separated by 20 years (Wiggins, 2003; Hopwood & Waugh, 2020). The case study (Wiggins, 2003) yielded from this study is now a classic in the psychological literature and the recently published follow-up (Hopwood & Waugh, 2020) shows promise of being the same.

References

American Psychiatric Association. (2013). *Diagnostic and statistical manual of mental disorders (DSM-5®)*. Washington, DC: American Psychiatric Pub.

Brabender, V. (1998). Teaching that first Rorschach course. In L. Handler & M. Hilsenroth (Eds.), *Teaching and learning personality assessment* (pp. 215–234). Mahwah, NJ: Laurence Erlbaum and Associates.

Brabender, V., & Bricklin, P. (2001). Ethical issues in psychological assessment in different settings. *Journal of Personality Assessment,* 77(2), 192–194.

Brabender, V., & Fallon, A. F. (2012). *Working with adoptive parents: Research, theory, and therapeutic interventions.* Hoboken, NJ: Wiley.

Brabender, V., & Mihura, J. L. (Eds.). (2016). *Handbook of gender and sexuality in psychological assessment.* New York: Routledge.

Comas-Diaz, L. (2012). *Multicultural care: A clinician's guide to cultural competence.* Washington, DC: American Psychological Association.

Dickens, C. (1839). *Nicholas Nickleby.* London: Chapman & Hall.

Finn, S. E., Fischer, C. T., & Handler, L. (2012). *Collaborative/therapeutic assessment: A casebook and guide*. Hoboken, NJ: John Wiley & Sons.

Fonagy, P., & Allison, E. (2014). The role of mentalizing and epistemic trust in the therapeutic relationship. *Psychotherapy, 51*(3), 372–380.

Hopwood, C. J., & Waugh, M. H. (Eds). *Personality assessment paradigms and methods: A collaborative reassessment of Madeline G.* Oxfordshire: Routledge.

Hyde, J. S., Bigler, R. S., Joel, D., Tate, C. C., & van Anders, S. M. (2019). The future of sex and gender in psychology: Five challenges to the gender binary. *American Psychologist, 74*(2), 171–193.

Kotov, R., Krueger, R. F., Watson, D., Achenbach, T. M., Althoff, R. R., Bagby, R. M.,... & Eaton, N. R. (2017). The Hierarchical Taxonomy of Psychopathology (HiTOP): A dimensional alternative to traditional nosologies. *Journal of Abnormal Psychology, 126*(4), 454–477.

Krishnamurthy, R., & Yalof, J. The assessment competency. In M. B. Kenkel & R. L. Peterson (Eds.), *Competency-based education for professional psychology* (pp. 87–104). Washington, DC: American Psychological Association.

Lingiardi, V., & McWilliams, N. (Eds.). (2017). *Psychodynamic diagnostic manual: PDM-2*. New York: Guilford Publications.

Lorenz, E. (2000). The butterfly effect. *World Scientific Series on Nonlinear Science Series A, 39*, 91–94.

Mangione, L., Borden, K. A., Abrams, J. C., Arbeitman, D., Fernando, A. D., Knauss, L. K.,... & VandeCreek, L. (2006). The "how to" of half-time internships: Exemplars, structure, and quality assurance. *Professional Psychology: Research and Practice, 37*(6), 651–657.

Meyer, G. J., Mihura, J. L., & Waugh, M. H. (2020). A psychodynamic perspective on Madeline G. In C. J. Hopwood & M. H. Waugh (Eds.), *Personality assessment paradigms and methods: A collaborative reassessment of Madeline G.* (pp. 35–111). New York: Routledge.

Momenian-Schneider, S. H., Brabender, V. M., & Nath, S. R. (2009). Psychophysiological reactions to the response phase of the Rorschach and 16PF. *Journal of Personality Assessment, 91*(5), 494–496.

Opie, I., & Opie, P. (1951). *Oxford dictionary of nursery rhymes*. Oxford: Oxford University Press.

Piotrowski, C., & Belter, R. W. (1999). Internship training in psychological assessment: Has managed care had an impact? *Assessment, 6*(4), 381–389.

Roysircar, G., & Krishnamurthy, R. (2018). Nationality and personality assessment. In *Diversity-sensitive personality assessment* (pp. 151–178). Oxfordshire: Routledge.

Singer, H., & Brabender, V. (1993). The use of the Rorschach to differentiate unipolar and bipolar disorders. *Journal of Personality Assessment, 60*(2), 333–345.

Ward, R. M. (2008). Assessee and assessor experiences of significant events in psychological assessment feedback. *Journal of Personality Assessment, 90*(4), 307–322.

Wiggins, J. S. (2003). *Paradigms of personality assessment*. New York: Guilford Press.

Yalof, J., & Brabender, V. (2001). Ethical dilemmas in personality assessment courses: Using the classroom for in vivo training. *Journal of Personality Assessment, 77*(2), 203–213.

8 Thoughts from a Contrarian Generalist

A Roundabout Journey to Where I Am Now

Robert F. Bornstein

I grew up in Manhattan, on East End Avenue, a somewhat obscure neighborhood that in the words of a *New York Times* article from a few years back, "hugs the edge of the Upper East Side like fuzz on a peach". East End Avenue is only 13 blocks long, running from 79th to 92nd street, and when I was a child there in the early 1960s, it had a distinct old-time feel. The streets were cobblestone, and there were no traffic lights, just stop signs. Things have changed since then—East End is now a semi-bustling area with lots of young parents and kids—but it still hasn't caught up to the rest of New York in many respects. It still has a bit of an old school ambiance.

Growing up in New York was great, but it left me stunningly naïve regarding some basic aspects of life. For example, one of the first times we ventured out for a day in the country ("the country" in this case being Westchester), I was shocked to discover that some people got their mail delivered to a box on a post at the end of their driveway, unlocked and completely unsecured. In New York, one's mail is held in a fortified, burglar-proof lockbox. Only when I got to college did I realize that for most people trick-or-treating involves going from house to house ringing doorbells. Where I grew up Halloween meant taking the elevator from floor to floor—you were never under any circumstances permitted to leave your building. (How I reconciled this latter experience with the events depicted in various Halloween TV specials I do not know, but somehow I did; Figure 8.1).

I was supposed to be a doctor

That was the plan from as early as I can remember, and I never questioned it, even for a moment. Off I went in the fall of 1977 to begin my first year at Amherst College, completely committed to majoring in biology. Things didn't work out exactly as I had planned; there were too many temptations, and I was having way too much fun to study. When I received my third C grade (it might actually have been my fourth) I was summoned to the office of the fellow who ran the pre-med program and told to find something else to do with my life. I switched to psychology,

DOI: 10.4324/9781003036302-8

Figure 8.1 Me riding a horse, probably around age two. I cannot explain this picture—there are very few horses in New York City, and why my parents decided to perch me on one is a mystery.

and decided to major in art as well, to try my hand at painting. The rest, as they say, is history.

In the midst of my transition from biology to psychology I made an interesting choice—one that I still don't understand completely, but which had a significant impact on my career in more ways than I can count. During my freshman year, while still in Amherst's pre-med program, I had managed to obtain a summer position as a research assistant in the Department of Biochemistry at Mount Sinai School of Medicine in New York, not too far from where I grew up. I figured that this sort of experience would help me get into medical school. Even though I switched from biology to psychology during my sophomore year at Amherst I continued doing my summer biochemistry research—all four summers, in fact—and I had the good fortune to work for an extraordinarily generous person, Terry Ann Krulwich, whose mission in life was (and still is, I believe) to give young people a leg up on their grad school applications by awarding them co-authorship on publications whenever possible. My understanding of biochemistry was modest at best—we were studying the dynamics of sodium-proton antiporters in membrane vesicles of alkalophilic bacteria—but I did my job as well as I could, and by the time I applied to clinical psychology doctoral programs in the fall of my senior year I had two (soon to be three) impressive-sounding publications under my belt. My first published paper was a product of my work at Mount Sinai (Krulwich et al., 1979). I applied to 24 clinical psychology PhD programs, was accepted at three, and began my clinical training at SUNY-Buffalo ("UB" as it is known locally) in the fall of 1981.

Graduate school and beyond

It didn't take long for me to realize that I had made the right decision in attending UB. On our first day of graduate training, at the opening reception for incoming doctoral students, I met Mary Languirand, who, as it happens, was in the same entering class as I was. Sparks soon flew, and Mary took an apartment in the building next door to mine so we could spend more time with each other. After about a year of that, we ditched our solo apartments, moved in together in 1983, and got married in 1990. We've been inseparable ever since. We've actually co-authored several books over the years, and Mary deserves a medal, or something, for putting up with me all this time. I'm not the easiest person to live with (Figure 8.2).

Buffalo in the early 1980s was a great place to be a grad student, and the Psychology Department at UB was a wonderful, welcoming environment for a young psychologist-to-be. I had the good fortune to be assigned to work with Joseph Masling, who was engaged in two fascinating research streams, one examining perception without awareness, and the other exploring the construct validity and clinical utility of the Rorschach Oral Dependency (ROD) scale. I began by helping Joe conduct some subliminal priming studies he had planned for us before I arrived, and my apprenticeship soon morphed into a collaborative relationship that has continued for nearly four decades. Like Terry Krulwich, Joe Masling was

Figure 8.2 A photo from the late 1980s; Joe Masling and I were guests at John Auerbach's wedding in New Haven, CT.

Figure 8.3 Attendees at the *Perception without Awareness* conference in March 1991. Front row: Anthony Marcel, Robert Bornstein, Joseph Masling, Paula Niedenthal, John Kihlstrom. Second row: Phil Merikle, John Bargh, Joel Weinberger, Larry Jacoby. Third row: Matthew Erdelyi, Thane Pittman, Howard Shevrin.

exceptionally generous in assigning research credit, and during my four years there we co-authored a half-dozen articles that have held up pretty well over the years. One of our first investigations—a study of the link between dependency and yielding—helped set in motion my own independent research program, and eventually led us to reconceptualize the dynamics of interpersonal dependency and dependent personality disorder (Figure 8.3).

It was an unremarkable study in its conception. In line with prevailing wisdom at the time, we had hypothesized that, being passive by nature, dependent college students would yield to the opinions of nondependent students in a laboratory negotiation task. But a quirk in our experimental design altered the outcome in an unanticipated way, and we found the exact opposite of what we had predicted: In two thirds of the dyads, the dependent person refused to change their initial opinion and simply would not yield. When we interviewed those participants after the fact and asked them why they had behaved as they did, a common theme emerged; the dependent students told us that impressing the experimenter by holding their ground was more important to them than getting along with a peer. We realized at that moment that dependency-related passivity, when it occurs, is not reflexive but strategic, and that dependent people are quite capable to behaving actively—sometimes even aggressively—to strengthen ties with potential caregivers. What began as a minor study in the mid-1980s (Bornstein et al., 1987) continues to shape our understanding of the dynamics of interpersonal dependency in intimate partner violence, child abuse, bereavement, resilience, health service use, adherence to medical and psychotherapeutic treatment regimens, and other areas (Porcerelli et al., 2009; Denckla et al., 2015; Kane & Bornstein, 2018; Bornstein, 2019a).

In the summer of 1985 we moved to Syracuse, where I completed my predoctoral internship at Upstate Medical Center, and Mary completed hers at the R. H. Hutchings Psychiatric Center (which, as luck would have it, was literally down the block from Upstate). While on internship I published the first of what would turn out to be many papers in the *Journal of Personality Disorders*. Theodore Millon was one of the founding editors of JPD (Allen Frances was the other), and from the beginning Ted handled all my submissions to the journal. In the 15+ years that Ted served as JPD editor he never turned down anything I sent him; he accepted every manuscript I submitted. I am grateful that, many years later, as Ted's health began to fail, I had the opportunity to tell him how much his support meant to me. It gave me the confidence to submit manuscripts to JPD and other journals, believing that I would be treated kindly and that I'd have a decent chance of having my work accepted for publication. By and large this has turned out to be true. Although like all researchers I have had the occasional negative experience with journal editors and grant reviewers, as I look back on my experience as an author, I am amazed at the degree to which colleagues have been helpful and supportive in evaluating and responding to my work.

Thinking outside the box

Like many professors, my decision to enter academia was based in part on pragmatic concerns. Tenure seemed like a good thing to have—a promise of stability in an uncertain world—and as best I could tell when I was pondering potential career paths, the essence of being a professor is that you get to spend most of your time talking to really smart people about things you find interesting to begin with (sort of like telling endless, meandering stories at a party except no one can walk away from you no matter how bored they are, because if they do you'll fail them). All that, and you get to dress like a slob. This was definitely the job for me.

I began my academic career at Gettysburg College in the fall of 1986, and quickly discovered I loved teaching. Gettysburg turned out to be a perfect environment for me to develop my research program, for two reasons. First, the college was in the process of trying to establish a national reputation among liberal arts institutions, and as a result they were enormously generous in supporting faculty members' scholarship. They did not care a whit about what topics I studied, so long as I was publishing in peer-reviewed journals.

Second, I was the only clinician in a department of nine faculty members. As a result, I interacted more-or-less exclusively with cognitive, social, and developmental psychologists. I was forced outside my comfort zone and spent a lot of time thinking about psychological phenomena (mental imagery, episodic memory, attribution theory, language acquisition) that I would probably have ignored had I been surrounded by clinicians. Over time I brought this perspective to my own research, so when I thought about personality, and personality assessment, I approached the topic with the mindset of an experimentalist. This "outsider perspective" (the same sort of outsider experience I had earlier gone through when I realized that not everyone rode the elevator to go trick-or-treating) has shaped every aspect of my professional life.

Gettysburg College's modest publication expectations coupled with its generous research support enabled me to take on high-risk, labor-intensive projects without worrying about my productivity, so my first major undertaking was a meta-analysis of research on the mere exposure effect. It is a deceptively simple phenomenon with a long history in social psychology: The more frequently we are exposed to particular stimuli (images, nonsense words, works of art, other people), the more we like them. I spent the better part of a year hand-calculating effect sizes for 200+ published studies of the exposure effect—there were no meta-analysis software packages at that time—and was lucky enough to have the end result published in *Psychological Bulletin* (Bornstein, 1989). The paper has been widely cited, made its way into many Intro Psych textbooks, and was crucial in establishing me as a serious academic. It also had the somewhat comical effect of causing colleagues who don't know me to assume I'm a social psychologist. When I meet people for the first time at professional meetings, and they realize I'm the guy who wrote that mere exposure paper, they're often disappointed to learn I'm actually a clinician.

In addition to doing mere exposure research, during my first few years in Gettysburg I continued to study perception without awareness, and was able to demonstrate that under certain conditions subliminal stimuli actually produced significantly stronger effects on behavior than the same stimuli consciously perceived (Bornstein, 1990; Bornstein & D'Agostino, 1992). These findings helped establish perception without awareness as a robust and reliable phenomenon (see Erdelyi, 2004), and in 1991 Thane Pittman and I organized a three-day conference, *Perception Without Awareness: Cognitive, Clinical, and Social Perspectives*, to bring together leading researchers in this area. I got to spend a weekend with some famous and soon-to-be-famous psychologists, and Thane and I co-edited a book based on talks given at the meeting (Bornstein & Pittman, 1992). I was in hog heaven—on top of the world (Figure 8.4).

Figure 8.4 With Ted Millon at the 2005 American Psychological Association
conference in Washington, DC. With Ted's support I received the Division 12/American Psychological Foundation Millon Award for Excellence in Personality Research that year.

As time went on my interests shifted back to the dependency research
that Joe and I had worked on while I was still a doctoral student, and
I began to conduct additional studies examining the construct validity of
the ROD scale (Bornstein, 1996). A few years later I completed a meta-
analysis showing that the behaviorally referenced criterion validity of
ROD scores was equal to or better than that of every widely used questionnaire measure of interpersonal dependency (Bornstein, 1999). I also
began conducting studies to assess the impact of various experimental manipulations on self-report and performance-based dependency scores, borrowing these manipulations from cognitive, social, and neuropsychology.
We examined, among other things, the impact of mindset priming and
induced mood states on self-report and performance-based measures of interpersonal dependency, finding that mood influenced performance-based
but not self-report dependency scores, whereas mindset priming had the
opposite effect. These findings eventually coalesced into the process dissociation approach to examining test score interrelationships (Bornstein,
2002a), an integrative framework wherein one illuminates the psychological processes that are engaged by various psychological tests by deliberately
altering these processes and assessing the impact of the manipulations on
test scores.

The other great thing about being surrounded by non-clinicians, beyond the ways it helped shape my research, was that it made me a better

teacher. I had to work hard to explain what I was doing to colleagues with no background (and minimal interest) in clinical psychology, so I was forced to figure out how to describe personality pathology to a memory researcher, and performance-based testing to someone whose expertise was in speech perception. Once I figured that out, explaining this sort of material to undergraduates was easy.

The big picture

In May 1992 I received a handwritten letter from Paul Meehl, in response to a survey that I was conducting to assess the views of journal editors and manuscript reviewers regarding advantages and disadvantages of reviewer anonymity. Most respondents reported being uncomfortable with the concept of "open reviews", but 91% indicated that they would continue to review manuscripts if such a system was put in place (Bornstein, 1993). Meehl was very much in favor of an open review system, and his letter was quite supportive; he encouraged me to continue this line of research and try to improve what he saw as a flawed manuscript evaluation process.

I was, as you might imagine, thrilled by Meehl's encouraging letter. He had long been something of a hero to me, and a role model as well. I not only admired the perceptiveness and creativity that characterized his work, but also the range of his contributions, which included everything from his seminal writings on clinical versus statistical prediction and construct validity to his more recent work on schizotypy, psychometrics, philosophy of science, and research design. I was most inspired—awed, really—by his courage, and his willingness to challenge the status quo. I had the same feeling after reading *Why I Do Not Attend Case Conferences* (Meehl, 1973) as when I read *The Catcher in the Rye* and saw the Ramones perform live for the first time: Are people really allowed to say this stuff?

Like Joe Masling's mentorship and Ted Millon's votes of confidence, Paul Meehl's example had a profound influence on my work. From that day forward I was determined to spend my time addressing a broad range of issues in psychology—whatever seemed interesting and important, the riskier the better—rather than working narrowly on a single topic. And I decided that it was important to say what I believed, even if what I believed might upset people.

Obstinacy, orderliness, and parsimony

When I was a graduate student one of my supervisors told me that my obsessiveness was going to interfere with my clinical work. Hearing that really bothered me. I was genuinely shocked to learn that someone thought I was obsessive (I guess my defenses were working overtime), but I now realize he was right. Years later, when I began teaching a doctoral-level personality disorders course, I invited my students to complete the International

Personality Disorders Examination (IPDE) screening questionnaire (Loranger et al., 1994), and I completed it along with them. I figured it would be fun to chat about our personality styles and quirks (it was), and that it would be a good ice-breaker to help facilitate class discussion among the quieter students (it did). By this point in life I had more self-awareness than I had when I was in graduate school, and I was not the least surprised to discover that my score on the IPDE Obsessive–Compulsive Personality Disorder (PD) scale was pretty elevated (five out of a possible eight). I also scored above threshold on the Avoidant PD scale (that seemed right), and on the Schizoid PD scale as well. This latter result was a bit unsettling, but I felt better after reading Nancy McWilliams' insightful (2006) essay on schizoid dynamics. If you ever want to know what schizoid people are like—I mean *really* like, not just a listing of symptoms and traits—read the McWilliams article.

In hindsight I realize that my schizoid tendencies have contributed greatly to my scholarly work. I am a divergent thinker, and I seem to discover (or perhaps a better term would be created) connections among ostensibly unrelated concepts. My obsessiveness has helped as well, I think, in that my attention to detail enables me to organize these divergent thoughts into coherent narratives. Without question, I exhibit two of the three key elements of Freud's (1908/1959) anal triad, and like orderliness, obstinacy has played a significant role in my work.

I'm stubborn, and as is true of many obsessive people, I can be oppositional as well. After years conducting empirical studies of psychoanalytic concepts (to little effect), co-editing with Joe Masling the *Empirical Studies of Psychoanalytic Theories* book series (with modest sales), and giving talks at psychoanalytic meetings regarding the importance of subjecting psychodynamic concepts to rigorous empirical verification (the typical audience for these talks being about five people), I was sufficiently annoyed that I decided it was time to state my case directly, bluntly, and undiplomatically. In 2001 I published *The Impending Death of Psychoanalysis*, with the support of Joseph Reppen, a very open-minded, innovative, forward thinking journal editor.

If my intent at the time was to piss people off, I succeeded. I received a pile of what can only be described as hate mail, and my argument (the essence of which was that the psychoanalytic community was destroying psychoanalysis by being unresponsive to the demands of modern clinical practice and research) was criticized vociferously. One critic actually psychoanalyzed me in print—I did not fare well, in her view—leading to a pretty funny exchange in the pages of *Psychoanalytic Psychology* (see Bornstein, 2002b). I stand by everything I said in that article, though perhaps I'd say it a bit less bluntly today. The article eventually evolved into a series of three papers offering a roadmap for the development of an empirically rigorous, clinically useful approach to psychoanalytic theory (Bornstein, 2001, 2005, 2007; Figure 8.5).

Figure 8.5 One of many great evenings out with Mary. This photo is also from the 2005 APA conference; we were celebrating the Millon Award.

A mid-career shift

Gettysburg College was a great place to begin my career, but after nearly 20 years living in a town of 7,000 people Mary and I were ready to move on, and when George Stricker retired from Adelphi University they decided to fill his line with an established researcher whose work was consistent with the department's longstanding commitment to psychodynamic theory, therapy, and research. That person turned out to be me, and in 2006 we relocated to Westbury, New York. Mary began re-establishing her clinical practice in Garden City, not too far from the Adelphi campus, and I joined the faculty of the Derner School of Psychology (Figure 8.6).

The transition was difficult in certain respects (our five-minute commute to work was replaced by a 45-minute battle with hellish traffic), and very gratifying in others (we were now surrounded by a wonderful group of clinicians and clinical doctoral students). The transition was also

Figure 8.6 With my students, Fallon Kane and Adam Natoli, at the 2016 Omicron Delta Kappa initiation ceremony at Adelphi University. Fallon and Adam nominated me for admission to ODK, and I was honored to be asked to speak at the event.

marked by a somewhat jarring shift in my role within the department. At Gettysburg I had been perceived by my experimental colleagues as being excessively clinical—preoccupied with issues that could not be studied empirically (like unconscious processes), and not sufficiently rigorous in my empirical work. A couple of people on the faculty actually cautioned students not to take my courses, lest they be led astray by my soft-headed thinking. At Adelphi I was perceived by many as being too rigidly empirical, and not sufficiently sensitive to the human side of psychology. A few of my more traditional psychoanalytic colleagues cautioned students not to take my courses, lest they be led astray by my mindless devotion to empiricism. Exact same research; diametrically opposed perceptions. Context is, indeed, everything.

These bumps in the road notwithstanding, I was welcomed into the Adelphi fold, and my approach to personality assessment, which had begun to take shape in Buffalo and Gettysburg, now coalesced into a cohesive framework. The process dissociation approach (Bornstein, 2002a) expanded to incorporate concepts and findings from biology, physics, and art (Bornstein, 2009), and ultimately became a broader, more integrative strategy for test score validation—the process focused (PF) model (Bornstein, 2011). In the PF model, I reconceptualized test score validity as the degree to which respondents can be shown to engage in a predictable set of psychological processes during testing, with those processes determined by the nature of the instrument(s) used and the context in which

Figure 8.7 Being asked to help draft the second edition of the *Psychodydnamic Diagnostic Manual* was one of the highlights of my career. Here I am with several key contributors to PDM-2 at the 2015 International Psychoanalytic Congress in Boston. To my left is John O'Neil; to my right are Vittorio Lingiardi, Bob Gordon, and Bill MacGillavray.

testing takes place. In contrast to the traditional approach wherein correlational methods are used to quantify the relationship between test score and criterion, the PF model incorporates experimental methods (often borrowed from cognitive and social psychology) to manipulate variables that moderate test score-criterion relationships, enabling researchers to draw more definitive conclusions regarding the impact of underlying psychological processes on test scores (see Berant et al., 2008, for an example). The emphasis on underlying process in the PF model also provides a more nuanced framework for understanding and interpreting test score discontinuities—divergences between scores on tests that use contrasting methods to assess similar constructs. This latter aspect of the PF model has implications for multimethod assessment and test score integration (Hopwood & Bornstein, 2014), and is a key component of evidence-based psychological assessment (Bornstein, 2017; Figure 8.7).

A reputation, once acquired, is difficult to change

One unintended consequence of my focus on performance-based testing, multimethod assessment, and the importance of scrutinizing divergences between questionnaire and performance-based test results is that I have come to be regarded as being dismissive of self-report evidence. Nothing could be further from the truth. I find self-report data to be extraordinarily valuable—the best way to understand how people perceive and present themselves. My quibble is not with self-report evidence, but with contemporary psychology's overreliance on self-reports, and our tendency to equate self-reports with the underlying constructs they purport to assess when we describe and interpret our results. We should all be more careful in this regard, myself included, contextualizing our findings by noting how the method(s) we used to obtain our results may have influenced the outcome.

Along somewhat similar lines, in recent years I have come to be perceived as someone who is skeptical regarding trait approaches to personality and personality pathology. It is true that I have written articles criticizing contemporary dimensional frameworks, especially as they are applied to conceptualizing personality pathology in the *Diagnostic and Statistical Manual of Mental Disorders* (DSM) and other diagnostic systems. These criticisms notwithstanding, my colleagues and I have also published evidence helping to document the heuristic value (Bornstein & Cecero, 2000), and clinical utility (Bornstein & Natoli, 2019) of the trait perspective, and I was an early advocate of applying a dimensional approach to PD assessment and diagnosis. In 1997 I proposed using a dimensional strategy to assess pathological dependency and dependent PD, and a year later I developed an overarching dimensional framework to conceptualize and diagnose personality pathology in DSM-5 and beyond, capturing the adaptive as well as the maladaptive elements of each personality style (Bornstein, 1998). In my view dimensional and categorical approaches are complementary, not contradictory, and I believe that they will oscillate in influence during the coming decades, as they have during the past 100 years, each enhancing the other as we learn more about the dynamics of normal and pathological personality functioning (Bornstein, 2019b; Figure 8.8).

Beyond academia

Using a deft combination of laziness and ineptitude I was able to avoid become a physician, a role for which I would have been profoundly ill-suited. I had no such luck when it came to presidential politics. In 2013 I was asked to run for President of the Society for Personality Assessment (SPA). I agreed, and was elected. I began my six-year term on the SPA Board of Trustees (two years as President-Elect, two as President, and two as Past President) in September 2013 (Figure 8.9).

Leading a professional society is not an ideal situation for an obsessive person—there are too many things that one cannot control—but with the help of selfless, creative, incredibly hard-working colleagues on the SPA board, I muddled through. Having the opportunity to present plenary talks at SPA's annual conferences in 2015 and 2016 was a wonderful experience (it's not often that one gets to address a captive audience of several hundred people). One of my priorities while I was on the SPA board was to increase student involvement in the society, so I invited the President of the SPA Graduate Student Association to speak during the opening session of the conference each year. I had the honor of introducing two

Figure 8.8 Celebrating with friends at a Society for Personality Assessment meeting: Joni Mihura, Bill Kinder, John Kurtz, and Radhika Krishnamurthy.

colleagues whose work I admire greatly—John Cacioppo at the 2015 SPA conference, and Greg Meyer in 2017—before their Master Lectures. Both talks were superb.

Of all that I accomplished while on the SPA board I am most proud of the letter I wrote to the SPA membership following the Pulse Nightclub shooting in Orlando, Florida on June 12, 2016, a tragedy that resulted in the death of 49 people and the wounding of 53 others. I received many heartfelt responses from SPA members who were touched by my letter, and I was deeply touched by their responses as well—by their willingness to share their feelings and experiences with me. Without question, the personal connections that I developed with SPA colleagues and friends were the most meaningful aspect of my time on the SPA board. The sentiments I expressed in my 2016 letter still hold true, so I decided to include it here (Figure 8.10).

I am a teacher first

If you asked me to describe my professional self in one word, that word would not be *psychologist*. It would be *teacher*. Teaching is the core of my professional identity, and what I care about most. Then why, some have asked, do I spend so much time writing? The answer, in my way of

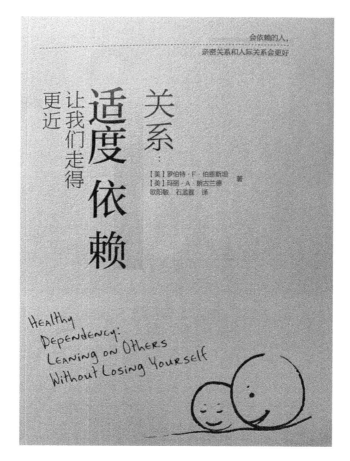

Figure 8.9 In 2003 Mary and I co-authored *Healthy Dependency*, which was published by Newmarket Press (Bornstein & Languirand, 2003). The
book was eventually translated into Korean, and into Simplified Man-
darin Chinese (which is the cover art pictured here).

thinking, is simple. Writing is teaching. When I stand near the front of a
classroom, I teach by talking with my students, describing new (or not-so-
new) ideas and findings, and answering their questions as best I can. When
I write a journal article or book chapter, I teach by explaining to my colleagues what I found in a study, what I believe about a particular issue, and
what I think is important in psychology today. It's the exact same process,
except that in one context teaching takes place verbally, and in the other
it takes place through writing.

I love what I do. I won the career lottery. Being a professor is the best
job in the world. If you don't believe me, try it yourself. But make sure you
have great students, supportive colleagues, and caring mentors. Without
them it won't be nearly as gratifying, and it won't be as much fun.

Society for Personality Assessment

June 12, 2016

Dear Colleagues,

I have been President of SPA for just over nine months. This is the third time I've written to SPA members in the wake of a senseless tragedy. The first two communications were private—one to our French colleagues following the attacks in Paris last November, the second to our colleagues in Belgium this past March.

Early Sunday morning a man brought two firearms to a nightclub in Orlando that is frequented by members of the LGBT community. He killed more than 50 people. He knew none of these people beforehand. He attacked them for what they symbolized in his mind, not who they were as individuals.

What do this weekend's events in Orlando have to do with personality assessment? Possibly nothing. But they provide us with an opportunity for reflection, and a chance to think about who we are and what we do. It's a good time to ask ourselves why we became psychologists, and how we became interested enough in personality assessment to make this a central part of our professional and personal lives.

The myriad challenges of academia and professional practice notwithstanding, it's important to remember that many years ago—at least for some of us it's that long—we chose to become mental health professionals because we wanted to improve the lives of others. It may sound a bit naïve, but it's true nonetheless: We do what we do to make the world a better place.

Psychologists—and personality psychologists in particular—bring a particular set of skills and insights to the study of human mental life. We specialize in understanding why people behave as they do in a complex and confusing world. Though we're better at describing human behavior than predicting it (prediction is a tough nut to crack), these events serve as reminders that we really can contribute to the greater good.

We should remind ourselves as well that we are role models, for our students, patients, and members of the public. Within SPA we disagree about many things, theoretical, empirical, and practical, and we do like to argue, which is one reason the annual meetings are so engaging. But we resolve our disagreements respectfully, and in the end we put aside differences and focus on our shared values, goals, and beliefs. Whatever we may say on the podium or in print, it's what we do, not what we say, that has the most lasting impact on those around us.

Sincerely,

Robert F. Bornstein, PhD
President, SPA Board of Trustees

6109 H Arlington Blvd., Falls Church, VA 22044, Tel: (703) 534-4772, Fax: (703) 534-6905
Email: manager@spaonline.org or assistant@spaonline.org Web site: www.personality.org

Figure 8.10 Letter to SPA members; June 12, 2016.

References

Berant, E., Newborn, M., & Orgler, S. (2008). Convergence of self-report scales and Rorschach indexes of psychological distress: The moderating role of self-disclosure. *Journal of Personality Assessment, 90*, 36–43.

Bornstein, R. F. (1989). Exposure and affect: Overview and meta-analysis of research, 1968–1987. *Psychological Bulletin, 106*, 265–289.

Bornstein, R. F. (1990). Critical importance of stimulus unawareness for the production of subliminal psychodynamic activation effects: A meta-analytic review. *Journal of Clinical Psychology, 46,* 201–210.

Bornstein, R. F. (1993). Costs and benefits of reviewer anonymity: A survey of journal editors and manuscript reviewers. *Journal of Social Behavior and Personality, 8,* 355–370.

Bornstein, R. F. (1996). Construct validity of the Rorschach Oral Dependency Scale: 1967–1995. *Psychological Assessment, 8,* 200–205.

Bornstein, R. F. (1997). Dependent personality disorder in the DSM-IV and beyond. *Clinical Psychology: Science and Practice, 4,* 175–187.

Bornstein, R. F. (1998). Reconceptualizing personality disorder diagnosis in DSM-V: The discriminant validity challenge. *Clinical Psychology: Science and Practice, 5,* 333–343.

Bornstein, R. F. (1999). Criterion validity of objective and projective dependency tests: A meta-analytic assessment of behavioral prediction. *Psychological Assessment, 11,* 48–57.

Bornstein, R. F. (2001). The impending death of psychoanalysis. *Psychoanalytic Psychology, 18,* 3–20.

Bornstein, R. F. (2002a). A process dissociation approach to objective-projective test score interrelationships. *Journal of Personality Assessment, 78,* 47–68.

Bornstein, R. F. (2002b). The impending death of psychoanalysis: From destructive obfuscation to constructive dialogue. *Psychoanalytic Psychology, 19,* 580–590.

Bornstein, R. F. (2005). Reconnecting psychoanalysis to mainstream psychology: Opportunities and challenges. *Psychoanalytic Psychology, 22,* 323–340.

Bornstein, R. F. (2007). Nomothetic psychoanalysis. *Psychoanalytic Psychology, 24,* 590–602.

Bornstein, R. F. (2009). Heisenberg, Kandinsky, and the heteromethod convergence problem: Lessons from within and beyond psychology. *Journal of Personality Assessment, 91,* 1–8.

Bornstein, R. F. (2011). Toward a process-focused model of test score validity: Improving psychological assessment in science and practice. *Psychological Assessment, 23,* 532–544.

Bornstein, R. F. (2017). Evidence based psychological assessment. *Journal of Personality Assessment, 99,* 435–445.

Bornstein, R. F. (2019a). Synergistic dependencies in partner and elder abuse. *American Psychologist, 74,* 713–724.

Bornstein, R. F. (2019b). The trait-type dialectic: Construct validity, clinical utility, and the diagnostic process. *Personality Disorders: Theory, Research, and Treatment, 10,* 199–209.

Bornstein, R. F., & Cecero, J. J. (2000). Deconstructing dependency in a five-factor world: A meta-analytic review. *Journal of Personality Assessment, 74,* 324–343.

Bornstein, R. F., & D'Agostino, P. R. (1992). Stimulus recognition and the mere exposure effect. *Journal of Personality and Social Psychology, 63,* 545–552.

Bornstein, R. F., & Languirand, M. A. (2003). *Healthy dependency: Leaning on others without losing yourself.* New York: Newmarket Press.

Bornstein, R. F., & Natoli, A. P. (2019). Clinical utility of categorical and dimensional perspectives on personality pathology: A meta-analytic review. *Personality Disorders: Theory, Research, and Treatment, 10,* 479–490.

Bornstein, R. F., & Pittman, T. S. (Eds.) (1992). *Perception without awareness: Cognitive, clinical, and social perspectives.* New York: Guilford Press.

Bornstein, R. F., Masling, J. M., & Poynton, F. G. (1987). Orality as a factor in interpersonal yielding. *Psychoanalytic Psychology, 4,* 161–170.

Denckla, C. A., Bornstein, R. F., Mancini, A. D., & Bonanno, G. A. (2015). Disambiguating dependency and attachment among conjugally bereaved adults. *Journal of Loss and Trauma, 20,* 468–483.

Erdelyi, M. H. (2004). Subliminal perception and its cognates: Theory, indeterminacy, and time. *Consciousness and Cognition, 13,* 73–91.

Freud, S. (1959). Character and anal erotism. In J. Strachey (Ed. & Trans.), *The standard edition of the complete psychological works of Sigmund Freud* (Vol. 9, pp. 167–176). London: Hogarth. (Original work published 1908.)

Hopwood, C. J., & Bornstein, R. F. (Eds.) (2014). *Multimethod clinical assessment.* New York: Guilford Press.

Kane, F. A., & Bornstein, R. F. (2018). Unhealthy dependency in perpetrators and victims of child maltreatment: A meta-analytic review. *Journal of Clinical Psychology, 74,* 867–882.

Krulwich, T. A., Mandel, K. M., Bornstein, R. F., & Guffanti, A. A. (1979). A non-alkalophilic mutant of *Bacillus alcalophilus* lacks the Na+/H+ antiporter. *Biochemical and Biophysical Research Communications, 91,* 58–62.

Loranger, A. W., Sartorius, N, Andreoli, A., Berger, P., Channabasavanna, S. M., Coid, B… & Ferguson, B. (1994). The international personality disorder examination. *Archives of General Psychiatry, 51,* 215–224.

McWilliams, N. (2006). Some thoughts about schizoid dynamics. *Psychoanalytic Review, 93,* 1–24.

Meehl, P. E. (1973). Why I do not attend case conferences. In P. E. Meehl (Ed.), *Psychodiagnosis: Selected papers* (pp. 225–302). Minneapolis: University of Minnesota Press.

Porcerelli, J. H., Bornstein, R. F., Markova, T., & Huprich, S. K. (2009). Physical health correlates of pathological and healthy dependency in urban women. *Journal of Nervous and Mental Disease, 197,* 761–765.

9 An Overdetermined Life in Psychoanalysis

Nancy McWilliams

The invitation to participate in this collection of autobiographical statements comes in my eighth decade, an apt time for reflection and self-analysis. I have written previously about my personal history in several psychoanalytic contexts, including in two published articles, one composed in response to Elliot Jurist's request for a paper in *Psychoanalytic Psychology* on the impact of my personal psychoanalysis on my life and career (McWilliams, 2013), the other written for the Danielson Institute about connections between spiritual/religious influences and my vocation (McWilliams, 2014). This invitation has instigated a more general overview of how I understand my own psychology and its relationship to my work, especially to my approach to personality assessment.

In the first section, I describe a childhood characterized by repeated loss and change. Because I attempt to reconstruct my feelings and coping strategies in each phase of my life, and because I have been introspective and self-reflective from a young age, the telling of my story is interwoven with my understanding of the effects of my history on my psychology and life decisions. Thus, even in the autobiography section, I have not been able to separate the facts from my interpretations of those facts. But I have tried to reserve for the second section the discussion of how my history has influenced my approach to the study of personality. There, I focus more narrowly on how my background has affected how I think about individual differences. Data and interpretation of the data are not entirely separable there, either, but for purposes of this project, this organization made the most sense to me.

Formative years

Early childhood

I was born in Abington, PA, 1945, the middle child of three girls, to well-educated white Protestant parents living in a Philadelphia suburb. When I was two, my father's job required a move to Springfield, MA, where he bought a house in the nearby bedroom community of Long-meadow, the site of my earliest memories. My parents were both New

DOI: 10.4324/9781003036302-9

Yorkers; according to my father, their move out of the city was a way of escaping my mother's overinvolved mother (who reportedly saw my father, the son of an Irish fire captain and best friend of Jimmy Hines of Tammany Hall, as not high-status enough for her daughter). Whatever the reason, they were part of the huge post-war middle-class move to the suburbs.

My father graduated from Columbia Law school in 1929. In the Great Depression, unable to find employment as an attorney, he took a job in an insurance company. He stayed in that field, where his work involved assessing the insurability of major corporate projects. Valued by his employers for his capacity to judge risk by discriminating people of integrity from con artists, he eventually rose to the vice presidency of a major insurance corporation. My mother was a graduate of Columbia Teachers College who worked with deaf children, teaching them to speak. She gave up her hope to combine a career with parenthood when my older sister proved to be a sickly infant. I knew her only in her domestic role, but I had a sense of her deep interest in psychology; she had once written a book of advice for adolescents. My parents were happy together, and my earliest memories are almost all positive.

I was reportedly an easy baby with a sunny disposition. I have a letter from my mother to her mother stating that on one dreary day, "even Nancy" was out of sorts. I was securely attached. A neuropsychoanalyst friend has speculated that congenitally, I may have high levels of oxytocin. I seem also to have been temperamentally sensitive; one of my favorite fairy tales was "The Princess and the Pea." I was also a very curious child, interested in everything; I would open the *World Book Encyclopedia* to a random page and read. At the same time, like most second-born children, I had a rebellious bent. I took physical risks, loved climbing trees, and was often describe affectionately as a tomboy. I had a mischievous streak and liked to subvert authority; one friend from kindergarten later told me her mother called me a "holy terror."

I was quite a confident girl. When I was seven, the family was spending August on the Connecticut shore. Walking around the area, I noticed that the local activity center was hosting some competitions, one of which was a boat-rowing contest. I watched how rowing was done, thought it looked pretty easy, and entered the contest, which had only two competitors in my age range. Not surprisingly, I came in second. I walked home sporting a red ribbon. When my mother asked about it, I announced that I had won second prize in a row-boat contest. "But Nancy, you've never rowed a boat," she said. "I have now," I replied.

My father was deeply loving, loyal, and a paragon of integrity. Having lost his beloved mother young, he appreciated female care-giving and over the course of his life made good marriages to three quite different women. He came from a family that included women with careers (his aunt and great-aunt had been teachers) and was unusually egalitarian for the times. His sister, who was in the first graduating class at Columbia Law School that included women (three of them), became an attorney and later a judge. My father did housework, greatly valued education irrespective of gender, and brought his daughters up to feel entitled to respect. (I was horrified when I learned in adulthood that in some of my friends' families, education for women was not a priority.) My father prided himself on being politically an Independent, often took contrarian positions, and gave his daughters a clear directive to think for ourselves.

My sisters have both been highly successful. My older sister got a PhD in Literature from the English department at Columbia University and was the first woman hired to teach on the faculty of Columbia College (only because "gender" had been a last-minute addition to the 1964 Civil Rights law, and the federal government could now withhold money from noncompliant universities). She eventually became Dean at a midwestern college serving low-income and minority communities. My younger sister received an MBA from Harvard Business School and started her own head-hunting company. She has taught at business schools, including Harvard.

According to a recent issue of the *APA Monitor* (October 2019, p. 84), only 20% of Americans surveyed in 1946 said that women are as competent as men, and only 25% considered women equally intelligent. This was the air we all breathed in the 1950s, but fortunately not in my family. I recall a teacher in third grade who asked us to draw what we wanted to be when we grew up. I told her I wasn't sure yet and asked what I should draw under the circumstances. She explained that girls could be mothers or nurses or teachers (note the "or"). I drew a teacher.

Our father was loving but had an unpredictable temper. He would go into sudden rages – never directed at his children but nonetheless frightening. In some states of mind, he could see no shades of grey; everything involved a right way versus a wrong way. He had a tendency to banish people permanently when they disappointed him. I realized in analysis how terrified I had been growing up that he would throw me out of his life as he had exiled his sister and some former friends. I spent my childhood trying to understand and cope with his erratic outbursts. My interest in diagnosis and individual differences is deeply rooted in oedipal dynamics; I wanted to understand Daddy, to please him, and also to heal him.

As a young child I developed an unconscious fantasy, later to emerge in my analysis, that my father would have liked me better if I had been a boy. It is not unreasonable that a man who already had a daughter would have wanted a son, but I don't think I was right. The idea that males were preferable to females came to me from all the cultural messages of the time affirming the privileged status of men, and also from my mother, for whom men were clearly more interesting than women. She was full of ideas about how to understand male behavior and support male egos. I remember explicitly wanting to be a boy until about age eight, when I learned that men (and not women) were drafted to fight wars. I decided I preferred to be a girl.

I did not find a way to make sense of my father until I was in my twenties, when I read Kurt Goldstein's writing (e.g., 1952) about the "catastrophic reactions" of children with brain injuries, which described his rages to a tee. Then I put together the fact that he had had the "sleeping sickness" (encephalitis lethargica) as a boy (this was known but not talked about much in the family). Despite a remarkable recovery and the survival of his prodigious intelligence (he was a bridge champion who paid for college with his winnings at poker and backgammon; he allegedly learned physics at Columbia without cracking a book), he had clearly sustained some neurological damage.

I recalled my father's complaint about a doctor who had asked him, because his eyes did not dilate properly – I think he was excluded from military service on those grounds – whether he had ever had syphilis. He had emphatically corrected the doctor, explaining that he had had encephalitis lethargica as a boy. (He told this story with indignation, as if the physician had been accusing him of moral turpitude. But the neurological sign the doctor had picked up, "Argyll Robertson pupil," is a known marker of brain damage and often a result of syphilis.) Like the other victims of the sleeping sickness epidemic, he eventually went back into a comatose state, in which he died at age 76. Seven years ago, I consulted with Oliver Sacks, who told me he had known only a few survivors of the encephalitis lethargica epidemic who had lived into their seventies before the secondary coma overtook them, and although quirky, they all seemed to be people of unusually strong character. That description would fit my father.

My mother was warm, easy-going, fun-loving, and compassionate. She nourished my sense of agency and self-esteem; I have not a single memory of being shamed by her. She was talented as well, an actress and singer with a trained coloratura voice (which she kept up via singing in the church choir). She was deeply interested in others, especially men; she idealized her father and devalued her mother. She had lost her younger sister when she was ten, and I think she reacted to that death with a determination to enjoy the moment, treat others well, and appreciate people as they are rather than complain of their limitations. I made similar vows to myself when she died in her forties. They involved a reaction-formation against my own aggression, but they were also about my trying to carry on what I saw as my mother's aborted mission to make the world a kinder place.

I do not know how much exposure my mother had to psychoanalytic ideas at Teachers College in the 1930s (though I have been told that the atmosphere was quite psychoanalytic there), but she frequently offered explanations of others' behavior that involved what I now see as psychodynamic insight. I remember many instances, often when someone had confused me or hurt my feelings, when she would speculate on that person's psychology as a way of helping me take his or her behavior less personally. My older sister remembers being exasperated by our mother's tendency to minister to the wounded birds among her boyfriends who, even after she had broken up with them, would turn up in our kitchen for long talks with Mother.

Loss

My mother died when I was nine, after a two-year struggle with cancer. My grandmother later told me that her goal for me in her dying months was to support and increase my capacity to do things on my own. I don't remember specific examples of that effort, but I do remember feeling that I was going to survive her death and expecting to be able to find my way in life without her. (This involved some not-so-adaptive counterdependency that I had to work through later in analysis.) I have extensive, detailed memories of my mother and feel the enduring influence of her love for me. As an adolescent, I could rarely sympathize with my friends' complaints about their mothers; I felt they were lucky to *have* mothers.

Two consequences of my childhood bereavement of which I am conscious are my valuing of female/maternal virtues and my appreciating the wisdom of those who have come before rather than being automatically attracted to the "newest thing." I idealized my mother as she was dying and after her death, identified strongly with her loving qualities, and set a premium on values such as caring for others and empathizing with alternative viewpoints. I identified also with my father's commitments to honesty and devotion, which helped me survive the loss. A few months before her death, I remember his telling me that she was going to die and encouraging my tears (a deviation from the family's usual Irish and Scots-Irish stoicism).

Like others bereaved in childhood, I learned an indelible lesson about life's capriciousness. The take-home message was that you had better appreciate what you have, and do what you want to do when you can do it, because who knows how much time you or anyone you love has. This awareness underlies all of my involvements, including a tendency to become overextended.

Summer camp

My mother died in July 1955. I was at a Girl Scout camp in the eastern Berkshire mountains. The administrators there, Meg Fardy and Dot Peavey, two women who fell in love with each other that summer and began a life-long partnership, took an interest in me and made it possible for me to stay on for the whole season, much to my father's gratitude. I returned every summer for many years, finding the place a critical source of continuity when discontinuities afflicted other parts of my life.

Over the years, these women influenced me greatly, eventually training me to be a counselor and then a camp director. They were very psychologically minded, especially Meg, who (I later found out) was an admirer of Theodor Reik.

I loved camp and the proto-feminist sensibility it embodied. There you were rewarded for being a good leader and also a good follower. It conveyed an ongoing assumption that girls could do anything that boys could, and if one was not strong enough to do a particular thing, a group of girls could get it done just fine. Qualities like initiative, resourcefulness, stoicism, and consideration for others were held in high regard. Before the women's movement a decade later, this was the only experience I had had of such an environment.

There was scant diversity in the white-bread, mostly Republican suburbs I inhabited during the school year, but at camp I met and grew close to girls from different racial, ethnic, religious, and socioeconomic backgrounds. Lesbian attachments were normalized, though not labeled as such and not acted out to my knowledge (there is not much privacy when four or five people share a tent, and in mid-century America, some desires went unformulated, especially by adolescent girls). Even the heterosexual campers there had passionate same-sex attachments, often having a recognized "sidekick." On being hired as a counselor, one took a "camp name" (one of the ways Girl Scout camps minimize the possibilities for ethnic prejudice in campers). Mine was "Sunny." There are still a few people who call me that.

At camp, we sang a lot, traditional Girl Scout songs but also folk songs, especially those written or popularized by Pete Seeger. The camp director corresponded with him about music; he occasionally gave concerts in the area to which the older campers went, and once he came to our camp to lead songs. This connection was quite subversive at the time – he was still blacklisted for communist sympathies – but we did not know it then; his music was a perfect vehicle for our idealism. I loved to sing and lead songs, was admired for my harmonies, and taught myself rudimentary guitar.

Latency and early adolescence

After my mother's death, my father was a wreck. He hired a housekeeper and continued to work, but he was undone by watching his children go through a maternal loss like the one he had endured shortly after his mother had nursed him devotedly through the encephalitic coma. He became more explosive and scarier. I was troubled by his yelling at my five-year-old sister that she had to go to school despite the stomach aches she had begun to suffer; I recall thinking about writing for advice to Dr. Paul Popenoe, the *Ladies Home Journal* expert on family matters (not a doctor, actually, and an enthusiastic eugenicist, I later learned).

During this difficult time, my father leaned on my older sister, age 16, who consequently missed some aspects of a normal adolescence by virtue of her being the dutiful, responsible helpmate.

I kept a low profile, played the piano a lot, read avidly, and spent hours at the houses of my friends. I developed a willful personal narrative that I was just fine without a mother. When salesmen would come to the door asking for her, I would reply, "My mother is *deceased*. What can I do for you?" I enjoyed making them uncomfortable. I also developed some grandiose aspirations in this period that included, at different times, curing cancer and becoming the first female President of the United States.

A painful aftereffect of this omnipotent self-representation is that although I have learned to lean on people I trust and to ask for what I need from them, I tend to bristle if others assume I need help when I have not asked. My poor husband Michael has had to learn very diplomatic ways of approaching me when he wants to offer care, as my reaction to unrequested solicitude tends to be defensive. I continue to work on this. Being patronized by men is especially intolerable to me, but my allergy to being infantilized extends to everyone.

I felt pretty lost in the months after my mother's death, but I was psychologically rescued by the loving African American woman my father had hired to care for us. Anna told me I would be okay, saying she had lost her mother at my age and knew how I felt. I adored her and took heart from what she said. Unfortunately, she became pregnant and exhausted, and after about four months, my father let her go. Ignorant of her condition, I saw this as another abrupt, inexplicable rejection of a person to whom he had previously been warm and generous. I still have an affectionate letter from Anna that she wrote to me after she was fired.

A few months after my mother's death, mutual friends introduced my father to a divorcée with a son two years younger than I was. She and he were married several months later and legally cross-adopted their youngest three children. She was a lovely person but quite different from my birth mother: an artist, reserved and conservative, with some underlying sadness that imbued her earnest effort to become a good parent to my younger sister and me. My older sister disliked her, perhaps feeling kicked out of her role as surrogate wife/mother, and kept her distance. My younger sister and I whole-heartedly welcomed her. Wanting to avoid the "wicked" connotations of "stepmother," I referred to her as my "second mother" when differentiating her from my biological parent.

One change after another followed my first mother's death: We moved to a bigger house that would accommodate a housekeeper, requiring a change of schools; then to a different school because I had been redistricted; then back to my first school when we moved into my second mother's house. I had good teachers, whose sensitive mothering of me I can see clearly in retrospect. I made friends in all these places. Then Dad's company was bought out again, requiring us to move to the New

York area. My father, who always based the choice of where to buy a house on the reputation of the local public educational system, was told that New Canaan, CT, had the best schools. We moved there when I was in sixth grade.

In New Canaan I had my first experience of feeling like a devalued outsider. Corporate mobility made newcomers plentiful there. At age 11 I was chubby and wore glasses, and my parents were not friends with the parents of the popular kids ("We aren't cocktail party types," my mother explained). It didn't help my social ambitions that I looked to teachers to be motherly figures at a time when my peers were starting to reject maternal attachments. I turned my upset at being socially marginal into righteous indignation about "conformity," "apathy," and other sins of the 1950s. I began referring to the popular girls as "snobs."

By eighth grade I had established myself well enough to feel more comfortable in the school community. My best friend there was a girl whose mother was Jewish. She raised my awareness of the subtle antisemitism in New Canaan; like me, she was interested in social justice generally. I remember writing an article for the school newspaper critiquing the "happy conformists" who would rather shiver in the cold in fashionable outfits than stay warm in less chic clothing. Just as I was becoming acclimated, my father's company went belly up. The best job he could find was in Reading, PA. We moved in the summer after my eighth-grade year.

High school

I was miserable at the prospect of another move. But I determined that this time I would not be the rejected new girl. I made a list – I wish I still had it – of things to remember in the new school (20 rules that included "Smile at everyone!" and "Don't latch on to anyone before you know their reputation"). I started at Wyomissing High School in ninth grade. Unlike New Canaan, Wyomissing was a very stable community; the senior yearbook featured pictures of the class from kindergarten on. New girls were interesting. I had gotten contact lenses and lost weight. Although I did not really feel it yet, I had gotten pretty. I was unprepared, albeit thrilled, to be welcomed to girls' houses after school and wooed by the most attractive boys in our class of 55 students.

My family had calmed and stabilized during my high school years, and my untroubled time in Wyomissing was critical for my recovery of a genuine (not compensatory) sense of confidence. I was much more interested in social relations than academics and did A-/B+ work. Our class was too small for cliques, and though many classmates were unhappy in such a limited environment, it was perfect for me. I am still in touch with high school friends and go regularly to reunions. (My second analyst, a woman I saw after I had had my second child and after my first analyst had died, once teased me about my tendency to maintain relationships, "Is there anyone you *haven't* kept up a connection with?"). Starting in ninth grade I fell in love, had a best friend, made the cheerleading squad, and eventually became president of the student council.

I had two highly formative teachers who taught me grammar, sentence structure, and style. They initiated a lifelong romance with words and a love of good writing. I cannot overstate their influence on my professional life: The fact that I write well has reaped incalculable rewards. My Latin teacher, Florence Schrack, another mother figure of whom I was deeply fond, had previously been John Updike's English Composition teacher. My charismatic English teacher, Russell Milford, had us write a theme in class every Friday. He would put a topic on the board and give us 45 minutes to write an essay on it. On Mondays, he would read a few of the best ones, detailing their merits. In our senior year, he required an Intensive Theme, my first real term paper. Still the social critic, I did mine on Sinclair Lewis and actually worked to do it well.

I loved my life in Wyomissing but with some reservations. It was even more of a monoculture than my previous communities. In this Pennsylvania Dutch-influenced Lutheran town, I was in a Presbyterian minority. There was only one Jewish student in our class, my friend Stuart, who was often the target of antisemitic microaggressions. In my sophomore year, the National Council of Christians and Jews started a program for teens in the Reading area and asked each high school to send one Christian and one Jew to an organizational meeting. Our principal called Stuart in and told him to "pick a Christian and go." Stuart picked me. We found ourselves in a diverse and passionate group of students inspired by the new Civil Rights movement. I quickly made friends there who were into politics, folk music, jazz, poetry, and other sexy involvements. I became close to Velvet Miller from Reading High School, my first intimate black friend, to whom I am still deeply attached.

In that same year, my Civics teacher assigned a paper on a social problem of our choice. I chose antisemitism. When I asked the high school librarian for help, she suggested the books of Carey McWilliams. I remember liking the name. This remarkable journalist and left-wing activist eventually became my father-in-law, but I am getting ahead of myself. In high school, I read his *Brothers under the Skin* and used its arguments in many debates about "the Negro problem." I frequently opined about social issues and remember competing in an oratorical contest via a speech I wrote entitled "Look for the Other Side," in which I urged listeners to think about viewpoints different from the ones that might seem obvious to them.

College

In mid-high school, I began thinking about college. My older sister, who had gone to Wellesley and hated its 1950s single-sex atmosphere and orientation toward meeting Mr. Right, had transferred to Barnard (I am the only family member who did not go to some branch of Columbia). She suggested Oberlin, the first college to have admitted women on an equal basis with men and black people on an equal basis with whites. She thought Oberlin would take women's intellects seriously. My mother worried that it was "a little pink," but she and my father believed I was old enough to choose where I wanted to go, and they knew the college had a good reputation for both academics and music. I am aware now of how much privilege I had growing up in affluent white communities in that era; it never occurred to me that I would not go to a high-quality Liberal Arts college of my choice, for which my parents would readily pay.

At Oberlin, I initially felt marginal again. There were so many New Yorkers with college-prep courses under their belts and enviable cultural sophistication. They would drop names of important intellectual influences (writers, playwrights, artists), and I had no names to drop. In the first week, my roommate and I passed a sign saying that Carey McWilliams would be in a freshman orientation show. This was my chance. "Oh," I said, affecting a casual attitude, "I know his work. I've read his books." "That's his son," she responded flatly, adding that the son was a professor in the Government department, had been a radical at Berkeley, and was dating a black student. Just the kind of person I had gone to Oberlin to be around.

I next saw that name on a poster for a chapel talk. Per my stereotypes, Berkeley radicals eschewed religion and certainly did not give sermons. I had to get a look at this guy. Carey gave a spellbinding talk: brilliant, funny, passionate. I decided to take a class from him, following my mother's advice to study with professors who had the best reputations as teachers, irrespective of their field. Although I initially intended to major in Classics (identifying with Mrs. Schrack), after taking Carey's fascinating introductory class in American Government, I decided to take all his courses. Eventually I majored in Government (political science) and listed him as my faculty advisor. For a long time, I was too intimidated by him to approach him, but in May of my sophomore year, I needed my advisor's consultation on a topic for my eventual honors thesis in political theory. Carey said I seemed to be naturally psychologically minded and suggested that I do a paper on the political theory of Sigmund Freud. He handed me a copy of *Civilization and Its Discontents*, with which I became mesmerized. Not having been raised in a psychoanalytically literate subculture, I knew very little about Freudian ideas, except that they involved sex (a topic in which I was quite interested). Thus began my psychoanalytic education.

The summer after my freshman year, while I was counseling at camp, my father phoned to say that my second mother had been diagnosed with cancer, the same kind that had killed my first mother. (Years later, I learned he had been wrong: My first mother died of ovarian cancer and my second mother of colon cancer, but they had similar invasions of the bowel and both had to undergo colostomies and radiation). It was pretty clear that my family was headed once more into months of suffering with hospitals, treatments, stress, and uncertainty. The clear message to me was that the best thing I could do for my family was to stay in college and do well, but I felt guilty not helping out at home, and I feared the worst.

After surgery, my mother improved for several months. I began to hope. But in the spring of my sophomore year, the cancer had become metastatic. I had planned a summer as an exchange student in Greece and was given strict instructions by both parents to take that opportunity and enjoy it as much as possible. I did so. It was a wonderful summer that gave me a permanent affection for the country, its beauty, its food, its music, and its language. I particularly warmed to being cared for by a loving Greek mother. My postponed grief engulfed me on the plane ride home, however, as I anticipated the taxi trip from the airport to Sloane Kettering Memorial Hospital, where my mother was now gravely ill.

In the fall term of my junior year, I was distracted and easily fatigued, a condition I did not then identify as depression. Carey, who had learned from one of my friends that I was facing the impending death of my second mother, reached out to me in the role of advisor. When she was put on the critical list, Dad urged me to stay in school and denied my request for air fare to visit. Carey bought me a ticket to New York and drove me to the airport so that I could see her one more time. I was deeply touched. My father was surprised when I turned up at the hospital but reacted warmly, appreciating my professor's generosity, which he immediately repaid. Carey and I started to see each other socially. Our first date turned out to be on the day my mother died.

With a contemporary perspective on the ethics of power, I can see the exploitive aspect of Carey's pursuing me when I was in such a vulnerable place. But at the time, I felt like a grownup making an informed choice. Liaisons between professors and students were often romanticized in those years, and I enjoyed the attention that came my way for being in an improbable relationship. At Oberlin, angst was a prerequisite for being seen as "deep," and my temperament is anything but melancholic. I had long felt dismissed as "wholesome," and I delighted in imagining that I was now seen as a sort of scarlet woman.

Carey's values inspired me, and I fed on his brilliance. He seemed utterly unthreatened by my own intelligence and ambition – a rarity then. A feminist before the resurgence of feminism, he thought men should be as involved with their children as women were, and was outraged that the wife of his department chair was not permitted to teach at Oberlin despite being a prominent scholar (there was a "nepotism" rule then that in practice affected only wives). It was a politically exciting time: Oberlin was a hub for the social movements of day. Carey, who had co-founded the student political party at Berkeley from which the Free Speech Movement arose, seemed to know everybody in the New Left, and activists often turned up in our living room. I remember, for example, Rennie Davis worrying there about what Mayor Daley might do in the face of the demonstrations planned for the Democratic National Convention in Chicago.

At a deeper level, I was of course looking for a parent, in the context of the loss of my mother and the knowledge that my father would be out of commission for a time as well, as he had been after his previous bereavement. I married Carey at Oberlin in September of my senior year. With considerable professional help, we eventually made our relationship into a solid partnership and brought up two daughters of whom I am infinitely proud. He died in 2005, still thriving in his work teaching at both Rutgers and Haverford. For purposes of this article, the most critical aspect of Carey's influence on me is that he recognized my interest in individual differences and started me on the path to being a psychoanalyst by introducing me to Freud (Figure 9.1).

Early adulthood

My father was apprehensive about my marrying my professor but told me he trusted my judgment. He attended our wedding with the woman who would become his third wife and a loving stepmother to my devastated younger sister. The family had to make yet another move because of my father's job, this time to a suburb of Chicago, a wrenching loss for her.

Figure 9.1 The author with her daughters.

Worse, on the basis of his teenage son's acting out resentment about the quick replacement of his mother, my father disowned my brother – one of his most tragic decrees. The fact that he could do this to a child he had loved and worked hard to parent sensitively suggests that my persistent fears of being thrown out of the family were not entirely a figment of my infantile imagination.

During my senior year at Oberlin, I decided I wanted to be a psychotherapist. I knew my temperament was suited to working intimately with people. I did not want to stay in political science, where I thought I would always be seen as Mrs. Wilson Carey McWilliams and would probably run into nepotism rules prohibiting married people from working in the same department. I had taken no psychology courses, but I was reading Freud and popular psychoanalytic writers of the time (Erik Erikson, Norman O. Brown, Karen Horney, Herbert Marcuse, Erich Fromm). I was particularly taken with the writings of Theodor Reik, the first scholar I had encountered who talked about female psychology not as a deviation from a male norm but as a distinct and valuable sensibility in its own right. Reading him now, I find his tone paternalistic, but at the time, his appreciation of the strengths in femininity was a revelation.

Graduate school and psychoanalytic training

A few months after we married, Carey accepted a job offer from Brooklyn College. In late August of 1967, we moved to Brooklyn. To accumulate enough credits in psychology to apply to a clinical program, I took non-matriculated courses at the college. When I told one of my teachers of my interest in Freud and my resonance to Theodor Reik's writing, she noted that Reik was still alive and in Manhattan. I decided to write to him, asking for a meeting. He responded immediately. I have told this story before (McWilliams, 2004, 2013); the short version is that Reik talked me into going into psychoanalysis. The clinic he had founded referred me to a mensch of an analyst, a social worker who ran a settlement house on the Lower East Side.

I went into treatment thinking I was doing so for sheerly professional reasons, but then it improved my personal life in countless ways (McWilliams, 2013). I was able to grieve my losses, work through my unconscious fear of men, reduce my counterdependency, improve my marriage, and embrace my previously dissociated wish to have children. I continued with my analyst when we moved to New Jersey. Carey had been invited to teach at Livingston College of Rutgers University, a new, experimental school oriented toward first-generation and minority students. Having been rejected by clinical programs at NYU and CCNY, I was then studying Personality at the City University of New York, a big commuter campus at which I was not particularly happy. I transferred to the Personality and Social doctoral program at Rutgers.

There I studied with Silvan Tomkins, the brilliant theorist of affect, and Dan Ogilvie, a student of Henry Murray's "personology" who was then exploring object relations theory. George Atwood joined the faculty in my second year there and Robert Stolorow in my third. Although I enjoyed witnessing the emerging collaboration between George and Bob, and became (and still am) close to George, I felt that they treated me with a subtle dismissiveness. I attributed this to my being female (George later told me I was wrong, noting that he and Bob had excluded many people from their conversations, including Sylvan, who was equally hurt by their intellectual bromance). My go-to explanation may not have been accurate, but it was also not entirely off-base. Unexamined sexism was everywhere when I was a graduate student, and I felt it keenly. Men would cluelessly make comments like, "You're pretty smart for a woman" or "You're a threat to my male ego, you know." There were no female professors in the Personality program, and everywhere, the voice of authority was inexorably male. It is part of my enduring psychology to be hyperaware of signs of the devaluation of women and to be competitive for a respected place at the grown-ups' table.

It interests me in retrospect that as a graduate student I was implicitly expecting to be accepted by George and Bob as an equal, enough so to be hurt when that did not happen. My sense of entitlement to such collegiality reflected my general self-confidence, the early 1970s habit of ignoring distinctions of authority, and the fact that they were about my age. But it was also a symptom of my own internalized sexism in the form of my feeling that, by virtue of my marriage to a full professor, I could claim Carey's status. I had been brought up in environments where a woman's social position was determined by the man to whom she was attached. As a faculty wife, I was accustomed to being in academic circles, and I had unreasonable, defensive expectations of being accepted as "one of the guys" when I hadn't yet finished my doctorate.

In New Jersey, it was possible then to be licensed as a practitioner on the basis of a degree in a field *related* clinical psychology. I had rejected the opportunity to be in the clinical program at Rutgers because most of its faculty were hostile to psychoanalysis. (This was before the existence of the multi-orientational PsyD program for which I now teach.) I was not trained in assessment tools as I would have been had I studied clinical psychology, but George gave me the Rorschach, and in the context of my having learned a lot in analysis about my deeper dynamics, I was astonished by how powerful that instrument was. Then we gave each other the Thematic Apperception Test, which similarly impressed me. I greatly admired George's capacity to capture the organizing narrative of an individual, the story that Sylvan would have called the person's "nuclear scene," by inferring an overall theme or personal myth from someone's life story and self-presentation. It comported with Reik's intuitive approach to comprehending unconscious uniqueness. I thought I had a gift for that kind of inference, for what would later be framed as a right-brained way of knowing (Schore, 2019).

When I completed my master's degree (my thesis was an empirical study of internalized sexism in women), I was eligible to apply for analytic training at the National Psychological Association for Psychoanalysis, the institute Theodor Reik had founded, with which my analyst was associated. NPAP was a product of Reik's having been excluded from the institutes of the American Psychoanalytic Association, which would admit only physicians (hence the adjective "Psychological" in NPAP's moniker). I studied to be an analyst there at the same time as I pursued work on my doctorate (on characterological altruism) and clinical training at the local mental health center. NPAP was much more egalitarian and theoretically diverse than other institutes of that era. I know this only with hindsight; at the time, I took the open-minded atmosphere of my training for granted.

The most important influence on me at NPAP was the supervision, individually and in a group setting, of Arthur Robbins, a kind of artist of the soul, a psychoanalyst/sculptor who had an almost clairvoyant perceptiveness and welcomed accounts of countertransference. I remember that after a few supervision sessions, Art observed that while I appeared highly conventional, he had come to understand that I was deeply unconventional. I felt seen. And I wanted to get what he had: a highly disciplined psychoanalytic intuition. At the time, I thought of what I was learning as "classical analysis." Freud's protégé Reik had trained Jules Nydes, who trained Art, and so I saw myself as in a direct Freudian line. I did not yet know that there was another version of "classical" that referred to the rigid ego-psychological techniques that the medical institutes then idealized.

During that same period of time, both my analytic treatment and the feminist movement were profoundly impactful. They assaulted my omnipotence, increased my humility, reduced my knee-jerk competition with other women, called into question things I had taken for granted, expanded my capacity to mentalize others, and raised my consciousness in general. Just as Girl Scout camp had counteracted some of my sexist internalizations, second-wave feminism connected me with my deep identification with maternal power and wisdom. Without that influence, I would have adopted more uncritically my idealized mother's hysterical defenses and deferred to prevailing masculine models of scholarship.

Reinforcing my experience in analysis, the movement encouraged me to speak in my own voice (Gilligan, 1982) rather than in the tone of male-dominated subcultures, to value the subjective and intuitive, to understand that just as the personal is the political, the personal is intricately interwoven into intellectual discourse: Subjectivity is better made explicit than denied. Feminism reinforced my natural skepticism toward both conventional cultural assumptions and arrogant claims to unprecedented knowledge. It supported my tendency to use my creativity in the service of synthesis and pedagogy rather than for purposes of proposing some new paradigm.

In line with feminist sensibilities, I have never been interested in developing "my own" theory of personality. Instead, I have tried to pass on the most valuable elements of the clinical tradition that taught me so many useful ways of understanding myself and others. In 1998 I participated in a conference in Crete with Eleanor Maccoby, the eminent researcher on sex differences. She asked me about my book on diagnosis, which had been recently published, and in response to my description, she commented on empirical evidence that female authors are characteristically integrative. The influence of feminism clearly liberated a deep identification with my mothers and their maternal forms of creativity.

Interpretation and implications

Personality themes

It is interesting to me, as I write this, to find the familiar themes of my psychology emerging in every developmental era. I have always known that in spite of my famously sunny temperament, my childhood bereavements and dislocations left me with a depressive sensibility, a sense of the inevitability of loss, an identification with suffering, and an orientation toward reducing it in others. I sometimes describe myself as a temperamental optimist and an intellectual pessimist. But I did not have a superordinate concept for many of the other qualities evident in this account until the early 1990s, when I read Otto Kernberg's (1984, p. 80) description of high-functioning hysterical personality, in which he foregrounds warmth, gender-related conflicts, and competitive strivings.

That I recognized myself in Kernberg's depiction, and that I felt understood rather than pathologized, reflect my good luck that neither my parents nor my analyst ever commented on my psychology in a disparaging or patronizing tone. Conventional clinical labels for personality syndromes, including hysterical dynamics (despite the condescension suffusing many depictions of them) consequently seem to me simply descriptive and not necessarily negative. I do not confuse personality disorders with personality *per se*; I view the former as being characterized by excessive, inflexible, maladaptive, or primitive expressions of the dynamics that define any relevant personality configuration. With the possible exception of psychopathy, I see any personality style in itself as no more pathological than hair color.

In my own story, as is typical for people with hysterical psychologies, oedipal overtones are everywhere. They make sense of my attraction to Freudian ideas – which spoke to me the first time I encountered them (Freud's theory may be a bad fit for many people, but it was a good fit for me). The defenses against gender-based feelings of inadequacy, along with desire and fear toward men, are everywhere here. They include inclinations toward exhibitionism (as in my courtship – and my comfort in writing this autobiography, for that matter), competition with both women and men (for different reasons), and efforts to be included in various boys' clubs and to prove myself as smart and capable as any male. Somehow, the underlying self-states of insufficiency and envy coexist with a genuine sense of good-enough-ness and competence that was fostered by both my parents and by the advantages of my privileged upbringing.

I would not want my comment about exhibitionism to be understood reductively; my tendency toward self-disclosure in professional writing is consciously intended to give individual experience the dignity it deserves. I especially want to rescue individuality from the popular habit of equating psychodynamics with psychopathology. To do so, I believe one has to speak honestly and without apology about one's own psychology. There is a moralistic tendency, evident throughout my account of my history, that underlies this position, an ongoing effort to be honest and upright, perhaps excessively and defensively so in some instances.

As a child I was rewarded for honesty and encouraged to speak the truth. In my adolescence, I was sometimes asked why I was so "sincere" (the word of the day – it would be "authentic" now); evidently my directness made some of my peers uncomfortable. I remember my mother telling me when I was quite young, as she tried to teach me about tact, that I could get away with saying just about anything if I figured out the right way to say it. That lesson has had innumerable payoffs in my professional life, in which I frequently find myself in the role of discerning an elephant in the room that others are relieved to have named.

The effort to be true has often been adaptive and is another piece of my attraction to psychoanalysis, which I see as all about trying to be conscious of difficult and painful truths. Theodor Reik's idea that moral courage is a distinctive virtue of a psychoanalyst has always appealed to me. I relate my own effort to embody such courage mainly to my father's personal rectitude. He once told me he had wanted to be a Protestant minister but had concluded that the life of a minister's wife was too difficult. I cannot remember his ever lying. When my first mother was critically ill in the hospital, however, he did tell me that if a staff member there asked me how old I was, I should say I was 12, just in case there was an age limit for visitors. I remember this vividly because it is the only time I can recall when he countenanced dishonesty.

Because where there is righteousness, there is usually unconscious culpability, I assume that my moralistic qualities are also symptomatic of oedipal guilt, some of which emerged in my psychoanalysis. Unconsciously fearing that my hostility had somehow killed off my mother, I tried after her death to be the best little girl I could possibly be. I wanted to keep my second mother safe. When I was a teenager, some of my classmates experienced me as insufferably self-righteous (they told me so years later). My adolescent rebelliousness took only nondomestic, political forms in those years; I was afraid of my father's retribution if I strayed from the paths of righteousness. I am grateful to my analyst for helping me to mellow in the direction of acceptance, forgiveness, and tolerance of myself and others.

Another recurring theme is marginality. Although I am comfortable in groups and have often assumed leadership positions, I have typically stayed a bit on the outside looking in. I identify with outsiders. My training in both clinical psychology and psychoanalysis were somewhat outside the mainstream. This tendency probably results from my having moved so much growing up and also from my deep identification with an African American caregiver and two lesbian mother-substitutes. As I age, I appreciate my more schizoid side. I have realized that I like being on the margins, or, more accurately, I like the freedom to go in and out of a sense of belonging. In opposition to my father's dogmatism, but also in identification with his contrarianism, I like to see things from alternative perspectives. I view personality and clinical engagement through both one-person and two-person lenses. I expect and enjoy the coexistence of apparently contradictory or paradoxical truths, a broadmindedness that somehow coexists with an opinionated streak. My niece notes that all the Rileys are know-it-alls and suggests that our family motto should be "Often wrong, never in doubt."

Related to marginality is my deep-rooted tendency to question authority – perhaps rooted in my observing my father's episodic craziness as well as on my being a second child. In a small way, I have been trying to speak truth to power throughout my professional career, whether that power resides in current academic prejudices, professional organizations, insurance companies, pharmaceutical corporations, or governmental bodies. In line with my respect for contradiction and paradox, I note that this cynicism toward authoritative knowledge coexists with a deep cherishing of emotional wisdom and commonsensical reflection, the legacy of my mother.

Relevance to personality assessment

My ambivalence about authority extends to objective measurement and technical expertise in the area of personality assessment. I worry that generalizing from statistical averages has the downside of obscuring the most distinctive aspects of individuals. I have been well trained in the evidence that subjectivity contaminates judgment, but when trying to understand any person's unique story, I tend to trust my gut more than research-derived algorithms. I listen "with the third ear" (Reik, 1948) to the metaphors, fantasies, and songs that enter my mind as I hear or read a person's story. I value subjective perceptions and am keenly aware that objectivity has its own limitations; for example, many randomized controlled trials define syndromes so narrowly that they no longer resemble naturalistic clinical phenomena.

In personality scholarship, I appreciate the Big Five approach to assessment (McCrae & Costa, 1989); I am impressed by its validity and reliability and by the extensive scholarship that has influenced it. I like the fact that it is dimensional (assessing more-and-less rather than present-versus-absent). And yet with the possible exception of the introversion-extraversion dimension, I have not found the Big Five traits particularly relevant clinically. In preparation for this article, I took the test online, scoring in the 74th percentile for extraversion, the 98th for emotional stability, and the 93rd agreeableness, conscientiousness, and intellect/imagination. The results do not surprise me, but I do not feel they exactly illuminate me, either.

I prefer to think about individuality, especially as it relates to clinical work, as being a product of the interaction of qualities that can be seen from at least ten different perspectives: temperament (e.g., Kagan, 1994), attachment style (e.g., Mikulincer & Shaver, 2007), dynamic patterns (e.g., Shedler, 2015), defenses (e.g., Perry, 2014), implicit organizing cognitions (e.g., Silberschatz, 2005), affective patterns (e.g., Tomkins, 1995), motivational (drive) constellations (e.g., Davis & Panksepp, 2018), the self-definition versus the self-in-relationship polarity (Blatt, 2008), recurrent relational themes (whether termed internalized object relations, inner working models, core conflictual relationship themes, schemas, RIGS, FRAMES, or any of the other labels for talking about these patterns; e.g., Luborsky & Crits-Cristoph, 1996), and level of severity of clinical manifestations (Kernberg & Caligor, 2005). I have given an empirical citation for each to make the point that there is an extensive research literature in all these domains. My clinical experience suggests that this kind of intersectional perspective provides a better evidence-base for clinical work than either the measurement of traits or the conduct of randomized controlled trials of manualized treatments for different symptomatic constellations.

I have always resonated to the psychoanalytic principle of overdetermination (Waelder, 1960); that is, the assumption that any problem important enough to warrant clinical attention has been created by multiple, interacting forces. This intellectual position is in some tension with the principle of parsimony that has greatly influenced the hypothesis-testing model privileged in academic psychology. Overdetermination applies to personality as well as symptoms; I see individuals as best understood by multiple examinatory lenses. Most psychoanalytic therapists shift fluidly from one perspective to another, reflecting on different features of individuality depending on what is alive in a particular patient in any clinical moment. We do not usually think in a systematic, superordinate way about these angles of vision on an individual's personality, though doing so can be a good exercise in formulating the psychology of a particular client and checking for our own blind spots.

In the 1990s, in response to questions about how I think about case formulation, I produced a similar list of interacting perspectives, which eventually became a textbook (McWilliams, 1999). I organized that volume in terms of assessing (1) what cannot be changed and thus needs to be accepted (e.g., temperament or brain damage [as in my father]), (2) developmental issues, (3) patterns of defense, (4) central affects, (5) identifications (including those issuing from culture, religion, race, and minority status), (6) relational patterns, (7) ways of regulating self-esteem, and (8) organizing beliefs.

The second edition of the *Psychodynamic Diagnostic Manual* (PDM-2) (Lingiardi & McWilliams, 2017) includes the *Psychodiagnostic Chart-2* (PDC-2), an instrument created by Robert Gordon and Robert Bornstein (2015) to help clinicians to get an initial overview of each patient's psychology. It focuses on level of severity (based on assessing identity integration, object relations, level of defense, and reality testing), personality style, and current mental functioning (12 areas, subsumed under cognitive and affective processes, identity and relationships, defense and coping, and self-awareness and self-direction), along with evaluation of symptoms and relevant issues of culture, context, and minority stress.

I hope this assessment tool will be useful for researchers in personality, clinical psychology, and counseling, who can apply it systematically to questions involving individual differences. I expect that practitioners will use it less for formal diagnosis than for thinking about patients in the clinical process. The PDC is the simplest version that could be derived from interrelated psychoanalytic ways of conceptualizing individuals, and yet it is anything but reductionistic. I hope also that neither the PDC nor the PDM as a whole will be used in ways that reify, oversimplify, or overly pathologize different ways of being human.

I have written previously (McWilliams, 2017) about the value of thinking in terms of dynamic themes. Although individuals can be accurately described by static or dimensional traits, I think they are more accurately depicted in terms of *polarities* central to their psychology, on which they often show qualities at both ends of the continuum that is most salient to them (e.g., closeness versus distance for people with a schizoid psychology, control versus dyscontrol for obsessive-compulsive individuals, idealization/grandiosity versus devaluation/shame for people with narcissistic dynamics, trust versus distrust for those with significant paranoia). Jung's positing the presence in the self of the converse or "shadow" side of each of his identified dynamisms (introversion coexisting with extroversion, the anima with the animus, and so on) has always appealed to me, illuminating what otherwise can seem to be inexplicable inconsistencies in a personality (e.g., "How could such a peaceable soul have behaved so violently?" or "How could such a skeptical person have been so gullible?").

Viewing myself in terms of organizing themes, I am struck with several polarities via which my own psychology can be conceptualized. I can find attitudes and behaviors in myself on both ends of each continuum. My predominant preoccupations include male versus female, power versus impotence, inclusion versus exclusion, visibility versus invisibility, independence versus dependence, pride/arrogance versus shame/humility, goodness versus badness, and truth versus falsehood. All these are inter-related psychodynamically, and all shed some light on why my work has taken the directions it has.

Some final reflections

I have found it illuminating to participate in this project. I appreciate having been asked to think through the connection between my indi-vidual psychology and my professional practice. I have tried to describe myself accurately, but I should remind readers of the old joke that the only problem with self-analysis is the countertransference. We know now that memory is always a work in process, not remotely comparable to looking back on a mentally filmed documentary of one's life. Unconscious choices about what to remember and not remember, and about how to understand our memories, are driven by our idiosyncratic interpretations of what hap-pens to us, considered in light of the themes that have come to dominate our subjectivity and protect our self-esteem. Our psychologies are prod-ucts of the epigenetic interactions of biological templates with successive human environments, filtered through evolving organizing assumptions.

Personality can be seen as both fixed and elastic. If, once established, our personality patterns did not admit of change, trauma would not damage us as profoundly as it can even late in life, and conversely, psychotherapy for personality disorders would be an exercise in futility. Nevertheless, it is the stability and consistency of individual psychology, including my own, that have impressed me more than its plasticity. In the early 1970s, when I was new to academic psychology, scholars who assumed the continuity – or sometimes even the existence – of stable personality differences viewed themselves as a somewhat beleaguered minority – one I was happy to join, given my inclinations toward marginality and the questioning of conventional authority. Thanks to the empirical study of individual traits, attachment research, and other intersecting intellectual movements, that situation has changed, as this project itself attests.

In closing, having established myself as a "both-and" more than an "either-or" kind of thinker, let me repeat my view that individuality ad-mits of many alternative conceptualizations, few of which are mutually exclusive, and each of which may be differentially applicable to different purposes. Those purposes also determine salience. For me, it is their clini-cal applicability, the utility of each perspective in helping me try to reduce mental suffering, that have shaped the ways I think about personality.

Acknowledgments

I thank Michael Garrett for his close reading and advice on this manu-script and my sisters, Susan Riley Solberg and Elizabeth Gordon Riley, for their fact-checking.

References

Blatt, S. J. (2008). *Polarities of experience: Relatedness and self-definition in personality development, psychopathology, and the therapeutic process.* Washington, DC: American Psychological Association.

Davis, K. L., & Panksepp, J. (2018). *The emotional foundations of personality: A neurobiological and evolutionary approach.* New York: Norton.

Gilligan, C. (1982). *In a different voice: psychological theory and women's development.* Cambridge, MA: Harvard University Press.

Goldstein, K. (1952). The effect of brain damage on the personality. *Psychiatry: Interpersonal and Biological Processes, 15*(3), 245–260.

Gordon, R. M., & Bornstein, R. F. (2015). Psychodynamic diagnostic Chart-2, adult version 8.1. In V. Lingiardi & N. McWilliams (Eds.), *Psychodynamic Diagnostic Manual: PDM-2* (2nd ed., pp. 1019–1023). New York: Guilford Press.

Kagan, J. (1994). *Galen's prophecy: Temperament in human nature.* New York: Basic Books.

Kernberg, O. F., & Caligor, E. (2005). A psychoanalytic theory of personality disorders. In M. F. Lenzenweger & J. F. Clarkin (Eds.), *Major theories of personality disorders* (2nd ed., pp. 114–126). New York: Guilford Press.

Lingiardi, V., & McWilliams, N. (Eds.). *Psychodynamic Diagnostic Manual (PDM-2)* (2nd ed.). New York: Guilford Press.

Luborsky, L., & Crits-Cristoph, P. (1996). *Understanding transference* (2nd ed.). Washington, DC: American Psychological Association.

McCrae, R. R., & Costa, P. T. (1989). The structure of interpersonal traits: Wiggins's circumplex and the five-factor model. *Journal of Personality and Social Psychology, 56*(4), 586–595.

McWilliams, N. (1994). *Psychoanalytic diagnosis: Understanding personality structure in the clinical process* (1st ed.). New York: Guilford Press.

McWilliams, N. (2013). The impact of my own psychotherapy on my work as a therapist. *Psychoanalytic Psychology, 30*(4), 621–626.

McWilliams, N. (2014). Reflections on the effects of a protestant girlhood. In G. S. Stavros & S. J. Sandage (Eds.), *The skillful soul of the psychotherapist: The link between spirituality and clinical excellence* (pp. 17–29). Lanham, MD: Rowman & Littlefield.

McWilliams, N. (2017). Integrative research for integrative practice: A plea for respectful collaboration across clinician and researcher roles. *Journal of Psychotherapy Integration, 27*(3), 283–294.

Mikulincer, M., & Shaver, P. R. (2007). *Attachment in adulthood: Structure, dynamics, and change.* New York: Guilford Press.

Perry, J. C. (2014). Anomalies and specific functions in the clinical identification of defense mechanisms. *Journal of Clinical Psychology, 70*, 406–418.

Reik, T. (1948). *Listening with the third ear: The inner experience of a psychoanalyst.* New York: Farrar, Strauss.

Schore, A. N. (2019). *Right brain psychotherapy.* New York: Norton.

Shedler, J. (2015). Integrating clinical and empirical perspectives on personality. The Shedler-Westen Assessment Procedure (SWAP). In S. K. Huprich (Ed.), *Personality disorders: Toward theoretical and empirical integration in diagnosis and assessment* (pp. 225–252). Washington, DC: American Psychological Association.

Silberschatz, G. (Ed.) (2005). *Transformative relationships: The control-mastery theory of psychotherapy.* New York: Routledge.

Tomkins, S. S. (1995). Script theory. In E. V. Demos (Ed.), *Exploring affect: The selected writings of Silvan Tomkins* (pp. 312–388). New York: Cambridge University Press.

Waelder, R. (1960). *Basic theory of psychoanalysis.* New York: International Universities Press.

10 Influences and Inspirations

Robert P. Archer

Personal and professional aspects of my life and career

I was born in Newark, New Jersey, and raised in St. Petersburg, Florida. My father, Robert Sinclair Henderson Archer, was a British World War I army veteran born in the city of Wallsend in Northumberland, England. My father immigrated from England to the United States in the 1920s and became a boilermaker in the industrial section of Northeast New Jersey prior to retiring to Florida in 1958. My father never shared his educational background with me, but I suspect that, like most of the people in Wallsend England which was at that time a center of British shipbuilding, he left school at an early age to work at the shipyard. My father maintained a heavy working-class English accent throughout his life, and I can remember "translating" my father's statements to friends who visited our home and had difficulty understanding his accent.

My mother, Mildred Elizabeth Keesey, was of Pennsylvania Dutch/ Irish ancestry and her father died in a steel mill accident. My mother and her sister were placed in foster care following the death of their father, until my grandmother was able to secure the two jobs that were necessary to generate sufficient funds to reestablish their home and family. Following her release from foster care, my mother left school at an early age to go to work in a paint factory to help support the household. My mother was a direct descendant of a Union Civil War Veteran, Daniel Keesey, who joined the 16th Pennsylvania Infantry Division in York Pennsylvania in April 1861 at age 16, initially as a 90-day enlistee. He was wounded in combat at the Battle of Monocacy in Maryland and was discharged from the Army of the Potomac at the conclusion of the Civil War in June 1865.

When I was eight years old, my father retired and our family moved to St. Petersburg, Florida, where I attended segregated public schools. I graduated from Dixie Hollins High School, the "Home of the Fighting Rebels" and it never occurred to any of us that our school name or motto could be problematic. I was an undisciplined student with a record of inconsistent performance. In classes that I enjoyed I would typically do well. My grades in my Latin, algebra, and chemistry classes, however, left much to be desired. To the surprise of many of my peers, and some

DOI: 10.4324/9781003036302-10

of my teachers, I was admitted to the University of South Florida where I received a BA and eventually, after a two-year break from college, an MA in Psychology and a Ph.D. in Clinical and Community Psychology.

I was the first member of my immediate family, and the only member of my high school peer group, to complete college. My approach to college was much different than my earlier educational efforts, largely due to my fears that I might not be "college material". I conscientiously completed all assignments and put in long hours preparing for classes. I selected psychology as my major during my junior year because I enjoyed the subject area, and loved Hall And Lindsey's *Theories of Personality* (1965), and as importantly because I developed a personal relationship with several of the psychology faculty through our shared interest and involvement in the antiwar movement of the late 1960s. I viewed the antiwar movement as my minor area of study, although at several points it was my major focus, particularly following the "police riot" at the 1968 Democratic Convention in Mayor Daley's Chicago.

I was classified as a Conscientious Objector (CO) by my draft board and between undergraduate and graduate school; I served for two years in mandatory "alternative service". In support of my CO application, my father wrote a letter to my draft board that stated, in part, that as a veteran of World War I, the "war to end all wars," he fully supported my conviction that warfare as a means of settling international conflicts was both ineffective in terms of achieving lasting conflict resolution and inherently immoral. My father never mentioned the details of his experiences in WWI beyond a few humorous stories meant to entertain me, and I only know he was stationed on the Western Front in France during his wartime service.

My alternative service was conducted as a special education teacher in a school in the Washington DC suburbs. The school used a behavioral approach, including a token economy system, to help provide educational services to learning-disabled and psychologically disabled students. As a special education teacher for those two years, I learned that I had limited talent and skill as a classroom teacher, but a great deal of interest in adolescent development and psychopathology.

I entered graduate school immediately following my completion of my CO obligation. Roughly half of the students who entered with my class did not complete the training. I was attracted to the personality assessment area during the first year of my program largely because of the influence of two individuals I will discuss in more detail later in this chapter: the mentorship by Charles Spielberger and the writings of Paul Meehl. Personality assessment seemed to me to be an area closest to a "hard science" of any of the clinical psychology's subfields, i.e., based upon empirical data and statistical analyses so that issues in personality assessment were ultimately resolved by the strongest data, not the best abstract argument.

I completed my Clinical Psychology Internship at the Medical University of South Carolina (MUSC) in Charleston, South Carolina, during the 1976–1977 academic year. I learned at MUSC that research projects, unlike my dissertation experience, could be engaging, exciting and (even) enjoyable. I entered MUSC thinking that I would spend my career as a clinician, and left my internship convinced that I should pursue an academic career that incorporated research and teaching, along with my clinical interests, into my daily activities. My subsequent 40-year career in medical school settings provided a splendid opportunity to engage in all three (i.e., clinical, research, and teaching) of these areas as well as a variety of engaging administrative responsibilities.

The factors that effect and shape an individual's life and career are often difficult to recognize at the moment that they are occurring, but hopefully easier to discern looking back over a career. Charles Spielberger's example has largely shaped my understanding of how a researcher goes about the process of establishing a productive research program. Paul Meehl's contribution has been in forming the way in which I view personality assessment, particularly responses to the MMPI but also more generally to all self-report measures of personality and psychopathology. My opportunities to collaborate with Auke Tellegen have caused me to reconsider the feasibility of restructuring the MMPI with the goals of limiting the influence of the First Factor on the MMPI (and potentially other self-report measures) and fostered the adoption of contemporary models of psychopathology in my thinking about the development of assessment instruments. In the following pages of this chapter I will try to describe the role of each of these individuals in more detail.

Influences that have shaped my approach to personality assessment research

Charles Spielberger

A major influence on my thinking about personality assessment relates to my experiences with Charles Spielberger. At the time that I worked as a research assistant for Dr. Spielberger in the mid-1970s, he was refining his development of the State-Trait Anxiety Inventory (STAI) which was published in 1983 by Spielberger, Gorsuch, Lushene, Yang, and Jacobs. The STAI would eventually be translated into over 50 languages and used in thousands of research studies. In addition to being a prolific researcher, Spielberger served as the leader of numerous national and international psychological associations including his service as the President of the American Psychological Association.

My firsthand observation of Charlie over several years convinced me he was one of the most hardworking individuals I had ever met. Charlie never ceased putting in long hours, to the chagrin of his research assistants who became exhausted trying to keep up with his workload. Later in my own career, as I met other individuals who had achieved levels of success similar to Spielberger's, I realized it was one trait that they all had in common, i.e., the ability to maintain a focused and intense level of concentration on a research program to an extent that would discourage most individuals. I am quite sure that I never came close to replicating Spielberger's intensity but having the opportunity to observe him reinforced my efforts to try to replicate his level of commitment. Further, I have always been thankful for learning a great deal about research methodology by serving as his research assistant.

The most important lessons I learned from Spielberger concerned the "nuts and bolts" of conducting research, most crucially the importance of developing a coherent and integrated research program of interrelated studies. Many graduate students harbor dreams of conducting "the" landmark research study that dramatically advances a field of science. While such single "one off" groundbreaking studies may exist, Spielberger emphasized the importance of building a body of knowledge through a comprehensive series of interconnected research studies as the much more feasible way in which researchers advance scientific knowledge. Such a focused research approach is greatly facilitated by the researcher developing a research team, including long term collaborators across institutions, and by developing and maintaining an in-depth knowledge of the cutting-edge issues within the field. It also certainly helps if the researcher is in an academic setting that provides the opportunity to involve graduate students in his or her research program in a manner that is of benefit to both researcher and students. The researcher's opportunity to work with graduate students serves to expand and extend their research within their field, while the graduate student receives the benefit of supervision from an individual at the forefront of a research area and senior authorship on a publishable dissertation project. This lesson about the importance of research specialization and continuity of focus became central to my own research program across my career.

Paul Meehl

As a graduate student at the University of South Florida I was introduced to the Minnesota Multiphasic Personality Inventory (MMPI) in a course on Psychological Assessment. My MMPI lineage can be traced as follows: Paul Mauger (who taught the assessment course) had been a student of James Butcher at the University of Minnesota, who in turn was a student of Grant Dahlstrom at the University of North Carolina, Chapel Hill, who in turn was a student of Starke Hathaway at the University of Minnesota. At the time of the assessment course Mauger was a recently hired assistant professor who came to USF with an enthusiastic embrace of the "Dust Bowl Empiricism" that marked the original development of the MMPI as illustrated by the external criterion keying method used to select items for basic scale membership. In addition to the MMPI, Mauger also introduced me to the writings of Paul Meehl.

While Paul Meehl was not involved in the original creation of the MMPI (he was in high school at the time of that work) his doctoral dissertation subsequently led to the development of the K correction procedure for the test (Meehl & Hathaway, 1946). Meehl became the Hathaway and Regents' Professor of Psychology at the University of Minnesota and served as a President of the American Psychological Association. Meehl's heavy contribution to the literature on the MMPI included his advocacy for an actuarial/statistical interpretive approach to the MMPI and the greater accuracy produced by statistical prediction approaches, in contrast to clinical prediction, whenever the actuarial data were available and suitable to the prediction task at hand. Beyond his contributions to the MMPI, Meehl is widely recognized for his seminal contributions to the concept of construct validity, the etiology of schizophrenia, and the philosophy of science and clinical inquiry. Across the many years I taught personality assessment to graduate students, Meehl's 1973 collection of writings entitled, *Psychodiagnosis: Selected Papers,* was a standard part of the course syllabus. To explain how Meehl's writings influenced my early thinking about personality assessment, it is necessary for me to go into some detail concerning his observations as well as some salient points about the development of the MMPI.

Paul Meehl's (1945) *the Dynamics of "Structured" Personality Tests,* which he termed his "empirical manifesto", served a crucial role in providing me with a framework for my understanding of test responses on objective instruments, particularly the MMPI. The development of the MMPI was, in part, a response to the failure of academic psychologists, often without benefit of significant clinical experience, to create clinically useful personality assessment measures. These early 20th century personality inventories were typically based heavily on the selection of face valid items deemed to be reflective of a specific psychological variable, such as depression or anxiety. Item selection was based on the test authors' rational judgments concerning item relevancy to the target or core construct. Rational scale construction involves the selection of items that logically or rationally appear to measure important areas of a construct based on the test developer's theory, clinical experience, and intuition. A fundamental assumption inherent in this test construction method was that the items selected actually measured what the authors assumed they measured. As noted by Hathaway and McKinley (1940, 1942), however, these early scales often failed to show evidence of construct validity when evaluated in clinical settings, e.g., individuals diagnosed as neurotic did not produce elevated test scores on scales of neuroticism when contrasted with responses from persons in the normal population. The dismal state of personality assessment by the 1930s was summarized by Hathaway as follows:

"it was so widely accepted that personality inventories were valueless that some program directors did not feel that any coursework in their nature and interpretation was worth the effort" (1960, p. xiii).

The MMPI (Hathaway & McKinley, 1943) was developed in part to address this weakness by creating scales using an empirically based methodology. The MMPI scales were assembled by contrasting item responses of patients placed in various psychiatric diagnostic groups with the responses derived from individuals in nonclinical samples. Item selection was driven by the extent to which individuals in the diagnostic criterion group answered an item in the keyed direction more frequently than individuals in the normative sample. Hathaway and McKinley (1944) summarized this procedure as follows: "every item finally chosen {for scale membership} differentiates between criterion and normal groups, and that is the reason for acceptance or rejection of the items. They are not selected for their content or theoretical import. Frequently the authors can see no possible rationale to an item in a given scale; it is nevertheless accepted if it appears to differentiate" (pp. 31–32).

Objective personality assessment measures have frequently been criticized on the grounds that the information provided by these tests is limited by the respondent's self-knowledge and self-awareness. Meehl noted that this relatively common approach to the understanding of personality inventories, still prevalent today, viewed the self-ratings provided by the test respondent as an acceptable substitute for the much more impractical option of taking behavioral samples of that respondent. To illustrate this point, Meehl (1945) observed that we may believe that shyness is related to a readiness to blush. Since we cannot conveniently monitor the individual across time to determine whether he blushes or not, a reasonable substitute might be to simply ask that person, "Do you blush easily?" In evaluating his response, we might believe that he will be aware of whether he blushes easily and that he will also be willing to accurately tell us about this susceptibility. To the extent that a respondent's self-awareness and willingness to accurately self-disclose are limited, the usefulness of his or her test responses is correspondingly limited.

Meehl explicitly rejected the hypotheses that self-ratings are a "feeble surrogate for a behavioral sample." (1945, p. 297). He asserted that self-ratings should be considered an intrinsically interesting and significant behavior, the usefulness of which is established based on empirical investigations of external correlates of that behavior. This perspective proposed by Meehl emancipated test interpreters from the restriction that respondents must be able to describe their behavior accurately as measured against some objective external standard. To illustrate this latter point, Meehl proposed that we consider two individuals, both of whom experience similar headaches on an average of once per month. One of these individuals is a hypochondriac, while the other is an individual without a history of symptoms of hypochondriasis. We examine their item endorsements and find that the hypochondriac endorses the item "I have frequent headaches" as true while their normal counterpart's response was that the statement is false, despite the fact that both individuals experience headaches with the same intensity and frequency. One way of viewing this is to conclude that this is a poorly worded item that creates ambiguity because these individuals with the same headache histories responded to the same item in different ways. In contrast, Meehl argued that the utility of the item is essentially defined by the extent to which hypochondriacal individuals endorsed that item in the keyed or scored direction more frequently than individuals from the normal population. Thus, the meaning or usefulness of an item is to be determined by the strength of its relationship to external criteria, not by the degree to which an individual's response might be seen as accurate or inaccurate for them. As noted by Meehl (1945), "Not only does this approach free from the restriction that the subject must be able to describe their behavior accurately, but a careful study of structured personality tests built on this basis shows that such a restriction would falsify the actual relationships between what a man says and what a man is ... that the majority of [MMPI] questions seem by inspection to require self-ratings has been a source of theoretical misunderstanding, since the stimulus situation seems to request a self-rating, whereas the scoring does not assume a valid self-rating to have been given. It is difficult to give any psychologically meaningful interpretation of some of the empirical findings on the MMPI unless the more sophisticated view is maintained." (p. 297).

Given Meehl's provocative view, it was quite possible for an individual to reveal important data concerning their personality without an active intent to do so and without the requirement of self-awareness. For me, a second-year graduate student, Meehl's radical empiricism led me to a quite different way of viewing the meaning of responses to objective personality assessment instruments. Meehl's view resonated with my growing caution concerning an exclusive reliance on theory in test construction, particularly on all-encompassing and over-arching theoretical frameworks, and an increasing preference for empirically supported approaches. As has often been noted, the first few years following Galileo's invention of the telescope revealed more truths about the nature of the universe than centuries of theoretical speculation.

Meehl (1971) eventually modified his radical empiricism which he came to view as "psychometrically simplistic" (p. 296). He observed that the reduced external validity values often found when MMPI scales were evaluated in new samples and populations might be attributable, at least in part, to the selection of items exclusively based on statistical criteria, regardless of whether the item "makes sense" from a conceptual or theoretical framework. In Meehl's evolved view, the automatic inclusion of "subtle" items in scale membership, i.e., items that bear little apparent relationship to a construct, often inadvertently introduces items reflecting error variance in these scales. This view has received substantial support in studies and reviews focused on the marked limitations of subtle MMPI items in predicting to external criterion (e.g., Butcher et al., 1989; Herkov et al., 1991; Tellegen et al., 2003). I have come to share the now widely held view that scale development based exclusively on a statistical method like criterion keying, without any attempt to link item selection to an explicit conceptual framework, is inherently prone to the selection of an unacceptably high number of unproductive items. Contemporary scale construction has been based on the belief that scale development is most usefully undertaken when scales are constructed using empirical methods of item selection that is also informed by a conceptual framework. Nevertheless, Meehl's emphasis on objective personality assessment measurement as a probabilistic indicator of an individual's complex psychological functioning, and the crucial role of research data in establishing the meaning of objective personality assessment measures, continues to heavily influence my own thinking and research program. Meehl's paper caused me to think more complexly about the process involved in responding to items on a test, and to move beyond the view that objective test respondents were simply being asked to provide accurate data concerning their history of psychological functioning. Meehl's later papers, particularly including *"Wanted: A Good Cookbook* (1956); *When Shall we use our Heads instead of the Formula?* (1957); *"Clinical versus Actuarial Prediction: A Theoretical Analysis and a Review of the Evidence"* (1954) and the follow-up *"Causes and Effects of my Disturbing Little Book"* (1986) helped to shape my belief in the importance of empircical and actuarial methods in personality assessment.

Before I leave the topic of Paul Meehl, I should note his influence on my becoming a forensic psychologist. In 1999 I presented an MMPI-A workshop at a conference in Florida and had some time left before I had to catch a flight back home. David Faust, who had completed an internship and postdoctoral fellowship at the University of Minnesota, was also presenting at the same conference on the practice of forensic psychology. I knew very little about forensic psychology, welcomed the opportunity to gain some knowledge in the area, and I decided at the last minute to sit in on his presentation. Faust cited Meehl multiple times during that workshop, stressing the importance of actuarial prediction and the pitfalls of clinical judgment in the practice of forensic psychology. His approach to psychology was consistently data-driven and empirically based. I could see the influence of Meehl throughout his presentation and I left with much enthusiasm about learning more about forensic psychology. I spent the next few years attending hundreds of hours of training sessions on forensic psychology. By 2003 I had begun to convert clinical my practice at Eastern Virginia Medical School (EVMS) exclusively to forensic evaluations, subsequently established a postdoctoral fellowship in forensic psychology at EVMS and eventually the EVMS Forensic Evaluation Program. After I retired from EVMS in 2016, I joined my daughter in her forensic practice in Virginia. Another debt that I owe to Paul Meehl, thanks to the outstanding workshop by David Faust over 20 years ago.

Auke Tellegen

The third, and most recent, influence on my work has been the contributions of Auke Tellegen and his colleagues, particularly in the development of the MMPI-2-Restrucutred Clinical (RC) Scales. Tellegen is Professor Emeritus in the Department of Psychology at the University of Minnesota and he served as a professor in that department from 1986 to 1999. Tellegen is the co-author of the MMPI-2 and MMPI-A, the MMPI-2-RF and MMPI-A-RF, and most recently the MMPI-3 (Ben-Porath and Tellegen, 2020). He is also the author of the Multidimensional Personality Questionnaire (MPQ), a self-report broadband test of normal personality. In addition to his unique expertise in personality psychology and measurement, Tellegen has made lasting contributions to the field of behavioral genetics and hypnosis. In 2000, Tellegen received the Bruno Klopfer Distinguished Contribution Award for Lifetime Achievement in Personality Assessment from the Society for Personality Assessment. In his invited address on that occasion, Tellegen presented an approach to identifying and containing the influence of the MMPI first factor on the MMPI basic scales. It was the first time in my career that I heard a specific proposal involving a method of addressing this crucial issue.

The presence of a common or First Factor had been well-known among personality assessment experts for many decades, particularly following Welsh's (1956) factor analysis of the MMPI and the identification of this First Factor in his Maladjustment Scale. Factor analytic studies spanning decades have uniformly revealed the presence of this major source of common variance across seemingly unrelated scales that has been variously labeled as General Maladjustment, Emotional Distress, Anxiety, or simply the First Factor. Archer, Belevich and Elkins (1994) also found the pervasive presence of this factor evident in the MMPI-A responses of adolescents.

Although the problems associated with the First Factor had been well represented in the MMPI, first factor effects can be found in numerous personality inventories developed using widely differing methodologies. Tellegen noted this issue in the mid-80s and stated: "It is generally the case that correlations between {different} measures of adjustment tend to be substantial, giving rise to a large-sometimes very large, general demoralization or subjective discomfort factor .... One challenge in developing new self-report scales is to find ways of not measuring this general factor. (1985, p. 692)". Friedman et al. (2001) noted that the effect of the first or common factor is that the discriminant utility of any scales developed for the assessment of emotional distress must take into account the influence of this factor as a major source of variance. As observed by Friedman et al.

(2001), no matter the specific label given to the first factor (e.g., Anxiety, General Maladjustment, Emotional Distress, etc.), the presence of this factor generally tends to decrease the sensitivity of a scale in discriminating one form of distress or psychopathology from another.

In the Restructured Clinical (RC) scales monograph, Tellegen et al. (2003) labeled this factor Demoralization. He observed that each of the MMPI-2 Clinical scales contained a substantial number of items that bear a large and inadvertent relationship with Demoralization. The effects of this factor, combined with the extensive item overlap found among the Basic scales, produced surprisingly high MMPI-2 Basic scale intercorrelations that compromised the discriminant validity of these scales. To illustrate this point, Tellegen et al. noted that the correlations found between MMPI scales Pt (Psychasthenia), typically viewed as a measure of neuroticism or anxiety, and scale Sc (Schizophrenia), intended to identify individuals suffering from schizophrenia, typically exceeded.80. If these scales were sensitive and specific measures of their respective underlying constructs, the marked correlations between these scales would be quite perplexing. The confounding influence of the first factor is not restricted to the MMPI-2 Basic scales but can be found in a variety of MMPI-2 and MMPI-A Content and Supplementary scales.

To address this perennial First factor problem, Tellegen et al. developed a measure of the first factor (i.e., the Demoralization scale). Tellegen stated, "We need to stress that we did not doubt the clinical significance of Demoralization and the need to measure it. However, we considered it preferable, conceptually and pragmatically, to assess Demoralization just once, with a separate Restructured Scale rather than repeatedly and confounded with other content, as seems to occur when clinicians interpret the overall elevation of the Clinical Scale profile" (2003, p. 12). To reduce the redundant effects of this factor, Tellegen also introduced the concept of seed or core components of the MMPI Basic scales which were uniquely associated with the basic measurement construct of each of the Clinical scales. Tellegen began with the assumption that demoralization was not a distinctive component or core of any of the basic clinical scales. The innovative approach developed by Tellegen was to isolate the demoralization items from the core constructs of each of the basic scales, resulting in shorter and more discriminant scales based on their distinctive components with the effects of the demoralization factors substantially reduced. To accomplish this goal, Tellegen conducted item level factor analyses of each individual clinical scale to yield the demoralization factor and to identify a distinctive core component of each clinical scale.

The eventual result of Tellegen's efforts to develop the Restructured Clinical scales was the creation new test instruments for adults, i.e., the MMPI-2-RF (Tellegen & Ben-Porath, 2008) and the MMPI-3 (Ben-Porath and Tellegen, 2020). Tellegen's development of the RC scales also resulted in my participation in the development of the Minnesota

Multiphasic Personality Inventory-Adolescent-Restructured (MMPI-A-RF) for adolescents (Archer et al., 2016). These more recent test instruments are shorter than the earlier counterparts (MMPI-2 and MMPI-A) while maintaining comparable levels of convergent validity but improved levels of discriminant validity. The test structure underlying these more recent instruments also utilizes a hierarchical organization of dimensional scales more consistent with contemporary views of the nature of psychopathology. The trade-off involved in developing these more recent versions of the MMPI is that the restructured forms of the MMPI bear important differences from their predecessors and are clearly more than simple test revisions. The innovative nature of the MMPI-2-RF, MMPI-A-RF, and forthcoming MMPI-3 made the massive literature available for the prior editions, particularly the interpretive literature that allows for an understanding of the correlates of scale evaluations, not directly applicable to these revisions. The revised test instruments come, therefore, at the cost of the need to develop independent research literatures based directly on these new tests. I anticipate that the MMPI-A-RF will generate a substantial research literature over the next decade, in a manner like the extensive research literature that has been established for the MMPI-2-RF.

My approach to personality assessment

The MMPI

I began using the MMPI with adolescents during my internship at the Medical University of South Carolina (MUSC) when I rotated to an adolescent inpatient unit at the MUSC hospital. I was very eager to use this opportunity to see how the MMPI might work with adolescent respondents. At that time (mid 1970s) it was the common practice to administer the MMPI to adolescents and evaluate their response patterns using the standard adult K-corrected norms. In the absence of any "official" set of adolescent norms from the test publisher, much confusion prevailed among clinicians and researchers concerning the most appropriate normative reference group from which to evaluate adolescents' MMPI profiles. This issue became the focus of my early research efforts, i.e., which norms were most useful in interpreting adolescent MMPI response patterns. In a series of studies published from 1984 through 1992, I and my colleagues found ample evidence that the practice of using adult norms to interpret adolescent profiles typically produced gross overestimates of psychopathology (e.g., Archer, 1984, 1987; Pancoast & Archer, 1988). Expanding this research focus, I became interested in trying to understand the differences in item endorsement frequencies found between adults and adolescents, as well as differences manifest in the responses of samples of normal adolescents versus adolescents who had received one or more psychiatric diagnoses (e.g., Archer, 1997; Archer et al., 2001; Archer, 2005). This, in turn, led to investigations on the effects of K correction style procedures for adolescent norms (Alperin et al., 1996; Fontaine et al., 2001) and examinations of the changes in typical adolescent response patterns across 40 years (e.g., Newsome et al., 2003). Survey research by Archer et al. (1991) indicated that the MMPI was the most frequently used objective personality assessment instrument in the evaluation of adolescents. This research was the beginning of my career long efforts to emulate Spielberger's methodological lesson: identify an area of research that you are passionate about and develop a research program based on a series of interconnected studies that advance knowledge in that area.

The development MMPI-A

Despite the popularity of the MMPI with this age group, the survey by Archer et al. (1991) also found that clinicians reported several concerns regarding the original form of the MMPI when used with adolescents. These concerns included the absence of contemporary adolescent norms, the presence of inappropriate or outdated language in the item pool, and the overall test length (566 items). To address these issues, the University of Minnesota Press created an advisory committee to consider the creation of an adolescent form of the MMPI including the development of adolescent norms based on a national sampling. The Committee initially consisted of James Butcher, John Graham, Grant Dahlstrom, me, and Beverly Kaemmer. The project was quickly expanded to include Auke Tellegen, Yossi Ben-Porath, and Carolyn Williams. The Committee recommended the development of an adolescent form and the collection of normative data from 1620 adolescents across multiple sites in the United States. In developing this test an explicit emphasis was placed on maintaining as much continuity as possible between the validity and basic clinical scales on original form of the MMPI and the revised form specifically designed for use with adolescents, i.e., the Minnesota Multiphasic Personality Inventory-Adolescent (MMPI-A). Within this context, however, opportunities were taken to improve or modify the MMPI item pool by revising or eliminating outdated items and developing new scales specifically relevant to adolescent development and/or psychopathology. The final version of the MMPI-A (Butcher et al., 1992) contained 478 items and was the first form of the test specifically designed for, and normed on, adolescents. The release of the MMPI-A in 1992 provided, for the first time, a standardized method for assessing adolescents resulting in improved assessment practices for both clinicians and researchers using this test instrument. It was also my first opportunity to become centrally involved in a substantive test revision including the development of new scales.

The final form of the MMPI-A included the original basic clinical scales with the deletion of items related to religious attitudes or practices, bowel or bladder functioning, and items deemed inappropriate for adolescents.

The revised test also included several new validity scales (the F scale sub-scales of F1 and F2, the Variable Response Inconsistency (VRIN), and the True Response Inconsistency (TRIN) scales). The MMPI-A also contained 15 Content Scales based on similar scales that had been developed for the MMPI-2 but also including several scales unique to the adolescent form. The MMPI-A included six Supplementary Scales that incorporated a combination of three pre-existing scales, i.e., the McAndrew Alcoholism Scale-Revised (MAC-R), the Anxiety (A) scale, and the Repression (R) scale, and three scales newly developed for the MMPI-A (the Alcohol/Drug Problem Acknowledgment (ACK) scale, the Alcohol/Drug problem proneness scale, and the Immaturity (IMM) scale. The Harris–Lingoes content subscales developed for the original MMPI were carried over to the MMPI-A.

Following the original release of the MMPI-A, a set of 31 Content Component subscales were subsequently developed by Sherwood et al. (1997) to identify meaningful item clusters within 13 of the 15 MMPI-A content scales, and the MMPI-A Personality Psychopathology Five (PSY-5) scales were developed by McNulty et al. (1997). Table 10.1 provides an overview of the MMPI-A scale and subscale structure.

The MMPI-A was rapidly adopted by clinicians and researchers. Archer and Newsom (2000) investigated the test use practices of 346 psychologists who worked with adolescents in a variety of settings and responded to our survey. The survey results indicated that the MMPI-A was the most widely used objective personality assessment instrument with adolescents, and the only objective personality assessment test included in the top 10 list of the most frequently used tests. Among the primary reasons for the popularity of the MMPI-A were the availability of contemporary adolescent norms, ease of administration, and a comprehensive research base available for the instrument. Among the most frequently cited disadvantages reported by the respondents were the length of the test instrument and the time required for administration, scoring, and interpretation. Baum et al. (2009) examined the literature on the MMPI-A and other objective test messages based on a review of articles, books, chapters, dissertations, and monographs appearing between 1992 and 2007. These authors concluded that the MMPI-A was the most widely researched objective personality assessment instrument used with adolescents. Archer et al. (2006) surveyed a group of forensic psychologists concerning their utilization of a wide variety of test instruments and reported that the MMPI-A was the most widely used self-report personality assessment instrument in evaluating adolescents in this specialized field.

Despite the popularity of the MMPI-A, several problems remained unresolved by this revised form of the MMPI. As previously noted, the developers of MMPI-A (and of the MMPI-2 which served as a basis for the MMPI-A) placed a crucial value on maintaining continuity between the original scales of the MMPI and these test revisions. The MMPI-A

Table 10.1 Overview of the MMPI-A scales and subscales

Basic Profile Scales (17 scales)
Standard Scales (13)
    L through *Si*
Additional Validity Scales (4)
    F_1/F_2 (Subscales of *F* Scale)
    VRIN (Variable Response Inconsistency)
    TRIN (True Response Inconsistency)

Content and Supplementary Scales (21 scales)
Content Scales (15)
    A-anx (Anxiety)
    A-obs (Obsessiveness)
    A-dep (Depression)
    A-hea (Health Concerns)
    A-aln (Alienation)
    A-biz (Bizarre Mentation)
    A-ang (Anger)
    A-cyn (Cynicism)
    A-con (Conduct Problems)
    A-lse (Low Self-esteem)
    A-las (Low Aspirations)
    A-sod (Social Discomfort)
    A-fam (Family Problems)
    A-sch (School Problems)
    A-trt (Negative Treatment Indicators)
Supplementary Scales (6)
    MAC-R (MacAndrew Alcoholism-Revised)
    ACK (Alcohol/Drug Problem Acknowledgment)
    PRO (Alcohol/Drug Problem Proneness)
    IMM (Immaturity)
    A (Anxiety)
    R (Repression)

Harris-Lingoes and Si Subscales (31 scales)
Harris-Lingoes Subscales (28)
    D_1 (Subjective depression)
    D_2 (Psychomotor retardation)
    D_3 (Physical malfunctioning)
    D_4 (Mental dullness)
    D_5 (Brooding)
    Hy_1 (Denial of social anxiety)
    Hy_2 (Need for affection)
    Hy_3 (Lassitude-malaise)
    Hy_4 (Somatic complaints)
    Hy_5 (Inhibition of aggression)
    Pd_1 (Familial discord)
    Pd_2 (Authority problems)
    Pd_3 (Social imperturbability)
    Pd_4 (Social alienation)
    Pd_5 (Self-alienation)
    Pa_1 (Persecutory ideas)
    Pa_2 (Poignancy)

Pa_3 (Naïveté)

Sc_1 (Social alienation)
Sc_2 (Emotional alienation)
Sc_3 (Lack of ego mastery, cognitive)
Sc_4 (Lack of ego mastery, conative)
Sc_5 (Lack of ego mastery, defective inhibition)
Sc_6 (Bizarre sensory experiences)
Ma_1 (Amorality)
Ma_2 (Psychomotor acceleration)
Ma_3 (Imperturbability)
Ma_4 (Ego inflation)
Si Subscales (3)
   Si_1 (Shyness/Self-Consciousness)
   Si_2 (Social Avoidance)
   Si_3 (Alienation–Self and others)

Content Component Scales (31)
$A\text{-}dep_1$ (Dysphoria)
$A\text{-}dep_2$ (Self-Depreciation)
$A\text{-}dep_3$ (Lack of Drive)
$A\text{-}dep_4$ (Suicidal Ideation)
$A\text{-}hea_1$ (Gastrointestinal Complaints)
$A\text{-}hea_2$ (Neurological Symptoms)
$A\text{-}hea_3$ (General Health Concerns)
$A\text{-}aln_1$ (Misunderstood)
$A\text{-}aln_2$ (Social Isolation)
$A\text{-}aln_3$ (Interpersonal Skepticism)
$A\text{-}biz_1$ (Psychotic Symptomatology)
$A\text{-}biz_2$ (Paranoid Ideation)
$A\text{-}ang_1$ (Explosive Behavior)
$A\text{-}ang_2$ (Irritability)
$A\text{-}cyn_1$ (Misanthropic Beliefs)
$A\text{-}cyn_2$ (Interpersonal Suspiciousness)
$A\text{-}con_1$ (Acting-Out Behaviors)
$A\text{-}con_2$ (Antisocial Attitudes)
$A\text{-}con_3$ (Negative Peer Group Influences)
$A\text{-}lse_1$ (Self-Doubt)
$A\text{-}lse_2$ (Interpersonal Submissiveness)
$A\text{-}las_1$ (Low Achievement Orientation)
$A\text{-}las_2$ (Lack of Initiative)
$A\text{-}sod_1$ (Introversion)
$A\text{-}sod_2$ (Shyness)
$A\text{-}fam_1$ (Familial Discord)
$A\text{-}fam_2$ (Familial Alienation)
$A\text{-}sch_1$ (School Conduct Problems)
$A\text{-}sch_2$ (Negative Attitudes)
$A\text{-}trt_1$ (Low Motivation)
$A\text{-}trt_2$ (Inability to Disclose)

Personality Psychopathology Five (PSY-5) Scales (5)
AGGR (Aggressiveness)
PSYC (Psychoticism)
DISC (Disconstraint)
NEGE (Negative Emotionality/Neuroticism)
INTR (Introversion/Low Positive Emotionality)

basic scales, therefore, were carried over from the original test instrument with minimal revision. The MMPI-A basic clinical scales consisted of items originally selected using the criterion-keying methodology employed by Hathaway and McKinley in the late 1930s based on diagnostic groups developed in the early 1920s. Further, in the development of the MMPI-A basic clinical scales, no effort was made to cross-validate the items selected for these scales, i.e., to re-examine the items performance in distinguishing between adolescents in clinical groups and normal adolescents in independent samples. These limitations resulted in the basic clinical scales continuing to be heterogeneous and multidimensional scales with extensive item overlap. These characteristics, in turn, resulted in the continuation of high levels of intercorrelation between MMPI-A basic scales that reflected substantial limitations in the discriminant validity of the scales. Archer and Klinefelter (1991), for example, factor analyzed MMPI-A items and scales found the presence of a large pervasive factor on both the item and scale level. Further, in terms of the MMPI-A Content scales, McCarthy and Archer (1998) performed a factor analysis of the 15 MMPI-A Content scales and found that one broad factor, corresponding to Welsh's General Maladjustment dimension, generally accounted for the majority of scale raw score variance. Further, the 478-items length of the MMPI-A, while shorter than the original test instrument, was identified as a significant disadvantage in comparison with shorter instruments that were available for the assessment of adolescents.

My involvement in developing the MMPI-A represented an attempt to adapt the original MMPI by means of statistically based refinements that serve to improve test performance in terms of internal and external validity. It also represented a movement toward a more conceptually based test, particularly reflected in the development of the 15 MMPI-A Content scales and the MMPI-A PSY-5 scales. The developers of the MMPI-A, including myself, purposefully avoided any attempt to substantially revise the basic clinical scales in order to maintain continuity with the research literature available for the original test instrument. Absent a clear vision concerning the potential goals and benefits of revising substantially the basic scales, a conservative approach appeared the most reasonable course.

MMPI-A-RF

The development of the MMPI-A-RF (Archer et al., 2016) began in 2007 with the appointment of an advisory committee to explore the potential for developing and adolescent instrument modeled after the approach utilized in developing the MMPI-2-RF (Archer, 2017). The steering committee consisted of Richard Handel and me at the Eastern Virginia Medical School, Yossi Ben-Porath at Kent State University, and Auke Tellegen at the University of Minnesota. The first step in evaluating the feasibility of a restructured form of the MMPI-A concerned the extent to which we could identify a clear demoralization factor in the MMPI-A and isolate the effects of this factor by developing a Demoralization Scale for the MMPI-A-RF. This process, combined with identifying the major distinctive or core components for each of the clinical scales, was crucial to the development of the Restructured Clinical (RC) scales for the MMPI-A-RF. Just as the MMPI-2 served as the template for the development of the MMPI-A, the MMPI-2-RF served as the template for the development of the MMPI-A-RF (Archer, 2017).

The final form of the MMPI-A-RF consists of 241 items drawn from the 478-items of the MMPI-A. The MMPI-A-RF normative sample is a subset of the MMPI-A normative sample. Specifically, 805 girls and 805 boys were drawn from the 1620 adolescents in the MMPI-A normative sample to generate a set of non-gendered norms for the MMPI-A-RF. The process for the development of the MMPI-A-RF, described in detail in the test manual (Archer et al., 2016), resulted in the creation of 48 scales including six validity scales and 42 substantive scales. Table 10.2 presents the MMPI-A-RF scale names, abbreviations, with short descriptions of each scale.

The 42 substantive scales of the MMPI-A-RF are organized into a three-tiered hierarchical structure that includes three Higher-Order (H-O) broad-based scales at the top of the hierarchy, nine Restructured Clinical (RC) scales at the mid-level, and 25 Specific Problem (SP) scales at the lowest level of the hierarchy corresponding to the most focused and narrow width scales. Item overlap was avoided for the scales within each hierarchical level. The SP scales are further organized into 4 general content groupings including five Somatic/Cognitive scales, nine Internalizing scales, six Externalizing scales, and five Interpersonal scales. While many of the SP scales have names identical to their counterparts on the MMPI-2-RF, it is important to note that the item composition of the scales typically differs, often substantively, from their MMPI-2-RF counterparts. It should also be noted that several of the MMPI-A-RF SP scales do not have a counterpart on the MMPI-2-RF, e.g., the Negative School Attitudes (NSA), Conduct Problems (CNP), and Negative Peer Influences (NPI) scales within the externalizing group of SP scales. The MMPI-A-RF also contains the Personality Psychopathology Five (PSY-5) scales developed by McNulty and Harkness based on their analyses of the 241 test items, and a set of 53 critical items representing 14 content categories based on a subset of the Forbey and Ben-Porath (1998) set of 81 critical items for the MMPI-A.

The central goal in the development of the MMPI-A-RF was to improve the discriminant validity of the MMPI-A-RF scales beyond levels achieved by the MMPI-A. This objective was achieved by reducing the ubiquitous and confounding influence of the demoralization factor and by eliminating the extensive item overlap that occurred within the MMPI-A basic scales. Archer (2006) noted that the creation of basic scales with

Table 10.2 MMPI-A-RF scale and descriptions

Validity Scales

VRIN-r (Variable Response Inconsistency) Random responding

TRIN-r (True Response Inconsistency) Fixed responding

CRIN (Combined Response Inconsistency)

Combination of fixed and random inconsistent responding

F-r (Infrequent Responses) Responses infrequent in the general population

L-r (Uncommon Virtues) Rarely claimed moral attributes or activities

K-r (Adjustment Validity) Uncommonly high level of psychological adjustments

Higher-Order (H-O) Scales

EID (Emotional/Internalizing Dysfunction) Problems associated with mood and affect

THD (Thought Dysfunction) Problems associated with disordered thinking

BXD (Behavioral/Externalizing Dysfunction) Problems associated with under-controlled behavior

Restructured Clinical (RC) Scales

RCd (Demoralization) General unhappiness and dissatisfaction

RC1 (Somatic Complaints) Diffuse physical health complaints

RC2 (Low Positive Emotions) A distinctive, core vulnerability factor in depression

RC3 (Cynicism) Non-self-referential beliefs that others are bad and not to be trusted

RC4 (Antisocial Behavior) Rule-breaking and irresponsible behavior

RC6 (Ideas of Persecution) Self-referential beliefs that others pose a threat

RC7 (Dysfunctional Negative Emotions) Maladaptive anxiety, anger, and irritability

RC8 (Aberrant Experiences) Unusual perceptions or thoughts associated with psychosis

RC9 (Hypomanic Activation) Over-activation, aggression, impulsivity, and grandiosity

Specific Problems (SP) Scales

Somatic/Cognitive Scales

MLS (Malaise) Overall sense of physical debilitation, poor health

GIC (Gastrointestinal Complaints) Nausea, recurring upset stomach, and poor appetite

HPC (Head Pain Complaints) Head and neck pain

NUC (Neurological Complaints) Dizziness, weakness, paralysis, and loss of balance

COG (Cognitive Complaints) Memory problems, difficulties concentrating

Internalizing Scales

HLP (Helplessness/Hopelessness) Belief that goals cannot be reached or problems solved

SFD (Self-Doubt) Lack of self-confidence, feelings of uselessness

NFC (Inefficacy) Belief that one is indecisive and inefficacious)

OCS (Obsessions/Compulsions) Varied obsessional and compulsive behaviors

STW (Stress/Worry) Preoccupation with disappointments, difficulty with time pressure

AXY (Anxiety) Pervasive anxiety, frights, frequent nightmares

ANP (Anger Proneness) Easily angered, impatient with others

BRF (Behavior-Restricting Fears) Fears that significantly inhibit normal behavior

SPF (Specific Fears) Multiple specific fears

Externalizing Scales
  NSA (Negative School Attitudes) Negative attitudes and beliefs about school
  ASA (Antisocial Attitudes) Various antisocial beliefs and attitudes
  CNP (Conduct Problems) Difficulties at school and at home, stealing
  SUB (Substance Abuse) Current and past misuse of alcohol and drugs
  NPI (Negative Peer Influence) Affiliation with negative peer group
  AGG (Aggression) Physically aggressive, violent behavior
Interpersonal Scales
  FML (Family Problems) Conflictual family relationships
  IPP (Interpersonal Passivity) Being unassertive and submissive
  SAV (Social Avoidance) Avoiding or not enjoying social events
  SHY (Shyness) Feeling uncomfortable and anxious around others
  DSF (Disaffiliativeness) Disliking people and being around them
Personality Psychopathology Five (PSY-5) Scales
  AGGR-r (Aggressiveness-Revised) Instrumental, goal-directed aggression
  PSYC-r (Psychoticism-Revised) Disconnection from reality
  DISC-r (Disconstraint-Revised) Under-controlled behavior
  NEGE-r (Negative Emotionality/Neuroticism-Revised) Anxiety, insecurity, worry and fear
  INTR-r (Introversion/Low Positive Emotionality-Revised) Social disengagement and anhedonia

---

extensive item overlap, heterogeneous content, and the pervasive influence of a shared first factor are attributable, at least in part, to the criterion keying method used by Hathaway and McKinley in the development of the MMPI basic scales. While scales heavily influenced by the demoralization factor might still be expected to show strong evidence of convergent validity as reflected in high correlations with predicted external criteria, such scales also might be anticipated to result in more limited discriminant validity, i.e., higher than anticipated correlations with measures of unrelated constructs. The MMPI-A-RF reduced the measurement redundancy that occurred among the MMPI-A basic scales by isolating the demoralization factor and reducing the influence of that factor on the "seed" or "core" components of the basic scales. This process, in turn, resulted in shorter RC scales, in comparison to the MMPI-A basic scales, with comparable levels of convergent validity but substantially improved discriminant validity values.

The MMPI-A-RF also makes a substantial break with MMPI precedent in terms of moving away from reliance on clinical scales based on the categories of mental disorder created by Kraepelin (1921) to a contemporary model of psychopathology that is reflected in a hierarchical organization of *dimensional* constructs ranging from very broad constructs to more narrowly focused constructs. The problems with categorical diagnostic models of psychopathology are well known and documented.

These issues include the high occurrence of comorbidity, or the extensive co-occurrence of diagnoses for an individual, particularly frequent among the personality disorder diagnoses. Limitations also involve the heterogeneity of the individuals included within a single diagnostic category that is produced by the often quite diverse combination of signs and symptoms that may be used to reach the necessary number of criteria to warrant that diagnosis. In addition to the problems inherent in the traditional diagnostic system, it became clear soon after the publication of the original MMPI that the test instrument was of quite limited usefulness in predicting to psychiatric diagnosis. Indeed, as noted by Graham (2012), the reasons that the MMPI was not particularly useful in terms of its original purpose of differential diagnosis, i.e., discriminating individuals in various psychiatric categories, may be attributed to several factors. Graham cited the high intercorrelations among the MMPI basic clinical scales, the extensive degree of item overlap in the scales, and the inherent limitations and lack of reliability found in traditional psychiatric diagnosis.

The MMPI-A-RF employs a new paradigm on the nature of psychopathology that is much more consistent with contemporary models. Specifically, the MMPI-A-RF scales reflect a hierarchical organization of dimensions of psychopathology, ranging from the broad Higher-Order (H-O) scales, through the more narrowly focused Restructured Clinical (RC) scales, to the most narrowly focused Specific Problem (SP) scales at the bottom or third level the of the hierarchy. This hierarchical organization of dimensional constructs, ranging from relatively broad to relatively narrow, reflects modern thinking about psychopathology and how psychopathology is viewed in contemporary theories. Figure 10.1 displays the substantive scales of the MMPI-A-RF organized into these three hierarchical levels.

My involvement in the MMPI-A-RF project reflected my own evolution from a "radical empiricist" in my early career as reflected in Paul Meehl's early writings to a researcher who places primary reliance on statistical methods strongly guided by an underlying conceptual framework. The conceptual emphasis in the MMPI-A-RF included efforts to carefully define key or core elements of target constructs used to develop scales and the use of a hierarchical organization to represent the interrelationship of scales within the test instrument. My involvement in the MMPI-A-RF also reflected the culmination of four decades of my research focus on various forms of, and issues related to, the MMPI. Finally, in keeping with the theme of this chapter, it is also a tribute to the effects of Charles Spielberger's mantra about developing a *program* of interconnected research studies that seek to systematically advance the field of inquiry.

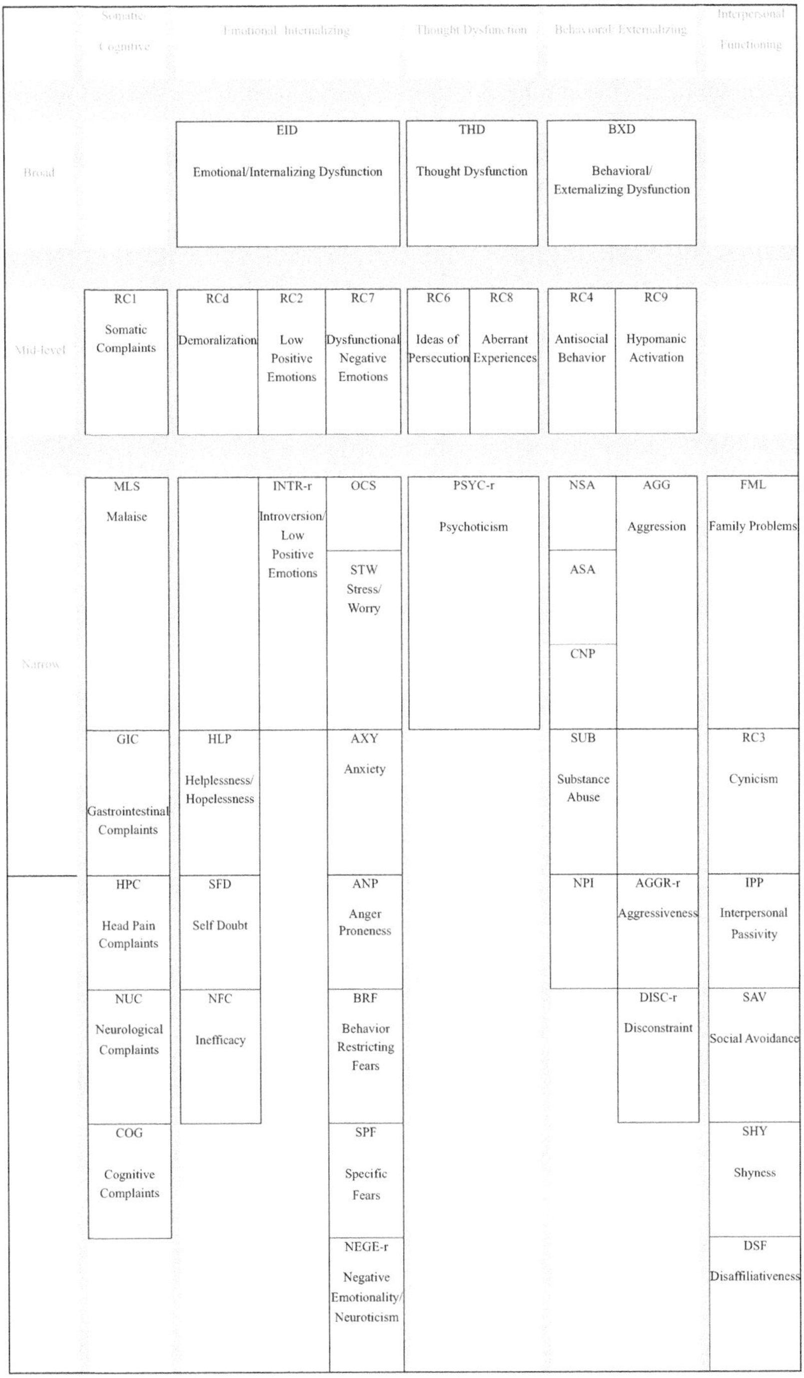

	Somatic/Cognitive	Emotional/Internalizing				Thought Dysfunction		Behavioral/Externalizing		Interpersonal Functioning

Broad

EID — Emotional/Internalizing Dysfunction	THD — Thought Dysfunction	BXD — Behavioral/Externalizing Dysfunction

Mid-level

RC1 Somatic Complaints	RCd Demoralization	RC2 Low Positive Emotions	RC7 Dysfunctional Negative Emotions	RC6 Ideas of Persecution	RC8 Aberrant Experiences	RC4 Antisocial Behavior	RC9 Hypomanic Activation

Narrow

Somatic/Cognitive	Emotional/Internalizing		Thought Dysfunction	Behavioral/Externalizing		Interpersonal Functioning
MLS — Malaise	INTR-r — Introversion/Low Positive Emotions	OCS	PSYC-r — Psychoticism	NSA	AGG — Aggression	FML — Family Problems
		STW — Stress/Worry		ASA		
				CNP		
GIC — Gastrointestinal Complaints	HLP — Helplessness/Hopelessness	AXY — Anxiety		SUB — Substance Abuse		RC3 — Cynicism
HPC — Head Pain Complaints	SFD — Self Doubt	ANP — Anger Proneness		NPI	AGGR-r — Aggressiveness	IPP — Interpersonal Passivity
NUC — Neurological Complaints	NFC — Inefficacy	BRF — Behavior Restricting Fears			DISC-r — Disconstraint	SAV — Social Avoidance
COG — Cognitive Complaints		SPF — Specific Fears				SHY — Shyness
		NEGE-r — Negative Emotionality/Neuroticism				DSF — Disaffiliativeness

Figure 10.1 Overview of the MMPI-A-RF scales organized into three hierarchical levels

Summary

The focus of this chapter has been on the influence of Paul Meehl, Charles Spielberger, and Auke Tellegen on my thinking about personality assessment, my involvement in the application of the MMPI with adolescents, and my role in the development of the MMPI-A and the MMPI-A-RF I have spent over 40 years researching and using the various forms of the MMPI with adolescents and adults. From the original publication of the MMPI in 1942 until the publication of the MMPI-A in 1992, the original form was widely used with adolescents. This practice resulted in several benefits as well as significant problems when adolescents were assessed with an instrument designed primarily for adults. From 1992 until 2016, the MMPI-A was the only form of the MMPI that was specifically designed for use with adolescents. Since late 2016, there have been two forms of the MMPI available for use with adolescents, i.e., the MMPI-A (based on the structure of the MMPI-2) and the MMPI-A-RF (developed from the MMPI-2-RF). My research career has been heavily involved with the application of these tests to understanding the developmental issues and forms of psychopathology experienced by adolescents (e.g., Archer, 2005). I have been extremely fortunate to have had the opportunity to become involved with a psychometric instrument of sufficient complexity to maintain my curiosity across these many years.

Although the focus of this chapter has been on the influence of Paul Meehl, Charles Spielberger, and Auke Tellegen, I would certainly be remiss if I did not mention several other individuals who were invaluable in supporting the development of my career and research program. Mr. Raymont Gordon and Mr. David Elkins served for many years as my research assistants at the Eastern Virginia Medical School and between them were involved in all my research program during my 34 years at EVMS. Ms. Scheryl Chadwick's service as my administrative assistant was invaluable in facilitating our progress on numerous research projects. It has also been my privilege to collaborate with Dr. Richard Handel, my colleague and fellow personality assessment enthusiast (and American Civil War buff) at the Eastern Virginia Medical School.

The family of Frank Harrell Redwood generously created an endowed professorship at EVMS that served to support my research and academic activities for many years at EVMS. Ms. Beverly Kaemmer at the University of Minnesota Press also provided grant support, encouragement, and access to invaluable data sources for our MMPI research projects. Finally, I would like to express my deepest gratitude for the support and long-standing patience of my wife, Dr. Linda R. Archer, and my daughter, Dr. Elizabeth M. Wheeler.

References

Alperin, J. J., Archer, R. P., & Coates, G. D. (1996). Development and effects of an MMPI-A K-correction procedure. *Journal of Personality Assessment, 67*, 155–168.

Archer, R. P. (1984). Use of the MMPI with adolescents: A review of salient issues. *Clinical Psychology Review, 4,* 241–251.

Archer, R. P. (1987). *Using the MMPI with adolescents.* Hillsdale, NJ: Lawrence Erlbaum Associates.

Archer, R. P. (1997a). Future directions for the MMPI-A: Research and clinical issues. *Journal of Personality Assessment, 68,* 95–109.

Archer, R. P. (2005). Implications of MMPI/MMPI-A findings for understanding adolescent development and psychopathology. *Journal of Personality Assessment, 8,* 257–270.

Archer, R. P. (2006). A perspective on the Restructured Clinical (RC) scale project. *Journal of Personality Assessment, 87(2),* 179–185.

Archer, R. P. (2017). *Assessing adolescent psychopathology: MMPI-A/MMPI-A-RF.* New York: Routledge.

Archer, R. P., Belevich, J. K. S., & Elkins, D. E. (1994). Item-level and scale level factor structures of the MMPI-A. *Journal of Personality Assessment, 62,* 332–345.

Archer, R.P., Buffington-Vollum, J.K., Stredny, R.V., & Handel, R.W. (2006). A survey of psychological test use patterns among forensic psychologists. *Journal of Personality Assessment, 87,* 84–94.

Archer, R. P., & Elkins, D. E. (1999). Identification of random responding on the MMPI-A. *Journal of Personality Assessment, 73,* 407–421.

Archer, R. P., Handel, R. W., Ben-Porath, Y. S., & Tellegen, A. (2016a). *Minnesota Multiphasic Personality Inventory – Adolescent – Restructured Form (MMPI-A-RF): Administration, scoring, interpretation, and technical manual.* Minneapolis: University of Minnesota Press.

Archer, R. P., Handel, R. W., Ben-Porath, Y. S., & Tellegen, A. (2016b). *Minnesota Multiphasic Personality Inventory – Adolescent – Restructured Form (MMPI-A-RF): User's guide for reports.* Minneapolis: University of Minnesota Press.

Archer, R.P., Handel, R.W., & Lynch, K.D. (2001). The effectiveness of MMPI-A items in discriminating between normative and clinical samples. *Journal of Personality Assessment, 77,* 420–435.

Archer, R. P., & Klinefelter, D. (1991). MMPI factor analytic findings for adolescents: Item- and scale-level factor structures. *Journal of Personality Assessment, 57,* 356–367.

Archer, R. P., Maruish, M., Imhof, E. A., & Piotrowski, C. (1991). Psychological test usage with adolescent clients: 1990 survey findings. *Professional Psychology: Research and Practice, 22,* 247–252.

Archer, R. P., & Newsom, C. R. (2000). Psychological test usage with adolescent clients: Survey update. *Assessment, 7,* 227–235.

Baum, L.J., Archer, R.P., Forbey, J.D., & Handel, R.W. (2009). A review of the Minnesota Multiphasic Personality Inventory-Adolescent (MMPI-A) and the Millon Adolescent Clinical Inventory (MACI) with an emphasis on juvenile justice samples. *Assessment, 16,* 384–400.

Ben-Porath, Y. S., & Tellegen, A. (2020). *Minnesota Multiphasic Personality Inventory-3 (MMPI-3): Manual for administration, scoring, and interpretation.* Minneapolis: University of Minnesota Press.

Butcher, J. N., Dahlstrom, W. G., Graham, J. R., Tellegen, A., & Kaemmer, B. (1989). *MMPI-2 (Minnesota Multiphasic Personality Inventory-2): Manual for administration and scoring.* Minneapolis: University of Minnesota Press.

Butcher, J. N., Williams, C. L., Graham, J. R., Archer, R. P., Tellegen, A., Ben-Porath, Y. S., & Kaemmer, B. (1992). *MMPI-A (Minnesota Multiphasic*

Personality Inventory - Adolescent): Manual for administration, scoring, and interpretation. Minneapolis: University of Minnesota Press.

Fontaine, J. L., Archer, R. P., Elkins, D. E., & Johansen, J. (2001). The effects of MMPI-A T-score elevation on classification accuracy for normal and clinical adolescent samples. *Journal of Personality Assessment, 76,* 264–281.

Forbey, J. D., & Ben-Porath, Y. S. (1998). *A critical item set for the MMPI-A (MMPI-2/MMPI-A test reports #4).* Minneapolis: University of Minnesota Press.

Friedman, A. F., Lewak, R., Nichols, D. S., & Webb, J. T. (2001). *Psychological assessment with the MMPI–2.* Mahwah, NJ: Lawrence Erlbaum Associates, Inc.

Graham, J.R. (2012). *MMPI-2: Assessing personality and psychopathology* (5th ed.). New York: University of Oxford Press, Inc.

Hall, C. S., & Lindzey, G. (1965). *Theories of personality.* New York: John Wiley and Sons.

Hathaway, S. R. (1960). Foreword. In W. G. Dahlstrom, G. S. Welsh, & L. E. Dahlstrom (Eds.), *An MMPI handbook: Vol. 1. Clinical interpretation* (pp. xiii–iv). Minneapolis: University of Minnesota Press.

Hathaway, S. R., & McKinley, J. C. (1940). A multiphasic personality schedule (Minnesota): I. Construction of the schedule. *Journal of Psychology, 10,* 249–254.

Hathaway, S. R., & McKinley, J. C. (1942). A multiphasic personality schedule (Minnesota):III. The measurement of symptomatic depression. *Journal of Psychology, 14,* 73–84.

Hathaway, S. R., & McKinley, J. C. (1943). *The Minnesota multiphasic personality inventory* (rev. ed.). Minneapolis: University of Minnesota Press.

Herkov, M. J., Archer, R. P., & Gordon, R. A. (1991). MMPI response sets among adolescents: An evaluation of the limitations of the Subtle-Obvious subscales. *Psychological Assessment: A Journal of Consulting and Clinical Psychology, 3,* 424–426.

Kraepelin, E. (1921). Ueber Entwurtzelung. *Zeitschrift fur die Gesamte Nuerologie und Psychiatrie, 44,* 921–928.

McCarthy, L., & Archer, R. P. (1998). Factor structure of the MMPI-A content scales: Item-level and scale-level findings. *Journal of Personality Assessment, 7,* 84–97.

McNulty, J. L., Harkness, A. R., Ben-Porath, Y. S., & Williams, C. L. (1997). Assessing the personality psychopathology five (PSY-5) in adolescents: New MMPI-A scales. *Psychological Assessment, 9,* 250–259.

McKinley, J. C., & Hathaway, S. R. (!944). The MMPI: V. Hysteria, hypomania, and psychopathic deviate. *Journal of Applied Psychology, 28,* 153–174.

Meehl, P. E. (1945). The dynamics of "structured" personality tests. *Journal of Clinical Psychology, 1,* 295–303.

Meehl, P. E. (1954). *Clinical versus statistical prediction: A theoretical analysis and a review of the evidence.* Minneapolis: University of Minnesota Press.

Meehl, P. E. (1956). Wanted: A good cookbook. *American Psychologist, 11,* 263–272.

Meehl, P. E. (1957). When shall we use our heads instead of the formula? *Journal of Counseling Psychology, 4,* 268–273.

Meehl, P. E. (1971). Prefatory comments to the dynamics of "structured" personality tests. In L.D. Goodstein & R.I. Lanyon (Eds.), *Readings in Personality Assessment* (pp. 245–253). New York: Wiley.

Meehl, P. E. (1973). *Psychodiagnosis: Selected papers.* Minneapolis: University of Minnesota Press

Meehl, P. E. (1986). Causes and effects of my disturbing little book. *Journal of Personality Assessment, 50,* 370–375.

Meehl, P. E., & Hathaway, S. R. (1946). The K factor as a suppressor variable in the MMPI. *Journal of Applied Psychology, 30,* 525–564.

Newsom, C. R., Archer, R. P., Trumbetta, S., & Gottesman, I. I. (2003). Changes in adolescent response patterns on the MMPI/MMPI-A across four decades. *Journal of Personality Assessment, 81,* 74–84.

Pancoast, D. L., & Archer, R. P. (1988). MMPI adolescent norms: Patterns and trends across 4 decades. *Journal of Personality Assessment, 52,* 691–706.

Sherwood, N. E., Ben-Porath, Y. S., & Williams, C. L. (1997). The MMPI-A content component scales: Development, psychometric characteristics, and clinical application. *MMPI-2/MMPI-A Test Report 3.* Minneapolis: University of Minnesota Press.

Speilberger, C. D., Gorsuch, R.L., Lushene, P.R., Vang, P.R., & Jacobs, G.A. (1983). *Manual for the state-trait anxiety inventory.* Palo Alto, CA: Consulting Psychologist Press.

Tellegen, A., & Ben-Porath, Y. S. (1985). Structures of mood and personality and their relevance to assessing anxiety with emphasis on self-report. In A. H. Tuma & J.D. Maser (Eds.), *Anxiety and anxiety disorders* (pp. 681–706). Hillsdale, NJ: Lawrence Erlbaum.

Tellegen, A., & Ben-Porath, Y. S. (2008). *Minnesota multiphasic personality inventory-2 restructured form: Manual for administration, scoring, and interpretation.* Minneapolis: University of Minnesota Press.

Tellegen, A., Ben-Porath, Y. S., McNulty, J. L., Arbisi, P. A., Graham, J. R., & Kaemmer, B. (2003). *The MMPI-2 restructured clinical scales: Development, validation, and interpretation.* Minneapolis: University of Minnesota Press.

Welsh, G. S. (1956). Factor dimensions A and R. In G. S. Welsh & W. G. Dahlstrom (Eds.), *Basic readings on the MMPI in psychology and medicine* (pp. 264–281). Minneapolis: University of Minnesota Press.

11 It Takes a Village to Raise an MMPI Author[1]

Yossef S. Ben-Porath

I began "practicing" personality assessment in my adolescence. No, I did not know the term, let alone use it to describe what I was doing. And, of course, I was not conducting formal assessments; but in the tenth grade, I compiled a list of 50 or so classmates and proceeded to write a description of each individual. Unfortunately, the list and paragraph-long descriptions are long gone. Less than a year after they were written, my family moved half-way across the world. Perhaps, I complied the list as a way to "stay in touch" with my classmates, most of whom, as it turned out, I would never see again. Be that as it may, as I recall, my observations included attributes such as how friendly and dependable they were, whether they were well-liked and why, whether they had or lacked confidence, how studious they were, and so on. These brief narratives most likely included additional features that I have forgotten. What I do recall rather vividly is writing them in a notebook. The writing process was free-flowing – no grid or checklists – but there certainly was a comparative aspect to my first exercise in capturing individual differences.

How did a 15-year-old, amateur personality assessor become a professor who specializes in the assessment of personality and psychopathology with the MMPI? Chris Hopwood invited me to explore this question via my first (and likely only) effort at autobiography. I begin with a brief recounting of my childhood and adolescence, followed by relevant experiences during my college and graduate school years, and then my 30-year (to date) professional career.

Childhood, adolescence, and early adulthood

Change was a constant while I was growing up. I was born in Jerusalem, Israel, the oldest child of Moshe and Edna Ben-Porath. After surviving Nazi occupation of his native Bukovina, my father's family fled the region and settled in Romania when the Soviets assumed control of his hometown, Chernivtsi (aka Chernovitz) following World War II. Two years later, at the age of 15, he boarded a ship bound illegally for British-controlled Palestine, seeking to fulfill his Zionist dream. The ship was intercepted by the British and its passengers interred in a camp in

DOI: 10.4324/9781003036302-11

Cyprus. As an unaccompanied minor, my father was allowed after three months to complete his journey, and he was placed by the Jewish Agency on a kibbutz on the shores of the Sea of Galilee. His brief experience as a kibbutznik came to an end several months later, with the outbreak of Israel's war of independence, when at the age of 16 he joined the fledgling Israeli Defense Force. Two years and many battles later, upon his discharge from military service, my father completed his high school equivalency and then enrolled at the Hebrew University of Jerusalem where he earned a Bachelor's and then a Master's degree in Physics.

My mom, the daughter of Zionists who had emigrated to the land of Israel in the 1920s, was born in Jerusalem. After completing her military service, she too enrolled at the Hebrew University, where she earned Bachelor's and Master's degrees in Microbiology. While still in school, both my parents worked at Hadassah Hospital, my dad as a physicist in the Radiology department and my mom as a microbiologist. Their birthdays were one day apart. They met when their respective co-workers planned a breakroom celebration of their birthdays for the same time. They married three months later, and I was born ten months after that.

A year later, we made the first of many moves as a family. My dad received a fellowship to study radiological techniques at MD Anderson and we spent the second year of my life in Houston, TX. We then moved back to Jerusalem for the next four years (my younger sister was born shortly after our return), until we moved yet again, this time to the Chicago, IL area where my dad obtained his PhD in Nuclear Physics, specializing in nuclear medicine at Loyola University, and my mom earned her PhD in Microbiology, specializing in virology at the University of Illinois at Chicago.

I celebrated my sixth birthday onboard the ship we took from Israel to the United States in the middle of my kindergarten year. About a month after our arrival, my parents were called to a meeting with my teacher, who somberly informed them that I would not be able to move on to the first grade owing to an abysmal score I had received on the readiness exam all kindergarten students were administered. She recommended that I be enrolled in special education classes. My father liked to recount how when he asked to see the test, he observed that I had scored approximately 40% on a four-option multiple choice exam administered in a language that I did not speak. He pointed out to the teacher that I had in fact performed well above the expected guessing level of 25% correct.

I did wind up getting promoted to the first grade. By the fall, we had moved to a different school district and my English had improved considerably, although I do recall wondering why my school was run by what I understood to be a prince (rather than principal). That misunderstanding was quickly cleared up. We were, as it turned out, the only Jewish family in the district. I recall my teachers making a point to incorporate some of the Jewish holidays in classroom decorations and even inviting my parents to come tell my classmates about Hannukah and Passover. By the end of our four and a half years in Chicagoland, English was no longer a problem, however, despite my parents' best efforts, I had forgotten most of my Hebrew. I did gain a baby brother ten years my junior a few months prior to our return.

We moved back to Israel once more, this time to a new city, Haifa. I found myself beginning the fifth grade understanding very little of what was said in class, trying to make new friends with whom I could not readily communicate. With daily tutoring, by the end of the fifth grade I had caught up with my classmates. I had also made some new friends. My dad began working for a company that manufactured medical imaging equipment. My mom was hired to establish a new Virology lab at the largest regional hospital. Both began teaching at the medical school affiliated with this hospital. The six years we lived in Haifa were the longest consecutive period of residence in the same city throughout my childhood. Some of the friends I made during this time remain among my closest. It was at the end of this period that I conducted the personality assessment exercise I described earlier in this chapter.

Our next stop was back in the United States; this time in northern New Jersey, approximately a 30-minute drive from New York City. My dad was tasked with establishing a US subsidiary of the technology company he worked for and my mom was hired as a visiting researcher at Roche Laboratories. I was 16 years old and completed my last two years of high school in New Jersey. From the rather tame environment of Haifa, I found myself thrust into the anything but tame mid-1970s of the greater NYC region. For once, language was not an obstacle, as I had retained my English, and as an avid reader (of mysteries and adventures back then) even developed it further while in Israel. I was not, however, a stellar student (too many distractions?). During my senior year I did have a life-changing experience. Inspired, at least in part, by my early informal assessment exercise, I enrolled in a psychology class, and decided that was the career I would pursue.

In one important way, my senior year was different from that of most my friends and classmates. To be allowed to leave Israel at the age of 16, I had to commit to return upon graduating from high school to begin my compulsory military service. Although the plan all along was that our family would move back to Israel at the end of our two years in New Jersey, my parents recommended that I apply to colleges and use my acceptance as evidence of college aptitude when the time came to apply again after completing my service. I was accepted as a Psychology major at several schools, but in the end had to inform them that I would not be enrolling.

As might be imagined, transitioning from high school life in the US during roaring 1970s to the military required some adjustment. Following an interesting stint on a desert island, during the latter half of my three-year service I was assigned to a liaison office in my adopted hometown of Haifa. My duties there included serving as a go-between for military personnel and their families. I would take phone calls from worried parents who had not heard from their sons or daughters (no cell phones back then), or in more serious cases assist families with getting their soldiers home in the event of illness or the loss of a loved one. Toward the end of my service, I was assigned to a team tasked with going to soldiers' homes to notify their loved ones when tragedy struck, and their son or daughter had lost their life. We then accompanied the families through the funeral process. These experiences were formidable and challenging on many levels. I vividly recall being struck by the wide range of reactions to this devastating news and noting that though cultural and religious factors played a significant role in these variations, they could not entirely explain sometimes strong intrafamilial differences. This opportunity to witness people coping with extreme stress and grief was illuminating. It solidified my interest in understanding individual differences.

To summarize my childhood, adolescence, and early adulthood: Change was a constant. The moves back and forth between Israel and the United States resulted in my being both bilingual and bicultural, feeling equally at home in both countries, and missing some of the unique features of each, while away from the other.

Undergraduate experiences

After completing my three-year compulsory military service, I took a year off to clear my head and go through the process of applying to colleges in Israel. I spent several months visiting the United States during this period, catching up with high school friends and traveling to different parts of the country. At the end of the college search process, I decided to attend the University of Haifa, where I had been admitted as a double major in Psychology and Political Science. Perhaps to compensate for late starts owing to military service, most undergraduate degree programs in Israel can be completed in three years. The year was 1981, I was 22 years old, not at all uncommon for first year students in Israel.

During my first semester, I enrolled in an Introduction to Psychology class taught by Shlomo Breznitz, a world-renowned stress researcher and an amazing instructor. His lectures were fascinating, delivered in a captivating style with no notes or any other cues. He would enter the classroom and deliver a well-structured, content-rich lecture on the many facets of psychology. Visual aids consisted of occasional chalkboard notations or figures he would draw. The textbook was an early edition of Hilgard et al. A random (or perhaps not) recollection from that class stemmed from my English-language facility. Just about all our textbooks were from the US, and my fluency in English was an advantage. My classmates would occasionally request assistance with unfamiliar terms. One such occasion involved the confusing term "inventory". My classmate had looked it up in in an English-Hebrew dictionary and could not understand how a list of supplies or the process of counting goods in a business was related to psychological testing. I explained the meaning of the term in this context. Interestingly, she did not request help with the term "multiphasic". This was my first, albeit brief encounter with the MMPI.

The University of Haifa Psychology Department had a subject pool. Intro students were required to participate. I signed up for an experiment run by Breznitz's lab, a study of decision-making under stress. The stressor involved a cold suppressor test, in which the participant's hand was immersed in a container of ice water for as long as could they could tolerate. I struck up a conversation with the RA who ran the experiment, an advanced student who after the session explained the procedure and paradigm and showed me around the lab. We stayed in touch and at the end of the semester I was enrolled as the newest RA in the lab. I did not have much contact with Breznitz, but the opportunity to work with advanced undergraduate and graduate students was invaluable. I learned that to earn a PhD in psychology (which I had already determined was my educational goal) would most likely require attending graduate school in the United States, and that research experience would boost my chances for admission. I remained active in the lab for the remainder of my undergraduate years, culminating in completion of an honor's thesis, which eventually was my second publication (Keinan et al., 1987). Another critical tip I picked up in the lab was that being able to run statistical analyses would significantly bolster my chances of graduate school admission and, importantly, the prospects of employment as a research assistant. I followed this advice and became well-versed in statistical analyses using SAS on an IBM mainframe computer.

By the end of my second year of college I knew I wanted to pursue PhD studies in the United States. Although fascinated by the stress research on which I was now working as an RA, I was leaning toward specializing in Industrial Organizational (I/O) psychology. During the first semester of my second year of studies, I had taken a psychological testing class, and became fascinated by the concept and mechanics of measuring individual differences. My interest in I/O psychology stemmed from the instructor's emphasis in the class, which reflected his background and training. This interest was short-lived. My plans, and the ultimate trajectory of my career were to change during my third and final undergraduate year.

Psychology majors at the University of Haifa were required complete a year-long practical experience during their senior year. I was assigned to a psychiatric hospital. Each student was paired with a patient with whom we visited once a week. A psychologist working at the facility served as our supervisor with whom we met individually, also on a weekly basis. I was paired with an 18-year-old man, I will call him "M," who had been an inpatient in a locked unit at the facility for several months by the time we first met. I was told he had been diagnosed with paranoid schizophrenia. Our first several meetings were awkward. M was reluctant to speak, and I did not know what to say. My supervisor suggested I attempt to engage him with card games, which did serve to break the ice. A few weeks into my experience M was granted permission to leave the unit (but remain on hospital grounds) in my company. We would walk and talk. He began to open up about his family and how abusive they had been to him in his childhood. M told me about his twin brother who had been beaten to death by his father, and how he, himself, would be locked in a closet for weeks. He explained that years of such maltreatment led eventually to his hospitalization.

My supervisor was psychodynamically oriented. I would spend our meetings describing that week's encounter and she would inquire about my feelings and thoughts. Several months into the experience, she startled me with a question. After I recounted a particularly harrowing tale of abuse M had shared, she asked me whether I was certain it was true. She went on to clarify she was not asking whether M believed it to be true, rather, she asked about my certainty in the story's truthfulness. I replied rather indignantly that I had no reason to question M's honesty. She re-iterated that she also was not questioning his honesty and asked whether I thought it possible that M was being perfectly honest, while at the same time his story was untrue. My confusion soon turned to anger as she went on to share with me details from M's chart, which quickly made clear that much of M's family history as I had come to believe it, including that he had had a twin brother, was untrue. I was angry at M, and at my supervisor. I asked her why she allowed me to be misled as I had been for so long. She explained that there could be no better way for me to learn about the power and impact of delusional thinking. Just as I believed and was horrified by M's childhood experiences, so did and was he. It took a while for me to forgive her for having "tricked" me in this manner. With time, I came to appreciate this as one of the most formidable experiences of my clinical training.

By the second semester of my senior year, I had decided to take a gap year before applying to graduate school. Owing in part to my practical ex-perience, I had begun to question my choice of I/O psychology as a career. I was very much looking forward to taking an Abnormal psychology class that semester, believing it would help me decide between I/O and Clinical psychology. To my great fortune, the instructor was a newly minted PhD, Moshe Almagor, who had just joined the faculty after completing his doc-toral studies at the University of Minnesota, where his mentor was Auke Tellegen. Clinical psychology in Israel at the time remained mainly psy-chodynamic. Here was a young, ponytailed professor, who taught psycho-pathology from the perspective of clinical science. When he announced, early on, he was looking for volunteers to work with him on a mood study I seized the opportunity. The year was 1984. Moshe and I remain close friends and research collaborators to this day.

The study involved a cross-cultural replication of Tellegen's two-factor mood model, using daily mood ratings provided by 85 participants over the course of 45 days. The research I had been involved with in the stress lab, including my honors thesis, was experimental. The mood study was my first encounter with data collection in the "real world" and with correlational research. For my gap year, Almagor and I decided to focus on a study of the association between personality and mood, using Tellegen's Multidimensional Personality Questionnaire (MPQ). This required that we translate the MPQ to Hebrew. Thus, I was an MPQ researcher before I was an MMPI researcher.

There is no better way to gain an appreciation for the nuances of personality test items than to endeavor to translate them into another language, for use in a different culture. We were able to directly adapt nearly all the (then) 300 MPQ items but three that involved snowstorms, frozen lakes, and tornadoes, all foreign experiences to Israeli test takers. These items were replaced with ones dealing with more familiar phenomena – sandstorms and cliffs. Seeing my name on the mimeographed copies of the translated test booklet was extraordinarily rewarding and motivating. My mind was made up, I wanted to get my PhD in Clinical psychology, and to specialize in the study of personality and mood. In other words, I wanted to follow in my undergraduate mentor's footsteps.

The first step would involve graduate school application. The process began early in the fall of 1984. I wound up invited to interview at several programs, but my top choice did not conduct interviews back then. It did require that you submit, along with your application package, your MMPI profile. The absence of an official Hebrew translation exempted me form this requirement. I was able to conduct some interviews by phone and decided to travel to the United States for others that were scheduled for the end of March. While at one of these schools I learned that I had been offered admission to the University of Minnesota's clinical program. As I was already in the United States, I decided to visit the school before making a commitment. I called and spoke with the clinical training director, Gloria Leon, and arranged to visit the first two days of April. I arrived on April 1, and found the twin cities blanketed in white, the result of a spring snowstorm. The visit went well and solidified my decision, I would get my degree at the University of Minnesota.

Graduate studies (and one)

It also snowed my first day of graduate school, in September 1985. The day began with introductions; my four classmates and I got to meet the core clinical faculty (in order of seniority): Paul Meehl, Norman Garmezy,

Auke Tellegen, James Butcher, Gloria Leon, and William Iacono. In addition to getting to meet each other, the purpose of these introductions was to assist the incoming class with our first task, deciding who we would like to worth with (Minnesota did not have a mentorship admission model at that time). I already knew I wanted to work with Tellegen; and scheduled a meeting with him the first week of classes. It has been an honor, and a true gift to be working with Auke ever since. Other noteworthy recollections of that first day are that Meehl essentially told us that unless we have a math minor with extensive experience with calculus, he would not be able to work with us. Butcher described a major project he was leading, a restandardization of the MMPI.

As an international student (it would be another 17 years before I became a US citizen), I was not eligible for most of the training fellowships available to graduate students in the department at the time. My parents were my primary funding source for the first year, but my dad advised I keep an eye out for opportunities. A life-changing one presented itself during my second quarter of studies at Minnesota.

During the second quarter that we took the first-year personality assessment class co-taught by Auke Tellegen and Jim Butcher. Tellegen taught the first three weeks of the course. He had us read Wiggins (1973) and covered some basic psychometrics. I recall particularly his emphasis on the impact of base rates and the importance of positive and negative predictive power. The rest of the course was dedicated to learning from Butcher all about the MMPI. The textbook was Graham (1977). The first mid-term during the MMPI portion of the class was considered a rite of passage in the clinical program. Among other minute details, we had to memorize the number of items on each of the Clinical Scales of the inventory.

The minute details behind us, we turned next to the art and science of MMPI interpretation. One day, Butcher told us we were in for a special treat, the author of our textbook would be visiting during our next class period. He was coming to town to testify in a high-profile court case. I had always been an avid newspaper reader. That is why I was aware of an ongoing murder trial involving the insanity defense. When Jack Graham attended our next class meeting, Butcher began the class as he usually did by handing out copies of an MMPI profile that we would be discussing that day. After we had gone through the usual process of considering the various scale and subscale scores, Butcher asked whether we thought anything was unique about the profile. I put two and two together and said I thought this looked like the MMPI of someone capable of brutal violence, perhaps even murder. Butcher and Graham exchanged a knowing look, but neither confirmed nor denied my "diagnosis."

I will never know whether my deep read of that MMPI profile had anything to do with this, but within a week or two of Graham's visit, Butcher stopped me in the hallway and said he had funding for a research assistant, but the position required familiarity with running SPSS analyses on a mainframe computer. As described earlier, during my undergraduate years I had learned how to use SAS on an IBM mainframe. I figured (correctly) that using SPSS can't be that different, and confidently assured Butcher that I was well qualified for the task. He hired me on the spot. To my good fortune, one of his advanced graduate students, Laura Keller, taught me what I needed to know about SPSS and the university's VAX mainframe computer. When Laura left for internship, I became the primary research assistant on the project, managing and analyzing several clinical datasets that Butcher had collected for the MMPI revision project. We also did some work with the normative sample after it had been put together by Grant Dahlstrom's team at the University of North Carolina.

Working on the MMPI restandardization project opened many doors for me. I will always be grateful to Jim for giving me this opportunity of a lifetime. One day, he told me that Jack Graham, Carolyn Williams, and he had been working on a set of content scales for the revised test and handed me a list of target scales and preliminary item assignments that they had agreed to. He asked that I run some item analyses. I identified for each of the provisional scales items that did not perform adequately. Next, we calculated correlations between the unassigned items and the provisional scales, and identified candidates for addition to the eventual scales, which were consistent in content with the targeted constructs. Using the clinical and normative datasets, I next ran reliability and validity analyses. Jim generously invited me to co-author the book introducing the MMPI-2 Content Scales.

Some time after I was hired to work on the project Auke Tellegen joined the restandardization committee, giving me the unexpected opportunity to work with him for the first, but certainly not the last time on the MMPI. I remembered that during our first-year personality assessment class Tellegen had described some of the shortcomings of the Clinical Scales and how he would go about addressing them. Later I would learn that the restandardization committee chose not to pursue these improvements, owing to concerns that updating both the test norms and the clinical scales may introduce too much change all at once. Instead, I worked with Tellegen on two of the major innovations of the MMPI-2, the uniform T scores, which we later introduced in an article (Tellegen & Ben-Porath, 1992), and development of the Variable Response Inconsistency (VRIN) and True Response Inconsistency (TRIN) scales, which were fashioned after similarly labeled scales he had developed for the MPQ.

The MMPI-2 was published in 1989, right around the time I completed my internship and earned my PhD. The University of Minnesota Internship Consortium was run by legendary neuropsychologist Manfred Meier and housed in the Department of Neurology of the University of Minnesota Medical School. Two six-month rotations, the first at a state hospital, the second at a community mental health center, were complemented by weekly didactics and monthly attendance at grand rounds for case conferences, where once, on a whim, I approached Paul Meehl and asked him what he was doing there (those who do not get the reference should look up "Paul Meehl case conferences"). The training was top notch, but without a doubt the greatest long-term benefit I reaped that year was the beginning of a life-long personal friendship and professional collaboration with my internship classmate Paul Arbisi.

Rather than go on the job market during internship, I decided to stay at Minnesota for another year, cobbling together an appointment as a Visiting Assistant Professor in the psychology department teaching three undergraduate classes, working on the MMPI project, and one day a week of post-doctoral clinical experience at the community mental health center where I had completed my second internship rotation. I also volunteered that year at the Minneapolis Walk-in Counseling Center. MMPI work now focused on development of the adolescent version of the inventory, the MMPI-A, and writing up MMPI-2 studies for publication. However, the most consequential experience I had that year was the beginning of my career-long involvement with continuing education. With the release of the MMPI-2, demand for training was high. Jim Butcher invited me to join the MMPI-2 Workshops and Symposium faculty, another opportunity for which I am grateful.

A primary task during my post-doctoral year was to find a job. I interviewed at a number of schools, and ultimately accepted an offer to join the faculty at Kent State University. My five years in Minnesota had been a period of intense intellectual development and professional growth. In addition to the experiences already described, I had the opportunity to take Paul Meehl's philosophy of science seminar, learn about psychophysiology from David Lykken (and have both Meehl and Lykken serve on my dissertation committee) and behavioral genetics from Matt McGue. I had the good fortune to interact with many highly talented graduate students, among them my classmates Anna Cerri, Paul Marshall, Niels Waller, and Marie Welborn, MMPI research mates Kyunghee Han, Laura Keller, Brad Roper, Wendy Slutske, and Nathan Weed, other students including Paul Arbisi, Alan Harkness, Scott Lilienfeld, and Carol Peterson, and many more who went on to pursue a range of successful careers. I also was able to continue to work with my undergraduate mentor Moshe Almagor, who taught in the psychology department each summer while I was there. But the time had come to leave the nest.

Kent State years

The chronology

I joined the Kent State faculty in August 1990. Chief among the factors that attracted me to Kent was the opportunity to collaborate with Jack Graham. We hit the ground running with a project he had begun to plan before I arrived, to collect data at what is now called Portage Path Behavioral Health, a large community mental health center that serves the Akron, Ohio region. Our goal was to conduct the first comprehensive empirical correlate study in decades; the first ever with the MMPI-2. Beginning in 1991, over a period of 21 months, every adult seeking services at the agency (who could) completed the MMPI-2 as part of their intake and was then followed over the course of their treatment. Intake workers provided their initial impressions, therapists identified treatment goals, completed a comprehensive rating form derived from the previous empirical correlate literature, and provided periodic updates on their clients' progress. We obtained valid MMPI-2 protocols and data on over 1,000 individuals. This dataset wound up being used in many doctoral dissertations, master's theses, journal articles, research monographs, and a comprehensive MMPI-2 empirical correlate book (Graham et al., 1999). Other comprehensive data collection projects launched in the 1990s included a chart review-based study of well over 2,000 psychiatric inpatients conducted in collaboration with Paul Arbisi, and a similarly designed investigation of several hundred criminal defendants. These datasets also proved to be very fruitful, yielding multiple studies and publications.

Funding for these and many other projects was provided by the MMPI Publisher, the University of Minnesota Press. Over the past 30 years, the Press has granted Kent State over 3.5 million dollars to conduct MMPI research, supporting the work and training of multiple post-docs, and dozens of graduate and undergraduate students. This funding was made possible by the long-time director of the Press's Test Division, Beverly Kaemmer. After taking the division's helm in the early 1980s, she negotiated an agreement with the test distributor (then, National Computer Systems, later renamed Pearson Clinical Assessment), which required that a proportion of the revenue generated annually by the MMPI would be dedicated to supporting a robust research and development program managed by the Press. The funds generated by this agreement were used first to develop the MMPI-2 in the 1980s, then to fund the comprehensive data collection projects just mentioned during the 1990s, and next to support efforts to modernize the MMPI, culminating in publication of the MMPI-3 in 2020. Dozens of more specifically focused research projects conducted throughout the United States were similarly funded by the Press. After decades of able leadership of the Test Division and management of the MMPI instruments, Bev retired in 2019.

In the late 1990s, Bev initiated an effort to update the MMPI-2 manual, which culminated in publication of the second edition, which I coauthored, in 2001. The updated manual incorporated new scales I had co-authored over the course of the 1990s, including the Infrequency Psychopathology (Fp) validity scale with Paul Arbisi, and the Personality Psychopathology-Five (PSY-5) scales with Alan Harkness and John McNulty. Fp was developed in response to Paul's experience as a psychologist working in the inpatient unit of the Minneapolis VA. After transitioning from the MMPI to the MMPI-2, he observed a dramatic increase in the proportion of seemingly invalid MMPI-2 protocols among his patients. We designed the Fp scale to be less sensitive to genuine psychopathology than F. Development of the PSY-5 Scales was initiated by Al. A research program he had begun as Auke Tellegen's advisee at the University of Minnesota led to the introduction of the first dimensional model of personality disorder-related psychopathology (Harkness & McNulty, 1994), presaging the very similar Alternative Model of Personality Disorder, introduced 20 years later in the DSM-5. In the early 1990s Al suggested that we develop MMPI-2 scales to assess these constructs. Fp and the PSY-5 scales were first published the same year (Arbisi & Ben-Porath, 1995; Harkness et al., 1995). By the time they were reviewed for inclusion in the MMPI-2 manual, a significant literature documenting their utility supported their addition to the test.

Another set of scales reviewed for the 2001 manual was developed by Auke Tellegen in the early to mid-1990s. I first saw Auke present these scales at an international MMPI meeting in Haifa, Israel in 1995. As described earlier, his proposed update of the MMPI Clinical Scales was rejected by the restandardization committee in the 1980s, owing to concerns about updating both the norms and the Clinical scales at the same time. Shortly after the MMPI-2 was published, Auke began implementing his proposal, yielding two sets of scales he called streamlined clinical scales and interpersonal scales. Although the scales appeared quite promising, at the time they were reviewed for inclusion in the 2001 manual empirical correlate data had yet to be established for these measures. After deciding to set them aside for the time being, Bev Kaemmer suggested that Auke and I use the MMPI-2 datasets collected with University of Minnesota Press funding at Kent to closely examine Auke's new scales.

The opportunity for another MMPI-related collaboration with Auke would have been more than sufficient for me to enthusiastically accept Bev's suggestion, which I did. However, by that time I had also become increasingly aware of the need to update the Clinical Scales. As described earlier, using the large and very detailed Portage Path (community mental health) dataset we collected in the early 1990s, Jack Graham, John McNulty, and I conducted a comprehensive MMPI-2 empirical correlate study. That project afforded me a look under the hood of the Clinical Scales, and this close-up view underscored some significant limitations, particularly insofar as their discriminant validity was concerned. Doubly motivated, I joined Auke in studying his new scales using our outpatient and inpatient datasets. We wound up making some final modifications to the streamlined Clinical Scales, which we eventually labeled the Restructured Clinical (RC) Scales. We also decided to set aside Auke's initial set of interpersonal scales for further work.

The RC Scales were added to the MMPI-2 in 2003. A research monograph (Tellegen et al., 2003) provided the rationale for, and a description of their development, detailed psychometric findings, and guidance for interpreting RC Scale findings in the context of the MMPI-2. My research team at Kent embarked on a series of RC Scale validation studies with samples representing a broad range of settings. This effort produced numerous peer-reviewed publications over the next several years. Some criticisms of the RC Scales were published as well. Auke and I, along with some of my research collaborators and students, provided data-based rebuttals.

While finalizing and studying the RC Scales, it became clear to Auke and me that the entire MMPI-2 could be improved substantially through a somewhat similar restructuring project. We began work toward this end, focusing first on the set of interpersonal scales Auke had developed, and then expanding the development effort to produce a comprehensive set of measures representing the constructs that could be reliably and validly assessed with the MMPI-2 item pool. This work, which culminated in the release of the MMPI-2-RF in 2008, has been described in detail elsewhere (Ben-Porath, 2012).

What has not been discussed in as much detail are the considerations that led us to recommend to the publisher a gradual modernization of the then 60-year-old inventory. The MMPI-2-RF was developed exclusively with MMPI-2 items. This allowed us to study the restructured version of the test with many already existing, rich MMPI-2 datasets and to continue to rely on the MMPI-2 norms, which had been collected some 20 years prior to the release of the MMPI-2-RF. On the basis of extensive data analyses, we had conducted over the course of several years prior to its release, Auke and I were very confident that the MMPI-2-RF would offer substantial improvements and a more efficient assessment instrument that could be linked both empirically and conceptually to the modern personality and psychopathology literature. However, the updated inventory also represented a major paradigm shift and its acceptance in applied settings was not a forgone conclusion. Rather than impose this change on MMPI-2 users, we recommended, and the publisher agreed that the MMPI-2-RF be positioned as an alternative, rather than a replacement for the MMPI-2.

The decision to limit the MMPI-2-RF to the MMPI-2 item pool meant that anyone with an MMPI-2 dataset had the ability to score the restructured form and conduct their own MMPI-2-RF research. Consequently, within a few years of its release a broad range of investigators had published MMPI-2-RF studies of their own. During the 12 years that separated release of the MMPI-2-RF and the 2020 publication of the MMPI-3, over 500 peer-reviewed studies were published. This empirical literature, coupled with a steady increase in the number of MMPI-2 users who chose to transition to the MMPI-2-RF, led Auke and me to propose, and the publisher and distributor to agree, that we take next step and update the then 30-year-old MMPI-2-RF norms and items pool. The process we followed and its outcome, the MMPI-3, are described in detail in the test manuals (Ben-Porath & Tellegen, 2020a, 2020b) and in a forth-coming textbook (Ben-Porath & Sellbom, 2022).

Behind the scenes

We have reached the present day of my professional journey. Capturing 30 years at Kent State in just a few paragraphs inevitably required that I pick and choose among many events and leave some stories untold. In the concluding pages of this chapter, I highlight several meaningful factors that played important roles in my professional development.

For more than 20 years, I have been extensively involved with didactic and practical assessment training in our clinical program. Our first-year clinical students complete a two-semester didactic sequence, which I co-teach with one of our neuropsychologists. In their second and third years of training, they see clients in our training clinic, where, often with the aid of a post-doc, I supervise all adult intake assessments. I regularly tell our non-MMPI students that, like it or not, they will become MMPI experts. Over the years, I've heard from many graduates that they did not fully value this skill until they became the go to MMPI experts at their setting.

I mentioned earlier that during my post-doctoral year at Minnesota, Jim Butcher invited me to join the MMPI Workshops and Symposia faculty. I have been involved extensively in continuing education for psychologists ever since. I cannot emphasize enough the critical role this has played in my career. There is no better way to learn than to teach. This is true at every level. To effectively teach psychologists how to use the MMPI in their practice, requires, on the one hand, an understanding of the instru-ment that far exceeds what is required for its application, and on the other, knowledge of how psychologists use the test in their assessments. Herein lies the other benefit of my involvement with continuing education, the opportunity to interact regularly with MMPI users and learn from them both how they use the inventory and how we might better meet their needs. Many of the innovations introduced first with the MMPI-2-RF and most recently with the MMPI-3 resulted from these interactions.

I would not have been able to engage in continuing education activities to the extent that I have (my CV indicates nearly 400 workshops to date), without the support of my academic department, and in particular my Chair over the past dozen years, Maria Zaragoza. Maria also supported my long-standing involvement with journal editing. Between 1997 and 2021 I served continuously as either Editor or Associate Editor of two of the leading journals in our field, Psychological Assessment and Assessment. In addition to the intrinsic reward of being able to contribute to shaping the discipline, exposure to the broad range of research submitted to these journals provided important perspective to my work with the MMPI.

During the first half of my career, I conducted well over 1,000 psychological assessments. As a consultant at the Court Psycho-Diagnostic Clinic in Akron, Ohio, I assessed one or two criminal defendants court ordered to undergo competency to stand trial and/or insanity evaluations each week. Kathy Stafford, the long-standing Clinic Director taught me how to do these evaluations and provided me a steady stream of challenging referrals. She also became a valued research collaborator. I also conducted hundreds of preemployment evaluations of candidates for public safety positions. This experience was invaluable when later in my career I collaborated with Dave Corey in developing the MMPI-2-RF and MMPI-3 Police Candidate Interpretive Reports. In addition to this very fruitful professional partnership, Dave has become a treasured friend.

The MMPI is a remarkably versatile instrument. Its original and primary application has always been in mental health settings, as a tool that assists in diagnosis and treatment planning. However, from its early days, the test was also used in medical settings and with time it came to be applied extensively in a range of forensic and public safety settings. To learn and meet the needs of MMPI users in these settings I have regularly attended a wide range of conferences, some of which would not have been on my radar. Coupled with my continuing education activities, this afforded me the opportunity to meet and develop collaborative relationships and, in some instances, personal friendships with many outstanding professionals. At the risk of some inadvertent omissions (for which I apologize), I would like to acknowledge those with whom I have had the privilege to publish on multiple occasions. They include correctional psychologists Maureen Black and Diane Gartland; forensic psychologists Dan Davis, Jay Flens, and Tasha Phillips; health psychologists Kathy Ashton, Andy Block, Leslie Heinberg, Ashliegh Pona, and Judith Scheman; neuropsychologists Kevin Bianchini, Kyle Boone, David Freeman, Roger Gervais, Paul Green, Kevin Greve, Manny Greifenstein, Robert Heilbronner, Paul Kaufmann, Glenn Larrabbee, Paul Lees-Haley, Jody Pickle, and Marty Rohling; and police and public safety psychologists Bruce Cappo, David Corey, Paul Detrick, Gary Fischler, Herb Gupton, and David Hill. I have also benefited tremendously from collaborations with academic colleagues Bob Archer, Mike Bagby, and Paul Ingram.

I have saved the most important contributors to my career for last. I mentioned earlier that one of the factors that led me to choose Kent State for my first and only position was the opportunity to collaborate with Jack Graham. Another important contributor was the very positive impression I formed of the graduate students with whom I had a chance to meet during my 1990 interview at Kent. My expectations in this regard could not have been better met. I have been truly blessed with the opportunity to work, and in many instances continue to work with some of the best and brightest. I list here in chronological order the graduate students (not all of them my advisees) with whom I've published more than once: Nancy Sherwood, Deanna Barthlow. Rob Gallagher, Rick Handel, Lyn Stein, Johnathan Forbey, Amy Windover, Martin Sellbom, Dustin Wygant, Carlo Veltri, Linda Baum, Wendy Dragon, Danielle Burchett, Tayla Lee, Stephanie Miller, Adam Crighton, Adam Hicks, Ryan Marek, Anthony Tarescavage, Bill Menton, Jessica Tylicki, Katy Martin-Fernandez, Jordan Hall, Andy Kremyar, and Megan Whitman. I've also been extremely fortunate to work with remarkably talented post-docs (in chronological order): John McNulty, Johnathan Forbey, Martin Sellbom, Curt Matson, Jacob Finn, Eleanor Shkalim, Anthony Tarescavage, and Bill Menton.

In 1965, Jim Butcher convened the first MMPI research symposium. This meeting has taken place annually ever since. In addition to showcasing the most up to date MMPI research, this conference has served as a student-friendly venue, and it has launched several successful MMPI research careers. I presented my first paper in 1988. These days, my former students Martin Sellbom and Dustin Wygant serve as program chairs. My current students are frequent presenters, as are many of my former students and their students, my academic grandstudents, and now even some of my great-grandstudents present at this meeting. I cannot overstate how rewarding it is to spend two days annually in the company of my academic progeny.

Concluding comments

Chris Hopwood requested that I write about personal and professional aspects of my life and career, my approach to personality assessment, and how my personality and experiences have contributed to this approach. In the preceding pages I hope to have conveyed that my work on the MMPI has been guided by cherished mentors, colleagues, and students, many of whom are also my friends. During my first 25 or so years at Kent, my undergraduate mentor, Moshe Almagor, taught courses in our graduate and/or undergraduate program nearly every summer. Our collaboration continues to date, as Moshe works on the Hebrew version of the MMPI-3 and our friendship is strong as ever. Last summer (2020) we celebrated Auke Tellegen's 90th birthday from a COVID-19-induced distance. Auke remains my mentor, my role model, and my dear friend. My graduate school and internship colleague Paul Arbisi remains a cherished research collaborator and friend.

I have had the good fortune of working with consummate professionals in the psychological testing industry. Foremost among them is Beverly Kaemmer, whose decades-long management of the MMPI has been key to its success and longevity. Though she has retired from professional life, Bev remains a dear friend. Doug Armato, Director of the University of Minnesota Press, Katie Nickerson, Bev's successor as its Test Division Manager, and Alicia Gomez, Product Development Editor, continue the tradition of collegial collaboration in our efforts to keep the MMPI at the forefront of psychological assessment.

Several key personnel at Pearson Clinical Assessment have also played important roles in my work on the MMPI. While still a graduate student, I got to know then MMPI Product Manager Carol Watson, who went on to lead Pearson's Clinical Assessment division for many years. Legendary MMPI Product Manager Krista Ketchmark was a key partner during the development and launch of the MMPI-2-RF, and current product manager Deb Ringwelski has continued this tradition during the development of the MMPI-3. Research Director John Kamp, and Lead Digital Content Developer Karen Perkins, have played critical roles in translating our ideas for innovating the MMPI-2-RF and now the MMPI-3 into user-friendly software-based reports.

My approach to personality assessment was shaped by the experiences recounted in this chapter. Rigorous and creative applied scientific research informed by basic research in the fields of personality and psychopathology, collaboration with expert clinicians, and practical experience using our measures, are in my view the foundations for developing, teaching, and optimally using personality assessment devices.

I began this chapter with a brief personal history. My parents, Moshe and Edna, are no longer living. My dad left us way too soon and was survived by mom for 20 years. Their professional careers were an inspiration, and their unconditional love remains a blessing for which I am eternally grateful. Both remain an integral part of who I am as a person and a professional.

Over the past 25+ years, my wife Denise's love, support, understanding, and tolerance of my long workdays and frequent professional travel have been the backbone of my success. Our children Adam, Rose, and Ella are now emerging adults, beginning to forge their own ways. I lovingly hope that their eventual careers are as rewarding as mine has been.

Epilogue

The day after I submitted this chapter, personal tragedy struck, and we lost our beloved daughter Rose, 19 years old, to a drug overdose. With profound sadness, I dedicate this chapter to her loving memory.

Note

1 Disclosure: I serve as a consultant to the MMPI Publisher, the University of Minnesota Press, and distributor, Pearson. I receive research funding from the University of Minnesota Press. As co-author of the MMPI-2-RF and MMPI-3 I receives royalties on sales of these tests.

References

Arbisi, P.A., & Ben-Porath, Y.S. (1995). An MMPI-2 infrequent response scale for use with psychopathological populations: The infrequency-psychopathology F(p) scale. *Psychological Assessment*, 7(4), 424–431.

Ben-Porath, Y.S. (2012). *Interpreting the MMPI-2-RF.* Minneapolis: University of Minnesota Press.

Ben-Porath, Y.S. & Sellbom, M. (2022). *Interpreting the MMPI-3.* Minneapolis: University of Minnesota Press.

Ben-Porath, Y. S., & Tellegen, A. (2020a). *Minnesota Multiphasic Personality Inventory-3 (MMPI-3): Manual for administration, scoring, and interpretation.* Minneapolis: University of Minnesota Press.

Ben-Porath, Y. S., & Tellegen, A. (2020b). *Minnesota Multiphasic Personality Inventory-3 (MMPI-3): Technical manual.* Minneapolis: University of Minnesota Press.

Graham, J.R. (1977). *The MMPI: A practical guide.* New York: Oxford University Press.

Graham, J.R., Ben-Porath, Y.S., & McNulty, J.L. (1999). *MMPI-2 Correlates for outpatient community mental health settings.* Minneapolis: University of Minnesota Press.

Harkness A.R., McNulty, J.L., & Ben-Porath, Y.S. (1995). The personality psychopathology five (PSY-5): Constructs and MMPI-2 Scales. *Psychological Assessment*, 7(1), 104–114.

Keinan, G., Friedland, N., & Ben-Porath, Y.S. (1987). Decision making under stress: Scanning of alternatives under physical threat. *Acta Psychologica*, 64(3), 219–228.

Tellegen, A., & Ben-Porath, Y.S. (1992). The new uniform T-scores for the MMPI-2: Rationale, derivation, and appraisal. *Psychological Assessment*, 4(2), 145–155.

Tellegen, A., Ben-Porath, Y.S., McNulty, J.L., Arbisi, P.A., Graham, J.R., & Kaemmer, B. (2003). *The MMPI-2 restructured clinical scales: Development, validation, and interpretation.* Minneapolis: University of Minnesota Press.

12 A Long Life

Twists and Turns

Phebe Cramer

I was born on December 30, 1935, in San Francisco, California. For most of my childhood, I lived in Oakland, which was a quiet, attractive city at that time. I walked the two blocks to my elementary school.

On December 7, 1941, the Japanese bombed Pearl Harbor. I was nearly six years old. My father, a civil engineer, was away on a Defense Department job. My mother was worried that the Japanese might come to the United States west coast, and so she moved us to stay with her family in Indianapolis. This was the first time I met my cousins and extended family, and it was a delightful holiday. After three months, we returned to the Bay Area.

Air raid drills and blackouts were regular occurrences. We all wore identification "dog tags" and practiced taking shelter at school. Food and gasoline were rationed, as were shoes. My grandmother, as her part for the war effort, knit sweaters for the troops.

During this time (1942 and following), my father was transferred to Utah, to build a steel mill for use by the Armed forces. He was not drafted into military service due to the critical nature of his job. My mother and I joined him in Utah in the summers, when I was out of school.

This was my introduction into the customs of the Mormons, where men still had more than one wife, sometimes living in adjoining sections of the same house. My parents looked for a house in which we could live, rather than staying in a hotel. I remember a house owner telling us that the house used to have another room, but when his son left, he took the room with him. The ways of the people there puzzled me.

When the war was over, I rode my bike the two miles to my Junior High School. When it came time for High School, I transferred to a private, all girls' school in Berkeley. This provided both an excellent academic experience, and also allowed me to take, as the physical education requirement, training at a local swimming club. Competitive swimming became a major focus of my life during my teenage years. During that time, I acquired ten American records and one world record, in the 100-yard butterfly. As always happens, all of these records were broken long ago.

After High School, I attended the University of California, Berkeley. This was a great change for me, going from a High School class of

DOI: 10.4324/9781003036302-12

35 students to the University, which at that time had 18,000 students. I had always been curious about why people did what they did. For this reason, I majored in Psychology, and worked as a research assistant at the Institute of Personality Assessment and Research (IPAR), with such prominent personality psychologists as Jack Block, Harrison Gough, Frank Barron, and Donald MacKinnon. My experiences at IPAR significantly shaped my ideas about personality assessment. Participants in the IPAR research studies were brought to the Institute for a weekend of intensive study. Each staff member used their own preferred assessment method to study the participants who came to the Institute, who were authors, mathematicians, and architects. My particular assessment method was the Dramatic Constructions test, modeled after the work of Erik Erikson, in which the participant used miniature figures and furniture to create a dramatic story. This approach, based on the imaginative, open-ended creation of the participants, has been an important influence in my subsequent work.

During my Junior year at the University, I married a fellow student who lived across the street from the house I shared with three friends. That marriage lasted two years.

After one graduate year of study of at Berkeley, I decided I wanted to pursue a different approach to the study of personality. I transferred to the Clinical Program at New York University (NYU), where I studied with Robert Holt, George Klein, and Donald Spence, among others. I also worked as a Research Assistant at the Research Center for Mental Health at NYU. The clinical orientation at NYU was psychoanalytic, and provided the background for the different approach to personality that I wanted. During that time, David Rapaport was a visiting scholar at NYU, and I had weekly individual meetings with him to discuss psychoanalytic writings. My association with the outstanding psychologists at Berkeley and NYU gave me a sense of esteem about the work I was doing. I admired them and felt gratified that I could work with them.

As part of the clinical program, I had a yearlong internship at Psychological Institute, part of the Columbia University Medical Center complex in uptown New York City. Following this, I pursued both a clinical and academic career. I worked as a clinical psychologist at Maimonides Hospital for one year, and then continued clinical work at an outpatient clinic in New York City. Beginning in 1963, I was appointed as an Assistant Professor at Barnard College, Columbia University, where I taught from 1963 to 1967 (on leave 1965–1966; Spring 1967). During this time, my research focused on cognitive processes.

In this connection I was offered a one year visiting scholar position at the Institute of Human Learning, University of California, Berkeley. This was followed by a year as a Visiting Professor and other positions at Berkeley that extended from 1965 to Spring 1970.

Up until this time, there had been only one woman in the Psychology Department. Jean Macfarlane had been hired in 1929, after receiving her PhD from Berkeley in 1922. When I was at Berkeley, there were no women in the Psychology Department. There were a few women in the research centers. Jeanne Block and Diana Baumrind were at the Institute of Human Development, and Ravenna Helson was at the Institute of Personality Assessment and Research. Not until the government threatened to withhold research funds were (a few) women hired as FTEs by the University.

In 1970, I accepted a position as Associate Professor of Psychology at Williams College, in Massachusetts. Williams had been an all-male college since 1793. When I joined the college, there were four other women on the faculty. Two of these were over 60 years old, in special non-FTE positions, and taught languages. The other two were Assistant Professors. Neither stayed at Williams. A female professor was thus a rarity. The male faculty were polite, if skeptical. It was the faculty wives who had difficulty accepting me into the community. They had assumed that I was coming to open a nursery school. This made social gatherings problematic for me.

I stayed at Williams for the next 40 years, teaching Developmental Psychology, Personality Assessment, and other clinical courses, and conducting a clinical practice. I always found the combination of teaching, doing research, and having a clinical practice to be mutually beneficial. Each provided experience and insight that enriched the other work. However, it meant that there was less time for leisure activities.

My clinical work was psychodynamically informed. That is, I paid attention to the interplay of early experience and current life, addressing both how the former influenced that latter. I explored how dreams were important reflections of current conflicts, and how defense mechanisms interfered with successful reality testing.

In 1972, I married John Savacool, a Professor in the French Department at Williams. He has passed on. We had two daughters – Mara and Julia – who have both gone on to have their own interesting careers.

With both parents actively involved in academic careers, it was necessary for us to share child rearing and household responsibilities. If I had late afternoon academic appointments, my husband would pick up the girls after school and stay with them at home. We took turns, on alternate weeks, doing the shopping and cooking. Being a responsive mother meant that I had less time for socializing and leisure time activities. Life had to be organized and focused on the necessities.

As they were growing up, my daughters became involved in competitive figure skating. In that connection, I studied and became a certified figure skating judge. To facilitate my daughters' training, I spent many hours in ice skating rinks, including weekly travels to Lake Placid, NY, where they were coached.

My scientific contributions fall into two broad areas. At first, my research publications were in Cognitive Psychology, focusing on priming, semantic generalization, and developmental processes. This includes my book, *Word Association* (1968) and 28 publications between 1964 and 1981, in journals such as the *Journal of Experimental Psychology, Journal of Experimental Child Psychology, Journal of Verbal Learning and Verbal Behavior,* and *Psychonomic Science,* for which I was a member of the Editorial Board from 1972 to 1977.

Beginning in 1986, my publications shifted to the broad area of personality, focusing especially on defense mechanisms, narcissism, and the developmental precursors of these. This work is presented in my book, *Protecting the Self: Defense Mechanisms in Action* (2006), and in the article "Seven pillars of defense mechanism theory", *Social and Personality Psychology Compass* (2008).

During the years at Williams, I published many articles on the topics of Defense Mechanisms, Narcissism, and longitudinal Personality Development. My work has especially focused on how defense mechanisms change with age, and how early experience influences the development of defenses and narcissism. I continue to publish on these topics. Also, given my reliance on the TAT for personality assessment, I published a book on the TAT: *Story Telling, Narrative, and the TAT (1996).*

I also served as Associate Editor for the *Journal of Personality* from 1992 to 1997 and as Associate Editor for the *Journal of Research in Personality* from 2009 to 2014. I have been active in the Society for Personality Assessment, attending yearly meetings and frequently presenting a paper.

After retirement from teaching at Williams in 2009, I have continued to carry out research, write papers, and give lectures. In 2014, I was awarded the Bruno Klopfer Distinguished Contribution award by the Society for Personality Assessment. In 2018 I was awarded the Henry A. Murray award for Distinguished Contributions to the Study of Lives, by the Association for Research in Personality.

My approach to personality assessment has been shaped by two factors. I have found it more meaningful to let persons tell their own story, rather than providing a set of scripted response alternatives. This approach is based on my clinical work and my own personal reaction to self-report measures, trying to select a representative response from a list of alternatives, some of which do, but not quite, represent my own point of view.

My approach has also been shaped by my own personality. If I were to locate myself on the Internalizer/Externalizer personality dimension, I would place myself on the internalizer end. This focus on the inner determinants of personality has led me to adopting assessment methods that allow the inner dimensions to be assessed. Each person, and their personality, is unique. There is not one mold, or set of molds, into which a person may be successfully placed. Despite personality tests that will describe a person as one type or another, these are summary statements that ignore the unique qualities of the individual.

I have been asked, what do I think has contributed to my success. I would say: good genes, hard work, persistence, and resilience (Figure 12.1).

Figure 12.1 The author.

One other thing about me: I like to travel. Beginning at age 12, I took my first big trip, going to Pre-Castro Cuba, to visit with friends of my mother. During my graduate school years, I travelled throughout Europe, visiting all the usual tourist attractions. I also spent several months living in Spain, where my father was working. More recently, I have done extensive travel, to Central and South America, Galapagos Islands, Tahiti, India, Burma, China and Mongolia. Most recently, I travelled through Alaska by boat.

13 Thomas A. Widiger

Personality Assessment

Thomas A. Widiger

The purpose of this chapter is to provide my personal and professional history, particularly in relationship to the development of my interest, training, and research concerning personality assessment. I begin with a presentation of my personal history and co-occurring collegiate history, noting in particular experiences that led to my work in personality assessment. This is followed by a section concerned with my perspective on personality assessment.

Personal, professional, and assessment history

When I entered college, I did not intend to become a psychologist. I was planning on becoming a novelist. Many of my friends were artists. In my sophomore year, I lived in a "hippie house" in my home town of Midland, Michigan, attending a junior college (Delta College). One of my favorite courses was English literature, taught by a very long-haired young professor who would at times visit our house to discuss Kurt Vonnegut, Joseph Heller, or Ken Kesey, while partaking in artifacts of a local head shop.

During Christmas break a major winter storm was going to roll in. So, we all got into a station wagon and headed for a commune in Missouri. It wasn't an easy life there. A friend and I stayed in a shack with no heat. We bathed in the primary house, but it was still just a tub of largely cold water. During the day we did various chores, clearing land and repairing various cabins. Nevertheless, one of our group stayed, joining the commune (he eventually left to work on oil rigs off the Texas coast). The rest of us returned home to finish college.

I changed my career plans after taking my first psychology course. I recognized that I did not really have any great ideas for a novel, and I became substantially more interested in psychology. At the end of the class I asked the professor for additional reading. He suggested R.D. Laing's (1960) *The Divided Self*, Sigmund Freud's (1900) *Interpretation of Dreams*, and Sandor Ferenczi's (1912) *Sex in Psychoanalysis*. For the life of me, I could not understand why he recommended Ferenczi's book. I found it unintelligible and/or coldly abstract. However, I read with considerable zeal the texts by Laing and Freud. I switched from literature to psychology.

DOI: 10.4324/9781003036302-13

Our house was eventually condemned beneath us. One of the problems was that it became well known that we would accept anyone's cat. Our house was not a "very, very very fine house." We had considerably more than just "two cats in the yard." There was eventually a notable fog of flees as one walked through the carpeted living room. But, of course, there were more problems than that. It didn't help that the police station was kitty-corner across the street. I don't think they enjoyed seeing us sitting on the porch roof, listening to Crosby, Stills, Nash, and Young sing "Our House."

I transferred to the University of Michigan for my junior year. I was though a general studies major, not a psychology major, largely to avoid having to fulfill a foreign language requirement. I had taken German in high school (the language of my grandparents on my father's side) but grew tired of it. Otherwise, I took all of the other courses that would be required for a psychology major, along with additional psychology electives.

My favorite class was an advanced undergraduate course in psychopathology. Many of the readings were chapters by Freud. I was a very active class participant, my hand frequently raised to join the discussion. I wanted though even more. Toward the end of the semester I approached the professor after class to ask if I could discuss further with him some writings by Freud. He clearly wasn't interested. He did not offer me a time to meet in his office. Instead, he suggested we talk as he walked back to his office. It was more like a run than a walk. I was essentially trotting next to him, trying to engage him in conversation. When we reached his office, he said, "Nice talk" and then shut the door in my face.

I actually couldn't blame him. I did not look like a serious scholar. I looked like any other hippie, with hair way down my back, dressed in tattered clothes. I was again living in a hippie house. We loved turkey and chicken pot pies, emptied over white bread laden with butter. All of the other residents were art majors. It was a beautifully decorated two-story home. The lamps, couches, vases, and curtains were from the 1940s to 1950s. The large front porch was colorfully painted with various artifacts hanging off the porch roof (including a hollow bomb). One day, Firesign Theater was in town for a show and they stopped by our house because they found it so intriguing. They toured the house and "we" happily gave them some of our stuff, hopefully for a future album cover (unfortunately, I was not there at the time!).

In some regards, though, we were not typical hippies. We also really enjoyed truck driving music (e.g. David Dudley, Red Sovine, Merle Haggard, and, of course, Commander Cody and the Lost Planet Airman). We attended not only rock festivals but also truck driving jamborees. There was one time when we failed to appreciate that hippies would not always be welcome at a truck driver festival. All of the attendees were situated at various park tables rather than sitting along the ground which was typically the case at a rock festival. A group next to us (not hippies) began to stack their empty beer cans in a growing pyramid. We delighted at the friendly competition, stacking our own beer cans and joking with them, as well as sharing our joint pleasure in the music. Apparently, though at least one of their group was being flirtatious with us and/or vice versa. I honestly don't have any real recollection of that. When the premier performer, Dave Dudley ("Six Days on the Road"), finally appeared, most everyone left their tables and moved closer to the stage. When the show was over, I had become separated from my group. As I walked back to our car I was suddenly pushed to the ground, kicked, and slugged, with angry exclamations, "Don't you ever try to pick up the sheriff's wife again!" I was not the one in our group flirting with her, but that didn't seem to matter to them. I think I was just one of our group that they had managed to find. I don't think I would ever really want to join a Fight Club.

A major limitation of being a general studies major was that I did not have an advisor. I had very strong, highly competitive grades and GRE score. I did not think that getting into graduate school would be a problem. However, when I got the applications, I discovered that I needed three letters of recommendation. I did not have a close relationship with any professor.

Fortunately, I was able to get a job as a research assistant for an educational psychology professor. I spent an additional year in Ann Arbor, helping him to develop individualized instruction programs. I got an excellent letter of recommendation from him, and then two additional letters from professors of classes that I had taken. I didn't ask the psychopathology professor, but I suspect the letters I did get from the two other professors were not particularly impressive. There wasn't much they could really say.

I applied to lots of doctoral programs. My top two choices were University of Michigan and University of Texas at Austin (albeit for the wrong reason: it was the home of the Armadillo World Headquarters). I got only one face-to-face interview (not to either Michigan or Texas), which I don't think went well. I was very nervous. My mouth was dry. There was a glass of water on his desk but I felt I shouldn't take a sip, as that would likely reveal my nervousness (as if it was not already obvious). Plus, I still had very long hair. They did not make me an offer. I was not surprised.

Miami University in Ohio was the only program to make me an offer (we only had a phone interview). I did finally cut my hair before I arrived. I went there to work with a systems family therapist, as that was my primary interest at the time. However, he left after my first year, which was frankly quite fortunate because his career became rather troubled. I then started to work with his replacement, a Jungian family therapist, but I never resonated well with that perspective.

Fortunately, a new professor was hired that year, Len Rorer, who taught the assessment sequence. The primary textbook was *Personality and Prediction: Principles of Personality Assessment* by Jerry Wiggins (1973). I loved that book (Pincus & Widiger, 2014; Widiger, 2020). I shifted my interest from marital therapy to personality assessment. Indeed, my Master's Thesis, although chaired by my family therapist mentor, was largely an assessment paper and the eventual publication was co-authored with Len (Widiger et al., 1980). I switched to Len for my dissertation. Admittedly though, my dissertation was not itself concerned with personality assessment (Widiger & Rorer, 1984). It was concerned in part with ethical issues in psychotherapy that grew out of my experience with systems therapy (e.g., therapists suggesting that they could impact persons without them even being aware that they were being hypnotized).

I took a Rorschach class from Karen Maitland-Schilling, for which we had to complete the Rorschach ourselves, administered by another student. A female friend of mine, with whom I spent many evenings sharing conversation and wine, administered the Rorschach to me and vice versa. It was not a particularly objective context for a Rorschach administration. Dr. Maitland-Shilling kept all of our Rorschach protocols in a filing cabinet in her office. One day, I asked to have my protocol so that I would make a Xerox copy. I never returned it.

My interest in personality assessment grew substantially during graduate school, for example, I drove, almost non-stop, from Oxford, Ohio to Miami, Florida to attend a day-long workshop run by James Butcher (Minnesota Multiphasic Personality Inventory; MMPI) and Theodore Millon (Millon Multiaxial Clinical Inventory; MCMI). I was intending to drive non-stop but finally had to succumb to getting at least some sleep at a rest stop off the highway. However, with that rest I arrived just an hour before the workshop was to begin. I sat in the front row but I was just so, so sleep-deprived that I had trouble keeping my eyes open. I knew that Drs. Butcher and Millon would notice this, so I shifted to the back row after lunch. Nevertheless, I loved it!

One of my most valued publications was an *Annual Review of Psychology* paper "on" personality assessment. Len had been invited to prepare a paper on personality assessment, and he invited me to co-author. Len though was quite a procrastinator (he eventually wrote a paper on how to treat procrastination, which I found rather ironic). He got a deferment for a year after having written very little during the first year. I was so afraid that it would never be done. But, we did manage to complete it (Rorer & Widiger, 1983). We began the paper by acknowledging that it had very little to do with personality assessment, concerned instead with philosophy of science (e.g., falsificationism and critical rationalism). Len was a graduate student of Paul Meehl and embraced Meehl's (1978) views on philosophy of science.

When I applied for internship, I was primarily interested in one that provided research opportunities. I had two face-to-face interviews for internship, which was actually very good for the time (very few internships at that time required face-to-face interviews). My interview at Cornell

University in Westchester went well, even though one interviewer thought I was from the University of Miami (in Florida).

A primary interest I had with Cornell was that one of the five original primary Rorschach theorists still worked there (i.e., Roy Schaefer). I was very interested in the Rorschach, although recognizing that it had a problematic research base (Widiger & Maitland-Schilling, 1980). However, when I arrived, I was informed that Shaefer had retired. Nevertheless, I enjoyed my Rorschach training at Cornell. I particularly valued one supervisor who did not want to know anything more about the patient than age and sex. Most supervisors wanted you to tell them essentially the entire story. They then "discovered" what was already known within the Rorschach. She, however, bravely went blind, a style of assessment training embraced as well by Meehl (1973) for the MMPI. I was so impressed, but never myself became anywhere near that skilled and in fact grew somewhat skeptical regarding the "skills" of others using the non-blind approach.

One of the leading psychiatrists at Cornell (in Westchester) was Otto Kernberg, and I became increasingly interested in personality disorders, including, of course, borderline. I recall attending a grand rounds conference in which Kernberg interviewed a patient of his on the stage. She would express her idealization, being treated by "THE" leading borderline clinician. He humbly responded by saying, essentially, "Actually, I'm not that good."

I became closely familiar with the psychiatric literature on personality disorders and quickly recognized that a lot of the methodology and findings in personality assessment research could be applied to these largely psychodynamic and/or psychiatric constructs. One such idea was to apply Bayesian statistics (learned from Wiggins, 1973) to the personality disorder diagnostic criterion sets. I presented the idea to the Director of Clinical Training, John Clarkin. He indicated that we didn't really have to collect new data as he was part of a research team that had already collected the necessary data. I met with the team shortly thereafter, one of whom was the psychiatrist Allen Frances, who worked at Cornell at Payne Whitney in New York City.

We eventually published our study on the use of Bayesian statistics for the diagnosis of personality disorders (i.e., Clarkin et al., 1983). But, more importantly for my own career, I had by then developed a strong collaborative relationship with Allen Frances, who was a leading personality disorder psychiatrist. We soon published a review paper on applying a variety of findings and principles from personality assessment to the assessment and diagnosis of personality disorders (Widiger & Frances, 1985).

By then I was an Assistant Professor at the University of Kentucky. One of my early collaborations with Frances was a critique of the MCMI as a measure of the DSM-III personality disorders, co-authored not only with

Allen but also with Janet Williams and Robert Spitzer (i.e., Widiger et al., 1985), key players in the developments of DSM-III and DSM-III-R (e.g., Spitzer et al., 1980). Our paper was rather critical of the MCMI's validity as a measure of the DSM-III personality disorders. Needless to say, Dr. Millon was not pleased. He sent me a "confidential" letter. I'm not sure that its confidentiality is in fact legally binding, but I continued to collaborate with Drs. Frances, Williams, and Spitzer.

Years later a past graduate student of Dr. Millon asked me to participate in a symposium concerning Millon's contributions to personology and personality assessment. I replied by indicating that I had been and would be rather critical of the MCMI and Millon's theoretical model. He replied that this was precisely why he was inviting me. He wanted a balanced symposium. So, I agreed to participate. However, when I was on the stage with the other presenters the Chair indicated that we were all there to celebrate Dr. Millon's work in a festschrift honoring his career. My heart sank. This was not the purpose of my talk, not by any means. I was later told that the intention of the symposium had changed, shifting from a balanced presentation to a celebratory festschrift. The talks in front of me indeed presented glowing reports of the life history and many influential contributions of Dr. Millon. I would agree that Dr. Millon is, hands down, among the most influential contributors to the field of personality disorder (e.g., co-editing the first personality disorders journal, key in the foundation of the International Society for the Study of Personality Disorders and, of course, writing the authoritative text at that time: Millon, 1981). When it was my turn though, I presented a very thoroughly damning critique of Dr. Millon's theoretical model, the MCMI, and the respective research. The audience replied largely with just silence. They were, well, not surprisingly, stunned. It was like I was stabbing Dr. Millon in the back at his festschrift celebration. Dr. Millon provided the discussion, during which he suggested that perhaps I should consider pursuing a different career. A month or so later the Chair of the symposium called me to indicate that he had secured an agreement from the *Journal of Personality Assessment* to publish the symposium. I agreed to do so (Widiger, 1999) only if he made it very clear in his introduction that I was asked to provide a critique.

One of my favorite experiences though was attending the annual meeting of the *Society for Personality Assessment*. At one such meeting early in my career I was attending a reception. I saw Jerry Wiggins across the room, standing there with a martini, speaking joyfully with a student. I couldn't help myself. I had to meet him and introduce myself.

I was so impressed at how engaging and warm he was. We instantly became friends, trading stories about Len Rorer, who had been a colleague of his at the Oregon Research Institute. There are many stories about Len Rorer. Let me just say that in his living room over the fireplace was a full-frontal nude painting of himself. Len would tell me that he was a member of a nudist colony, which he said was largely a front for "swinging." I am reluctant to tell any more stories (none involve me personally, although I was once invited). Jerry told me about a party he was at with Len in Oregon. Len and his wife (at that time, they eventually divorced) liked to take their clothes off at parties and dance naked. Toward the end of the party Anna Anastasi got her car stuck hanging somewhat off a cliff. Len ran out and jumped up and down on the trunk, naked. Len's behavior eventually resulted in a forced early retirement. I attended the colloquium honoring his contributions and intended to attend a dinner that evening. Len made it clear that he had no plans to attend the dinner (it was cancelled). Roger Knudson, another faculty member, stated at the colloquium that he remembered well to this day the first time he met Len, but he could not remember what Len was wearing.

My close collaborator, Allen Frances, eventually became Chair of the fourth edition of the American Psychiatric Association's *Diagnostic and Statistical Manual of Mental Disorders* (DSM-IV; APA, 1994). Allen invited me to serve as its Research Coordinator. A primary mandate for DSM-IV was to have the effort be much more transparent and empirically based. Toward that end, all of the proposals had to be preceded by an objective and comprehensive literature review, modeled closely after the meta-analytic approach that required an explicit method section, specifying explicit criteria for study inclusion and exclusion. Many qualitative reviewers cherry-pick the studies in order to provide a rather one-sided view of the literature. This was not to be done for DSM-IV. Indeed, it was at times quite difficult to get the leading nosologic researchers to commit to this approach and the work that was involved. Borrowing from my experience from Rorer and Widiger (1983), many of these reviews were also submitted to hostile critics of the proposals and certainly most were submitted to peer-reviewed journals for which they received critical review (Widiger & Trull, 1993). The point being is that one should embrace critical review rather than attempt to suppress it or ignore it, as it is through the success in overcoming these critiques that true progress occurs (Meehl, 1978). One of the members of DSM-IV refused to submit such a review and his proposal was rejected. In the end, all of the reviews were published in a three-volume *DSM-IV Sourcebook* series (Widiger et al., 1994, 1996, 1997). One regret, though, is that I subsequently felt that we should have published critical reviews along with them.

Many of the proposals were also field-tested in studies funded by the National Institute of Mental Health (NIMH). As such, they had to test alternative proposals against one another, as well as against the prior edition, DSM-III-R. I was in charge of the field trial for the proposed revisions to antisocial personality disorder, which pitted DSM-III-R antisocial with the very well-regard Psychopathy Checklist-Revised (Hare, 1991). One of the sites in the field trial was headed by Lee Robins (1966), the primary author of DSM-III antisocial and another site was headed by Robert Hare.

There were additional sites as well (Widiger et al., 1996). The final edition of the *DSM-IV Sourcebook* included the results from all of the field trials, re-analyses of existing data sets funded by the MacArthur Foundation, and the final decision papers by respective Work Group Chairs (Widiger et al., 1998).

My initial work as the Research Coordinator required that I take a two-year leave of absence from the University of Kentucky to work more closely with Allen Frances at Payne Whitney Clinic in Manhattan, New York. During the first year I was visited by Paul Costa, who with Jeff McCrae, had developed the highly influential measure of the Five Factor Model (FFM), the NEO Personality Inventory-Revised (NEO PI-R; Costa & McCrae, 1992). At the time, I was still largely focused on the interpersonal circumplex (IPC), consistent with the work of Jerry Wiggins (Wiggins & Pincus, 1989). However, I was having trouble with the coverage of some of the DSM personality disorders by the IPC, particularly the borderline, obsessive-compulsive, and schizotypal personality disorders (Widiger & Hagemoser, 1997 represents this concern well, although published some years later).

Paul introduced me to the FFM. It clearly solved my problems. The FFM includes the interpersonal traits. Agreeableness versus antagonism and extraversion versus introversion are essentially 45-degree rotations of the IPC defining axes of agency and communion (McCrae & Costa, 1989). However, the FFM goes beyond the IPC to include as well the fundamental dimensions of neuroticism, conscientiousness, and openness. The borderline, obsessive-compulsive, and schizotypal personality disorders do involve interpersonal styles, but these are not their fundamental traits. Neuroticism (or negative affectivity) is very central to the borderline personality disorder, maladaptive conscientiousness (compulsivity) is clearly central to the obsessive-compulsive, and openness (cognitive-perceptual aberrations) is central to the schizotypal (Lynam & Widiger, 2001). Thereafter Paul and I developed a strong collaboration, although it was sometime until we published our initial paper on the FFM of personality disorder (Widiger & Costa, 1994), as well as the first edition of our text, *Personality disorders and the five-factor model of personality* (Costa & Widiger, 1994).

The predominant model of general personality structure is the FFM (Costa & McCrae, 2017). The FFM has amassed a considerable body of empirical support (Widiger, 2017), including childhood antecedents (Mervielde et al., 2005), multivariate behavior genetics with respect to its structure (Jarnecke & South, 2017), temporal stability across the life span (Roberts & DelVecchio, 2000), and cross-cultural replication (Allik & Realo, 2017). The FFM is also associated with a wide array of important life outcomes, both positive and negative (Ozer & Benet-Martinez, 2006; Roberts et al., 2007).

The FFM is aligned with the Big Five, the lexical model of personality structure (Goldberg, 1993). The lexical approach to constructing a descriptive model of personality rests on the compelling premise that what is of most importance, interest, or meaning to persons when describing themselves and others will be naturally encoded into the language. Language is a sedimentary deposit of the observations of persons over the many years of the language's evolution. Fundamental domains of personality are constructed as persons compile more and more words to describe the various nuances, distinctions, and gradations of each respective domain, and the structure of personality is provided by the empirical relationship among the large body of trait terms. The Big Five domains, as identified by Goldberg (1993), are surgency (FFM extraversion), agreeableness, constraint (FFM conscientiousness), emotional instability, and intellect (FFM openness).

Since my meeting with Paul Costa much of my research has been largely focused on the further conceptualization and understanding of the personality disorders from the perspective of the FFM (Widiger, 2000, 2003; Widiger & McCabe, in press; Widiger & Simonsen, 2005; Widiger & Trull, 2007). This work was influential in helping to shift the DSM personality disorder nomenclature toward a dimensional trait model. Indeed, Section III of DSM-5 now includes a dimensional trait model, consisting of the domains of negative affectivity, detachment, psychoticism, antagonism, and disinhibition (Krueger et al., 2012). As stated in DSM-5 (APA, 2013, p. 773), "these five broad domains are maladaptive variants of the five domains of the extensively validated and replicated personality model known as the 'Big Five,' or the Five Factor Model of personality."

Upon my return to the University of Kentucky I was very pleased to hear that Krista Trobst was applying for a faculty position, I was thrilled in part because Krista made it clear that her husband, Jerry Wiggins, would come with her. All he wanted was office space and to teach a graduate course on personality assessment, in which he would try out his new book. I must admit though some apprehension. Jerry did not attend many conferences but if we happened to be at the same one, we would have martinis and delightful conversations. Would Jerry want to drink most every evening as we would do at a conference? I could not handle that. But, perhaps Jerry would have the same concern. In any case, it did not work out. Jerry and Krista went instead to York University in Canada.

Jerry though did finish his book. Well, largely finished it. The book was *Paradigms of Personality Assessment* (Wiggins, 2003). I read penultimate transcripts. However, before it was entirely finished, very sadly, Jerry suffered a debilitating stroke. Krista and Jerry elicited my help in finishing the book. I didn't do much. Just sort of help to tie loose ends together. In any case, I strongly recommend this book to anyone interested in personality assessment. Jerry identified five basic paradigms in personality assessment: the psychodynamic (e.g., Rorschach), interpersonal (e.g., interpersonal circumplex), personological (life history interview), multivariate (e.g., five factor model), and empirical (e.g., MMPI). He emphasized that he respected and valued all five paradigms, essentially equally, and that was really quite clear in his writing.

The second half of the book was an assessment of a very engaging and colorful woman, "Madeline G.," by leading experts for each of the five paradigms. Paul Costa and Ralph Piedmont (a post-doc working with Paul at the National Institute of Aging) interpreted her NEO PI-R (Costa & McCrae, 1992) as well as the informant version completed by her common-law husband. Madeline, at the time, was a fast-rising community activist lawyer recently hired at a major law firm. Much of her assessments were quite positive. However, a curious finding was the substantial discrepancy between her self-report NEO PI-R and the informant report. Her common-law husband had a much more negative view. Ralph Piedmont was a marital counselor and he made much about discrepancies in self and spousal reports (Piedmont, 1998).

With the delay of the book's publication due to Jerry's stroke, it eventually became evident that Madeline's life was actually not so rosy. Her common-law husband left her (resulting in a significant depression) and she lost her job at a prestigious law firm. Much of this was presaged in her NEO PI-R assessments. This text and her multiple assessments were so intriguing that follow-up assessments were conducted of Madeline 17 years later. Myself and Cristina Crego interpreted her self-report NEO PI-R as well as another informant NEO PI-R report by a very close colleague (Widiger & Crego, 2019b).

My assessment approach

As noted earlier, my work since my meeting and collaboration with Paul Costa has been largely concerned with validating and extending the perspective that the DSM personality disorders are readily understood as maladaptive variants of the FFM personality traits (Widiger, 2000, 2003; Widiger & McCabe, in press; Widiger & Simonsen, 2005; Widiger & Trull, 2007). I have also been personally involved in the development of a variety of FFM and other measures. One measure is a brief one-page self-report and/or a clinician rating form of the FFM (i.e., the Five Factor Model Rating Form; FFMRF; Mullins-Sweatt et al., 2006; Samuel et al., 2013).

A subsequent variant of the FFMRF has explicit and distinct adaptive and maladaptive components at both poles of all five domains of the FFM, again within a one-page rating form (i.e., the Five Factor Form; FFF; Rojas & Widiger, 2014) recognizing that there are indeed maladaptive variants for all ten poles of the five FFM domains (Crego et al., 2020; Widiger & Crego, 2019a). The FFF includes 30 items, each of which aligns with a respective facet of the FFM as assessed by the NEO PI-R (Costa & McCrae, 1992). For example, the FFF trust item includes "cynical, suspicious" (maladaptive) and "cautious, skeptical" (adaptive) at one pole; at the opposite pole are "trusting" (adaptive) and "gullible" (maladaptive). Similarly, for the FFM facet achievement-striving, the respective FFF item contrasts being "workaholic, acclaim-seeking" (maladaptive) and "purposeful, diligent, ambitious" (adaptive) with being either "carefree, content" (adaptive) or "aimless, shiftless, desultory" (maladaptive). Subsequent validations studies include Rojas and Widiger (2018) and Rojas et al. (2018).

All but two of my measures are self-report inventories, the exception being semi-structured interviews for the FFM (Trull et al., 2001) and for the DSM-IV personality disorders (Widiger et al., 1995). All of my FFM measures would be said to be within the multivariate paradigm (Wiggins, 2003). However, some could also be said to fall as well within the empirical paradigm, as many of them were developed in a manner consistent with the empirical paradigm perspective. Eight Five Factor Model Personality Disorder (FFMPD) inventories have been developed, including the Elemental Psychopathy Assessment (EPA; Lynam et al., 2011), the Five Factor Schizotypal Inventory (FFSI; Edmundson et al., 2011), the Five Factor Histrionic Inventory (FFHI; Tomiatti et al., 2012), the Five Factor Avoidant Assessment (FFAvA; Lynam et al., 2012), the Five Factor Borderline Inventory (FFBI; Mullins-Sweatt et al., 2012), the Five Factor Obsessive-Compulsive Inventory (FFOCI; Samuel et al. (2012), the Five Factor Dependency Inventory (FFDI; Gore et al., 2012), and the Five Factor Narcissism Inventory (FFNI; Glover et al., 2012). Each was constructed by first identifying which facets of the FFM (included in the NEO PI-R; Costa & McCrae, 1992) appear to be most relevant for each respective personality disorder. It was useful to construct the FFMPD scales on the basis of respective DSM-IV personality disorders to ensure that the ultimate collection would fully cover traits included within the existing diagnostic nomenclature. The facet selections were based on researchers' FFM descriptions of each personality disorder (i.e., Lynam & Widiger, 2001), clinicians' descriptions (i.e., Samuel & Widiger, 2004), and FFM-personality disorder research (e.g., Samuel & Widiger, 2008). Potential items were then written to assess for each respective facet scale. Items were selected in part on the basis of their empirical relationship with both the respective FFM facet and personality disorder (e.g., Glover et al., 2012; Gore et al., 2012; Samuel et al., 2012). Oltmanns et al. (2018) developed and validated an informant version of the FFNI. These measures can be used to assess either the respective personality disorder from the perspective of the FFM or, alternatively, one can select scales from across the measures to assess for clinically important maladaptive variants of respective pole(s) of the FFM (Widiger et al., 2012). A Special Section of *Psychological Assessment* was devoted to these scales (Bagby & Widiger, 2018). A large number of subsequent validation studies have been conducted (Bagby & Widiger, 2018; Crego et al., 2018).

An additional measure developed within my lab is the FLUX scale, a self-report measure of the fluctuation between grandiosity and vulnerability. A prevailing view of narcissism is that persons fluctuate between states of grandiosity and vulnerability, yet existing measures of grandiose and vulnerable narcissism (including the FFNI) do not assess for nor even recognize this potential fluctuation. Grandiose and vulnerable narcissism are typically assessed as if there are stable personality traits (i.e., either grandiose or vulnerable consistently over time). The FLUX was constructed precisely to assess for a characteristic fluctuation between grandiosity and vulnerability (Oltmanns & Widiger, 2018a).

Finally, there is also the Personality Inventory for ICD-11 (PiCD; Oltmanns & Widiger, 2018b) The PiCD provides an assessment of the five domains of the World Health Organization's (WHO) maladaptive trait model to be included in the forthcoming eleventh edition of the International Classification of Diseases (ICD-11; WHO, 2018). These five domains are negative affectivity, detachment, dissociality, disinhibition, and anankastia that are again said by its authors to be aligned with the FFM: "Negative Affective with neuroticism, Detachment with low extraversion, Dissocial with low agreeableness, Disinhibited with low conscientiousness and Anankastic with high conscientiousness" (Mulder et al., 2016, p. 85).

Items for the PiCD were written to assess these domains and were selected not only on the basis of convergent validity but also on the basis of discriminant validity. Potential PiCD items were submitted to a series of factor analysis that identified items that loaded optimally on its respective domain without also loading on a different domain (Oltmanns & Widiger, 2018b). A subsequent validation study was provided by Oltmanns and Widiger (2019) and a recent Special Section of *Psychological Assessment* was largely devoted to further studies of the PiCD (Bagby & Widiger, 2020). An informant version of the PiCD is currently in development.

I would suggest that the empirical approach to scale construction should be embraced by all test authors, selecting items on the basis of their internal consistency with other items for that scale, convergent validity with a respective criterion measure, and discriminant validity (not correlating with other constructs; Wiggins, 2003). Some suggest this is perhaps "cheating," as the empirical process selects items on the same basis by which they would eventually be validated. However, it can be quite difficult to anticipate how an item will perform empirically. Better to know in advance. The pure empirical approach would select items solely on the basis of their correlation with a respective criterion. The potential advantage of this approach is that one will obtain items that will have no face validity and therefore cannot easily be faked. However, items that have no apparent face validity for the construct being assessed may have strong convergent validity for untoward and problematic reasons; for instance, gender bias (Lindsay & Widiger, 1995). In any case, failure to consider empirically based information may come back to bite the test author when the scale (and/or certain items) perform in a manner that is highly problematic yet could have been anticipated during scale construction (Crego et al., 2015; McCabe & Widiger, in press).

Most any FFM measure can also be said to incorporate a good deal of the interpersonal perspective. As noted earlier, two of the FFM domains align very closely and comfortably with the defining axes of the IPC. Much of what will be learned from an IPC assessment of personality disorders can and will be learned by the agreeableness and extraversion domains of the FFM. However, there are some aspects of the IPC that are not well represented by the respective FFM domains (e.g., the complementarity of communion domain; Bluhm et al., 1990).

I would even boldly suggest that the FFM is not incompatible with the psychoanalytic perspective. I have never fully understood the apparent opposition, if not antagonism, of psychodynamic researchers with the FFM trait model. I consider the FFM to be simply descriptive, much like the DSM. Just as Dr. Spitzer removed theoretically specific aspects from the DSM-III to facilitate that the classification being usable by alternative, if not competing, theoretical perspectives (Spitzer et al., 1980), so too can the FFM be used by alternative theoretical perspectives. Indeed, psychodynamic constructs, as included within the California Q-Set (Block, 1961), the Shedler-Westen Assessment Procedure (Shedler & Westen, 2004), and the DSM-5 Section III self-other deficits (Bender et al., 2011) can all be readily understood within the FFM personality structure (see McCrae et al., 1986; Mullins-Sweatt & Widiger, 2007; and Widiger & McCabe, in press, respectively).

In fact, I have always had difficulty considering the Rorschach, as scored by the performance criteria emphasized within the predominant Exner system (Exner & Erdberg, 2005) to be particularly psychodynamic. It has long been unclear to me how the percent or ratio of color, form, texture, or shading is consistent with the psychodynamic understanding of personality disorders or defense mechanisms. I always preferred myself the more clearly psychodynamic interpretation of content and free association during the inquiry phase to be more consistent with the psychodynamic perspective (Aronow et al., 1994). On the other hand, the Aronow et al. approach to Rorschach interpretation and scoring, and most any interpretation and scoring of the Thematic Apperception Test (Morgan & Murray, 1935) are quite clearly substantially more compatible and congruent with the psychodynamic perspective than any FFM measure.

Conclusions

It is certainly an honor and pleasure to provide any aspect of one's life history. I am very grateful for this opportunity. A priority was to be factual, acknowledging some of my own failures. I did not follow a smooth path to graduate school. I also attempted to provide some entertainment, acknowledging some of the more amusing anecdotes from my past. Ultimately, I attempted to provide a clear statement as to my assessment perspective and its foundations in my training and past experiences. I hope you enjoyed it, or at least found it of some interest.

References

Allik, J., & Realo, A. (2017). Universal and specific in the five factor model. In T. A. Widiger (Ed.), *The Oxford handbook of the five factor model* (pp. 173–190). New York: Oxford University Press.

American Psychiatric Association. (2004). *Diagnostic and statistical manual of mental disorders* (4th ed.). Washington, DC: Author.

American Psychiatric Association. (2013). *Diagnostic and statistical manual of mental disorders* (5th ed.). Washington, DC: Author.

Aronow, E., Reznikoff, M., & Moreland, K. (1994). *The Rorschach technique: Perceptual basics, content interpretation, and applications.* Boston, MA: Allyn & Bacon.

Bagby, R. M., & Widiger, T. A. (2018). Five factor model personality disorder scales: An introduction to a special section on assessment of maladaptive variants of the five-factor model. *Psychological Assessment, 30,* 1–9.

Bagby, R. M., & Widiger, T. A. (2020). Assessment of the ICD-11 dimensional trait model: An introduction to the Special Section. *Psychological Assessment, 32,* 1–7.

Bender, D. S., Morey, L. C., & Skodol, A. E. (2011). Toward a model for assessing level of personality functioning in DSM–5, part I: A review of theory and methods. *Journal of Personality Assessment, 93,* 332–346.

Block, J (1961) *The Q-sort method of personality assessment and psychiatric research* Springfield, IL: Charles G Thomas.

Bluhm, C., Widiger, T. A. & Miele, G. (1990). Interpersonal complementarity and individual differences. *Journal of Personality and Social Psychology, 58,* 464–471.

Clarkin, J., Widiger, T. A., Frances, A., Hurt, S., & Gilmore, M. (1983). Prototypic typology and the borderline personality disorder. *Journal of Abnormal Psychology, 92,* 263–275.

Costa, P. T., & McCrae, R. R. (1992). *Revised NEO Personality Inventory (NEO PI-R) and NEO Five-Factor Inventory (NEO-FFI) professional manual.* Odessa, FL: Psychological Assessment Resources.

Costa, P. T., & McCrae, R. R. (2017). The NEO inventories as instruments of psychological theory. In T. A. Widiger (Ed.), *The Oxford handbook of the five factor model* (pp. 11–37). New York: Oxford University Press.

Costa, P. T., & Widiger, T. A. (Eds.). (1994). *Personality disorders and the five-factor model of personality.* Washington, DC: American Psychological Association.

Crego, C., Gore, W. L., Rojas, S. L., & Widiger, T. A. (2015). The discriminant (and convergent) validity of the Personality Inventory for DSM-5. *Personality Disorders: Theory, Research, and Treatment, 6,* 321–325.

Crego, C., Oltmanns, J. R., & Widiger, T. A. (2018). FFMPD scales: Comparisons to the FFM, PID-5, and CAT-PD-SF. *Psychological Assessment, 30,* 62–73.

Crego, C., Oltmanns, J. R., & Widiger, T. A. (2020). Obtaining and losing the maladaptive bipolarity of the five factor model through factor analysis. *Personality Disorders: Theory, Research, and Treatment, 11,* 119–130.

Edmundson, M., Lynam, D. R., Miller, J. D., Gore, W. L., & Widiger, T. A. (2011). A five-factor measure of schizotypal personality traits. *Assessment, 18,* 321–334.

Exner Jr, J. E., & Erdberg, P. (2005). *The Rorschach: A comprehensive system.* New York: John Wiley & Sons Inc.

Ferenczi, S. (1912) *Selected papers. Volume 1: Sex in psychoanalysis.* New York: Basic Books.

Freud, S. (1900). *The interpretation of dreams.* London, New York: G. Allen & Unwin, ltd.

Glover, N., Miller, J. D., Lynam, D. R., Crego, C., & Widiger, T. A. (2012). The five-factor narcissism inventory: A five-factor measure of narcissistic personality traits. *Journal of Personality Assessment, 94,* 500–512.

Goldberg, L. R. (1993). The structure of phenotypic personality traits. *American Psychologist, 48,* 26–34.

Gore, W. L., Presnall, J., Lynam, D. R., Miller, J. D., & Widiger, T. A. (2012). A five-factor measure of dependent personality traits. *Journal of Personality Assessment, 94,* 488–499.

Hare, R. D. (1991). *The hare psychopathy checklist-revised manual.* North Tonawanda, NY: Multi-Health Systems.

Jarnecke, A. M., & South, S. C. (2017)). Behavior and molecular genetics of the five-factor model. In T. A. Widiger (Ed.), *The Oxford handbook of the five factor model* (pp. 301–318). New York: Oxford University Press.

Krueger, R. F., Derringer, J., Markon, K. E., Watson, D., & Skodol, A. E. (2012). Initial construction of a maladaptive personality trait model and inventory for DSM-5. *Psychological Medicine, 42,* 1879–1890.

Laing, R. D. (1960). *The divided self: An existential study in sanity and madness.* Harmondsworth: Penguin.

Lindsay, K., & Widiger, T. A. (1995). Sex and gender bias in self-report personality disorder inventories: Items analyses of the MCMI-II, MMPI, and PDQ-R. *Journal of Personality Assessment, 65,* 1–20.

Lynam, D. R., Gaughan, E. T., Miller, J. D., Miller, D. J., Mullins-Sweatt, S., & Widiger, T. A. (2011). Assessing the basic traits associated with psychopathy: Development and validation of the elemental psychopathy assessment. *Psychological Assessment, 23,* 108–124.

Lynam, D. R., Loehr, A., Miller, J. D., & Widiger, T. A. (2012). A five-factor measure of avoidant personality: The FFAvA. *Journal of Personality Assessment, 94,* 466–474.

Lynam, D. R., & Widiger, T. A. (2001). Using the five factor model to represent the DSM-IV personality disorders: An expert consensus approach. *Journal of Abnormal Psychology, 110,* 401–412.

McCabe, G. A., & Widiger, T. A. (2020). Discriminant validity of the AMPD. *Psychological Assessment, 32*(12), 1158–1171.

McCrae, R. R., & Costa, P. T. (1989). The structure of interpersonal traits: Wiggins's circumplex and the five-factor model. *Journal of Personality and Social Psychology, 56,* 586–595.

McCrae, R. R, Costa, P. T, & Busch, C. M. (1986). Evaluating comprehensiveness in personality systems: The California Q-Set and the five-factor model. *Journal of Personality, 54,* 430–446.

Meehl, P. E. (1973). Why I do not attend case conferences. *Psychodiagnosis: Selected papers* (pp. 225–302). Minneapolis: University of Minnesota Press.

Meehl, P. E. (1978). Theoretical risks and tabular asterisks: Sir Karl, Sir Ronald, and the slow progress of soft psychology. *Journal of Consulting and Clinical Psychology, 46*, 806–834.

Mervielde, I., De Clercq, B., De Fruyt, F., & Van Leeuwen, K. (2005). Temperament, personality, and developmental psychopathology as childhood antecedents of personality disorders. *Journal of Personality Disorders, 19*, 171–201.

Millon, T. (1981). *Disorders of personality, DSM-III, Axis II.* New York: John Wiley.

Morgan, C. D., & Murray, H. A. (1935). A method for investigating fantasies: The Thematic Apperception Test. *Archives of Neurology & Psychiatry, 34*, 289–306.

Mulder, R. T., Horwood, J., Tyrer, P., Carter, J, & Joyce, P. R. (2016). Validating the proposed ICD-11 domains. *Personality and Mental Health, 10*, 84–95.

Mullins-Sweatt, S. N., Edmundson, M., Sauer-Zavala, S., Lynam, D. R., Miller, J. D., & Widiger, T. A. (2012). Five-factor measure of borderline personality traits. *Journal of Personality Assessment, 94*, 475–487.

Mullins-Sweatt, S. N., Jamerson, J. E., Samuel, D. B., Olson, D. R., & Widiger, T. A. (2006). Psychometric properties of an abbreviated instrument of the five-factor model. *Assessment, 13*, 119–137.

Mullins-Sweatt, S. N, & Widiger, T. A. (2007). The Shedler-Westen assessment procedure from the perspective of general personality structure. *Journal of Abnormal Psychology, 116*, 618–623.

Oltmanns, J. R., Crego, C., & Widiger, T. A. (2018). Informant assessment: The informant five-factor narcissism inventory. *Psychological Assessment, 30*, 43–61.

Oltmanns, J. R., & Widiger, T. A. (2018a). Assessment of fluctuation between grandiose and vulnerable narcissism. Development and initial validation of the FLUX scales. *Psychological Assessment, 30*, 1612–1624.

Oltmanns, J. R., & Widiger, T. A. (2018b). A self-report measure for the ICD-11 dimensional trait model proposal: The Personality Inventory for ICD-11. *Psychological Assessment, 30*, 154–169.

Oltmanns, J. R., & Widiger, T. A. (2019). Evaluating the assessment of the ICD-11 personality disorder diagnostic system. *Psychological Assessment, 31*, 674–684.

Ozer, D. J. & Benet-Martinez, V. (2006). Personality and the prediction of consequential outcomes. *Annual Review of Psychology, 57*, 401–421.

Piedmont, R. L. (1998). *The revised NEO personality inventory: Clinical and research applications.* New York, NY: Plenum Press.

Pincus, A. L., & Widiger, T. A. (2014). Wiggins, Jerry S. (1931–2006). *The encyclopedia of clinical psychology, 1–2.* Wiley Online Library. https://doi.org/10.1002/9781118625392.wbecp402

Roberts, B. W., & DelVecchio, W. F. (2000). The rank-order consistency of personality traits from childhood to old age: A quantitative review of longitudinal studies. *Psychological Bulletin, 126*, 3–25.

Roberts, B. W., Kuncel, N. R., Shiner, R., Caspi, A., & Goldberg, L. R. (2007). The power of personality: The comparative validity of personality traits, socioeconomic status, and cognitive ability for predicting important life outcomes. *Perspectives on Psychological Science, 2*, 313–345.

Robins, L. N. (1966). *Deviant children grown up.* Baltimore, MD: Williams & Wilkins.

Rojas, S. L., Crego, C., & Widiger, T. A. (2019). A conceptual dismantling of the Five Factor Form: Lexical support for the bipolarity of maladaptive personality structure. *Journal of Research in Personality, 80*, 62–71.

Rojas, S. L., & Widiger, T. A. (2014). The convergent and discriminant validity of the Five Factor Form. *Assessment, 21,* 143–157.

Rojas, S. L., & Widiger, T. A. (2018). Convergent and discriminant validity of the Five Factor Form and the Sliderbar Inventory. *Assessment, 25,* 222–234.

Rorer, L., & Widiger, T. A. (1983). Personality structure and assessment. *Annual Review of Psychology, 34,* 431–463.

Samuel, D. B., Mullins-Sweatt, S. N., & Widiger, T. A. (2013). An investigation of the factor structure and convergent and discriminant validity of the Five Factor Model Rating Form. *Assessment, 20,* 24–35.

Samuel, D. B., Riddell, A. D. B., Lynam, D. R., Miller, J. D., & Widiger, T. A. (2012). A five-factor measure of obsessive-compulsive personality traits. *Journal of Personality Assessment, 94,* 456–465.

Samuel, D. B., & Widiger, T. A. (2004). Clinicians' descriptions of prototypic personality disorders. *Journal of Personality Disorders, 18,* 286–308.

Samuel, D. B., & Widiger, T. A. (2008). A meta-analytic review of the relationships between the five-factor model and DSM-IV-TR personality disorders: a facet level analysis. *Clinical Psychology Review, 28,* 1326–1342.

Shedler, J., & Westen, D. (2004). Dimensions of personality pathology: An alternative to the five-factor model. *American Journal of Psychiatry, 161,* 1743–1754.

Spitzer, R. L., Williams, J. B. W., & Skodol, A. E. (1980). DSM-III: The major achievements and an overview. *American Journal of Psychiatry, 137,* 151–164.

Tomiatti, M., Gore, W. L., Lynam, D. R., Miller, J. D., & Widiger, T. A. (2012). A five-factor measure of histrionic personality traits. In A. M. Columbus (Ed.), *Advances in Psychology Research* (Vol. 87, pp. 113–138). Hauppauge, NY: Nova Science Publishers.

Trull, T. J., Widiger, T. A., & Burr, R. (2001). A structured interview for the assessment of the five factor model of personality: Facet-level relations to the Axis II personality disorders. *Journal of Personality, 69,* 175–198.

Widiger, T. A. (1999). Millon's dimensional polarities. *Journal of Personality Assessment, 72,* 365–389.

Widiger, T. A. (2000). Personality disorders in the 21st century. *Journal of Personality Disorders, 14,* 3–16.

Widiger, T. A. (2003). Personality disorder diagnosis. *World Psychiatry, 2,* 131–135.

Widiger, T. A. (2020). Bruno Klopfer award address: Five-factor model personality disorder scales. *Journal of Personality Assessment, 102,* 1–9.

Widiger, T. A. (Ed.). (2017). *The Oxford handbook of the five-factor model.* New York: Oxford University Press.

Widiger, T. A., Cadoret, R., Hare, R., Robins, L., Rutherford, M., Zanarini, M., Alterman, A., Apple, M., Corbitt, E., Forth, A., Hart, S., Kultermann, J., Woody, G., & Frances, A. (1996). DSM-IV antisocial personality disorder field trial. *Journal of Abnormal Psychology, 105,* 3–16.

Widiger, T. A., & Costa, P. T. (1994). Personality and personality disorders. *Journal of Abnormal Psychology, 103,* 78–91.

Widiger, T. A., & Crego, C. (2019a). The bipolarity of normal and abnormal personality structure; Implications for assessment. *Psychological Assessment, 31,* 420–431.

Widiger, T. A., & Crego, C. (2019b). Madeline from the perspective of the five-factor model. In C. Hopwood & M. Waugh (Eds.), *Personality assessment* and paradigms: A collaborative reassessment of Madeline G. (pp. 132–144). New York: Elsevier.

Widiger, T., & Frances, A. (1985). The DSM-III personality disorders. Perspectives from psychology. *Archives of General Psychiatry, 42*, 615–623.

Widiger, T. A. Frances, A. J., Pincus, H. A., First, M. B., Ross, R. R., & Davis, W. W. (Eds.) (1994). *DSM-IV sourcebook* (Vol 1). Washington, DC: American Psychiatric Association.

Widiger T. A., Frances, A. J., Pincus, H. A., First, M. B., Ross, R. R., & Davis, W. W. (Eds.). (1996). *DSM-IV sourcebook* (Vol 2). Washington, DC: American Psychiatric Association.

Widiger, T. A., Frances, A. J., Pincus, H. A., Ross, R. R., First, M. B., & Davis, W. W. (Eds.). (1997). *DSM-IV sourcebook* (Vol. 3). Washington, DC: American Psychiatric Association.

Widiger, T. A., Frances, A. J., Pincus, H. A., Ross, R., First, M. B., Davis, W. W., & Kline, M. (Eds.). (1998). *DSM-IV sourcebook* (Vol. 4). Washington, DC: American Psychiatric Association.

Widiger, T. A., & Hagemoser, S. (1997). Personality disorders and the interpersonal circumplex. In R. Plutchik & H. R. Conte (Eds.), *Circumplex models of personality and emotions* (pp. 299–325). Washington, DC: American Psychological Association.

Widiger, T., Knudson, R., & Rorer, L. (1980). Convergent and discriminant validity of measures of cognitive styles and abilities. *Journal of Personality and Social Psychology, 39*, 116–129.

Widiger, T. A., Lynam, D. R., Miller, J. D., & Oltmanns, T. F. (2012). Measures to assess maladaptive variants of the five factor model. *Journal of Personality Assessment, 94*, 450–455.

Widiger, T., & Maitland-Schilling, K. (1980). Toward a construct validation of the Rorschach. *Journal of Personality Assessment, 44*, 450–459.

Widiger, T. A., Mangine, S., Corbitt, E. M., Ellis, C. G., & Thomas, G. V. (1995). *Personality Disorder Interview-IV. A Semistructured interview for the assessment of personality disorders*. Odessa, FL: Psychological Assessment Resources.

Widiger, T. A., & McCabe, G. A. (2020). The Alternative Model of Personality Disorders (AMPD) from the perspective of the five-factor model. *Psychopathology, 53*(3), 149–156.

Widiger, T. A., & Rorer, L. (1984). The responsible psychotherapist. *American Psychologist, 39*, 503–515.

Widiger, T. A., & Simonsen, E. (2005). Alternative dimensional models of personality disorder: Finding a common ground. *Journal of Personality Disorders, 19*,110–130.

Widiger, T. A., & Trull, T. J. (1993). The scholarly development of DSM-IV. In J. A. Costa e Silva & C. C. Nadelson (Eds.), *International review of psychiatry* (Vol. 1, pp. 59–78). Washington, DC: American Psychiatric Press.

Widiger, T. A., & Trull, T. J. (2007). Plate tectonics in the classification of personality disorder: shifting to a dimensional model. *American Psychologist, 62*, 71–83.

Widiger, T. A., Williams, J., Spitzer, R., & Frances, A. (1985). The MCMI as a measure of DSM-III. *Journal of Personality Assessment, 49*, 366–378.

Wiggins, J. S. (1973). *Personality and prediction: Principles of personality assessment*. Malabar, FL: Krieger Publishing Company.

Wiggins, J. S. (2003). *Paradigms of personality assessment.* New York: Guilford.

Wiggins, J. S., & Pincus, A. L. (1989). Conceptions of personality disorders and dimensions of personality. *Psychological Assessment: A Journal of Consulting and Clinical Psychology, 1,* 305–316

World Health Organization (2018). *ICD-11, the 11th revision of the international classification of diseases.*

14 Evolving Convictions through Dogged Pursuit of Answers and Large Dollops of Luck

My Piece in the World of Personality and Psychopathology Assessment[1]

Lee Anna Clark

In retrospect, the first indicator of how my interests might lead me to become a scientist was "discovering" Chicago's Museum of Science and Industry. Denver, where I lived from age 3 through high school, had a Museum of Natural History[2] and an Art Museum, both of which I found rather boring as a child, but on a summer vacation to Chicago—a departure from our usual camping trips to Yellowstone, the Grand Canyon, Mesa Verde, Petrified Forest, and other national forests and parks in Colorado and neighboring states—we likely went to the Art Institute, Shedd Aquarium, and Adler Planetarium, but all I remember is the Museum of Science and Industry, which had fascinating exhibits with which you could interact and experiment. I was riveted and could have stayed for hours.

Backing up to the beginning, I was born in Vermont, lived in St. Louis from age 3 months to 3 years and thence grew up in Denver. My father was a Congregational[3] pastor, my mother a pastor's wife and homemaker with an MFA in Theater who started back to school for her Ph.D. in Theater when I was 12—but her fascinating biography must await another opportunity. I was a tomboy (thanks partly to my older brother), school-smart (but average, at best, in "people skills"), sensitive (but not very self-aware or insightful), competitive, and self-disciplined. I took piano lessons from age 5 to 15, but my real musical love was the cello, which I studied from age 8 through college, and continued to play until graduate school, including performing Boccherini's Cello Concerto in D major with a community orchestra. "Fun fact": Stephen Finn—author of another autobiography in this volume—and I played together for fun in a trio in graduate school, with Steve on the flute.

My most influential mentors as a child were my cello teacher, Fred Hoeppner, long-time first-chair cellist in the Denver Symphony, who

DOI: 10.4324/9781003036302-14

taught me as much about life as about playing cello, and my high-school English teacher, Lynn Pettyjohn, who was the Yearbook Sponsor during the three years that I worked my way up to Editor in my senior year, and who helped me take my first steps to being comfortable with who I was, instead of being unhappy over who I wanted to be, but was not—one of the popular kids.

Also in retrospect, the single most important event that put me on the path to becoming who I am today was a conversation I happened to overhear: One classmate telling another about the American Field Service summer-abroad program. It sounded like an exciting opportunity, so I applied and was selected. To this day I feel a little guilty that the classmate from whom I learned about the program, and who I assume also applied, was not selected. I was hoping to be sent to France, but much to my surprise, I was assigned to a family in Ashikaga, Japan, about an hour-and-a-half north of Tokyo. The family's two daughters, the younger of whom was my age, spoke "high-school English," but the parents knew little. That summer's immersion in Japanese culture—a complex blend of ancient and modern elements—including learning enough Japanese to have simple conversations, was the most challenging experience of my young life. I determined then and there that I would study Japanese in college and return to the country so I could absorb it more fully.

College and "Gap" years

Following my best friend from high school, I went to Cornell University, where I studied Japanese with Eleanor Jorden, then America's premier Japanese linguistic scholar. I was accepted into Cornell's College Scholar Program, which allows students to design their own interdisciplinary major. I focused on psycholinguistics hoping to plumb the depths of the what, how, and why of language and its use. I received a Danforth Fellowship to Berkeley in linguistics, but deferred admission because the opportunity arose to teach English in Japan to students in the first two "general-studies" years at Sapporo Medical School, on the northern island, Hokkaido. Another "fun fact": I went to Japan the summer after the Winter Olympics in Sapporo and lived on the back side of the mountain where some of the skiing events had been held. Wednesdays and Saturdays were half-days in Japanese schools and in the winter, I often took the tram after classes to ski at the newly renovated area.

After three wonderful years, it was time to return to the U.S. for graduate school. Over that period, however, linguistics as a field had become dominated by Noam Chomsky's cognitive approach, which I found dry and far from my interest in the cultural and individual interfaces with language, so I returned to Cornell instead where Professor Jorden graciously (and luckily for me) hired me as a Teacher Associate in the seminal intensive Japanese language program she had founded, while I figured out what I wanted to be when I grew up. I ended up getting an M.A. in Japanese Studies while I applied to graduate school in Psychology and was admitted to the University of Minnesota's Clinical Psychology program to work with James Butcher, a foremost cross-cultural scholar focused on translations of the Minnesota Multiphasic Personality Inventory (MMPI).

Like many who knew me, you may ask, "Why clinical psychology?— given my then-average people skills, self-awareness, and insight (the latter two of which likely contain part of the answer)." The main reason was that I saw myself headed towards academia but, in addition, I was more interested in individual people than in groups (e.g., social or industrial/organizational psychology) or how the brain worked (e.g., cognitive psychology) or developed (e.g., developmental psychology). I also had a pragmatic streak: If academia didn't work out, I would have a professional skill on which to fall back.

Graduate school

Given that I had taken only three psychology courses in college—one semester of Intro and two related to language—the first semester of graduate school was an exhilarating, steep learning curve. Assessment was a major emphasis, with courses in intellectual assessment, objective (i.e., MMPI) and projective testing, plus measurement, and I found myself more drawn to those courses and to psychopathology, than to those in intervention. My most memorable graduate-school experience was Auke Tellegen's personality-assessment seminar, which delved into personality theory (rather than test administration and interpretation taught in the clinically oriented classes). Tellingly, the particular class that I remember most clearly was when someone asked Tellegen how he had come to develop the Multidimensional Personality Questionnaire,[4] and he spontaneously gave a long exposition of the process, including how it had led to his theoretical leap to link two primary mood dimensions—negative and positive affect—with two major personality dimensions—Eysenck's Neuroticism (N) and Extraversion (E), which Tellegen termed Negative Affectivity (NA) and Positive Affectivity (PA; see Tellegen, 1985).

Before going further, it is important to situate these events in the context of the knowledge base of the time: (1) My psychopathology class used the Second Edition of the *Diagnostic Manual of Mental Disorders* (*DSM*; American Psychiatric Association, 1968), a spiral-bound pamphlet about a half-inch thick and 5½" × 8" in size. (2) the term 'five-factor model of personality" had not appeared in the literature (although a replicable five-factor structure of personality had been identified; see Goldberg, 1990, for a history); (3) whether, or the extent to which, personality and psychopathology were related was not a focus of research. In fact, they were widely considered distinct and largely unrelated fields (although this had not always been the case historically; see Watson & Clark, 1994) and (4) that psychopathology was a categorical phenomenon was essentially an unquestioned fact. Through the 1970s, barely over 100 papers were published exploring the idea that psychopathology might be better conceptualized as interrelated dimensions.

In the first week of graduate school, I met David Watson, a third-year student of Tellegen's in the Personality Psychology program. We became friends, began dating a year later and, in due time, moved in together. Not long thereafter, fortune smiled on me again, and I received a Fulbright Fellowship to return to Japan to work on a Japanese translation of the MMPI. The Fellowship provided $3,000 for an accompanying spouse and, although we had not been talking about marriage, it certainly seemed that we were on that trajectory, so I said to David, "No one will ever pay us $3,000 to get married again." On February 14, he proposed and I accepted.

During our year in Japan, David and I not only worked on our dissertations, but also began work on Watson and Clark (1984) and Watson et al. (1984). The latter was based on David's dissertation, but required my involvement because the data were collected using Japanese language materials and students. I mention these articles because they were the first of an ongoing research collaboration that has yielded ~90 co-authored publications to date, and because the former was our "break-out" publication on major personality dimensions and their relations to psychopathology.

Around the time we returned from Japan, the Third Edition of the *DSM-III* (American Psychiatric Association [APA], 1980) was published, and I was excited to see that personality disorders (PDs) had been put on a separate "Axis" from the "clinical disorders," because this meant that PD lay at the intersection of my two interests—clinical and personality psychology. Moreover, I was pleased to see that (a) the beginning of the PD chapter began with a reasonable definition of personality traits as "enduring patterns of perceiving, relating to, and thinking about the environment and oneself, [that] are exhibited in a wide range of important social and personal contexts," and (b) the definition of traits was followed by a definition of PDs as constituted of traits that were "inflexible and maladaptive and cause either significant impairment in social or occupational functioning or subjective distress" (p. 305, APA, 1980). That the DSM model was based on these two definitions pleased me because it meant that it would be relatively straightforward to research the clinical–personality intersection.

Or so I thought... until I noted the jarring disconnect between, on the one hand, the DSM definitions of traits and PDs and, on the other hand, the specific criteria by which PDs were diagnosed. It puzzled me that PDs were not *assessed*, and thus diagnosed, in the same the way that they were *defined*. That is, although PDs were defined as traits, many of the criteria by which they were assessed/diagnosed were not themselves traits, although some were trait indicators. For example, "physically self-damaging acts, e.g., suicidal gestures, self-mutilation, recurrent accidents or physical fights" (p. 323, APA, 1980) seemed much more like a clinically relevant set of behaviors than a trait (or even a compilation of four indicators of trait aggressiveness or of a tendency to self-harm). Moreover, even when a criterion was clearly a trait (e.g., "hypersensitivity"), it was often assessed using as few as four indicators (e.g., p. 309, APA, 1980) which, from a measurement perspective, was essentially a four-item scale and therefore not likely to be highly reliable.

Through classes in measurement and assessment, I knew that scales' reliability in turn limited their validity, so I wondered how one might assess/diagnose the *DSM-III* PDs reliably and validly, given that the official criteria didn't seem likely to be up to the task. Further, in other cases, only a description of the trait and *no* indicators were provided (e.g., "excessive devotion to work and productivity to the exclusion of pleasure and the value of interpersonal relationships"; p. 328, APA, 1980), so it also was unclear how one would ensure reliable and valid assessment of such criteria. Even worse, some criteria confounded distinct traits; for example, Histrionic PD criterion A, "Characteristic disturbances in interpersonal relationships" included both "egocentric, self-indulgent, and inconsiderate of others" and "dependent, helpless, constantly seeking reassurance." Although one certainly could imagine that an individual might have both of these characteristics, they seemed more like manifestations of at least two different traits than of a single one.

Assuming that there must be measures that either the APA or researchers working in the area had developed, just as there were for then-called Axis I disorders (cf. *Hamilton Rating Scale for Depression*; Hamilton, 1960), I began searching the literature for such measures. The relatively few that I found varied widely in approach, including assessing traits (Tyrer & Alexander, 1979), behaviors (Livesley, 1985), and a mix of symptoms, traits, and behaviors (Baron et al., 1981). Recognizing a research opportunity because of the newness of the Axis II concept, the more elaborated descriptions and criteria of *DSM-III* PD diagnoses compared to those in *DSM-II*, and the consequent paucity of measures in the field, I decided that my first major research project would be to develop a comprehensive, trait-based self-report measure of personality pathology—blissfully unaware of the project's complexity and that 12 years would pass before the measure's publication.

Postdoctoral fellowship

After two years spent on our dissertations and my clinical internship in Seattle, David and I landed postdoctoral fellowships at Washington University School of Medicine's Psychiatry Department with Irving Gottesman and Greg Carey. During this period, articles had begun to appear that both noted the important contribution of the new PD model and critiqued not only its poor reliability but also its poor discriminant validity (e.g., similar, even identical, criteria appeared in multiple PDs), its unclear boundary with normality, and the considerable within-diagnosis heterogeneity of various PDs (e.g., Frances, 1980). It was recognized early on that these problems stemmed in large part from imposing a categorical system on the constructs of personality and its pathology, which are dimensional (Widiger & Frances, 1985). This strengthened my conviction that developing a measure to assess trait dimensions relevant to PD was an endeavor worth pursuing.

However, in reading this emerging and fast-growing literature (from ~200 articles/year in the early 1980s to ~450/year by the end of the decade), I realized that I could not develop a measure until I had identified the dimensions that collectively described the domain, necessitating preliminary studies. Moreover, David and I wanted to take advantage of being at Washington University, where the *DSM-III*'s descriptive approach to diagnosis began with the Feighner Criteria (see Kendler et al., 2010, for an historical accounting) and the Research Diagnostic Criteria (Spitzer & Robins, 1978), so together we embarked on a project that applied Tellegen's two-factor personality–mood connection (Negative Affect[ivity]/N and Positive(Affect[ivity]/E) to the puzzle of anxiety–depression comorbidity. We found that both anxiety and depression symptoms and disorders related broadly to trait NA/N, whereas depression symptoms and disorders related more specifically to trait PA/E (Watson et al., 1988). I circle back to these results after relating an important series of other events that took place simultaneously with our graduate school and postdoctoral years.

Beginning a family

Looping back in time, our first child, Bartholomew Clark Watson, was born in November 1980, the year we returned from Japan. We were still poor graduate students and daycare wasn't a viable option—it didn't even cross our minds. Rather, we divided the day into morning and afternoon shifts, during which one of us would work on TA duties or go to the computer center to analyze our dissertation data (personal computers were still very rare), while the other had childcare duties.

Besides work and childcare, we had an informal Sunday afternoon volleyball game with other students and young faculty members in the department, many of whom became well-known academicians themselves, including Judy Garber, Steve Hollon, Phil Kendell, and Rob deRubeis. We took Bart along in a baby carrier and put him on the floor in a recessed area of the gym, protected by an upright piano that was there for who knows what reason. He usually obliged us by sleeping through the hour or two that we played. As he grew older—and the weather warmer—we sometimes took him to the computer center with us, where he amused himself playing with discarded punch cards in a large collection barrel (you tossed in cards on which you'd made an error because each card had to be punched in perfectly on a single try; "Undo" did not yet exist). We kept an eye out to make sure that nobody dumped a large box of cards into the barrel, unaware that a small child was sitting inside. I also took Bart with me to a conference when he was 4 months old and still nursing. Jim Butcher reportedly had great fun babysitting while I gave my presentation. Figure 14.1 is a picture of Bart on the airplane, clearly in pre-car-seat days. Finally, two other graduate students, Ann Masten and Kelly Bemis Vitousek—both of whom also became well-known academicians—happened to have girls within four months of Bart's age. We had "birthday get-togethers" once a month before I left for internship, our final year of graduate school, during which we both finished our dissertations. Figure 14.2 shows the three children at their April 1981 "party."

Wash U had an affiliated daycare center in which we placed Bart throughout our postdoctoral years, and our daughter, Erica Watson Clark, was born in October of our second year there. I stayed home with her for the first three weeks, but then started taking her in to work with me. I would rock her in the baby carrier with my foot while I worked, for

Figure 14.1 Bart on the plane to a conference in Hawai'I.

Figure 14.2 Bart and "friends" at a monthly "party".

the first time, on a desktop computer (see Figure 14.3). At six weeks, she also started going to the daycare center half-time for the remainder of our postdoctoral years. That spring, I went on the job market, as there were many more positions in clinical than in personality psychology. We had

Figure 14.3 Lee Anna at work rocking Erica.

decided we would not live apart and that if I was offered a position, we would work out whatever we could for David.

I received several interview invitations and near the end of the call, the person would ask if I had any questions or anything else to discuss. I responded that, yes, I would be bringing my five-month-old daughter with me, so I would need to have some kind of babysitting arrangement and a half-hour break every few hours to nurse her. After a brief silence on the other end, the caller would regroup and say that that could be arranged. I let them know that she was used to daycare and was an outgoing child, so an arrangement such as having graduate students in rotating shifts play with her or be there while she napped would be fine. I figured that if the department was not OK with my having children and balancing family life with work, then it was not a good fit for us, so we would remain postdocs for another year and keep looking until we found a more suitable department. Fortunately, I received a couple of offers and Southern Methodist University also offered David a position working on Jaime Pennebaker's grant, so I began life as a faculty member in Dallas in August 1984.

First faculty position—the developmental phase

The "Model" Era

Returning to the project we started at Wash U, the finding that both anxiety and depression symptoms and disorders related broadly to trait NA/N, whereas depression symptoms and disorders related more specifically to trait PA/E (Watson et al., 1988) raised a number of intriguing questions regarding relations between personality dimensions and psychopathology: Were basic, temperamental (i.e., strongly biologically based) aspects of personality traits risk factors for depression and/or anxiety? Did anxiety and depressive disorders have a temporary or lasting effect on one's personality traits? Were there still more basic factors underlying both personality and psychopathology? Alternatively, did measurement artifacts spuriously inflate or otherwise affect the correlations between NA/PA and anxiety/depression? If so, could these be eliminated by improving how we measured personality and/or psychopathology? The results also raised questions regarding relations between affective personality traits and mood states: Were affective traits simply mood-state averages or was there more than a statistical relation? Again, it is important to remember that, although tremendous progress has been made on answering these questions in the 35 intervening years, all of this was unknown in the mid-1980s.

As came to be a hallmark of our research over the years—both independently and collaboratively—we first wanted to ensure that we understood what we were measuring as clearly and as precisely as possible. Thus, during this phase of our careers, together with Tellegen, we developed and published the Positive and Negative Affect Schedule (Watson et al., 1988) which, by early March 2021, had been cited over 40,000 times (per Google Scholar). We also wanted to develop trait measures of Negative and Positive Affectivity that focused more on the affective core of these dimensions than traditional measures of Neuroticism and Extraversion, especially the latter, which has a strong interpersonal/ social component (see Watson & Clark, 1997). This work led to the General Temperament Survey (GTS), which also incorporated the third of the "Big Three" dimensions, Disinhibition (vs. Constraint). In addition to existing as a stand-alone measure, the GTS scales were incorporated into the measure I was developing to assess dimensions of personality pathology. They are used most often in that context, which also is where I discuss them.

The breakthrough in understanding depression–anxiety comorbidity in relation to personality came gradually and was developed in a series of articles and chapters written between 1988 and 1991 (Watson et al., 1988; Clark, 1989; Clark & Watson, 1991a, 1991b). As noted earlier, building on Tellegen's work distinguishing NA and PA, it was relatively easy to establish that NA was a common factor underlying depression and anxiety (along with many other types of psychopathology, as is now well-known; see Watson & Clark, 1984, for an early paper that addresses this), and that PA was a distinctive factor underlying depression (e.g., Watson et al., 1988), but the asymmetry bothered me and I kept searching for an anxiety-specific factor. In Clark (1989), a broad review of anxiety–depression overlap, the first glimmers of such a factor appeared when I examined symptom-level differences in studies of patients with anxiety and/or depression. The only consistently differentiating symptoms were associated with autonomic symptoms (e.g., as in panic attacks) and agoraphobic avoidance.

Heartened by this finding, and the fact that there rarely were sufficient indicators of autonomic arousal to form their own factor in self-report measures of anxiety, we developed the Mood and Anxiety Symptom Questionnaire (MASQ; Watson & Clark, 1991) to test the hypothesis that the anxiety-specific factor that I was seeking was autonomic arousal. Moreover, David Barlow, who chaired the Anxiety Disorders Work Group (WG) for *DSM-IV* (APA, 1994), asked us to review the literature on anxiety-depression overlap to help the WG determine whether the data supported inclusion of a "mixed anxiety-depression" diagnosis in the upcoming DSM revision. Long-story short, our review concluded that a tripartite structure of a general distress factor common to both anxiety and depressive disorders, an anxiety-specific factor of physiological hyperarousal, and a depression-specific factor of anhedonia/low PA best captured the data (Clark & Watson, 1991d). Subsequent work using the MASQ by both ourselves (Watson, Clark et al., 1995; Watson, Weber et al., 1995), others (e.g., Brown et al., 1998) has provided support for the model, including in youth (e.g., Joiner & Lonigan, 2000), as well as showing robust relations with personality traits NA and PA (e.g., Clark et al., 1994). Later work, primarily by David, has refined the model (e.g., Mineka et al., 1998; Watson, 2005) and expanded its measurement (e.g., Watson et al., 2012).

The schedule for nonadaptive and adaptive personality

As mentioned, the "tripartite era" started with a project at Wash U to take advantage of being where the *DSM-III*'s descriptive approach to diagnosis had begun. We focused on this work as long as we did for two main reasons: First, the era of dimensional models of psychopathology and their links with personality was just beginning, the issues were challenging and intriguing, and they connected well with my interest in personality. Moreover, it was exciting to be at the forefront of what proved to be a fast-developing research domain. Second, although my primary interest still lay in personality pathology, I had realized that a sole focus on that research domain, including the development of a comprehensive, trait-dimensional PD measure, was going to take a while and that I needed to be mindful of having a sufficient body of work to obtain tenure. Accordingly, I bifurcated my time and effort on the anxiety-depression comorbidity problem and the measurement of personality pathology. Thus, I now go back in time to the beginning of my first faculty position to trace the latter line of research.

Ironically, although the publication of *DSM-III* with its novel PD diagnostic system was the instigation for my PD research, it also was a major barrier to developing a trait-based measure of personality pathology. This is because, as mentioned earlier, its definition and diagnostic method were incommensurate. Thus, my first task was to determine just exactly what trait dimensions were needed, collectively, to describe the PD domain comprehensively. I decided to tackle this problem using an ingenious technique that Tellegen had developed. In brief, using multiple indicators of an indeterminant number of dimensions, raters independently sort the indicators into groups based on similarity. This yields a co-occurrence matrix that can be factor analyzed like a correlation matrix and its factor structure examined. As indicators, I used all of the individual *DSM-III* PD criteria, creating multiple indicators from complex criteria, and including indicators from alternative conceptualizations of personality pathology, as well as criteria from longer term, more trait-like "Axis I" disorders, such as dysthymia and generalized anxiety disorder (see Clark, 1990, for details).

The result was 23 relatively homogeneous dimensions, and I was gratified to see that each dimension contained indicators from multiple PDs and, conversely, that every PD contained indicators of multiple dimensions, providing support for the ideas that the *DSM-III* PD categories (1) were heterogeneous with regard to their component traits and (2) were comorbid because they had certain traits in common. Now I finally had a starting point: The set of traits for which I needed to develop measures. I used these 23 groupings to write self-report items to assess each dimension. Through an iterative process involving multiple stages of data collection, analysis, and refinement of not only the scales, but also the trait concepts they were intended to assess, I ultimately derived a set of 15 internally consistent, relatively independent trait measures that, when factor analyzed, broadly formed Tellegen's/Eysenck's "Big Three" higher order dimensions of NA, PA, and Disinhibition (vs. Constraint; DvC). I wanted the measure's name to be both memorable and accurately reflective of its scope, so I decided to call it the *Schedule for Nonadaptive and Adaptive Personality (SNAP)*. In 1993, 12 years after I began work on the *DSM-III*-inspired measure (and six years after *DSM-III-R* appeared), I concluded negotiations with the University of Minnesota Press to publish the instrument—a choice made easy by the fact that the Press was also working with Auke to publish the *Multidimensional Personality Questionnaire* (see Tellegen & Waller, 2008). Perhaps not coincidentally, I also was granted tenure in 1993.

Mid-career—the validation phase

In a conceptual sense, the publication of the tripartite model (Clark & Watson, 1991c) and the SNAP in 1993, ended the early, "developmental" phase of my career. I then entered a second, "validation" phase, during which I expanded—broadened and deepened—my research in both mood, anxiety, and depression and in personality pathology. The primary aims of this research were building the nomological nets around the SNAP and around the tripartite model of anxiety and depression, and using the data to refine and/or revise them as needed. Over the next 15 years (and actually starting in the late 1980s), my research efforts included establishing and developing external collaborations and facilitating my students' research. It was also the era during which I was most involved in professional organizations, in administration, and in family life—raising two children through the teenage years and the transition from high school to college to early adulthood. I elaborate on each in turn, after which I discuss why this phase might also be titled "The Waiting Phase."

Key collaborators

The first of the important external collaborations that developed over my career was with a faculty member at the University of Texas Southwestern Medical Center at Dallas, where I was given a Clinical Assistant Professor position in 1988, via which I gave guest lectures, attended Grand Rounds, participated in dissertation committees, and so on. This collaboration, which continues productively to this day, is with Robin Jarrett, who researches cognitive-behavioral therapy for depression. Importantly, Robin, who was far more integrated than I into the worlds of NIMH and psychiatry, introduced me to both, which proved to be highly generative.

The first major effect of Robin sharing this knowledge stemmed from her telling me about NIMH Workshops and advising me to watch for a workshop on personality disorders, which I could ask to attend as an observer. Fortuitously, a workshop on the assessment of personality disorders was announced soon thereafter and I contacted Jack Maser, then-Program Officer for NIMH's Personality Disorder (PD) section. In an amazing stroke of luck, Jack was a long-time friend of Tellegen, and, accordingly, not only invited me to attend, but to present at the workshop! I was thrilled at the opportunity and consider that 1988 meeting a significant turning point in my career, because I was introduced to many of the major figures in the field—including, for example, John Gunderson, Gerald Klerman, Armand Loranger, Tom McGlashan—and, in turn, I introduced them to the idea of a trait-dimensional system for personality disorders, in which they showed considerable interest. Little did any of us know then that I would keep harping on the idea for the next 30 years.

Three other significant collaborations also began between 1986 and 1990, the first based on an earlier chance meeting. The Epidemiological Catchment Area (ECA) study was ongoing during my postdoctoral years at Wash U and the ECA research team offered training in the Diagnostic Interview Schedule, the study's primary assessment tool. At the training session I attended, I met a team from the University of Iowa, headed by Bruce Pfohl, a psychiatrist who was developing an interview for PD assessment. Due to this common interest, Bruce and I kept in touch, and when he was President of the Iowa Psychiatric Society, he invited me to present at their 1986 Annual Meeting in Iowa City, at which two noteworthy things occurred: First, I met Peter Tyrer, a well-known international figure in personality pathology from England. Peter had been beating a PD-dimensional drum since the late 1970s, decades ahead of the field as a whole, and had developed an informant interview assessing 24 trait dimensions relevant to PD, on which he presented at the convention. Peter and I immediately felt each other to be kindred spirits and developed a lifelong friendship. Second, as I jogged in City Park one morning (only a few minutes from our downtown hotel) I mused, "I could see myself living here" (hold that thought…).

The third collaboration was with W. John Livesley, a British psychiatrist in Canada who had begun publishing on PD trait dimensions in 1986, and who came to my attention as I reviewed the literature in preparation for grant applications. I contacted John (to put a noteworthy timestamp on this event, I used a typewriter to write the letter and mailed it via what we now call snail mail), we began corresponding, and eventually arranged a long-distance phone call (a significant event in the late 1980s, as they were notably more expensive than local calls). I still remember his crisp,

British voice answering the phone, "Livesley here." We first met at the next NIMH PD Workshop in 1991 and also went on to have a lifelong collaboration and friendship.

To conclude this section, I circle back to Robin Jarrett, as there is no question that my ongoing collaboration with her—and with my RA at the time, Jeffrey Vittengl, whom I invited to work with Robin and me beginning in the late 1990s, in large part because of his data-analytic prowess—has been the most productive of my career in terms of numbers of publication. In the 25 or so years that we have worked together, we have only met in person a handful of times. However—although our conference calls were irregular at first, and there were times when I was so busy with my own work that I tried to take a step back or even step away altogether—Robin was always patient and steadfast, and would gently bring me back into the fold. Eventually, the three of us settled into a weekly conference call that has continued now for many years. We have collaborated on ~40 publications, ~2 dozen of which also include Michael Thase, all based on data from Robin's, or Robin's and Michael's, NIMH-funded, randomized clinical trials involving CBT for depression. We recently agreed to work together on data from my own NIMH-funded grant on PD assessment so our collaboration, like the snow in the Yuletide song, "shows no sign of stopping."

Student research

In 1993, I was approached by Don Fowles, a Professor at the University of Iowa, whom I had met through the *Society of Research in Psychopathology* (SRP; more on that later), who asked whether I (and, of course, David also) might be interested in joining the faculty at the University of Iowa. Although we were quite happy at SMU, we were ready for a change, particularly because we were dissatisfied with the public schools in Dallas, to the point that we had enrolled our children in a private school. We disliked doing that in principle, preferring the broader range of social influence that public schools offered (not to mention the cost!), yet were not willing to sacrifice our children's formal education to that principle. Moreover, Iowa had a well-known Ph.D. program, whereas SMU had had only a terminal master's program until a few years earlier and its fledgling Ph.D. program was still building its reputation, *and* Iowa was offering to bring us in as Full Professors. Remembering how much I had liked Iowa City when I visited there in the mid-1980's, I agreed to interview and the rest, as they say, is history.

Thus, in 1993, we began the most settled period of our professional lives, remaining at U Iowa until 2010. As indicated by this section's heading, it was after moving to Iowa with its strong Ph.D. program that I began to focus much of my work around student interests, which had the important effect of considerably broadening my research, as the students were interested in a wide variety of topics related to personality and its pathology. Initially, the expansion was simply to different populations and test forms: Jennifer Linde broadened my target research group to include adolescents and their parents (Linde et al., 2013); Elena Harlan and (much later) Yuliya Kotelnikova developed short forms (Harlan & Clark, 1999; Kotelnikova et al., 2015; Kotelnikova et al., 2019); Rebecca Ready and (again much later) Hallie Nuzum added informants (Nuzum et al., 2019; Ready et al., 2000). Nuzum also explored the language of test items (Nuzum et al., 2019), whereas Ready also examined whether mothers' personality traits interact with their infants' temperament to predict parental behavior, as did Robert Latzman with mothers and their adolescent sons' (in both cases, they do interact; respectively, Ready et al., 2000; Latzman et al., 2009). Len Simms experimented with computer adaptive testing (Simms & Clark, 2005).

Other students started developing the nomological network of personality traits. Sarah Reynolds examined the overlap of personality pathology with the five-factor model of personality domains and facets (Reynolds & Clark, 2001). Kevin Wu first led me to examine relations between personality traits and daily behaviors (Wu & Clark, 2003) and also to explore how personality pathology overlapped with clinical syndromes (Wu et al., 2007), as did Alex Casillas (Casillas & Clark, 2002) and Carrie Weaver (Kotelnikova et al., 2019). Eunyoe Ro got me interested in functioning (Ro & Clark, 2009, 2013; Clark, & Ro, 2014) and disability (Ro et al., 2017, 2018). Rob Latzman involved me in examining personality and executive functioning (Latzman et al., 2010, 2016) and externalizing behaviors (Latzman et al., 2011, 2013), as did Lilian Dindo (Dindo et al., 2009), who also examined the tenyear predictive power of toddlers' personality for academic achievement (Dindo et al., 2017), and relations of marital adjustment with both partners' personalities and personality perceptions (Brock et al., 2016). Leigh Sharma led me on a deep dive into "impulsivity" (Sharma et al., 2013), including laboratory tasks of the construct (Sharma et al., 2014) and Theresa Morgan into dependency (Morgan & Clark, 2010). Although some readers may find this listing tedious and skip over it, I have taken the time and space to provide this information in some detail because, despite the fact that renowned scholars often give a nod to how much their students influenced their research, one typically has to take their word for it. I thought my students deserved more prominent recognition of the vital importance of their contributions than just a token nod.

Professional organizations

I am devoting a section to professional organizations in which I was an active member because I believe these are reasonably good indicators of one's professional identity and thus another way to convey who I am as a scientist. Like most graduate students, I first attended conferences with my advisor, Jim Butcher—a major player in the international world of person-ality assessment owing to his cross-cultural MMPI research—specifically, the Annual Symposium on Recent Developments in the Use of the MMPI, and two International Conferences on Personality Assessment. These were heady experiences, because Jim introduced me to other well-known scholars in those professional circles, and often invited me to join their dinners and other informal gatherings.

Finding a Home. By the time I started my first faculty position, however, my interest in personality assessment had moved away from the MMPI. I first joined the *American Psychological Association* (hereafter "our APA"), eventually becoming a member of several Divisions, most importantly 12 (Clinical), Section III, the *Society for a Science of Clinical Psychology* (SSCP), which has evolved into a parallel entity that one can join independently from our APA. There often are heated debates on its listserv about severing ties with our APA, which many SSCP members see as a guild with more interest in serving its licensed practitioners than in advancing science.[5]

During the period that I was most actively involved in SSCP, including serving in its Presidential sequence from 2007 to 2009, I participated in its becoming more closely aligned with APS. Nevertheless, I still preferred working toward increasing the scientific basis of practice from within over separatism. However, when an independent investigation concluded that our APA had colluded with the U.S. Department of Defense and aided the CIA in justifying torture, I quit our APA (but not SSCP) and will rejoin only when I am convinced that the organization as a whole clearly has its values more closely aligned with science and its ethical applications.

In 1992, I was invited to join the *Society for Research in Psychopathology* (SRP), one of the few organizations that has criteria for joining and to which you have to be elected (vs. simply paying the annual dues). It quickly became clear to me that SRP was "home," the organization in which I would focus my efforts: I served eight years on its Executive Board, was a member of various committees, chaired hosting the 2007 meeting in Iowa City, and served in its presidential sequence from 2010 to 2013.

In writing this chapter, I realized that the reason I felt at home in SRP was that my primary interest lies in understanding psychopathology—What does it mean to call a personality pathological?—and SRP is the organization whose members' most closely share that interest. Their methods differ (e.g., many are experimentalists, whereas I work through assessment)[6] and the research domains differ (i.e., few study personality pathology), but everyone's primary focus is directly on understanding psy-chopathology, and that is "home" for me. Perhaps in return, I was awarded the 2017 Zubin Award for Lifetime Contributions to the Understanding of Psychopathology.

Personality and Personality Disorder Organizations. In 2002, a group of 15–20 faculty interested in personality psychology gathered at a small conference in Dartmouth, New Hampshire, over the course of which we decided to find a new organization, the *Association for Research in Personality* (ARP). The impetus for this was that the main other organization for personality research was the *Society for Personality and Social Psychology* was the primary conference for (non-clinical), which is dominated by social psychologists, so personality psychologists feel like poor relatives at a wedding, out of place and overlooked. Being in ARP keeps me apprised of and grounded in basic personality research, which is important because understanding normal personality is the basis for identifying its pathology.

The *International Society for the Study of Personality Disorders* (ISSPD), which I joined in 1996, and its North American branch, NASSPD, which emerged in 2012 from the smolders of ARPD (a story in its own right; see Supplemental Material A) are the final two organizations important in my career. My involvement in ISSPD ramped up slowly—for many years I only attended the biennial conferences—but through working on *DSM-5* (APA, 2013) and *ICD11* (World Health Organization [WHO], 2019), my involvement grew and I was elected to its Executive Board in 2012. Over the next four years, I helped transform it from an Executive-Board-controlled to a member-run organization. In 2020, I became its Federation Vice-President, tasked with working with its regional affiliates—Australia-Asia, Europe, Latin America, and North America, with a Middle Eastern region being developed—to help coordinate and integrate their efforts with those of the parent organization. Although much of the work presented at ISSPD is based on "WEIRD" (Western, educated, industrialized, rich, and democratic) cultures, being involved in ISSPD reminds me that the conceptualization and assessment of personality pathology must be broad enough to incorporate the perspectives of cultures worldwide. Getting to know and sharing experiences with interesting people from around the globe at biennial conferences in Copenhagen, Florence, Heidelberg, Melbourne, Montreal, The Hague, and Vancouver is an enriching benefit.

NASSPD is near the end of its first decade and, despite several setbacks (e.g., the unfortunate timing of the tragic Boston Marathon bombing just days before its first conference in Boston), it has developed into a robust organization with a strong core of members. Although dominated by research on borderline personality disorder (as is ISSPD), it is working to broaden its scope to include the growing number of PD researchers who focus on the *DSM-5* Alternative Model of Personality Disorder (AMPD; APA, 2013) and the *ICD-11*'s fully dimensional PD model. I served on NASSPD's inaugural Board of Directors, but stepped down when it became clear that the organization was continuing to be Board-controlled rather than member-run. I strongly believe that professional organizations should reflect their memberships' interests, which is best ensured by their being able to vote on its officers and Board members.

The Hierarchical Taxonomy of Psychopathology (HiTOP) Consortium. I end this section with a brief description of an informal group of scientists working to develop a robust dimensional system for assessing and diagnosing psychopathology as an alternative to the dominant categorical models of *DSM-5* and *ICD-11.* It is informal in that it has no bylaws, no formal officers, and an organic collection of nine (to date) WGs focused on developing various aspects of the model (e.g., Measure Development, Genetics, Revisions, and Clinical Translation). It has held several small conferences in connection with other conferences and held its first stand-alone conference—by virtue of being virtual—in Spring, 2021. The Hi-TOP model (Kotov et al., 2017) was first published by a "core" group of 40 members (including me) and currently has 145 members (see http://renaissance.stonybrookmedicine.edu/HITOP for the most recent list).

The consortium and its WGs have now published multiple papers, of which I have participated in eight, with another under review, and a great many other papers have been published from a HiTOP perspective by its members and others, as well as a growing number of critiques. According to a PsycINFO search conducted on March 21, 2021, 70 articles now use the term HiTOP or Hierarchical Taxonomy of Psychopathology in their entry. At this point, only time will tell how HiTOP will develop.

Mentoring

Although involvement in professional organizations is not typically associated with mentoring, it certainly was for me. The female-to-male ratio is generally increasing in academia, and notably so in psychology, but when I began my career, the field was still quite male dominant. However, over the years, my advisees and the students on whose various committees I've served, have been mostly female, 70–80% across both graduate and undergraduate students. In addition, I became an informal adviser to many more women, extending to professional contacts, both female colleagues across the university and in professional organizations, especially SRP. Women students would stop by my office to tell me about problems they were having with their advisors, and colleagues around the country would e-mail me to set up phone calls (now Zoom meetings) to ask my advice about everything from difficulties in their departments to balancing work and family life.

Regarding the latter, my advice was always some variant of encouragement and practicality, and I would share my own stories of dealing with situations similar to their own. A particular one that comes to mind was a postdoc who was ready to go on the job market and also happened to be pregnant. She wondered whether she should submit applications or wait a year or two. I responded that if I were in her shoes I would apply and pointed out that the job-search process would help screen out schools that might be a poor fit because they did not seem open to women who also had a life outside of academia. She did apply and her husband went with her to her last interview because she was getting close to her due date. She got the job and is now a full professor and Director of Clinical Training.

I also heard from women I met at conferences that I had served as a role model for them. It pleased me no end to learn that I was helping others (and, I'd like to think, the field), by just being myself, doing and loving what I did.

Family life

I last discussed our children in connection with when I began my first faculty position at SMU. Luckily, we found a facility that accepted children under two, and David's position was flexible so if one of them were ill, he was able to be the caregiver. By the time Bart started first grade, however, David had a Visiting Professor position, so we arranged our teaching schedules to ensure that one of us was always available if needed. Over time, the kids started participating in various activities—both took piano lessons and played organized sports; Erica sang in a church choir. They kept life busy, and we did our best to keep it manageable.

When we moved to Iowa City, Bart was entering junior high school and Erica fifth grade. Kids' activities ramp up at these ages, so chauffeuring to practices and attending various events became a regular part of our schedules. They expanded their activities—in particular, joining "traveling" soccer teams—so we were at the soccer fields nearly every Saturday, almost year-round because the indoor season started up soon after the outdoor season ended. During tournament season, we were gone for whole weekends. To "make matters worse," I became quite involved in their soccer organization and, as President, helped lead the club through the transition from a loose federation of area teams to the Iowa City Alliance soccer club, with a full-time, salaried head coach; some part-time, paid assistant coaches; standard uniforms, and so on. I even trained to be a referee, earned my license, and learned first-hand how hard refereeing is! You would be correct if you surmised that there were weeks when I spent many hours on soccer.

I had to be very efficient to stay on top of my scholarship during these years, although, fortunately, the pace of academic life was slower than it is now. For example, in today's world, a submitted manuscript is in the hands of the journal instantaneously, whereas then, it took several days. Likewise, manuscripts were sent directly to reviewers without their first being asked whether they would accept, so if they refused the review and returned the manuscript, it could be several weeks between when the journal sent it out and got it back. So I somehow managed to keep moving forward.

Administration

When we had been at U Iowa about five years, I was nominated for several administrative positions. I looked into them, decided that the cost-benefit ratio was too steep, and declined. Then I was nominated for the position of Associate Provost (AP) for Faculty. The idea of being in upper administration was more intriguing to me, so I applied, although I really didn't expect to get the position because I had virtually no administrative experience. Thus, it was much to my surprise when I was offered the position. To this day I wonder whether the key factor was when the search committee learned about my soccer administrative experience and thought to themselves, "If she can manage soccer parents, she can manage faculty."

The seven years that I spent in the Provost Office were a rich learning experience, and I offer but a précis. The first year was intimidating and the second year challenging, but more fulfilling, as I grew into the position. It was exciting to have the opportunity to get to know the University President and other upper-level administrators, plus my counterparts at the other Big Ten Universities. In years three and four, the position kept my interest because the University was making changes to various faculty-related policies that were in my portfolio and I dealt with several faculty grievances in which my expertise in psychopathology was highly relevant. The position was extremely time-consuming, and because—unlike many who take on administrative roles—I did not want to give up my scholarship, I became much more familiar with 2 and 3 AM than I liked. I stayed through six years to finish my term, and then a seventh because the University had a new Provost, and it didn't seem right for him to have to learn the job with an inexperienced person as AP for Faculty, after which I was more than ready to get back to the department and full-time scholarship.

The waiting phase

I promised an explanation of this label at the beginning of this section and waited until now to provide it, because it is a retrospective label. That is, as I was living through the years described above, I certainly did not think of it as such. However, as I look at my CV for those years and reflect back on how much time I spent on professional organizations, in administration, on family and its spin-off activities, and focused on my students' research more than my own, I realize that all of that activity served, in part, to keep me "moving in place" while the field came around to thinking about psychopathology in general—and personality pathology in particular—in dimensional rather than categorical terms. At some level, I must have felt that I had run dimensions up the flagpole and no one saluted, shot my wad and nobody jumped. But, at another level, I also must have believed that the field would come around eventually and that it would be better for me to be patient and contribute to the field in other ways than to keep hammering the same nail over and over with little effect or perhaps even backlash. Not that I totally stopped beating the drum, of course (to continue the mixed-metaphor theme of the paragraph;-). A plug for dimensions was in every conference presentation and every student-generated publication, and certainly in many family dinner conversations.

In 2004, NIMH and the American Psychiatric Association co-sponsored a small conference on "Dimensional models of personality disorder: Etiology, pathology, phenomenology, and treatment," co-chaired by Tom Widiger and Eric Simonsen in which they presented a paper "Finding a common ground" on which I was invited to give a commentary. This was one of a series of conferences that NIMH and APA co-sponsored to set a research agenda for DSM-V (sic at that time). It also was the first clear sign that a dimensional approach to personality disorder diagnoses was being considered. There was remarkable agreement at the conference on the idea and, even though the attendees were almost surely not a representative sample of PD researchers, I left feeling optimistic about PD in *DSM-V.*

In 2006, I was invited to the Borderline Personality Disorder Phenotypes Conference, a small gathering of perhaps a dozen scholars. By that time, rumblings about revising the DSM were getting louder and clearer, and I had heard that Andy Skodol, whom I had known for years and who also was at the conference, had been selected to lead the Personality Disorders WG. I let Andy know that I would be very interested in serving, and the very fact that I subsequently was invited, along with like-minded Bob Krueger and John Livesley, among others, was another indication that a dimensional approach to diagnosing PD was on the table, or at least had not been ruled out. Moreover, early on, co-Chairs David Kupfer and Darrell Regier indicated that a "paradigm shift"—or at least notable movement toward greater inclusion of dimensional approaches—was a very real possibility. I began to have some hope that my career-long goal of having a PD diagnostic system that reflected the "true" nature of PD, as well as how PD and its component traits were defined and assessed/ diagnosed might be realized.

Late career – the culmination phase

It is important to state that my conceptualization of a dimensional system for PD diagnosis and how one might revise the *DSM-IV* categorical system to reflect how personality pathology is manifested in the real world had changed significantly since 1980. When *DSM-III* was first published, I naïvely accepted that its 11 PD types were known entities. A quarter of a century later, however, not only I, but many others in the field, knew this was not true; indeed, the changes in the PD section with each *DSM* revision made clear that there was not a known set of disorders in nature that simply needed definition. Rather, as Steve Hyman put it so well recently, not only personality pathology, but mental disorder in general, "cannot reasonably be understood as discrete categories—and certainly not as natural kinds"; in fact, per research findings to date, they are better conceived as "heterogeneous quantitative deviations from health" (Hyman, 2021, p. 6).

Moreover, research in personality itself had advanced considerably since 1980, when the field was still debating whether normal- and maladaptive-range personality traits were distinct domains or reflected different ranges on the same set of continuous dimensions. There is now near universal consensus on the latter. How many personality traits there are was also an ongoing discussion. Were there as many as the 22 in Jackson's (1994) Personality Research Form or as few as three per Eysenck, Tellegen (who later recognized up to seven; Tellegen & Waller, 1987) and, initially, Costa and McCrae (1980), who expanded their number from three to five to match the "Big Five" (McCrae & Costa, 1985), all subsequently divided into 30 facets via the *NEO Personality Inventory Revised* (NEO-PI R; Costa & McCrae, 1985). Other measures had 15 (*SNAP2*; Clark et al., 2014), 18 (*Dimensional Assessment of Personality Pathology–Basic Questionnaire*; Livesley, 2010) or 24 (*Personality Assessment Schedule*; Tyrer, 1979).

Debates about the higher order structure of personality traits came abruptly to an end when Markon et al. (2005) demonstrated they all could be integrated into a hierarchical model of two to five trait domains. Thereafter, discussions regarding the number and composition of lower order "aspects" (DeYoung et al., 2013), "facets" (Costa & McCrae, 1985), and "nuances" (Mõttus et al., 2017) continued, but with little passion, as it was widely accepted that the various levels and divisions all derived from the same broad personality trait structure.

Further, conceptualization of personality pathology had expanded from a sole focus on maladaptive traits to include personality dysfunction, distinct from traits. This was "old news" in the clinical world, but rare in the PD research literature until the 2000s (e.g., Parker et al., 2002, 2004; Livesley & Jang, 2005; Verheul et al., 2008), made prominent with the publication of the AMPD and the *ICD-11* PD diagnosis. It became a focus of my research with the publication of Ro and Clark (2009; see also Ro & Clark, 2013; Clark & Ro, 2014; Clark et al., 2018; Nuzum et al., 2019). In the course of this work, I re-discovered the functioning-trait distinction in basic personality work, dating back to Gordon Allport (1937), who stated "Personality is something and personality does something" (Allport, 1937). Importantly, Allport stressed that the two aspects of personality—the traits that a personality "has" and the functions that a personality "does"—form an integrated, organized, coherent system.

Accordingly, an important question is the extent to which these two aspects of personality are distinct and can be measured independently which, in turn, raises the question of the extent to which existing measures of personality traits and personality functioning are "contaminated" with each other. When I first became interested in this question, I assumed that "too much" overlap, "too high" a correlation between personality trait and functioning measures was because the latter were "contaminated" with trait variance, given the long history of development and refinement of trait measures, but when a student asked why it couldn't be the other way around—that personality trait measures were "contaminated" with functioning variance—I realized I needed to test that assumption. Thus, some of my current research probes the degree of functioning in trait measures and vice versa. I want to examine the range in degree of overlap across different measures and, ultimately, to posit a small range of "theoretically optimal" overlap and to develop a set of trait and functioning scales that fall within that range. It may be a fool's errand, but it is worth the effort.

Finally, Dan McAdams' Presidential address at the 2017 ARP biennial meeting focused on his "three-layer" theory of personality: Traits are the foundational layer, goals and motivations the middle layer, and life narratives the top layer. Catalyzed by his talk, I began to connect the middle and top layers of personality with personality pathology and to integrate both the middle (e.g., Clark, 2017) and top (e.g., Adler & Clark, 2019; Lind et al., 2020) layers into my work.

DSM-5

The actual *DSM* revision process was slow getting underway because (1) great care was taken to ensure that WG members had no conflicts of interest that might compromise their judgment; and (2) the *DSM*-revision leadership wanted a diversity of opinions represented on the WGs, including international (non-North American) representatives, various disciplinary perspectives and theoretical orientations, as well as gender- and race/ethnicity-based diversity.[7] When our WG finally met, our first action was to change our name to "Personality and Personality Disorders" to indicate clearly that our approach would be grounded in the personality spectrum from adaptive to pathological personality. Otherwise, however, although our discussions were cordial, our opinions were broadly diverse.

There was an initial strong push by one subset for taking a prototype approach, with narrative descriptors, which others, including me, thought would be disastrous—highly unreliable and not well-supported empirically. Not surprisingly (at least to some of us), our first published draft of a prototype model met with highly mixed reviews and we went back to the drawing board. Thereafter, we began to wend our way—although not without both major and minor disagreements in the process—toward the current AMPD. I do not herein relate in any detail how we arrived there, as that rather tortuous process is reasonably well described by Zachar, Krueger and Kendler (2016). Rather, I focus on my role in, and perspective on, what I see as four key points: (1) The development of the AMPD's two-part model: Criterion A, personality dysfunction, and Criterion B, pathological expression of personality traits; (2) deliberate exclusion of a "clinical significance criterion"; (3) effect of the imposition of higher level

DSM-5 revision structures and processes; and (4) my own short-term and longer term reactions to the final decision of the APA Board of Trustees not to adopt the WG's proposal as *DSM-5's* primary PD diagnostic system.

AMPD's Two-Part Model. That the diagnosis should consist of two main criteria was fairly readily agreed upon. There was considerable research demonstrating that the *DSM-IV* PDs could be characterized using personality trait dimensions, so including a trait-based criterion was a no-brainer. The WG also readily agreed that a personality-functioning component was needed. In both cases, we discussed the particulars extensively. Regarding Criterion A, some WG members' theoretical perspective was broadly psychodynamic, based on the clinical-research literature, whereas others' perspective was based on evolutionary psychology. The latter perspective holds that personality pathology is not simply trait extremity—significant statistical deviation—but rather represents something dysfunctional in individuals—a view commensurate with the *DSM-5* definition of mental disorder.[8]

As articulated in Livesley and Jang (2005), the "something dysfunctional" is a failure to fulfill one or more of personality's three basic functions: (1) Providing a stable, integrated view of self, both per se and in relation to others; (2) facilitating development of adaptive attachments and affiliative relationships; and (3) facilitating prosocial and cooperative behaviors in the broader social group. In this view, there are degrees of failure, so personality functioning is also on a highly adaptive to strongly maladaptive continuum. The WG agreed that we first needed a definition of personality dysfunction that was acceptable to both perspectives, and started an iterative process toward that goal.

Regarding Criterion B, although we expected that the trait structure would broadly align with the five-factor model of personality, we felt we could not adopt an existing measure for practical (e.g., intellectual-property rights) and political (personal loyalties) reasons, so we compiled everyone's view of what traits should be included and, from those, intended to derive a model that would be broadly acceptable to the group and could serve as the starting point for developing a research-based self-report measure. Some WG members primarily wanted the trait set to include all traits represented in previous *DSM* PDs, whereas others drew from their own and others' research in normal and maladaptive personality.

Both tasks—deriving a consensual definition of personality dysfunction and set of traits on which to develop a research-based measure—proved to be more controversial than anticipated, so we ultimately divided the WG into two subgroups, one responsible for each criterion. At that time, the University of Minnesota Press still owned the SNAP's copyright and, per our contract, I could not participate in developing any potentially competing measure. Therefore—quite ironically, given that I had focused on getting the *DSM* to adopt a trait-based PD diagnostic system throughout my career—after the initial stage of developing the target trait set,

I worked with the Criterion A group and was not involved in developing the resultant AMPD trait model.

Criterion A's chief architect was Donna Bender, whose orientation was more clinical/psychodynamic, whereas I view personality dysfunction from the adaptive-failure model's perspective. Therefore, I saw my task as working to structure the criterion in a way that it could be operationalized and subsequently developed into a psychometrically sound measure. How well we succeeded has been and continues to be researched and discussed in the published literature (e.g., Zimmerman et al., 2015; Hopwood et al., 2018; Morey, 2019; Sleep et al., 2019a, 2019b; Morey et al., 2020; Sharp & Wall, 2021). The Criterion B subgroup's outcome is well known—the *Personality Inventory for DSM-5* (PID-5; Krueger et al. (2012)—and needs no further commentary. Accordingly, the WG's next published draft presented a fully dimensional two-criterion model. Space limitations prevent me from describing how the AMPD ended up a "hybrid" model, but it was a significant part of the process, so it is included in Supplemental Material B.

Exclusion of a "Clinical Significance Criterion" in the AMPD. Beginning with *DSM-III*, to set a threshold between disorder and non-disorder, the definition of mental disorder included that the condition is associated with distress or disability. In *DSM-IV,* a criterion was added to address this issue, typically worded "…causes clinically significant distress or impairment in social, occupational, or other important areas of functioning" (APA, 2000, p. 8), with "causes" notably stronger wording than the definition's "associated with." In *DSM-5,* the definition was eased, stating "*usually* associated with…" (emphasis added).[9] A primary reason for the easing was that in 2001, the World Health Assembly had published the International Classification of Functioning, which made a distinction between the functioning of the body (including the brain/mind) and the physical and psychosocial disabilities that were associated with bodily/psychological dysfunction. A main argument for separating mental/physical dysfunction from psychosocial/physical disability was the large range of individual differences in the degree of disability associated with the "objectively" same level of bodily/ psychological dysfunction, such that it seemed inaccurate to say that the dysfunction caused the disability (see Clark et al., 2017 for a discussion of this issue). Nonetheless, most WGs did not change the clinical significance criterion.

I had become interested in the concept of functioning because of a student's research (see Ro & Clark, 2009), and that interest increased through the *DSM* revision process, including serving on the Impairment and Disability Study Group. To me, the adaptive-failure perspective on Criterion A essentially reflected the ICF perspective because it was based on the notion that personality had a psychological function which was impaired in PD. The WG agreed, and therefore decided not to include the *DSM-IV* clinical significance criterion in our proposal.

Imposition of Higher-Level DSM-5 Revision Structures and Processes. At the beginning of the *DSM* revision process, WGs were essentially told that they were free to develop their proposals as they thought best. Although many WGs chose only to "tweak" their criteria and others considered moderate changes, the P&PD group was one of a few that proposed sweeping changes. Although we received various forms of pushback, described previously, none was as major as the imposition of the *Scientific Review Committee* (SRC) and the *Clinical and Public Health Committee* (CPHC). Prior to the creation of these committees, WG proposals had been evaluated by the Task Force, which included the co-Chairs, Research Director, Text Editors, and the Chairs of the WGs and other Study Groups, and which generally had been supportive of our radical proposal—asking for revisions but not undermining its major goals.

In contrast, the SRC required that "extensive, high-quality research" support any proposed major revision and the CPHC's purview was the "clinical utility and public health consequences" of implementing proposed revisions (Zachar et al., 2016, p. 5). Given that the P&PD WG's proposed diagnostic model was completely new in its particulars, so we could point specifically only to the small amount of research that the WG itself had done (e.g., Krueger et al., 2012; Morey & Skodol, 2013), we focused on the 30-years' worth of research documenting the invalidity of the *DSM-IV* PD categories and supporting a dimensional approach to PD in general. To no one's surprise, therefore, it was rated poorly by the SRC, leaving us to hope that the CPHC would take the data presented into account and thereby support inclusion of the untested proposal. We were sorely disappointed and, to add insult to injury, several CPHC evaluators openly admitted that they knew very little about PD, which seemed highly inappropriate to our WG's members, given our collective expertise in the field.

Reactions to the relegation of the WG's PD proposal to Section III. Despite the handwriting on the wall, we still held our collective breaths when the day of final reckoning—the vote of the APA Board of Trustees—arrived, with the result that the proposal would be placed in a new Section III, "Emerging Models and Methods," in the back of the manual, along with the dimensional assessment measures that various WGs had developed, the Cultural Formulation Interview, and several proposed diagnoses for further study (e.g., Internet Gaming Disorder, Nonsuicidal Self-Injury). My initial reactions ranged from fury to extreme dismay that, once again, my dream of a dimensional PD diagnostic system in the *DSM* had been thwarted.

Gradually, however, as months and then years went by, I gained perspective on both the experience and its outcome. I also followed the voluminous research on the AMPD conducted since 2013, documenting its limitations and raising unresolved questions (e.g., What "should be" the degree of overlap between personality functioning and traits?), and realized that had the proposal been placed in the main section of the *DSM-5*, the backlash might have been more devastating to the model (and to me!) than the APA's decision was; that having the model in Section III gave the field the opportunity to produce the kind of research that the SRC wanted to see, to improve the model and "prove" the worthiness of its approach. Indeed, there are indications that if presented with enough of the right type of research, the Steering Committee may be open to moving the AMPD into Section II.

ICD-11

In 2009, not long after the DSM revision process got underway, the WHO began its process of revising the ICD, which was then in its 10th Edition.[10] A Senior Project Officer of the revision approached the *DSM-5* Task Force co-Chairs and asked if I might serve as a liaison between the *DSM* P&PD WG and *ICD*'s PD WG, I suspect because the *ICD* PD WG Chair was my old friend, Peter Tyrer. The *DSM-5* Task Force co-Chairs were amenable, so I took on this role and was again heartened to find that a dimensional approach was being seriously considered. As the *DSM-5* process came to a close, my involvement in the *ICD-11* increased, and I became a full WG member.

Despite the AMPD's fate, the *ICD-11* PD WG decided to move ahead with a dimensional model. Because the *ICD* is the official system that all of its 194 member states (i.e., countries) have agreed by treaty to use in reporting morbidity and mortality data, its diagnoses must be amenable to cultural variation. Accordingly, the WG decided to require that only the severity of personality dysfunction would be required for a diagnosis of Mild, Moderate, and Severe PD.[11]

The biggest debate in the WG was whether severity should be based only on interpersonal dysfunction or should also include dysfunction in aspects of the self. The essence of the debate concerned possible difficulties in diagnosing self-dysfunction due to wide cultural variation in the concept of "the self." The debate was resolved by including both aspects but allowing diagnosis based on either or both (as in the AMPD). Similarly, the WG decided to include four of the five traits of the AMPD (excluding psychoticism, because schizotypal disorder is coded in the *ICD-11* schizophrenia section, not in the PD section) and including anankastia, a British term for obsessive-compulsive traits (e.g., rigid perfectionism, perseveration, behavioral and emotional overcontrol), plus substituting the term "dyssocial" for "antagonism."

Unlike the AMPD process, there was relatively little "drama" in developing the *ICD-11* PD diagnoses, other than a last-minute addition of a "borderline pattern" qualifier to the five trait qualifiers, based on concerns of officers of the three prominent *Societies for the Study of Personality Disorder* (International, European, and North American) that lack of the term borderline in PD diagnosis would be a major barrier to obtaining third-party payments for treatment of many patients with severe PD. In May 2019, at the 72nd World Health Assembly, *ICD-11* was officially endorsed. Thus, my career-long quest to help bring about an official instantiation of a dimensional PD diagnostic system was at last brought to a satisfying end, almost 40 years after the publication of *DSM-III*.

So what now?

Of course, the story doesn't stop there, with a big "The End" on the last page. Nor were the years from 2004 to the present *completely* dominated by the *DSM* and *ICD* revision processes. During those years, I also obtained a large NIMH grant to determine the most efficient way to diagnose PD using a combination of personality trait and functioning measures. Many of those data have been presented at conferences and a few have been published, but many more await my having the time to write them up. Moreover, if you've read this far, you won't be surprised that I wasn't about to stop pursuing full development of a dimensional PD diagnostic system with the release of the *ICD-11*. We are now working on a self-report measure for the new system, which I hope will inform its evolution as it is adapted for worldwide use.

Further, David and I moved from the University of Iowa to Notre Dame in 2010 to participate in evolving the Psychology Department's counseling psychology program into a clinical psychology program. The new program was accredited by our APA in 2011 and re-accredited in 2016. It is now in the process of taking its next big step of establishing a Research, Training, and Service Consortium with a full-fledged training clinic for our graduate students to provide clinical services to the community, coordinated with a research center for children and families and another for prevention and treatment of suicide and self-harm.

From 2016 to 2020, I served as Department Chair, saw the department through an external review, and oversaw the transition of our corner of academia to online instruction and meetings in the early months of the COVID-19 pandemic. I had long thought that Department Chair was the most difficult role in any University, and that belief was fully confirmed during those four years, as I experienced on a daily basis what it felt like to be flattened between the faculty road and the administrative rubber.

Those also were the years that our children finished their formal schooling, started working in "the real world" as the Chief Economist of the Brewer's Association[12] and as a prosecuting attorney. They also married and blessed us with four granddaughters, with whom we hope to spend more time in the coming years, and leave to the next generation of scholars the task of moving how the field thinks about and measures not just PD, but all of psychopathology toward dimensions. It is gratifying to me that as I wind down my career, many others in and outside of the Hi-TOP Consortium are launching theirs, and that they are doing so already cognizant of the inadequacies of categorical models and ready to do something about it.

Notes

Access to the Support Material for this chapter can be found at: www.routledge.com/9780367477431.

 1 Disclosure: Lee Anna Clark is the author and copyright owner of the Schedule for Nonadaptive and Adaptive Personality-2nd edition (SNAP-2, © 2014) and its family of measures. There is no licensing fee for use of the measures for non-commercial, unfunded research or for clinical use if clients are not charged. For all other uses, a mutually acceptable licensing fee is negotiated and such fees are used to support students' research.

     The work described in this chapter has been supported by the University of Minnesota Press, the National Institute of Mental Health (grants 1-R01-MH043282-01 and R01-MH083830 from to Lee Anna Clark), and the three institutions at which I have a faculty member, Southern Methodist University, University of Iowa, and University of Notre Dame. It also would not have been possible without the help of many graduate and undergraduate students who have served as research assistants over the course of my career, the support of my parents and siblings, my children, Bart Clark Watson and Erica Watson Clark Crisp, of course, that of David Watson, my collaborator, spouse, co-parent, and partner in every aspect of life.

 2 Now the Museum of Nature and Science.

 3 Officially "Congregational Christian" which, due to a 1957 merger with the Evangelical and Reformed Church became the United Church of Christ.

 4 Originally the Differential Personality Questionnaire.

 5 Of course, SSCP is not unique regarding these concerns, which played a big part in founding the *Association for Psychological Science* (APS) of which I also am a member, albeit not heavily involved.

 6 See Supplemental Material A for why home is not an assessment-focused organization.

 7 Our 11-member WG was evenly divided between psychiatrists and psychologists, had two international participants (Renato Alarcón, originally from Peru, and Roel Verheul, from the Netherlands), two women (Donna Bender and me), one racial/ethnic minority member (Carl Bell), six others (Andy Skodol, Chair; John Oldham, Co-Chair; Robert Krueger, John Livesley, Leslie Morey, and Larry Siever).

 8 clinically significant disturbance in an individual's cognition, emotion regulation, or behavior that reflects a dysfunction in the psychological, biological, or developmental processes underlying mental functioning" (APA, 2013; p. 20).

 9 Interestingly, *DSM-III* also "hedged" this requirement, worded "...typically associated with..." (APA, 1980, p. 6).

10 However, the U.S. did not ratify *ICD-10* until 2014, about 25 years behind the rest of the world, and so still used *ICD-9* until then.

11 PD, severity unspecified, also is available for cases with insufficient information to determine severity, and Personality Difficulty also has a non-diagnostic (i.e., subclinical) descriptive code.

12 https://www.brewersassociation.org/

References

Allport, G. W. (1937). *Personality: A psychological interpretation*. New York: Holt.

American Psychiatric Association (1968). *Diagnostic and statistical manual* (2nd ed.). Washington, DC: Author.

American Psychiatric Association (1980). *Diagnostic and statistical manual* (3rd ed.). Washington, D.C.: Author.

American Psychiatric Association (1987). *Diagnostic and statistical manual* (3rd ed.-Rev.). Washington, D.C.: Author.

American Psychiatric Association (1994). *Diagnostic and statistical manual* (4th ed.). Washington, D.C.: Author.

Baron, M., Asnis, L., & Rhoda, G. (1981). The Schedule for Schizotypal Personalities (SSP): A diagnostic interview for schizotypal features. *Psychiatry Research, 4*, 213–228.

Brown, T. A., Chorpita, B. F., & Barlow, D. H. (1998). Structural relationships among dimensions of the *DSM-IV* anxiety and mood disorders and dimensions of negative affect, positive affect, and autonomic arousal. *Journal of Abnormal Psychology, 107*, 179–192.

Cattell, R. B., Cattell, A. K., & Cattell, H. E. P. (1993). *16PF fifth edition questionnaire.* Champaign, IL: Institute for Personality and Ability Testing.

Chorpita, B. F. (2002). The tripartite model and dimensions of anxiety and depression: An examination of structure in a large school sample. *Journal of Abnormal Child Psychology, 30*, 177–190.

Clark, L. A. (1989). The anxiety and depressive disorders: Descriptive psychopathology and differential diagnosis. In P. C. Kendall & D. Watson (Eds.). *Anxiety and depression: Distinctive and overlapping features* (pp. 83129). New York: Academic Press.

Clark, L. A. (1990). Toward a consensual set of symptom clusters for assessment of personality disorder. In J. N. Butcher & C. D. Spielberger (Eds.), *Advances in personality assessment* (Vol. 8, pp. 243–266). Hillsdale, NJ: Erlbaum.

Clark, L. A., Cuthbert, B. N., Lewis-Fernandéz, R., Narrow, W., & Reed, G. M. (2017). Three approaches to understanding and classifying mental disorder: ICD-11, DSM-5, and RDoC. *Psychological Science in the Public Interest, 18*, 72–145.

Clark, L. A., & Watson, D. (1991a). General affective dispositions in physical and psychological health. In C. R. Snyder & D. R. Forsyth (Eds.), *Handbook of social and clinical psychology* (pp. 221–245). Elmsford, New York: Pergamon Press. Available online (Chapter 12): http://scholarship.richmond.edu/bookshelf/157/

Clark, L. A., & Watson, D. (1991b). Theoretical and empirical issues in differentiating depression from anxiety. In J. Becker & A. Kleinman (Eds.), *Psychosocial Aspects of Depression* (pp. 39–65). Hillsdale, NJ: Erlbaum.

Clark, L. A., & Watson, D. (1991c). Tripartite model of anxiety and depression: Psychometric evidence and taxonomic implications. *Journal of Abnormal Psychology, 100*, 316–336.

Clark, L. A., & Watson, D. (1991d). Tripartite model of anxiety and depression: Psychometric evidence and taxonomic implications. *Journal of Abnormal Psychology, 100*, 316–336.

Clark, L. A., Watson, D., & Mineka, S. (1994). Temperament, personality, and the mood and anxiety disorders. *Journal of Abnormal Psychology, 103*, 103–116.

Costa, P. T., Jr., & McCrae. R. R. (1985). *The NEO personality inventory manual.* Odessa, FL: Psychological Assessment Resources.

Frances, A. (1980). The DSM-III personality disorders section: A commentary. *The American Journal of Psychiatry, 137*, 1050–1054.

Goldberg, L. R. (1990). An alternative "description of personality": The big-five factor structure. *Journal of Personality and Social Psychology, 59*(6), 1216–1229.

Hopwood, C. J., Good, E. W., & Morey, L. C. (2018). Validity of the *DSM-5* levels of personality functioning Scale–Self report. *Journal of Personality Assessment, 100*, 650–659.

Hyman, S. (2021). Psychiatric disorders: Grounded in biology, but not natural kinds. *Perspectives in Biology & Medicine, 64*, 6–28.

Jackson, D.N. (1984). *Personality research form manual* (3rd ed.). Port Huron, MI: Research Psychologists Press.

Joiner, T. E., Jr., & Lonigan, C. J. (2000). Tripartite model of depression and anxiety in youth psychiatric inpatients: Relations with diagnostic status and future symptoms. *Journal of Clinical Child Psychology, 29*, 372–382.

Kendler, K. S. Muñoz, R. A. & Murphy, G. (2009). The development of the Feighner Criteria: A historical perspective. *American Journal of Psychiatry, 167*, 134–142.

Kotov, R., Krueger, R. F., Watson, D., Achenbach, T. M., Althoff, R. R. Bagby, M., Clark, L. A. … & Zimmerman, M. (2017). The Hierarchical Taxonomy of Psychopathology (HiTOP): A dimensional alternative to traditional nosologies. *Journal of Abnormal Psychology, 124*, 454–477.

Krueger, R. F., Derringer, J., Markon, K. E., Watson, D., & Skodol, A. E. (2012). Initial construction of a maladaptive personality trait model and inventory for *DSM-5*. *Psychological Medicine, 42*, 1879–1890.

Livesley, W. J. (1985). The classification of personality disorder: II. The problem of diagnostic criteria. *The Canadian Journal of Psychiatry / La Revue Canadienne De Psychiatrie, 30*, 359–362.

Livesley, W. J., & Jang, K. L. (2005). Differentiating normal, abnormal, and disordered personality. *European Journal of Personality, 19*, 257–268.

McCrae, R. R., & Costa, P. T, Jr. (1985). Updating Norman's "adequate taxonomy": Intelligence and personality dimensions in natural language and in questionnaires. *Journal of Personality and Social Psychology, 49*, 710–721.

Mineka, S., Watson, D. W., & Clark, L. A. (1998). Psychopathology: Comorbidity of anxiety and unipolar mood disorders. *Annual Review of Psychology, 49*, 377–412.

Morey, L. C. (2019). Thoughts on the assessment of the DSM–5 alternative model for personality disorders: Comment on Sleep et al. (2019). *Psychological Assessment, 31*, 209–311.

Morey, L. C., Good, E. W., & Hopwood, C. J. (2022). Global personality dysfunction and the relationship of pathological and normal trait domains in the DSM-5 alternative model for personality disorders. *Journal of Personality, 90*(1), 34–46.

Morey, L. C., & Skodol, A. E. (2013). Convergence between *DSM-IV-TR* and *DSM-5* diagnostic models for personality disorder: Evaluation of strategies for establishing diagnostic thresholds. *Journal of Psychiatric Practice, 19*, 179–193.

Sharp, C. & Wall, K. (2021, online ahead of print). *DSM-5* level of personality functioning: Refocusing personality disorder on what it means to be human. *Annual Review of Clinical Psychology, 17*, 487–504.

Skodol, A. E., Gunderson, J. G., Shea, M. T., McGlashan, T. H., Morey, L. C., Sanislow, C. A., Bender, D. S., Grilo, C. M., Zanarini, M. C., Yen, S., Pagano, M. E., & Stout, R. L. (2005). The Collaborative Longitudinal Personality

Disorders Study (CLPS): Overview and implications. *Journal of Personality Disorders, 19,* 487–504.

Sleep, C. E., Lynam, D. R., Widiger, T. A., Crowe, M. L., & Miller, J. D. (2019a). An evaluation of DSM–5 section III personality disorder criterion A (impairment) in accounting for psychopathology. *Psychological Assessment, 31,* 1181–1191.

Sleep, C. E., Lynam, D. R., Widiger, T. A., Crowe, M. L., & Miller, J. D. (2019b). Difficulties with the conceptualization and assessment of Criterion A in the *DSM-5* alternative model of personality disorder: A reply to Morey (2019). *Psychological Assessment, 31,* 1200–1205.

Spitzer R. L., Robins, E. (1978). Research diagnostic criteria: Rationale and reliability. *Archives of General Psychiatry, 35,* 773–782.

Tellegen, A. (1985). Structures of mood and personality and their relevance to assessing anxiety, with an emphasis on self-report. In A. H. Tuma, & J. D. Maser (Eds.), *Anxiety and the anxiety disorders* (pp. 681–706). Hillsdale, NJ: Lawrence Erlbaum Associates, Inc.

Tellegen, A., & Waller, N. G. (2008). Exploring personality through test construction: Development of the multidimensional personality questionnaire. In G. J. Boyle, G. Matthews & D. H. Saklofske (Eds.), *The SAGE handbook of personality theory and assessment, Vol 2: Personality measurement and testing* (pp. 261–292). Thousand Oaks, CA: Sage Publications, Inc.

Tyrer, P., & Alexander, J. (1979). Classification of personality disorder. *The British Journal of Psychiatry, 135,* 163–167.

Watson, D. (2005). Rethinking the mood and anxiety disorders: A quantitative hierarchical model for DSM-V. *Journal of Abnormal Psychology, 114,* 522–536.

Watson, D., & Clark, L. A. (1984). Negative affectivity: The disposition to experience unpleasant emotional states. *Psychological Bulletin, 95,* 465–490.

Watson, D., & Clark, L. A. (1991). *The Mood and Anxiety Symptom Questionnaire (MASQ).* Department of Psychology, University of Iowa, Iowa City, IA. Permission required for use; contact db.watson@nd.edu

Watson, D., & Clark, L. A. (1992). Affects separable and inseparable: A hierarchical model of the negative affects. *Journal of Personality and Social Psychology, 62,* 489–505.

Watson, D., & Clark, L. A. (Eds.). (1994). Personality and psychopathology [Special issue]. *Journal of Abnormal Psychology, 103,* 3–5.

Watson, D., Clark, L. A., & Carey, G. (1988). Positive and negative affectivity and their relation to anxiety and depressive disorders. *Journal of Abnormal Psychology, 97,* 346–353.

Watson, D., Clark, L. A., & Tellegen, A. (1984). Cross-cultural convergence in the structure of mood: A Japanese replication and a comparison with U. S. findings. *Journal of Personality and Social Psychology, 47,* 127–144.

Watson, D., Clark, L. A., & Tellegen, A. (1988). Development and validation of brief measures of positive and negative affect: The PANAS scales. *Journal of Personality and Social Psychology, 54,* 1063–1070.

Watson, D., O'Hara, M. W., Naragon-Gainey, K., Koffel, E., Chmielewski, M., Kotov, R., Stasik, S. M., & Ruggero, C. J. (2012). Development and validation of new anxiety and bipolar symptom scales for an expanded version of the IDAS (the IDAS-II). *Assessment, 19,* 399–420.

Watson, D., Weber, K., Assenheimer, J. S., Clark, L. A., Strauss, M. E., & Mc-
Cormick, R. A. (1995). Testing a tripartite model: I. Assessing the convergent
and discriminant validity of anxiety and depression symptom scales. *Journal of
Abnormal Psychology, 104,* 3–14.

Widiger, T. A., & Frances, A. (1985). The *DSM-III* personality disorders: Perspectives from psychology. *Archives of General Psychiatry, 42,* 615–623.

Zimmerman, J., Böhnke, J.R., Eschstruth, R., Mathews, Alessa, Wenzel, K., &
Leising, D. (2015). The latent structure of personality functioning: Investigating Criterion A from the Alternative Model for Personality Disorders in *DSM-
5. Journal of Abnormal Psychology, 134,* 532–548.

15 My Journey to Become a Clinical Psychologist

Roger L. Greene

Early years

I was born on September 5, 1944, in Salina, Kansas to Merrill and Belva Greene. I had one brother, Everett, five years older than I, and one younger sister, Merrie, two years younger. My Dad was a brakeman on the Rock Island Railroad; my Mom, a housewife. In the summer of 1948, the Rock Island Railroad transferred my Dad to Limon, Colorado, 90 miles east of Denver. In the early 1950s, the Railroad wanted to transfer my Dad again. After careful consideration, Dad turned down the transfer, deciding with my mom to raise their family in Limon. My Dad began a new job as the distributor of the Denver Post in the Limon area and, over time, also became a wholesale milk distributor for Limon and the surrounding areas of eastern Colorado.

The Limon of my youth was a small town, population around 1,500, far from the scenic Rocky Mountains that everyone associates with Colorado. Limon's claim to fame was that two transcontinental railroads (the Rock Island and the Santa Fe) and two transcontinental highways (US 24 and US 40) crossed at Limon. The two highways merged on the east side of Limon and split on the west side to go on to Colorado Springs (24) and to Denver (40). Limon essentially was one or two blocks wide along this two to three-mile strip, populated with gas stations, restaurants, and motels. Virtually all of the families in Limon either worked in one of these businesses or on outlying farms and ranches.

My early childhood consisted of school, helping my Dad, and playing. I would often ride my bicycle to see my friends around the neighborhood and then return home for meals. The Big Sandy River, which ran through town, was usually dry except for when it rained and occasionally flooded. My friends and I spent many a day playing in the creek bed.

In sixth grade, I took my first paying job, a Denver Post paper route of about 60 customers. When I needed a new bike to deliver the papers, the local hardware store let me buy one for $10/month for six months—my introduction to the world of high finance. After school, I would ride my bike about a mile to the service station to pick up the papers. After rolling them and loading them onto my bike, I set off to deliver them.

DOI: 10.4324/9781003036302-15

A few years later, for four summers beginning the year before my junior year of high school, I worked in a service station, earning $60 for six ten-hour days. I pumped gas, cleaned the windshields, and handled the credit cards—literally by hand. The service station owners taught me an important life lesson: Every job had to be done correctly, regardless of how long it took.

My education in Limon was unremarkable—at least from my perspective. Twenty-two of us who started the first grade in 1950 were a significant part of our senior class of 39 in 1962. No one wondered who was going to be in each year's new class. Classes were easy for me in a school that did not stress academics. For example, I wrote one essay throughout my high school years and was assigned one book, *A Tale of Two Cities*, to read. Luckily, I was a voracious reader and read a lot of the books in our school and local library.

More than academics, Limon High School was known for its athletic teams. The football team was undefeated during my entire four years in high school, winning the state championship every year in the classification for schools with enrollments under 200 students. Most of the starting lineup, including me, were on the all-state team in our junior and senior years. Limon also won state championships in basketball and track in most of our high school years.

College years

After high school, I enrolled at the University of Colorado. What a rude awakening. My classes ranged from 30 to 500 students, most of whom had gone to the largest high schools in Denver. No longer did I know everyone in all of my classes. And there were vast differences in how my new classmates and I had been prepared for the academic challenges of college. Nevertheless, I found some familiarity: I was able to socialize with three of my high school classmates who also attended the University of Colorado.

Two themes of my educational career appeared as an undergraduate and continued throughout my academic career. The first theme was that I was not aware of resources in college that I could access to guide the decisions I would need to make. For example, my advisor was a baseball coach who had little knowledge of or interest in academic decisions. I was on my own. So with basic trust and optimism, I would forge ahead and make changes as they became necessary. I went to college because it was expected, and to the University of Colorado where my brother, with whom I roomed off campus, was a student. I liked mathematics in high school, so I started taking the mathematics sequence in the fall of my freshman year. The first semester, during which I took algebra and geometry, went well. The first half of the second semester covered solid geometry. I earned an "A." I received an "F" in calculus, so I got a "C" for the semester. Because the next three semesters were all calculus, I realized that mathematics would not be a fruitful path to follow. For two semesters in my sophomore year, I took business courses that were uninteresting and too easy. At the start of my junior year, I had to declare a major.

Then the second theme of my academic career appeared: serendipity. At a choice point, wondering what to do, a serendipitous event would open a new career path. I would follow the new path until the next serendipitous event occurred. For example, I was invited to join the honors program in the Department of Psychology based on my grade in Introduction to Psychology. I did not know that the Department of Psychology had a national reputation until years later, but I saw no reason not to major in Psychology, and off I went. The honors seminar in psychology was taught by Michael Wertheimer, and the abnormal class by Victor Raimy. The other classes in the major were taught by assistant professors. Toward the end of my junior year, I had a question that I wanted to ask the Chair of the Department of Psychology. I went into the office to make an appointment and was informed that the Chair did not see undergraduates, so I was referred to an assistant professor.

At the end of my junior year, serendipity, this second theme, occurred again. I needed to go to summer school to earn enough hours to graduate at the end of my senior year. I was looking for classes to take when I saw a brochure from the Western Interstate Commission on Higher Education (WICHE) that described a summer work-study program designed to recruit students into the field of psychology. The program offered the number of units I needed to graduate and paid a stipend, so I applied and was accepted. After a week of classroom orientation, I was assigned to a locked ward at Colorado State Hospital in Pueblo for eight weeks. Even though antipsychotic medications had been in use for nearly a decade, I had no idea of what expect other than what I had learned in my abnormal psychology class and in orientation. The ward looked very ordinary, with patients sitting around in a day room, and with long hallways with rooms. One noteworthy experience happened during the first week or so of being on the ward. A very overweight woman (300 lbs.+) was walking around the ward nude. We were told that any time the staff dressed her, she would undress herself, flush her clothes down the toilet, and stop up the ward's sewer system. The staff's choices were to lock her in her room or allow her to walk around nude. Their decision was obvious.

In addition to this odd initiation to an inpatient ward, I was struck by the case conferences. A case conference, chaired by the ward psychiatrist, was attended by 30 or more individuals, including ward staff and groups of students (nursing, psychology) in a crowded room. After a brief review of the patient's history, the ward psychiatrist would interview the patient about the patient's most intimate details. Patients seemed comfortable responding to those intrusive questions, or at least they did not balk at doing so. I do not recall meeting a psychologist during my time at the hospital.

Mary Sharon Haug and I married in 1964. Although we had gone through grade school and high school in the same class, we did not start dating formally until our senior year. After high school, she went off to Colorado State College in Greeley, while I went to the University of Colorado in Boulder. Five other couples in our high school class also married. One couple got divorced, two of us lost our wives to breast cancer—I lost Mary Sharon in 2004. The other couples are still living and married. There may be something said for knowing your future spouse for a long time before getting married.

My senior year at Colorado was unremarkable. Thanks to the WICHE self-study program, I had the hours I needed to graduate in 1966. In that early spring, I started looking for a job. The Placement Bureau had few interesting interviews for students with BAs in psychology. I had several interviews with recruiters who would hire BAs—I would have 15 minutes to learn about my recruiter's organization while the recruiter would review my qualifications. I do not recall that I attended, or even if there was, an orientation seminar for this process. Because the job opportunities did not look good, I again wondered what I would do. I then remembered that someone at Colorado State Hospital, during my summer experience there, had mentioned that New Mexico Highlands University in Las Vegas, NM had a good master's program in psychology. Based on that information, I applied to and was accepted into their program.

Graduation at the University of Colorado, a massive event, took place in the football stadium. All 2,500–3,000 liberal arts degree candidates were seated in the end zone. When it came time to have our degrees conferred, we all stood up, our degrees were conferred, and we sat back down. I stood in line to receive my diploma that was handed to me by a clerk.

Graduate education

I entered the master's program at New Mexico Highlands University with no idea of what to expect. There were 12–15 students in my class and we took all of our classes together throughout the year, reminding me of my small classes in Limon. The only choices I had through the year were the topic of my master's thesis and who would chair it. We had three-quarter sequences in assessment (WAIS/WISC; MMPI; Rorschach [Beck]), statistics, and experimental (physiological; perception; learning; history). The faculty were well trained and very committed to teaching, a luxury rarely available in a doctoral program. My only formal training in assessment in my graduate career occurred at Highlands University. The professor focused primarily on the Rorschach so the MMPI course consisted essentially of reading Dahlstrom, Welsh, and Dahlstrom's *An MMPI Handbook: Clinical Interpretation.* Because New Mexico State Hospital was in Las Vegas, we had a readily available clinical population to assess. We administered a traditional battery of a WAIS, MMPI, and Rorschach to all patients.

In the early spring I was offered a position as an instructor in the Department. As a result, I did not have to decide what to do when I graduated. I spent three years teaching introductory psychology, social psychology, personality theory, and intellectual assessment. I took a class in Fortran programming during the master's program using an IBM 1,620 computer. I actually used computer scoring of the tests for introductory psychology. The 60–80 students would take the exam using a pencil to remove perforated numbers in each column of the punch card. The students were very impressed that their score and the distribution of scores were available about an hour after the exam.

The Department of Psychology at Highlands University was responsible for the Western Interstate Commission on Higher Education (WICHE) summer work-study program for the State of New Mexico. As the newest faculty member, I was put in charge of coordinating this program in which I had participated only a few years earlier.

Another event may have been serendipitous or not. A friend in the business program and I became interested in buying the McDonald's franchise in Santa Fe. He pursued most of the details and reached the point of learning that we needed to obtain a loan for $100,000 to secure the franchise. At the time, McDonald's was selling hamburgers for only 15 cents; after much deliberation we were not sure if we would be able to cover the loan—How many hamburgers would we have to sell?—and stopped the process. I lost track of my friend for years until I saw that he had been named President of Highlands University. I decided to pursue my career in psychology, so it seems that everything turned out well for both of us.

I knew that I wanted to get a doctorate and reviewed literature on doctoral programs, probably from the APA. I was not concerned about getting into a doctoral program since I had done very well in my master's program, had three years of teaching experience, and one publication. I applied to Washington State University because their information stated that they prepared students for academic careers. I also applied to Texas Tech University because it was nearby. I do not recall applying to any other programs. Texas Tech turned me down, so it was easy to accept the offer from Washington State.

The Washington State decision worked well for me. The program provided excellent training, and I was supported by a NIMH fellowship. The Department had a strong behavioral emphasis that even filtered into the clinical program. I had taken a number of similar courses at New Mexico Highlands University that made the course work easier. The only course work that transferred were the assessment courses in which the program had little interest. The behavioral emphasis in the Department probably decreased interest in assessment, and clinical training focused on clinical judgment. I spent most of my research time focused on the psychophysiological interests of my major professor. Academically, I focused on statistics, developmental psychology, and computer programming in addition to the clinical training.

A student colleague became interested in Masters and Johnson's therapy for sexual dysfunctions. Because he needed one more male therapist before the clinical program would provide the training, I volunteered. We completed two-years of training that had a strong behavioral focus. I was impressed by both the training we were provided as well as the cases that the four therapist teams successfully treated.

Thanks to the NIMH fellowship, I was able to spend two months studying with Eugene Gollin, a developmental psychologist at the University of Colorado. Mary Sharon and Holly—who was born in 1968 in Las Vegas, NM—were able to stay with our parents in Limon who could spend time with their first granddaughter. I commuted to Boulder during the week, and returned to Limon for the weekends.

When it came time for an internship, my major professor wanted me to apply to the University of Oklahoma Medical School, because of the superb training that he had received there. I did so. I also applied to the University of Arizona Medical School, which was starting a new internship; I was assured that the internship would be accredited before I finished. I do not recall whether I applied to other programs. During that time, internships were allowed an entire week to let students know if they had been selected. When selection time came, the University of Arizona called early in the week to inform me that I had been selected. I then contacted the University of Oklahoma to determine my status. I was told that the Director of Training was going to be gone all week. They thought that I had been accepted and the Director would let me know early in the next week. Giving no thought to the potential quality of training, Mary Sharon and I decided that we would like to spend a year in Tucson; I accepted the University of Arizona offer. When I informed my major professor of my decision, he said, "You dumb ★★★★★ get out of my office and do not come back." I knew enough to leave. When I returned the next week, he said, "You still are a dumb ★★★★★ but you can come back to finish your dissertation." In sum, his assessment that I was choosing an unknown internship over a known, high-quality internship was accurate.

My internship at the University of Arizona Medical School was the traditional four-month rotations in child, inpatient, and outpatient treatment. The child rotation, where I started, was not prepared to train interns. It took almost six weeks to get our first client, and our training was pieced together slowly. But by year's end, the child rotation was working satisfactorily. The inpatient setting was unusual, at least to me, because we were supervised by a psychiatrist. He was an excellent clinician and taught us much about the psychiatric side of inpatient treatment. The other aspect of the inpatient rotation was that we had 33 hours of meetings a week, so the days were long. We rotated through the emergency room at the county hospital in Tucson, attached to a psychiatry resident.

This experience provided another opportunity to see psychiatry in action with a wide variety of patients with acute psychopathology. The outpatient rotation was six hours a day of various group activities with patients who were being treated to keep them from being sent to the state hospital.

Early in the internship, the Director asked if I knew one of the experimental faculty at Washington State University. This faculty member had taught a three-week section of proseminar that was required of all first-year students. He also occasionally joined a group of graduate students and faculty that met for beer at a local bar on Friday afternoons. Otherwise I had no contact with him. The Director had called him to vet me for their University of Arizona internship. This faculty member's assessment of me was "He seems to be fine." I later used this anecdote when training clinical students on the importance of being socially appropriate with everyone in their training programs because they do not know who might be called upon to obtain background information. I also should mention that the internship, despite its initial assurances, was not accredited before we graduated—that did not occur for two more years, and the accreditation was not retroactive. My decision to go to the University of Arizona resulted in my graduating from an unaccredited program. Internship accreditation was not as important in that era as would it become in the next two decades.

After my internship, I started two lines of search for my next career step. My first choice was a postdoctoral position in neuropsychology; I applied to the program at the University of Wisconsin with Charles Matthews. My second choice was an academic position; I applied to APA-accredited clinical training programs that had openings. Early in this process, I started receiving rejection letters from programs to which I had not applied— quite puzzling. That did not inspire confidence in my search. My major professor later told me that he had sent a cover letter and my vita to every clinical training program in the United States. I interviewed at four universities and received only one offer, Texas Tech University. I was also accepted into the postdoctoral program at Wisconsin that was in the process of renewing their grant support. I was assured that it would be funded, but they just did not know the exact timeline. I had a wife and a daughter to support with an academic position in hand, and the one position I really wanted was in limbo. After living in limbo for two weeks, I accepted the position at Texas Tech University. Two weeks later Wisconsin called me to say that they had received funding and I explained the decision I had made. This decision appears to be the first one in which I considered all of the possibilities rather than following my heart. I am surprised in looking back at this decision in the context of all of my decisions thus far in my academic career, that I did not accept the postdoctoral position. It was one of the top postdoctoral programs in neuropsychology in the country, and it had been my dream for years. But the path that I chose worked out eminently better than I ever expected, so it clearly was not a bad decision.

Early career and sundry experiences

At the time, the transition process we had gone through did not seem unusual because it all was necessary. We had lived in seven different residences and four cities by the time we left graduate school in Pullman in 1973, we went to internship in Tucson, and then took my new position at Texas Tech University in 1974. Holly was between five and six during this process and we assumed that she would not be too affected by it. Holly came home from her kindergarten class at the end of the school year in Lubbock, and told us "I like it here, can we stay?" We did not move again until Holly got married in 1992 and I accepted a new position in California.

As a new assistant professor at Texas Tech, I was assigned to classes that the other faculty preferred to avoid. I taught undergraduate abnormal psychology, supervised clinical practice in our Clinic, and graduate-level classes in personality theory and assessment (WAIS/WISC; MMPI; neuropsychology). I could not have been happier with the choices if I had made them myself.

In addition to my primary focus on the MMPI, I also taught neuropsychological assessment every year, then a rapidly growing field. I had a colleague who was a neuropsychologist in the Department of Psychiatry at the TTU School of Medicine. I collaborated with him on a number of research projects until he left in the late 1980s. He was working on a grant proposal looking at age and clinical population differences in neuropsychological functioning. One of our populations was people with alcoholic problems in the Department's treatment program. When we approached these individuals to ask them to participate in the project, they did not know us and were not eager to volunteer. We decided that, if one of us worked in the treatment program, we would have better success. As you can probably guess by now, I volunteered and added another clinical setting to my academic career. I worked quarter-time in the program for over ten years. I interpreted all of the MMPIs that were written for and given to the patients (~2,500). This assignment made me learn to use language that was easily understood and to convey less desirable characteristics such as defensive, hostile, and so on, in terms that patients would find acceptable. I incorporated this language style into the next edition of my MMPI-2 computer interpretive software (Greene & Brown, 1998). I also ran two inpatient groups and one outpatient group per week. I thoroughly loved working in substance abuse and it was my favorite group of patients with whom to work. I even took my sabbatical in the alcohol treatment program at the Mayo Clinic in Rochester during the first six months of 1987.

My willingness to volunteer when asked resulted in my working in a number of departments in the Texas Tech University School of Medicine, in addition to the Department of Psychiatry. As soon as I arrived at Texas Tech, I worked in a Developmental Disabilities Clinic that was attached to the Department of Pediatrics. One morning a week I assessed toddlers under the age of three, and another morning, school age children for suspected learning disabilities. I got lots of experience administering the Bayley Developmental Test of Intelligence with the first group and the Wechsler Intelligence Scale for Children with the other. After five years, the Clinic was closed for reasons I never knew.

I next worked in the Orthopedics Department where a resident wanted to start a pain clinic and use the MMPI. One afternoon a week I would see the referrals for a clinical interview as part of the evaluation process. When we first opened the clinic, we had asked a nurse to give the MMPI to the patient. When one of them gave the MMPI booklet back to us that had been torn into small pieces, it was clear that I need to be explaining the use of the MMPI to them. Most people in this setting were willing to take the MMPI, but they wanted it to be very clear their pain was not in their head. The pain clinic closed after two years when the resident graduated. Throughout the years that I was at Texas Tech, I performed neuropsychological evaluations for the Neurology Department for both inpatients and outpatients.

I had become very interested in Jungian psychology in graduate school when a fellow student shared his enthusiasm in many long discussions. I read most of Jung's *Collect Works* after I arrived at Texas Tech. My fellow student had started his training in Jungian analysis, and he encouraged me to start the training. The first requirement to apply for training was five-years of dream analysis. The closest analyst was in Dallas, so every Thursday for five years I would take a noon flight to Dallas for an hour of analysis and return by 5:00. My first analyst was a psychiatrist who cautioned that my interest in assessment might not sit well with the selection committee for training. He also told me frequently that I needed to get more unconscious material into my dreams, a suggestion that I had no idea of how to implement. I switched to another analyst after a few years who was an Episcopalian priest. His focus on dreams emphasized the religious/ spiritual themes, while the psychiatrist was more focused on clinical issues. Both of my analysts focused on the mythological roots of my dreams and would recommend that I read the mythology that was relevant. The priest, after making the recommendation, would summarize the mythology for me. As I was approaching the completion of my five years of dream analysis, I sat down and looked at the required course work. The first year focused on the study of mythology in the original language. The thought of needing to learn at least Greek and to study mythology for a year was enough to convince me that I was no longer interested in Jungian training.

I had become interested in running in graduate school. That interest persisted for the next 30+ years. The marathon craze started in the mid-1970s and I decided that I need to run a marathon. Finishing your first marathon is very empowering because you have completed something that you thought might be impossible. Then you have to run your second marathon to convince yourself that the first marathon was not a fluke. Then you are hooked. I ran around 30 miles a week up to my last marathon in 2003. I completed 12 marathons. I also added three 50-miles runs toward the end of my running (see Table 15.1). You slow down with age, but you still can run longer distances rather easily.

I started officiating basketball during my Tucson internship in Tucson to supplement our income. I continued officiating basketball in Lubbock and became a member of the Southwest Basketball Officials Association. The secretary of our local chapter assigned all games. There were five classifications of high school (1A, 2A, 3A, 4A, 5A). New officials started at the lowest classification, and one would gradually work up in classification after gaining experience and earning favorable ratings. December games consisted of tournaments for the first few weeks. District games began in January and lasted until the end of February when district championships started. There were two basketball games (girls' and boys' varsity) every Tuesday and Friday. The minimum for officiating a game was $15 and then there was an increasing scale based on attendance. At 1A and some 2A schools you never exceeded $15 because of the size of the school. Travel to games took from 60 to 90 minutes and you were expected to arrive an hour before the 6:30 tipoff. The total time to arrive an hour before the game, officiate the games, and travel would vary from 6 to 8 hours for $30. Clearly, it was not an activity in which you engaged for the money. I did get to visit a large sample of the smaller high schools in west Texas that were not much different from Limon.

I have many stories to tell from my officiating experiences. For example, Three Way High School held homecoming at a basketball game because they did not have enough students to field a football team. A representative boy and girl from 1st grade to the 12th marched in their finest clothes and the queen was crowned. Three Way also had to cancel a game one year when one boy was out of town and, as a result, they did not have five players to start the game—that is the definition of a small school!

The district championship for Muleshoe and Dimmit High Schools boys' game was also a classic. These schools played for the district championship each year and the winner would go on to win the state championship for 2A. When we arrived to call the game, the principal of Muleshoe High School, the home team, met us and told us that the gym would be packed and that they would do their best to keep the fans off the court during the game because of the expected overflow crowding. The principal also arranged for a police escort after the game. We called the girls game first as customary and the police escort arrived toward the end of that game. He could be best characterized as Barney Fife's twin—short, skinny, and might have weighed 90 pounds. The game was as close and exciting as expected. With under 30 seconds left, Dimmit was ahead by one point, and Muleshoe was bringing the ball up court. My co-official called walking on the Muleshoe player, obvious from anywhere on the

Table 15.1 Running results

| Date | City | Event | Distance/Time | | | | | |
			5.0m	10K	10.0m	15K	13.1m	26.2m
5/10/86	Lubbock	Run for Texas		51:33				
9/27/86	Lubbock	Red Raider Road Race		49:52			2:06:05	4:21:12
12/14/86	Dallas	White Rock						4:17:11
2/28/87	Fort Worth	Cowtown Marathon		49:24				
10/10/87	Lubbock	Red Raider Road Race					1:53:58	
11/17/87	Lubbock	Buffalo Springs Wallow		50:57				
9/24/88	Lubbock	Red Raider Road Race						
12/4/88	Dallas	White Rock					1:57:00	4:07:05
10/14/89	Lubbock	Red Raider Road Race		46:54				
10/29/89	Chicago	Old Style Marathon						4:30:34
7/4/90	Brownfield	Firecracker 10 Mile			1:26:11			
9/26/90	Albuquerque	Duke City Marathon						4:09:46
9/29/90	Lubbock	Red Raider Road Race		53:13				
10/13/90	Minneapolis	Twin Cities Marathon						4:16:03
12/2/90	Dallas	White Rock					1:59:05	4:12:17
4/20/91	Lubbock	Run for the Arts				1:14:27		
12/21/91	Lubbock	Lubbock Invitational						4:30:33
2/8/92	Birmingham	50 Mile Run						10:22:29
1/29/95	San Francisco	1/2 Marathon					2:08:14	
4/1/95	Sacramento	American River 50 Mile						11:53:00
12/14/96	Huntsville	Sunmart 50 Mile						11:30:02
1/1/98	Fort Worth	Eastside YMCA New Year's Run	49:24					
7/12/98	San Francisco	Marathon						5:19:00
12/5/99	Dallas	White Rock Marathon						5:38:00
2/20/00	Austin	Motorola Marathon						5:21:00
11/27/03	Dallas	Turkey Trot			1:40:08			
12/14/03	Honolulu	Honolulu Marathon					3:13:28	6:43:06

court. Dimmit won the game. Although much commotion ensued, our Barney Fife escort was not to be seen. We quietly left the court.

Later career and the MMPI—Relationships and scholarship

My approach to teaching graduate-level courses was to hand out an outline of my lectures. I wanted the students to listen and think rather than to focus on writing their notes. After several years, one of the students suggested that I turn the outlines into a text for the MMPI. This suggestion started an additional path in my career. I drafted a cover letter along with my class outlines. I did not know to whom I should send the proposal, so I opened my desk drawer to the stack of business cards that the book representatives would leave after encouraging me to select their books for my classes. I randomly chose six of them and forwarded the proposal. I received one acceptance—from Grune & Stratton. Now I had to write the book, *The MMPI: An interpretive manual* that was published in 1980. The book was updated three times (1991: *The MMPI-2/MMPI: An interpretive manual*; 2000: *The MMPI-2/MMPI: An interpretive manual* [2nd ed.]; 2011: *The MMPI-2/MMPI-2-RF: An interpretive manual* [3rd ed.]).

As I wrote the book, one aim was to include numerous tables and charts to make the MMPI interpretive process as explicit as possible for the reader. I also wanted to base my writing on published research rather than on clinical lore. In reviewing the MMPI research, I was amazed by how little published work existed for statements that were cited frequently as interpretations for specific scales or codetypes. These gaps in the literature kept my graduate students busy for the next 30 years. In addition, I insisted that all of my students attend and make presentations at national societies every year and work on manuscripts for publication. My goal for all my students was a dissertation of publishable quality. A large number of them successfully published their work.

Assessing the validity of the MMPI had interested me from my first and only course, back in my master's program at New Mexico Highlands University. It made sense to me to evaluate how the person took the MMPI before interpreting the test results. For example, it caught my attention that individuals taking the MMPI frequently would ask why the test repeated so many items, so I focused on the MMPI's 16 repeated items. Because no published data addressed this issue, I initially looked at how often these 16 pairs of items were endorsed inconsistently in MMPI samples that I had available. I also developed the Carelessness scale (Greene, 1978), which consisted of 12 pairs of empirically selected items that were judged to be psychologically opposite in content. Interestingly, these items did not arouse the concerns that were expressed about the 16 pairs of repeated items. The Carelessness scale was the precursor of the Variable Response Inconsistency scale that was later developed for the MMPI-2. A graduate student in my MMPI class who had offered to review and provide feedback for my forthcoming book—for which she was given a copy—suggested a table outlining the steps needed to assess the validity of an administration of the MMPI. This table was the first version of my system for assessing MMPI validity that would evolve over the next 30 years.

After my *MMPI Manual* appeared in 1980, professional groups and APA internships began to invite me to speak for two days on the interpretation of the MMPI results. Following my usual practice of teaching with outlines, I brought copies of my *Manual* to these first presentations for the participants to use and either buy or return at the program's end. Two problems arose. First, as you might imagine, the logistics of transporting so many books were quite a chore. Second, a surprising number of books at each presentation turned up missing, neither paid for nor returned. Consequently, I reverted to outlines with slides to help the attendees stay oriented to the handouts. Starting in 1985 until I retired in 2011, I averaged about ten two-day presentations on the MMPI per year (see Table 15.2 for two example years), including four or five presentations per year to Army and Naval internships as well as to an occasional Air Force internship. In addition, continuing education groups would ask me to make four or five presentations in various cities around the country. One presentation a

Table 15.2 Workshops in 1998 and 2005

1998

Federal Correctional Institute, Dublin CA, (January)
Eisenhower Army Medical Center, Augusta GA (February)
Society for Personality Assessment, Boston (February)
American Academy of Forensic Psychologists, Milwaukee (March) [with Stuart Greenberg]
University of California, San Francisco (May) [with Phil Erdberg and Bill Lynch]
University of Alaska, Anchorage (June)
National Naval Medical Center, Bethesda (September)
Tripler Army Medical Center, Honolulu (September)
Palo Alto Veterans Administration Medical Center, Palo Alto (December)

2005

Dallas Psychological Association, Dallas (January)
Georgia Psychological Association, Atlanta (February)
American Academy of Forensic Psychology, Dallas (February)
Washington Bar Association, Seattle (April) [with Stu Greenberg]
Tripler Army Medical Center, Honolulu (April)
Annual Rorschach Workshop, Asheville NC (September)
Tripler Army Medical Center, Honolulu (October)
Eisenhower Army Medical Center, Augusta GA (October)
Georgia Psychological Association, Atlanta (October) [with Stu Greenberg]
Central Kansas Mental Health, Manhattan (November)
National Naval Medical Center, Bethesda (December)

---

year would focus on forensic uses of the MMPI-2, often sponsored by the American Academy of Forensic Psychology.

The annual Symposium on Recent Developments in the Use of the MMPI hosted by Jim Butcher became an annual event for me in the early 1980s. This Symposium, usually in February or March, alternated for years between St. Petersburg, FL and Honolulu, with an occasional meeting in Minneapolis. Needless to say, it was not hard to convince me to attend. At the 1983 meeting in Minneapolis, I was attending a presentation by Dave Nichols on the Wiggins content scales, when he recommended my text in an answer to a question from the audience. I had not yet met him, so I introduced myself. It became readily apparent that we had similar research interests. We clicked. A life-long relationship working on MMPI issues developed from this interaction. We researched and published so many scholarly articles together that it was impossible for us to be sure which of us had come up an idea for a paper. That was never an issue between us.

The University of Minnesota Press invited a small group to Minneapolis to be introduced to the MMPI-2 shortly before its debut at APA in August 1989: Jim Butcher, Alex Caldwell, Grant Dahlstrom, Jack Graham, myself, Kevin Moreland, and Dave Nichols. I had often dreamed in graduate school of participating in truly graduate-level seminars. This group surpassed my wildest expectations.

I had the good fortune to be working in assessment when assessment was esteemed widely and a major agenda item of annual meetings. Assessment psychologists were well represented in the administrative side of APA: Ray Fowler was the CEO, and Ray Fowler (1988), Joe Matarazzo (1989), and Charles Spielberger (1991) all served as presidents. It was awe inspiring to be on a first name basis with these accomplished psychologists. In addition, the Society of Personality Assessment was growing, and I had the pleasure of serving on the Board of Trustees from 1993 to 1998, and as Associate Editor of the Journal of Personality Assessment from 2002 to 2004. In 2010, I was awarded the Klopfer Award for lifetime achievement in assessment.

In the mid-1980s, Bob Colligan, Bob Archer, and I began discussing the idea of creating a new self-report inventory. The original MMPI had been in existence for 40 years; the MMPI2 was designed to update the MMPI. We were sure that we could create a better inventory. We developed some of our ideas and began looking for an interested publisher. The Psychological Corporation called and invited us to make a presentation. It did not go well. We thought that we were going to discuss the parameters of the project; they were looking for a finished proposal. We then approached Psychological Assessment Resources (PAR) about our project, and spent several years developing our strategy. We were never able to bring the plan to fruition because of legal issues with Mayo Clinic, where Bob Colligan worked, and PAR's reluctance to financially back the project. But our wish for a new self-report inventory was realized in 1991 when PAR published Les Morey's Personality Assessment Inventory.

At this same time, PAR approached me to be the founding editor of *Assessment*, a new journal that they wanted to develop. I, like many in the field at the time, thought that there already were too many journals and that, as a result, the quality of the publications had been decreasing. After I declined PAR's offer, PAR asked Bob Archer to be the journal editor, and he accepted. *Assessment* debuted in 1992. My declining this offer was another one of the few times in my career when I did not automatically make a decision.

In April 1989, I was one of five psychologists selected by the American Psychological Association to testify in congressional hearings before the House Armed Services Committee into the explosion on the USS Iowa's gun turret 2. The US Navy's first investigation concluded that one of the crewmen had caused the explosion. The families of the victims, media, and members of Congress heavily criticized this conclusion. Two FBI psychologists testified at the House Armed Services Committee hearing before us. Based on their equivocal death analysis, the FBI psychologists concluded that the crewman had died of his own actions by trying to make the explosion look like an accident. One of the Representatives asked the psychologists if they had ever made a mistake in their investigations. They responded, "The FBI does not make mistakes." I was one of the four psychologists who testified that, based on the evidence that we were provided, it did not look probable that the crewman would have caused the explosion. The fifth psychologist testified that it might have been possible that the crewman would have caused the explosion. In the end, the Armed Service Committee Investigations of both the House and Senate concluded that the Navy's conclusion contained major flaws and then ordered new investigations. These final investigations determined that the explosion was caused by powder being rammed too far and fast into the gun turret.

I worked my way through the academic ranks and was promoted to associate professor with tenure in 1979, and professor in 1988. I served as Director of Clinical Training from 1980 to 1986. I was a tenured as full professor with no administrative responsibilities from 1986 until 1992 which has to be the best job in the world. I had been very pleased with my academic career at Texas Tech and, during that period, had only entertained two potential job positions. I was friends with two of the psychologists at the Mayo Clinic, and several times we talked about my taking a position with them. I do not remember specifically what was going on in my life at these times—probably Holly was close to finishing high school—but it was not a good time to move. I also interviewed to be the Director of the Internship Program for the Air Force at Wilford Hall, San Antonio. I ultimately declined the position because the program was still scoring the MMPI by hand with no assurances of access to computer resources.

In 1992, I accepted the position of Chair and Director of Clinical Training at Pacific Graduate School of Psychology in Palo Alto. I had an administrative position of some capacity in this program for ten years until I retired in 2003.

I also continued my focus on the MMPI-2, attending to three specific issues. First, Dave Nichols and I continued working on trying to make sense of the multitude of MMPI scales—there actually were more MMPI scales than items. For example, The MMPI-2 Extended Score Report contains 140 scales: 9 validity scales; 10 clinical scales; 9 restructured clinical scales; 15 content scales; 15 supplementary scales; 5 Psy-5 scales; 31 subscales of the clinical scales; 27 content component scales; and 17 sets of critical items. Using a variety of conceptual and statistical strategies, we developed the MMPI-2 Structural Summary that was published by Psychological Assessment Resources in 1995 (Greene & Nichols, 1995; Nichols & Greene, 1995).

Second, I worked on a system to match MMPI-2 profiles to prototypes that would facilitate profile interpretation. MMPI-2 interpretation is based on codetypes that frequently are difficult to interpret because of the number of elevated scales and the similarity of their elevations. I developed algorithms to account for an MMPI-2 profile's elevation(s), patterns of elevated scales, and linear relationships among the scales. The integration of these proprietary algorithms was introduced in the 1998 edition of my computer interpretive software, providing an empirical index of the degree of fit with approximately 100 two- and three-point codetypes (Greene & Brown, 1998).

Third, the ongoing interest in assessing validity that Dave Nichols and I shared moved from consistency of MMPI-2 item endorsement to the accuracy of item endorsement. We investigated this issue using Paulhus' distinction between impression management, whereby the person intentionally creates a favorable description that will change depending upon the setting, and self-deception, whereby the person believes the favorable description is accurate across all settings. The Lie (L) scale of the MMPI-2 is an excellent measure of impression management and our research showed that it was a taxon, i.e., a dichotomous category in that the person does or does not do impression management. The Correction (K) and Superlative (S) were at best adequate measures of self-deception. We investigated numerous scales and sets of items within the MMPI-2 but were unable to create a viable scale of self-deception.

One of my weekly highlights while I was in Palo Alto was taking care of two-year-old toddlers at our church. We would have from 5 to 15 toddlers each week and we got to play with and enjoy them for an hour or so while their parents were in church. We would then return them to their parents until the next week. I continued this practice of weekly care of toddlers at our churches for nearly 30 years. I vowed when the first parent, whom I had cared for, brought their child, I would retire. This event was about to happen in Palo Alto when we retired and moved to Plano in 2003 to be near our own grandchildren (Figure 15.1).

Figure 15.1 The author reading to toddlers.

Around 2000, John Exner asked me to join his Rorschach Research Council. I was very surprised and honored because I had administered the Rorschach a few times in my master's program but never in the ensuing 30 years. The Research Council met for two days in the spring and fall each year, alternating between Asheville, NC, and major cities around the country. I quickly learned that dinner after the first day would be at the best steak restaurant wherever we were. A few hours in each meeting would be focused on scoring issues. I could be sure that John and Don Viglione would discuss why "bugs" were a popular response and "insects" were an unusual response. It was a hard idea to explain to students who were learning to score the Rorschach. After a number of years of hearing this discussion, I finally realized that John used empirical categories to support his "bug" assertions—most people say "bug" and few say "insect"—and Don based his views on conceptual categories.

In 2006, Irv Weiner asked me to be his coauthor for the *Handbook of Personality Assessment*, a book that John Wiley wanted to publish. I always had great respect for Irv's scholarly work, which I had first encountered in graduate school. He was the long-term editor of the *Journal of Personality Assessment* and very active in the entire field of assessment. I was honored that he asked me, and I accepted. The *Handbook of Personality Assessment* (Weiner & Greene, 2008) was published in 2008 and updated in a second edition in 2017 (Weiner & Greene, 2017). This seemed like a nice way to mark the end of my career.

I devoted the last decade of my career trying to invoke a paradigm shift in the field of assessment, because the techniques for assessing psychopathology have not changed across the last 50–70 years (MMPI, MMPI-2, MMPI-RF), (MCMI, MCMI-II, MCM-III, MCMIIV). In no other area of science or technology has so little change been seen in the 70 years. I (Greene, 2011) proposed a computer-based system for assessment wherein individuals would be evaluated in a number of distinct areas (e.g., depression, hypersensitivity, anger, alienation) in a comprehensive evaluation. This system would allow individuals to indicate which areas are important to them and should be reviewed in greater depth and which areas are not important and can be given less attention. It also would be individualized so that no individual would receive the same set of items within or across areas. Individuals would be administered only the items within each area that are needed to evaluate it adequately. Once individuals have indicated a specific area is not important to them, the assessment process will continue on to the next area until the entire evaluation has been completed. This computer-based system would allow for areas to be added when need for them is demonstrated and areas to be deleted if they are unrelated to any outcome variables of interest. I can say that the response to my proposal has been underwhelming. Kuhn (1955) stated that a paradigm shift required the advocates of the current paradigm to die. I thought that price was too high, but I was willing to retire.

References

Greene, R. L. (1978). An empirically derived MMPI carelessness scale. *Journal of Clinical Psychology, 34,* 407410.

Greene, R. L. (1980). *The MMPI: An interpretive manual.* New York: Grune & Stratton.

Greene, R. L. (1991). *The MMPI2/MMPI: An interpretive manual.* Boston, MA: Allyn & Bacon.

Greene, R. L. (2000). *The MMPI-2: An interpretive manual* (2nd ed.). Boston, MA: Allyn & Bacon.

Greene, R. L. (2011a). Some considerations for enhancing psychological assessment. *Journal of Personality Assessment, 93,* 198–203.

Greene, R. L. (2011b). *The MMPI-2/MMPI-2-RF: An interpretive manual* (3rd ed.). Boston, MA: Allyn & Bacon.

Greene, R. L., & Brown, R., Jr. (1998). *MMPI2 adult interpretive system version 2.0* [Computer software]. Lutz, FL: Psychological Assessment Resources.

Greene, R. L., & Nichols, D. S. (1995). *MMPI2 structural summary* [Computer software]. Lutz, FL: Psychological Assessment Resources.

Kuhn. T. (1954). *The structure of scientific revolutions.* Chicago, IL: University of Chicago Press.

Nichols, D. S., & Greene, R. L. (1995). *MMPI2 structural summary interpretive manual.* Lutz, FL: Psychological Assessment Resources.

Weiner, I. B., & Greene, R. L. (2008). *Handbook of personality assessment.* New York: Wiley.

Weiner, I. B., & Greene, R. L. (2017). *Handbook of personality assessment* (2nd ed.) New York: Wiley.

16 From Stable Traits to Spinning Vectors

A Measurement Driven Journey[1]

D. S. Moskowitz

When asked to write an autobiographical book chapter, a person might decide to present the material linearly, in the order of the person's life history. I have taken a different approach. Much of the material in this chapter is organized thematically based on issues that have been of concern to me. Early in the chapter, I introduce the concept of small events, a concept which is explored in more detail in the discussion of what a trait is and how we can measure traits better. The middle of the chapter is concerned with the conceptualization and measurement of consistency, which had an important role in understanding the person–situation debate. Much of the material in the last third of the chapter discusses how growth in understanding the person–situation debate became growth in our understanding of intra-individual variability.

Small events

As I write, I am sitting at my desk with the coronavirus raging outside. We are under a shelter at home order, and yet I do not feel disconnected from others. Throughout the day, there are small events that connect me with others. I appreciate the oatmeal that my husband prepares for us to share for breakfast. I praise and make suggestions for changes to my doctoral student who writes to me about preparing her thesis for submission to a journal. My house cleaner, whom I have not seen for several weeks, calls to inquire about my health. One of my sisters e-mails me to set up an online chat with our third sister. We smile, laugh and joke during an online visit that focuses on complaining about getting groceries during the pandemic. My daughter calls to chat about the events of her day. This description of my day suggests that I am often agreeable, but not always. Sometimes my agreeable behavior co-occurs with submissive behavior, as indicated by my waiting for friends and family to contact me rather than my initiating contact with them. Sometimes my agreeable behavior co-occurs with dominant behavior as occurs in events with students when I both praise them and try to shape their manuscripts. I am variable in my display of agreeableness, which to a large extent depends on the behavior of others. I work with the presumption that our personalities are the result

DOI: 10.4324/9781003036302-16

of the accumulation of many events. Most often these events are small, as in the previous example of the events of my day, but sometimes the events are large, such as the pandemic. Moreover, it is not only the expression of mean levels of behaviors that is important for understanding personality; the patterning of behaviors in these events also has significance. In this chapter, I will describe a method for assessing personality through small events. This method originated from the person-situation debate and is currently reflected in expanding interest in intra-individual variability.

Early influential personal and career events

A long time ago, in a galaxy far, far away (perhaps not that long ago and not that far away), I was a senior in high school, and I went on a date with a recent graduate from my high school. He was smart, witty, conscientious and kind. We went to a Dodgers-Mets baseball game. On the way home we stopped by New York's JFK airport to watch the airplanes take off and land. We laughed a lot, had an excellent time, and have not been separated for long periods of time since that day. David Zuroff is the best collaborator a person could have, and the best husband.

My professional life was not as easy to establish. When we look around psychology classes or psychology departmental faculty meetings in the present time it is hard to imagine psychology classes filled primarily with male students taught primarily by male professors. During the period when women were not highly represented in psychology, it was believed that there were graduate programs who had quotas on the number of women who could be accepted, which was the beginning of the more difficult career tracks for women than men.

When David and I started searching for jobs after graduate school, we became familiar with the frightening concept of "the faculty wife." Both members of a couple might have excellent credentials, but if one of them were offered a position, it would be the husband who was hired. At the time of the job offer, the wife would often be told that something might develop in her area. Until then, she could work part-time teaching courses. The young couple, flush with the offer for the husband and assured that something would develop for the wife, accepts the position. However, the wife soon learns that part-time instructors are paid a pittance of a salary, and there are no facilities for her research unless she can squeeze into a corner of her husband's lab space. I spent my first six years post-PhD in positions that were some variants of the faculty wife before I was appointed to a full-time tenure track position. Now, I try to remember the contributions of women who came before me who had limited access to resources yet persevered in their research and their academic careers. I try to appreciate efforts that have been made to improving the status of women and to accommodating the needs of academic couples. While there are still problems, progress on these issues has been made.

I feel appreciation towards Professor Virginia Douglas, former chair, and the Department of Psychology at McGill for seeing my potential and making it possible to conduct much of the research reported in this chapter. The congenial relationships among faculty have been supported for the most part by frequent agreeable, communal behaviors and low levels of status-seeking agentic behaviors, at least among colleagues.

Feminism not only changed the gender composition of Departments of Psychology, but it also affected how I named myself on my manuscripts and publications. Early in my career, I read an article by Sara Kiesler demonstrating that articles written by men received better evaluations than articles written by women even when the texts were identical. I applied the implications of that article to my own work and started identifying myself on my articles with my initials (D. S.). A consequence of concealing my identity was that I came to be referred to as "he" in the literature. This was a reasonable presumption given that the base rate would indicate that more men than women wrote articles. I had also been advised to maintain the use of one name in my articles so my body of work would be identified together. Consequently, I remain "D. S." despite many readers of my publications knowing my sex. Hopefully, the present cohort and future cohorts will not have to hide aspects of their identity to maximize positive evaluations of their work.

A core issue in personality assessment

The controversy seems so long ago, and yet strong feelings remain. During the 1970s, I was a graduate student at the University of Connecticut taking courses with Julian B. Rotter and J. Conrad Schwarz on personality theory and personality measurement. Walter Mischel's (1968) slim book on *Personality and Assessment* was having a profound effect on the study of personality. Mischel asserted that there was a lack of consistency in personality, and this absence of consistency indicated that traits did not exist. This position was endorsed by many psychologists in a major paradigm shift. As one colleague later said to me, Mischel's critique of personality almost destroyed the field. It affected everything: who received appointments; what was considered suitable to study; what got published; who got grants, and who got tenure.

A confluence of influences

Professor rotter

In lectures given during his personality theory course, Professor Julian B. Rotter emphasized the importance of using clear language when constructing personality theory. In *Social Learning Theory and Clinical Psychology* (Rotter, 1954), he proposed three core constructs: expectancies, reinforcement values, and behavior potentials which could be defined as specific to a particular situation, but which could also be defined as generalizing across elements of situations. For example, locus of control was a personality construct developed by Rotter (1966) which was defined as a generalized expectancy indicating the degree to which persons hold the belief that they, rather than external forces, have influence over the outcomes of events in their lives. Instead of a generalized expectancy, one could define a personality construct as specific to a situation such as the expectancy that studying will improve a student's grades, or yet more specifically, that carefully doing homework problems will improve math grades. Based to a large extent on Professor Rotter's lectures, I came to believe that the definition of a personality characteristic should include consideration of whether the characteristic made predictions to specific situations or to generalizations that crossed sets of situations. It seemed possible that specificity and generality could be incorporated into the measurement of personality characteristics.

Professors schwarz, wiggins, and cronbach

Concurrently with Professor Rotter's course on personality theory, I was taking a personality assessment course with J. Conrad Schwarz that included some material on psychometrics. I was excited reading the text by Jerry Wiggins (1973) on *Personality and Prediction.* I was also intrigued by *Generalizability Theory,* developed by Cronbach et al. (1972) which provided a way of estimating the sources of variation that influence error and, importantly, the relative strengths of these components of error. For example, we might ask whether rater or time was a greater influence over error. From another perspective, we could try to identify the sources of generalizability influencing scores on a measurement method.

Epstein: the power of aggregation

According to the Spearman-Brown prophesy formula, increasing the number of items on a test increases reliability (Brown, 1910; Spearman, 1910). This formula was first articulated in the context of assessing how change in the length of a test would affect test reliability when test reliability meant split-half reliability, that is, how scores on one half of the test correlated with scores on the other half of a test. Split-half reliability has generally been calculated to assess internal consistency, the extent to which test items co-occur. The Spearman-Brown formula can be used to estimate change in consistency as a function of fewer or greater number of items on a test.

Seymour Epstein (1979) extended the application of the Spearman-Brown formula to consistency over days. In each of several studies using university students, he measured participants' emotions on multiple days using methods such as self-ratings and ratings by others. He split the data in half to examine how the average odd day score correlated with the average even day score. Increasing the number of days on which scores were based led to an increase in split-half reliability. For example, consider the calculation of split-half reliability for a 6-item (i.e., day) test. The odd day score would average scores on Day 1, Day 3, and Day 5, while the even day score would average scores on Days 2, 4, and 6. The number of days on which a score was based would increase up to some limit imposed by the number of days the test was administered. Epstein found that for many measures, increasing the number of days on which a score was based increased the correlation between the odd day scores and the even day scores. Epstein suggested that finding a substantial correlation between scores based on odd and even days was evidence for the existence of traits and suggested that traits emerge when scores are averaged.

I realized that Epstein's formulation could be extended by merging his ideas with the ideas of Rotter (1954) and Cronbach and associates (1972). It was not only that there had to be more days of measurement to establish consistency; there had to be consideration of all the potential elements of consistency, such as generality over items, generality over occasions, and generality across situations.

Studying consistency

Over the next 15 years, I conducted several studies with different assessment methods and different age groups to illustrate several ways personality characteristics could be consistent. In each study some type of consistency was found, but these multiple types of consistency did not necessarily co-occur. Having examined consistency using a naturalistic study of preschool aged children (Moskowitz, 1982) and a laboratory study of young adults (Moskowitz, 1988), I next wanted to examine consistency among adults in naturalistic settings. I focused on three types of consistency that I had worked with in prior studies: cross-situational generality (i.e., behavioral consistency across events), temporal stability (i.e., behavioral consistency over time), and coherence (i.e., consistency across situation-relevant behaviors).

Observing young children in a naturalistic setting

In one project, I conducted a study using behavioral observations to examine consistency across occasions (temporal stability) for dominance and dependency among preschool age children (Moskowitz, 1982). Children were observed over eight weeks for a total of approximately four hours. Stability over occasions of observations was poor to modest when scores were based on 1 week or approximately 20–30 minutes of observation.

Generality across occasions improved when behavioral observation scores were based on a greater number of weeks of observations, that is a greater amount of observation time. In other words, there was greater temporal stability when there was more observation time for each child.

Using the same data set, I found that generality across behaviors representing a personality characteristic (coherence) improved when using a greater number of behaviors. In addition, generality across trained observers was found to be greater when using an increased number of observers (Moskowitz & Schwarz, 1982).

Observing young adults in the laboratory

Similar results were found for university age students assessed with behavior observation data collected in a laboratory setting. Participants were recruited as pairs of same-sex friends. Each person was observed working with a partner on six problem-solving tasks; participants engaged in each task on separate occasions. On two occasions the partner was the friend; on two occasions the partner was a same-sex stranger (someone else's friend), and on two occasions the other participant was an opposite-sex stranger who was the friend of someone else in the study. I could examine generality across task and kind of partner and generality across observers under more controlled circumstances than possible in a naturalistic setting. In this study of university students (Moskowitz, 1988), as well as in the previously described study of preschool age children, there is not a single dimension of consistency to be exclusively considered when justifying personality characteristics. From the consistency and specificity of personality debate, I learned several principles:

Lesson 1, There are different types of consistency, all of which can be relevant to justifying the existence of personality characteristics;

Lesson 2, Aspects of personality constructs can be consistent when there is suitable consideration during the construction of the personality measure of the relevant dimensions of consistency;

Lesson 3, Pay attention to whether there are sufficient data to find consistency.

Which personality characteristics to study

I wanted to improve upon these studies of consistency by examining personality characteristics that were systematically selected from a defined domain. If unexpected results were obtained, it might be possible to look back at the relations among the characteristics to discover what had led to discrepant results.

Selecting behaviors

I used the Interpersonal Circle Model to derive behaviors. The Interpersonal Circle is a structurally less demanding version of a model known as the Interpersonal Circumplex. A circumplex loads characteristics onto eight equally spaced octants while the Interpersonal Circle uses four octants defined by two intersecting yet independent dimensions. The Interpersonal Circumplex has a long history of use; for a summary, see Fournier et al. (2011). Wiggins (1991) named the two major dimensions *agency* and *communion*, although other names have been used such as affiliation and dominance. Wiggins defined agency as strivings for mastery and power which would enhance and protect the differentiation of the individual. Higher scores on this dimension indicate efforts by the person to individuate the self and have influence and control over tasks and over others. Agentic behavior is expressed in frequent dominant acts and infrequent submissive acts. Communal behavior reflects strivings to seek stronger connections with others or with a group. Communal behavior is reflected in frequent agreeable behaviors and infrequent quarrelsome behaviors.

Items were generated by interviewing team members at the research and development site of a large telecommunications firm. The personality characteristics were described, and people were asked to provide behavioral examples of the characteristics. I obtained additional items by reviewing questionnaires. To obtain diverse reactions to the items, this initial pool was refined using ratings from experts, graduate students, and university managers. More information about item selection can be found in Moskowitz (1994). A list of items on each scale can be found in Appendix A. These items are referred to as the Social Behavior Inventory.

In the interpersonal circle model, a specific behavior can be classified in terms of its relation to both agency and communion. The item "I went along with the other," falls within the agreeable and submissive quadrant of the interpersonal circle and is rated highly on the communal dimension and low on the agentic dimension. The item, "I criticized the other" is rated highly on the agentic dimension and low on the communal dimension thereby falling within the dominant-quarrelsome quadrant.

The Social Behavior Inventory (SBI) items have primarily been used with an event contingent recording (ECR) methodology, a type of intensive repeated measures collected in naturalistic settings to assess a person's agentic (dominant to submissive) behaviors and communal (agreeable to quarrelsome) behaviors. The SBI items are brief, easily administered, and easily understood. While once known as the science of behavior, much contemporary psychological research focusses on cognition and affect. In contrast, the SBI focusses on behaviors, specifically interpersonal behaviors. When used with ECR, the 12 items for each dimension of behavior (dominance, agreeableness, submissiveness, and quarrelsomeness) are divided equally among four forms; thus, there were three items per dimension of behavior per form. The items for the four forms are approximately balanced for frequency of item endorsement. In addition, the items can be used with other methods such as one-occasion self-reports, one-occasion reports by others, and daily diaries (Figure 16.1).

Dominant Behavior Scale

I set goal(s) for the other(s) or for us.

I gave information.

I expressed an opinion.

I criticized the other(s)**.

I took the lead in planning/organizing a project or activity.

I asked for a volunteer.

I spoke in a clear firm voice.

I asked the other(s) to do something.

I got immediately to the point.

I tried to get the other(s) to do something else.

I made a suggestion.

I assigned someone to a task.

Submissive Behavior Scale

I waited for the other person to act or talk first.

I went along with the other(s) **.

I did not express disagreement when I thought it.

I spoke softly.

I let other(s) make plans or decisions.

I gave in.

I spoke only when I was spoken to.

I did not say what I wanted directly

I did not state my own views.

Figure 16.1 Social behavior inventory items.

I did not say how I felt.

I avoided taking the lead or being responsible.

I did not say what was on my mind.

Agreeable Behavior Scale

I listened attentively to the other.

I went along with the other(s)**.

I spoke favorably of someone who was not present.

I compromised about a decision.

I complimented or praised the other person.

I smiled and laughed with other(s).

I showed sympathy.

I exchanged pleasantries.

I pointed out to the other(s) where there was agreement.

I expressed affection with words or gestures.

I made a concession to avoid unpleasantness.

I expressed reassurance.

Quarrelsome Behavior Scale

I did not respond to other(s)' questions or comments.

I criticized the other(s) *.

I raised my voice.

I made a sarcastic comment.

I demanded that the other(s) do what I wanted

I discredited what someone said.

I confronted the other(s) about something I did not like.

I gave incorrect information.

I stated strongly that I did not like or that I would not do something

I ignored the other(s)' comments.

I withheld useful information.

I showed impatience

*This item appears on both the dominant scale and the quarrelsome scale.

** This item appears on both the submissive scale and the agreeable scale.

Figure 16.1 (Continued)

Social behavior inventory

In its first version, the SBI had two scales, dominant behavior and agreeable behavior. People generally made positive comments about themselves which led these scales to have poor discriminant validity. To address this issue, in subsequent studies, I used a four-scale version of the SBI with one scale for each pole of the Interpersonal Circle. I used a scoring procedure called ipsatization that was developed by Horowitz and his collaborators (Horowitz et al., 1988). The ipsatized trait score reflected the frequency with which items relevant to the trait were checked, adjusted for a participant's general rate of responding.

To contextualize or to decontextualize

When used with an event-contingent recording procedure, the SBI items can be contextualized by adding items about situational cues that occur concurrently with the behavioral items. The SBI can be decontextualized by specifying an instructional set that refers to a substantial reference time period, such as during the past six months.

Event-contingent recording

In event-contingent recording, data are recorded subsequent to the occurrence of a specified event. This requires the identification of events with a discernible beginning and an end. The explicit identification of events of interest permits the maximization of the collection of data about these focal events and the minimization of the amount of time between the event and the recording of information about the event. In my research, this method has been found to be particularly suitable for data collection about social interactions. ECR has also been found to be suitable for events involving poor health such as smoking.

When I started working with ECR data I was very concerned about the feasibility of the method. Would community adults follow the procedure? Would community adults remain in the study for almost three weeks, the length of the ECR procedure? About 80% of the sample who began the first study remained in the study, and they appeared to have followed directions. Thus, I concluded that I had demonstrated the feasibility of the method, and I considered the study a success.

SBI/ECR/NS

As I sat at my desk to run analyses on the first version of the SBI with four scales, I was scared. I had put a great amount of time and resources into developing the SBI/ECR/NS (Social Behavior Inventory using Event Contingent Recording in Naturalistic Settings) combination. I expected that my grant would not and should not be renewed if I had little to show to the granting agency funding my research. My index finger lingered over the keyboard. Suddenly, it dropped, and I pressed the submit key to make the program run.

Almost immediately the essential results were known (Moskowitz, 1994). The pattern of correlations was as would be expected for a measure of the Interpersonal Circle Model. There was high agreement in the assignment of items to scales. The SBI/ECR/NS agency scale was correlated with the Interpersonal Adjectives Scale – Revised agency scale (IAS-R, Wiggins, 1995). The two measures of communion were correlated with each other. As expected, agency and communion measures were not significantly correlated. The analyses established the basic convergent and discriminant validity of these measures. I had demonstrated feasibility and some validity for the SBI/ECR/NS. There was a future for the SBI at least when combined with event-contingent recording.

Varied formats and reliability

There is evidence for moderate to high generality across items when the SBI is used for self-reports and for reports by their friends. Inter-rater reliability is moderate to high when the SBI is used by independent observers (Mongrain et al., 1998; Sadler & Woody, 2003). These findings provide support for the consistency of agency and communion across both items and across reports by familiar and unfamiliar others.

Comments on scoring the SBI/ECR/NS

I have constructed several kinds of scores when using the SBI/ECR/NS. Some of these scores are at the level of the event, that is, event-level behavior scores, and some scores are at the level of the person, i.e., mean behavior scores across events, reflecting the person's dispositions. A third kind of score refers to within-person intraindividual variability and includes the within person scores of flux, pulse, and spin.

Constructing scores

The dimensions of agency and communion can be thought of as a Cartesian (x,y) coordinate system defining the space of interpersonal behavior. Polar coordinates of angular displacement and extremity (r, θ have also been used by circumplex researchers to define the space of interpersonal behavior. Figure 16.2 illustrates the relation between the two dimensions. Social behavior during an interpersonal interaction is shown as a vector which initiates at the origin and extends to the point in interpersonal space (x,y) corresponding to the observed levels of agency and communion. Alternatively, the vector can be characterized in terms of its degree of rotation (angular displacement, θ) from the horizontal axis and its length (r).

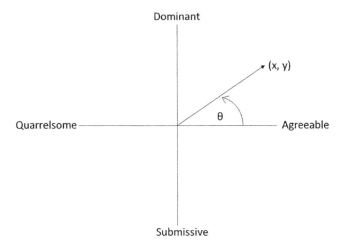

Figure 16.2 Relation between agency and communion.

Event-level behavior scale scores

When used with an ECR methodology, event-specific scores suitable for multi-level modelling can be constructed. The event-specific scores can be analyzed for various contextual effects, such as social roles, relationship closeness, perceived qualities of the other person, and physical qualities of the environment such as exposure to bright light (aan het Rot et al., 2008. Thus, a method which had originally been developed to study consistency has become a useful method for studying variability in a person's behavior.

Person-level scores

My collaborators and I recommend using the event-level scores with the appropriate multi-level statistics to examine person-level variables. For an example of using the same data to analyze both within-person and between-person scores, see the study of attachment by Sadikaj et al. (2011), who demonstrated a within-person association between negative affect and the perceived person's agreeable behavior. At the person-level they demonstrated that this effect is stronger for individuals who have an anxious attachment orientation. They contextualized these findings by noting that the effects were stronger when interacting with the romantic partner.

Flux, pulse and spin scores

Flux, pulse and spin are person-level scores that can be calculated in addition to communal and agentic behavior scores. Communal and agentic behavior scores for each interaction are treated as Cartesian coordinates and then transformed to polar coordinates from which an angular position score expressed in radians is calculated. Conceptually, flux refers to variability around a person's mean score; four flux scores can be calculated, one for each of the circumplex poles. Pulse is the standard deviation around the person's mean extremity score. Interpersonal spin is the standard deviation of the angular position scores across events (for formula for the circular standard deviation, see Mardia, 1972; Figure 16.3).

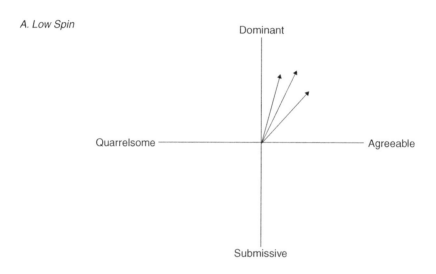

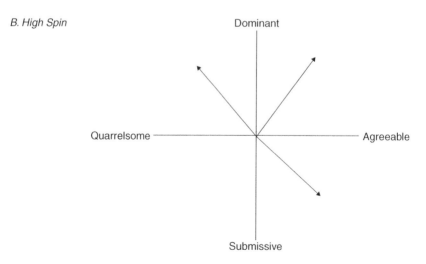

Figure 16.3 Patterns of within-person variability.

What can interpersonal spin tell us?

Relationships at work

We demonstrated that higher spinners report greater distance from their contacts in the workplace. Co-workers are less satisfied and engage less often in pleasant activities with higher spinners. Co-workers avoid higher spinners with whom they are well acquainted because they feel more negative affect when interacting with these individuals (Côté et al., 2012).

Personal relationships

We also found that dynamic personality constructs such as spin can improve our understanding of personality characteristics that influence individuals' couple relationships. In a longitudinal study with three measurement points collected over seven-months, higher spinners had lower need satisfaction, and lower need satisfaction was associated with a decline in relationship satisfaction from the end of the ECR period to T3, which was about three months later. Higher spin was also associated with lower perceived autonomy support, and lower support was associated with decreased progress in a couple's goal completion from T2 to T3. The effects of spin were independent of the effects of mean levels of behavior. These findings extend the understanding of intraindividual variability in interpersonal behavior (Sadikaj et al., 2015).

The interpersonal grid: Why another measure was needed

Correspondence and reciprocity are two major principles of Interpersonal Theory. According to the correspondence principle, people are likely to respond with agreeable behavior when other people are agreeable towards them. The reciprocity principle predicts that individuals will respond to others with submissive behavior when others behave dominantly towards them. There is support for these principles, but it also seems possible that the identification of moderators of these principles could lead to better nuanced theory. To investigate the relation between self-reports of behavior and reports of others' behavior required the development of a measure suitable for measuring perceptions of others.

I first considered having participants rate others in each interpersonal event using the SBI. There were two problems with that approach. First, the procedure would become longer to complete and that might reduce compliance among participants. Second, I was concerned about shared method variance. We might find that relations between self-report and reports about others were caused by similarities in the method instead of the content of the SBI. We have used the Interpersonal Grid (IG; Moskowitz & Zuroff, 2005) to collect information about participants' perceptions of others concurrent with reports of participants' affect and their own behavior. The IG is useful when the investigator requires a very brief method to assess information about perceptions of the other, that includes a rapid report of perception of the other in each event (Figure 16.4).

The tale of the between and the within

For the analyses of SBI/ECR/NS, I initially relied on my graduate school training in statistics, which was primarily concerned with using ANOVA techniques to conduct between-subjects analyses. The first papers I wrote with SBI/ECR/NS data used a one-between (gender of participant) x one-within (the categorical variable, social role status) design for each event. Since ANOVA does not handle missing data well, I had to throw out many subjects who had missing data. This seemed like a waste of information, but a necessity given the constraints of the analyses.

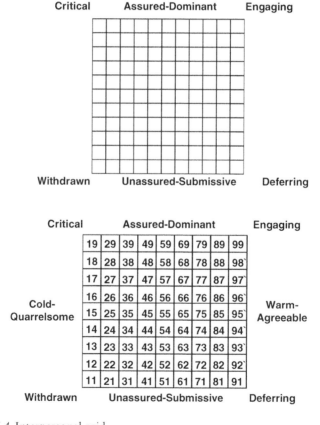

Figure 16.4 Interpersonal grid.

Analyzing repeated measures was a problem for the ECR data. Each participant was generating approximately 45 events, and each of these events had several associated measurements. Doing the calculations was difficult and time-consuming; sometimes I had to run analyses overnight. However, this was a technical problem that resolved itself as computers could be configured with faster processors and more memory. There was another problem that was a consequence of using naturalistic data; our data were unbalanced in that participants had unequal numbers of interpersonal events which led to biased estimation of regression coefficients.

The plan for analyses evolved. A colleague suggested that we could get better estimates by using weighted least squares regressions rather than ordinary least squares analyses. Forging ahead, so I could start at the beginning I gained experience using weighted least squares (WLS) rather than Ordinary Least Squares (OLS).

The programming for undertaking these models was arduous. For the first published project, we were working with about 6.5 records per day × 20 days × 89 participants or about 11,570 events. It took a lot of computer memory to run studies with that size data base. For each individual I had to regress one variable on another variable; then extract the intercepts and b's for each individual, and merge the file with the b's and intercepts into a file with the other variables. It was not a pleasant task. Fortunately, Stéphane Côté, an undergraduate at the time who was working in my lab, spent a summer reading the SAS manual to find an efficient way to manipulate the data to prepare for WLS.

Subsequently, I heard about a new statistical technique called multilevel modelling. It had been used in educational research, such as studies of children nested in classes or classes next in schools. The statistical models were not yet well known in personality assessment, but it was easy to see the importance of the concept of individuals nested in some other level, such as individuals nested in couples.

As I began to become familiar with various new statistical techniques, I started to feel a sense of unease. There was a plethora of statistical analyses which permitted the modelling of the individual when there were many data points. For example, we could use time series analyses, or weighted least squares, or multilevel analyses, or structural equation modelling (SEM), or multilevel SEM. For which kinds of designs were each of these methods best suited?

I was discovering that I was not alone. There seemed to be great confusion among experienced and novice researchers who were interested in analyzing measurements based on intensive repeated measures. With the encouragement of Lisa Harlow, who was the editor of the quantitative psychology book series at Erlbaum, I edited a book with Scott Hershberger about intraindividual variability analyses (Moskowitz & Hershberger, 2002). This was a very practical book written at an introductory level about techniques such as weighted least squares, categorical mixed designs, multilevel structural equations, and analysis of categorical data models. In particular, the chapters about multilevel modeling were useful in understanding the theory and the practice for analyzing various designs. The book sold well. Surprisingly, people started addressing me as an expert in this area when instead I had been trying to reduce my ignorance.

Event-contingent vs. Signal-contingent recording

Many people have asked me why I use event-contingent recording rather than signal-contingent recording. In signal-contingent recording, forms are completed on receipt of a signal. Many researchers use signal-contingent recording when they want information about how close in time the completion of the record form was to the occurrence of the signal which many or may not be close in time to the focal event. In contrast, with event-contingent recording a pertinent event initiates completion of a form. The event can occur at any time. If the participant is following instructions, the record of the event will be close in time to the occurrence of the event. With signal contingent recording, the participant may miss relevant events that do not occur close in time to a pre-existing schedule of signals. In other words, with measures of affect it is sensible to ask the question or some variant of the question, "how are you feeling now?" notwithstanding whether or not that moment occurs with an interpersonal event for the participant. The parallel question, "how are you behaving now?" is likely to miss interpersonal events that do not occur at the time of a signal.

Defining situations

One vexing problem throughout the history of personality psychology has been how to define situations. Many of the situations that individuals encounter include a large interpersonal component. Thus, it seemed plausible that the interpersonal circle could be used as a domain for sampling situations as well as a domain for sampling personality characteristics. Sampling from each of the quadrants of the interpersonal circle seemed like it could provide information of similar breadth about personality characteristics and situational characteristics.

We conducted a 20-day ECR study (Moskowitz & Zuroff, 2008) in which we included both the SBI and the IG. The SBI scores were included to measure the participant's reports of their own interpersonal behaviors in each event. The IG was included to obtain participants' reports along the dimensions of agency and communion about people with whom they were interacting. While it might have been preferable from a modeling perspective to use the same scale for self-reports and perceptions of others, I used different scales to reduce shared method variance. The IG is a good choice for collecting SBI–ECR–NS data as it is brief and does not greatly increase the burden on participants.

We used the data collected from working adults to construct behavioral profiles analogously to work done by Shoda et al. (1994) with children with behavior disorders. My student, Marc Fournier, used these data to create dichotomous item scores for situations. Scores greater than the midpoint of the scale (6 out of 11) were used to identify situations that were high or low on perceived agency and situations that were high low on perceived communion. The agency and communion scores were then used to create a fourfold table of interpersonal situations of similar conceptual breadth. The four quadrants of the interpersonal circle were that the other person was perceived as agreeable-dominant, agreeable-submissive, quarrelsome-dominant, or quarrelsome-submissive. We used these scores to create a behavioral profile for each person consisting of eight scores which captured how agentically and how communally the person reported behaving in each of these four situations. In other words, we constructed behavior-situation profiles by averaging behavior data for each participant for each of the four situations for agency and communion.

We (Fournier et al., 2009) examined the variance in behavior-situation profiles attributable to between-person and to within-person effects. We found that the between-person variance accounted for about 50% of the total variance. We also found that within-person variance accounted for about 50% of the total variance of the behavior-situation profiles. This indicated that within-subject sources of variance and between-subject sources of variance contributed approximately equally to the total variance of the behavior-situation profiles. This is important, because we usually focus our attention on between-person analyses, asking questions such as how much are highly dominant individuals different from less dominant individuals. However, our findings suggest that there may be within-person patterns of interest. For example, is there a pattern of behavior in which persons are elevated on dominance in response to quarrelsome dominance, but are not dominant in response to agreeable dominance.

We calculated the temporal stability of the behavior-situation profiles. To do so, the data were split in half, and two sets of scores were calculated for each person; the correlation for each pole of the circumplex was then calculated by correlating the two sets of scores coming from the same person. This procedure was repeated 1,000 times to estimate the reliability of each of the behavior-situation profiles for each of the behavior scales. The stability of the behavior-situation profiles scales ranged from 0.24 for dominant behavior to 0.52 quarrelsome behavior; all were statistically significant. These findings indicate that a personality dimension can be characterized by more than its mean. Dimensions of personality can also be characterized by patterning of the behavior in relation to a set of situations.

Applications to the study of interpersonal behavior

Tryptophan I

I had come across the work of a researcher who was investigating the effects of administering tryptophan on the social behavior of monkeys. I was curious as to whether the SBI/ECR/NS could detect the effects of tryptophan on the social behavior of humans. Tryptophan is an amino acid that raises brain serotonin. David Zuroff mentioned that there was a neurochemist at McGill, Professor Simon Young, who studied the effects of tryptophan on humans. When Simon and I met, there did seem to be connections between our areas of work, and we started to sketch a study. In addition, we recruited David Zuroff for his general statistical expertise, Lawrence Annable for expertise in clinical statistical design, and Gilbert Pinard, Professor and psychiatrist, who evaluated participants' suitability for the study – a necessity, as tryptophan is a prescribed medication in Canada. When we described the planned study to colleagues, several suggested that the effect of tryptophan on healthy individuals would be too small to be observed. Fortunately, the funding agency took a different view. During one phase of the study, participants ingested tryptophan three times a day with meals for 12 days and in the other phase, participants ingested a placebo pill on same schedule for 12 days. There was also a two-day washout period between phases of the study. Participants completed the SBI-ECR-NS during both phases.

Our findings (Moskowitz et al., 2001) contradicted doubts that we would not find any effects of tryptophan supplementation. Using the SBI/ECR/NS measurement of social behavior with event-contingent recording, we instead found that recruits from the community given tryptophan supplements did show changes in social behavior. In particular, tryptophan decreased quarrelsome behavior when tryptophan was given first, suggesting that a decrease in quarrelsome behavior when tryptophan was given first may have carried over into the subsequent placebo period. We speculated that tryptophan may have changed the person's interaction patterns, such that a reduction in quarrelsome behavior caused by tryptophan was maintained by changes in the behaviors of others towards participants. Tryptophan may have initiated the change in behavior while the reactions of other people to the changed behavior maintained the new patterns of behavior. We suspected that one reason for the sensitivity of our measures was the many measurements of behavior that we obtained for each individual. Aggregating scores across many points decreases error variance, thereby increasing the likelihood that effects are found.

Tryptophan II

Simon Young's student, Marije aan het Rot, conducted another double-blind cross-over study with tryptophan supplementation (aan het Rot et al., 2006). This time the participants were irritable and angry individuals whom we expected to have lower than normal levels of brain serotonin. We again found that tryptophan supplementation decreased quarrelsome behavior. In addition, irritable individuals became more agreeable and saw others as more agreeable. If we assume that the irritable individuals had lower levels of brain serotonin, the results of this study are also consistent with the possibility that tryptophan first changes behavior, and then these changes are maintained by changes in the person's interaction patterns with others (Young et al., 2014).

Paroxetine

To further our understanding of how serotonin influences interpersonal behavior and how naturalistic measures might detect these influences, we conducted a study using the SBI/ECR/NS procedure to examine whether this procedure is sufficiently sensitive to detect change during pharmacotherapy. I was particularly interested in integrating this work with the use of the flux, pulse, and spin variables. We found that administration of the SSRI paroxetine over a five-month period reduced intraindividual variability in the interpersonal behavior of individuals with Social Anxiety Disorder. My former student, Lance Rappaport, and colleagues found that participants demonstrated reduced intraindividual variability in interpersonal behaviors while taking paroxetine (Rappaport et al., 2018). Thus, the measurement methodology did appear to be sensitive to change in a serotonin-related medication.

Borderline personality disorder

My students and I have considered whether the SBI/ECR/NS method could contribute novel findings to the understanding of individuals who had symptoms of psychopathology. One characteristic attributed by clinicians to Borderline Personality Disorder (BPD) is erratic, variable behavior, but it has been difficult to quantify erratic behavior. My former student, Jennifer Russell, along with our collaborators examined whether the intraindividual variability constructs developed by David Zuroff and myself could quantify differences in within-person variability for women with BPD and women who were healthy controls. We found differences in the means of variables. Individuals with BPD were less dominant and more submissive than the nonclinical control women. In addition to the difference in means, women with BPD displayed more intraindividual variability on several variables including greater flux in quarrelsome and agreeable behaviors, and they exhibited more spin than nonclinical control participants (Russell et al., 2007).

Gentiana Sadikaj, another graduate of my lab, developed this work further by showing the possibility of studying sequences that could become cycles in the behavior and social perceptions of individuals with BPD. She demonstrated that individuals with BPD reported more quarrelsome behavior and more negative affect during interactions in which they perceived others as more quarrelsome than usual. Greater negative affect reactivity to perceptions of another person's quarrelsome behavior partly accounted for the increased quarrelsome behavior reported by individuals with BPD during these interactions. This pattern of results suggests a cycle in which the perception of cold-quarrelsome behavior in another person triggers elevated negative affect and quarrelsome behavior in individuals with BPD, which subsequently leads to perceptions of others as quarrelsome, and the cycle begins again (Sadikaj et al., 2010).

Genetics

My colleagues, Genta Sadikaj and Jennifer Bartz, approached me with the idea that we could collect genetics data from couples who had previously participated in one of my lab's ECR studies. We found that a variation of the CD38 gene – CD38.rs379686 – was associated with an individual's communal behavior in interactions with their romantic partner. Individuals with the CC genotype were more communal towards their romantic partners, and they reported that their partners were more communal towards them. Combining SBI/ECR/NS with genetics data may be a powerful combination for better understanding of how people maintain relationships.

Interpreting scores

There was something missing from the use of the SBI/ECR/NS. For many years, when I had taught a Tests and Measures course for undergraduates, I would lecture that it was necessary to have a normative sample to provide adequate norms to interpret an individual's test scores. If I had a normative sample for an IQ test, I could use the information to calculate the standard error of measurement (SE) to determine whether the person's score was in the normal range. However, it is difficult to obtain representative normative samples, and normative scores drift over time and should be recalculated. It seemed likely that we would not be able to interpret SBI/ECR/NS scores based on norms.

Then, Professor Aaron Pincus and his students and collaborators had a good idea. They realized that they could take advantage of the repeated measurements provided by the ECR for interpreting individual's scores. They could compare people to themselves. Thus, using this approach, they began to create idiographic norms rather than using nomothetic norms. For example, they calculated whether there was greater variance in scores when individuals were at work or with a spouse. They calculated interpersonal complementarity (reciprocity between the person and perceptions of the other) and asked whether the within-person correlation between self-reports of dominance and perceptions of the other person's submissiveness was stronger at home or at work (Pincus et al., 2014). If we can envision personality assessment which uses idiographic norms, there is still work to be done. We would have to decide which questions to ask and whether the questions should also be idiographic, attuned to individuals, or standardized across identifiable groups.

Small events can matter

The topic of major life events is well developed; divorce, a new job, and moving can be very stressful. Brief encounters of significance can also occur. For example, when I was struggling at the beginning of my career, Professor Martha Wilson of the University of Connecticut said to me in passing that women should not evaluate themselves against the biological clock used by men. The memory of those words in that brief encounter has provided support for my pursuit of career goals ignoring the timeline for men. For example, I was appointed Associate Professor and Full Professor at a later age than my male contemporaries. My overarching career goal though has been to conduct rigorous, innovative work and that has been possible at any age in my career (Figure 16.5).

Figure 16.5 The author.

Why does ECR appeal to me?

There are probably two main reasons for the appeal of ECR. First I like the amount of control I have over the measurements. I can construct scores which are very specific, e.g. representing very specifically defined situations. Alternatively, I can aggregate scores to represent different degrees of generality. I can construct scores which refer to different lengths of time or to different patterns in the data, such as long or short cycles. In other words, this approach has been appealing to me, because it permits me to construct measures which can be molecular, precise and closely defined.

Second, I enjoy conducting studies which are big and bold. Early on in my career I conducted a behavioral observation study which involved nine observers coding data about 56 children for ten hours per week. Child-observer pairings and observer-observer pairings were rotated to avoid observer drift. This study required political acumen as well as organizational skills and knowledge of measurement and research design. It was a combination I cheerfully enjoyed. During the early ECR studies many people confidently told me that I would not be able to get people to volunteer for or to complete the ECR procedure. In fact, members of my lab have successfully run more than 500 participants through the procedure for these studies. I like the challenge of what I do.

Conclusion

Students often ask the question, "How did you develop your line of research?" I try to be honest in my response and reply "I never planned my research as a series of studies. Instead, I read the literature, examined my own results, and asked, "What is the next logical study?" The development of my line of research emerges only when I look back at my work to see what I have done.

Several years ago, I attended a McGill University commencement. The main address was given by Professor Stephen Weinberg, Nobel Prize winning physicist. His advice to the young scientists at commencement may be valuable to people in many fields who are asking, "What's next?" (Weinberg, 2004). He recommended jumping into messy areas, as that is where the action is likely to be. He also recommended forgiving one's self for wasting time. It is hard to know in advance which problems are solvable at a particular historical moment given available tools and theory. He also told the graduates to be kind to themselves if they discover that they were on an unproductive path. He recommended learning about the history of their fields. Understanding the context of their work would help them to see their own work as contributing to that which has come before, and why there were good reasons at the time to go down the path that they chose.

With respect to the assessment of personality, it surprises me that where I started my thinking is so different from where I am now. I jumped into a very messy area which turned out to be very productive. I started off doing work that impacted on people's understanding of consistency. This work has turned out to interweave theory, models, and measurement in ways that give both researchers and clinicians new tools. Working in this area necessitated identifying a model which could be integrated with prior work to support the future growth of research on personality assessment. The understanding of consistency impacted on our understanding of traits. Then the improved measurement of consistency became merged with models which provided new constructs which have led to new insights into personality.

My early work on traits led me to be among the researchers to pioneer the development of tools to capture the running stream of people's interpersonal behavior, a methodology which repeatedly measures individuals using validated tools to assess interpersonal behavior in vivo. I developed the Social Behavior Inventory to assess a person's own interpersonal behavior and the Interpersonal Grid to assess the behavior of a person's interaction partners. With these tools, my students, my collaborators, and I have shown how our perceptions of others and our own interpersonal social behaviors are patterned across our most significant role relationships, including those we have with friends, coworkers, supervisors and romantic partners.

Looking towards the future

New developments in design and new technologies may make possible ECR research with larger sample sizes. In the year 2000, I did not expect that 20 years later virtually everyone would carry a smart phone in their pocket or their purse, that the device would be optimized for collecting intensive repeated measures data, and that the cost of the device would be paid for by the person providing the data. Rather than being an expensive data collection strategy as it was in the year 2000; once the app has been built, the procedure has become a financially inexpensive data collection methodology.

Building from the bottom up, each small event can contribute some knowledge about the person. However, it is important to remember that creating knowledge takes time. Moreover, we need to think not only about the between-person analyses with respect to the number of people participating in the measurement procedure, but also with respect to how many occasions of measurement are needed to get reliable measurement with results that generalize across some relevant interval of time. In other words, we need to better understand occasions of measurement for within-person analyses.

Models of individuals are becoming more complex, such as building models of individuals using multiple time scales (McKee et al., 2018). My hope is that the SBI and the IG permit other fields as well as personality psychology to integrate more complex models of stability and variability to study the events of our everyday lives.

Notes

1 The preparation of this chapter was supported by grant number 410-2010-1168 from the Social Sciences and Humanities Research Council of Canada to D. S. Moskowitz (PI). I have no conflicts of interest to disclose.
Many thanks to my collaborators and former students who have worked on the projects I describe. To name a few former students, I am grateful for help from Gentiana Sadikaj, Kayleigh-Ann Clegg, Elizabeth Foley, Ella Vanderbilt, Emily Todorov, Eun Jung Suh, Kirk Brown, Jennifer Russell, Julie Desaulniers, Nina Sand, Lance Rappaport, Marc Fournier, Michael Quek, and Stéphane Côté. Comments by Gentiana Sadikaj and Kayleigh-Ann Clegg were particularly valuable during the preparation of this chapter. Photo of the author by Nasuna Stuart-Ulin.

References

aan het Rot, M., Moskowitz, D. S., Hsu, Z. & Young, S. N. (2015). Eating a meal is associated with elevations in agreeableness and reductions in quarrelsomeness. *Physiology & Behavior, 144,* 103–109. https://doi.org/10.1016/j.physbeh.2015.03.014.

aan het Rot, M., Moskowitz, D. S., Pinard, G., & Young, S. N. (2006). Social behaviour and mood in everyday life: The effects of tryptophan in quarrelsome individuals. *Journal of Psychiatry and Neuroscience, 31*(4), 253–262.

aan het Rot, M., Moskowitz, D. S., & Young, S. N. (2008). Exposure to bright light is associated with positive social interaction and good mood over short time periods: A naturalistic study in mildly seasonal people. *Journal of Psychiatric Research, 42,* 311–319.

aan het Rot, M., Russell, J. J., Moskowitz., D. S. & Young, 2008). Alcohol in a social context: Findings from event-contingent recording studies of everyday social interactions. *Alcoholism: Clinical and Experimental Research, 32,* 459–471.

Alden, L. E., & Phillips, N. (1990). An interpersonal analysis of social anxiety and depression. *Cognitive Therapy and Research, 14*(5), 499–512.

Berenson, K. R., Downey, G., Rafaeli, E., Coifman, K. G., & Paquin, N. L. (2011). The rejection–rage contingency in borderline personality disorder. *Journal of Abnormal Psychology, 120*(3), 681–690.

Brown, W. (1910). Some exact experimental results in the correlation of mental abilities. *British Journal of Psychology, 3,* 296–322.

Conte, H. R., & Plutchik, R. (1981). A circumplex model for interpersonal personality traits. *Journal of Personality and Social Psychology, 40*(4), 701–711.

Côté, S., Moskowitz, D. S., & Zuroff, D. C. (2012). Social relationships and intraindividual variability in interpersonal behavior: Correlates of interpersonal spin. *Journal of Personality and Social Psychology, 102*(3), 646–659.

Cronbach, L. J., Gleser, G. C., Nanda, H., & Rajaratnam, N. (1972). *The dependability of behavioral measurements: Theory of generalizability of scores and profiles.* New York: Wiley.

Epstein, S. (1979). The stability of behavior: On predicting most of the people much of the time. *Journal of Personality and Social Psychology, 37*(7), 1097–1126. https://doi.org/10.1037/0022-3514.37.7.1097

Fleeson, W., & Noftle, E. E. (2008). Where does personality have its influence? A supermatrix of consistency concepts. *Journal of Personality, 76*(6), 1355–1386.

Fournier, M. A., Moskowitz, D. S., & Zuroff, D. C. (2008). Integrating dispositions, signatures, and the interpersonal domain. *Journal of Personality and Social Psychology, 94*(3), 531–545.

Fournier, M. A., Moskowitz, D. S., & Zuroff, D. C. (2009). The interpersonal signature. *Journal of Research in Personality, 43*(2), 155–162.

Fournier, M. A., Moskowitz, D. S., & Zuroff, D. C. (2011). Origins and applications of the interpersonal circumplex. In L. M. Horowitz & S. Strack (Eds.), *Handbook of interpersonal psychology* (pp. 57–74). Hoboken NJ: Wiley.

Gifford, R. (1991). Mapping nonverbal behavior on the interpersonal circle. *Journal of Personality and Social Psychology, 61*(2), 279–288.

Gifford, R. (1994). A lens-mapping framework for understanding the encoding and decoding of interpersonal dispositions in nonverbal behavior. *Journal of Personality and Social Psychology, 66*(2), 398–412.

Horowitz, L. M., Dryer, D. C., & Krasnoperova, E. N. (1997). The circumplex structure of interpersonal problems. In R. Plutchik & H. R. Conte (Eds.), *Circumplex models of personality and emotions* (p. 347–384). American Psychological Association. https://doi.org/10.1037/10261-015

Horowitz, L. M., Rosenberg, S. E., Baer, B. A., Ureno, G., & Villasenor, V. S. (1988). Inventory of interpersonal problems: Psychometric properties and clinical applications. *Journal of Consulting and Clinical Psychology, 56*(6), 885–892.

Kenny, D. A., & La Voie, L. (1984). The social relations model. *Advances in Experimental Social Psychology, 18,* 141–182.

Kiesler, D. J. (1983). The 1982 interpersonal circle: A taxonomy for complementarity in human transactions. *Psychological Review, 90*(3), 185–214.

Lorr, M., & McNair, D. M. (1965). Expansion of the interpersonal behavior circle. *Journal of Personality and Social Psychology, 2*(6), 823–830. https://doi.org/10.1037/h0022709

Mardia, K.V. (1972). *Statistics of directional data.* London: Academic Press.

McKee, K. L., Rappaport, L. M., Boker, S. M., Moskowitz, D. S., & Neale, M. C. (2018). Adaptive equilibrium regulation: Modeling individual dynamics on multiple timescales. *Structural Equation Modeling: A Multidisciplinary Journal, 25*(6), 888–905.

Mischel, W. (1968). *Personality and assessment.* New York: Wiley.

Mongrain, M., Vettese, L. C., Shuster, B., & Kendal, N. (1998). Perceptual biases, affect, and behavior in the relationships of dependents and self-critics. *Journal of Personality and Social Psychology, 75*(1), 230–241.

Moskowitz, D. S. (1982). Coherence and cross-situational generality in personality: A new analysis of old problems. *Journal of Personality and Social Psychology, 43*(4), 754–768.

Moskowitz, D. S. (1988). Cross-situational generality in the laboratory: Dominance and friendliness. *Journal of Personality and Social Psychology, 54*(5), 829–839.

Moskowitz, D. S. (1994). Cross-situational generality and the interpersonal circumplex. *Journal of Personality and Social Psychology, 66*(5), 921–933.

Moskowitz, D. S., & Fournier, M. A. (2015). The interplay of persons and situations: Retrospect ad prospect. In M. Mikulincer, P. R. Shaver, L. M. Cooper, & R. J. Larsen (Eds.), *APA Handbook of personality and social psychology, Volume 4: Personality processes and individual* differences (pp. 471–489). American Psychological Association. http://dx.doi.org/10.1037/14343-021.

Moskowitz, D. S., & Hershberger, S. L. (2002). *Modeling intraindividual variability with repeated measures data: Methods and applications.* Mahwah: Lawrence Erlbaum Associates Publishers.

Moskowitz, D. S., Pinard, G., Zuroff, D. C., Annable, L., & Young, S. N. (2001). The effect of tryptophan on social interaction in everyday life: A placebo-controlled study. *Neuropsychopharmacology, 25*(2), 277–289. https://doi.org/10.1016/S0893-133X(01)00219-6

Moskowitz, D. S., & Schwarz, J. C. (1982). The comparative validity of behavioral count scores and knowledgeable informants' rating scores. *Journal of Personality and Social Psychology, 42*(3), 518–528.

Moskowitz, D. S., Suh, E. J., & Desaulniers, J. (1994). Situational influences on gender differences in agency and communion. *Journal of Personality and Social Psychology, 66*(4), 753–761.

Moskowitz, D. S., & Zuroff, D. C. (2004). Flux, pulse, and spin: Dynamic additions to the personality lexicon. *Journal of Personality and Social Psychology, 86*(6), 880–893.

Pincus, A. L., Sadler, P., Woody, E., Roche, M. J., Thomas, K. M., & Wright, A. G. (2014). Multimethod assessment of interpersonal dynamics. In C. J. Hopwood & R. F. Bornstein (Eds.), *Multimethod clinical assessment* (pp. 51–91). New York: Guilford Press.

Rappaport, L. M., Moskowitz, D. S., & D'Antono, B. (2014). Naturalistic interpersonal behavior patterns differentiate depression and anxiety symptoms in the community. *Journal of Counseling Psychology, 61*(2), 253–263.

Rappaport, L. M., Russell, J. J., Hedeker, D., Pinard, G., Bleau, P., & Moskowitz, D. S. (2018). Affect, interpersonal behaviour and interpersonal perception during open-label, uncontrolled paroxetine treatment of people with social anxiety disorder: A pilot study. *Journal of Psychiatry & Neuroscience, 43*(6), 407–415. https://doi.org/10.1503/jpn.170141

Rotter, J. B. (1954). *Social learning and clinical psychology.* Englewood Cliffs, NJ: Prentice-Hall Inc.

Rotter, J.B. (1966). Generalized expectancies for internal versus external control of reinforcement. *Psychological Monographs, 80*(1), 1–28.

Russell, J. J., Moskowitz, D. S., Zuroff, D. C., Sookman, D., & Paris, J. (2007). Stability and variability of affective experience and interpersonal behavior in borderline personality disorder. *Journal of Abnormal Psychology, 116*(3), 578–588.

Sadikaj, G., Moskowitz, D. S., Zuroff, D. C., & Bartz, J. A. (2020). CD38 is associated with communal behavior, partner perceptions, affect and relationship adjustment in romantic relationships. *Scientific Reports, 10*(1), 1–14.

Sadikaj, G., Rappaport, L. M., Moskowitz, D. S., Zuroff, D. C., Koestner, R., & Powers, T. (2015). Consequences of interpersonal spin on couple relevant goal progress and relationship satisfaction. *Journal of Personality and Social Psychology, 109*(4), 722b.

Sadikaj, G., Russell, J. J., Moskowitz, D. S., & Paris, J. (2010). Affect dysregulation in individuals with borderline personality disorder: Persistence and interpersonal triggers. *Journal of Personality Assessment, 92*(6), 490–500.

Sadler, P., & Woody, E. (2003). Is who you are who you're talking to? Interpersonal style and complementarily in mixed-sex interactions. *Journal of Personality and Social Psychology, 81,* 80–96.

Shoda, Y., Mischel, W., & Wright, J. C. (1994). Intraindividual stability in the organization and patterning of behavior: Incorporating psychological situations into the idiographic analysis of personality. *Journal of Personality and Social Psychology, 67*(4), 674–687.

Spearman, C. (1910). Correlation calculated with faulty data. *British Journal of Psychology, 3*(3), 271–295.

Stiglmayr, C. E., Grathwol, T., Linehan, M. M., Ihorst, G., Fahrenberg, J., & Bohus, M. (2005). Aversive tension in patients with borderline personality disorder: A computer-based controlled field study. *Acta Psychiatrica Scandinavica, 111*(5), 372–379.

Tchalova, K., Sadikaj, G., Moskowitz, D. S., Zuroff, D. C., & Bartz, J. A. (2019). Variation in the μ-opioid receptor gene (OPRM1) and experiences of felt security in response to a romantic partner's quarrelsome behavior. *Molecular Psychiatry,* 1–11.

Weinberg, S. (2004). Four golden lessons. *Nature, 426(389)* (27 November 2003). https://doi.org/10.1038/426389ab

Widiger, T. A., & Hagemoser, S. (1997). Personality disorders and the interpersonal circumplex. In R. Plutchik & H. R. Conte (Eds.), *Circumplex models of personality and emotions* (pp. 299–325). American Psychological Association. https://doi.org/10.1037/10261-013

Wiggins, J. S. (1973). *Personality and prediction: principles of personality assessment.* Malabar, FL: Krieger Publishing Company.

Wiggins, J.S. (1979). A psychological taxonomy of trait-descriptive terms: The interpersonal domain. *Journal of Personality and Social Psychology, 37*(3), 395–412.

Wiggins, J. S. (1991). Agency and communion as conceptual coordinates for the understanding and measurement of interpersonal behavior. In W. Grove & D. Ciccetti (Eds.), *Thinking clearly about psychology: Essays in honor of Paul Everett Meehl* (pp. 89–113). Minneapolis: University of Minnesota Press.

Wiggins, J. S. (1995). *Interpersonal adjective scales: Professional manual.* Odessa, FL: Psychological Assessment Resources.

Young, S. N., Moskowitz, D. S., & aan het Rot, M. (2014). Possible role of more social behavior in the clinical effect of antidepressant drugs. *Journal of Psychiatry and Neuroscience, 39*(6) 60–65. https://doi.org/10.1503/jpn.130165.

17 A Brief History of "Me"

Lorna Smith Benjamin

Writing an autobiography violates every related standard I can recall from childhood. For example: "Don't be self-centered. Do what needs to be done and don't complain. Don't get any ideas to the effect you are special. Don't whine or expect help: just get the job done".

Early years and World War II

That is the sort of message my two older (foster) brothers and I received on an everyday basis. Everybody hustled and even in our advanced years, everybody still is "productive" and, heaven forbid, not *dependent*. This is the prototype for East Coast Protestants in the 1940s. Born in 1934 of hard-working parents raised on adjacent farms in Palmyra New York, I was an only child until 1941, when suddenly I had a baby sister and two older foster brothers. The baby was a biological sibling.

My brothers were adopted. The US had joined World War II by then and things had changed in ways that even "us little kids" could see. Almost everybody's Dad had gone to the war and the women often were very busy with a war-related tasks too. Examples I knew about included working in factories, ferrying airplanes from factories in the US to their overseas base, and in my mother's case, teaching school. Her assignment happened to be 5th grade, and I happened to be in that grade. That situation was, let us say, challenging. Some of the moms served the military too, either as full-fledged soldiers or as adjunct military. For example, one of our neighbors, just an ordinary citizen as far as we knew, ferried war planes from the US to Europe. "Us kids" collected old steel and rubber tires to be reprocessed and used again. And there were air raid drills too. That was because U Boats (submarines) had been seen in the St. Lawrence River and in Lake Ontario. That was inland USA. And several cities along its coast were attractive targets for a determined enemy. At the time, nobody I knew had any ambivalence about what the US stands for. And our generous Marshall Plan to help Europe rebuild after the war was equally admirable. In the early 1950s, I took a bicycle trip with American Youth Hostels through Europe and felt extraordinarily welcome in France and Italy. Those folks could not do enough for an American, a person from

DOI: 10.4324/9781003036302-17

the country that had liberated them. That attitude now is a dim memory, and the change is completely understandable, given changes in American behavior since then.

I was lucky in that my father had been deemed vital to the war effort at home and so he did not leave. I also was fortunate because he was kind and attentive and very supportive in ways that encouraged confidence and competence. He worked at Kodak Rochester and during the very dangerous London Blitz, Kodak of Rochester offered care for children of employees at Kodak London. That is how I got the brothers one day in 1941. We all were treated equally in the family and the standards for responsibility-taking were clear and enforced. The brothers stayed until the end of the war and returned to Europe late in 1945. Eventually they both came back to the US, one sponsored by my mother and the other came later "on his own." They both have done well in life: One was an airline pilot and the other gained a PhD in statistics, was/is a consultant, and teaches bridge to passengers on transatlantic ships. My baby sister stayed in Rochester and looked after our parents as the rest of us sallied forth. For a while, she was an administrator at Kodak (as was my father) and now lives in an attractive, very pleasant retirement center in Rochester.

Life in academia

My life as an academic had an unlikely beginning at Brockport Central High School. Despite its isolation, the quality of education was more than adequate preparation for the years to come. Since then, I have marveled at that and have decided it was due to New York State's many well-managed branches of its Teacher's College and its control of quality by assessing all college bound students by "Regents Examinations." Later on, when I encountered students who graduated from well known, exclusive private Eastern schools, I did not feel underprivileged. I understood and could use principles and basic science and grammar and had a solid introduction to French. However, I could not keep up with east coast discussions that required the ability to cite famous authors and writings in literature and science. In sum, I think my little country school taught the "basics" quite well enough and that is important to me, and in some ways, remarkable. The quality probably was maintained because the State of New York cared about education. During our country high school years, there were final examinations for every class that had been designed in Albany, the capitol of New York State. The process was solemn and on everybody's mind throughout the school year. During the Regents exam week, each morning, the teachers would go to the main office and a giant safe was opened and stacks of Regent's exams for each class were distributed. Education clearly was a priority for New York State and as a graduate of a public school, I am grateful.

I also graduated from the Eastman School of Music's Saturday program. That, of course, was not a public school. My favorite part of the musical training was to attend the ancillary summer music camp called Tally Ho. Each week we got to work under a different nationally recognized conductor and on Sundays there was a big concert where the results of the week's work were open to the public. In addition to making a few life-long friends, I loved the chance to experience how "big time" conductors work. Perfectionism regarding exacting detail about what should happen when and why were clearly embedded in marvelous descriptions of the bigger picture. The need for intense focus and repetition as well as meticulous concern for continuity and coherence was clear. Basically, hard work mastering such minutiae paid off in subsequent fine symphonies of sound from a bunch of high school kids at summer camp. The integrative skills and self-discipline have worked well in academia.

The other lesson I had at Tally Ho and at the Eastman School of Music is that some people are, quite simply, astonishingly talented. What some of those kids could do was truly breathtaking and inspirational. Many of those, of course, went on the be professional musicians. One of them turned out to be my college roommate for two years. In her ultimate career, Margaret Jean Harris Smith first was a pianist and then an organist. Margaret, true to form, selected the perfect husband. Skilled in playing the organ, she married a brilliant theologian who became a much respected and beloved pastor. A perfect match, they now are spending these years together in an attractive residential home. The most recent time I was with Margaret was when she gave a recital at the National Cathedral in Washington D.C. It reminded me of how she had been 50 years earlier during her Senior Recital at Oberlin. In person, she always is funny in a sly and quiet way; at her Senior Recital, she actually got the solemn "long haired" audience to giggle during one of her selections. It is truly remarkable how gifted people in the arts can activate all kinds of important affects and thoughts in their audiences.

Off to college in Ohio and then to the monkeys at Wisconsin

I chose Oberlin because, unlike most other colleges and universities, Oberlin allowed girls in the marching band. The fact that Oberlin was an elitist school well populated with students who had been to prestigious East Coast Private schools, was not apparent to me at first. But there they were. I was totally overwhelmed, stunned with assignments such as read 500 pages for homework in the first week in the first semester at Oberlin. Eventually, I did figure out how to fit in and do well there; by graduation time, I was in excellent standing. After college I returned home to Rochester for a year and worked as a teacher in an underprivileged part of the city. During that year I applied for graduate schools and in the end, chose to work with Harry Harlow and his baby monkeys. Harry told me to look at what was available in the lab and do whatever I wanted to do.

I did exactly that and my dissertation was a realization of my fantasy of bringing respectable science to clinically relevant problems. I chose to study thumbsucking in monkeys. My study compared learning theory to psychoanalytic theory when accounting for thumbsucking. Learning theory won, hands down. I did get that study published but the paper has languished in the collection of dissertation studies rarely to be read or cited. But I enjoyed it and harvested a lot of extra information from the data base that yielded five very different publications related to child development in my first three postdoctoral years.

My choice to work with Harry Harlow and his monkeys rather than accept offers from some other great places apparently delighted Harry. Quite a few times he told me that he had been giving speeches and various colleagues at institutions that I had been admitted to complained about my choosing to work with him instead of them. The one he most often cited with a grin was Harvard. I never regretted choosing to work with Harry and the monkeys. Harry liked to challenge students and we both favor hostile repartee, so we got along very well. He was uncommonly generous in offering resources to me, and I took full advantage of his offers. As a result, I had five publications just a few years after getting the PhD. Carl Rogers also was on the faculty at Wisconsin and I am grateful to have had him as a supervisor for 6 months in my post-doctoral years, supported by an NIMH fellowship.

At the University of Wisconsin, I also got to know even more famous people, including men who had been invited to speak to the Department of Psychiatry. I was assigned to meet visiting speakers at their hotel and bring them to the University; or take them back to their hotel. Or take them to lunch. Examples include Rollo May and Franz Alexander. I hasten to add there was never any misbehavior on their part. I cannot say that inappropriate behavior with young women was not an issue in the 1960s. It was. But not with these classy men. Not even a hint. I do believe that now sexual approaches are a bigger danger for young females, possibly because television has desensitized everyone about sexuality and violence via constant exposure to very explicit scenes that do not please people with a solid secure base, but activate damaged individuals in unhealthy ways.

I had married a professor and nepotism rules were in full bloom; so after the dissertation work, I stayed in the margins of academia. I did not mind that at all. I could stay home with my babies for half of each work-day and used any free time to read journals and to teach myself to program the Control Data 1604 computer at the University of Wisconsin. Early Fortran was closely related to machine language and therefore quite easy to generalize. Using it taught me skills with patterns that have lasted a lifetime. For example, programming helped me learn to organize a paper or a book in ways that allow consideration of exacting detail, but also stand on and reveal underlying, coherent themes. I am grateful to the Wisconsin Alumni Foundation and NIMH for making funds available to give a marginal person like me access to the giant computer. This all was before laptops or even desktops were widely available.

In 1963, my first daughter was born and the second came in 1965. Both girls responsibly took advantage of White privileges in that they rapidly completed college and married well. One has raised three remarkable children, all engineers. The other is a veterinarian who also has a PhD in immunology. She is a faculty member at a California veterinary school. I am also lucky enough to enjoy my sons-in-law utterly without ambivalence. They all are more than one could hope for. My three grandchildren are likewise beautiful, kind, well-educated and highly functional. If one were to survey our family with a critical attitude, I would be the "clinker," because I divorced long ago and have never remarried. One consequence is that I am wary of people who cannot/will not manage alcohol or drugs. As a psychotherapist, I only work with patients with substance abuse as a primary concern if they will attend AA or NA for managing substance abuse and commit to working in psychotherapy to try to restore their options in life.

A bit about the impact of developmental experience on professional perspectives

The theme of sexual obsession and inappropriate violence is worth space here in the context of a personal developmental report. It starts with little boys acting big during childhood. It continues with bravado in high school, often for the benefit of male peers. And it continues ever after. I have thought quite a bit about it, given I was raised in a neighborhood of boys only and have known men in many different contexts. I also have thought about why it is that I have never been approached sexually unless I wanted to be. I hasten to add that I have always been picky about it. I thank my parents for being completely sane about sexuality. Perhaps that is because of their farm based developmental histories. One does get confronted with "primitive basics" on a regular basis on a farm. All it takes to be sane about it is to acknowledge that we humans are just another member (a lucky version) of the animal kingdom. Sexuality is (1) important for reproduction of the species and (2) important in organizing bonding in the primate troupe which has to stick together and coordinate selected behaviors in order to survive and thrive. We are a group animal because none of us has the strength or skill needed to survive alone in the jungle. Harlow summarized: "A lone monkey is a dead monkey."

Anyone who does not appreciate the meaning of that should reflect carefully on the fact that mass killings (not necessarily including those apparently sanctioned by states at war) usually are perpetrated by suicidal loner young adult males. Why would that be? I think that testosterone is a powerful mobilizer of sexual and aggressive behaviors and we do a dreadfully poor job helping young men cope with it. From a "biological" perspective, I suggest sexuality usually is controlled by interest and joy in belonging to "the troupe" and by control of group process by senior individuals (male or female) in the community. But social rules and traditions per se mean little unless they are directly associated with secure attachment to other human beings. Attachment is a regulator and without it, a "loner" is lethally dangerous if there is access to weapons of destruction.

One can never know answers to What If (I had done this instead of that). It is best to be with what was and is and be grateful. I am. Following graduation and six years of part time training and work as a post-doctoral fellow in the University of Wisconsin Department of Psychiatry, I was admitted to the academic track as Assistant Professor and gradually progressed to Full Professor of Psychiatry. I enjoyed supervising the residents and post-doctoral fellows and had time to do research and publish too. Eventually I accepted opportunities to give a few job-talks and decided to accept the University of Utah's offer in large part because of the opportunity for good skiing, which I loved. I have been reasonably productive at University of Utah and never regretted that choice. Presently I live in the mountains and am grateful for the clean air and beautiful scenery. I still work part time at the University and, most importantly, have room to accommodate grandchildren and their friends in my house. I have some really interesting visitors from time to time!

The editor requested information about the development of one's scholarly life. My story about that returns again and again to my father. I benefited a lot from his fix-it attitude and "skill sets" but don't use them much anymore because I don't have to; and am lazier. But his instruction gave me a "can do" and "why not" mental set and it has served well in unexpected ways. I have dared to create a valid and reliable measurement system of social interactions (Structural Analysis of Social Behavior, SASB). I believe its validity is solid; its reliability is high, and its potential usefulness to clinicians and patients is enormous. SASB has not been recognized as much as it would have been if I were male. Hopefully, its merits nonetheless eventually will be widely recognized.

I also have organized my thoughts about what is an effective version of psychodynamic therapy in another book. Like SASB, Interpersonal Reconstructive Therapy exists in the literature, but barely. Again, part of the problem likely is its female sponsorship. Another issue is that SASB and IRT are a bit complex by today's standards. Each demands creative work with principles and concepts that cannot be assessed by multiple choice exams or marginal check boxes. Eventually psychology may go beyond quick and easy measurement and then SASB and IRT will appeal more to young psychologists. To be clear about my meaning of "quick and easy," note that by imagining that a Randomized Control Trial (RCT) is all you need to establish effectiveness of a psychological principle or approach is crude at best. One simple illustration of how to upgrade psychotherapy research is to show a relationship between activation of the mechanisms of change and changes in symptoms. That model involves a dynamic study of "cause" and is much closer to the drug protocol that has served so long as the alleged Gold Standard to establishing effectiveness of a treatment. Interpersonal Reconstructive Therapy has met that standard.

Conclusion

In conclusion, I feel grateful I have been given so many advantages that started simply by living in a neighborhood that had good public educational programs and being able to receive an excellent college education (Oberlin College) that clearly taught the importance of learning "why" and "how" as distinct from mastering facts. And for being able to study and learn with teachers who worked in small groups and more often used discussion instead of lecturing. That was followed by learning much about primate behavior working with Harry Harlow in his amazing Primate Laboratory at the University of Wisconsin. All that background enriched the elegant training in psychotherapy from certified Psychoanalysts in the Wisconsin Department of Psychiatry. What was most important during those post-doctoral years was that they showed their work, could talk about what they were doing and why, and could make helpful remarks when reviewing their trainee's recordings of sessions. That model for teaching psychotherapy is very much like training to become a professional musician, and I sing its praises. The part of that that seems often to be missing from psychotherapy training is the modeling by the master. Under the heading of protecting patient confidentiality, the work of supervisors is rarely seen. For the good of all, it would be better to be certain about trainee's ability to protect confidentiality and allow experts routinely to show qualified trainees what has worked for them. Absent modeling and clear discussion of it under safe conditions, everyone more or less has to "reinvent the wheel." And so we still have ox carts instead of Mercedes.

18 The Numbers and the Story

Leslie C. Morey

I was born in Chicago Heights, Illinois, in 1956, around the beginning of Dwight Eisenhower's second term as president of the United States. I don't remember much of anything about Ike's presidency, but I do have some vague memories of the 1960 presidential election that pit John F. Kennedy against Richard Nixon, as it exposed a bit of a rift in my household. My father, a highly practical midwestern Protestant (albeit one with quite a good sense of humor about things) was a lifelong Republican, while my mother, born in Paris and a survivor of the Occupation, being much more oriented towards a continental sophistication, was drawn to the charisma and excitement generated by the Kennedys. In many respects, my parents seemed to have one of those "opposites attract" relationship, but the challenges of sustaining those types of relationships are often formidable, and it was not to last. However, I think I have benefited by inheriting parts of each parent, giving me a somewhat "bipartite" approach to my work that reflects a combination of the pragmatic/empirical/analytic/scientific with the expansive/intuitive/synthetic/artistic. This has allowed me to be comfortable in both of the two lands of "Clinicia" and "Psychometrika" described by Cronbach (1954) shortly before I was born, a divide that has thus been around longer than I have.

Two events that profoundly affected me at roughly the same time were the JFK assassination and the dissolution of my parent's marriage. Both left me with a heightened awareness that things were not as predictable as they might seem, and that it was important to be able to adjust to a "new normal". Although these were significant disruptions, I nonetheless I had a reasonably happy childhood that was enhanced by close relationships with family and neighborhood friends that produced many good memories. For example, right in the midst of all this disruption, I remember sitting with my older sister watching this new group called the Beatles play on the Ed Sullivan show; as a seven-year old, I was watching with curiosity but with considerably less enthusiasm than my sister. I will say that somewhere around the Sgt. Pepper album, my enthusiasm started to increase, and the explosion of the "progressive rock" era which that album catalyzed led me to pick up the bass guitar, an avocation that continues to this day despite rather limited progress in my abilities. I do continue to regularly gig as a

DOI: 10.4324/9781003036302-18

bassist with multiple bands, although to paraphrase Samuel Johnson, a 60+ professor playing bass on stage is like a dog walking on its hind legs: it may not be done well, but people are surprised to find it done at all.

I also remember enjoying my first few years of school, where I had good friends and a number of solid mastery experiences. Apparently one of those mastery experiences (interesting given my eventual profession) was a knack for doing very well on standardized tests, and I seem to recall being in meetings where my performance on these tests was discussed in hushed tones. Ultimately, those meetings led to a decision that I would "skip" 3rd grade, progressing directly from 2nd to 4th. One result of that was that my older sister had to teach me multiplication and cursive writing over the summer. Since she went on to become an award-winning junior high mathematics teacher, I might deserve some credit as her first test subject (don't tell her that I'm still not very good at either multiplication or cursive writing). However, another result was that I was placed into a new peer group where I was younger, smaller, probably less mature, and considerably less well accepted than I had been with my former cohort. This led me to experience much of the remainder of primary school as somewhat of an "outsider". My enthusiasm for school waned and I became an indifferent student. The "outsider" experience was further buttressed in those years as both of my parents remarried, creating new nuclear families into which I did not comfortably fit. I do think that those experiences have worked to help me make important empathic connections with many of the patients and clients I've seen over the years, who commonly come to the mental health system with a similar conviction that they don't fit in anywhere.

I believe that one adaptation to these experiences was to become more of an introvert than I had been previously; another was an increasing significance of my neighborhood friends in my life. I came to spend nearly all of my spare time with this group, playing sports and games. With respect to sports, Chicago was primarily a baseball town, albeit a bifurcated one (White Sox here). In the summer, we'd play pickup games of baseball nearly daily; in the long Chicago winters, we would have to move indoors but often played a baseball simulation board game that was based upon the actual statistical performance of major league players (Strat-o-matic baseball, for the initiated). This game involved rolling three dice—one to determine a column, the remaining two to determine a row—and individual cards for each player were provided that were to be consulted for the results (e.g., strike out, home run). Thus, at an early age, I became intimately familiar with key quantitative concepts that have served me well over the years: matrices, multivariate normal distributions, and the harsh realities of probability. With respect to the latter, I learned quickly that although prediction was never going to be made with complete certainty, it was nevertheless unwise to ignore the probabilities, and that even very small increments in prediction became meaningful over many observations/

games (this latter lesson was underscored, in baseball and in personality research, by Abelson in 1985—just because Cohen in 1977 called an effect size "small" doesn't mean that such effects can't be worth millions of dollars in salary differences). Because I tended to understand these concepts a bit better than did my friends, I confess that I won more than my share of those simulated games. Furthermore, being an introvert, the process of how these dice could be used to bring an immediacy to the performance of long dead baseball players like Babe Ruth and Ty Cobb fascinated me, and I did a fair amount of reading in baseball history. As an illustration of my commitment, I got a paper route delivering the *Chicago Tribune* (Sundays were dreaded), and saved my proceeds to buy an item that I doubt many 12-year olds at the time were coveting—the newly released *Baseball Encyclopedia* (Macmillan, 1969), a groundbreaking 2,337-page tome that contained the complete longitudinal statistical record of every player that ever played major league baseball. As peculiar as that preoccupation may seem, I truly believe that the endless hours I spent scrutinizing that volume gave me a knack for being able to translate what might appear to be a dry series of numbers into a story about a *person*—again, that combination of the empirical with the synthetic. Looking at a record, I could tell you whether that player was fast or slow, impulsive or patient, burly or slight, a late bloomer or a disappointment who never reached his potential.

To me, this is what personality assessment has always been about. We attempt to determine the most useful things (constructs) to know about a person given the question we have been asked; we use procedures that attempt to quantify or scale those aspects into numbers (measurement); and then we combine those numbers with all available information in a way that tells the story of the respondent as it relates to the original question (assessment). This bridging of the numbers and the story reflect the attempt to span the divide described by Cronbach (1954), and facilitating that effort is largely how I've spent my entire career. By the way, I still have my prized 1969 first edition Macmillan.

I continued to meander through school with little distinction. Heading towards the end of high school, I had little direction although college was clearly an expectation, so I completed some applications, which stipulated that I indicate my preferred major subject. In discussing things with my dad, he and I both recognized that I was "good with numbers", and being ever-practical, he strongly encouraged me to go into accounting, where well-paying jobs were plentiful. Not having any better plans myself, I checked that box and dutifully headed off to Dekalb, Illinois to attend Northern Illinois University. This transition was considerable—thrust with thousands of other freshmen into a new social context in which everyone had to forge new relationships and identities, it was a new beginning, and it may have been just what I needed. Being new to college and not particularly mature (I began college having just turned 16), I and my newfound friends may or may not have done a few (or more) ill-considered things, but despite this (and somewhat inexplicably), I found myself doing better academically than I had done since 2nd grade. I was getting top scores in accounting classes that others were failing in droves. Flushed with success, I increasingly wanted to broaden my intellectual horizons—certainly not a value that I had held throughout much of primary school—and the breadth requirements for the general degree allowed me to explore them. Thus, in my first semester of my sophomore year, I took Introductory Psychology to fulfill a social science requirement.

I think I might have had a high school course that touched upon psychology, but at the time it made little impact on me. However, I liked the college version, taught by an energetic graduate student, and I wanted to learn more. Consulting my university catalog, I discovered that I would only need a few more courses to receive a minor in psychology, which I thought might be a nice complement to my less humanistic accounting major, and I signed up for two additional psychology courses for the spring semester: *Personality Theory*, and *Psychological Tests and Measurement*. It is no exaggeration to say that those two courses changed my life.

These two courses simultaneously appealed to the aforementioned bipartite aspects of my own personality—the expansive ideas of the great theorists like Jung, Adler, Kelly, Cattell, and Dollard & Miller, as covered in the classic Hall and Lindzey (1970) text, and the empirical realities of the state of the art in assessment, represented in the venerable Anastasi (1976) book. In personality, I was exposed to interpretations of the human experience as varied as the existentialists and the radical behaviorists, and watched the three Gloria films (Shostrom, 1966) for the first time with wonder (by the way, my personal reactions to each of those films have changed considerably over the years). I felt that these theorists were struggling with the fundamental questions of the ages, with plenty of those questions remaining unanswered. While the personality course seemed to be reasonably well received by my classmates, I was a clear outlier in the test and measurement class, in that I seemed to be the only student who was remotely interested in the material. Whereas the other students scattered for cover at the first sign of a regression equation, I was (apparently idiosyncratically) excited by the concepts and the opportunities for the advancement of knowledge therein. Not surprisingly because of my concomitant appreciation for my personality course, I was particularly intrigued by the area of personality assessment, and discovered to my amazement that the most popular instruments of the time impressively violated many of the most basic psychometric doctrines with which my classmates had struggled so mightily during the beginning sections of the class. I could not understand how instruments with such shortcomings could see such widespread use. However, I remember that the Anastasi text provided a ray of hope: a brief section on a then novel personality instrument, one that seemed to incorporate many of the important developments in the assessment field—the Personality Research Form (PRF:

Jackson, 1967). The PRF was cited as a promising new state-of-the-art instrument that, beginning with a formal personality theory as laid out by Henry Murray (1938), held the promise of avoiding many of the pitfalls of earlier measures through the use of the "construct validation" approach to test development. I felt that here lay the path towards addressing some of those fundamental questions raised in the personality class, and in the classic college sophomore tradition, I thought that perhaps I was just the person to do it. Much like my bass playing, I have subsequently persisted in this line for decades despite rather less progress than originally hoped.

Given this commitment, psychology became my major field of study and accounting became my minor. This was much to my father's chagrin, who sent me clippings from the *Chronicle of Higher Education* regarding the dire job prospects for college professors, in part because the Vietnam War and its educational draft deferment had greatly increased the popularity of graduate school. Nonetheless, a future in accounting was not in the cards, although I will admit that the accounting minor came in handy many years later when I became a Psychology Department Head. Instead, with youthful overconfidence I sent out my applications to graduate programs in clinical psychology, armed with a solid GPA and strong GRE scores given my aforementioned affinity for standardized tests. My personal statement was reasonably specific, in that I hoped to be able to study and measure problematic forms of personality in ways that would lead to better customized interventions for specific types of patients—basically, the patient/treatment matching hypothesis that would come to prominence some time later. Not well mentored and sorely overestimating the competitiveness of my applications, I was crushed by the near total lack of enthusiasm for my applications. Ultimately, I was placed on a couple of alternate lists for admission, and somewhat at the last minute I was admitted to the University of Florida, with no commitment for funding. Faced with zero alternatives, I accepted immediately; if nothing else, simply escaping northern Illinois winters for the sunnier climes of Florida would be worth it.

The summer before graduate school I worked overtime hours in a factory in an effort to save up money that would help me pay my graduate school expenses, given the uncertain funding status. Working right up until the last minute, I arrived in Gainesville the day before classes were to begin, and I presented to Hugh Davis, the training director for Clinical Psychology, to check in. I don't think the department quite knew what to do with me since I had been admitted off the alternate list, and when I applied there was really nobody in the department who matched my interests in personality and psychopathology assessment. However, Hugh was committed to trying to arrange funding support for all students. Apparently, the department had promised a research assistant to a newly arrived assistant professor, so Hugh asked me if I knew anything about computers. Now, note that this was 1977, four years before the release of the IBM PC and in the heyday of punched card readers, and the way that Hugh pronounced the word "computer" made it apparent that he considered such objects to fall squarely within the realm of science fiction. I replied gamely that I had a class in PL/1 and had used SPSS and SAS (which were quite new at the time) to some extent for undergraduate projects. He said "well, since I've never heard of any of those, you must know something, so you're assigned to Roger Blashfield as an RA". I then searched the maze that was Shands Teaching Hospital for Blashfield's office in the psychiatry department, and found this young faculty member moving in boxes of books, as he had also just arrived that day—so my first official RA duty was helping him carry books to move into his office.

Although at the time I certainly did not realize it, I could not have asked for a mentor who better matched my interests, as well as my personality. With respect to my interests, consider my academic pedigree as inherited from Roger, presented in Figure 18.1. Roger had two co-advisors in his doctoral training at Indiana University: Richard Price and Alex Buchwald. These two mentors represented the culmination of two great lines in psychology—the line of grand ideas fathered by William James, and the methodologically precise experimental approach founded by Wilhelm Wundt. Through these two lines fall some of the most famous names in psychological assessment, such as Terman and Merrill of Stanford-Binet fame, and Hathaway and Meehl representing the MMPI tradition. Roger's specific interest was in the classification of mental disorders, including the study of classification through the use of then-novel multivariate statistical techniques that were being made feasible through the availability of computers. Given that such classifications (a) must be founded upon quality measurement, and (b) were necessary to facilitate individualized treatments (Blashfield & Draguns, 1976), I could not have asked for a better mentor match if I had actually had the good sense to pursue such a match in my applications. Throughout my career I have been the fortunate beneficiary of quite a few fortuitous opportunities, but none more significant than my seemingly random pairing with Roger.

My first projects with Roger involved working with empirical classification techniques known collectively as cluster analysis, studying the methods themselves with Monte Carlo simulations of data with known classification structures, and also reviewing the efforts to apply such methods to psychiatric data (e.g., Blashfield & Morey, 1979, 1980). This empirical work taught me early lessons that were quite enlightening: slight variations in the application of these methods could and would generate quite different solutions to the same data set, and the methods could be applied to random data to create meaningless but nonetheless systematic classifications (since the algorithms on which the methods were based were themselves systematic). Roger introduced me to the concept of naive empiricism (e.g., Blashfield, 1984), the misguided belief that simply because a method was quantitative and involved complex calculations, it

Figure 18.1 The author's academic lineage.

must therefore be the royal road to scientific insight. Roger often invoked the "law of the hammer", which was that if you give a small boy a hammer, he comes to believe that everything he sees is a nail. We have seen the operation of this "law" time and again in psychology—the widespread and indiscriminate application of empirical methods (whether it be cluster analysis, factor analysis, structural equation modeling, neural networking, item response theory, or whatever the next methodological fad might be) to problems regardless of their suitability or appropriateness for addressing the larger questions involved. My experiences with the nuances and limitations of these multivariate approaches led me to be quite skeptical of any given result without some replication across methodological specifics, across different indicators, and across samples. In particular, I learned not to overvalue the results of any analyses focused exclusively on the internal properties of a collection of variables (e.g., item intercorrelations). One of my favorite examples of the "law of the hammer" is coefficient alpha (Cronbach, 1951), an estimate of internal consistency that is invariably cited as an indicator of "reliability" of a measure (i.e., freedom from random error) in most psychology journal articles. The fact is, internal consistency (i.e., high item intercorrelation) is not only insufficient for validity, but it is also unnecessary for validity, and furthermore we were told almost 70 years ago that it might actually impede validity (Loevinger, 1954), a lesson we are apparently rather slow to learn. The notion that we cannot sum uncorrelated indicators to meaningfully predict something flies in the face of the entire logic of multiple regression, another technique subject to considerable abuse. There are numerous examples of essentially uncorrelated indicators that can be summed to predict outcomes in mental and physical health, such as different psychosocial stressors or risk factors for cancer or heart disease. Nonetheless, we continue to read journal articles describing "good" or "inadequate" coefficient alpha results, evaluative statements that are meaningless unless there is a good reason to expect high values (e.g., replications across observers).

Rather than focusing upon the internal structure of a data set, I came to believe that the primary significance of any analytic result lay in its ability to predict external criteria. The approach was underscored in my graduate personality assessment course, taught by Roger, as I found considerable inspiration in the text: Wiggins' (1973) classic *Personality and Prediction*. As such, I began to develop techniques to formally evaluate internal replication as well as external prediction (Morey et al., 1983). In keeping with my general bipartite approach, I felt that the antidote to naive empiricism was a solid theoretical underpinning that could guide our construction, expectations, and interpretations of the empirical results. Throughout all this, Roger provided a steady grounding and a gently guiding hand. For me, this style of an advisor was probably particularly important because of my somewhat uneven relationships with authority. Roger was notably person-centered in a Rogerian manner in both his clinical supervision and in his research mentoring; he worked with me to develop and encourage my interests, rather than dictate to me which of his projects I should be working on. This was probably beneficial for both of us, as despite Hugh Davis's confidence in me I proved to have rather dismal programming skills which I continue to exercise to this day, using archaic programming languages to the amusement of my sons who specialize in this field. Instead of treating me as underqualified IT staff, Roger was interested in developing me as a full collaborator, and he placed a considerable amount of trust in my ability to contribute my share. My most vivid memory of that unmerited trust was his allowing me to deliver a paper on a panel at the meeting of the Classification Society in 1979, a conference that Roger hosted and which thus focused upon classification in mental health. The capstone of the convention was a symposium on empirical classification in mental health; the presenters were Paul Meehl (of MMPI fame), Robert Spitzer (of the impending DSM-III fame), Maurice Lorr (developer of the Profile of Mood States, among other methods), and me, insignificant graduate student, placed there by Roger who by any standard should have been the one presenting with these luminaries. I suppose it was good that I was young and stupid, because I had the audacity to follow these presenters and hammer on the point that, in the absence of theory as a guide, empirical classification approaches were as likely to yield meaningless results as not. I am uncertain whether this message was fully appreciated by Meehl as a fixture of dustbowl empiricism, or by Spitzer as the impetus behind the pointedly "atheoretical" DSM-III. However, Roger knew that this would be a tremendous opportunity for my career development, and while the result from Meehl was limited to a quick "nice talk" and a handshake, the interaction initiated a series of conversations with Bob Spitzer, as I described how the criterion-based approach of DSM-III was allowing me to treat the criterion sets as de facto psychological measurements, opening up a realm of possible investigations into criterion psychometrics and its relationship to clinical judgment. This work led to a series of papers that were among the first to evaluate the DSMs in this manner (Morey & Blashfield, 1980; Morey, 1988a, 1988b, 1988c), and allowed me to advance the notion that the goal of describing Meehl's own concept of the "nomological net" (Cronbach & Meehl, 1955) for the DSM provided an outline for classification research in mental health (Morey, 1991).

Roger's facilitation of my involvement with Classification Society meetings also resulted in yet another fortuitous opportunity of the type upon which my career has been built. Roger helped arrange a meeting for me with a young researcher named Harvey Skinner, who had been a graduate student of Douglas Jackson. Jackson's influence on Skinner can be seen in the latter's groundbreaking work in the application of the construct validation approach to psychiatric classification (e.g., Skinner, 1981, 1986). This meeting evolved into an ongoing relationship, and ultimately I had the good fortune to have Harvey serve as a co-mentor for my dissertation, enabling my access to a remarkable data set gathered at the Addiction Research Foundation in Toronto for the purpose of studying the classification of alcohol-related disorders (e.g., Morey et al., 1984). Harvey's insights into the construct validation approach and his more psychological, dimensional set of analytic techniques provided a nice complement to Roger's knowledge of categorical techniques and the psychiatric model, and their mentoring taught me to be open to the merits of diverse approaches to the problems of measurement, classification, and assessment (Figure 18.2).

Figure 18.2 The author with Roger Blashfield and Harvey Skinner.

In addition to Roger and Harvey, I also benefited from strong courses and supervision from clinical psychology faculty such as Hugh Davis, Mary Mc-Caulley, Wiley Rasbury, Jacque Goldman, and Paul Satz, as well as from faculty in Psychiatry, particularly John Kuldau and Gus Newman. There were also important relationships, in some cases long-lasting, with members of my graduate school cohort. I remember that I and a few similarly authority-challenged members of my cohort petitioned the chair of the department, Nate Perry, to have greater graduate student representation in decision making, particularly with respect to hiring and colloquium speakers. In an attempt to mollify us, Perry granted us permission to invite and host a speaker entirely of our choosing. After some discussion, we invited and hosted Jane Loevinger, and our little group spent a few days with her, which all parties enjoyed—the guest of honor included, as she seemed particularly pleased that her invitation had come directly from the graduate students. Loevinger, of course, was the godmother of construct validation (Loevinger, 1957) and listening to her talk informally about issues in the field was electrifying, including one of the most cogent analyses of the limits of behaviorism that I had heard before or since. One of my co-conspirators in this episode was my classmate Mark Waugh; he and I later published a fairly widely-cited paper together on the MMPI and personality disorder (Morey et al., 1985), both as newly minted assistant professors; after a bit of a hiatus, we recently reprised that collaboration with a joint publication more than 30 years later (Waugh et al., 2017).

To finish my doctoral training, I completed a clinical internship in the Department of Psychiatry at the University of Texas Health Sciences Center at San Antonio. It was very much a clinical internship, with no research component, and it involved considerable time demands. One notable aspect of the internship was that it was divided equally into four rotations, involving child outpatient, child inpatient, adult outpatient, and adult inpatient experiences. This provided a remarkably broad range of developmental presentations as well as severity of psychopathology, and by the end of the internship I felt I had seen most everything in the DSM. Although in my subsequent career I have focused mostly on adult psychopathology, I found the training in assessment and therapy with children particularly valuable, with insightful supervision from faculty such as Wayne Ehrisman and Jim Stedman. Although much of childhood assessment focuses upon cognitive issues, the assessment of psychopathology in this age group is fascinating as it is typically quite multi-method in nature by necessity (e.g., self-report, interview, performance, informant report), more so than is generally the case with adults, and the utility of the various methods can vary quite broadly by age and by case. Most of my supervisors were encouraging, or at least tolerant, of my preoccupations with assessment and allowed me to delve deep into the recesses of the testing materials cabinet to see what I could find and try. In one experiment that I thought was quite exciting, I attempted to combine an older projective assessment technique (the Make-A-Picture Story or MAPS; Schneidman, 1947) with a child therapy approach, the Mutual Story-Telling Technique (MST; Gardner, 1970). Briefly, the MAPS involves a series of background pictures and the respondent is to populate the picture with one or more of a variety of provided cardboard figures (mostly human), and then tell a story about the scene; the MST approach has the child tell a largely unprompted story, and then the therapist provides an alternative version of that story than reflects a healthier resolution or a more mature adaptation than the one used by the child. I found this real-time integration of assessment and intervention to be quite well received by the kids I used it with, and I felt that it noticeably sped alliance formation and therapeutic progress. It seemed that the intervention benefited from the standardization and data provided by the assessment, while the assessment was refined by real-time feedback provided through the intervention. Thus, this reflected an early effort towards the concept of collaborative or therapeutic assessment (e.g. Finn et al., 2012), a popular current paradigm that seeks to enhance and formalize the therapeutic impact of assessment—a long-standing career goal that I described back in that largely unsuccessful personal statement for my graduate school applications.

During my internship, I began the process of applying for jobs. Although post-doctoral fellowships were not as commonplace then as they are now, I was primarily interested in a faculty position—I felt I had been a student long enough, and that it was time to "reverse the voice" (Loevinger, 1966) and place myself in the instructor role. Thus, once again I sorely overestimated the competitiveness of my application, and again I was chagrined by the large collection of rejection letters I quickly assembled. Although I had little response from doctoral-granting programs, I did spark some interest from smaller universities, and eventually I was quite pleased to receive and accept a tenure-track offer as an Assistant Professor of Psychology at the University of Tulsa, and I began teaching there in fall of 1981. One of the most exciting aspects of the Tulsa job was that, following a recommendation that had been provided by outside consultant Janet Spence a few years previously, the psychology department was planning to initiate a doctoral program in clinical psychology, and I would have the opportunity to have a prominent role in the design and shaping of that program.

It was my first experience in a faculty position, and I loved it. I enjoyed stimulating and often tangential conversations with all six other colleagues in the department. A special treat was eating in the faculty dining room and lunching with different spontaneously formed sets of faculty members every day, drawn from every department in the university—an experience that may only be possible in a smaller university. Although the teaching load was heavy and nearly every course was a new preparation for me, I worked on setting a groundwork for my research, meeting with various mental health agencies in an effort to explore possibilities for data collection. However, two events in this first year of my new job occurred nearly simultaneously that necessitated some reconsideration of plans. First, university administrators decided that hiring yet another outside consultant was necessary to work out the final details of the doctoral program, and they selected a well-known organizational psychologist from Johns Hopkins, Robert Hogan, to provide input. Hogan's consultative feedback to the administration was that Tulsa did not need a doctoral program in clinical psychology; instead, the department needed a doctoral program in industrial/organizational psychology, and it needed to hire Hogan to head it. And, the administration complied. This was an early exposure to prototypical university administration of the type that, despite my having served as Director of Clinical Training and as Department Head, has led me to view administrative jobs with distaste. The relentless treadmill of career advancement in university administration makes any long-term planning impossible. What many administrators desire is to develop an impressive sounding "innovation/initiative/reform/strategic plan" that is their ticket to their next, higher position in the academic food chain, dean to provost to president to chancellor, and there is no glory in simply pursuing plans laid out by previous administrations. This meant that in year two of my new job I would have Bob Hogan with his apparent skepticism towards clinical psychology as my department head, and there would be no doctoral program in clinical for the foreseeable future.

The other contemporaneous event was a phone call from Gary Tischler in the Department of Psychiatry at Yale. Gary was the Director of the Yale Psychiatric Institute (YPI), and also the chair of an American Psychiatric Association task force charged with evaluating the effectiveness of the then-new (and fairly controversial) DSM-III classification. Gary was interested in enhancing the research profile of YPI and was particularly hoping to stimulate research on the DSM-III itself, and it just so happened that I was one of the few people who was not involved with the development of the DSM-III that had published empirical findings on it (e.g., Morey, 1980; Morey & Blashfield, 1980). He asked me if I would be interested in coming to New Haven and discussing the possibility of taking a faculty position in Psychiatry. I was, and I did—Yale was calling, and to a budding academic that lure was irresistible. Although I loved my job at Tulsa, the portents were unsettling and the best choice of action seemed clear. Regardless, I am pleased to report that Tulsa, under Hogan's leadership, indeed did eventually develop what has turned out to be an excellent clinical doctoral program, one with strong expertise in assessment.

I moved on to Yale as an Assistant Professor of Psychiatry and was handed the responsibility for developing the Evaluation Service at the Yale Psychiatric Institute. The history of YPI was a storied one; it began as the Institute of Human Relations (Winternitz, 1930) developed within the School of Medicine, one of the first and most influential multidisciplinary institutes to focus upon human behavior, and home to Dollard and Miller (a sociologist and experimental psychologist, respectively) among others. Perhaps because it was located in a medical school, over the years the discipline of psychiatry increasingly determined the direction of the institute, and it was eventually turned into a psychiatric hospital and renamed. As a hospital, it came to focus upon long term, dynamically oriented treatment of severe mental disorder, with Theodore Lidz and Stephen Fleck providing intellectual leadership with investigations into the interpersonal origins and interventions with schizophrenia (e.g., Lidz et al., 1965). When I arrived at YPI, such psychosocial interpretations of schizophrenia had become distinctly unfashionable with the increasingly biopharmacological trend in psychiatry, and the Institute had shifted to focus upon severe personality disorders, particularly among young adults and older adolescents. However, it continued to provide long term treatment for these conditions, with an average length of stay of around 450 days while I was there, and this treatment included individual psychotherapy four days a week.

To facilitate Tischler's goal of restoring the national research profile of YPI, my job was to develop and implement a standardized battery that would provide diagnoses and other psychological information at admission, and then re-evaluate all patients periodically during their hospitalization, typically every three to four months. In addition to providing a valuable clinical service, this provided me with a rich data set which was ideally suited to my interests in diagnosis and assessment, in particular with personality disorders as represented on the then still-novel "Axis II" of the DSM-III. The "implementation" of this service was, in fact, me; during my time at YPI, I administered structured interviews, questionnaires, and various other measures to *every* patient admitted to the Institute, and re-evaluated all of them, every three to four months. I attended every case conference held on all of these patients in order to provide results from my evaluation, and I also listened to input provided by the still-multidisciplinary YPI staff (attending psychiatrists, residents, nurses, social workers, occupational therapists, psychologists and psychology interns). Often the staff would include input from other Yale faculty; on occasion Lidz or Fleck might attend conferences although they were emeritus at that point, but more regularly I was fortunate to hear input from Sid Blatt or from fellow new hire Rebecca Smith Behrends. In the re-evaluation meetings, I was able to hear about how the preceding months had gone for the patients; who had made impressive progress, who had eloped, who had been placed in seclusion, who had manifested suicidal thoughts or gestures. Consistent with an aforementioned theme, this allowed me to connect the "numbers" of my evaluation consisting of diagnoses or test scores with the "story" of the person as it evolved during those 450 days. It also refined my views of diagnostic validity, resembling what Spitzer (1983) later described as the "LEAD standard" for mental health diagnosis and assessment: longitudinal evaluation performed by expert clinicians who utilize all the data available. The LEAD standard was a recognition that there was no "gold standard" of validity in psychiatry—there is no particular biological test or behavior against which we can gauge validity of our assessments. Rather, validation involves elaborating a broad nomological network, and many of the nodes in that network can only be gleaned with the passage of time—hence, the "longitudinal" element of the LEAD standard. Being privy to the data and the story of these patients for almost two years of their life, I was completely and continuously immersed in both the science and the practice of assessment. In my job, there was no divide of the type described by Cronbach (1954)—every day involved an integration and a mutual informing of theory, data, and application, and I believe my expertise as both an assessment researcher and as a clinical assessor grew by leaps and bounds during my years at YPI.

One of my closest comrades at YPI was a psychiatric post-doctoral fellow, Wayne Fenton. Wayne was beginning an impressive research career, and was also a particularly empathic clinician, and I especially appreciated his capacity to cut through theoretical or medical jargon to arrive at a grounded, often irreverent, but invariably common-sense formulation of an issue. Wayne was also a guitarist, so he and I would get together and play, typically acoustically, and he was my primary musical partner while I was in New Haven. Towards the end of Wayne's fellowship, he accepted a position as the research director of Chestnut Lodge Hospital, like YPI one of a handful of remaining long-term psychiatric hospitals in the country and then run by noted researcher Thomas McGlashan. Wayne moved his family to the Washington DC area but needed to complete his fellowship, and so he lived with me for three months, where he enjoyed sleeping amidst my ever-expanding collection of basses and guitars in the music room of my rambling house on Howard Avenue in New Haven. After moving to Washington, he and Tom McGlashan collaborated on a number of important papers, and as the feasibility of long-term psychiatric hospitalization diminished, Wayne oversaw the closing of Chestnut Lodge and then moved to the National Institute of Mental Health, where he became the first director of Division of Adult Translational Research as well as the Associate Director of Clinical Affairs. Because I was serving on a grant panel and some national committees that met regularly in Washington, I would see him frequently. We perused music shops and he would bring me to his house to survey his latest guitar purchase. Over Labor Day weekend in 2006, Wayne was providing backup coverage for a 19-year-old psychotic patient whose parents were urgently requesting an emergency appointment. Wayne had only met this patient once previously and had little background data with which to work, but with his characteristic compassion and his dedication to helping the severely mentally ill, he agreed to meet with the patient in his private office on this holiday weekend. Within 30 minutes of the scheduled appointment, Wayne was found dead in his office and the patient was apprehended nearby, admitting to the fatal assault (Oransky, 2006). I miss him to this day, and I offer this story both in tribute to my friend, but also as a tragic reminder of the overwhelming challenges in predicting specific events in mental disorders, and the profound importance of even slight increments in predictive probabilities that our assessments might yield.

Although my time at Yale was an unparalleled learning laboratory for assessment, I was beginning to chafe at the drawbacks of being a non-physician junior faculty member in a medical school as compared to a traditional psychology department, and I ultimately accepted an offer to join the Department of Psychology at Vanderbilt University. I spent 15 years at Vanderbilt, with a one-year leave as a Visiting Professor at Harvard Medical School working with the National Technical Center for Substance Abuse Needs Assessment. I rose from Assistant to Associate to Full Professor at Vanderbilt, and enjoyed my return to teaching and supervising many strong graduate and undergraduate students. I particularly benefited from collaborating with Hans Strupp and his students, with Hans being one of the top psychotherapy process researchers in the history of the field. His psychotherapy projects and my interests in the interaction of assessment with treatment led to a number of interesting explorations of this issue (e.g., Talley et al., 1990), as once again I was provided with the opportunity to make a longitudinal study of the relationship of assessment data to what happens during and after psychotherapy.

Two other enduring research projects began during my years at Vanderbilt, both post-tenure as I was now provided the luxury of pursuing longer-term projects that might have limited immediate returns. The first of these began when I was contacted by Bob Smith, the president and founder of the test publishing company Psychological Assessment Resources (PAR), to see if I might be interested in preparing a proposal for the development of a multi-scale clinical inventory. I'm not certain exactly why he contacted me; I suppose it was because I had published a number of studies on the MMPI, the MCMI, and the DSM, all of which were to some extent critical of the limitations of those methods. I regarded this phone call as the ultimate "put up or shut up" moment—if I was going to be a critic, could I demonstrate that I could do any better? Once again, I approached the project with typical overconfidence, but PAR was apparently convinced by what I had to say, and the work culminating in the publication of the Personality Assessment Inventory (PAI; Morey, 1991) was begun. The years spent developing the PAI provided a living laboratory in test construction and a truly humbling experience. I went into the project feeling confident that I knew the psychometric rules; I was equipped with the construct validation gospels provided by giants such as Loevinger (1957), Cronbach and Meehl (1955), and Jackson (1970), so how difficult could it be to make the perfect instrument? The answer: it was not difficult, it was impossible. I approached the item selection with a checklist of desirable properties, and I eventually discovered to my chagrin that many of these properties were inversely related to each other. This perhaps should have been easier to anticipate, but I didn't fully appreciate until my eyes were blurry from staring at mounds of spreadsheets that indicators with good convergent validity tended to have poor discriminant validity; indicators with good sensitivity to problems tended to have poor specificity; items that were helpful for discriminating normality from pathology were not helpful in discriminating among different forms of pathology; and so forth. I learned painfully that no item is perfect—rather, our best strategy is to assemble groups of items that all serve somewhat different purposes, in order to collectively cover the limitations inherent in any single item. Perhaps the most useful lesson learned in my years of test development is encapsulated in this sentence: "An overreliance on a single item parameter (for item selection) typically leads to a scale with one desirable psychometric property and numerous undesirable ones" (Morey, 2013, p. 413). Although not perfect, I am pleased with how the PAI turned out, as it has held up pretty well in thousands of subsequent research studies of exceptionally diverse applications. All told, it was another example of my good fortune in being the beneficiary of a fortuitous opportunity, and I am grateful to Bob Smith and John Schinka, the research director at PAR in those early days, for their belief in and support for the ambitious plans of an overconfident young test developer.

The second fortuitous opportunity that I was afforded shortly thereafter involved an invitation to participate as a collaborator in an NIMH proposal for a multisite longitudinal study of individuals with personality disorder. Four distinguished investigators, three of them psychiatrists and all four housed within departments of psychiatry, had begun discussing the need for such a project, but they felt that a fifth investigator who represented a more psychological approach to personality and measurement was needed to balance the group and enhance the attractiveness of the application to diverse reviewers. Thus, I was invited to join John Gunderson (Harvard), Tom McGlashan (Yale), Andy Skodol (Columbia), and Tracie Shea

(Brown) as the fifth Principal Investigator in preparing the application for the project that ultimately became known as the Collaborative Longitudinal Personality Study (CLPS; e.g., Gunderson et al., 2000). Once funded, the project allowed us to follow groups of patients with specific personality disorder diagnoses for ten years, and also following a comparison group of patients with Major Depression but no significant personality pathology. It was such a privilege to be able to gather rich longitudinal data and ponder its meaning with this all-star group of colleagues, and I think our group (Figure 18.3) was unique in its openness and camaraderie. I also think NIMH got a good return on its investment, as the CLPS project yielded more than 100 research articles and developed an outstanding "next generation" of personality disorder investigators across all the sites, including rising stars such as Emily Ansell, Donna Bender, Carlos Grilo, Chris Hopwood, John Markowitz, Anthony Pinto, Doug Samuel, Chuck Sanislow, and Shirley Yen. With respect to my primary contributions and lessons learned, I believe that the data reshaped my thinking about the best approach to classification of personality disorders, with a number of important conclusions. First, the project finally quantified just how much validity is lost when constructs that are fundamentally dimensional are forced into categories, when measured against a diverse array of validating outcomes (Morey et al., 2007). Second, the drawbacks of attempting to "carve nature at its joints" in too fine a manner became apparent, as models incorporating large numbers of low-level indicators tended to overfit data and perform more poorly on cross validation than models focusing upon higher order domains (e.g., Morey et al., 2012). Third, models that incorporated a combination of normative personality trait dimensions with dimensionalized personality pathology demonstrated appreciably better validity that either normal traits or pathology in isolation (e.g., Hopwood et al., 2011; Morey et al., 2012). Finally, of particular salience to assessment, study results indicated that personality can indeed be independently evaluated even in the midst of powerful state conditions such as severe depression (Morey et al., 2010), and that different assessment methods (e.g., self-report vs. interview vs. observation) can be differentially suited for measuring different features of the same disorder (Hopwood et al., 2008). Some of these conclusions challenged prevailing assumptions about personality diagnosis and assessment, and it was gratifying to be able to gather the data that allowed our project to reach these conclusions.

Shortly after the CLPS project began data collection, I moved from Vanderbilt to the Department of Psychology at Texas A&M University and continued my participation in the project from there. I was approached by a colleague from A&M to send a CV because the clinical program was looking for a senior faculty member with expertise in assessment. After two terms as Director of Clinical Training at Vanderbilt, with Strupp retiring and the departmental commitment to clinical training apparently waning, I felt that it was time for a change. I did, however, mandate that

Figure 18.3 The CLPS PIs: McGlashan, Morey, Skodol, Gunderson, and Shea.

A&M include in my offer letter the proviso that I would not be asked to serve as Director of Clinical Training, as I felt I had completed my administrative penance. However, I was apparently insufficiently explicit in my negotiations, as within a few years of arriving, I found myself winning a straw ballot to be the next Department Head, despite actively campaigning against myself. I ultimately agreed to the Dean's request that I serve one term as Head. I think that I was an effective advocate for the department's interests, as we were able to increase our faculty size by roughly 50% and hired a number of outstanding new faculty during my tenure—including a particularly strong group with broad assessment interests (Morey, 2010). Having absolutely no aspirations for further administrative appointments was also quite freeing, as I mainly desired to help the department wrest resources from the university administration. Thus, pleasing the upper administration was not a particular priority; in fact, I was comfortable with the notion of getting fired from the job, another indicator of my aforementioned authority problems. Ultimately, I survived my term and I believe that I left the department in better shape than when I began the job, so I count that mission as accomplished.

At A&M, I was provided with yet another of those fortuitous opportunities on which my career has seemingly been based: I was invited to participate as a member of the Work Group on Personality and Personality Disorders for the development of DSM-5. As with the PAI, this was another "put up or shut up" moment—having criticized the DSM in print for the previous 30 years, it was time to attempt to show that it could be done better. With a collection of diverse but noteworthy intellects, Work Group meetings were stimulating, far-ranging, and in some cases quite heated. The tensions pulled in a number of different directions, but I believe that one of the most central involved that enduring conflict between the empirical and the clinical, and I felt that I played a useful role in that group as someone who had been straddling that divide for my entire career. Ultimately, the end product of that group turned out to be quite innovative as well as decidedly controversial, and in an unprecedented move the Board of Trustees of the American Psychiatric Association rejected the Work Group proposal, simply continuing the categorical DSM-IV representation of personality disorder and placing the Work Group's recommendation in an appendix as an "Alternative Model for Personality Disorders" (Skodol et al., 2013; Zachar et al., 2016). I continue to believe that this model represents an elegant solution to the problem of personality disorder classification; a severity dimension that represents maturation of key personality functions (e.g. empathy, self-direction) or lack thereof, and trait dimensions that represent commonly identified trait domains that underlie personality in general. From combinations of severity and trait domains, the traditional categorical personality disorder concepts can be precisely described (Morey & Skodol, 2013), providing continuity with a research literature that has been based on that tradition for decades. To me, this model provides an integrated framework with which to consider the psychiatric and the psychological, the static and the longitudinal, the normal and the abnormal, the psychometric and the clinical. To this point, the American Psychiatric Association has still not formally accepted this approach, but I am confident that it will ultimately be adopted in some form. The entire experience brings to mind one of Blashfield's favorite quotes from R. E. Kendell (1975) who pointed out that any consensus psychiatric classification is "'bound to be conservative and theoretically unenterprising because, like a convoy, its rate of progress is dictated by that of its slowest members." It may be some years before that convoy catches up with the Work Group, but my reading of the recent research literature on personality disorder suggests that the field has left the extant categorical model far behind.

In compiling this narrative, I have been reminded time and again of the remarkable good fortune I have had throughout my career. I must add to that list the opportunities over the past 40 years that I have had to work with wonderful students, at the graduate, undergraduate, and intern levels. At the risk of undeservedly leaving someone out, I will not provide a string of names of these many students, but you know who you are, and I am proud of you all. Some of my most gratifying experiences have been to attend professional conferences (which I don't do that frequently) and be surrounded by some of my former students who have gone on to successful careers, where they introduce me to their students, and in some cases to students of their students—my academic great-grandchildren, as it were.

For example, Figure 18.4 includes photos taken at the Society for Personality Assessment conference, in which I am surrounded by my academic progeny—every one of them extending the academic line shown earlier in Figure 1. As I approach retirement, I have no compulsion to "work until I drop" in a desperate effort to get the important tasks done. I am entirely comfortable with turning over that task to the researchers, clinicians, administrators, and scholars that I may have influenced in some way over the years; I'm confident that they're up to the task.

Figure 18.4 Morey with his academic progeny, Society for Personality Assessment; top, 2012; bottom, 2017.

I'm generally a fairly private person, and I have provided relatively little discussion of my family, but my family is supremely important to me and they have played a key role in keeping me sane and grounded. Out of respect for their privacy, I will refrain from extensive details concerning my wife Janice and my three sons Michael, Charlie, and Jack, other than to say that they have been a treasured source of support, love, aggravation, consternation, pride, and joy over the past decades. Loevinger (1966) might be pleased to know that the travails I inflicted on my parents have now largely been re-experienced with reversal of voice, which is both enlightening and only fitting. With the boys having hit adulthood, Janice and I have naturally been pondering retirement plans. Personally, I am thinking that it is time to finally hit it big as a bass player, while Janice's wish has been to act upon her lifelong commitment to help abandoned or mistreated animals. We have made a head start on this latter plan by opening a registered non-profit animal sanctuary, with a particular focus upon pigs. As I write this, we have 15 rescue pigs enjoying the good life in our lovely pasture, along with a smattering of other animals. I am pleased to report that my studies lead me to believe that pigs demonstrate personality variability comparable to that displayed by humans. Furthermore, with respect to socially desirable traits, pigs might compare favorably to academics, subject of course to measurement method variance.

In concluding, I suppose the best summary of the preceding material is that throughout my career I've been fortunate to have been presented with remarkable opportunities, and in a number of instances I was able to use those opportunities to help realize significant goals. In particular, I was lucky to have mentors, colleagues, and students who facilitated those opportunities which enabled me to be proactive in pursuing them, rather than passively waiting for them to occur. In doing so, I've attempted to draw upon the bipartite nature of my own personality to attempt to bridge similar divisions in my field. I will relate one last anecdote that was a memorable and particularly satisfying indicator that I may have had some measure of success in straddling this divide. It was shortly after the publication of the PAI, and I was doing a number of workshops to introduce the then-novel instrument. At one of these early workshops, I glanced at the list of registered attendees before starting, and noted with apprehension that one of the participants was Theodore (Ted) Blau, one of the most prominent forensic psychologists in the field and the first clinician in independent practice to be elected president of the American Psychological Association. I had never met Ted before, but I surmised that he was most likely attending the workshop to learn about this novel instrument and, as forensic psychologists tend to do, develop a good understanding of its potential weaknesses suitable for use in court. At any rate, I went through my usual presentation, which consisted of extensive background about the test construction and the theoretical underpinnings of the constructs that it measured (typically more detail than most attendees wanted), progressing to a discussion of the scales, and ultimately culminating in some case presentations. Consistent with the theme that hopefully has emerged in this chapter, the case presentations involved demonstrating how the numbers provided in the form of test scores could be translated into a *person*—a complete story with overtones of development, current experience of the world, and the various future directions that this story might take, depending upon possible intervening events whose salience was suggested by the test data. Ted never said a word during all of this, and I was having little success gauging his reaction. Finally, I completed my presentation and thanked the participants for coming. At that point, Ted stood up, faced the audience, and pronounced: "Friends, THAT is a scientist-practitioner!" I particularly value that memory because, in my career goals, I suppose that is really all I ever intended to be.

References

Abelson, R. P. (1985). A variance explanation paradox: When a little is a lot. *Psychological Bulletin*, *97*(1), 129–133.

Anastasi, A. (1976). *Psychological testing* (4th ed.). Toronto: Macmillan.

Blashfield, R. K. (1984). *The classification of psychopathology: Neo-Kraepelinian and quantitative approaches*. New York: Plenum.

Blashfield, R. K., & Draguns, J. G. (1976). Toward a taxonomy of psychopathology: The purpose of psychiatric classification. *British Journal of Psychiatry*, *129*, 574–583.

Blashfield, R. K., & Morey, L. C. (1979). The classification of depression through cluster analysis. *Comprehensive Psychiatry*, *20*, 516–527.

Blashfield, R. K. & Morey, L. C. (1980). A comparison of four clustering methods using MMPI Monte Carlo data. *Applied Psychological Measurement*, *4*, 57–64.

Cohen, J. (1977). *Statistical power analysis for the behavioral sciences*. New York: Academic Press.

Cronbach, L. J. (1951). Coefficient alpha and the internal structure of tests. *Psychometrika*, *16*(3), 297–334.

Cronbach, L. J. (1954). Report on a psychometric mission to Clinicia. *Psychometrika*, *19*(4), 263–270.

Cronbach, L. J., & Meehl, P. E. (1955). Construct validity in psychological tests. *Psychological Bulletin*, *52*(4), 281–302.

Finn, S. E., Fischer, C. T., & Handler, L. (2012). *Collaborative/therapeutic assessment: A casebook and guide*. Hoboken, NJ: John Wiley & Sons.

Gardner, R. A. (1970). The mutual storytelling technique: Use in the treatment of a child with post-traumatic neurosis. *American Journal of Psychotherapy*, *24*(3), 419–439.

Gunderson, J. G., Shea, M. T., Skodol, A. E., McGlashan, T. H., Morey, L. C., Stout, R. L., Zanarini, M. C., Grilo, C. M., Oldham, J. M., & Keller, M. B. (2000). The collaborative longitudinal personality disorders study: Development, aims, design, and sample characteristics. *Journal of Personality Disorders*, *14*, 300–315.

Hall, C. S., & Lindzey, G. (1970). *Theories of personality*. New York: John Wiley & Sons.

Hopwood, C. J., Malone, J. C., Ansell, E. B., Sanislow, C. A., Grilo, C. M., McGlashan, T. H., Pinto, A., Markowitz, J. C., Shea, M. T., Skodol, A. E., Gunderson, J. G., Zanarini, M. C., & Morey, L. C. (2011). Personality assessment in DSM-V: Empirical support for rating severity, style, and traits. *Journal of Personality Disorders, 25*, 305–320.

Hopwood, C. J., Morey, L. C., Edelen, M. O., Shea, M. T., Grilo, C. M., Sanislow, C. A., McGlashan, T. H., Daversa, M. T., Gunderson, J. G., Markowitz, J. C., & Skodol, A. E. (2008). A comparison of interview and self-report methods for the assessment of borderline personality disorder criteria. *Psychological Assessment, 20(1)*, 81–85.

Jackson, D. N. (1967). *Personality research form manual.* Port Huron, MI: Research Psychologists Press.

Jackson, D. N. (1970). A sequential system for personality scale development. In C. D. Spielberger (Ed.), *Current topics in community and clinical psychology* (Vol. 2, pp. 62–97). New York: Academic Press.

Kendell, R. E. (1975). *The role of diagnosis in psychiatry.* London: Blackwell Scientific Publications.

Loevinger, J. (1954). The attenuation paradox in test theory. *Psychological Bulletin, 51*(5), 493–504.

Loevinger, J. (1957). Objective tests as instruments of psychological theory. *Psychological Reports, 3*, 635–694.

Loevinger, J. (1966). Three principles for a psychoanalytic psychology. *Journal of Abnormal Psychology, 71*(6), 432–443.

Lidz, T., Fleck, S., & Cornelison, A. R. (1965). *Schizophrenia and the family.* New York: International Universities Press.

Macmillan (1969). *The baseball encyclopedia.* Toronto: Macmillan.

McNair, D., Lorr, M., & Doppleman, L. (1971). *POMS manual for the profile of mood states.* San Diego, CA: Educational and Industrial Testing Service.

Morey, L. C. (1980). Differences between psychologists and psychiatrists in use of DSM-III. *American Journal of Psychiatry, 137*, 1123–1124.

Morey, L. C. (1988a). Personality disorders under DSM-III and DSM-III-R: An examination of convergence, coverage, and internal consistency. *American Journal of Psychiatry, 145*, 573–577.

Morey, L. C. (1988b). The categorical representation of personality disorder: A cluster analysis of DSM-III-R personality features. *Journal of Abnormal Psychology, 97*, 314–321.

Morey, L. C. (1988c). A psychometric analysis of the DSM-III-R personality disorder criteria. *Journal of Personality Disorders, 2*, 109–124.

Morey, L. C. (1991). Classification of mental disorder as a collection of hypothetical constructs. *Journal of Abnormal Psychology, 100*, 289–293.

Morey, L. C. (2010). Leading North American programs in clinical assessment research: An assessment of productivity and impact. *Journal of Personality Assessment, 92*(3), 207–211.

Morey, L. C. (2013). Measuring personality and psychopathology. In I. Weiner (Ed.), *Handbook of psychology* (2nd ed., pp. 395–427). New York: John Wiley.

Morey, L. C., Blashfield, R. K. & Skinner, H. A. (1983). A comparison of cluster analytic techniques within a sequential validation framework. *Multivariate Behavioral Research, 18*, 309–329.

Morey, L. C., Hopwood, C. J., Markowitz, J. C., Gunderson, J. G., Grilo, C. M., McGlashan, T. H., Shea, M. T., Yen, S., Sanislow, C. A., Ansell, E. B.,

& Skodol, A. E. (2012). Comparison of alternative models for personality disorders, II: 6-, 8- and 10-year follow-up. *Psychological Medicine, 42,* 1705–1713.

Morey, L. C., Shea, M. T., Markowitz, J. C., Stout, R. L., Hopwood, C. J., Gunderson, J. G., Grilo, C. M., McGlashan, T. H., Yen, S., Sanislow, C. A., & Skodol, A. E. (2010). State effects of major depression on the assessment of personality and personality disorder. *American Journal of Psychiatry, 167,* 528–535.

Morey, L. C., Skinner, H. A., & Blashfield, R. K. (1984). A typology of alcohol abusers: Correlates and implications. *Journal of Abnormal Psychology, 93,* 408–417.

Morey, L. C., & Skodol, A. E. (2013). Convergence between DSM-IV-TR and DSM-5 diagnostic models for personality disorder: Evaluation of strategies for establishing diagnostic thresholds. *Journal of Psychiatric Practice, 19,* 179–193.

Morey, L. C., Waugh, M. H. & Blashfield, R. K. (1985). MMPI scales for DSMIII personality disorders: Their derivation and correlates. *Journal of Personality Assessment, 49,* 245–251.

Murray, H. A. (1938). *Explorations in personality.* New York: Oxford Press.

Oransky, I. (2006). Obituary: Wayne S. Fenton. *The Lancet, 368,* 1568.

Skinner H. A. (1981). Toward the integration of classification theory and methods. *Journal of Abnormal Psychology, 90,* 68–87.

Skinner, H. A. (1986). Construct validation approach to psychiatric classification. In T. Millon & G. L. Klerman (Eds.), *Contemporary directions in psychopathology: Toward the DSM-IV* (pp. 307–330). New York: The Guilford Press.

Skodol, A. E., Morey, L. C., Bender, D. S., & Oldham, J. E. (2013). The ironic fate of personality disorders in DSM-5. *Personality Disorders: Theory, Research and Treatment, 4,* 342–349.

Spitzer, R. L. (1983). Psychiatric diagnosis: are clinicians still necessary? *Comprehensive Psychiatry, 24(5),* 399–411.

Shostrom, E. L. (Producer; 1966). *Three Approaches to Psychotherapy [Film].* Santa Ana, CA: Psychological Films.

Shneidman, E. S. (1947). The *Make-A-Picture-Story* (MAPS) projective personality test: a preliminary report. *Journal of Consulting Psychology, 11(6),* 315–325.

Talley, P. F., Strupp, H. H., & Morey, L. C. (1990). Matchmaking in psychotherapy: An investigation of patient-therapist matching. *Journal of Consulting and Clinical Psychology, 58,* 182–188.

Waugh, M. H., Hopwood, C. J., Krueger, R. F., Morey, L. C., Pincus, A. L., & Wright, A. G. C. (2017). Psychological assessment with the DSM-5 Alternative Model for Personality Disorders: Tradition and innovation. *Professional Psychology Research and Practice, 48(2),* 79–89.

Wiggins, J. S. (1973). *Personality and prediction: Principles of personality assessment.* Reading, MA: Addison-Wesley.

Winternitz, M. (1930). The institute of human relations at Yale University. *New England Journal of Medicine, 202,* 57–59.

Zachar, P., Krueger, R. F., & Kendler, K. S. (2016). Personality disorder in DSM-5: an oral history. *Psychological Medicine, 46(1),* 1–10. https://doi.org/10.1017/S0033291715001543

19 Circle Songs and Sands of Time

Aaron L. Pincus

I am grateful to be included in this collection of autobiographical essays by many of the most accomplished figures in personality assessment science and practice. It might not have turned out this way, as I imagined myself pursuing a career as a veterinarian throughout my childhood and adolescence. Even so, I do recall much pondering about why people (including myself) think, feel, and behave as they do. My first experience with psychological assessment was testing as gifted at an early age in an ethnically diverse elementary school in Los Angeles. A well-developed program for gifted students afforded me both special educational opportunities and a ready-made group of friends who were similarly intellectually inclined. This was my ticket to ride. I was not particularly good at sports, nor was I musically or artistically talented. Scholarly pursuits are where I excelled, and it has been that way my entire life. In the pages that follow, I elaborate on my scholarly development, my career as a psychologist, my approach to personality assessment, and the people and places that inspired, influenced, and helped me. I can see that I have accomplished much in my career. But ultimately, I could not have done it without an amazing group of mentors, colleagues, collaborators, and students. In many ways, this chapter is written to honor and thank them.

What a long strange trip it's been: my scholarly life and career

In this section, I detail my scholarly development and professional career. I completed my Bachelor's degree in psychology (with high honors) at the University of California—Davis (UCD) in 1985, my Master's degree in personality psychology at the University of California—Berkeley (UCB) in 1987, and my doctorate in clinical psychology at the University of British Columbia (UBC) in 1992. I have spent my entire faculty career, starting in 1992, at the Pennsylvania State University (PSU).

DOI: 10.4324/9781003036302-19

Something new is waiting to be born

Consistent with my vision of a veterinary career, I began my undergraduate studies at UCD as a declared zoology major in 1981. I chose Davis because of its preeminent School of Veterinary Medicine. Over the first year and a half, a few things became clear to me. First, all eight biological science majors, including zoology, were constructed and delivered solely to weed students out of qualifying to take the MCAT. Second, after several dismissive meetings with different zoology faculty, I found they were completely disinterested in engaging or mentoring undergraduate students in zoological science. Finally, and in contrast, the Psychology Department and faculty were very student oriented and the climate in Young Hall was inviting, inclusive, and respectful. In the middle of my sophomore year, I changed my major to psychology. Among the first courses I took were Tom Natsoulas' Psychology of Consciousness, Charles Tart's Altered States of Consciousness, and Bruce Hackett's Sociology of Utopian Societies. The courses were unusual but ideal for me given I had recently discovered the Grateful Dead and a community of Davis Deadheads, and we were already studying these topics ad hoc.

However, it was my introduction to personality theory, taught by psychobiographer Alan Elms that truly captivated me. His course included books by Freud, Jung, Erickson, and Skinner. Elms also assigned portions of Harry Stack Sullivan's (1953) *Interpersonal Theory of Psychiatry*, a book that really spoke to me. As I delved into interpersonal theory, I quickly came across Leary's (1957) *Interpersonal Diagnosis of Personality* and its derivation of the interpersonal circle. I found Sullivan's books (which were notes taken at his lectures) among the most insightful and penetrating psychological works I had ever read. Leary's work spoke of the levels of personality and personality dynamics, and the interpersonal circle was a powerful conceptual and empirical operationalization of interpersonal functioning. Both books continue to catalyze insights over 60 years since their publications. Through Elms' course I discovered that the goal of understanding how and why people think, feel, and behave as they do in a theoretically coherent and integrated fashion that we call "personality" was what I was looking for. It was the beginning of an enduring love affair. Later, I would take both Elms' undergraduate course in psychobiography, and later still Mac Runyan's graduate seminar in psychobiography when I arrived at UCB.

And know the truth must still lie somewhere in between

Unlike contemporary undergraduate courses in personality that tend to emphasize empirical research, my undergraduate courses exposed me to as much personality theory as I could devour. I was accepted into the personality psychology graduate program at UCB in 1985. For two years at the Institute for Personality Assessment and Research (IPAR)[1] I took a deep dive into personality traits (from Allport to the Big Five) and personality assessment as an integrative attempt to understand the whole person. IPAR had an amazing collection of assessment luminaries including Harrison Gough, Jack Block, Ravenna Helson, Kenneth Craik, Gerald Mendelsohn, and a young Oliver John in his first years as a faculty member. I participated in among the last series of multimethod, multiday weekend live-in assessments started by Donald Mackinnon. In my time, groups of MBA students from Stanford University and UCB stayed over for a weekend and completed questionnaires and interviews, as well as participating in leaderless group discussions (with observers), informal get-togethers with assessors, and many other assessment tasks. I recall all the new graduate students following Harrison Gough around during informal gatherings as he was the master of casually engaging participants while keenly assessing them at the same time. I learned quite a bit about "bedside manner" just watching Gough do his thing. At the end, each of us assessors integrated the results for one or more of the participants. I summarized one MBA student I interviewed who had previously worked as a musician, a chef, and other short-lived roles. I concluded that he would excel in the MBA program, but then probably move on to something else entirely.

In my first year, Gough taught his final graduate seminar on the California Psychological Inventory prior to retirement. Every personality graduate student in the program took it. I recall sitting amongst my older peers feeling increasingly anxious that I did not understand what anyone was saying about the concept of construct validity. IPAR also was a beacon for numerous visitors who came for short periods and entire sabbaticals. I attended talks and gatherings with Robert Hogan, Leonard Horowitz, Lew Goldberg, Arnold Buss, and many others.

During these two years, I continued reading Sullivan's works and contemporary empirical research employing the Interpersonal Circle. Furthermore, Leary's book was never far from reach and seemed to speak to everything I queried its pages about. Sullivan and Leary really spoke of personality and psychopathology, as well as normality and abnormality, in fully integrated ways and this began to strongly influence my thinking. I became convinced that personality and clinical psychology were inseparable and any partitioning of them was ill conceived. I did not understand why so many psychology departments had separate clinical psychology and personality psychology tracks. I spoke with Sheldon Korchin, the head of Berkeley's clinical psychology program at the time, about the possibility of letting me work in both tracks and obtain clinical training. It was basically a non-starter. I became increasingly concerned about how to apply personality theory, personality traits, and personality assessment in the absence of a clinical context. Sure, I could study creative people like MacKinnon and Helson did or personality development like Block did. But Sullivan and Leary spoke intimately about personality and psychopathology in such an integrated and compelling way, and I knew that was what I wanted to do.

Given I found interpersonal theory and its elegant operationalization centered around the Interpersonal Circle (Figure 19.1) an attractive intellectual path, I started exploring the contemporary interpersonalists. I was intrigued with Robert Carson's and Don Kiesler's discussions of interpersonal complementarity (Carson, 1969; Kiesler, 1983). I was moved by Jerry Wiggins' distillation of interpersonal traits (Wiggins, 1979) and the interpersonal circle's ability to integrate across the fields of personality, clinical, and social psychology (Wiggins, 1980, 1982). My mind was blown by Lorna Smith Benjamin's complex yet comprehensive Structural Analysis of Social Behavior (SASB; Benjamin, 1974). For my Master's thesis, I contacted Don Kiesler to see if I could acquire his Impact Message Inventory (IMI), which mapped the interpersonal circle in terms of the thoughts, feelings, and impulses to act that are evoked when interacting with a specific target person. This was the first time I reached out to well-established scholar, and to my delight he responded supportively and sent me a prepublication copy of the IMI manual. I used it in my master's study, a scenario-based assessment of reactions (impact messages) to various interpersonal experiences. It was not a great study and my analyses were rudimentary, but it was a start.

As I was completing my Masters, and having been rebuffed regarding clinical training, I decided to apply to the clinical psychology doctoral programs at Virginia Commonwealth University (VCU) to work with Don Kiesler and UBC to work with Jerry Wiggins. It was not an easy decision to leave Berkeley and I remember walking with Oliver John, who grilled me as to why I was considering it. I interviewed at both schools and was accepted into UBC's clinical psychology doctoral program. Only years later would I learn that Wiggins and Kiesler discussed me after my interviews. They felt that I was very well-versed in personality theory but not particularly strong in methodology and statistics. They concluded that working with Wiggins would most help me develop the methodological and quantitative skills that I lacked. Thus, I was accepted at UBC but not at VCU. In 1987, I visited the Canadian consulate in San Francisco and applied for a student visa. That summer, I moved to Vancouver.

Strike another match, go start anew

The move to UBC and working closely with Jerry Wiggins was the best thing that ever happened to me professionally. After stints at Stanford University and the University of Illinois, Wiggins was by then a prominent elder statesman of personality assessment. I did not really grasp just how prominent a scholar and how beloved a figure he was at the time (see Pincus & Widiger, 2015), but I quickly realized that we really worked well together.

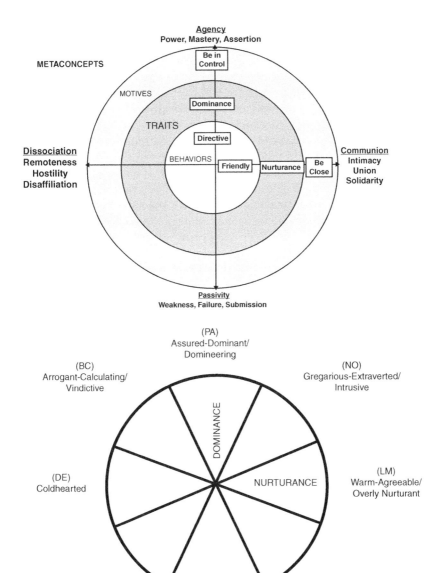

Figure 19.1 TOP—The agency and communion meta-framework; BOTTOM—
Interpersonal Circumplex (Traits/Problems).

I had to adjust to a more formal professional climate than Berkeley's program. Gone were the seminar rooms full of big comfortable couches and easy chairs, the laid-back attitude regarding course starting times, and faculty beginning seminars with "well, what did you think of what you read?" I arrived about five minutes late to my first seminar meeting, which was taught by Lynn Alden. When it was over, she sternly told me not to be late again. Wiggins worked hard and played hard. He arrived early every weekday and followed a fairly strict routine of writing in the morning, eating a packed lunch in the personality reading room at noon, and engaging in teaching and other scholarly business in the afternoon. As is well-known, no day was complete for Wiggins without an evening vodka martini. As a mentor, Wiggins was amazingly accepting, supportive, and challenging. He wanted me to fully join the scholarly community and facilitated my professional development in every way possible. He helped me learn to write well; after all, his writing earned him the nickname "The Mozart of Personality" (a small cameo of Mozart was pinned to Wiggins' office nameplate). He funded me on his grants and supported my successful application for a prestigious Killam Graduate Fellowship. He provided numerous opportunities to network by including me in projects and introducing me at conferences where it was his penchant to stake out a table at the hotel bar and hold court as various scholars came and went over the course of the evenings. My first year was a transition and Wiggins rarely told me what to do directly. Instead, he modeled the attitude and discipline to get ahead and the magnanimity to get along.

By my second year, Wiggins and I were working on research linking the Five-factor Model and DSM personality disorders. As was typical, after a discussion of the work over lunch he headed back to his office and casually remarked over his shoulder "I think canonical correlation would be a good analysis." That was it, I had my marching orders. I had not heard of canonical correlation and spent the next week learning about it and ultimately mastering the mainframe SPSS script for it that was embedded in the byzantine MANOVA command structure. We published the first empirical paper linking Five-factor Model personality traits and personality disorders (Wiggins & Pincus, 1989) which included the canonical analyses. Lew Goldberg (one of the paper's reviewers) concluded it was a "methodological tour de force." Wiggins was invited to present the work on a symposium chaired by Jeff McCrae at the 1989 American Psychological Association Convention. He offered the slot to me. I recall looking out at a large audience (with Wiggins in the front row) and feeling very nervous but also receiving a positive reception.

This initial paper also included the first empirical placement of DSM personality disorders on the interpersonal circle, and we were also deeply immersed in a major interpersonal circle project. The previous year, Len Horowitz published the Inventory of Interpersonal Problems, which included several unidimensional scales. Alden and Wiggins suggested that if the items were indeed interpersonal, we should be able to construct a circumplex measure of interpersonal problems to complement the Interpersonal Adjective Scales (Wiggins, 1979). I learned to construct circumplex measures and evaluate circular structure by working on this project, and the paper introducing the Inventory of Interpersonal Problems Circumplex Scales (IIP-C; Alden et al., 1990) remains my most highly cited paper. This was followed quickly by my earliest first-authored paper locating DSM personality disorders on the interpersonal problems circumplex (Pincus & Wiggins, 1990). I was fulfilling my goal of applying personality theory and personality assessment in the clinical context of personality disorders. The following year, Wiggins helped to expand my training by inviting me to coauthor an overview of personality structure and assessment for the *Annual Review of Psychology* (Wiggins & Pincus, 1992). Working on this review helped me place our work in the context of the broader field.

During this time, I also began my clinical training. The training clinic was small, and my supervision was focused on behavior therapy and cognitive therapy. It was not until I began my predoctoral internship at University Hospital—UBC Site that I began training in interpersonal and psychodynamic psychotherapy. Perhaps because I was well versed in personality theory, I took to it right away. At the time, John Livesley was the chair of the psychiatry department. He had developed Day House, a day treatment program for patients with personality disorders that was run out of an old two-story house across from the hospital. In addition to maintaining a large outpatient caseload throughout the internship, my first rotation was at Day House. There I served as a co-therapist for daily psychodynamic group therapy and was involved in other aspects of the treatment program. Now everything was coming together. I was conducting research on personality disorders, assessing patients for personality disorders, and treating patients with personality disorders. The hospital employed a large assessment core battery to help determine services for new outpatients and Day House added its own assessments as well. I even collected a small clinical sample as part of my dissertation data at the hospital.

After 4 months I had to shift rotations to inpatient assessment services, where I received referrals for new patients admitted to the large inpatient unit. This deepened my assessment training as I typically had to select an assessment battery to best answer the referral questions. I often included the IIP-C, the MMPI-2, the WAIS, and various interviews. It was fascinating and challenging. One memorable case involved a 19-year-old Native American male who was found wandering down a rode barefoot with headphones on and appeared disoriented. When I brought him from the ward to my office, he was very agitated. He banged on the hallway walls and walked quickly ahead of me. When we arrived at my office, he started pulling books off my shelf, which he fortunately stopped when I asked him to. As we began the WAIS, I noticed he had a cold and no concept of hygiene. Through many uncovered sneezes and snorts, it was a messy affair. Ultimately my report ruled out psychosis and suggested a diagnosis of ADHD and fetal alcohol syndrome. The assessment was the only way to successfully sort his complex presentation and diagnosis. I cannot remember if I caught his cold.

At the end of the assessment rotation, I was scheduled to move to the Alzheimer's Clinic for my final four-month rotation. I had heard from other interns that the work was repetitive (administering the same tests to new patients every day), and the interns were asked to only report test scores without interpretation. By this time, I had gone on the job market, received offers for assistant professor positions at the University of Miami and PSU, and accepted the latter's position. I pleaded with Livesley to allow me to skip the Alzheimer Clinic rotation and return to Day House for the final four months of internship. After all, I had a job and my work focused on personality assessment and personality disorders, not Alzheimer's disease. He agreed and I continued my psychodynamic group therapy training at Day House.

I completed my internship and headed to Pennsylvania to begin my faculty position in 1992. Because UBC required two dissertation defenses—a departmental defense and a separate university defense, I had to fly back to Vancouver early that Fall to complete the latter. During the questioning period, Wiggins brought up some recent preliminary work shared by John Digman which involved factor analyses of the Big Five personality traits in multiple samples that consistently resulted in 2 higher-order factors. The complete work was published much later. I had not seen Digman's work, and after puzzling over Wiggins' question, I declared that I did not have an answer. Wiggins smiled, pointed at me, and said "I can still get ya!" Afterward, we went to the faculty club to celebrate with vodka martinis.

My time at UBC is also important because I met my wonderful wife of 29 years, Kim, in the psychology department in 1990. Kim was a former police constable from Mississauga, Ontario, who had left the force and landed as a full-time research assistant for John Yuille's studies of the accuracy of children's testimony in child abuse cases. According to Kim, she had her eyes on me for some time and tried to get my attention on several occasions. I had seen her having lunch with another graduate student who I knew was recently divorced and erroneously concluded they were dating, so I did not get the messages she was sending me. One day Kim stopped by my office wearing a leather mini skirt. She told me she was driving down to California to visit relatives in Sacramento and knowing I arrived from northern California, wondered if I wanted to join her. After pondering things for a minute, I replied "nice skirt!" I agreed to join Kim and we decided to camp on the coasts of Washington and Oregon on the way down. On the day we left, I realized that we would be spending the nights together in a two-person tent. So that trip was basically our first date and soon we were in love.

As my internship year and job search moved along, it became clear that I would be returning to the United States. One night while we were sitting on the couch, Kim (a Canadian citizen) turned to me, smiled, and said, "If I'm coming with you, we'll just have to get married!" We agreed there and then, and I never gave it a second thought. Soon we were off looking for rings and preparing to tell our families about the wedding no one was being invited to. In April of 1992, we had a small ceremony in my Vancouver studio apartment officiated by a justice of the peace and two witnesses. John Coltrane's *A Love Supreme* played in the background as we read the vows we wrote ourselves. Kim is my soulmate and we have supported each other through many trials and achievements. We continue to share a wonderful life together. To say I could not have done it without her is a massive understatement.

Some rise, some fall, some climb

The pre-tenure period is one of the most stressful times in anyone's academic career. I began as one of four new assistant professors of psychology at PSU in 1992. Somehow, in five years, I had to establish my lab and demonstrate significant scientific productivity, develop and teach undergraduate personality and graduate personality assessment courses, and obtain my post-doctoral supervised clinical hours to be eligible for state licensure. During my tenure review, I had a dream that sums up how it felt:

> Kim and I were huddled in a small wooden shack in the middle of nowhere. A violent storm was boiling outside with huge black clouds and spears of red lightning bolts hitting the ground and exploding all around. Somehow, we needed to get out of the shack and to a safe place, but to do so meant running and dodging the lightning.

That is how it often felt, but I just kept working at everything. By the time I was awarded tenure in 1998, I was the only one of the original four assistant professors left at PSU. One successfully moved on to another university while the other two dropped out of academia. Criteria for successful tenure and promotion have certainly changed since 1998. At that time, I think three works stand out that probably got me across the finish line. One was my first chapter reviewing interpersonal theory and the interpersonal circle (Pincus, 1994), although it admittedly stuck close to prior accounts and did not really push the theoretical or methodological envelope. The others were papers in the *Journal of Personality and Social Psychology* written with my long-time collaborator Michael Gurtman (Pincus & Gurtman, 1995; Pincus et al., 1998). The 1998 paper was a massive psychometric and structural integration of the interpersonal circle, Benjamin's SASB, and the Five-factor Model. The revise and resubmit decision came with 14 pages of single-spaced reviews. The action editor, Jerry Burger, said in his letter that the amount of reviewer feedback generated by my submission suggested that I must be on to something. As a pre-tenure faculty, I had no choice but to dig in, revise the manuscript, and try to respond to all 14 pages of comments. Talk about dodging red lightning bolts! Fortunately, I had just enough time to resubmit and receive an acceptance letter prior to my official tenure review.

One other notable achievement that occurred just before my tenure review was a direct benefit of working with Jerry Wiggins. Wiggins helped me network and made sure to introduce me to many other scholars in personality and clinical psychology. Among them, a group of contemporary interpersonalists including Wiggins, Lynn Alden, Robert Carson, Len Horowitz, and Lorna Smith Benjamin, who were meeting intermittently to discuss forming an "interpersonal psychology society." I was invited to join this group and together we ultimately founded and incorporated the non-profit Society for Interpersonal Theory and Research (SITAR: https://sitarsociety.org/). By 1998, we had dues paying members and held our first conference in Snowbird, Utah. I do not remember much about what I or others presented, but I do remember meeting many people who would become colleagues and collaborators and feeling like the society had potential. Most relevant for my tenure review, I became the president-elect and the following year I served as SITAR's second president, following Len Horowitz. I am proud that SITAR continues today and was ready to host their 23rd annual meeting in 2020 in Seattle until the pandemic that year cancelled most scientific conferences.

There were days, and there were days, and there were days between

PSU does not promote faculty to Full Professor very quickly. I spent 12 years as an Associate Professor. Too long in my opinion. When I was hired in 1992, I was told that tenure and promotion was about doing well in research, teaching, and service to the University and the field. But soon after I was tenured and promoted to Associate Professor, PSU developed a "grant mentality" and one major criterion for promotion was the sum total of external funding acquired. In these "days between" my tenure and my promotion to full professor, I began the two enduring scholarly efforts that I consider my major contributions to personality assessment: (i) extending and expanding interpersonal theory and assessment into a comprehensive framework for conceptualizing personality and psychopathology, and (ii) improving the assessment of pathological narcissism. Also, regarding teaching and learning personality assessment, I have developed, taught, and continuously revised my graduate seminar in personality assessment to keep up with changes in assessment science and practice. One thing that has influenced my approach to personality assessment is consistent clinical practice and supervision of clinical trainee's assessments and psychotherapy.

To practice and supervise competently, I continued to expand my own training in assessment and psychotherapy. Instead of focusing solely on research grants, I chose to integrate science and practice and ensure I was the best clinical supervisor and educator I could be. That did not put me on the fast track for promotion, but it was much more satisfying personally.

After becoming fully acquainted with Benjamin's SASB and doing some initial research (e.g., Pincus et al., 1998; Pincus et al., 1999; Ruiz et al., 1999), I took my first sabbatical in 2000 and spent a semester as a visiting scholar at the University of Utah working with Lorna Smith Benjamin. The plan was to write a "how to" book on the applications of SASB assessment including both the SASB Intrex Questionnaires and SASB observational coding. Additionally, I sat in on Benjamin's weekly clinical practicum and her weekly inpatient interview (grand rounds) at University of Utah Hospital. She was a very generous host. We spent time together at her downtown Salt Lake City office and her beautiful home in Park City. Once a week she would take me out to dinner at one of her favorite restaurants, where any offers from me to pay were gently pushed aside. I had a small office in the psychology department that had a wide window looking up at the Wasatch Mountains. Even better, Benjamin gave me a key to her department office, which was one of two 10th floor panoramic rooftop suites. I used it regularly, but I never ran into her there. Like their creator, both Intrex scoring and SASB coding are complex. That semester we wrote four chapters, but simply did not have enough time to finish the book. Regardless of the book's fate, I mastered both assessment methods and their software; and the immersion into Benjamin's work as a clinician and clinical supervisor, along with our informal discussions, were immensely influential.

Contemporary integrative interpersonal theory and assessment

By 2003, I was confident in my evaluation of the advantages and limitations of interpersonal theory and assessment and began developing conceptual and methodological extensions. A new review of interpersonal theory (Pincus & Ansell, 2003) presented revised and novel basic assumptions. Perhaps the most important assumptions being a reformulated definition of the "interpersonal situation" as the basic unit of analysis for studying personality and psychopathology, and the incorporation of mental representations of self and other into interpersonal theory, inspired by object relations theory and Benjamin's (2003) concept of "Important People and their Internal Representations." This was also the first publication to assert that interpersonal theory's focus on the meta-constructs of agency and communion and their assessment based on the dimensions of the interpersonal circle (Wiggins, 1991), was capable of integrating other theoretical perspectives on personality, personality development, and psychopathology, including attachment theory (e.g., internal working models are interpersonal), social cognitive theories (e.g., interpersonal schemas are, well, interpersonal), psychodynamic theories (e.g., mental representations of self and other are interpersonal), and even evolutionary theories (e.g., dominance hierarchies and social bonds are interpersonal).

That same year, I coauthored a major review of contemporary circular analytic methods as they applied to interpersonal assessment and assessment more generally (Gurtman & Pincus, 2003). The chapter stands out as a methodological primer for applying circular analytic methods for research and practice. It is divided into applications to address four major questions: (i) *How do I evaluate circular structure in my domain of interest?*, (ii) *How do I use the circumplex to describe individuals?*, (iii) *How do I use the circumplex to describe and compare groups?* (see also Wright et al., 2009), and (iv) *How do I use the circumplex to evaluate constructs and their measures?* Notably we published an applied example that same year, presenting a clinical interpersonal assessment of Madeline G (Pincus & Gurtman, 2003) as part of Wiggins' (2003) well-known collaborative case study.

In the next two years, I worked extensively on two chapters that pushed the scope of interpersonal theory even further by incorporating my extensive clinical work with personality disorders. Contemporary Integrative Interpersonal Theory (CIIT; Pincus, 2005a) was formally introduced. Because personality and psychopathology are interpenetrating in CIIT, this chapter fully articulated a personality metatheory, a personality structure, personality processes (e.g., motivational, regulatory, etc.), and their development. Along with a close companion chapter (Pincus, 2005b), I also provided definitions of normal and disordered personality functioning and called for a distinction between what personality pathology is (definition of personality disorder) and how it is expressed (description of individual differences in personality disorders). This distinction proved prescient as it was operationalized later in the DSM-5 Alternative Model for Personality Disorders (AMPD) and the ICD-11 personality disorder classification.

I returned to a more traditional review of interpersonal theory and research the following year (Pincus & Gurtman, 2006). That year also includes one of my least known but most enjoyable publications to write. I was asked to review the new movie Charlie and the Chocolate Factory starring Johnny Depp as Willy Wonka. Wonka was a fine example of a person high on schizotypy and that was the direction my review took (Pincus, 2006). Over the next few years, my attention was divided between CIIT and the assessment of pathological narcissism. My works on the former include a steady stream of empirical papers with various operationalizations of the interpersonal circle (e.g., Erickson et al., 2009) and chapters applying CIIT to psychotherapeutic practice (Pincus & Cain, 2008; Anchin & Pincus, 2010). Finally, a small commentary (Pincus et al., 2009) was the first to argue that CIIT provides a framework for articulating both the person *and* the situation by asserting that the most important features of situations are the perceived agentic and communal characteristics of self and other. This line of thinking is extensively incorporated in future articulations of CIIT.

Assessment of pathological narcissism

During the "days between" my tenure and my promotion to full professor, my ongoing clinical work and supervision focusing on personality disorders led to a growing concern. My clinical experiences with narcissistic patients and the extensive clinical literature on pathological narcissism were not well represented in DSM-IV/5 diagnostic criteria for narcissistic personality disorder, nor by the bulk of narcissism measures used in personality and social psychology research that assess narcissism as a normal personality trait. The initial publication that started a resurgent interest in better defining and assessing the construct of narcissism appeared in 2003 (Dickinson & Pincus, 2003). Although it would be five years before I started working on the assessment of pathological narcissism extensively, this paper remains one of my most highly cited.

I remained concerned that current diagnostic and psychometric assessments of narcissism would result in many false negatives, and this would lead to problems with the therapeutic alliance and difficulties implementing symptom focused treatments. My lab began an extensive literature review of the conceptualizations of narcissism across psychiatry, clinical psychology, and social-personality psychology (Cain et al., 2008) which identified over 50 different labels distinguishing two phenotypic expressions: narcissistic grandiosity and narcissistic vulnerability. Narcissistic grandiosity reflects the self-enhancing nature of motivation in narcissistic individuals and narcissistic vulnerability reflects the self-, emotion-, and behavior- regulation deficits that impair functioning when needed recognition or victory is not experienced. A clinical model of pathological narcissism was then formally presented that suggested states of narcissistic grandiosity and narcissistic vulnerability may oscillate and coexist over time (Pincus & Lukowitsky, 2010).

In the late 2000s, no existing self-report measure of narcissism comprehensively assessed grandiosity and vulnerability. Thus, we constructed the Pathological Narcissism Inventory (PNI; Pincus et al., 2009) to fill this gap. The PNI was constructed to assess 4 facets of narcissistic vulnerability (entitlement rage, hiding the self, contingent self-esteem, devaluing) and 3 facets of narcissistic grandiosity (exploitativeness, grandiose fantasy, self-sacrificing self-enhancement). Importantly, the inventory was constructed such that the two higher-order factors (grandiosity and vulnerability) are positively intercorrelated (Wright et al., 2010). It is important to note this expected intercorrelation as many future investigations accounting for both grandiosity and vulnerability make explicit assumptions that they are orthogonal dimensions. The PNI does not assume this, rather grandiosity and vulnerability share a pathological narcissistic core and their overlap can be controlled for in empirical evaluations if desired. I don't necessarily think the PNI is the gold standard for clinical assessment, but I am gratified to see that over the last 12 years this theory and measure of narcissism has raised awareness and changed how most clinical and empirical examinations of pathological narcissism are framed and discussed (e.g., Kaufman et al., 2020; Pincus, 2020).

Days between revisited

Although I was not on the fast track to promotion, I was starting to receive recognition from the scholarly field. In 2007, I was awarded the Theodore Millon Award for mid-career contributions to personality psychology from the American Psychological Foundation and APA Division 12. Pearson's fete honoring Millon that evening on the 54th floor of a San Francisco high rise was amazing. In 2008, I was invited to speak at the Hertz Memorial Symposium honoring the passing of Jerry Wiggins at the Society for Personality Assessment (SPA) annual meeting, where I also organized a symposium in Wiggins' honor. I was a latecomer to SPA but have been back every year since. Joining SPA, meeting new colleagues and collaborators, and connecting broadly with personality assessment science and practice has further advanced my assessment skill set.

In 2008 and 2009, I began working on and ultimately submitted a proposal for a large two-year, $1,000,000 RC1 grant, entitled *Tools for Articulating Within-Person Dynamic Models Of Interpersonal Interaction*, with colleagues David Conroy from the Department of Kinesiology and Nilam Ram from the Department of Human Development and Family Studies. To collect intensive repeated measures data on a fairly long and large scale, we proposed a multi-burst experience sampling study using smartphones with an age-stratified community-dwelling adult sample ranging from 18 to 89 years of age. I was hiking a local mountain with Kim when my phone rang. There was barely enough cell service, but over a crackling signal I could make out Nilam Ram saying "1st percentile," which in grant lingo means we need to get started right now. Soon after, I met with my department head, delivered the news about our grant, and he agreed to begin what would be a successful review for promotion to full professor in the spring of 2010.

One step done and another begun

With the new grant, I was able to fund a full year sabbatical which I spent helping run our grant-funded study. It took a village. First, we had to learn how to program smartphones as the work predates modular plug and play app construction and web-based hosting options now available. Then we had to recruit 140 participants who were willing to come to the lab 6 times in 12 months (before and after three 21-day bursts of experience sampling data collection on smartphones we provided). Although it was often stressful, the study was successful (Ram et al., 2014) and continues to generate new results (e.g., Brinberg et al., 2021). I learned to think about temporal dynamics of personality in new ways that could be modeled with new analytic methods. After completing the study's active data collection, I spent the next eight years working on numerous longitudinal and intensive repeated measures experience sampling studies focusing on a range of topics including personality disorders, the AMPD, interpersonal interactions, and pathological narcissism (e.g., Wright et al., 2011; Roche et al., 2014, 2016; Dowgwillo et al., 2019),

More important to me were the personal and professional changes that slowly evolved over the last decade as various new experiences impacted me. Soon after my promotion I was asked to serve two years on the College Promotion and Tenure Committee. The decisions were serious, so our reviews were seriously comprehensive. Reading the candidates' dossiers, I was struck with how faculty from all over the Liberal Arts (from Japanese comparative literature to economics) were tremendously accomplished. It really helped me calibrate my self-concept. I might be good, but a lot of folks are better. A few years later, I had a similar experience serving as editor-in-chief for the journal *Assessment* from 2014 to 2018. I was again reminded of what a small slice of the professional pie I personally occupy and that there are many others who are much more talented than me. Around 2016 I began a stint as our clinical program's director of clinical training. It lasted one year and then I gave it up. Being responsible for a large accredited clinical doctoral program but not actually in charge of the people who make up the program was beyond my stress tolerance levels and I quickly realized that I am not cut out for administration. This crash and burn experience led me to begin an ongoing study and practice of Stoic philosophy, which has consolidated many personal changes that had begun after 2010. This is the decade I rejected ego and realized what I can and cannot control. Erik Erikson is right when he speaks of generativity. This was the decade that I truly shifted from prioritizing myself and identifying with the university to prioritizing my graduate students and clinical supervisees and working on being a better person rather than chasing honorary post-promotion titles like "distinguished professor." I think this created a level of professional freedom and personal serenity I had never experienced before. Combined with my new view of temporal dynamics, this has led to further advances in interpersonal theory and the assessment of pathological narcissism.

Contemporary integrative interpersonal theory and assessment

During the past decade, I have continued to expand interpersonal theory and incorporate temporal dynamics into interpersonal assessment, which together, have given rise to a new interpersonal model. Early in the decade

I began to apply CIIT to psychopathology more generally (Pincus et al., 2010; Lukowitsky & Pincus, 2011; Pincus & Wright, 2011). I introduced the concept of interpersonal pathoplasticity to describe how individual differences in interpersonal style could impact the presentation, course, and treatment of symptom disorders (e.g., Przeworski et al., 2011). I began incorporating dynamic patterning of interpersonal behavior into conceptions of personality pathology and its treatment (Pincus & Hopwood, 2012; Hopwood et al., 2013; Cain & Pincus, 2016). By 2013, I confidently asserted that CIIT can serve as a meta-theory for psychological science (Pincus & Ansell, 2013). On the interpersonal assessment side, several advances were notable (Pincus, 2010; Pincus et al., 2014a). First, Pam Sadler developed the Continuous Assessment of Interpersonal Dynamics (CAID) method to assess dyadic interactions in terms of timeseries of self and other's agency and communion at half-second intervals (Lizdek et al., 2012). Second, it became increasingly easy and affordable to conduct experiencing sampling using event-contingent recording paradigms studying interpersonal perception and behavior in social interactions in daily life (e.g., Roche et al., 2014). Finally, we introduced multi-surface interpersonal assessment guidelines (MSIA; Dawood & Pincus, 2016) to aid in assessment of convergence and divergence in an individual's responses across multiple interpersonal circle measures. Research using MSIA can also paint detailed interpersonal portraits of other constructs (e.g., Dowgwillo & Pincus, 2017). We added to the stable of interpersonal circle measures by constructing the Interpersonal Sensitivities Circumplex (ISC; Hopwood et al., 2011) and the Interpersonal Influence Tactics Circumplex (IIT-C; Bliton & Pincus, 2020).

The most exciting development has been my recent work with Christopher Hopwood and my former student Aidan Wright advancing CIIT's Interpersonal Situation Framework (Hopwood et al., 2019; Pincus et al., 2015, 2020). The interpersonal situation includes self and a proximal other or mental representation of an other, creating an interpersonal field of influence (Figure 19.2). Self and other both have agentic and communal motives, goals, dispositions, and affective experiences linked with satisfaction and frustration of motives and goals. Self and other must perceive and construe the behaviors unfolding between them. Normal personality can perceive and construe interpersonal behavior and emotion accurately and normatively, whereas personality pathology involves deficits and distortions in interpersonal perception and construal (Pincus et al., 2020). The interpersonal situation can be empirically operationalized with intensive repeated measures data (Dowgwillo et al., 2019) using methods like CAID and experience sampling assessment. After eight years of experience sampling studies, I recently shifted focus to faster timescales and outfitted my lab for a series of planned studies using the CAID method. The most recent overview of CIIT and interpersonal assessment covers all these advances

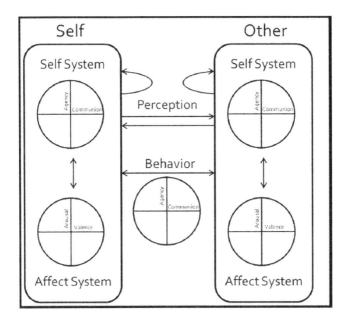

Figure 19.2 The interpersonal situation.

in detail (Dawood et al., 2018) and an applied example is presented in the collaborative reassessment of Madeline G (Pincus et al., 2020).

Assessment of pathological narcissism

In the last decade, the interest in pathological narcissism was further catalyzed by the initial decision to drop narcissistic personality disorder from DSM-5. Due to a large outcry (e.g., Pincus, 2011), this decision was reversed, but the entire revision of personality disorders was not adopted in the main text. Instead, the AMPD was moved to Section III leaving the DSM-5 with two different models for diagnosing personality disorders. The clinical theory of narcissism (Pincus et al., 2015) and the PNI and its short forms (Schoenleber et al., 2015) gained in popularity, but many additional new measures of narcissism were also introduced. As I said earlier, I do not view the PNI as a gold standard measure, but virtually all new measures of narcissism attempt to assess both grandiosity and vulnerability, and if not, there is explicit recognition of which phenotype is assessed and which is not. In addition to empirical studies using the PNI, I am most pleased with clinical papers describing assessment and treatment of actual cases (Pincus et al., 2014b, 2016) and how the phenomenology described in them are consistent with emerging research on the patterning of grandiose and vulnerable states over time (Edershile & Wright, 2021). Pathological narcissism has a complex and varying clinical presentation (Dawood & Pincus, 2018; Pincus, 2020; Pincus & Wright, 2021) and we need to employ newly emerging assessment and statistical methods to better identify and treat it. My work on pathological narcissism has sparked renewed interest in its assessment and treatment, and I look forward to the directions the field takes as it grapples with this long-standing form of personality pathology.

All Graceful instruments are known: my approach to personality assessment

This was a more challenging question than readers might think. Although I have deep expertise in a particular assessment paradigm, I do not limit myself to that perspective in any of my roles as practitioner, supervisor, and instructor. The best label I can offer for my approach to personality assessment is "integrative" and the aims of my approach are summarized in Table 19.1. I aim for *an accurate description of the person based on an integration of assessment paradigms*. Depending on the type of assessment and the referral questions, I might employ different measures and methods. For example, if the assessment most needs a symptom and diagnostic profile I might select the PAI, but if the assessment most needs a broad portrait of personality, psychopathology, and functioning I may use the MMPI-3. To assess cognitive-perceptual functioning and construal, depending on the nature of the referral, I might include the WAIS-IV or I might include the R-PAS. Similarly, to assess major personality trait dimensions I might use MSIA or the NEO-3 or the PID-5. As paradigms mature, instruments are

Table 19.1 Aims and aspects of my approach to personality assessment

---

1 Generate an accurate description of the person based on an integration of assessment methods and paradigms.
2 Embrace life-long learning and training to ensure use of the most up to date theories, measures, and methods.
3 Assess personality dispositions and personality dynamics.
4 Employ multimethod assessment and examine convergences and divergences across methods.
5 Understand the whole person in the context of their life history.
  a Conduct some form of clinical and life history assessment.
  b Develop interpretations that integrate theory cohesively with the perspective that personality and psychopathology are interpenetrating.
6 If it is a clinical assessment, collaborate with the patient regarding any additional questions they hope the assessment might speak to.
7 Generate relevant assessment reports.
  a Do not minimize psychopathology when it is indicated.
  b Include responses to each specific referral question.

---

revised, new instruments are developed, and new technologies become widespread, I also aim for *life-long learning and training to ensure I am using the most up to date theories, measures, and methods.*

I strongly believe that advances in technology and analytics allow for traditional approaches to personality assessment (i.e., self-report inventories, performance-based tests, interviews) to be augmented by experience sampling (prompted and event-contingent surveys, wearable physiological sensors, GPS locations), and even objective coding of the interpersonal exchanges between the person being assessed and others. I see a bright future for personality assessment in the coming age of personalized models of psychopathology (Wright & Woods, 2020), personalized assessment (Roche & Pincus, 2016; Wright & Zimmerman, 2019), and personalized treatments (Baune, 2019). Increasing the precision and personalization of clinical practice are tasks that are ready made for personality assessment. In my approach, I aim to *assess personality dispositions and personality dynamics.* CIIT is well positioned in this regard (Hopwood, 2018; Pincus et al., 2020), but this can be extended to many other traits, symptoms, emotions, and behaviors. Given my description so far, a logical extension of my approach to personality assessment is the aim to *employ multimethod assessment and examine convergences and divergences across methods.*

To best interpret and communicate assessment results, I integrate and interpret results with the aim of *understanding the whole person in the context of their life history.* There are two corollaries to this aim. First and most obvious, I aim to *conduct some form of clinical and life history assessment.* Second, my interpretations aim to *integrate theory cohesively with the perspective that personality and psychopathology are interpenetrating.*

The final two aims are contingent on the type of referral and the referral questions. For clinical referrals, I aim to *collaborate with the patient regarding any additional questions they hope the assessment might speak to.* Finally, I aim to *generate relevant assessment reports* that do not minimize psychopathology when it is indicated and include responses to specific referral questions.

The recent contemporary interpersonal reassessment of Madeline G. (Pincus et al., 2020) presents a model multimethod interpersonal assessment. This includes a life history, self- and informant-reports to derive MSIA profiles, as well as CAID-coded samples of interpersonal interactions with the assessor. If possible, I would add a week or two of experience sampling assessment of social interactions in daily life. Integrating these sources of information would provide comprehensive, contextualized assessment of the individual's interpersonal dispositions and dynamics within and across interpersonal situations.

See here how everything lead up to this day

I will first discuss the influential experiences, mentors, and collaborators I have had the honor of working with.[2] I will then briefly discuss my personality.

Once in a while you get shown the light: mentors and experiences

Alan Elms was my first true mentor in psychology. Not only did I take his classes, he also gave me his time and even let me serve as the teaching assistant for his personality course when I was a senior. Thank you for teaching me the importance of theory, for instilling in me a love for understanding the whole person and their life story, introducing me to Harry Stack Sullivan, and for accepting me and trusting me even when my freak flag was flying its highest.

My time at IPAR was highly influential. It was not a single mentor but the entire atmosphere of the place. Some of the support staff, faculty, and full-time scholars had been there for decades. The continuous stream of visiting scholars provided endless learning opportunities. Participating in weekend live-in assessments felt like I was part of an ongoing and vital history. I came away with a superior understanding of the concept of personality traits, a preference for multimethod personality assessment, and an appreciation for assessing and understanding the whole person.

Having Jerry Wiggins as my doctoral mentor was, in retrospect, an honor. I just did not know it at the time. Just being a "Wiggins student" opened many doors beyond the ones Wiggins personally opened for me. To this day, he serves as a model for how I work with my graduate students and I try to provide for them the same kind of mentorship Wiggins provided to me. In the end, by going to UBC, I did strengthen my methodological and statistical skills. However, Wiggins also modeled professionalism in scholarship and an ideal way to be a mentor. I aim to provide the same for my students and supervisees. I have chosen just a few Wiggins tales to tell here.

When I returned to Vancouver in 1992 for my University dissertation defense, I saw that the university-appointed examiner joining my committee, a faculty in counseling psychology, was carrying the latest issue of *Journal of Counseling and Development*. I groaned inside because I knew why the examiner had brought it. UBC regulations state that no part of a dissertation should be previously published material. The issue in hand had just come out and the small 5th chapter of my dissertation was published in it (Pincus & Wiggins, 1992). While I know this was brought up to the rest of the committee when I was out of the room, I do not know exactly what was said. What I do know is that the issue was never raised with me and my belief is that Wiggins protected me and found a calm but convincing way to recommend the examiner "not go there."

A decade later in 2002, as Wiggins was finishing his final book, *Paradigms of Personality Assessment*, he suffered a severe stroke that paralyzed him, robbed him of coherent language, and destroyed at least some of his identity. His wife, Krista Trobst, Tom Widiger, and I helped to finish the book as described in its coda. Later, Krista invited me to visit Wiggins in the hospital. It was difficult. Krista assured me that he recognized me, and she did her best to translate his strained and awkward efforts to speak. The one thing that I thought I heard, and Krista announced Wiggins said was, "lead our field." I went out to the courtyard and cried. That was the last time I was with Wiggins before his death in 2006. I attended a fitting memorial service at their home later that year. The drink of the day, and night, was the vodka martini. In preparing for the memorial service, personal anecdotes were requested via the internet on various listservs. My favorite one received was, "At conferences, the Wiggins entourage always seemed to be having the most fun!"

Lorna Smith Benjamin is another mentor I was lucky to learn from. Of all my mentors, Benjamin is the most clinically focused. She maintained a significant clinical practice and wanted clinical science to inform and be informed by the clinic. Her theoretical work exemplifies the integration of personality and psychopathology. My fuzzy memory says it was Benjamin that cautioned her supervisees not to minimize psychopathology in their case conceptualizations if indicated. I have appropriated that directly. On my sabbatical, I could barely keep up with her. Benjamin is the only person I have ever met who I thought might have a 300 IQ. She taught me to keep theory and research clinically informed, and I agree with her that clinical science needs to bridge with the clinic, not just other corners of the academy. Benjamin also introduced me to the business side of clinical practice and scholarship. I left that sabbatical convinced I should remain clinically active and allow it to inform my scholarly work.

I am not Ted Millon's student, but I am a student of Ted Millon. Anyone interested in personality disorders should become familiar with his work (Pincus & Krueger, 2015). I first met Millon in 1992 when I interviewed for assistant professor at the University of Miami. When I walked into his office, he stood tall, shook my hand, looked me over, and said "I see you are a unique individual, but you are also taking this seriously." You can put a suit and tie on a hippie, but he is still a hippie. Millon threw a party at his palatial home when I interviewed and we got along well. I did get an offer from Miami, but ultimately chose PSU. However, Millon and I remained in contact. The day I won the Millon Award in 2007, Kim and I had dinner with the Millons, along with Steve Strack and his wife Lennie. Later that night at the dessert Fete, we sat at the Millons' table while the who's who of personality and clinical psychology visited. At some point Kim and I excused ourselves to take in the amazing views of San Francisco and sample some scrumptious desserts. We kept in touch until Millon's passing in 2014. Millon taught me to think big. He is another mentor who sees personality and psychopathology as interpenetrating.

SPA is my favorite professional organization and I am proud to be an SPA Fellow. It is just the right size, allowing for a good deal of interaction at its meetings. It is very welcoming to students, and several of my students have served as officers in the graduate student association. SPA provides a resource rich environment to develop collaborations with colleagues new and old. I have participated in many emergent "project" meetings over the years at SPA meetings, planning out chapters, data collection, and more. It also provides workshops for assessment training and continuing education. Participating in SPA exposes me to the variety of assessment paradigms, methods, and measures, keeping me up to date on developments I need to know about. I cannot help but approach assessment with an integrationist's perspective. SPA allows me to learn from the best and the diversity and utility of assessment methods and perspectives impresses me every year.

Together, more or less in line: collaborators

Michael Gurtman sent Wiggins some of his earliest work on the inter-personal circle when I was a graduate student. Of course, Wiggins shared it with me. Gurtman was also one of the early members of SITAR and I would see him annually. Thus, we began working together early in my career. I really like our collaborations because they span from the theoretical to the methodological to the applied. Working with Gurtman taught me that circular structures and measures allow for a vast and unique array of analyses and options for graphic representation. More importantly, I made a lifelong friend. Beyond our scholarly collaborations, I want to thank Michael Gurtman for hosting me almost every summer for a Cubs series. Thank you also for touring me all around Chicago, from the Art Institute to Wrigleyville to our favorite Chinese restaurant. You are a beautiful person and a great friend. Go Cubs!

Christopher J. Hopwood was just finishing his doctorate when we met at the 2006 SITAR meeting. We have been collaborating, often with my former student Aidan Wright, ever since. Hopwood is amazingly prolific, widely recognized, and astute and informed about an enormous range of issues in personality and clinical science. Unfortunately, since his move to UCD, we no longer go to the annual Michigan State vs. Penn State football game. Aidan Wright was an undergraduate and graduate student in my lab and is now an associate professor at the University of Pittsburgh. He is deservedly well-known in his own right. He has received multiple awards (too many to list here) and is contributing novel theoretical and quantitative works in clinical and personality psychology at the highest level. I will simply say that working with Wright when he was a graduate student felt the most like Wiggins and me with the roles reversed. I am lucky Hopwood and Wright have time to continue collaborating on CIIT and the interpersonal situation framework. Our collaborations are hard work, but also exciting because with each draft, the creative gain is clear and satisfying. Something catalytic happens when we work together, it is more than the sum of the parts.

My experience sampling research collaborations with Nilam Ram and David Conroy really opened my eyes to the potential of mobile applications for personality assessment and the importance of assessing constructs over time. This fits very well with my experience conducting psychotherapy, where I am often targeting a contextualized and temporally dynamic process for intervention.

Finally, I just want to mention to Robert Hogan. Despite his repeated recommendations, I never cut my hair (Figure 19.3).

Figure 19.3 The author.

The music plays the band: my personality

Here is some objective test information about me. Both self and spouse-report Five-factor Model profiles describe me as high in Neuroticism, Openness, and Conscientiousness, average in Agreeableness, and low in Extraversion. Self-report on the interpersonal circle results in an angular location of 103°, suggesting dominant and slightly cold interpersonal traits. My MBTI profile is ENTJ (but I only made it to E by 1 point). Additionally, here is some subjective information about me. I am a true blend of my left-brain mother, from whom I inherited intellect and a mostly adaptive obsessive-compulsive personality style, and my right brain father, from whom I inherited a strong emotional life but, alas, none of his artistic skill. I am also a Libra, a practicing Stoic, and a Deadhead. What does all this have to do with my approach to personality assessment? To quote the Dalai Lama from a talk of his that I attended, "That's a good question! I don't know!"

Notes

1 Now the Institute for Personality and Social Research (IPSR).
2 Limited space precludes discussion of my wonderful students.

References

Alden, L. E., Wiggins, J. S., & Pincus, A. L. (1990). Construction of circumplex scales for the inventory of interpersonal problems. *Journal of Personality Assessment, 55,* 521–536.

Anchin, J. C., & Pincus, A. L. (2010). Evidence-based Interpersonal psychotherapy with personality disorders: Theory, components, and strategies. In J. J. Magnavita (Ed.), *Evidence-based treatment of personality dysfunction: Principles, methods, and processes* (pp. 113–166). Washington, DC: American Psychological Association.

Baune, B. (2019). *Personalized psychiatry.* New York: Academic Press.

Benjamin, L. S. (1974). Structural analysis of social behavior. *Psychological Review, 81,* 392–425.

Benjamin, L. S. (2003). *Interpersonal reconstructive therapy: Promoting change in nonresponders.* New York: Guilford Press.

Bliton, C. F., & Pincus, A. L. (2020). Initial construction and validation the inventory of interpersonal influence tactics circumplex (IIT-C) scales. *Assessment, 27,* 688–705.

Brinberg, M., Ram, N., Conroy, D. E., Pincus, A. L., & Gerstorf, D. (2021). Dyadic analysis and the reciprocal one-with-many model: Extending study of interpersonal processes with intensive longitudinal data. *Psychological Methods.* Advanced online publication. https://doi.org/10.1037/met0000380

Cain, N. M., & Pincus, A. L. (2016). Treating maladaptive interpersonal signatures. In Livesley, W. J., Dimaggio, G. S., & Clarkin, J. F. (Eds.), *Integrated treatment for personality disorder: A modular approach* (pp. 305–324). New York: Guilford Press.

Cain, N. M., Pincus, A. L., & Ansell, E. B. (2008). Narcissism at the crossroads: Phenotypic description of pathological narcissism across clinical theory, social/ personality psychology, and psychiatric diagnosis. *Clinical Psychology Review, 28,* 638–656.

Carson, R. C. (1969). *Interaction concepts of personality.* Chicago, IL: Aldine.

Dawood, S., Dowgwillo, E. A., Wu, L. Z., & Pincus, A. L. (2018). Contemporary integrative interpersonal theory of personality. In V. Zeigler-Hill and T. Shackleford (Eds.), *The SAGE handbook of personality and individual differences— Vol. 1: The science of personality and individual differences* (pp. 171–202). Los Angeles, CA: Sage.

Dawood, S., & Pincus, A. L. (2016). Multi-surface interpersonal assessment in a cognitive-behavioral therapy context. *Journal of Personality Assessment, 98,* 449–460.

Dawood, S., & Pincus, A. L. (2018). Pathological narcissism and the severity, variability, and instability of depressive symptoms. *Personality Disorders: Theory, Research, and Treatment, 9,* 144–154.

Dickinson, K. A., & Pincus, A. L. (2003). Interpersonal analysis of grandiose and vulnerable narcissism. *Journal of Personality Disorders, 17,* 188–207.

Dowgwillo, E. A., & Pincus, A. L. (2017). Differentiating dark triad traits within and across interpersonal circumplex surfaces. *Assessment, 24,* 23–44.

Dowgwillo, E. A., Pincus, A. L., Newman, M. G., Wilson, S. J., Molenaar, P. C. M., & Levy, K. N. (2019). Two methods for operationalizing the interpersonal situation to investigate personality pathology and interpersonal perception in daily life. In L. I. Truslow & J. M. Rahmaan (Eds.), *Personality disorders: What we know and future directions for research* (pp. 31–106). Hauppauge, NY: Nova Science Publishers.

Edershile, E. A., & Wright, A. G. (2021). Fluctuations in grandiose and vulnerable narcissistic states: A momentary perspective. *Journal of Personality and Social Psychology.* Advanced online publication. https://doi.org/10.1037/pspp0000370

Erickson, T. E., Newman, M. G., & Pincus, A. L. (2009). Predicting unpredictability: Do measures of interpersonal rigidity/flexibility and distress predict intraindividual variability in social perceptions and behavior? *Journal of Personality and Social Psychology, 97,* 893–912.

Gurtman, M. B., & Pincus, A. L. (2003). The circumplex model: Methods and research applications. In J. Schinka & W. Velicer (Eds.), *Comprehensive handbook of psychology, Volume Two: Research methods in psychology* (pp. 407–428). Hoboken, NJ: John Wiley & Sons.

Hopwood, C. J. (2018). Interpersonal dynamics in personality and personality disorders. *European Journal of Personality, 32,* 499–524.

Hopwood, C.J., Ansell, E.A., Pincus, A.L., Wright, A.G.C., Lukowitsky, M.R., & Roche, M.J. (2011). The circumplex structure of interpersonal sensitivities. *Journal of Personality, 79,* 707–740.

Hopwood, C.J., Pincus, A.L., & Wright, A.G.C. (2019). The interpersonal situation: Integrating personality assessment, case formulation, and intervention. In D.B. Samuel & D.R. Lynam (Eds.), *Using basic personality research to inform personality pathology* (pp. 94–121). New York: Oxford University Press.

Hopwood, C.J., Wright, A.G.C., Ansell, E.B., & Pincus, A.L. (2013). The interpersonal core of personality pathology. *Journal of Personality Disorders, 27,* 270–295.

Kaufman, S. B., Weiss, B., Miller, J. D., & Campbell, W. K. (2020). Clinical correlates of vulnerable and grandiose narcissism: A personality perspective. *Journal of Personality Disorders, 34,* 107–130.

Kiesler, D. J. (1983). The 1982 interpersonal circle: A taxonomy for complementarity in human transactions. *Psychological Review, 90,* 185–214.

Leary, T.F. (1957). *Interpersonal diagnosis of personality.* New York: Ronald Press.

Lizdek, I., Sadler, P., Woody, E., Ethier, N., & Malet, G. (2012). Capturing the stream of behavior: A computer-joystick method for coding interpersonal behavior continuously over time. *Social Science Computer Review, 30,* 513–521.

Lukowitsky, M. R., & Pincus, A. L. (2011). The pantheoretical nature of mental representations and their ability to predict interpersonal adjustment in a nonclinical sample. *Psychoanalytic Psychology, 28,* 48–74.

Pincus, A. L. (1994). The interpersonal circumplex and the interpersonal theory: Perspectives on personality and its pathology. In S. Strack and M. Lorr (Eds.), *Differentiating normal and abnormal personality* (pp. 114–136). New York: Springer.

Pincus, A. L. (2005a). A contemporary integrative interpersonal theory of personality disorders. In M. Lenzenweger & J.F. Clarkin (Eds.), *Major theories of personality disorder* (2nd ed., pp. 282–331). New York: Guilford.

Pincus, A. L. (2005b). The interpersonal nexus of personality disorders. In S. Strack (Ed.), *Handbook of personology and psychopathology* (pp. 120–139). New York: Wiley.

Pincus, A. L. (2006). The schizotypy of Willy Wonka [Review of the motion picture Charlie and the Chocolate Factory]. PsycCritiques—*Contemporary Psychology: APA Review of Books, 51,* Article 23.

Pincus, A. L. (2010). Introduction to the Special Series on integrating personality, psychopathology, and psychotherapy using interpersonal assessment. *Journal of Personality Assessment, 92,* 467–470.

Pincus, A. L. (2011). Some comments on nomology, diagnostic process, and narcissistic personality disorder in the DSM-5 proposal for personality and personality disorders. *Personality Disorders: Theory, Research, and Treatment, 2,* 41–53.

Pincus, A. L. (2020). Complexity, pleomorphism, and dynamic processes in Narcissistic personality disorder. *Journal of Personality Disorders, 34,* 204–206.

Pincus, A. L., & Ansell, E. B. (2003). Interpersonal theory of personality. In T. Millon & M. Lerner (Eds.), *Comprehensive handbook of psychology Vol. 5: Personality and social psychology* (pp. 209–229). New York: Wiley.

Pincus, A. L., & Ansell, E. B. (2013). Interpersonal theory of personality. In J. Suls & H. Tennen (Eds.), *Handbook of psychology Vol. 5: Personality and social psychology* (2nd ed., pp. 141–159). Hoboken, NJ: Wiley.

Pincus, A. L., Ansell, E. B., Pimentel, C. A., Cain, N. M., Wright, A. G. C., & Levy, K. N. (2009). Initial construction and validation of the Pathological Narcissism Inventory. *Psychological Assessment, 21,* 365–379.

Pincus, A. L., & Cain, N. M. (2008). Interpersonal psychotherapy. In D. C. S. Richard & S. K. Huprich (Eds.), *Clinical psychology: assessment, treatment, & research* (pp. 213–245). New York: Academic Press.

Pincus, A. L., Cain, N. M., & Halberstadt, A. L. (2020). Importance of self and other in defining personality pathology. *Psychopathology.* Advanced online publication.

Pincus, A. L., Cain, N. M., & Wright, A. G. C. (2014). Narcissistic grandiosity and narcissistic vulnerability in psychotherapy. *Personality Disorders: Theory, Research, and Treatment, 5,* 439–443.

Pincus, A. L., Dickinson, K. A., Schut, A. J., Castonguay, L. G., & Bedics, J. (1999). Integrating interpersonal assessment and adult attachment using Structural Analysis of Social Behavior (SASB): Validation and recommendations. *European Journal of Psychological Assessment, 15,* 206–220.

Pincus, A. L., Dowgwillo, E. A., & Greenberg, L. (2016). Three cases of Narcissistic Personality Disorder through the lens of the DSM-5 alternative Model for personality disorders. *Practice Innovations, 1,* 164–177.

Pincus, A. L., & Gurtman, M. B. (1995). The three faces of interpersonal dependency: Structural analyses of self-report dependency measures. *Journal of Personality and Social Psychology, 69,* 744–758.

Pincus, A. L., & Gurtman, M. B. (2003). Interpersonal assessment. In J.S. Wiggins (Ed.), *Paradigms of personality assessment* (pp. 246–261). New York: Guilford Press.

Pincus, A. L., & Gurtman, M. B. (2006). Interpersonal theory and the interpersonal circumplex: Evolving perspectives on normal and abnormal personality. In S. Strack (Ed.), *Differentiating normal and abnormal personality* (2nd ed., pp. 83–111). New York: Springer.

Pincus, A. L., Gurtman, M. B., & Ruiz, M. A. (1998). Structural analysis of social behavior (SASB): Circumplex analyses and structural relations with the interpersonal circle and the five-factor model of personality. *Journal of Personality and Social Psychology, 74,* 1629–1645.

Pincus, A. L., & Hopwood, C. J. (2012). A contemporary interpersonal model of personality pathology and personality disorder. In T. A. Widiger (Ed.), *Oxford handbook of personality disorders* (pp. 372–398). New York: Oxford University Press.

Pincus, A. L., Hopwood, C. J., & Dawood, S. (2020). A contemporary interpersonal reassessment of Madeline G. In C. J. Hopwood & M. Waugh (Eds.), *Personality assessment paradigms and methods: A collaborative reassessment of Madeline G.* (pp. 112–131). New York: Routledge.

Pincus, A. L., Hopwood, C. J., & Wright, A. G. C. (2015). The situation through an interpersonal lens. *European Journal of Personality, 29,* 407–408.

Pincus, A. L., Hopwood, C. J., & Wright, A. G. C. (2020). The interpersonal situation: An integrative framework for the study of personality, psychopathology, and psychotherapy. In D. Funder, J. F. Rauthmann, & R. Sherman (Eds.), *Oxford handbook of psychological situations* (pp. 124–142). New York: Oxford University Press.

Pincus, A. L., & Krueger, R. F. (2015). Theodore Millon's contributions to conceptualizing personality disorders. *Journal of Personality Assessment, 97,* 537–540.

Pincus, A. L., & Lukowitsky, M. R. (2010). Pathological narcissism and narcissistic personality disorder. *Annual Review of Clinical Psychology, 6,* 421–446.

Pincus, A. L., Lukowitsky, M. R., & Wright, A. G. C. (2010). The interpersonal nexus of personality and psychopathology. In T. Millon, R. Kreuger, & E. Simonsen (Eds.), *Contemporary directions in psychopathology: Scientific foundations for DSM-V and ICD-11* (pp. 523–552). New York: Guilford.

Pincus, A. L., Lukowitsky, M. R., Wright, A. G. C., & Eichler, W. C. (2009). The interpersonal nexus of persons, situations, and psychopathology. *Journal of Research in Personality, 43,* 264–265.

Pincus, A. L., Newes, S. L., Dickinson, K. A., & Ruiz, M. (1998). A comparison of three indexes to assess the dimensions of structural analysis of social behavior. *Journal of Personality Assessment, 70,* 145–170.

Pincus, A. L., Roche, M. J., & Good, E. W. (2015). Narcissistic personality disorder and pathologogical narcissism. In P. H. Blaney, R. F. Krueger, & T. Millon (Eds.), *Oxford textbook of psychopathology* (3rd ed., pp. 791–813). New York: Oxford University Press.

Pincus, A. L., Sadler, P., Woody, E., Roche, M. J., Thomas, K. M., & Wright, A. G. C. (2014). Multimethod assessment of interpersonal dynamics. In C. J. Hopwood & R. F. Bornstein (Eds.), *Multimethod clinical assessment* (pp. 51–91). New York: Guilford.

Pincus, A. L., & Widiger, T. A. (2015). Jerry S. Wiggins. In R. Cautin & S. O. Lillienfeld (Eds.), *The encyclopedia of clinical psychology*. Hoboken, NJ: Wiley. http://onlinelibrary.wiley.com/book/10.1002/9781118625392.

Pincus, A. L. & Wiggins, J. S. (1990). Interpersonal Problems and conceptions of personality disorders. *Journal of Personality Disorders, 4*, 342–352.

Pincus, A. L., & Wiggins, J. S. (1992). An expanded perspective on interpersonal assessment. *Journal of Counseling and Development, 71*, 91–94.

Pincus, A. L., & Wright, A. G. C. (2011). Interpersonal diagnosis of psychopathology. In L. M. Horowitz & S. Strack (Eds.), *Handbook of interpersonal psychology: theory, research, assessment, and therapeutic interventions* (pp. 359–381), Hoboken, NJ: Wiley.

Pincus, A. L., & Wright, A. G. C. (2021). Narcissism as the dynamics of grandiosity and vulnerability. In S. Doering, H-P. Hartmann, & O. F. Kernberg (Eds.), *Narzissmus: Grundlagen - Störungsbilder - Therapie* (2nd ed., pp. 56–62). Stuttgart, Germany: Schattauer Publishers.

Przeworski, A., Newman, M. G., Pincus, A. L., Kasoff, M., Yamasaki, A. S., & Castonguay, L. G. (2011). Interpersonal pathoplasticity in individuals with generalized anxiety disorder. *Journal of Abnormal Psychology, 120*, 286–298.

Ram, N., Conroy, D. E., Pincus, A. L., Lorek, A., Reber, A. L., Roche, M. J., Coccia, M., Morack, J, Feldman, J., & Gerstorf, D. (2014). Examining the interplay of processes across multiple time-scales: Illustration with the Intraindividual Study of Affect, Health, and Interpersonal Behavior (iSAHIB). *Research in Human Development, 11*, 142–160.

Roche, M. J., Jacoboson, N. C., & Pincus, A. L. (2016). Using repeated daily assessments to uncover oscillating patterns and temporally-dynamic triggers in structures of psychopathology: Applications to the DSM–5 alternative model for personality disorders. *Journal of Abnormal Psychology, 125*, 1090–1102.

Roche, M. J., & Pincus, A. L. (2016). Precision assessment: An individualized and temporally dynamic approach to understanding patients in their daily lives. In U. Kumar (Ed.), The *Wiley handbook of personality assessment* (pp.192–204), Hoboken, NJ: Wiley Blackwell.

Roche, M. J., Pincus, A. L., Rebar, A. L., Conroy, D. E., & Ram, N. (2014). Enriching psychological assessment using a person-specific analysis of interpersonal processes in daily life. *Assessment, 21*, 515–528.

Ruiz, M. A., & Pincus, A. L., & Bedics, J. (1999). Using the SASB introject surface to differentiate borderline personality disorder features in a nonclinical sample. *Journal of Personality Disorders, 13*, 187–198.

Schoenleber, M., Roche, M. J., Wetzel, E., Pincus, A. L., & Roberts, B. W. (2015). Development of a brief version of the Pathological Narcissism Inventory. *Psychological Assessment, 27* 1520–1526.

Sullivan, H. S. (1953). *The interpersonal theory of psychiatry*. New York: Norton.

Wiggins, J. S. (1979). A psychological taxonomy of trait descriptive terms: The interpersonal domain. *Journal of Personality and Social Psychology, 37,* 395–412.

Wiggins, J. S. (1980). Circumplex models of interpersonal behavior. In L. Wheeler (Ed.), *Review of personality and social psychology* (Vol. 1, pp. 265–294). Beverly Hills, CA: Sage.

Wiggins, J. S. (1982). Circumplex models of interpersonal behavior in clinical psychology. In P. C. Kendall & J. N. Butchner (Eds.), *Handbook of research methods in clinical psychology* (pp. 183–221). Hoboken, NJ: John Wiley & Sons.

Wiggins, J. S. (1991). Agency and communion as conceptual coordinates for the understanding and measurement of interpersonal behavior In D. Cicchetti & W. M. Grove (Eds.), *Thinking clearly about psychology: Essays in honor of Paul E. Meehl: Volume 2 personality and psychopathology* (pp. 89–113). Minneapolis: University of Minnesota Press.

Wiggins, J. S. (2003). *Paradigms of personality assessment.* New York: Guilford Press.

Wiggins, J. S., & Pincus, A. L. (1989). Conceptions of personality disorders and dimensions of personality. *Psychological Assessment, 1,* 305–316.

Wiggins, J. S., & Pincus, A. L. (1992). Personality: Structure and assessment. In M. R. Rosenzweig & L. W. Porter (Eds.), *Annual Review of Psychology, 43,* 473–504.

Wright, A. G. C., Lukowitsky, M. R., Pincus, A. L., & Conroy, D. E. (2010). The hierarchical factor structure and gender invariance of the Pathological Narcissism Inventory. *Assessment, 17,* 467–483.

Wright, A. G. C., Pincus, A. L., Conroy, D. E., & Hilsenroth, M. J. (2009). Integrating methods to optimize circumplex description and comparison of groups. *Journal of Personality Assessment, 91,* 311–322.

Wright, A. G. C., Pincus, A. L., & Lenzenweger, M. F. (2011). Development of personality and the remission and onset of personality pathology. *Journal of Personality and Social Psychology, 101,* 1351–1358.

Wright, A. G. C., & Woods, W. C. (2020). Personalized models of psychopathology. *Annual Review of Clinical Psychology, 16,* 49–74.

Wright, A. G. C., & Zimmermann, J. (2019). Applied ambulatory assessment: Integrating idiographic and nomothetic principles of measurement. *Psychological Assessment, 31,* 1467–1480.

Index

Note: **Bold** page numbers refer to tables; *italic* page numbers refer to figures and page numbers followed by "n" denote endnotes.

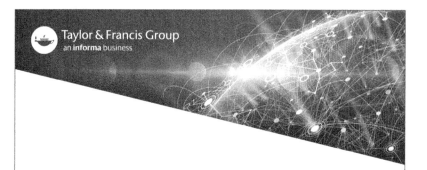